Money, Capital Mobility, and Trade

Robert A. Mundell

Money, Capital Mobility, and Trade

Essays in Honor of Robert A. Mundell

edited by
Guillermo A. Calvo, Rudi
Dornbusch, and Maurice
Obstfeld

The MIT Press
Cambridge, Massachusetts
London, England

This book was set in Palatino by Best-set Typesetter Ltd., Hong Kong

Printed and bound in the United States of America.

Library of Congress Cataloging-in-Publication Data

Money, capital mobility and trade : essays in honor of Robert A. Mundell / edited by Guillermo A. Calvo, Rudi Dornbusch, and Maurice Obstfeld.
    p. cm.
 Includes bibliographical references and index.
 ISBN 0-262-03282-1 (hc. : alk. paper)
 1. International economic relations. 2. International finance. 3. International trade.
I. Mundell, Robert A. II. Calvo, Guillermo. III. Dornbusch, Rudiger. IV. Obstfeld, Maurice.

HF1359 .M666   2001
332'.042–dc21

00-060069

Contents

Contributors

Caroline Betts
University of Southern California

Michael D. Bordo
Rutgers University

Roberto Chang
Rutgers University

Michael B. Devereux
University of British Columbia

Rudi Dornbusch
Massachusetts Institute of Technology

Barry Eichengreen
University of California, Berkeley

Robert P. Flood
International Monetary Fund

Francesco Giavazzi
Bocconi University

Alberto Giovannini
Banca di Roma

Linda S. Goldberg
Federal Reserve Bank of New York

Matthew T. Jones
International Monetary Fund

Ronald W. Jones
University of Rochester

Henryk Kierzkowski
Graduate Institute of International Studies, Geneva

Michael W. Klein
Tufts University

Philip R. Lane
Trinity College, University of Dublin

Ronald I. McKinnon
Stanford University

Nancy P. Marion
Dartmouth College

Enrique G. Mendoza
Duke University

Maurice Obstfeld
University of California, Berkeley

Torsten Persson
Stockholm University

Andrew K. Rose
University of California, Berkeley

Shouyong Shi
Queen's University

John B. Taylor
Stanford University

Martín Uribe
University of Pennsylvania

Andrés Velasco
Harvard University

Holger Wolf
Georgetown University

Acknowledgments

This Festschrift volume grew out of a conference in honor of Robert Alexander Mundell's sixty-fifth birthday, held at the World Bank and the International Monetary Fund on October 23 and 24, 1997. The conference preceded, by two years, the award to Mundell of the Nobel memorial prize in economics.

Several institutions provided generous financial support for the conference: the Economic Development Institute of the World Bank; the International Monetary Fund; the Center for International and Development Economics Research at the University of California, Berkeley, through a grant from the Ford Foundation; the Center for International Economics at the University of Maryland; and the World Economy Laboratory at the Massachusetts Institute of Technology.

The conference would never have gotten off the ground without Sara Guerschanik Calvo's energy in arranging primary financial support and organizing the logistics. We cannot thank her enough for her untiring efforts and her constant thoughtfulness.

Numerous conference participants made contributions as discussants, presenters, panel members, and lunch or dinner speakers. Although their words are not directly reproduced in this volume, their active participation nonetheless helped make Bob Mundell's sixty-fifth birthday celebration a truly memorable occasion. In this connection, we warmly thank Robert Bartley, Stanley Black, Alessandra Casella, Richard Clarida, Michael Connolly, Raquel Fernandez, Ronald Findlay, Stanley Fischer, Jeffrey Frankel, Jacob Frenkel, Peter Garber, Manuel Guitian, Arnold Harberger, Mohsin Khan, Paul Krugman, Leonardo Leiderman, Patrick Minford, Michael Mussa, Assaf Razin, Carmen Reinhart, Kenneth Rogoff, Joseph Stiglitz, Alexander Swoboda, Vinod Thomas, John Williamson, and Alan Winters.

Dulce Afzal's contribution to the on-site management of the conference was vital and is appreciated. We are grateful for Carol McIntire's unfailing efficiency and good cheer in assisting with conference correspondence and participants' travel arrangements. Annie Wai-Kuen Shun helped assemble the manuscript at Berkeley, and we are indebted to her for her cheerful assistance in several complex tasks. Finally, we thank Andrea Werblin, Lindsey Kistler, Melissa Vaughn, Sandra Minkkinen, and Terry Vaughn for shepherding the volume through MIT Press.

Nobel Prize Background Survey

The Royal Swedish Academy of Sciences has decided to award the Bank of Sweden Prize in Economic Sciences in Memory of Alfred Nobel, 1999 to Professor Robert A. Mundell, Columbia University, New York, USA for his analysis of monetary and fiscal policy under different exchange rate regimes and his analysis of optimum currency areas.

Robert A. Mundell was born in Canada in 1932. After completing his undergraduate education at the University of British Columbia and the University of Washington, he began his postgraduate studies at the London School of Economics. Mundell received his Ph.D. from MIT in 1956 with a thesis on international capital movements. After having held several professorships, he has been affiliated with Columbia University in New York since 1974.

Robert Mundell's most important contributions were made in the 1960s. During the latter half of this decade, Mundell was among the intellectual leaders in the creative research environment at the University of Chicago. These were exciting times at Chicago and many of his students from this period have become successful researchers in the same field, building on Mundell's foundational work.

Mundell's scientific contributions are original. Yet, they quickly transformed research in international macroeconomics. Characterized by uncommon foresight about the future development of international monetary arrangements, they became increasingly relevant in the policy-oriented discussion of monetary and fiscal policy and exchange rate systems. The impact of Mundell's ideas was enhanced by the simplicity and clarity of his exposition, whether in algebraic or geometric form. A sojourn at the research department of the International Monetary Fund, 1961–1963, apparently stimulated Mundell's choice of research problems; it also gave his research additional leverage among economic policymakers.

This survey begins by describing Robert Mundell's most important contributions: his analysis of stabilization policy in an open economy and his development of the theory of optimum currency areas. After a brief account of some of his work in other fields, it is asked how well Mundell's research—several decades later—stands up to contemporary scrutiny.

1. Stabilization Policy

In a series of papers published in the early 1960s—reprinted in his book *International Economics* (1968)—Robert Mundell developed his analysis of monetary and fiscal policy in open economies.

a. The Mundell-Fleming Model

In a pioneering article on the short-run effects of stabilization policy, Mundell (1963a) addresses the short-run effects of monetary and fiscal policy in an open economy. Mundell extended the so-called IS-LM model for a closed economy, originally developed by the 1972 economics laureate John Hicks, by introducing foreign trade and capital movements. The model highlights the response of capital movements to interest differentials and the response of net exports to the relative prices of domestic and foreign goods—the real exchange rate. The analysis is deceivingly simple, with sharp and numerous conclusions. Mundell demonstrated that the effects of stabilization policy hinge on the international mobility of financial assets. In particular, he demonstrated that the policy effects depend crucially on the exchange rate regime: under a floating exchange rate, monetary policy becomes powerful and fiscal policy powerless, whereas the opposite is true when the exchange rate is fixed. To illustrate the model and its results, it is useful to consider a particular special case.

Perfect Capital Mobility
In the interesting special case with perfect capital mobility, Mundell's model for a small open economy is summarized by three equilibrium conditions:

$$Y = G + A(Y, r, e) \tag{1}$$

$$D + R = L(Y, r) \tag{2}$$

$$r = r^*. \tag{3}$$

According to equation (1), national income Y is given by aggregate demand, the sum of public expenditures G and private demand A. Private demand, in turn, depends (positively) on national income and (negatively) on the domestic interest rate r. As prices are assumed to be sticky in the short run, the exchange rate e determines the relative price between domestic and foreign goods; hence private demand also depends—through net exports—(positively) on e. The left-hand side of equation (2) defines the supply of money (the money stock) as $D + R$, the sum of the central bank's holdings of domestic government bonds D and foreign securities (foreign exchange reserves) R. In equilibrium, the money supply corresponds to the private demand for money L, which depends (positively) on national income and (negatively) on the interest rate. Under perfect capital mobility, domestic and foreign financial assets are perfect substitutes. According to (3), arbitrage on the market for financial assets will then bring about parity between the domestic interest rate r and the foreign interest rate r^* (given static expectations about the exchange rate). If the domestic interest rate falls below (rises above) the foreign rate, an incipient outflow (inflow) of capital equates the two rates.

The stabilization policy instruments G (fiscal policy) and D (monetary policy) are exogenous variables controlled by the government and the central bank. Finally, the relation between the exchange rate e and the currency reserve R depends on the type of exchange rate regime.

Fixed Exchange Rates

Under a *fixed exchange rate*, the central bank defends a certain, given level of the exchange rate. At this level, the central bank must satisfy the public's demand for foreign currency by intervening in the foreign exchange market, which leads to shifts in its reserves. Formally, e is thus given exogenously, whereas R becomes endogenous under a fixed exchange rate.

Expansive fiscal policy measures—such as increasing public expenditures G—raise the level of domestic activity and national income without being impeded by crowding out in the form of rising interest rates and a stronger exchange rate. Formally, national income Y is determined directly by equation (1), since r is given by the world market and e by the exchange-rate commitment. This means that the money supply in the economy adjusts to changes in the demand for domestic liquidity as the central bank intervenes in the foreign-exchange market, by varying R, so as to stabilize the exchange rate. Formally, R is determined recursively by equation (2), for a given D.

Monetary policy measures—variations in D by means of so-called open market operations, i.e., sales or purchases of government bills or bonds—now turn out to be futile. The exchange rate cannot be kept stable at a given interest rate unless neutralizing interventions are undertaken on the currency market. An expansive monetary policy (higher D), for example, tends to reduce the domestic interest rate. But this immediately generates an outflow of capital, expanding the demand for foreign currency; when the central bank provides this foreign currency, it reduces domestic liquidity. In this way, changes in D are entirely offset by counteracting changes in R. As in the case of other financial-market disturbances, monetary policy does not affect the total supply of money, but only the composition of the central bank's assets.

Floating Exchange Rates

A floating exchange rate, on the other hand, is determined by the market: the central bank refrains from currency interventions and maintains currency reserves at a given level. Formally, R is thus an exogenous constant, whereas e becomes endogenous in the model. Monetary policy now becomes a powerful tool. An expansive monetary policy now raises economic activity because tendencies toward an outflow of capital and lower interest rates now weaken the exchange rate, which in turn encourages net exports. Formally, national income Y is determined recursively by equation (2), whereas equation (1) pins down the exchange rate e.

Fiscal policy becomes powerless, however. Its effect on demand, when monetary policy is unchanged (no change in the value of D), is wholly offset by counteracting changes in the net-export component of private demand A, in response to capital flows and exchange rate changes. As in the case of disturbances in private demand, changes in G only affect the composition of aggregate demand.

Analytical Foresight

Floating exchange rates and high capital mobility accurately describe today's monetary regime in many countries. But in the early 1960s, when Mundell published his contributions, an analysis of their consequences must have seemed like an academic curiosity. Since the late 1940s, almost all countries had been linked together in a global system of fixed exchange rates, as a result of the so-called Bretton Woods agreement. Furthermore, international capital movements were highly curtailed, largely by extensive capital and foreign-exchange controls. During the 1950s, however, Mundell's own country—Canada—had begun to ease these restrictions and allowed its currency to float against the U.S. dollar. His farsighted analysis became increasingly relevant over the next ten years, as international capital markets opened up in the course of the 1960s and the Bretton Woods system broke down in the early 1970s.

Extensions
Mundell also considered other versions of the model. For instance, when capital mobility is less than perfect, the arbitrage relation in (3) above is replaced by a capital-flow equation; now, the powerless policy instruments regain some of their effects on economic activity. In the case of two large economies, the world interest rate is not given, but determined in world financial markets; policy then has international spillover effects, the directions of which depend on the policy instrument and the exchange rate regime.

The Fleming Connection
Marcus Fleming (who died in 1976) was Deputy Director of the research department of the International Monetary Fund for many years; he was already a member of this department during the period of Mundell's affiliation. At approximately the same time as Mundell, Fleming (1962) presented similar research on stabilization policy in open economies. As a result, today's textbooks refer to the Mundell-Fleming model. In terms of depth, range, and analytical power, however, Mundell's contribution predominates.

b. Monetary Dynamics

In contrast to the dominant research tradition in this period, Mundell did not stop at the short-run effects of stabilization policy. Monetary dynamics is the key theme in a number of significant articles. Several of these articles are reprinted in the aforementioned book *International Economics* (1968); a few others are gathered in a second volume entitled *Monetary Theory* (1971).

The Principle of Effective Market Classification

Mundell emphasized differences in the speed of adjustment on different markets: the principle of effective market classification. Later on, such differences were highlighted by his own students and others—for instance, Rudiger Dornbusch (1976) and Pentti Kouri (1976)—to show how the exchange rate can temporarily "overshoot" in the wake of certain disturbances. This principle is a common theme in many of Mundell's writings.

International Adjustments and the Balance of Payments

An important problem in Mundell's work concerned the adjustment of the economy to imbalances in the balance of payments. In the postwar period, research on these imbalances had accentuated the effects of relative prices on the *flows* in foreign trade. Moreover, it had been based on *static, real* economic models. Inspired by David Hume's classic mechanism for international price adjustment (the *gold-specie flow*) which focused on *monetary* factors and *stock* variables, Mundell instead formulated *dynamic* models to describe how prolonged imbalances could arise and be eliminated.

In several contributions, Mundell (1960, 1968) demonstrated how, under fixed exchange rates, an economy will gradually adjust over time as surpluses and deficits in the balance of payments generate changes in the money stock. With sluggish capital movements, for example, an expansive monetary policy will reduce interest rates and raise domestic expenditures. The subsequent balance of payments deficit will generate monetary outflows, which in turn lower domestic demand, thereby pushing the balance of payments back toward equilibrium. Over time, the price level will also adjust and the real economic effects of monetary policy will disappear.

This work on monetary dynamics was extended by Mundell's own students and by other researchers. The approach became known as the *monetary approach to the balance of payments*; important contributions are collected in Frenkel and Johnson (1976). For a long time, the monetary approach was regarded as a kind of long-run benchmark for analyzing stabilization policy in open economies. The insights from this analysis have frequently been adopted in practical economic policymaking—particularly by IMF economists.

Under floating exchange rates, tendencies toward payments imbalances instead trigger changes in the exchange rate, but the adjustment of the economy over time is governed by the same forces. Once again,

Mundell's contributions paved the way for a new literature: the monetary approach to exchange rates. A number of papers on this topic are included in a special issue of the *Scandinavian Journal of Economics* (1976).

Assigning Policy Instruments to Targets

Mundell's analysis of monetary dynamics focused on another aspect that contrasted sharply with the prevailing theory of stabilization policy. This theory, which had been formulated by Jan Tinbergen and James Meade (economics laureates in 1969 and 1977, respectively), referred to a world where all economic policies in a country are determined simultaneously and coordinated by the same hand.

By contrast, Mundell (1962) used a simple dynamic model to examine how each of two instruments, the national budget and the interest rate, should be directed toward either of two targets, external and internal balance, in order for the economy to converge toward these objectives over time. This implies that each of two different authorities—the government and the central bank—is given decentralized responsibility for its own stabilization policy instrument. Mundell's conclusion was simple and straightforward. To prevent the economy from becoming dynamically unstable, responsibility should be assigned in accordance with the relative effects of the two instruments on the relevant markets; i.e., assignment should be guided by the principle of effective market classification. In Mundell's specific fixed-exchange rate model, monetary policy should be assigned to equilibrium in the balance of payments (external balance) and fiscal policy control of aggregate demand (internal balance).

Mundell's analysis emphasized the link between targets and instruments, rather than the rationale for decentralization itself. But by explaining the conditions for decentralization, he anticipated the idea which, long afterward, has become generally accepted, namely that the central bank should be given decentralized responsibility for price stability.

Influence on Research

Mundell's dynamic models were highly stylized and his analyses frequently relied on simple phase diagrams. For many reasons, his contributions nevertheless proved to be a watershed for research in international macroeconomics. He introduced a meaningful dynamic approach, by making an unambiguous distinction between stock and flow variables, and by clearly describing the stock-flow interaction during an economy's dynamic adjustment to a stable long-run equilibrium. Mundell's research also initiated the necessary rapprochement between Keynesian short-run analysis, where prices are assumed to be rigid, and classical long-run analysis, where prices are assumed to be flexible. Subsequent research has continued to build on this intellectual heritage. Nowadays, analytical work in international macroeconomics conventionally relies on dynamic models, which incorporate better microeconomic foundations, additional types of financial assets, and richer models of the dynamic adjustment of prices and the current account.

The Incompatible Trinity

The short-run and long-run analyses carried out by Mundell arrive at the same fundamental restrictions for monetary policy. With (i) *free capital mobility*, monetary policy can be oriented toward an (ii) *external target*—such as controlling the exchange rate—or (ii) a *domestic target*—such as controlling the price level—but not both at the same time. This so-called incompatible trinity has become self-evident for academic economists; today, this insight is also shared by the majority of participants in the practical debate on stabilization policy.

2.   Optimum Currency Areas

As indicated above, fixed exchange rates within the framework of the Bretton Woods system predominated the world economy in the early 1960s. At the time, a few researchers did in fact address the advantages and disadvantages of fixed versus floating exchange rates, even though this was regarded as rather academic subject matter. A national currency, however, was considered an axiom. In his article on optimum currency areas, Mundell (1961) radically reformulated the problem of different exchange rate systems, by posing a new and fundamental question. Under what circumstances is it advantageous for a number of regions to relinquish their monetary sovereignty in favor of a common currency?

Labor Mobility

In effect, Mundell merely notes the advantages of a common currency: lower transaction costs in trade and less uncertainty about relative prices. The disadvantages are described in a more elaborate way. He emphasizes the difficulty of maintaining full employment when changes in demand or other "asymmetric shocks" require a reduction in real wages in a particular region. Mundell stressed the importance of high labor mobility to offset such disturbances. Indeed, he characterized an optimum currency area as a set of regions among which the propensity to migrate is high enough to ensure full employment when one of the regions faces an asymmetric shock.

Later Work
Other researchers, such as Ronald McKinnon (1963) and Peter Kenen (1969), developed Mundell's approach by identifying additional criteria for optimum currency areas: capital mobility, regional specialization, and a common tax-transfer system. The way Mundell formulated the problem has continued to influence generations of economists.

Increasing Relevance
Over the years, inquiries into what constitutes an optimum currency area have continued to gain relevance in practical economic policymaking. Due to increasingly higher capital mobility in the world economy, regimes with a temporarily fixed, but adjustable, exchange rate have become more fragile; such regimes are also being called into question. Many observers view a currency union or a floating exchange rate—the two cases Mundell's article dealt with—as the most realistic alternatives. Needless to say, Mundell's problem and analysis have also attracted attention in connection with plans to introduce a common European currency. Researchers who have examined the economic advantages and disadvantages of EMU have adopted his approach as an obvious starting point. Indeed, one of the key issues in this context is labor mobility in response to asymmetric shocks.

3.   Other Contributions

The Mundell-Tobin Effect
Mundell has made other renowned contributions to macroeconomic theory. He has shown that higher inflation can induce investors to lower their cash balances in favor of increased real capital formation; see Mundell (1963b). As a result, even expected inflation has real economic effects. A similar argument was introduced by 1981 economics laureate James Tobin (1965). Accordingly, this effect of inflation has been labeled the Mundell-Tobin effect.

Mobility of Goods and Factors

Mundell has also made significant and lasting contributions to the theory of international trade. He has shown how international mobility of labor and capital tends to equalize the prices of goods among countries, even if foreign trade is limited by trade barriers; see Mundell (1957). This result can be seen as the mirror image of the well-known Heckscher-Ohlin-Samuelson result that free trade of goods tends to bring about equalization of factor rewards among countries, even if international capital mobility and migration is restricted. Free international factor mobility is a perfect substitute for free trade in commodities, in the sense that global production and consumption will be the same in both cases. The prediction from these results is obvious. Trade barriers stimulate international mobility of labor and capital, whereas restrictions on the international mobility of these factors stimulate trade in goods.

4.   Mundell's Contributions in Retrospect

In retrospect, Mundell's theory of stabilization policy undoubtedly has its limitations. The original Mundell-Fleming model, as in all macroeconomic research at the time, made highly simplified assumptions about the importance of expectations in financial markets; it also assumed complete price rigidity in the short run. These limitations have been addressed. Dornbusch (1976) for example, showed that gradual price adjustment and rational expectations can be incorporated into the analysis without significantly changing the results.

Neither Mundell's short-run analysis nor his dynamic models are derived from rigorous microeconomic foundations. They disregard, for instance, the intertemporal aspect of firms' and households' decisions. This is a drawback particularly in fiscal policy analysis, where it precludes adequate analyses of the effects of budget deficits—which sometimes weaken rather than strengthen the exchange rate (contrary to the predictions of the Mundell-Fleming model).

Later research has addressed these shortcomings as well. In a recent and noteworthy monograph, Obstfeld and Rogoff (1996) demonstrate how models with better microeconomic foundations and rational expectations can be used to study the effects of stabilization policy originally examined by Mundell; the authors are careful to point out the extent to which their results coincide with Mundell's. In its dynamic orientation, the "new open economy macroeconomics" is obviously influenced by the Mundellian tradition. New modeling techniques have not really replaced the Mundell-Fleming model, however, which —in its modern incarnation—remains the workhorse for policy-oriented analysis.

As indicated above, Mundell's approach to the problem of optimum currency areas is still very influential, both among academics and policymakers. In addition to the approach, in general, his emphasis on labor mobility remains particularly relevant today.

5. Summary

Robert Mundell has established the foundation for the theory that still dominates in practical considerations of monetary and fiscal policy in open economies. His work on monetary dynamics and optimum currency areas has inspired generations of researchers. Although dating back several decades, Mundell's contributions remain outstanding and constitute the core of teaching in international macroeconomics.

Mundell's research has had such a far-reaching and lasting impact because it combines formal—but still accessible—analysis, intuitive interpretation, and results with immediate policy applications. Above all, Mundell chose his problems with uncommon—almost prophetic—accuracy in terms of anticipating the future development of international monetary arrangements and international capital markets. Mundell's contributions serve as an excellent illustration of the value of basic research. At a given point in time, academic achievements may seem rather esoteric; not long afterward, however, they may take on great practical importance.

—Torsten Persson for the Nobel Prize Committee for Economic Sciences
Reprinted by permission of the Royal Swedish Academy of Sciences from http://www.nobel.se/announcement-99/economics99.html

6. References

Dornbusch, R. (1976). "Expectations and Exchange Rate Dynamics." *Journal of Political Economy* 84: 1161–1176.

Frenkel, J.A., and Johnson, H.G. (eds.) (1976). *The Monetary Approach to the Balance* of *Payments*. London: Allen and Unwin.

Fleming, J.M. (1962). "Domestic Financial Policies under Fixed and under Floating Exchange Rates." *IMF Staff Papers* 9: 369–379.

Kenen, P.B. (1969). "The Theory of Optimum Currency Areas: An Eclectic View." In Mundell, R.A., and Swoboda, A.K. (eds.), *Monetary Problems of the International Economy.* Chicago: University of Chicago Press.

Kouri, P.K. (1976). "The Exchange Rate and the Balance of Payments in the Short Run and in the Long Run." *Scandinavian Journal of Economics* 78: 280–304.

McKinnon, R.I. (1963). "Optimum Currency Areas." *American Economic Review* 53: 717–724.

Mundell, R.A. (1957). "International Trade and Factor Mobility." *American Economic Review* 47: 321–355.

Mundell, R.A. (1960). "The Monetary Dynamics of International Adjustment under Fixed and Flexible Exchange Rates." *Quarterly Journal of Economics* 74: 227–257.

Mundell, R.A. (1961). "A Theory of Optimum Currency Areas." *American Economic Review* 51: 657–665.

Mundell, R.A. (1962). "The Appropriate Use of Monetary and Fiscal Policy for Internal and External Stability." *IMF Staff Papers* 9: 70–79.

Mundell, R.A. (1963a). "Capital Mobility and Stabilization Policy under Fixed and Flexible Exchange Rates." *Canadian Journal of Economics* 29: 475–485.

Mundell, R.A. (1963b). "Inflation and Real Interest." *Journal of Political Economy* 71: 280–283.

Mundell, R.A. (1968). *International Economics.* New York: Macmillan.

Mundell, R.A. (1971). *Monetary Theory.* Pacific Palisades: Goodyear.

Obstfeld, M., and Rogoff, K. (1996). *Foundations of International Macroeconomics.* Cambridge, MA: MIT Press.

Scandinavian Journal of Economics 78 (1976), no. 2.

Tobin, J. (1965). "Money and Economic Growth." *Econometrica* 33: 671–684.

Introduction

The chapters that make up this volume originated as papers for a conference honoring Robert A. Mundell on his sixty-fifth birthday, including several papers that were prepared in Bob's honor but could not be presented because of a crowded agenda. The conference took place on October 23 and 24, 1997, on the premises of the World Bank and the International Monetary Fund. The venue was appropriate in view of Mundell's early association with the Fund's research department and his influence on the fundamental theoretical paradigms used today by everyone involved in trade and open macro policy. The timing was apt as well. Bob's birthday coincided with a massive speculative attack on the Hong Kong currency board dollar link—one that was beaten off in the end, but not before the Hong Kong stock market and stock markets around the world had taken a considerable bath.

Why did high officers of the Fund and Bank pause in the midst of a global financial crisis to join in honoring Bob Mundell? The answer is simple. As a writer and a teacher, Mundell has had as much impact on international economics as any postwar scholar. His analytical contributions to the field are on a par with those of Kindleberger, Meade, and Samuelson, all of whom were his teachers. International crises come, unfortunately, and fortunately go, but the occasion to honor properly an international economist of Mundell's stature is a much rarer event. Mundell's achievements were recognized on a bigger stage two years later when he was awarded the 1999 Nobel prize in economic sciences.

The chapters that follow range over many of Mundell's interests, including open-economy macro, international economic organization, trade, and history. Among the chapters' authors are many of Mundell's academic children, grandchildren, and great-grandchildren, as well as leading scholars of distinct lineage.

The lead chapter, by Caroline Betts and Michael Devereux, looks at a classical Mundellian theme, the effects of monetary and fiscal policy. The setting is different from the one Mundell explored in his own work. The framework includes imperfectly competitive producers in a two-country dynamic general equilibrium model typical of recent innovative approaches to open-economy macroeconomics. Betts and Devereux find that monetary surprises cause persistent movements in real exchange rates, the terms of trade, consumption, output, and the trade balance. They show that their class of models can give an empirically plausible account of cross-country output and consumption correlations, real exchange rate persistence, and the high variability of real exchange rates and terms of trade compared to that of output. A key message of the analysis: the choice of invoicing currency by exporters—domestic or foreign—has a huge impact on the international effects of monetary policy; invoicing, however, matters little for the effects of fiscal policy. The situation is reversed with regard to the completeness of asset markets, which matters for fiscal policy but not for monetary policy.

The role of gold in the international monetary system is another topic with which Mundell has famously associated himself. In chapter 2, Michael Bordo and Barry Eichengreen chronicle the vicissitudes of gold as an element in the international system, arguing that the gold-exchange standard was supported in the past by political factors largely absent today. They present evidence of a negative effect on the central bank demand for gold of floating exchange rates and higher international capital mobility; they explain continuing holding of gold by monetary authorities as the result of inertia and network externalities. Accelerating official sales of gold since the Mundell conference seem to bear out the message of this chapter.

Having pioneered the analysis of exchange rate regime choice in terms of optimum currency areas, Mundell has not been a supporter of the floating rates that emerged in the early 1970s and was an early advocate of the single European currency that has finally been launched. In chapter 3, Roberto Chang and Andrés Velasco take up an aspect of the choice of exchange rate regime that is not emphasized in Mundell's work but that has been highlighted by recent currency crises. Their chapter analyzes the links among bank fragility, the chosen monetary arrangements, and the vulnerability of the financial sector to collapse. They compare currency board arrangements, a fixed-exchange-rate-cum-domestic-lender-of-last-resort model, and a floating exchange rate. They find that in their model, a combination of flexible exchange rates with a domestic lender of last resort welfare-dominates other regimes by precluding internal as well as external crises.

Rudiger Dornbusch and Holger Wolf provide in chapter 4 a comparative analysis of European monetary reforms from 1945 to 1959, motivated in part by the situation facing the former Soviet bloc "tran sition" economies after their emergence from communist rule. They focus on the elimination of large monetary overhangs and argue that in the short run, avoidance of hyperinflation required "a courageous dissolution of the inherited *stock* imbalances"—for example, by blocking deposits and the forcible conversion of short-term government liabilities into long-term ones. Longer-term success, Dornbusch and Wolf argue, depended on durable fiscal restraint and structural reforms.

In chapter 5, Barry Eichengreen and Andrew Rose offer an empirical contribution on emerging-market banking crises. An outpouring of recent literature has analyzed the causes and consequences of banking problems in broad samples of countries. Eichengreen and Rose restrict their focus to developing countries, but not to developing countries experiencing banking problems. They find that vulnerabilities in domestic financial systems, coupled with adverse global economic conditions, tend to lead to banking crises. In particular, industrialized country interest rates tend to rise sharply in the year preceding banking crises. There is also some evidence of a role for the OECD business cycle in generating crises. Eichengreen and Rose conclude that there is much weaker evidence for the view that domestic macroeconomic mismanagement is the prime source of banking crisis risk.

Robert Flood and Nancy Marion present another perspective on international financial instability in their wide-ranging and comprehensive survey of theories and empirical work on currency crises, which appears as chapter 6 of the volume. In addition to summarizing what has been done, they present new results, deriving the optimal degree of commitment to a currency peg within a framework that draws from both "first-generation" and "second-generation" approaches to modeling crises. Their cross-generational framework stresses the important role of speculators and also recognizes that other policy goals constrain the government's commitment to a fixed exchange rate.

Mundell has not shied away from giving policy advice during his career, both in the monetary realm and with respect to supply-side fiscal measures. In chapter 7, Francesco Giavazzi and Alberto Giovannini ask why the interaction between economists and policy makers over macro stabilization issues often is so much more fruitful than their interaction over structural microeconomic issues. The question is inspired in part by the current situation in Europe, where forms of fiscal and monetary discipline have for years been enshrined in the Maastricht Treaty but the critical topic of labor market flexibility, central to Mundell's optimum currency area discussion, is barely on the table. Drawing on the experience of Italian reform, Giavazzi and Giovannini argue that small interest groups, inherently difficult to circumvent in the political process, cause large micro distortions. They also point to inertia in the functions of government. They propose that economists should participate in debates over reform as strategic players, not just as dispassionate cost-benefit analysts.

Mundell's 1957 article in the *American Economic Review* highlighted the connection between international factor mobility and trade. The empirics of that connection is the ultimate subject of chapter 8, by Linda Goldberg and Michael Klein. The authors start by developing a theoretical model of the effects of foreign direct investment (FDI) on the sectoral allocation of factors of production. Using disaggregated sectoral data from several Latin American countries, they next study the empirical effects of FDI on the allocation of labor and capital across industries. Their analysis suggests that for some sectors, inward FDI leads to an expansion of manufacturing trade, whereas for other sectors, FDI leads to trade contraction. These effects vary by country.

In chapter 9, Matthew Jones and Maurice Obstfeld revisit historical pre–World War II current account data for thirteen countries, which they revise to reflect a consistent accounting of the ambiguous role of international gold flows. The revised data, which are available on the home page of the National Bureau of Economic Research (http://www.nber.org), incorporate a theoretically coherent separation of monetary from nonmonetary gold flows in historical current account data. Jones and Obstfeld apply their adjusted data to examine the long-run link between saving and investment under alternative monetary and capital market conditions. Regressions along the lines of Feldstein and Horioka reveal significant cross-sectional saving-investment correlations over some spans of the classical gold standard. The relationship becomes much stronger after World War I, however, with an apparent interregnum during the fleeting attempt to restore the international gold standard after 1925.

The volume returns to the pure theory of international trade in chapter 10 with a chapter by Ronald Jones and Henryk Kierzkowski on the international fragmentation of production processes. The Jones-Kierzkowski model follows up on Mundell's early writing on factor mobility (as well as on Jones's own early contributions) by exploring the implications of trade in factors of production and intermediate goods. The authors find that the effects of fragmentation on the internal distribution of income and on national income levels are complex. Some factors, and even entire countries, may lose. However, even when fragmentation lowers the wage-rental ratio, it can also have effects akin to those of general technological progress, raising the real wage absolutely.

Philip Lane returns to the "new open-economy macroeconomics" in chapter 11. Lane's chapter is an empirical contribution to the literature inspired by the basic Mundell-Fleming open-economy macromodel. Lane develops an intertemporal model of a small open economy in which sticky domestic prices are set by imperfectly competitive producers. The model allows monetary disturbances to generate movements in the current account, but in contrast to the Mundell-Fleming framework, tracks the dynamic implications for the international net asset position. Using a vector-autoregressive model identified through structural restrictions, Lane estimates monetary shocks econometrically and shows that they have had a significant role for the U.S. current account.

Chapter 12, by Ronald McKinnon, begins by asking how Mundell evolved into a fierce advocate of currency union, starting from the more balanced view on the costs and benefits of currency union expressed in his "Optimum Currency Areas" article of 1961. McKinnon argues that this striking transformation in Mundell's outlook—accomplished over less than a decade—reflected a newer, "forward-looking" mode of thought. At a 1970 conference in Madrid, McKinnon recalls, Mundell presented two papers, one of them a plan for European currency union based on a single currency to be called the "Europa." The other was an analytical piece arguing (presciently but controversially in light of subsequent literature) that fixed exchange rates can come close, despite incomplete asset markets, to producing the optimal international allocation of risk that complete forward-looking securities markets can achieve. Disturbed by the currency-market instability of the late 1960s, Mundell by 1970 also took a much more alarmist view of the costs of exchange volatility than he had a decade before. The extreme currency volatility that forward-looking expectations can produce has been a constant theme in the work of Mundell's academic progeny, work that largely grew out of the flex-price dynamic framework of Mundell's *Monetary Theory*, a very different book from its largely Keynesian predecessor volume, *International Economics*. In light of the realization of Mundell's once remote monetary goal for Europe, McKinnon goes on in this chapter to discuss the euro's prospects and the desirability of a dollar-based common monetary standard in East Asia.

In his 1960 *Quarterly Journal of Economics* article on the dynamics of adjustment under alternative exchange regimes, Mundell proposed a theory of balance-of-payments crises in which speculators' assessment of the evolution of key economic variables determines confidence in the currency. Enrique Mendoza and Martín Uribe examine in chapter 13 the quantitative implications of Mundell's account from the perspective of a dynamic general equilibrium model in which speculative devaluation probabilities reflect rational expectations. The model explains key features of the process of real currency appreciation and widening external deficits that often predates collapses of fixed exchange rates.

Shouyong Shi revisits another distinctive Mundellian theme, the employment effects of import tariffs, in chapter 14. His innovative framework is a nonmonetary intertemporal optimization model in which the process of job search in the labor market is explicitly modeled. In that framework a tariff raises the terms of trade but also raises the reservation wage and thus may lower employment in both the short and long runs, contrary to the typical presumption that tariffs raise levels of employment. Shi concludes that even with persistent unemployment, tariff increases may be highly counterproductive as a policy to combat joblessness.

The final chapter, by John Taylor, focuses on questions related to Mundell's research on the fiscal-monetary policy mix. Taylor asks first whether a central bank's interest rate rule should respond to real variables such as unemployment or real growth. He goes on to look at the advisability of assigning fiscal policy to real variables if monetary policy is constrained (for example, by law) from reacting to nonfinancial variables. Within a multicountry simulation model along Mundell-Fleming lines, Taylor finds that interest rate rules that respond to real variables lead to better macroeconomic performance. He concludes that fiscal policy could compensate in principle were the central bank barred from reacting to real variables, but the fiscal adjustments required would be too sharp to be made promptly in practice.

Though they cover a broad variety of Bob Mundell's economic interests and contributions, the fifteen chapters in this volume leave untouched numerous other areas in which Bob's writings have inspired key scholarship or policy advice. Paradoxically, part of the reason is simply the fruitfulness of the ideas themselves. For example, the high volume of empirical work on optimum currency areas in the runup to the euro's introduction made it difficult come up with a single piece on the subject distinctive enough to merit inclusion! Notwithstanding its failure to do justice to Mundell's entire *oeuvre*, the editors hope this book will convey to readers some sense of how deeply he has shaped modern open-economy macroeconomics.

1

The International Effects of Monetary and Fiscal Policy in a Two-Country Model

Caroline Betts and
Michael B. Devereux

Introduction

In Mundell 1968 (chap. 18), Robert Mundell develops a model of the international transmission effects of monetary and fiscal policy shocks in a two-country version of what is now known as the Mundell-Fleming model. Mundell shows that under floating exchange rates, positive monetary policy innovations tend to have a "beggar-thy-neighbor" effect, raising domestic output but, through the effects of real depreciation, lowering foreign output. On the other hand, fiscal policy shocks tend to increase output in both countries.

The intuition behind the Mundell model remains at the center of a vast literature on the international policy transmission mechanism that has developed in the decades since floating exchange rates became a reality. It formed the background for the celebrated Dornbusch (1976) model. Extended versions of the model were used heavily in the mid-1980s to study the problems of international macroeconomic policy coordination (e.g., McKibbin and Sachs 1986). More recently, Taylor (1993) used a further extended Mundell-type model in an empirical analysis of international monetary policy in a multicountry environment.

Although the Mundell-Fleming model has remained highly influential in both academic and policy circles, developments in macroeconomics beginning in the late 1970s questioned the use of models in which the underlying preferences and technology were not fully specified and long-run budget constraints were not satisfied. The reworking of macroeconomic models to encompass dynamic economic theory is now at an advanced stage. But only recently have open-economy macroeconomists reached the stage where they can readdress Mundell's questions within a more modern framework. An important paper in this regard is that of Obstfeld and Rogoff (1995)[1] (henceforth OR). They argue that to understand short-run macroeconomics in the open economy, it is important to move beyond the Mundell-Fleming model toward a dynamic, utility-maximizing framework, where long-run budget constraints are satisfied.

This chapter develops the OR agenda in the direction of readdressing the issues analyzed in Mundell 1968. We set up a two-country, dynamic general equilibrium model in which prices adjust only slowly and investigate the main characteristics of the international macroeconomic transmission mechanism within this framework. We explore two important dimensions of the model: (a) the currency of export price invoicing, and (b) the degree of completeness of assets markets. In particular, we develop a framework in which export prices may be set in terms of the foreign currency (which we call "pricing-to-market"), rather than in domestic currency, as assumed by Mundell 1968 and OR. Since prices are sticky, this produces deviations from the law of one price (LOOP), which is consistent with the strong recent evidence of deviations from LOOP in traded goods (e.g., Engel and Rogers 1996). The model's second key feature is that we allow the structure of international asset markets to vary between an environment of complete markets, in which there is perfect cross-country coinsurance, and a more limited asset markets environment, in which noncontingent bonds are the only asset that may be traded across countries.

We first set out some stylized facts concerning the monetary policy transmission mechanism using G-7 data. We show that empirically, positive U.S. monetary policy shocks tend to raise output in both the United States and other G-7 countries. That is, monetary policy has positive international transmission effects on output. In addition, we show that a positive U.S. monetary policy disturbance causes a persistent real exchange rate depreciation and a persistent fall in U.S. short-term interest rates relative to G-7 interest rates.

We may summarize our results in two parts. First, the theoretical analysis of the policy transmission mechanism reveals a sharp dichotomy between the importance of the invoicing currency (or pricing-to-market) and the importance of asset market incompleteness. We find that for the analysis of the international monetary transmission mechanism, the structure of assets markets has very little importance. The monetary transmission mechanism differs only slightly between the complete markets environment and the incomplete markets environment. On the other hand, the degree of pricing-to-market is critical to the monetary transmission mechanism. The effects of monetary policy on output, consumption, the real exchange rate, and the terms of trade are all reversed when we move from a situation of domestic currency export price invoicing to a situation of pricing-to-market.

In the analysis of fiscal policy, we find by contrast that the degree of pricing-to-market is of very little consequence. The international transmission effects of fiscal spending are not sensitive to the currency of export price invoicing. All major aggregates move both qualitatively and quantitatively in the same way under either pricing regime in response to fiscal spending shocks. However, the structure of international asset markets is critical to the analysis of the transmission of fiscal spending. We find that with complete international asset markets, fiscal spending shocks have no real or nominal exchange rate effects and no terms-of-trade effects at all. Moreover, with complete asset markets, fiscal spending shocks have an identical impact on consumption and output for all countries. But with limited international asset markets, a domestic fiscal spending expansion will cause a terms-of-trade deterioration and a real and nominal exchange rate depreciation and also cause domestic and foreign consumption and output to move in opposite directions. Thus the degree of international insurance available in assets markets is of central importance to the effects of fiscal policy transmission.

The second aspect of our results concerns the match between our empirical results on the international monetary transmission mechanism and the findings of our theoretical model. We argue that the version of the model with pricing-to-market does a good job of matching the basic stylized facts of the international monetary policy transmission mechanism as documented by vector auto-regression (VAR) results. With pricing-to-market, monetary policy shocks tend to produce a positive comovement of output across countries, a persistent real exchange rate depreciation, and a decrease in the international interest rate differential.

The chapter is organized as follows. The next section gives our empirical results, and the following section develops the basic model. Subsequent sections discuss calibration, report the quantitative results of the model, and offer some conclusions.

Empirical Evidence

The chapter's goal is to establish both empirical evidence and a theoretical model concerning the international transmission of macroeconomic policy. In this section, we present some empirical evidence regarding the effects of monetary policy shocks on output levels, real exchange rates, and interest rates.[2]

We use monthly, seasonally adjusted data from the IMF's International Financial Statistics database for the G-7 countries on industrial production, interest rates, aggregate (CPI) price indices, and bilateral nominal exchange rates with the United States. Using the data for six countries—Canada, France, Germany, Italy, Japan, and the United Kingdom—we then construct a simple G-7 aggregate industrial production index, an average price level, an average short-term, market-based nominal interest rate, and an average nominal bilateral exchange rate with the United States. We also employ U.S. data for each of the first four of these variables and two measures of U.S. monetary policy instruments: nonborrowed reserves of the Federal Reserve system and the federal funds rate. Using the aggregate foreign price index, the U.S. price index, and the average nominal exchange rate of the G-7 aggregate, we construct a multilateral "real exchange rate" between the G-7 aggregate and the United States.

We construct and estimate two vector auto-regressions for the purpose of examining the conditional correlation between two measures of orthogonal shocks to U.S. monetary policy and the interest rates of both the United States and the G-7 aggregate, the real exchange rate between the United States and the G-7 aggregate, and the output levels of the United States and the G-7 aggregate.

We employ a perfectly standard methodology for estimating and identifying the VARs in which the innovation to each variable is orthogonalized, and we omit a full description of it here.[3] The basic idea is that we estimate a reduced-form VAR, then identify the Choleski decomposition of this VAR, in which all shocks (including the monetary policy shock) are orthogonalized and in which the monetary shock is ordered first in the empirical model. In other words, we identify an empirical model in which orthogonal shocks to U.S. monetary policy instruments may be construed as exogenous policy innovations, in the sense that the Fed sets values for these shocks independent of current information on outputs, interest rates, and the real exchange rate between the United States and the G-7 aggregate but conditional on all information on lagged values of these variables.

The two VARs that we estimate are specified as follows. The first is specified in the following vector of endogenous variables, which are ordered as indicated in the vector $\mathbf{X} = [NBR, I - I^*, Y, Y^*, RER]'$. Here,

NBR denotes nonborrowed reserves of the U.S. Federal Reserve, *I* and *I** denote the U.S. and G-7 aggregate short-term net nominal interest rates, *Y* and *Y** are U.S. and G-7 aggregate industrial production indices, and *RER* = *EP**/*P* denotes the real exchange rate of the United States with respect to the G-7 aggregate. In particular, *E* is the U.S. dollar price of a unit of G-7 aggregate currency, *P* and *P** are the U.S. and G-7 aggregate consumer price indices respectively, and *RER* is therefore the U.S. consumption goods price of a G-7 aggregate consumption good. All variables are in natural logarithms, except the nominal interest rate differential, which is a level. The second VAR is specified in the vector of endogenous variables **X** = [*FF*, *I**, *Y*, *Y**, *RER*]'. Here, *FF* denotes the Federal Funds Rate and *I** denotes the G-7 aggregate short-term, market-based net nominal interest rate.

In addition, all variables are Hodrick-Prescott filtered, and both VARs are estimated with an optimized (by standard criteria) lag length of four. In choosing to H-P filter the data, we are assuming that each of the variables in the VAR is likely to be characterized by a stochastic trend component. Obviously, there are many potential pitfalls in applying the H-P filter, especially if the variables are actually stationary. For example, Cogley and Nason (1995) present results indicating that the H-P filter induces correlation and business cycle dynamics even if none are present in the original data. Equally, however, there are many pitfalls involved in actually testing for stochastic nonstationarity and assuming a VAR specification based on, for example, first-differencing the data and possibly incorporating error correction terms to account for estimated cointegrating vectors between the relevant series. These pitfalls are largely associated with the power properties of such tests.

We choose to employ the H-P filter so as to maintain consistency with data typically used to evaluate business cycle models. We feel that it is unlikely that our variables are cointegrated (for example, because of the presence of productivity trends in the output or real exchange rate series). Estimating the same VARs using first-differenced data did not change the results qualitatively, although the impulse response functions, which map out the dynamic effects for each of the endogenous variables of money shocks, exhibited greater variability.

Figures 1.1a–1.1d and figures 1.2a–1.2d illustrate the results that we obtain for the first and second VAR specifications, respectively. These are the impulse response functions for the real exchange rate, the relevant interest rate variable, and industrial outputs to a one-standard-deviation expansionary innovation to the relevant monetary policy

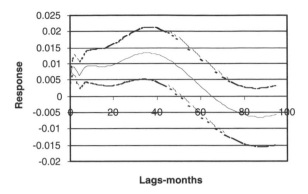

Figure 1.1a
EP^*/P response to U.S. money shock

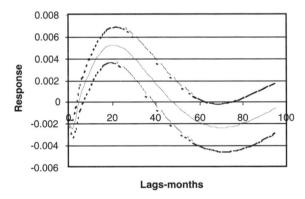

Figure 1.1b
Y response to U.S. money shock

instrument. Clearly the qualitative and even the quantitative features of the responses of interest rates, industrial output levels, and the real exchange rate are virtually identical across the two specifications. First, a large, persistent, and significant real exchange rate depreciation is associated with either monetary impulse (a one-standard-deviation positive innovation to NBR and a one-standard-deviation negative innovation to the federal funds rate). Second, a positive innovation to *NBR* has a large and significant "liquidity effect" on the nominal interest differential, whereas a negative innovation to the federal funds rate has a large and significant liquidity effect on the G-7 aggregate interest rate. Third, U.S. output first experiences a very small and barely

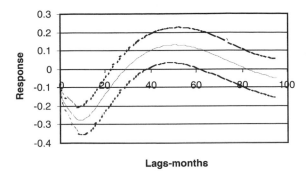

Figure 1.1c
$I - I^*$ response to U.S. money shock

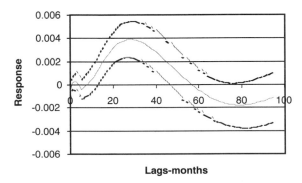

Figure 1.1d
Y^* response to U.S. money shock

significant initial decline that is immediately reversed, and becomes a positive and highly significant increase.[4] Finally, it is evident that in either specification of monetary policy shocks, the foreign output response, although delayed for a period of six to eight months, is ultimately positive and significant.

We found these responses to be robust to several changes in ordering of the endogenous variables and to alternative specifications of the model. In particular, we found that when we estimated the same VARs separately for each G-7 country in relation to the United States, we obtained results qualitatively identical to those that we report here.[5]

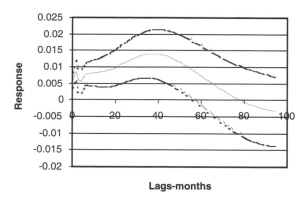

Figure 1.2a
EP^*/P response to U.S. money shock

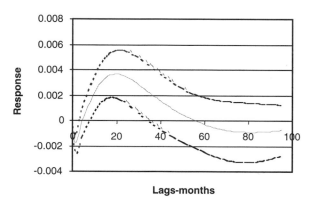

Figure 1.2b
Y response to U.S. money shock

Based on earlier empirical work of our own (Betts and Devereux 1996, 1998) as well as that of others (Eichenbaum and Evans 1995 and Schlagenhauf and Wrase 1995) and the additional results that we have reported here, we regard the positive output responses, real exchange rate depreciation, and liquidity effects for interest rates following monetary policy innovations as stylized facts to be accounted for by any good model of the international monetary policy transmission mechanism. We now develop a model that, among other things, can account for the positive output transmission of monetary policy shocks.

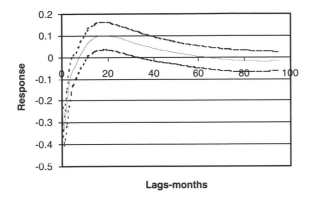

Figure 1.2c
$I - I^*$ response to U.S. money shock

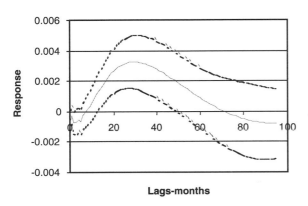

Figure 1.2d
Y^* response to U.S. money shock

A Two-Country Model of the Policy Transmission Mechanism

Modern approaches to the analysis of international macroeconomic policy transmission rely heavily on formal modeling of the type developed in OR. In this section we develop a model that can be used to explore the questions posed by Mundell, except that it is based explicitly on formal utility and profit maximization in an intertemporal setting, and the imposition of intertemporal budget constraints on all agents.

The model has two countries, which we denote "home" and "foreign." Within each country exist consumers, firms, and a government. Government spends directly on goods and services and issues fiat money. To keep the analysis simple, we will not formally distinguish between the central bank and the fiscal authority.

We assume that there is continuum of goods varieties in the world economy of measure 1 and that the relative size of the home and foreign economy's share of these goods is n and $(1 - n)$, respectively. We choose units so that the populations of the home and foreign country are also n and $(1 - n)$, respectively. In addition, in each country, a fraction s of goods varieties are invoiced in the currency of the buyer, and the remaining $(1 - s)$ goods varieties are priced in the currency of the seller. As we describe in greater detail below, firms that produce s goods varieties are also assumed to be able to segment markets, country by country, whereas firms that produce $(1 - s)$ goods varieties cannot. Thus it is possible for the prices of s goods in the home and foreign market to exhibit deviations from LOOP, whereas the prices of $(1 - s)$ goods must always satisfy LOOP.

Let the state of the world be defined as z_t. In each period t, there is a finite set of possible states of the world. Let z^t denote the history of realized states between time 0 and t, that is, $z^t = \{z_0, z_1, \ldots, z_t\}$. The probability of any history, z_t, is denoted by $\pi(z^t)$.

Typically, we will write the features of the model for the home country economy alone. The conditions for the foreign country are analogously defined in all cases, except those that are explicitly derived.

Consumers

We assume that preferences are identical across countries. In the home country, consumers have preferences given by

$$EU = \sum_{t=0}^{\infty} \sum_{z^t} \beta^t \pi(z^t) U\left(C(z^t), \frac{M(z^t)}{P(z^t)}, (1 - h(z^t))\right),$$

(1.1)

where

$$C(z^t) = \left(\int_0^1 c(i, z^t)^{1-1/p} di\right)^{p/(p-1)},$$

and

$$c(i, z^t) = \left(\sum_0^N x(i, j, z^t)^{1-1/\lambda}\right)^{\lambda/(\lambda-1)}.$$

In addition, we assume the specific functional form given by

$$U\left(C, \frac{M}{P}, 1-h\right) = \frac{C^{1-\sigma}}{1-\sigma} + \frac{\varsigma}{1-\varepsilon}\left(\frac{M}{P}\right)^{1-\varepsilon} + \eta \ln(1-h).$$

The consumer derives utility from a composite consumption good $C(z^t)$, real home-country money balances $M(z^t)/P(z^t)$, and leisure, where $h(z^t)$ represents hours worked. The composite consumption good is an aggregate of a continuum of differentiated varieties, where $c(i, z^t)$ represents the consumption of variety i. Within each variety, there is a further disaggregation into N types, so that $x(i, j, z^t)$ represents the consumption of variety i, type j good. We introduce types of good within each variety in order to allow for a distinction between two key parameters in the model: the elasticity of substitution between home and foreign goods and the parameter governing price markups over marginal costs.

Households also value real home-currency money balances, where the home CPI is defined as

$$P(z^t) = \left[\int_0^n p(i, z^t)^{1-\rho} di + \int_n^{n+(1-n)s} p^*(i, z^t)^{1-\rho} di \right.$$
$$\left. + \int_{n+(1-n)s}^1 \left(e(z^t)q^*(i, z^t)\right)^{1-\rho} di \right]^{1/(1-\rho)}.$$

The CPI depends on the price of n home goods and $1 - n$ foreign goods. Of these foreign goods, s goods are priced in domestic currency and have prices denoted $p^*(i, z^t)$, and $1 - s$ goods are priced in foreign currency and satisfy LOOP, so that the home-country price must be $e(z^t)q^*(i, z^t)$, where $e(z^t)$ is the exchange rate (price of foreign currency), and $q^*(i, z^t)$ is the foreign-country price of variety i. Within each variety, there is a further subprice index defined as

$$p(i, z^t) = \left[\sum_0^N p(i, j, z^t)^{1-\lambda}\right]^{1/(1-\lambda)}.$$

The representative consumer in the home country receives income in wages from employment, rents from holdings of physical capital, profits from the ownership of domestic firms, and income from asset holdings and existing money balances, and accepts transfers and/or pays taxes to the domestic government. Households then consume, accumulate capital and money balances, and purchase new assets.

We explore the consequences of two asset market structures. In the first type, there exist full and complete state-contingent asset markets. Agents can buy nominal state-contingent bonds. The home-country budget constraints are then written as

$$P(z^t)C(z^t) + M(z^t) + \sum_{z^{t+1}} w(z^{t+1}, z^t)b(z^{t+1}) + P(z^t)V(z^t)$$

$$= W(z^t)h(z^t) + R(z^t)K(z^t) + \Pi(z^t) + M(z^{t-1}) + b(z^t) + TR(z^t), \tag{1.2}$$

where

$$K(z^t) = \phi\left(\frac{V(z^{t-1})}{K(z^{t-1})}\right)K(z^{t-1}) + (1 - \delta)K(z^{t-1}). \tag{1.3}$$

The home consumer purchases a portfolio of state-contingent home-currency-denominated nominal bonds at price $w(z^{t+1}, z^t)$. In addition, she purchases a composite investment good $V(z^t)$, which requires the same basket of goods as the consumption index and forms next period's capital holdings. Since the investment good is constructed in the same way that the composite consumption good is, they have the identical composite price $P(z^t)$. The consumer also receives net transfers $TR(z^t)$ from the government and nominal, domestic currency profits from all domestic firms, which are denoted by $\Pi(z^t)$. In addition, $R(z^t)$ denotes the nominal rental return on a unit of capital, and δ denotes the depreciation rate of capital.

Investment is used to accumulate household capital according to equation (1.3). Accumulating capital is subject to adjustment costs. An increase in investment of one unit raises the next-period capital by $\phi'(.) < 1$ units. The function $\phi(.)$ must satisfy the conditions $\phi'(.) > 0$ and $\phi''(.) < 0$.

In the second type of asset market structure, following OR, we assume that the only assets that can be traded are non-state-contingent one-period home-currency-denominated nominal bonds. In this economy, the home consumer's budget constraint is written as

$$P(z^t)C(z^t) + M(z^t) + w(z^t)B(z^t) + P(z^t)V(z^t) = \tag{1.4}$$
$$W(z^t)h(z^t) + R(z^t)K(z^t) + \Pi(z^t) + M(z^{t-1}) + B(z^{t-1}) + TR(z^t),$$

again subject to equation (1.3), where $w(z^t)$ is the time t nominal bond price. The key difference between (1.3) and (1.4) is that in the latter, the consumer can smooth out the effects of income fluctuations only over time and not across states of the world.

The consumer's optimal consumption, money holdings, investment, and labor supply may be described by the following familiar conditions. First, in the complete markets environment we have the following conditions

$$w(z^{t+1}, z^t)C(z^t)^{-\sigma} = \beta\pi(z^{t+1})\frac{P(z^t)}{P(z^{t+1})}C(z^{t+1})^{-\sigma}, \tag{1.5}$$

$$\frac{M(z^t)}{P(z^t)} = \left[\varsigma C(z^t)^{\sigma} \frac{1+i(z^t)}{i(z^t)} \right]^{1/\varepsilon}, \tag{1.6}$$

$$\frac{\eta}{1-h(z^t)} = \frac{W(z^t)}{P(z^t)C(z^t)^{\sigma}}, \tag{1.7}$$

$$\frac{C(z^t)^{-\sigma}}{\phi'\left(\frac{V(z^t)}{K(z^t)}\right)} = \beta\sum_{z^{t+1}}\pi(z^{t+1})C(z^{t+1})^{-\sigma}\left[\frac{R(z^{t+1})}{P(z^{t|1})} + J(z^{t+1}, z^t)\right], \tag{1.8}$$

where

$$J(z^{t+1}, z^t) = \frac{1}{\phi'\left(\frac{V(z^{t+1})}{K(z^{t+1})}\right)}\left[\phi\left(\frac{V(z^{t+1})}{K(z^{t+1})}\right) - \phi'\left(\frac{V(z^{t+1})}{K(z^{t+1})}\right)\frac{V(z^{t+1})}{K(z^{t+1})} + (1-\delta)\right].$$

Equation (1.5) describes the state-contingent choice of intertemporal consumption smoothing, and (1.6) gives the consumer's implied demand for money. The term $i(z^t)$ represents the nominal interest rate, where

$$\frac{1}{1+i(z^t)} = \sum_{z^{t+1}}w(z^{t+1}, z^t).$$

Equation (1.7) describes the labor supply choice, and (1.8) results from the optimal choice of investment in the presence of adjustment costs.

In the incomplete markets environment, equations (1.6), (1.7), and (1.8) continue to hold, where in (1.6), the nominal discount factor is now defined as

$$\frac{1}{1+i(z^t)} = w(z^t).$$

Equation (1.5) is replaced by

$$w(z^t)C(z^t)^{-\sigma} = \beta\sum_{z^{t+1}}\frac{P(z^t)}{P(z^{t+1})}C(z^{t+1})^{-\sigma}. \tag{1.9}$$

Cross-Country Consumption Insurance

The different asset market structures principally affect the possibilities for cross-country consumption insurance. In the complete markets environment, it is easy to establish that optimal risk sharing will imply

$$\frac{C(z^t)}{C^*(z^t)} = \Lambda \left(\frac{Q(z^t)e(z^t)}{P(z^t)} \right)^{1/\sigma}, \tag{1.10}$$

where Λ is a constant reflecting initial wealth differences. This says that if purchasing power parity (PPP) holds, then consumption levels are equated up to the constant Λ as agents confront identical commodity prices. Here Q represents the foreign price. Movements in the real exchange rate or departures from PPP, however, will be reflected in different consumption rates. Despite the presence of complete insurance markets, it is not efficient to fully equalize consumption rates across countries unless PPP holds. As we see below, the presence of pricing-to-market will lead to persistent deviations from PPP.

In the bond market economy, on the other hand, there is no possibility for state-contingent consumption insurance. However, the (home-currency) nominal interest rate facing domestic and foreign agents is equal. Thus, we have

$$
\begin{aligned}
w(z^t) &= \beta \sum\nolimits_{z^{t+1}} \pi(z^{t+1}) \frac{P(z^t)}{P(z^{t+1})} \frac{C(z^{t+1})^{-\sigma}}{C(z^t)^{-\sigma}} \\
&= \beta \sum\nolimits_{z^{t+1}} \pi(z^{t+1}) \frac{Q(z^t)}{Q(z^{t+1})} \frac{e(z^t)}{e(z^{t+1})} \frac{C^*(z^{t+1})^{-\sigma}}{C^*(z^t)^{-\sigma}}.
\end{aligned} \tag{1.11}
$$

Whereas in the complete markets economy, deviations from PPP determine cross-country differences in the levels of consumption, in the bond market economy they drive a wedge between home- and foreign-country consumption growth rates. This is the critical difference between the two asset market structures.

Government

Governments in each country print money, levy taxes and purchase goods to produce a composite government consumption good. To economize on notation, we assume the government does not issue bonds and so must always balance its within-period budget. It is assumed that the government composite good is produced using the same aggregator that private consumption and investment goods use. The home-country government budget constraint is then

$$M(z^t) - M(z^{t-1}) = P(z^t)G(z^t) + TR(z^t), \tag{1.12}$$

where $G(z^t)$ represents the government composite good. We assume that the share of government spending in GDP is set by policy at rate θ_t.

Firms

Firms in each country hire capital and labor to produce output. Each type of good of each variety has a separate, price-setting firm. The number of firms within each variety, N, is sufficiently large that each firm ignores the impact of its pricing decision on the aggregate price index for that variety. A firm of variety i, type j, has production function given by

$$y(i, j, z^t) = k(i, j, z^t)^\alpha \ell(i, j, z^t)^{1-\alpha} - v, \tag{1.13}$$

where $k(i, j, z^t)$ is capital usage and $\ell(i, j, z^t)$ is labor usage. Firms must also bear a fixed cost of production v.

All firms will choose factor bundles to minimize costs. Thus, we must have

$$W(z^t) = MC(z^t)(1-\alpha)\frac{y(i, j, z^t)}{\ell(i, j, z^t)}, \tag{1.14}$$

$$R(z^t) = MC(z^t)\alpha\frac{y(i, j, z^t)}{k(i, j, z^t)}, \tag{1.15}$$

where $MC(z^t)$ is nominal marginal cost, which must be equal for all firms within the home economy. From (1.13), (1.14), and (1.15), it is clear that all firms in the home economy will have the same capital-labor ratio.

Pricing

We assume that firms must set nominal prices in advance. There are two features to the price-setting mechanism. The first concerns the currency of pricing. As we noted above, a subset s of firms set prices in the buyer's currency. Thus a home firm in this category will set a price p for sale to home consumers but a price q, denominated in foreign currency, for sale to foreign consumers. An unanticipated change in the exchange rate will cause a deviation from LOOP, which would require that $p = eq$. To avoid the arbitrage opportunity that this deviation implies, the firm must be able to segment its home and foreign markets.

We denote this type of pricing behavior as pricing-to-market (PTM). The remaining $(1 - s)$ of firms are unable to segment their markets by country and must set a unified price. In this case, we assume they price in their home currency. Thus a home firm in this category will set its price p, the same price charged to both home and foreign consumers.

The second feature of price setting is the way in which prices adjust. Following Calvo (1983), Yun (1996), and Kimball (1996), we assume that firms change their prices at random intervals dictated by a Poisson arrival rate. Each sector changes its price with probability $(1 - \gamma)$ in any period. Thus the average time between price changes for any one firm is $1/(1 - \gamma)$. Then, by the law of large numbers, exactly $(1 - \gamma)$ times the number of sectors (and therefore firms) in the economy will be changing their price in any given period.

The exact price-setting problem that the firm faces will depend on the degree of market completeness. Take first the case of complete markets. Given preferences as stated above, the firm will at any period face a price elasticity of demand equal to λ. Since its current price choice will affect its future expected profits, the firm will face the problem of choosing prices to maximize state-contingent profits. Take the case of a PTM firm in the home economy. Its state-contingent profits, in present value, may be written as

$$\sum_{t=0}^{\infty} \sum_{z^t} \varphi(z^t)\gamma^t \big[p(i, j, z^t)x_d(i, j, z^t) + e(z^t)q(i, j, z^t)x_d^*(i, j, z^t) \\ - MC(z^t)\big(x_d(i, j, z^t) + x_d^*(i, j, z^t)\big)\big],$$

(1.16)

where

$$\varphi(z^t) = \prod_{j=1}^{t} w(z^j, z^{j-1}),$$

for $t = 1, 2, \ldots$, is the period 0 price of a delivery of \$1 in state z^t, with $\varphi(z^0) = 1$, and $x_d(i, j, z^t)$ is the demand schedule of firm i, j by home consumers, etc.

With incomplete markets, the appropriate objective function for the firm is less clear. We will assume that the firm chooses prices so as to maximize the expected present value of profits, using the market nominal discount factors.[6] The firm's objective function in this case is then

$$E_0 \sum_{t=0}^{\infty} \Omega(z^t) \gamma^t \big[p(i, j, z^t) x_d(i, j, z^t) + e(z^t) q(i, j, z^t) x_d^*(i, j, z^t)$$
$$- MC(z^t) \big(x_d(i, j, z^t) + x_d^*(i, j, z^t) \big) \big]$$

(1.17)

where

$$\Omega(z^t) = \prod_{j=1}^{t} w(z^{j-1}),$$

for $t = 1, 2, \ldots$, with $\Omega(z^0) = 1$.

A PTM firm that is changing its price in a given period t will choose its prices for the domestic and foreign markets p and q, respectively, to maximize (1.16) or (1.17), depending upon the asset market structure. From the structure of the model described above it is clear that each firm will face a constant price elasticity of demand equal to λ. Now define as $\tilde{p}(i, j, z^t)$ the price set by firm j, in sector i, when it newly sets its price at time t, given the history z^t. Choosing $\tilde{p}(i, j, z^t)$ to maximize (1.16) gives the condition

$$\tilde{p}(i, j, z^t) = \left(1 - \sum_{z^{t+1}} \omega(z^{t+1}, z^t) \right) \frac{\lambda}{\lambda - 1} MC(z^t)$$
$$+ \sum_{z^{t+1}} \omega(z^{t+1}, z^t) \tilde{p}(i, j, z^{t+1}),$$

(1.18)

where

$$\omega(z^{t+1}, z^t) = \frac{\gamma w(z^{t+1}, z^t) \sum_{k=t+1}^{\infty} \sum_{z^k} \varphi(z^k) \gamma^{k-t-1} x(i, j, z^k)}{\sum_{k=t}^{\infty} \sum_{z^k} \varphi(z^k) \gamma^{k-t} x(i, j, z^k)}.$$

That is, the optimal newly set price of the firm is a function of current and expected future marginal costs.

Likewise, the newly set price for the foreign market can be described by the condition

$$\tilde{q}(i, j, z^t) = \left(1 - \sum_{z^{t+1}} \vartheta(z^{t+1}, z^t) \right) \frac{\lambda}{\lambda - 1} \frac{MC(z^t)}{e(z^t)}$$
$$+ \sum_{z^{t+1}} \vartheta(z^{t+1}, z^t) \tilde{q}(i, j, z^{t+1}),$$

(1.19)

where

$$\vartheta(z^{t+1}, z^t) = \frac{\gamma w(z^{t+1}, z^t) \sum_{k=t+1}^{\infty} \sum_{z^k} \varphi(z^k) \gamma^{k-t-1} x^*(i, j, z^k)}{\sum_{k=t}^{\infty} \sum_{z^k} \varphi(z^k) \gamma^{k-t} x^*(i, j, z^k)}.$$

Note that in comparing (1.18) and (1.19), we see that in a perfectly deterministic environment, the firm would always set its price so that $\tilde{p} = e\tilde{q}$, that is, LOOP would hold. This results from the fact that the elasticity of demand is constant and the same in the home and foreign market. Furthermore, this will be true of all goods as a result of the symmetry across firms. As a result, in a deterministic environment without monetary or fiscal policy shocks, PPP will hold. But in the presence of exchange rate uncertainty, the newly set prices will show systematic deviations from LOOP.

Although we have examined only the case of a PTM firm in the home economy, it is clear that a non-PTM firm's price will be described solely by a condition similar to (1.18).

In the incomplete asset markets case, the pricing decision will be described exactly as in (1.18) and (1.19), save for the fact that the weights ω and ϑ will differ by the different definition of the discount factor. Since all our results are derived by linear approximation, this makes no difference in what follows.

The structure of firms is entirely symmetric, so it is clear that all home firms, in any sector, will set the same value of $\tilde{p}$ and $\tilde{q}$. In addition, for any sector i, we have the price given by (slightly abusing notation) $p_t(i) = (1 - \gamma)\tilde{p} + \gamma p_{t-1}(i)$. Then defining the home-country price index for home-priced goods as

$$p(z^t)^{1-\rho} = \int_0^n p(i, z^t)^{1-\rho} \, di$$

and using the law of large numbers, we see that

$$p(z^t)^{1-\rho} = (1-\gamma)\tilde{p}(z^t)^{1-\rho} + \gamma p(z^{t-1})^{1-\rho}. \tag{1.20}$$

In a parallel manner, if we define the index of prices of foreign-currency-invoiced goods by home-country sectors as

$$q(z^t)^{1-\rho} = \int_{n(1-s)}^{ns} q(i, z^t)^{1-\rho} \, di,$$

we may show that

$$q(z^t)^{1-\rho} = (1-\gamma)\tilde{q}(z^t)^{1-\rho} + \gamma q(z^{t-1})^{1-\rho}. \tag{1.21}$$

Market Clearing

Within a country, all firms use the same capital-labor ratio. Therefore we may aggregate across firms and sectors to define the aggregate output in the home economy as

$$y = K^\alpha h^{1-\alpha} - vN.$$

Output must equal aggregate demand for the home country. Total demand comes from the following sources. First, there is demand for the consumption goods of the non-PTM firms, by both home and foreign consumers. Then there is the demand for the consumption goods of the PTM firms by home consumers and foreign consumers separately. Second, there is demand for investment goods of both non-PTM and PTM firms. Finally, there is the demand by government for the output of all firms. The market-clearing equation for the home country may then be written (for ease of notation we ignore the state notation here)

$$(K^\alpha h^{1-\alpha} - vN) = (1-s)\left[\left(\frac{p}{P}\right)^{-\rho} n(C+V+G)\right.$$

$$+ \left(\frac{p}{eQ}\right)^{-\rho} (1-n)(C^* + V^* + G^*)\right]$$

$$+ s\left[\left(\frac{p}{P}\right)^{-\rho} n(C+V+G)\right.$$

$$+ \left(\frac{q}{Q}\right)^{-\rho} (1-n)(C^* + V^* + G^*)\right]. \tag{1.22}$$

The expression on the left-hand side gives the level of average output per capita for the home country. This is smaller the higher is the fixed cost per sector, vN. The first expression on the right-hand side indicates that demand for the non-PTM good depends on its price relative to the price the home consumer faces, P, and separately, the price the foreign consumer faces (in home-currency units), eQ. Here we are using the properties of demand implied by the constant elasticity of substitution (CES) aggregator for C, V, and G.[7] Likewise, for the PTM firms, the second expression indicates that demand depends on prices facing the home consumer and the foreign consumer separately.

A similar market-clearing equation holds for the foreign country:

$$\left(K^{*\alpha} h^{*1-\alpha} - vN\right) = (1-s)\left[\left(\frac{eq^*}{P}\right)^{-\rho} n(C+V+G)\right.$$

$$+\left(\frac{q^*}{Q}\right)^{-\rho}(1-n)(C^*+V^*+G^*)\right]$$

$$+s\left[\left(\frac{p^*}{P}\right)^{-\rho} n(C+V+G)\right. \qquad (1.23)$$

$$+\left(\frac{q^*}{Q}\right)^{-\rho}(1-n)(C^*+V^*+G^*)\right].$$

Note finally that using the defined subprice indices above, we may write the CPI definitions for the home and foreign country as

$$P(z^t) = \left[np(z^t)^{1-\rho} + (1-n)sp^*(z^t)^{1-\rho} + (1-n)(1-s)eq^*(z^t)^{1-\rho}\right]^{1/(1-\rho)}, \qquad (1.24)$$

$$Q(z^t) = \left[(1-n)q^*(z^t)^{1-\rho} + nsp(z^t)^{1-\rho} + n(1-s)(p(z^t)/e(z^t))^{1-\rho}\right]^{1/(1-\rho)}. \qquad (1.25)$$

Equilibrium

We may characterize the equilibrium of the two-country economy by collecting the equations set out above. First, for the case of complete asset markets, equations (1.3), (1.6) (with (1.5) substituted in for $w(.,.)$), (1.7), (1.8), (1.14), (1.15), (1.18), (1.19), (1.20), and (1.21), all with their counterparts for the foreign economy, as well as equations (1.10), (1.22), (1.23), (1.24), and (1.25), give twenty-five equations. This represents a dynamic system in the twenty-five unknown variables given by $X(z^t)$, where

$$X(z^t) = \{C, C^*, h, h^*, V, V^*, K, K^*, W, W^*, R, R^*, p, q, p^*, q^*, P, Q, \tilde{p}, \tilde{q},$$
$$\tilde{p}^*, \tilde{q}^*, MC, MC^*, e\}.$$

In the economy with incomplete markets, equation (1.10) is replaced with equation (1.11). Moreover, because there is not full risk sharing, we must determine the initial allocation of consumption across countries, which requires use of the balance-of-payments equation (1.4). Given (1.13), we may rewrite (1.4) as

$$P(z^t)C(z^t) + q(z^t)B(z^t) + P(z^t)V(z^t) + P(z^t)G(z^t)$$
$$= \int_0^{n(1-s)} p(i, z^t)y^1(i, z^t)di + \int_{n(1-s)}^n \left[p(i, z^t)y^2(i, z^t)\right. \qquad (1.26)$$
$$+ e(z^t)q(i, z^t)y^3(i, z^t)\right]di + B(z^{t-1})$$

Equation (1.26) is explained as follows. The left-hand side is the value of current home-country expenditure on consumption, investment, and government goods, plus the value of new bond purchases from the rest of the world. The right-hand side measures the value of output of all home-country firms, plus the value of initial bonds. Note that home-country firms consist of non-PTM firms and PTM firms, and these must be summed separately. The variable $y^l(i, z^t)$, for instance, measures the output of all firms in sector i, when i is a non-PTM sector.

In general, there will be no easy way to aggregate output values across firms to simplify the right-hand side of (1.26), because different sectors will be changing prices at different times. However, in solving the model, we take a linear approximation around an initial steady state. In that linear approximation, we can aggregate across sectors directly.

To conclude, we write that the solution for the economy with incomplete markets represents twenty-six equations in the variables $X'(z^t)$, where

$$X'(z^t) = \{C, C^*, h, h^*, V, V^*, K, K^*, W, W^*, R, R^*, p, q, p^*, q^*, P, Q, \tilde{p}, \tilde{q},$$
$$\tilde{p}^*, \tilde{q}^*, MC, MC^*, e, B(z^t)\}.$$

We solve the model by linearizing around an initial zero-shock steady state.

Calibration

The calibrated parameters for the baseline case are reported in table 1.1. The rationale for the calibration is as follows. For a quarterly frequency, β is chosen to equal 0.99, which gives a 4 percent steady-state annual real interest rate (abstracting from long-run growth). The value of η is

Table 1.1
Calibrated parameters for baseline case

β	0.99	α	0.36	n	0.5
σ	7	δ	0.025	s	0, 1.
ε	8.2	v	1.1	γ	0.75
ς	1	μ	0.06	ϕ	0.025
η	3	μ^*	0.06	ϕ'	0.02
ρ	1.9	θ	0.2		
λ	10	θ^*	0.2		

chosen so that the representative agent in both countries elects to work 30 percent of available time, the standard calibration in real business cycle models.

The parameters ε and σ govern the consumption and interest elasticity of money demand. The consumption elasticity of money demand is equal to σ/ε. The interest elasticity of money demand is $\beta/\varepsilon(1 + \mu)$. These two elasticities are critical for the response of the real and the nominal exchange rate to monetary shocks. Mankiw and Summers (1986) estimate a consumption elasticity of money demand almost precisely equal to unity. Other estimates have been reported, both higher and lower. Helliwell, Conkerline, and Lafrance (1990) report a large number of estimated money demand elasticities for G7 countries that are typically used in macro models. These differ somewhat across countries, but for many countries the income elasticity for narrower definitions of money is below unity. For instance, the reported Fair and Taylor (1983) model uses an estimated elasticity for M1 of 0.85 for the United States and 0.55 for Japan.

We choose parameters for our baseline case so that $\sigma/\varepsilon = 0.85$, consistent with Fair and Taylor's estimate. Estimates of the interest elasticity of M1 vary from a value of 0.02 reported in Mankiw and Summers 1986 to values around 0.25 reported in Helliwell, Conkerline, and Lafrance 1990. We choose a value of 0.12, which is approximately halfway between these estimates. With the annual money growth rate equal to 6 percent, this requires a relatively low intertemporal elasticity of substitution, that is, $\sigma = 7$.

We set the markup parameter λ so that markups are equal to those found by Basu and Fernald (1994) for U.S. data, that is, in the region of 10 percent. This requires a high elasticity of substitution between goods within sectors. On the other hand, we set the elasticity of substitution between sectors so that the elasticity of substitution between foreign and domestic goods (ρ) is equal to 1.5, the number used in Backus, Kehoe, and Kydland 1994. The steady-state depreciation rate of capital is set at 10 percent per year, so that $\delta = 0.025$. The fixed-cost parameter v is then set to produce average profits of zero, in accordance with evidence of very small pure profits in the U.S. economy.

The share of government in GDP is set at 0.2, and the relative size parameter is set at 0.5, so that each country is of equal size. The price adjustment parameter is set so that the firm's average frequency of price adjustment is approximately four quarters. This requires $\gamma = 0.75$.

In the steady state, the adjustment cost function ϕ must equal the rate of depreciation. In addition, we also need to set the elasticity of Tobin's q (which is $1/\phi'$) with respect to investment. The higher is this elasticity, the greater time it takes to adjust the capital stock. Following Baxter and Crucini 1993, we set this elasticity so that the variability of investment relative to output in the simulated model is at reasonable levels.

Finally, we vary the pricing to-market parameter, s, between 0 and 1.

Quantitative Evaluation of the Model

We now explore the characteristics of the calibrated model by deriving the theoretical impulse responses to monetary and government spending shocks. The figures show the response of eight key variables: the real exchange rate, output levels, the nominal interest rate differential, consumption, the terms of trade, prices, investment levels, and the nominal exchange rate. The responses for other variables, such as the trade balance or interest rate differentials can be inferred from the variables illustrated in the figures. Results are derived for both complete and incomplete markets and for the economy with and without PTM.

Monetary Shocks

Figures 1.3–1.6 describe the impact of an unanticipated, permanent one percentage point expansion in the home country money supply, beginning in a steady state. Figures 1.3 and 1.4 represent the $s = 0$ case, for complete and incomplete markets, respectively, and figures 1.5 and 1.6 the $s = 1$ case, for complete and incomplete markets, respectively.

As to be expected, when $s = 0$, there is no real exchange rate effect of a monetary disturbance, since even with sticky prices, PPP holds at all times. The monetary expansion causes an immediate permanent depreciation in the nominal exchange rate in exact proportion to the increase in money (figure 1.3b). It follows, since uncovered interest rate parity must hold in this economy, that the monetary shock does not change the interest rate differential. Since prices take some time to adjust to the money shock (figure 1.3e), the nominal exchange rate depreciation causes a change in the terms of trade. How do the terms of trade respond? In the $s = 0$ case, export prices are invoiced in home currency and import prices in foreign currency. Thus a nominal depreciation causes a deterioration in the terms of trade (figure 1.3d). The fall in the

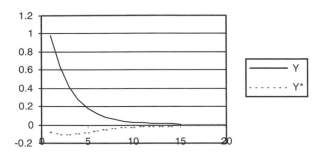

Figure 1.3a
Output

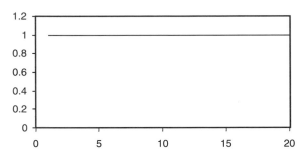

Figure 1.3b
Nominal exchange rate

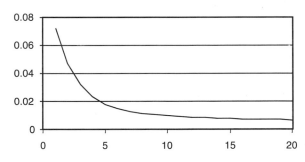

Figure 1.3c
Consumption

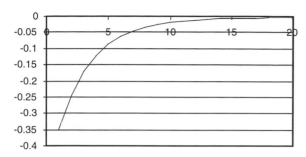

Figure 1.3d
Terms of trade

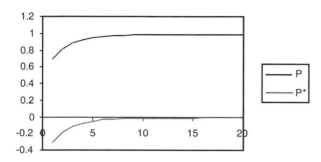

Figure 1.3e
Price levels

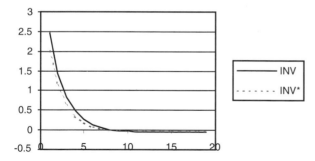

Figure 1.3f
Investment

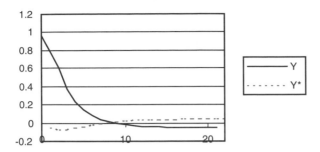

Figure 1.4a
Output

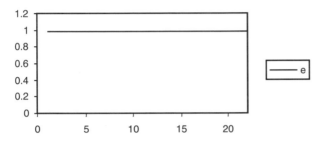

Figure 1.4b
Nominal exchange rate

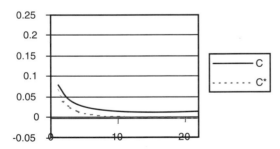

Figure 1.4c
Consumption

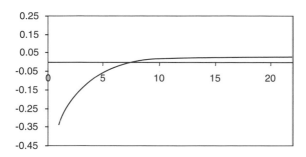

Figure 1.4d
Terms of trade

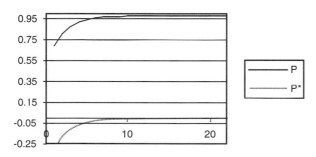

Figure 1.4e
Price levels

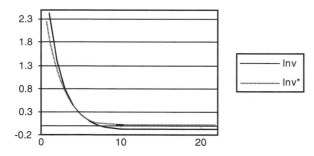

Figure 1.4f
Investment

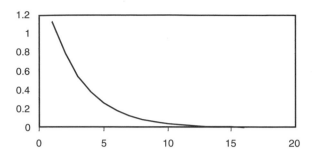

Figure 1.5a
Real exchange rate

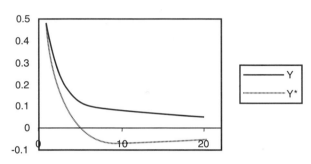

Figure 1.5b
Output

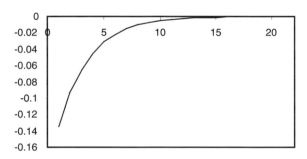

Figure 1.5c
Interest rate differential

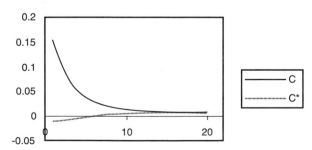

Figure 1.5d
Consumption

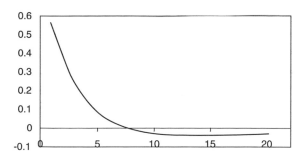

Figure 1.5e
Terms of trade

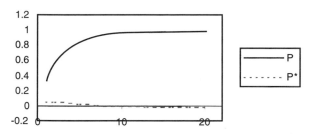

Figure 1.5f
Price levels

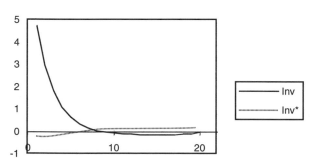

Figure 1.5g
Investment

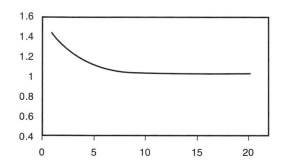

Figure 1.5h
Nominal exchange rate

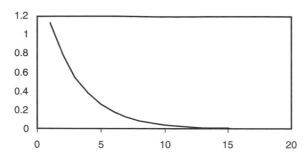

Figure 1.6a
Real exchange rate

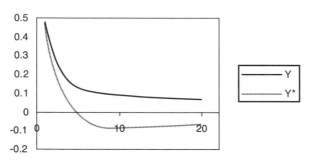

Figure 1.6b
Output

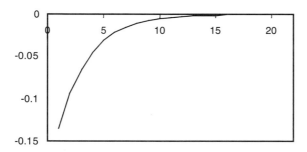

Figure 1.6c
Interest rate differential

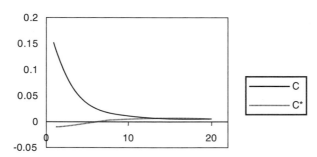

Figure 1.6d
Consumption

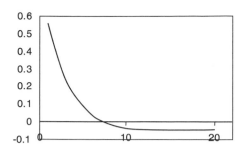

Figure 1.6e
Terms of trade

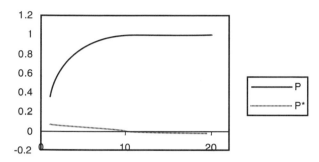

Figure 1.6f
Price levels

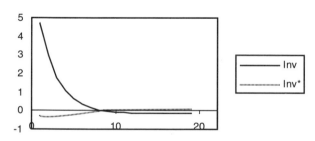

Figure 1.6g
Investment

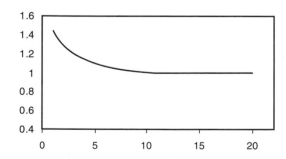

Figure 1.6h
Nominal exchange rate

terms of trade causes an "expenditure switching" of world demand away from the foreign country toward the home country. As a result, home output rises and foreign output falls (figure 1.3a). The international transmission of monetary policy in the $s = 0$ case is negative, for reasons essentially identical to Mundell 1968. Note that even though output levels move in different directions, consumption moves in the same way in both countries because of complete risk sharing (figure 1.3c). Consumption rises immediately but then gradually falls back to its steady-state level.

This illustrates the importance of differentiating output responses from consumption or welfare responses, a point emphasized by OR. In fact, in this complete markets economy, the home country will have lower welfare than the foreign country as a result of the monetary expansion, since home agents must work to produce a higher level of home output, which will be shared equally with consumers abroad.[8]

Finally, note that investment will rise in both countries (figure 1.3f). Since real interest rates can be inferred directly from the rate of growth of consumption (which in this case is equated across countries), we can deduce from figure 1.3c that the home monetary expansion reduces real interest rates in both countries. This stimulates an increase in investment expenditure.

How important are financial markets in generating these results? Let us now investigate the effects of monetary policy shocks when there is only trade in noncontingent nominal bonds. This is the market structure that is used in OR. Obstfeld and Rogoff show that an unanticipated monetary expansion will lead to a less than proportional rise in the nominal exchange rate and a home-country trade surplus, which leads to a permanent increase in home consumption, relative to foreign consumption. Figure 1.4 illustrates the result for our model in the case of incomplete markets. As before, of course, there is no impact on the real exchange rate when $s = 0$. The nominal exchange rate now rises slightly less than proportionally to money. Again, the terms of trade fall, precipitating an expenditure switching toward the home-country output, with a negative international transmission. But now there is a slightly larger increase in home consumption than foreign consumption (figure 1.4c), as the first-period home-country trade account surplus increases home assets, leading to a permanent carrying forward of home wealth into the future. The relatively large increase in home consumption implies that steady-state output is lower in the home economy (figure 1.4a) because of the wealth effects of consumption on labor supply.

We notice that in comparing figure 1.3 with figure 1.4, the asset market structure makes little difference to the central properties of the international monetary transmission mechanism. Although consumption does not respond in identical ways here, the pattern of response is almost identical in both countries. Quantitatively, the difference in the exchange rate's response between the two asset market structures is very small (1 as opposed to 0.99). Because of the persistence of the initial current account surplus, the home country will have a permanently larger steady-state consumption, as emphasized in OR. But quantitatively, the difference in consumption levels is miniscule. A 1 percent surprise increase in the home-country money supply increases steady-state home-country consumption by less than 0.01 percent of its initial level.

Figures 1.5 and 1.6 illustrate the case of monetary policy under pricing-to-market for complete and incomplete markets, respectively. Since PPP does not hold in the short run, the real exchange rate now responds to an unanticipated monetary shock. The shock immediately causes a real and nominal exchange rate depreciation (figures 1.5a and 1.5h). In fact the nominal exchange rate now "overshoots," rising more in the short run than in the long run. This causes a fall in the nominal interest rate differential (figure 1.5c). The movement in the real exchange rate causes consumption responses to diverge, even in the complete markets case (figure 1.5d), since with $s = 1$, optimal risk sharing is conditioned on movements in the real exchange rate (see equation (1.10)).

The response of the terms of trade is now the opposite of the $s = 0$ case. All exports are invoiced in foreign currency and imports in domestic currency. An exchange rate depreciation therefore raises the relative price of exports, that is, it improves the terms of trade (figure 1.5e). The monetary shock also now has an opposite impact on foreign output than in the $s = 0$ case. The presence of full pricing-to-market implies that there is no immediate pass-through from exchange rates to prices. Thus, an exchange rate depreciation has no expenditure-switching impact. Rather, there is a balanced expansion in demand for the goods of both the home and foreign country. Output of the home and foreign country rise by equal amounts initially (figure 1.5b). Following this, home-country output remains higher for a period, because the monetary disturbance expands home-country investment.

Finally, we see that investment rises in the home country while falling slightly in the foreign country (figure 1.5g). In the presence of departures from PPP, there is no longer equality of real interest rates between countries. As can be deduced from the changes in consumption growth rates, home real interest rates fall, while foreign rates rise slightly.

Thus the currency of pricing is a critical factor in the direction of the international transmission of monetary policy on output. Unlike the Mundell 1968 or the OR specification, an exchange rate depreciation with local currency invoicing of export prices does not generate negative international output transmission. In general, comparing the effects of monetary policy across the two different pricing regimes, we see there are substantial differences in international transmission. The direction of movements in output, consumption and investment, and the terms of trade are reversed when we move from the $s = 0$ case to the $s = 1$ case.

However, comparing figures 1.5 and 1.6, as well as figures 1.3 and 1.4, it is apparent that the asset market structure makes almost no difference to the international monetary transmission mechanism, with our without pricing-to-market.

It seems valid to conclude that for monetary policy transmission, the critical dichotomy is the currency of invoicing. Relative to this, the structure of international assets markets is much less important.

When we compare figures 1.5 and 1.6 to the empirical impulse responses for output levels, real exchange rates, and nominal interest rates as described in figures 1.1 and 1.2, a number of things are apparent. First, the theoretical monetary transmission mechanism in the $s = 1$ case captures the positive cross-country correlation of output in the data. Second, the theoretical results for the $s = 1$ case also reflect the positive and persistent impact of the money shock on the real exchange rate. Finally; the model with $s = 1$ also seems to capture well the effects of monetary policy shocks on nominal interest rate differentials. Thus the empirical international monetary transmission mechanism seems to be in accord with the economy in which pricing-to-market is predominant.

Government Spending Shocks

We now turn to the analysis of government spending policies, as illustrated in figures 1.7 and 1.8. The first thing to note is that in the case of complete markets, government spending shocks have identical effects on all home and foreign variables. Unlike in the classic Mundell model, government spending is not exclusively allocated to home-country goods but involves purchases of the composite consumption good.[9] That is, an increase in either country's government spending increases the demand for all goods produced in the home and foreign country. When markets are complete, both the home and foreign country share equally the wealth effects of financing this increased expenditure. The responses of output, consumption, and investment are then identical to those in a closed economy (e.g., Barro 1987). Both home and foreign output rise, stimulated by an increase in employment and investment, and consumption falls. There is no response in either the real or the nominal exchange rate (even in the $s = 1$ case), and there are no effects on the terms of trade or the trade balance. Moreover, because of the absence of exchange rate effects, the currency of invoicing is irrelevant. The degree of pricing-to-market has no consequences at all for the impact of fiscal policy shocks in the complete markets economy.

If markets are incomplete, however, government spending shocks have quite a different impact. An expansion in home-country government spending now leads to a permanent increase in the home consumer's tax bill, which is not shared with foreign consumers through coinsurance arrangements, as in the complete markets case. Home-country consumers reduce their consumption (figure 1.7c) and expand labor supply in response to the fall in real wealth. Home output rises, and since employment is higher, home investment is stimulated, leading to further increases in output over time (figure 1.7a).

When $s = 0$, the government spending shock has no real exchange rate effects, but the rise in home output leads to a terms-of-trade deterioration for the home economy (figure 1.7d), which is exacerbated over time as home output continues to rise. Thus, the government spending increase causes a permanent increase in home output and a permanent fall in the terms of trade.

What impacts are there for the foreign country? Initially, the rise in government spending will increase foreign output, since demand for foreign products rise, and prices are sticky. However, as prices adjust, the wealth effects of higher terms of trade and higher consumption begin to come into force. Foreign labor supply falls, and foreign output falls to a permanently lower level (figure 1.7a). Thus, the initial stimulation of foreign output is reversed in the new steady state. By contrast,

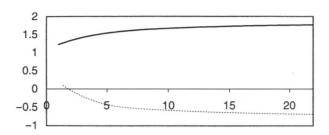

Figure 1.7a
Output

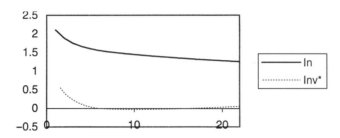

Figure 1.7b
Investment

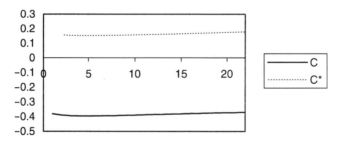

Figure 1.7c
Consumption

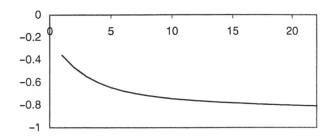

Figure 1.7d
Terms of trade

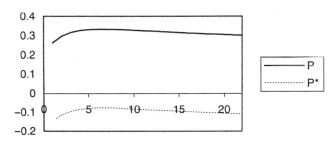

Figure 1.7e
Price level

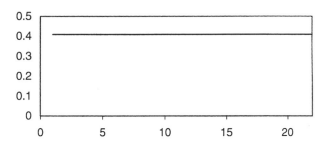

Figure 1.7f
Nominal exchange rate

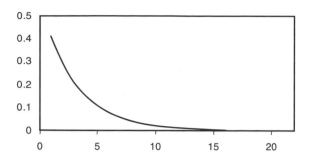

Figure 1.8a
Real exchange rate

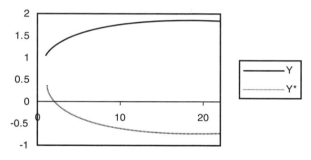

Figure 1.8b
Output

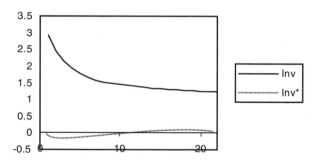

Figure 1.8c
Investment

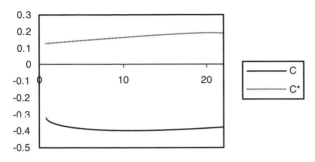

Figure 1.8d
Consumption

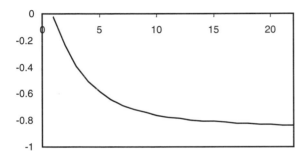

Figure 1.8e
Terms of trade

with permanently higher terms of trade, foreign consumption is higher in the new steady state.

A fiscal expansion also affects the nominal exchange rate (as shown also by OR). To restore money market equilibrium in the face of an increase in foreign consumption and a fall in domestic consumption, the domestic CPI must rise and the foreign CPI must fall. From the PPP conditions, this requires a nominal exchange rate depreciation that is both immediate and permanent.

Figure 1.8 illustrates the effects of fiscal policy with pricing-to-market ($s = 1$). The impact is almost the same as the $s = 0$ case, save for the response of the real and nominal exchange rate. With no immediate pass-through of the exchange rate to domestic and foreign prices (figure 1.8f), the foreign price level does not move at the time of the shock, and the rise in the home price level is smaller than in the $s = 0$ case. As a result, both the fall in home consumption and the rise in

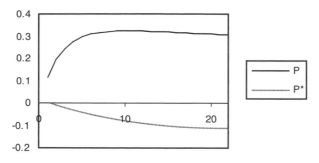

Figure 1.8f
Price level

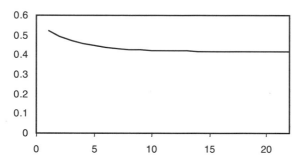

Figure 1.8g
Nominal exchange rate

foreign consumption are slightly smaller than in the $s = 0$ case (figure 1.8d). The nominal exchange rate then rises by more in the short run than in the long run (figure 1.8g), and the real exchange rate immediately depreciates (figure 1.8a). The reduced effect on consumption implies a smaller movement in labor supply, which reduces the magnitude of the output responses for both countries (figure 1.8b).

Nevertheless, the main features of the international transmission of fiscal shocks remain unaffected by changes in the currency of invoicing. We still see an immediate, positive cross-country transmission in output initially and a negative transmission in consumption. The terms of trade deteriorate, and the nominal exchange rate depreciates.

In contrast to the case for money shocks, however, the structure of asset markets is now of key importance for understanding the international transmission of fiscal shocks. If asset markets are complete, there are no exchange rate effects, no terms-of-trade effects, and no differential output or consumption responses to a home-country fiscal policy disturbance.

Discussion

We may then draw the following conclusions from our analysis. When we reexamine the central questions of Mundell 1968 in light of modern intertemporal optimizing sticky-price models, the impact of money shocks on the international transmission process relies not on the structure of asset markets but rather on the currency of invoicing, or the degree of pricing-to-market. When export prices are preset in the currency of the buyer rather than that of the seller, the international transmission of monetary policy is significantly altered. However, when asset markets are limited to noncontingent bonds trade rather than allowing full consumption coinsurance, the implications for the monetary transmission process are quite minor. One way to interpret the result is that moving from the simple assumption of capital mobility, used by Mundell and the subsequent literature, to a world of more sophisticated financial integration does not significantly alter the macroeconomic effects of monetary policy.

The consequences for fiscal policy are just the opposite. Approximately, the currency of invoicing has no implications for fiscal policy shocks. Changes in the currency of invoicing leave the main elements of the international policy transmission mechanism unchanged. On the other hand, changes in the asset market structure have substantial effects on the nature of the fiscal policy transmission mechanism. If agents cannot coinsure across countries, the effects of fiscal policy are fundamentally different than those in the complete markets environment.

Conclusions

This chapter has built on a number of recent contributions in international macroeconomics to examine a time-honored question in the field: the international transmission effects of monetary and fiscal policy. Mundell's (1968) contribution became the benchmark for thinking about this problem. Our results indicate that when we reexamine the effects of monetary and fiscal policy in a modern framework, paying careful attention to asset markets and pricing, we find some important differences from earlier analysis, and we obtain some clear insights that would not have been available using earlier approaches. In particular, we find that the critical issue pertaining to the international effects of monetary policy is the currency of export pricing, whereas the critical issue regarding the effects of fiscal policy is the structure of asset markets.

Notes

1. This new literature has grown very quickly. An important early paper was Svensson and van Wijnbergen 1989. More recent contributions include Bergin 1995, Corsetti and Pesenti 1998, Chari, Kehoe, and McGrattan 1997, Kollman 1997, Hau forthcoming, Senay 1998, Stockman and Ohanian 1997, and Tille 1998. Lane 1998 provides an insightful survey into this area.

2. Since we do not have a widely agreed identifying scheme for government spending shocks, in the empirical investigation we restrict our attention to the effects of monetary shocks.

3. For a review of this methodology, see Betts and Devereux 1998.

4. This initial negative response, although very small in our results, is consistent with evidence established in the closed-economy versions of this empirical characterization of monetary policy shocks presented by Christiano and Eichenbaum 1995, and with open-economy versions such as Schlagenhauf and Wrase 1995.

5. These results are available upon request from the authors.

6. Since we are not allowing for state-contingent pricing, the difference between the objective functions turns out to be unimportant for the pricing decision in any case.

7. We assume that governments minimize the cost of producing a given amount of the final government good G, or G^*.

8. This statement is based on the assumption that changes in the supply of real-money balances have welfare effects sufficiently small that they can be ignored.

9. Tille 1998 examines the impact of government spending in a two-country model under the alternative assumption that government spending is biased more toward domestic goods.

References

Backus, D. K., P. J. Kehoe, and F. Kydland. 1994. "Dynamics of the trade balance and the terms of trade: the J-curve." *American Economic Review* 84:84–103.

Barro, R. G. 1987. The neoclassical approach to fiscal Policy. In *Modern business cycle theory*, ed. R. G. Barro. Cambridge: MIT Press.

Basu, S., and J. Fernald. 1994. Constant returns and small markups in US manufacturing. International Finance discussion paper 483, Board of Governors of the Federal Reserve, Washington, D.C.

Baxter, M., and M. Crucini. 1993. Explaining savings investment correlations. *American Economic Review* 83:416–36.

Bergin, P. 1995. Mundell-Fleming revisited: Monetary and fiscal policies in a two country dynamic equilibrium model with wage contracts. University of California at Davis. Mimeographed.

Betts, C., and M. B. Devereux. 1996. The exchange rate in a model of pricing-to-market. *European Economic Review* 40:1007–21.

Betts, C., and M. B. Devereux. 1998. The international transmission of monetary policy: A model of real exchange rate adjustment with pricing-to-market. University of British Col. Mimeographed.

Calvo, G. 1983. Staggered prices in a utility maximizing framework. *Journal of Monetary Economics* 12:983–98.

Chari, V. V., P. J. Kehoe, and E. R. McGrattan. 1997. Monetary policy and the real exchange rate in sticky price models of the international business cycle. Discussion paper 5876, National Bureau of Economic Research, Cambridge, Mass.

Christiano, L. J., and M. Eichenbaum. 1995. Liquidity effects, monetary policy, and the business cycle. *Journal of Money, Credit, and Banking* 27:1113–36.

Cogley, T., and J. N. Nason. 1995. Effects of the Hodrick-Prescott filter on trends and difference stationary time series: Implications for business cycle research. *Journal of Economic Dynamics and Control* 19:253–78.

Corsetti, G., and P. Pesenti. 1998. Welfare and macroeconomic interdependence. Yale University, New Haven, Conn. Mimeographed.

Dornbusch, R. 1976. Expectations and exchange rate dynamics. *Journal of Political Economy* 84:1161–76.

Eichenbaum, M., and C. Evans. 1995. Some empirical evidence on the effects of monetary shocks on exchange rates. *Quarterly Journal of Economics* 110:995–1010.

Engel, C., and J. H. Rogers. 1996. How wide is the border? *American Economic Review* 86:1112–25.

Fair, R., and J. Taylor. 1983. Solution and maximum likelihood estimation dynamic, nonlinear rational expectations models. *Econometrica* 51:1169–85.

Hau, H. 2000. Exchange rate determination: The role of factor prices and market segmentation. *Journal of International Economics* 50:421–47.

Helliwell, J., J. Conkerline, and R. Lafrance. 1990. Multi-country modelling of financial markets. In *Financial sectors in open economies: Empirical analysis and policy issues*, ed. Peter Hooper. Federal Reserve Board, Washington, D.C.

Kimball, M. 1996. The quantitative analytics of the basic neo-monetarist model. *Journal of Money Credit and Banking* 27:1241–77.

Kollman, R. 1997. The exchange rate in a dynamic optimizing current account model with nominal rigidities: A quantitative investigation. Working paper 97-7, International Monetary Fund, Washington, D.C.

Lane, P. 1998. The new open economy macroeconomics: A survey. Trinity College, Dublin, Ireland. Mimeographed.

Mankiw, N. G., and L. H. Summers. 1986. Money demand and the effects of fiscal policies. *Journal of Money, Credit and Banking* 18:415–29.

McKibbin, W., and J. Sachs. 1986. Coordination of monetary and fiscal policies in the industrial economies. In *International aspects of fiscal policies*, ed. Jacob Frenkel, 73–120. Chicago: University of Chicago Press.

Mundell, R. A. 1968. *International economics*. New York: Macmillan.

Obstfeld, M., and K. Rogoff. 1995. Exchange rate dynamics redux. *Journal of Political Economy* 103:624–60.

Schlagenhauf, D. E., and J. M. Wrase. 1995. Liquidity and real activity in a simple open economy model. *Journal of Monetary Economics* 35:431–61.

Senay, O. 1998. The effects of goods and financial market integration on macroeconomic volatility. *The Manchester School Supplement* 66:39–61.

Stockman, A., and L. Ohanian. 1997. Short run independence of monetary policy under pegged exchange rates and effects of money on exchange rates and interest rates. *Journal of Money, Credit and Banking* 29:783–806.

Svensson, L., and S. van Wijnbergen. 1989. Excess capacity, monopolistic competition and international transmission of monetary disturbances. *Economic Journal* 99:785–805.

Taylor, J. B. 1993. *Macroeconomic policy in a world economy: From econometric design to practical operation*. New York and London: Norton.

Tille, C. 1998. The role of consumption substitutability in the international transmission of shocks. Federal Reserve Bank of New York. Mimeographed.

Yun, T. 1996. Nominal price rigidities, money supply endogeneity, and business cycles. *Journal of Monetary Economics* 37:345–70.

2

The Rise and Fall of a Barbarous Relic: The Role of Gold in the International Monetary System

Michael D. Bordo and
Barry Eichengreen

Introduction

Robert Mundell is renowned, even notorious, for advocating a role for gold in the international monetary system. Far from plumping for the sort of textbook gold standard that never has and never will exist, however, Mundell has always based his case on a nuanced view of the historical role of gold. The gold standard, in his view, always functioned as a gold-exchange standard in which specie was supplemented by foreign-exchange reserves issued by the leading international economic and financial power. There was nothing unstable or undesirable about this system so long as the price of gold was appropriately set. In particular, the gold-exchange standard allowed the world to economize on the costs of producing specie reserves and functioned smoothly when the reserve-currency country followed responsible policies.

Moreover, Mundell has always emphasized continuity in the evolution of international monetary arrangements, pointing to similarities in the structure of the prewar and interwar gold-exchange standards. He suggests that the Bretton Woods System of pegged-but-adjustable exchange rates is best understood as a gold-exchange standard (or more precisely as a gold-dollar standard) until the United States severed the gold-dollar link at the end of the 1960s.[1] The post-1973 shift to managed floating is seen as an aberration in which the stability and predictability of fixed exchange rates were allowed to go by the board, but even these developments have produced less real change than meets the eye. Floating, in this view, because it gave monetary authorities the license to pursue inflationary policies, has actually increased the demand for reserves, particularly the demand for reserves of dollars and gold. The persistence of gold in the portfolios of central banks points to a latent demand for monetary reform in which exchange rates are again pegged and the global supply of liquidity is managed by a world monetary authority that uses gold as one form of backing for its liabilities.

In this chapter we relate our own account of the rise and fall of the gold-based international monetary system to Mundell's interpretation. We seek to understand the motives for recent central-bank sales of gold, and we ask whether the yellow metal is likely to retain a monetary role in the twenty first century.

We report new evidence on the determinants of central banks' demands for gold using data spanning more than a century of international monetary history. We estimate the canonical model of the demand for reserves, which relates central bank holdings to country size, exposure to international transactions, and balance-of-payments volatility.[2] This procedure allows us to test propositions that flow from Mundell's analysis and to speculate on the future monetary role of gold.

Although our analysis is broadly consistent with Mundell's, we hold a less universalist view of the gold-exchange standard and argue that the international monetary system is accurately portrayed as a gold-exchange standard for at most seven decades from 1900. We emphasize the fact that the system was buttressed for most of its existence by special factors that have no counterparts today, early on by the insulation from political pressures enjoyed by central banks and later by capital controls that limited international financial flows. More generally, we are less confident than Mundell of the stability of a multiple reserve-asset system.[3]

We argue that the disintegration of the gold-exchange standard in the 1930s and the collapse of the Bretton Woods system between 1971 and 1973 both reveal the fragility of this system. In our view, more was responsible for stability problems in these two periods than an inappropriately set price of gold that limited the supply of international liquidity. Rather, the collapse of the interwar system and the collapse of Bretton Woods both reflected flaws in the structure of the gold-exchange standard, specifically, the tendency for such a system to amplify and propagate the effects of unstable policies in the reserve-currency countries, and the further tendency for the repercussions of those policies to destabilize the monetary system itself.

Finally, we consider some hypotheses to explain the persistence of gold holdings by monetary authorities for twenty years after the breakdown of the Bretton Woods system and after the Second Amendment to the Articles of Agreement of the International Monetary Fund severed the formal link to gold. We distinguish three proximate explanations: network externalities which encourage the maintenance of the same international monetary practices as one's neighbors and therefore cause existing practices to become locked in; simple inertia in central bank behavior; and inertia in statutory requirements. We find some support for all three hypotheses. We suggest that this evidence as well as recent official gold sales bode ill for the future monetary role of gold.

Perspectives on the Past

In this section we review the development of the international monetary system from the late nineteenth-century gold-exchange standard through the post–World War II gold-dollar standard.

The Gold Standard

The international gold standard developed out of the commodity-money standards that prevailed for many centuries up through and including the nineteenth. Prior to its advent, economies relied on a variety of commodity standards—silver standards, copper standards, and bimetallic standards among them. The pivotal development prompting the emergence of the gold standard in the nineteenth century was, in a sense, the industrial revolution, or more broadly the technological and organizational advances associated with the advent of modern economic growth. With advances in shipbuilding and armaments technologies, warfare became more expensive, increasing the financial requirements of the state. This increase in requirements led to the issue of public debt and the development of financial institutions that served as bankers to the state. Out of these arrangements emerged modern central banks. In return for extending them exceptional privileges, governments asked their bankers to discharge a range of public functions. These eventually included overseeing the monetary system, which in practice meant acting as steward of the gold standard. The development of the steam engine brought steam power to the mint and made practical the minting and issuance of token subsidiary coinage, facilitating the transition from silver and bimetallism to gold.[4] The development of double-entry bookkeeping, the establishment of the accountancy profession, and improvements in information technology—all corollaries of the industrial revolution—encouraged the spread of fractional-reserve banking, which allowed specie and specie-backed currency and coin to be supplemented with bank deposits and other near monies. Central banks followed suit, buying up circulating gold in exchange for token coin and paper money that then provided the basis for the domestic circulation.[5]

Once this movement toward the gold standard was initiated, it gained momentum. The shift to gold fed on itself through the operation of network externalities. There were advantages, in other words, to maintaining the same monetary arrangement as other countries. Doing so simplified trade. It facilitated foreign borrowing.[6] And a common standard minimized the confusion caused by the intercirculation of coins minted in neighboring countries. Thus, when Germany went over to gold in 1871, using the reparations received from its victory over France in the Franco-Prussian War, it brought Denmark, Norway, Holland, Sweden, and the members of the Latin Union in its train. Once this influential group had joined together on the gold standard, other countries were drawn to follow.

The Gold-Exchange Standard

Circa 1880, when this process really got under way, and it could for the first time be said that there existed a gold-based system of international scope, the system in place is accurately portrayed as a gold standard, not a gold-exchange standard.[7] In 1880, the foreign exchange reserves of central banks and governments amounted to less than 10 percent of their gold reserves.[8] (See figure 2.1)[9] The practice of holding foreign exchange was the exception, not the rule.[10] But the share of foreign exchange in world official reserves then began its steady rise (as seen most clearly in Lindert's data, as in figure A.2.1). Its upward trajectory was then interrupted by the Baring Crisis and the 1893 panic. By the turn of the century, however, the accumulation of foreign-exchange reserves was again proceeding, this time at an even faster pace than before. On the eve of World War I, the ratio of foreign exchange to gold reserves was 50 percent above its 1880 level.[11] This pattern suggests that the shift from the gold to the gold-exchange standard can be regarded as a post-1895—even a post-1900—phenomenon.[12]

Central banks were naturally attracted by the possibility of substituting interest-earning foreign assets for gold in their portfolios, although in some cases the monetary statutes under which they

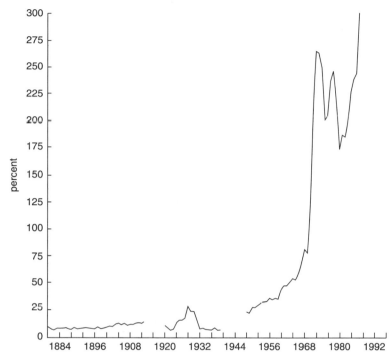

Figure 2.1
Ratio of foreign exchange reserves to gold reserves
Note: Gold standard: sixteen countries, Bloomfield 1963 and Lindert 1967, 1969.
Interwar: twenty-one countries, League of Nations.
Postwar: twenty-one countries, gold—official value, IFS.

operated provided only limited leeway for doing so. But as with the rise of the gold standard, the technological and organizational advances associated with the transition to modern economic growth encouraged the practice. The emergence of a global economy charac-terized by high levels of international trade and lending encouraged countries seeking to capitalize on the existence of international markets but for whom the accumulation of gold reserves was prohibitively expensive to opt for the more economical option of holding interest-bearing exchange reserves.[13] The growth of deep, broad, and liquid financial markets in London, Paris, Amsterdam, Zurich, and Berlin and of an efficient gold market in London reduced the costs of shifts between gold and interest-bearing assets. Improvements in trans-portation and communication, notably the growth of cable traffic, allowed governments and central banks headquartered in remote

locations to undertake more frequent portfolio shifts. The emergence
of a truly international capital market encouraged the practice of
holding foreign exchange reserves, lenders often requiring governments borrowing abroad to hold their loan proceeds on deposit in the
financial center where their bonds were underwritten and marketed.[14]

By the turn of the century, then, there existed a truly global gold-
exchange standard. A large literature seeks to understand its operation.
One strand of work, originating with Hume (1752/1952), focuses on
the adjustment mechanism and specifically on the importance of relative prices as opposed to income and wealth effects in bringing about
changes in the level of spending and in the distribution of gold
reserves. Later treatments in this spirit build on Mundell 1963, 1971.

In contrast, the modern literature, inspired by work on reputation
and time inconsistency, focuses on the political and economic factors
that lent credibility to the authorities' commitment to gold convertibility.[15] In the early twentieth century, credibility derived from the
protection central banks enjoyed from pressure to subordinate
exchange-rate policy to other goals. In many countries the right to vote
was limited until after World War I, circumscribing the ability of those
subject to unemployment to object when monetary policy was targeted
at other variables. Neither trade unions nor parliamentary labor parties
had developed to the point where workers could insist that other goals
temper defense of the exchange rate. Central banks and governments
were therefore free to do what was necessary to defend their currency
pegs.[16]

The credibility of that commitment had the effect of loosening the
constraints on policy. Because capital tended to flow in stabilizing
directions, it was only rarely necessary to apply harsh monetary measures in response to temporary disturbances. As in Svensson's (1994)
model of target zones, the existence of the exchange rate band defined
by the gold import and export points, plus a credible commitment to
defend it, gave the authorities leeway to vary interest rates in response
to shocks.[17]

The adequacy of the global supply of liquidity was a major issue
through the middle of the 1890s. The world price level trended downward from 1873 through 1893, provoking populist agitation against the
gold standard, as given classic expression in William Jennings Bryan's
"cross-of-gold" speech. At that point a series of gold discoveries, most
notably in Western Australia and South Africa, relaxed the constraint.
This may have been less the stabilizing response of the system to the

rising real price of gold than a corollary of the continued expansion of the international economy of which the gold standard was a part.[18] In other words, discoveries may have been the product not so much of any induced response to changes in the real gold price as of the penetration of agriculture into what had previously been sparsely settled regions of the world. (Recall Sutter's Mill, where two generations earlier the great California gold rush had been set off by the penetration of settled agriculture into what came to be known subsequently as the Gold Country. The immediate event precipitating the discovery was the construction of a lumber mill on the American River.) The irony, then, is that the equilibrating response—flow supplies of gold—reflected the fact that the global gold standard was superimposed on a disequilibrium system of changing migratory patterns and a changing geography of agricultural production.[19]

The fortuitous elasticity of the flow supply of new gold limited the need to supplement specie with foreign exchange. Nevertheless, the share of international reserves accounted for by foreign exchange continued to rise, from 16 percent in 1903 to 21 percent in 1910.[20] Exchange reserves held in sterling, francs, and marks loomed large relative to the gold reserves of the British, French, and German central banks. (Exchange reserves were 75 percent of the reserve-currency countries' gold reserves in 1913, according to Lindert 1969.) Questions quietly arose about the ability of the reserve-currency countries to honor their commitment to convert foreign exchange into gold in the event that foreign claimants all suddenly developed cold feet.[21]

How long this system would have lasted will never be known, for it was disrupted by the approach of World War I. Mounting political and military tensions raised doubts about whether countries would honor their unconditional commitment to redeem their foreign liabilities. As war loomed, they began shifting from foreign exchange into gold, the share of foreign balances in global reserves (thirty-five countries) falling from 26 percent in 1910 to 23 percent in 1913 (Lindert 1967).

The Interwar Gold-Exchange Standard

The international system reconstructed following World War I was similar to its prewar predecessor. Gold convertibility again provided the basis for the monetary circulation. The combination of a fixed gold price with the freedom to import and export gold held exchange rates within narrow bands.

The principal differences between the prewar and interwar systems were four. First, countries now withdrew gold coin from circulation and concentrated it in their central banks (or at institutions like the Bank of England, which held it on their behalf).[22] Second, the dollar emerged as sterling's rival for the status of leading reserve currency, reflecting the growing economic and financial power of the United States and the creation in 1913 of the Federal Reserve System, a central bank with the capacity to guarantee the liquidity of the market. Third, in a number of major countries, most notably the United States and United Kingdom, wages and prices no longer responded to changes in market conditions as freely as before.[23] Fourth and finally, compared with their prewar predecessors, interwar central banks responsible for managing the monetary system had more varied motives, came under more political pressure, and possessed less credibility. Universal male suffrage and the rise of trade unionism and parliamentary labor parties politicized monetary policy. Authors like Cassel, Keynes, and Hawtrey articulated theories linking monetary policy to employment and advertized their wares in popular publications and official testimony.

Mundell has argued that the fatal flaw in the interwar system was the failure of countries to set the gold price appropriately and to properly manage the global supply of liquidity.[24] The interwar gold standard was an engine for deflation, in this view. Although prices had risen significantly in the United States between 1914 and 1925, the dollar price of gold was left unchanged; according to Mundell, this rendered the dollar overvalued in terms of gold by as much as 35 to 40 percent. Other countries that restored their prewar parities, most notably Britain, experienced even more inflation over this interval than the United States. Higher commodity prices in conjunction with an unchanged nominal price of gold meant that the global supply of liquidity was inadequate. Central banks strapped for reserves raised their discount rates in the desperate effort to obtain them, imposing deflationary pressure under whose weight the gold standard edifice eventually crumbled.

This view must come to grips with the fact that the gold cover ratio (the ratio of gold to the sum of notes and central bank sight deposits) was in fact little changed, having fallen only from 48 percent in 1913 to 41 percent in 1925.[25] Forty-one percent was still considerably in excess of the gold required by statute, which lay in the 29 to 34 percent range.[26] Although price levels were higher than a decade earlier, so were gold stocks, reflecting mining and the concentration of monetary

gold in the vaults of central banks. Indeed, the $3 billion of gold coin
withdrawn from circulation provided the entire increase in gold cover
required by statute between 1913 and 1928. And if the stock of gold
was not enough, it could then be supplemented by rebuilding the
foreign exchange component that countries had liquidated during the
war and in its wake. In the event, the share of foreign exchange in
central bank reserves rose from 29 percent in 1924–1926 to 42 percent
in 1927–1928, somewhat higher than the 1910 benchmark of 36
percent.[27] In any case, it is hard to argue that a global liquidity shortage constrained the growth of notes and sight liabilities in the second
half of the 1920s, when they expanded at an annual average rate of 4
percent.[28]

Admittedly, there was the question of whether this configuration was
dynamically stable. Penetration of overseas regions of recent European
settlement having run its course, there were few prospective gold discoveries on the horizon, rendering the flow supply of new gold relatively inelastic.[29] For incremental liquidity the system depended on its
ability to pyramid additional foreign exchange reserves on a relatively
static base of monetary gold.[30] Contemporaries were not oblivious to
the exchange-overhang problem—to the fact that the system depended
on exchange reserves for incremental liquidity, but that augmenting
them could at the same time undermine confidence in the ability of the
reserve-currency countries to convert them—that had arisen in the first
decade of the twentieth century. Only after World War II was this
problem given a name, the "Triffin Dilemma", but it was well known
before. Writing in 1929, for example, monetary expert Feliks Mlynarski
warned that

banks which had adopted the gold exchange standard will become more and
more dependent on foreign reserves, and the banks which play the part of gold
centers will grow more and more dependent on deposits belonging to foreign
banks. Should this system last for a considerable time the gold centers may fall
into the danger of an excessive dependence on the banks which accumulate
foreign exchange reserves and vice versa the banks which apply the gold
exchange standard may fall into an excessive dependence on the gold centers.
The latter may be threatened with difficulties in exercising their rights to
receive gold, whilst the former may incur the risk of great disturbances in their
credit structure in the case of a sudden outflow of reserve deposits.[31]

The immediate problem, however, was neither the prospective
foreign exchange overhang nor the putative gold shortage. Rather, it
was the international distribution of reserves. Between 1927 and 1930,

the gold reserves of three countries—France, Germany, and the United States—rose from 56 percent to 63 percent of the world total. These trends reflected unstable monetary policies on the part of the newly created Federal Reserve System, sterilization of reserve inflows by the Bank of France, and efforts by the Reichsbank to rebuild its reserve position following the German hyperinflation.[32] The actions of these three central banks thereby imparted powerful deflationary impulses to the rest of the world. In addition, the United Kingdom suffered from persistent competitiveness problems that forced the Bank of England to follow contractionary monetary policies to maintain gold convertibility. The United Kingdom's weak position threatened the stability of one of the key reserve countries and hence the system itself.

Meanwhile, the decline in central bank credibility, reflecting increasing pressures to pursue domestic stabilization goals, meant that capital no longer flowed in stabilizing directions. Before the war, when a central bank allowed the exchange rate to weaken in response to a temporary shock, interest rates would fall, stimulating the economy, since currency traders expected the currency to appreciate subsequently, given the credibility of the commitment to hold it within the gold points. Now that the depth of that commitment had come into question, however, any weakening of the exchange rate might only excite expectations of a further weakening, with counterproductive interest-rate effects.[33] Thus the scope for stabilizing monetary policy was limited. In addition, the existence of two competing reserve currencies, sterling and the dollar, that were close substitutes in portfolios heightened the system's fragility by providing easy opportunities for shifting between them.

As soon as doubts surfaced about the stability of the reserve currencies, central banks scrambled to liquidate their exchange reserves and replace them with gold. The share of foreign exchange in global reserves plummeted from 37 percent at the end of 1930 to 13 percent at the end of 1931 and 11 percent at the end of 1932 (Nurkse 1944, appendix II). This collapse of the foreign-exchange component of the global reserve base exerted deflationary pressure on the world economy. Despite the fact that there was only so much gold to go around, central banks around the world wanted more. To attract it, they jacked up interest rates in the face of an unprecedented slump.

It is unnecessary to choose between unstable policies and an unstable international system as the cause of the Great Depression. The two sources of instability interacted and compounded one another. More than any other episode, the Depression revealed the fragility of the gold-exchange standard and the tendency for its operation to aggravate policy mistakes.[34]

With the liquidation of foreign exchange reserves, the gold-exchange standard collapsed back into a gold standard of the late-nineteenth-century variety. This shift was only temporary, however; between 1931 and 1936 the residual gold bloc collapsed, and the remaining gold-standard countries went onto floating rates. Recent research suggests that this was not entirely bad; abandoning gold convertibility allowed countries to adopt reflationary monetary policies and halt the downward spiral of prices and economic activity.[35]

At the same time, there is a sense in which the gold-exchange standard was never really abandoned. Although U.S. President Roosevelt unpegged the dollar from gold in 1933, he repegged it in 1934 at $35 a fine ounce. His decision to effectively put the dollar back on gold, albeit at a devalued rate, worked to preserve the currency's status as a reserve asset.

The Postwar Gold-Dollar Standard

Given U.S. economic preponderance, the dollar was the basis for international monetary relations after World War II. The disagreements between the United States and United Kingdom delegations at Bretton Woods are well known. What is relevant for our purposes is that the British delegation strongly opposed the reestablishment of a gold-based international monetary system, whereas the United States insisted on a role for gold. In part this divergence of opinion is explicable in terms of self-interest: Following World War II the United States held a majority of the free world's monetary gold reserves. But American attitudes cannot be understood without reference to the fact that gold convertibility had been a continuous fact of economic life in the United States, with the exception of nine short months in 1933–1934. The gold price of $35 established by Roosevelt in January 1934 remained the terms under which the United States stood ready to convert dollars under the Bretton Woods system. Tradition cast a long shadow.

Bretton Woods departed from the prewar and interwar gold standards in four ways. Pegged exchange rates became adjustable, subject to the existence of a "fundamental disequilibrium." Controls on capital- and (for a transitional period) current-account transactions were permitted to limit international capital flows. (This was a way of providing the central bank with the credibility needed to operate a system of pegged exchange rates despite the politicization of the monetary policy making; the circle was squared by using controls to loosen the link between exchange rate management and internal financial conditions.) A new institution, the International Monetary Fund (IMF), was created to provide surveillance of national economic policies. And limits were imposed on the rights of private citizens, as distinct from governments and central banks, to hold, import, and export gold.

These innovations addressed the major worries that policy makers inherited from the 1930s. They were concerned that an alternative should exist to deflation for eliminating payments deficits. They insisted on a mechanism for containing destabilizing capital flows. They sought to economize on gold in order to prevent a global liquidity shortage. And they recognized the need for a mechanism to influence governments whose policies threatened to destabilize the international system.

But none of these innovations eliminated the fundamental problem with the gold-exchange standard, namely, the need to accommodate the expanding world economy's demand for liquidity without at the same time destabilizing the system. Under the gold-exchange standard, this demand could be met only by pyramiding a growing quantity of foreign exchange reserves on an inelastic gold base. As early as 1947, Triffin had pointed to this problem as the weak link in the Bretton Woods chain.[36] The flow supply of new gold had always been inelastic, but this was especially so in a policy-making environment in which governments now resisted any fall in the price level (rise in the real price of gold). Economic growth was unusually rapid in the post–World War II quarter century, further aggravating the excess demand for reserves.

The problem, then, was that the acceptability of foreign-exchange reserves hinged on the willingness and ability of the reserve-currency country to convert its liabilities into gold. But under the postwar gold-dollar standard, increases in the demand for reserves were met mainly by increases in the ratio of dollars to monetary gold. As the foreign liabilities of the reserve-currency country grew, the credibility of its commitment to keep them as good as gold might be cast into doubt.

There was no obvious way around this dilemma. If the reserve-currency country neglected its deficits, its external liabilities would continue to mount relative to its gold reserves, aggravating the confidence problem. If it imposed restrictive policies, it would starve the world of reserves and stifle trade and growth. If it revalued its gold as Rueff, Harrod, Busschau, Gilbert, and Mundell advocated, raising the gold/exchange-reserve ratio by increasing the nominal price of the yellow metal, it would be regarded as reneging on its commitment to convert its liabilities into gold at a fixed price.[37] This would reduce the willingness of governments and central banks to hold its liabilities and undermine the system as a whole (as happened with sterling after 1949 and 1967).[38]

In any case, such a solution would only postpone the inevitable. In a rapidly growing world, it was only a matter of time before the gold scarcity would resurface, precipitating a crisis.[39] Opposition to gold revaluation was shared by most officials and academics, who believed that the creation of Special Drawing Rights (SDRs) was preferable to attempting to resurrect the gold-exchange standard (Williamson 1977, p. 35).

Keynes had sought to meet this problem by empowering his clearing union to issue "bancor," an international reserve asset that could be used to supplement supplies of the yellow metal.[40] The more conservative U.S. design for the IMF limited countries' right to draw from the IMF to a third of what Keynes proposed and linked those drawings to the gold that governments deposited with the IMF, thereby effectively eliminating its capacity to create paper gold.

As a result, the share of foreign exchange in global international reserves rose over the first two post–World War II decades. From the early 1960s, members of the Bellagio Group, of which Mundell was a member, sounded warnings and advocated the creation of a synthetic reserve asset. Such arguments found official expression in the 1963 IMF *Annual Report* and in a 1964 report of a G-10 study group.

The response, an amendment to the IMF Articles of Agreement creating the SDR, came finally in 1968. The delay reflected divisions between France and the United States and within the U.S. government itself. The Johnson administration recognized that the creation of the SDR might prevent a crisis of the dollar, but it also worried that the creation of a rival might reduce the U.S. currency's international role. Ultimately the United States conceded that something had to be done, because the alternative to the gold-exchange standard was generalized disorder. For the French, on the other hand, the collapse of the gold-exchange standard would make possible a return to a pure gold standard of the nineteenth-century variety and an end to America's "exorbitant privilege" of underwriting its external deficits courtesy of foreign central banks and governments.[41] Consequently, while other countries favored the creation of SDR, the French insisted that the scheme be activated only after the United States first eliminated its payments deficit. By the time the United States satisfied this precondition in 1969 and the SDR scheme was finally activated, issuing SDRs served only to aggravate worldwide inflation.

The first Triffin-like crisis occurred in March 1968, after the collapse of the Gold Pool established by the United States and seven other countries to reduce the pressure on U.S. reserves. The subsequent creation of a two-tier arrangement within which participants agreed to neither sell nor buy gold from the market transformed the Bretton Woods system. The two-tiered market demonetized gold at the margin and cut the link between gold production and other market sources of gold and official reserves. Together with the pressure that the United States placed on other monetary authorities to refrain from converting their dollar holdings into gold, it shifted the world onto a de facto dollar standard.[42] The final collapse of the system then followed, precipitated by mounting world inflation triggered in part by expansionary U.S. monetary policy, itself a reflection of the growing preference of the monetary authorities for full employment over price stability and budget deficits associated with the Vietnam War and spending on social programs.

As with the breakdown of the interwar standard four decades earlier, Bretton Woods collapsed in the face of growing imbalances between the policies of its principal members. The United States was unwilling to follow the stable financial policies required of the reserve center country, and the major European countries, for their part, were increasingly reluctant to import U.S. inflation.[43] The collapse of the system was symbolized by closure of the U.S. gold window on August 15, 1971, a decision triggered by French and British intentions to convert their dollars into gold.[44] The rest is history, as they say: half-baked reforms failed to rise, and by 1973 the Bretton Woods system was no more.

Speculations about the Future

A striking aspect of the subsequent system of generalized floating is the continued role of gold. Gold reserves, in ounces, remained basically unchanged for two decades after 1971, notwithstanding the elimination of the last official link between currencies and gold by the Second Amendment to the IMF Articles of Agreement. The dollar value of monetary gold stocks soared, rising six-fold at market prices. The other side of this coin (as it were) is that the value of monetary gold reserves failed to keep pace with the value of world trade, which expanded enormously over the period: The global gold/import ratio fell from 15 percent to 10 percent over the first two post–Bretton Woods decades. It follows that the ratio failed to keep pace with the growth of total reserves (figure 2.1). Still, the persistence of gold in the reserve portfolios of central banks is remarkable.

Only after 1989 did this hold begin to weaken.[45] Between 1990 and 1997, central banks sold off about 5 percent of their gold reserves. The share of gold in their international reserves has fallen to less than 25 percent from some 35 percent in 1989 (market value). In 1992–1993 the Netherlands and Belgium sold some 9 million and 5 million ounces, respectively (roughly one-quarter and one-third of their total reserves). Belgium sold a further 5.6 million ounces in 1995. Canada reduced its gold reserves from 17 million to 4 million ounces between 1988 and 1995. The Reserve Bank of Australia quietly disposed of nearly 80 percent of its gold. The Argentine Central Bank sold virtually all its gold reserves in the first half of 1997. In October 1997 a group of experts appointed by the Swiss government proposed that Switzerland sell more than half its gold reserves. The following month the Bundesbank announced that for some time it had been lending part of its gold reserves on the London bullion market.

Together these moves raise the question of whether we are now witnessing a break with the past. To answer that question, we must first understand the reasons for the persistence over the earlier period of the practice of gold reserves. We consider four hypotheses.[46]

Memory and Habit

The most popular explanation is memory and habit, specifically, memories of the association of gold with monetary stability and habits derived therefrom. The public—and for that matter monetary policy makers—may not understand the connection between gold reserves and price stability, but their recollection of the historical record leads them to believe that such a connection exists. This belief renders politicians reluctant to modify or revoke the statutes requiring the central bank to hold gold reserves for fear of encouraging reckless policies. It renders central bankers reluctant to liquidate their gold reserves for fear of exposing themselves to similar accusations.

It follows that as the gold standard becomes ancient history, memories should fade and with them the association of gold with price stability. As central banks display a growing commitment to policies of stable money even under fiat money standards, the idea that gold is necessarily associated with price stability should weaken and disappear. Parliaments and presidents who were hesitant to revoke statutes requiring the central bank to hold gold reserves may then finally gain the courage to do so.[47]

Lobbying by Gold Mining Interests

Mining interests lobby for central banks to continue to provide part of the demand for the world's gold stock. They oppose central bank sales of gold for fear that these will drive down the market price of their industry's product. Organizations like the World Gold Council circulate publications arguing the case for the maintenance of gold reserves. But as economic growth proceeds and extractive industries like gold mining account for a progressively smaller share of GNP, there is reason to think that their lobbying efforts will have less effect. Thus, the declining effectiveness of pressure from the gold interests may explain why a number of central banks have begun to draw down their gold reserves.[48]

Collective Responsibility

A third possibility is that central bankers feel collective responsibility for supporting the practice of holding gold reserves. If one important central bank begins selling off its gold, others might scramble to do likewise before the market price collapsed, and the practice would disintegrate. Hence, central banks, particularly those holding relatively large quantities of gold, realize that their individual actions may have undesirable systemic repercussions.

This "not-on-my-watch" hypothesis has the merit of consistency with the model of network externalities invoked above to explain the rise of the gold standard. It is consistent with the observation that those central banks that have been in the vanguard of gold sales have been medium-sized or relatively small, the implication being that they are least likely to set off a collective scramble out of gold. And it can explain why the process of liquidating gold reserves, once it gets underway, may be sudden and discontinuous.[49]

Gold as a War Chest

Gold has traditionally been held as a war chest. Countries concerned that potential belligerents will not redeem their monetary obligations have an incentive to hold reserves in the form of an asset that is not subject to such risk. Recall the shift out of foreign exchange by Germany and other countries in the years leading up to World War I. It can be similarly argued that East-West tensions encouraged the maintenance of gold reserves after World War II, and that the end of the Cold War has facilitated the decline of the practice.[50]

Evidence

To analyze these issues systematically, we estimated demand-for-reserves functions, relating the log of reserves to measures of economic size (log GNP), openness (the import/GNP ratio), and balance of payments variability (the three-year moving standard deviation of the log of exports).[51] We gathered annual data on these variables from 1880 through 1995 for a sample of twenty-one countries.[52] We included fixed effects for individual years, since specification tests suggested these were appropriate. And to shed light on compositional issues, we estimated separate equations for the demand for gold or for the ratio of gold to total reserves, depending on the hypothesis under consideration.[53]

Table 2.1 reports the results for the benchmark specification for total reserves and gold reserves. GNP and the import share enter with their expected signs. The income elasticity of demand for both gold and total reserves is unity or just above. Greater openness as measured by the import share translates into greater demand for both gold and total reserves over the entire period. Although export variability enters positively as a determinant of the demand for gold but negatively as a determinant of the demand for total reserves, both coefficients differ insignificantly from zero at conventional confidence levels. Although standard arguments suggest that the demand for reserves should increase with balance-of-payments variability, there are notorious difficulties with measuring balance-of-payments variability independently

Table 2.1
The demand for international reserves: Benchmark specification (constant, log GNP,
import share, export variability)

A. Dependent variable: Total reserves

Period	Constant	Log GNP	Import share	Export variability	R^2	n
Total	−3.87	1.02	1.94	−0.03	0.99	1,499
1882–1995	(−13.43)	(240.08)	(12.65)	(−0.90)		
Gold	−1.85	0.79	0.27	4.93	0.73	376
1882–1913	(−4.96)	(27.32)	(1.21)	(0.86)		
Interwar	−5.02	1.11	4.13	4.25	0.77	278
1923–1939	(−9.19)	(28.28)	(5.84)	(3.88)		
Interwar	−4.81	1.11	3.52	3.66	0.80	194
1925–1935	(−8.98)	(26.47)	(4.61)	(3.52)		
Bretton Woods	−3.43	1.02	3.80	−3.78	0.99	323
1951–1970	(−9.57)	(170.28)	(11.22)	(−3.88)		
Bretton Woods	−3.89	1.02	3.83	−3.52	1.00	241
1959–1970	(−17.91)	(181.70)	(10.42)	(−3.90)		
Floating	−3.47	1.00	2.93	−0.04	0.99	480
1973–1995	(−16.41)	(172.05)	(10.93)	(−1.23)		

B. Dependent variable: Gold reserves

Period	Constant	Log GNP	Import share	Export variability	R^2	n
Total	−4.66	1.06	2.47	0.11	0.99	1,497
1882–1995	(−10.66)	(164.90)	(10.58)	(2.11)		
Gold	−2.79	0.87	0.28	6.67	0.78	374
1882–1913	(−7.75)	(31.06)	(1.28)	(1.17)		
Interwar	−7.34	1.29	6.23	4.94	0.66	278
1923–1939	(−9.09)	(22.27)	(5.97)	(3.05)		
Interwar	−6.22	1.21	4.03	3.40	0.72	194
1925–1935	(−8.56)	(21.22)	(3.90)	(2.42)		
Bretton Woods	−4.11	1.04	4.04	−6.65	0.98	323
1951–1970	(−6.44)	(97.32)	(6.71)	(−3.84)		
Bretton Woods	−5.23	1.04	3.89	−6.04	0.99	241
1959–1970	(−12.85)	(98.83)	(5.65)	(−3.57)		
Floating	−7.08	1.05	4.57	0.15	0.96	480
1973–1995	(−17.30)	(93.52)	(8.80)	(2.50)		

Sources: See appendix 2.2.
Notes: *t*-statistics in parentheses. Two-tailed critical values are 1.96 at the 95% confidence
level and 2.58 at 99% level. Fixed effects are included. Variable definitions: Dependent
variables are log values. Import share = imports/GNP. Export variability = three-year
moving standard deviation of log exports.

of the reserve changes that are the variable to be explained. In particular, export variability will be inadequate when shocks to the balance of payments stem mainly from the capital account, whereas actual variability will not be appropriate when it is expected (as opposed to actual) balance-of-payments shocks that motivate the demand for reserves. Although for all these reasons it is unsurprising that the coefficient on export variability is not well defined, this coefficient still displays the expected positive sign and generally differs from zero at standard confidence levels, except in the Bretton Woods period in the case of gold and under Bretton Woods and the post–Bretton Woods float in the case of total reserves. We take these changes over time (specifically, the declining significance of our export revenue–based payments variability measure) as evidence of the growing importance of capital-account shocks as the period progressed.

To substantiate our interpretation of the timing of successive stages in the development of the gold-exchange standard, we conducted Chow tests for breaks in the demand for reserves.[54] Separately for the prewar era (1882–1913), the interwar period (1923–1939), the Bretton Woods period (1951–1970), and the floating period (1973–1995), we tested for a structural break in each year. The resulting series of test statistics are shown in figures 2.2–2.5. We are interested in identifying the years in which the test statistic peaks, which is the most likely period of structural shift.

Figure 2.2 suggests a break in the demand for foreign exchange reserves in the second half of the 1890s and in the ratio of gold reserves to total reserves in 1900–1901. (Critical values are 2.37 at the 95 percent confidence level and 3.32 at the 99 percent level.) This break in demand is consistent with our interpretation dating the emergence of a global gold-exchange standard as late as 1895 or 1900.

Figure 2.3, for the interwar period, suggests breaks in the demand for international reserves in 1931, when Britain and other countries abandoned gold convertibility, severing the link between domestic nominal variables and central bank gold reserves, and again around 1935, when the residual Gold Bloc began to splinter. The break in the determinants of the gold/total reserve ratio is centered on 1931; there is no comparable break in the mid-1930s, by which time the foreign-exchange component of the system had been largely liquidated.

Figure 2.4, for the Bretton Woods period, suggests stability in the determinants of the share of gold in total reserves when the sample is limited to 1959–1970 (a period sometimes referred to as that of the

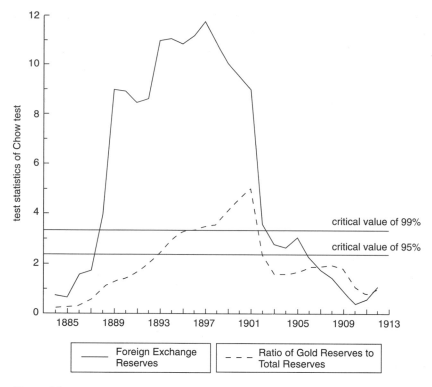

Figure 2.2
Test of structural break: The gold standard period

convertible Bretton Woods system). Over the longer period 1951–1970, in contrast, there are breaks toward the beginning of the period, not surprisingly given that foreign exchange was scarce in the early 1950s, after which the dollar shortage receded.

Finally, figure 2.5, for 1973–1995, shows considerable evidence of instability. The Chow tests for a shift in the demand for gold and the share of gold in total reserves peaks around 1987–1988, just before gold sales get under way.[55]

One explanation for changes over time in the share of reserves held in gold, suggested by Mundell's writings, emphasizes the volatility of monetary policy in the reserve-currency countries.[56] We measured volatility as a three-year moving standard deviation of the log of the monetary base and took the reserve-currency countries to be Britain under the gold standard; the United States, the United Kingdom, and France in the interwar period; the United States under Bretton Woods;

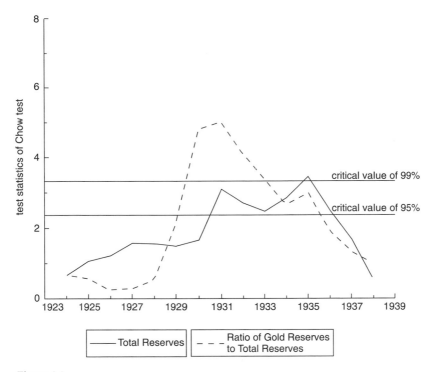

Figure 2.3
Test of structural break: The interwar period

and the United States, Germany, and Japan under the post–Bretton Woods float.[57] When we measure policy using changes in the monetary base, volatility enters positively for the heyday of the Bretton Woods system (1959–1970), a period when the United States came in for criticism for neglecting its responsibilities as a reserve-currency country, but with a zero coefficient otherwise (see table 2.2).[58]

When we measure volatility by the twelve-month standard deviation for each year of the exchange rate of the reserve-currency country or countries, we similarly find that volatility encouraged central banks to hold gold rather than foreign exchange in the post–Bretton Woods period of floating (1973–1995), but not before (see table 2.3).[59] This lends support to the Mundellian view that policy instability in the reserve-currency countries provided a motive for holding gold rather than foreign exchange. Plausibly, the relevant measure of instability was monetary policy related under Bretton Woods and exchange rate related thereafter.

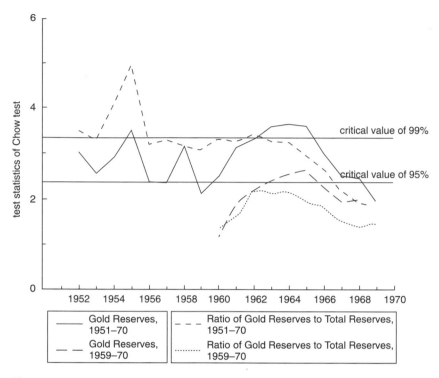

Figure 2.4
Test of structural break: Bretton Woods

To test Mundell's hypothesis that global inflation after the advent of floating rates stimulated the demand for gold, we add a world-inflation proxy to our specification.[60] In table 2.4 we report regressions for the demand for gold and the ratio of gold to total reserves. World inflation enters as predicted only in the post–Bretton Woods years, as if only then was inflation sufficiently persistent that actual inflation predicted future inflation and correspondingly affected the demand for reserves (table 2.4).[61] An alternative specification, in which we instead added a high-inflation dummy variable that takes on a value of unity when the inflation rate exceeded 3 percent, produced basically the same result. These regressions suggest that the shift from high inflation in the period 1973–1983 to low inflation in 1984–1995 reduced the demand for gold as a share of total reserves by about 8 percent. For the post–Bretton Woods float, then, the results support Mundell's view that the rise in inflation in the 1970s increased the demand for gold reserves, whereas the decline in inflation since the early 1980s reduced it.

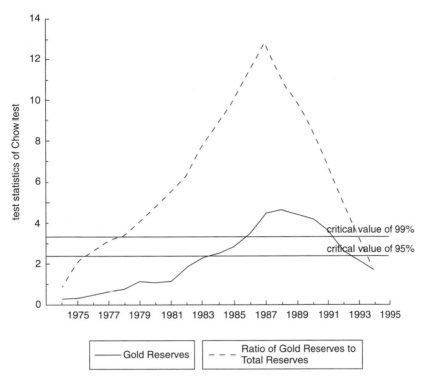

Figure 2.5
Test of structural break: Floating exchange rate period

To analyze the sources of persistence in the demand for gold reserves, we added three final regressors. One is the lagged dependent variable, which we interpret as a measure of simple inertia or historical persistence.[62] Interpretation of the coefficient on the lagged dependent variable is not straightforward, of course: A large coefficient could indicate that a greater propensity to hold gold reserves in the past has the effect of encouraging the central bank to hold more gold reserves in the present, but it could also simply be picking up the effects of random factors that cause some countries to hold more gold than others. Some countries may hold unusually high quantities of gold, in other words, because of persistent error terms rather than hysteresis in portfolio behavior per se.[63] A standard approach to estimation in this case is to instrument the lagged dependent variable (Liviatan 1963). Since the instrumental variables are uncorrelated in the probability limit with the disturbance, substituting the instrumented value of lagged reserves will yield consistent estimates.[64] Here the obvious

Table 2.2
The demand for international reserves, including money supply (M0) volatility

A. Dependent variable: Total reserves

Period	Constant	Log GNP	Import share	Export variability	Money supply volatility	R^2	n
Total 1882–1995	−3.74 (−65.58)	1.02 (477.59)	1.78 (12.02)	−0.04 (−1.37)	1.43 (4.25)	0.99	1,499
Gold 1882–1913	−2.12 (−8.65)	0.82 (30.07)	0.53 (2.52)	12.11 (2.35)	1.23 (0.67)	0.72	376
Interwar 1923–1939	−4.50 (−10.51)	1.10 (28.73)	3.31 (5.29)	3.17 (3.33)	0.11 (0.17)	0.76	278
Interwar 1925–1935	−4.55 (−9.69)	1.10 (26.79)	2.99 (4.41)	2.92 (3.18)	0.93 (1.06)	0.80	194
Bretton Woods 1951–1970	−3.86 (−21.68)	1.02 (172.58)	3.78 (11.24)	−4.08 (−4.36)	−2.66 (−2.30)	0.99	323
Bretton Woods 1959–1970	−4.15 (−25.75)	1.02 (183.23)	3.79 (10.38)	−3.28 (−3.68)	0.16 (2.00)	1.00	241
Floating 1973–1995	−3.74 (−22.29)	1.01 (179.26)	2.84 (10.60)	−0.02 (−0.49)	0.78 (1.33)	0.99	480

B. Dependent variable: Ratio of gold reserves to total reserves

Total 1882–1995	0.88 (41.06)	-0.02 (-22.37)	0.04 (0.65)	-0.06 (-5.10)	-0.48 (-3.74)	0.27	1,499
Gold 1882–1913	0.46 (6.39)	0.05 (5.73)	-0.03 (-0.53)	-1.23 (-0.80)	-0.10 (-0.18)	0.09	376
Interwar 1923–1939	0.46 (2.88)	0.02 (1.71)	0.14 (0.61)	0.05 (0.13)	0.10 (0.41)	0.01	278
Interwar 1925–1935	0.69 (3.42)	0.01 (0.55)	-0.26 (-0.89)	-0.28 (-0.70)	-0.01 (-0.03)	0.01	194
Bretton Woods 1951–1970	0.36 (4.65)	0.01 (2.51)	0.14 (0.98)	-0.70 (-1.74)	-0.75 (-1.51)	0.08	323
Bretton Woods 1959–1970	0.20 (3.14)	0.00 (2.16)	0.20 (1.40)	-0.03 (-0.10)	0.25 (8.07)	0.28	241
Floating 1973–1995	0.00 (0.03)	0.01 (3.53)	0.25 (3.29)	0.02 (2.22)	0.13 (0.78)	0.06	480

Sources: See appendix 2.2.

Notes: t-statistics in parentheses. Two-tailed critical values are 1.96 at the 95% confidence level and 2.58 at 99% level. Year dummies are not included. Variable definitions: Ratio of gold reserves to total reserves = log (gold reserves)/log (gold reserve + foreign reserves). Money supply volatility = three-year moving standard deviation of log M0 of major countries; gold standard (UK), interwar (U.S., UK, and France), Bretton Woods (U.S.), floating (U.S., Germany, and Japan).

Table 2.3
The demand for international reserves, including exchange rate volatility

A. Dependent variable: Gold reserves

Period	Constant	Log GNP	Import share	Export variability	Exchange rate volatility	R^2	n
Total 1923–1995	-4.58 (-32.59)	0.97 (184.14)	4.06 (9.88)	-0.14 (-2.27)	0.02 (3.87)	0.97	1,073
Interwar 1923–1939	-7.03 (-11.28)	1.27 (22.61)	5.42 (5.83)	3.79 (2.70)	0.00 (0.90)	0.65	278
Interwar 1925–1935	-5.89 (-9.50)	1.19 (21.44)	3.50 (3.72)	2.50 (2.02)	0.00 (0.77)	0.71	194
Bretton Woods 1951–1970	-5.29 (-15.74)	1.04 (97.05)	4.09 (6.19)	-6.87 (-4.02)	-0.47 (-1.74)	0.98	273
Bretton Woods 1959–1970	-5.35 (-16.12)	1.04 (99.03)	3.81 (5.53)	-6.43 (-3.84)	-0.45 (-1.59)	0.99	241
Floating 1973–1995	-7.47 (-23.04)	1.05 (97.82)	4.66 (9.13)	0.14 (2.39)	0.08 (2.24)	0.96	480

B. Dependent variable: Ratio of gold reserves to total reserves

Total 1923–1995	0.64 (22.16)	−0.01 (−11.38)	0.12 (1.42)	−0.04 (−3.57)	0.00 (4.74)	0.17	1,073
Interwar 1923–1939	0.45 (2.80)	0.03 (1.77)	0.19 (0.80)	−0.01 (−0.03)	0.00 (1.05)	0.01	278
Interwar 1925–1935	0.65 (3.30)	0.01 (0.63)	−0.19 (−0.64)	−0.35 (−0.89)	0.00 (1.05)	0.02	194
Bretton Woods 1951–1970	0.32 (4.06)	0.01 (2.41)	0.20 (1.25)	−0.60 (−1.47)	−0.07 (−1.14)	0.08	273
Bretton Woods 1959–1970	0.32 (4.14)	0.01 (2.46)	0.22 (1.35)	−0.52 (−1.31)	−0.10 (−1.54)	0.10	241
Floating 1973–1995	−0.02 (−0.42)	0.01 (3.57)	0.24 (3.18)	0.02 (2.26)	0.01 (1.90)	0.06	480

Sources: See appendix 2.2.

Notes: t-statistics in parentheses. Two-tailed critical values are 1.96 at the 95% confidence level and 2.58 at 99% level. Year dummies are not included. Variable definitions: Exchange rate volatility = standard deviation of monthly exchange rates of major currencies; interwar (pound/dollar); interwar (pound/dollar), postwar (index of trade weighted dollar).

Table 2.4
The demand for international reserves, including world inflation

A. Dependent variable: Gold reserves

Period	Constant	Log GNP	Import share	Export variability	World inflation	R^2	n
Floating[1] 1973–1994	−7.45 (−21.15)	1.05 (95.01)	4.66 (9.11)	0.15 (2.46)	0.03 (1.41)	0.96	480
Floating[2] 1973–1994	−7.41 (−22.37)	1.05 (96.32)	4.64 (9.06)	0.14 (2.41)	0.21 (1.57)	0.96	480
Floating[3] 1973–1994	−7.36 (−22.39)	1.05 (94.76)	4.67 (9.14)	0.15 (2.48)	0.16 (1.27)	0.96	480

B. Dependent variable: Ratio of gold reserves to total reserves

Period	Constant	Log GNP	Import share	Export variability	World inflation	R^2	n
Floating[1] 1973–1994	−0.10 (−2.01)	0.01 (4.53)	0.23 (3.04)	0.02 (2.72)	0.02 (4.40)	0.09	480
Floating[2] 1973–1994	−0.06 (−1.23)	0.01 (4.14)	0.23 (2.99)	0.02 (2.43)	0.07 (3.64)	0.08	480
Floating[3] 1973–1994	−0.07 (−1.51)	0.01 (4.59)	0.23 (3.09)	0.03 (2.87)	0.08 (4.52)	0.09	480

Sources: See appendix 2.2.
Notes: *t*-statistics in parentheses. Two-tailed critical values are 1.96 at the 95% confidence level and 2.58 at 99% level. Year dummies are not included. Variable definitions: (1) World inflation = the GDP weighted average of the G-5 (U.S., UK, France, Germany, and Japan) inflation rate; (2) World inflation = 1 if the GDP weighted average of G-5 inflation rate exceeds 3%, 0 otherwise; (3) World inflation = 1 if high inflation period (1973–1983), 0 otherwise.

instruments are lagged incomes, the lagged import ratio, and lagged export variability. Intuitively, including only the predicted, or systematic, component of lagged reserves enhances the plausibility of our interpretation that the lagged value is picking up inertia in the demand for reserves rather than persistent random effects.

Our second ancillary variable is a measure of network externalities, namely, the global gold reserve ratio. If the attractions of holding gold rise with the number of other countries that do the same and with the amount of gold they hold, then a given country's holdings should increase with the global ratio.

Our third ancillary variable measures statutes requiring central banks to hold reserves. If the demand for gold reserves is persistent because statutory requirements are persistent, then this variable should have an independent effect after controlling for other determinants of the demand for reserves. We use a dummy variable for the presence or absence of statutory gold reserve requirements.[65]

When included one at a time (table 5), each of these ancillary variables enters with its expected positive sign and a coefficient that differs from zero at standard confidence levels. When included together, all three variables matter, although lagged holdings and statutory requirements tend to dominate.

The instrumented lagged dependent variable enters with large coefficients in the gold-reserves equation, suggesting considerable persistence. Statutory requirements are highly significant determinants of the demand for gold in the Bretton Woods years and marginally significant in the interwar years. The fact that the coefficient on this variable is insignificant for our 115 years as a whole reflects its significant negative coefficient for the period 1880–1913. Over much of this period, two of the most important gold-standard countries, the United States and France, were not required to hold gold by statute.[66] Their inclusion produces the negative coefficient for the gold-standard years. The effect of the global gold ratio is ambiguous: although generally positive in sign, its coefficient differs insignificantly from zero in the demand-for-gold-reserves equation but does differ significantly from zero in the ratio-of-gold-to-total-reserves equation.

On balance, we conclude that there is some evidence supporting all three historical explanations for the persistence of gold reserves: simple inertia, network externalities, and statutory requirements.

To analyze the impact on the demand for reserves of the shift from fixed to floating rates, we added a dummy variable for the exchange

Table 2.5
The demand for international reserves, including instrumented lagged dependent variable, global gold ratio, dummy for statutory gold reserve requirements

A. Dependent variable: Gold reserves

Period	Constant	Log GNP	Import share	Export variability	Lagged dependent	Global gold	Statutory requirements	R^2	n
Total 1882–1970	−0.51 (−0.67)	−0.02 (−0.19)	0.02 (0.08)	0.48 (0.48)	1.03 (12.65)	0.48 (0.81)	0.14 (1.93)	0.98	955
Gold 1882–1913	3.11 (1.25)	0.15 (0.50)	0.30 (1.39)	−3.20 (−0.64)	0.85 (2.47)	−3.49 (−1.05)	−0.66 (−8.27)	0.81	374
Interwar 1923–1939	−1.91 (−0.72)	0.11 (0.32)	1.00 (0.62)	1.41 (0.88)	0.96 (3.55)	0.93 (0.61)	0.17 (1.02)	0.67	278
Interwar 1925–1935	−0.20 (−0.07)	0.10 (0.32)	−0.67 (−0.42)	0.08 (0.06)	0.90 (3.56)	−0.25 (−0.16)	0.24 (1.48)	0.74	194
Bretton Woods 1951–1970	−3.45 (−1.48)	0.28 (0.99)	1.50 (1.14)	2.20 (0.83)	0.76 (2.82)	1.00 (0.92)	0.97 (7.91)	0.87	303
Bretton Woods 1959–1970	−6.21 (−1.46)	0.58 (1.03)	2.40 (0.99)	2.54 (0.86)	0.50 (0.93)	2.33 (1.37)	0.88 (6.10)	0.89	221

B. Dependent variable: Ratio of gold reserves to total reserves

Total 1882–1970	−0.55 (−2.95)	0.06 (2.62)	0.04 (0.61)	0.05 (0.18)	−0.06 (−2.57)	1.13 (7.46)	−0.13 (6.68)	0.25	955
Gold 1882–1913	−0.17 (−0.18)	0.11 (1.33)	0.01 (0.13)	0.07 (0.04)	−0.08 (−0.73)	0.51 (0.44)	0.01 (0.37)	0.10	374
Interwar 1923–1939	0.13 (0.23)	−0.11 (−1.22)	−0.15 (−0.42)	−0.14 (−0.32)	0.13 (1.58)	0.86 (2.24)	0.09 (2.01)	0.06	278
Interwar 1925–1935	0.27 (0.38)	−0.14 (−1.25)	−0.55 (−1.20)	−0.50 (−1.02)	0.14 (1.45)	0.91 (1.91)	0.15 (2.97)	0.09	194
Bretton Woods 1951–1970	−0.19 (−0.32)	−0.11 (−1.01)	−0.02 (−0.04)	1.27 (2.08)	0.13 (1.24)	0.50 (1.87)	0.30 (10.84)	0.34	303
Bretton Woods 1959–1970	−0.35 (−0.32)	−0.07 (−0.32)	0.12 (0.17)	1.24 (1.78)	0.09 (0.44)	0.50 (1.25)	0.27 (8.63)	0.31	221

Sources: See appendix 2.2.

Notes: t-statistics in parentheses. Two-tailed critical values are 1.96 at the 95% confidence level and 2.58 at 99% level. Year dummies are not included. Two-stage least-squares estimates. Variable definitions: Lagged dependent variable is instrumented by the benchmark specification. Global gold ratios are calculated using our data; gold standard (16 countries), interwar and post-war (21 countries). Dummy for statutory gold reserve requirements = 1 if requirements are present, 0 otherwise.

rate regime (equaling zero for countries with pegged rates, one for those with floating rates).[67] Table 2.6 shows the effect of the exchange rate regime on the demand for gold and the demand for total reserves. The exchange rate regime matters in the gold standard years (when it enters negatively and significantly for 1882–1913 and 1923–1939 in the equations for both gold and total reserves). This is not surprising; the ability of poor countries with a history of running fiat money systems to accumulate the reserves necessary for the operation of a specie standard was one of the principal constraints on going on gold (Eichengreen and Flandreau 1996). The negative coefficient is again evident in the post–1972 period, especially in the equation for gold; the results thus suggest that countries with floating currencies had a significantly lower propensity to hold gold.[68]

To account for the impact on the demand for reserves of the relaxation of capital controls, we added dummy variables for two measures of capital controls: current account restrictions and capital account restrictions. Tables 2.7–2.8 present the results. Countries with such restrictions in place appear to have a significantly greater propensity to hold reserves in general and gold reserves in particular, a result driven largely by behavior in the post–Bretton Woods period.[69] The post–Bretton Woods years are the period of highest capital mobility, so these results support the argument that countries' growing ability to borrow abroad—an ability presumably not shared by countries with capital controls in place—diminished their need to hold reserves. In the equations where the dependent variable is gold reserves, current account restrictions enter with a strongly positive sign, as if the removal of controls leads countries to reduce their gold reserve holdings in particular. A possible interpretation is that countries that seek to integrate themselves into the world economy attach less value to the war chest argument for holding gold.

These results paint a less than rosy picture of the future monetary role for gold. Experience to date suggests that the move to floating rates and international capital mobility has progressively diminished central banks' appetite for gold. Habit, network externalities and lingering statutory requirements have all encouraged the authorities to hold onto their gold reserves for longer than might otherwise be expected. But although these effects introduce persistence into the demand for gold, such sources of persistence tend to die out over time. Each of these sources of inertia in central bank gold holdings is likely to have weaker effects in the future than in the past.

Conclusion

Recapitulating all our results would make a long chapter even longer. The briefest summary would emphasize four points.

First, the gold-exchange standard was a relatively recent arrangement that emerged only around 1900 in response to a set of historically specific factors, factors that also help to account for its smooth operation. How long those factors would have continued to support it will never be known, for a great war and then a great depression intervened before they could be put to the test.

Second, a system that relied on inelastically supplied precious metal and elastically supplied foreign exchange to meet the world economy's incremental demand for reserves was intrinsically fragile, prone to confidence problems, and a transmission belt for policy mistakes. Proposals to finesse the liquidity problem through periodic adjustments in the price of gold were not feasible, given the damage this would do to the credibility of the authorities' commitment to maintain convertibility at the prevailing price.

Third, network externalities, statutory restrictions, and habit all contributed to the persistence of the practice of holding gold reserves. But the hold of even factors as powerful as these inevitably weakens with time. And the effects of their erosion are reinforced by the rise of international capital mobility, which increases the ease of holding other forms of reserves, both unborrowed and borrowed, and by the shift to greater exchange-rate flexibility, which according to our results diminishes the demand for reserves in general.

Fourth and finally, network externalities, in conjunction with central bankers' collective sense of responsibility for the stability of the price of what remains an important reserve asset, suggest that the same factors that have long held in place the practice of holding gold reserves, when they come unstuck, may become unstuck all at once.

Table 2.6
The demand for international reserves, including an exchange rate regime dummy variable

A. *Dependent variable: Total reserves*

Period	Constant	Log GNP	Import share	Export variability	Exchange rate regime	R^2	n
Total 1882–1995	−3.81 (−13.52)	1.02 (243.87)	1.77 (11.54)	−0.01 (−0.24)	−0.36 (−6.24)	0.99	1,499
Gold 1882–1913	−1.81 (−5.22)	0.80 (29.48)	0.03 (0.13)	4.12 (0.77)	−0.90 (−7.40)	0.77	376
Interwar 1923–1939	−4.58 (−7.78)	1.09 (27.53)	4.25 (5.90)	3.76 (3.34)	−0.31 (−2.21)	0.77	278
Interwar 1925–1935	−4.34 (−7.65)	1.09 (25.52)	3.64 (4.68)	3.03 (2.85)	−0.34 (−2.59)	0.81	194
Bretton Woods 1951–1970	−3.68 (−9.95)	1.02 (184.78)	3.63 (11.56)	−3.69 (−4.12)	0.55 (3.63)	0.99	323
Bretton Woods 1959–1970	−4.11 (−19.23)	1.02 (191.21)	3.71 (10.61)	−3.60 (−4.19)	0.72 (3.61)	1.00	241
Floating 1973–1995	−3.35 (−15.19)	1.00 (172.46)	2.70 (9.87)	−0.03 (−0.96)	−0.23 (−3.15)	0.99	480

B. *Dependent variable: Gold reserves*

Total 1882–1995	-4.60 (-10.73)	1.06 (167.32)	2.26 (9.73)	0.13 (2.61)	-0.41 (-4.76)	0.99	1,497
Gold 1882–1913	-2.76 (-8.02)	0.87 (32.59)	0.09 (0.41)	6.24 (1.15)	-0.70 (-5.82)	0.80	374
Interwar 1923–1939	-6.74 (-7.76)	1.26 (21.62)	6.47 (6.09)	4.29 (2.58)	-0.44 (-2.08)	0.67	278
Interwar 1925–1935	-5.48 (-7.21)	1.17 (20.50)	4.21 (4.04)	2.43 (1.70)	-0.53 (-3.08)	0.74	194
Bretton Woods 1951–1970	-4.40 (-6.44)	1.04 (101.95)	3.74 (6.46)	-6.46 (-3.91)	0.56 (1.97)	0.98	323
Bretton Woods 1959–1970	-5.52 (-13.45)	1.04 (101.51)	3.68 (5.48)	-6.10 (-3.70)	0.84 (2.18)	0.99	241
Floating 1973–1995	-6.97 (-16.29)	1.05 (93.48)	4.33 (8.14)	0.16 (2.67)	-0.27 (-1.91)	0.96	480

Sources: See appendix 2.2.

Notes: t-statistics in parentheses. Two-tailed critical values are 1.96 at the 95% confidence level and 2.58 at 99% level. Year dummies are included. Variable definitions: Exchange rate regime dummy = 0 if a country has a fixed exchange rate regime, 1 if a country has a floating exchange rate regime.

Table 2.7
The demand for international reserves, including a capital controls dummy variable (current account restrictions)

A. *Dependent variable: Total reserves*

Period	Constant	Log GNP	Import share	Export variability	Capital controls	R^2	n
Total 1951–1994	−4.12 (−6.38)	1.01 (220.18)	3.05 (15.34)	−0.04 (−1.36)	0.22 (3.77)	0.99	826
Bretton Woods 1951–1970	−3.99 (−6.37)	1.01 (104.17)	3.45 (10.72)	−1.41 (−0.86)	−0.06 (−0.82)	0.98	306
Bretton Woods 1959–1970	−3.75 (−12.88)	1.02 (110.73)	3.42 (9.90)	−1.40 (−0.91)	0.02 (0.32)	0.99	224
Floating 1973–1994	−3.89 (−19.10)	1.01 (182.63)	2.81 (11.03)	−0.09 (−2.83)	0.52 (6.19)	0.99	480

B. *Dependent variable: Gold reserves*

Period	Constant	Log GNP	Import share	Export variability	Capital controls	R^2	n
Total 1951–1994	−5.91 (−4.73)	1.05 (88.75)	4.15 (10.86)	0.07 (1.24)	0.61 (5.47)	0.94	811
Bretton Woods 1951–1970	−5.62 (−4.16)	1.07 (35.78)	3.88 (6.01)	−3.68 (−1.16)	−0.01 (−0.10)	0.86	303
Bretton Woods 1959–1970	−7.01 (−7.51)	1.10 (35.17)	3.85 (5.21)	−2.96 (−0.94)	0.23 (1.45)	0.88	221
Floating 1973–1994	−7.17 (−15.51)	1.01 (77.43)	4.26 (8.59)	−0.03 (−0.44)	1.27 (7.64)	0.95	470

Sources: See appendix 2.2.
Notes: *t*-statistics in parentheses. Two-tailed critical values are 1.96 at the 95% confidence level and 2.58 at 99% level. Year dummies are included. Variable definitions: Capital controls dummy = 1 if a country has restrictions on its current account, 0 otherwise.

Table 2.8
The demand for international reserves, including a capital controls dummy variable (capital account restrictions)

A. Dependent variable: Total reserves

Period	Constant	Log GNP	Import share	Export variability	Capital controls	R^2	n
Total 1951–1994	-4.29 (-6.86)	1.01 (230.37)	3.14 (16.25)	-0.04 (-1.49)	0.39 (7.60)	0.99	826
Bretton Woods 1951–1970	-3.93 (-6.31)	1.01 (104.85)	3.44 (10.78)	-1.27 (-0.80)	-0.15 (-1.87)	0.98	306
Bretton Woods 1959–1970	-3.70 (-12.73)	1.02 (110.73)	3.39 (9.87)	-1.09 (-0.73)	-0.06 (-0.78)	0.99	224
Floating 1973–1994	-4.28 (-22.39)	1.01 (204.49)	3.11 (13.20)	-0.07 (-2.65)	0.71 (11.21)	0.99	480

B. Dependent variable: Gold reserves

Period	Constant	Log GNP	Import share	Export variability	Capital controls	R^2	n
Total 1951–1994	-4.95 (-3.88)	1.05 (86.69)	3.95 (10.11)	0.15 (2.59)	-0.12 (-1.13)	0.93	811
Bretton Woods 1951–1970	-4.52 (-3.58)	1.06 (37.95)	3.71 (6.16)	-1.65 (-0.56)	-0.84 (-5.81)	0.87	303
Bretton Woods 1959–1970	-5.88 (-6.65)	1.08 (36.59)	3.34 (4.78)	-0.37 (-0.12)	-0.75 (-4.60)	0.89	221
Floating 1973–1994	-7.01 (-13.84)	1.04 (72.57)	4.28 (8.04)	0.11 (1.72)	0.34 (2.39)	0.95	470

Sources: See appendix 2.2.
Notes: t-statistics in parentheses. Two-tailed critical values are 1.96 at the 95% confidence level and 2.58 at 99% level. Year dummies are included. Variable definitions: Capital controls dummy = 1 if a country has restrictions on its capital account, 0 otherwise.

Appendix 2.1   Alternative Measures of Reserves

Table A.2.1
Gold and foreign exchange reserves: Aggregate

A. Gold standard

Years	Series 1		Series 2	
	GR	FR	GR	FR
1880	545.1	49.4	1,000.0	104.9
1881	547.3	38.3	1,069.6	82.0
1882	589.3	37.6	1,139.1	84.4
1883	598.1	48.1	1,208.7	97.8
1884	635.5	50.3	1,278.3	120.8
1885	667.7	53.0	1,347.8	149.2
1886	720.8	60.0	1,417.4	126.9
1887	804.3	58.4	1,487.0	114.7
1888	823.5	56.8	1,556.5	115.2
1889	860.2	75.2	1,626.1	220.3
1890	812.0	57.2	1,695.7	257.5
1891	839.8	64.2	1,765.2	195.6
1892	893.9	70.8	1,834.8	155.0
1893	854.5	70.2	1,904.3	109.6
1894	988.8	78.8	1,973.9	154.9
1895	1,024.2	79.1	2,043.5	138.3
1896	1,069.2	78.3	2,113.0	183.0
1897	1,089.3	96.4	2,182.6	215.0
1898	1,102.8	83.5	2,252.2	191.7
1899	1,163.9	92.7	2,321.7	195.1
1900	1,247.0	112.1	2,391.3	224.5
1901	1,320.0	130.1	2,460.9	295.5
1902	1,381.1	128.4	2,530.4	378.2
1903	1,388.0	162.8	2,600.0	501.3
1904	1,404.5	175.1	2,828.6	567.0
1905	1,743.0	193.9	3,057.1	753.3
1906	1,761.1	224.2	3,285.7	908.8
1907	2,031.1	218.5	3,514.3	808.6
1908	2,226.7	256.5	3,742.9	776.4
1909	2,343.4	271.1	3,971.4	851.0
1910	2,355.8	301.9	4,200.0	1,097.0
1911	2,371.9	315.2	4,433.3	1,086.7

Table A.2.1
(continued)

Years	Series 1		Series 2	
	GR	FR	GR	FR
1912	2,436.1	310.0	4,666.7	1,040.0
1913	2,599.7	370.9	4,900.0	1,130.0

Note: Series 1: 16 countries, Bloomfield 1963 and Lindert 1967, 1969. Series 2: 35 countries, gold reserves (interpolated between benchmarks), Lindert 1969. Figures in millions of U.S. dollars.

B. Interwar

Years	Series 1	
	GR	FR
1920	6,215.7	652.5
1921	6,789.2	545.6
1922	7,262.9	450.7
1923	8,889.3	633.8
1924	8,589.1	1,109.0
1925	8,749.0	1,359.3
1926	8,806.5	1,343.8
1927	9,165.5	1,571.6
1928	10,005.2	2,849.5
1929	9,858.5	2,323.6
1930	9,590.7	2,268.2
1931	9,486.1	1,443.9
1932	9,957.0	719.9
1933	12,294.4	988.2
1934	18,196.4	1,241.3
1935	19,719.7	1,329.9
1936	24,880.0	1,598.0
1937	23,427.6	1,907.4
1938	23,942.6	1,462.8
1939	24,588.0	1,598.4

Note: Series 1: 21 countries, League of Nations 1930. Figures in millions of U.S. dollars.

Table A.2.1
(continued)

C. Postwar

	Series 1		Series 2		Series 3		Series 4	
Years	GR	FR	GR	FR	GR	FR	GR	FR
1948	30.1	6.9	30.0	6.9	32.5	15.3	32.2	15.3
1949	30.4	6.6	30.3	6.6	33.0	12.6	32.7	12.6
1950	30.5	8.3	30.4	8.3	33.4	15.0	33.2	15.0
1951	30.4	8.2	30.2	8.2	33.6	15.2	33.3	15.2
1952	30.7	8.8	30.4	8.8	33.6	15.8	33.3	15.8
1953	31.2	9.7	30.8	9.7	34.1	17.2	33.8	17.2
1954	31.9	10.3	31.8	10.3	34.7	18.3	34.8	18.3
1955	32.2	10.5	32.1	10.5	35.2	18.6	35.1	18.6
1956	32.8	11.6	32.5	11.6	35.9	20.0	35.8	20.0
1957	33.9	11.5	33.6	11.5	37.1	19.4	37.1	19.4
1958	34.5	12.2	34.4	12.2	37.8	19.6	37.9	19.6
1959	34.4	12.1	34.2	12.1	37.8	19.4	37.8	19.4
1960	34.9	14.9	35.3	14.9	37.9	22.1	38.6	22.1
1961	35.5	16.7	35.8	16.7	38.8	23.3	38.9	23.3
1962	35.4	16.6	35.7	16.6	39.2	23.7	39.2	23.7
1963	36.2	18.1	36.6	18.1	40.2	26.6	40.3	26.6
1964	36.8	19.7	37.1	19.7	40.7	28.4	40.9	28.4
1965	37.9	19.8	38.3	19.8	41.8	29.4	41.9	29.4
1966	36.9	21.2	37.3	21.2	40.8	32.0	41.0	32.0
1967	35.2	23.8	35.5	23.8	39.4	35.2	39.6	35.2
1968	33.4	26.9	39.9	26.9	38.8	39.1	46.4	39.1
1969	33.6	25.9	33.8	25.9	39.0	39.8	39.2	39.8
1970	32.4	39.6	34.2	39.6	37.1	56.2	39.6	56.2
1971	33.1	71.7	38.9	71.7	36.1	87.1	41.4	87.1
1972	33.7	89.3	56.9	89.3	.	110.9	61.1	110.9
1973	38.1	99.9	98.4	99.9	35.8	116.8	95.3	116.8
1974	40.1	99.7	163.5	99.7	35.8	144.0	155.7	144.0
1975	48.9	98.0	122.7	98.0	35.7	158.7	122.2	158.7
1976	54.6	111.1	117.9	111.1	35.5	186.6	117.8	186.6
1977	63.7	150.3	145.8	150.3	36.1	228.5	139.9	228.5
1978	80.6	198.2	200.6	198.2	36.3	245.5	180.1	245.5
1979	100.1	217.4	406.0	217.4	33.1	272.9	368.0	272.9
1980	141.5	244.2	467.0	244.2	33.4	321.3	441.7	321.3
1981	119.1	221.3	315.0	221.3	33.4	329.7	326.2	329.7
1982	111.0	204.2	361.0	204.2	33.3	327.9	394.0	327.9
1983	107.2	215.3	301.4	215.3	33.3	362.3	346.2	362.3

Table A.2.1
(continued)

C. Postwar

Years	Series 1		Series 2		Series 3		Series 4	
	GR	FR	GR	FR	GR	FR	GR	FR
1984	100.8	228.1	243.9	228.1	33.2	407.1	298.5	407.1
1985	108.6	258.8	259.3	258.8	33.3	404.8	283.3	404.8
1986	125.0	304.7	309.0	304.7	33.3	418.6	304.1	418.6
1987	148.2	454.6	379.2	454.6	33.1	507.6	322.8	507.6
1988	131.5	473.0	322.5	473.0	33.1	542.7	288.6	542.7
1989	129.8	498.8	314.9	498.8	32.9	591.0	287.1	591.0
1990	135.9	588.0	302.3	588.0	32.9	637.7	254.1	637.7
1991	133.5	574.6	276.0	574.6	32.8	671.8	231.9	671.8
1992	122.5	567.7	257.5	567.7	32.5	693.7	224.8	693.7
1993	122.9	597.6	297.0	597.6	32.3	765.9	262.1	765.9
1994	128.3	670.8	290.7	670.8	32.1	824.4	240.9	824.4
1995	130.2	770.9	291.1	770.9	31.8	949.9	236.3	949.9
1996	117.7	842.9	275.6	842.9	31.7	1,087.1	232.3	1,087.1

Sources: See appendix 2.2.
Note: Series 1: 21 countries, gold—official value, IFS. Series 2: 21 countries, gold—market value, IFS. Series 3: World, gold—book value, IFS. Series 4: World, gold—market value, IFS. Figures in billions of U.S. dollars for Series 1 and 2, billions of SDRs for Series 3 and 4.

Table A.2.2
Gold and foreign exchange reserves: Individual countries (1880–1939)

A. Gold standard

Years	Argentina GR	Argentina FR	Australia GR	Australia FR	Belgium GR	Belgium FR	Canada GR	Canada FR	Denmark GR	Denmark FR	Finland GR	Finland FR	France GR	France FR	Germany GR	Germany FR
1880	.	.	50.1	.	15.0	22.4	6.0	0.2	14.0	2.6	3.5	7.4	109.9	.	53.8	6.0
1881	.	.	49.4	.	15.5	14.1	6.6	0.3	14.0	3.3	3.5	6.4	115.7	.	47.5	4.5
1882	.	.	42.2	.	15.0	18.0	6.6	0.0	14.0	2.8	3.5	5.6	186.8	.	50.7	1.6
1883	.	.	43.2	.	14.5	26.1	7.2	0.0	14.0	2.8	3.5	6.4	178.9	.	66.2	2.5
1884	.	.	51.3	.	13.5	28.9	7.5	0.0	13.0	3.0	3.5	6.1	210.5	.	63.8	2.0
1885	.	.	61.3	.	14.0	28.4	6.7	1.0	13.0	2.3	3.5	5.3	222.9	.	63.5	6.7
1886	.	.	58.8	.	11.0	33.0	6.0	0.0	14.0	5.0	3.5	5.4	245.3	.	90.0	5.6
1887	.	.	72.0	.	11.0	31.6	6.0	0.0	15.0	7.2	3.5	4.1	225.8	.	111.8	3.7
1888	.	.	80.5	.	11.0	28.9	7.4	0.1	16.0	4.0	3.5	4.1	199.4	.	145.0	3.0
1889	.	.	75.8	.	13.0	34.0	6.0	0.0	16.0	4.1	3.5	6.0	256.6	.	140.4	3.0
1890	.	.	86.6	.	12.0	31.7	6.7	0.0	17.0	3.1	3.5	5.4	227.8	.	123.6	1.7
1891	.	.	85.1	.	13.0	34.7	5.8	0.0	16.0	2.7	3.5	4.5	275.3	.	137.7	4.7
1892	.	.	86.0	.	16.0	37.9	6.7	0.0	17.0	3.7	3.5	4.8	329.9	.	144.2	3.5
1893	.	0.0	86.3	.	15.0	39.5	7.7	0.3	17.0	4.2	3.5	3.6	329.0	.	123.3	1.7
1894	.	0.0	100.5	.	20.0	41.7	8.0	0.0	18.0	6.3	3.5	6.3	399.2	.	145.4	1.9
1895	.	0.0	104.6	.	17.5	41.9	8.2	0.0	19.0	4.4	3.5	9.2	379.7	.	164.8	2.0

Year																
1896	.	0.0	115.1	.	17.5	43.4	8.6	0.4	19.0	2.6	3.5	10.3	371.6	.	161.7	2.0
1897	.	0.0	103.6	.	17.5	50.9	8.3	1.1	18.0	3.5	3.5	11.4	374.7	.	139.4	3.6
1898	.	0.0	93.2	.	18.0	35.9	9.0	0.0	20.0	1.3	3.5	13.0	349.8	.	136.5	8.6
1899	.	1.8	90.0	.	18.0	41.9	9.6	0.0	20.0	1.3	4.0	9.8	370.0	.	136.5	7.9
1900	.	0.3	108.4	.	18.0	50.7	11.8	0.0	20.0	1.2	4.0	9.9	455.3	.	134.5	19.1
1901	.	1.0	96.3	.	17.0	66.5	11.6	0.0	19.0	4.6	4.0	10.8	483.4	.	155.9	13.5
1902	.	0.6	102.6	.	17.0	63.8	12.9	2.3	20.0	3.3	4.0	14.8	499.4	.	170.8	15.3
1903	36.9	1.9	97.4	.	18.0	63.3	16.1	0.2	21.0	2.0	4.0	15.7	463.2	.	153.4	12.9
1904	48.5	4.9	94.2	.	18.0	67.0	17.6	0.0	23.0	2.4	4.0	12.7	505.9	.	162.6	13.1
1905	87.0	8.6	104.6	1.5	19.0	57.9	19.6	0.0	25.0	2.3	5.5	17.0	557.9	1.0	176.6	16.2
1906	99.1	9.7	110.4	1.5	20.0	63.6	23.8	0.0	25.0	1.4	5.5	18.6	514.9	5.3	160.1	20.0
1907	101.4	0.6	115.4	1.1	20.5	46.7	25.1	5.0	21.4	1.9	5.5	17.0	507.7	16.8	150.7	8.5
1908	122.2	6.7	121.3	2.3	21.0	62.8	27.1	19.7	19.8	2.9	5.0	14.3	673.6	1.9	186.5	36.6
1909	166.4	13.1	128.0	5.2	21.5	58.3	27.5	0.3	20.0	3.7	4.5	20.6	673.6	13.0	189.0	44.6
1910	179.4	16.2	146.7	5.2	24.0	56.4	33.4	2.5	18.5	5.1	7.5	21.9	622.5	9.1	187.3	58.6
1911	182.3	10.3	162.9	3.5	36.0	55.3	37.5	15.5	24.1	5.7	7.5	20.9	614.1	1.9	176.3	40.7
1912	215.0	18.6	139.6	2.3	42.0	71.6	33.8	1.9	18.6	7.2	7.5	17.4	601.9	4.3	206.5	25.6
1913	225.0	5.0	152.1		48.0	77.7	45.4	13.2	20.6	6.2	7.0	20.9	677.5	3.2	256.5	49.6

Table A.2.2
(continued)

Years	Italy GR	Italy FR	Japan GR	Japan FR	Netherlands GR	Netherlands FR	Norway GR	Norway FR	Sweden GR	Sweden FR	Switzerland GR	Switzerland FR	UK GR	UK FR	U.S. GR	U.S. FR
1880	.	.	.	.	19.0	.	6.0	2.8	2.5	8.0	.	.	134.3	0.0	131.0	0.0
1881	.	.	.	.	4.0	.	6.0	2.4	2.5	7.3	.	.	119.7	0.0	163.0	0.0
1882	.	.	.	.	6.0	.	6.0	2.8	2.5	6.8	.	.	107.1	0.0	149.0	0.0
1883	.	.	.	.	10.0	.	6.0	3.2	2.5	7.1	.	.	108.0	0.0	144.0	0.0
1884	.	.	.	.	15.0	.	6.0	3.0	4.0	7.3	.	.	111.4	0.0	136.0	0.0
1885	.	.	.	.	26.0	.	6.0	2.5	4.0	6.8	.	.	117.8	0.0	129.0	0.0
1886	.	.	.	.	24.0	.	6.0	2.7	4.0	8.3	.	.	102.2	0.0	156.0	0.0
1887	30.0	.	.	.	22.0	.	7.0	3.3	4.0	8.5	.	.	106.1	0.0	190.0	0.0
1888	20.4	.	.	.	24.0	13.0	8.0	4.4	4.0	12.3	.	.	101.2	0.0	203.0	0.0
1889	19.8	.	.	.	22.0	3.3	8.0	4.2	5.0	10.9	.	.	104.1	0.0	190.0	0.0
1890	20.7	.	.	.	20.0	6.8	8.0	2.7	5.0	9.3	.	.	106.1	0.0	175.0	0.0
1891	21.8	.	.	.	16.0	9.5	8.0	2.7	5.0	8.1	.	.	118.7	0.0	134.0	0.0
1892	20.9	.	.	.	14.5	9.3	7.0	3.5	5.0	7.9	.	.	124.1	0.0	119.0	0.0
1893	19.2	.	.	.	18.1	9.8	7.0	1.6	5.0	10.0	.	.	128.5	0.0	95.0	0.0
1894	14.6	.	.	.	19.7	9.8	8.0	1.7	6.0	11.1	.	.	166.9	0.0	79.0	0.0
1895	16.8	.	.	.	17.3	6.7	8.0	2.6	7.0	12.3	.	.	189.8	0.0	88.0	0.0
1896	17.7	2.7	.	.	12.7	2.0	7.7	2.1	5.5	12.8	.	.	215.6	0.0	113.0	0.0

Year															
1897	24.6	2.9	48.5	·	12.7	2.9	7.8	5.1	8.5	15.0	·		173.3	0.0	149.0	0.0
1898	25.4	4.0	45.0	·	20.8	3.0	8.6	3.8	8.5	13.9	·		163.5	0.0	201.0	0.0
1899	27.2	2.8	55.2	·	18.2	2.2	8.6	3.5	8.5	21.5	·		157.2	0.0	241.0	0.0
1900	26.8	2.0	33.9	·	23.5	4.1	7.8	2.6	10.0	22.2	·		162.1	0.0	231.0	0.0
1901	26.4	3.9	35.8	·	27.7	4.4	8.2	3.3	12.5	22.1	·		174.2	0.0	248.0	0.0
1902	26.6	5.5	54.7	·	22.7	4.0	8.2	1.5	14.0	17.4	·		173.3	0.0	255.0	0.0
1903	39.2	6.0	69.5	42.2	20.2	2.5	6.7	2.0	16.0	14.0	·		167.4	0.0	259.0	0.0
1904	38.5	3.9	48.4	41.6	27.2	7.2	6.8	3.3	17.0	19.0	·		167.9	0.0	225.0	0.0
1905	40.5	6.1	239.1	52.2	31.9	8.4	7.6	3.6	18.0	20.6	·		173.7	0.0	237.0	0.0
1906	46.7	6.7	246.9	65.9	28.0	2.5	8.3	5.4	19.0	23.6	·		162.5	0.0	291.0	0.0
1907	334.5	7.6	222.2	79.6	34.0	2.3	7.3	7.5	19.0	18.3	14.6	5.3	169.8	0.0	282.0	0.0
1908	363.3	6.5	195.1	57.0	40.6	6.5	7.9	6.8	21.0	25.1	22.7	8.6	181.0	0.0	218.0	0.0
1909	369.0	7.3	222.7	57.8	48.6	7.3	8.1	7.3	22.0	26.0	23.9	9.4	182.0	0.0	236.0	0.0
1910	373.1	9.4	235.5	67.9	50.2	3.0	9.2	6.8	22.0	28.5	30.0	11.4	179.6	0.0	240.0	0.0
1911	396.0	11.9	181.7	77.8	56.4	6.6	10.3	6.2	24.0	52.5	31.0	4.7	185.9	0.0	246.0	0.0
1912	401.5	12.2	175.0	92.3	65.0	6.5	10.3	6.9	28.0	36.8	33.4	5.2	188.8	0.0	269.0	0.0
1913	402.6	10.9	187.9	115.8	60.9	5.5	11.9	8.9	28.0	43.4	32.8	8.2	180.6	0.0	263.0	0.0

Sources: Bloomfield 1963 and Lindert 1967, 1969.
Note: Figures in millions of U.S. dollars.

Table A.2.2
(continued)

B. Interwar

Years	Argentina GR	Argentina FR	Australia GR	Australia FR	Belgium GR	Belgium FR	Brazil GR	Brazil FR	Canada GR	Canada FR	Chile GR	Chile FR
1920	990.6	.	807.1	.	.	.	.	.	175.0	130.4	58.6	71.9
1921	728.6	.	856.6	.	.	.	.	.	155.7	100.2	38.5	46.1
1922	619.0	.	1,026.7	.	.	.	.	.	236.4	110.3	40.1	47.8
1923	802.9	.	1,068.2	188.6	98.0	6.6	41.6	18.3	180.3	103.9	39.0	46.8
1924	738.9	.	1,070.5	313.6	87.7	9.7	49.2	32.8	206.3	110.5	34.7	45.5
1925	720.0	.	1,461.0	448.8	90.4	10.0	55.4	21.1	226.0	209.0	35.1	53.2
1926	923.2	.	1,222.0	246.3	104.6	75.4	68.0	47.9	230.0	259.0	12.3	57.1
1927	1,101.5	.	1,182.9	351.2	100.0	73.0	99.8	42.8	229.0	210.0	9.2	49.2
1928	1,320.3	.	1,190.2	451.2	125.8	78.9	148.7	28.7	190.8	156.8	9.1	58.7
1929	950.5	95.7	941.9	183.7	163.5	85.3	148.4	26.9	149.8	71.4	9.1	49.8
1930	886.0	73.8	347.2	181.1	191.5	135.4	13.8	31.9	193.6	34.9	8.9	43.3
1931	468.5	41.7	241.0	241.8	355.0	0.0	7.4	14.4	137.7	37.6	8.8	15.4
1932	339.4	0.0	119.7	253.5	361.2	0.0	5.9	26.2	120.7	0.0	5.7	5.5
1933	224.4	0.0	8.5	588.1	489.4	0.0	4.8	22.5	116.8	0.0	6.7	6.2
1934	325.3	0.0	10.0	784.0	583.3	0.0	3.1	11.0	130.3	0.0	13.2	1.5
1935	1,561.6	164.6	9.8	596.1	636.9	0.0	6.8	25.9	113.4	4.0	7.3	0.1
1936	1,574.7	389.8	4.0	756.0	816.2	0.0	7.1	22.9	111.9	9.0	7.4	0.2
1937	1,690.1	272.0	4.0	962.0	722.3	32.4	9.7	4.1	109.0	15.0	7.4	0.2
1938	1,817.4	105.4	3.9	788.2	725.6	8.0	9.4	27.8	112.3	27.8	7.5	0.2
1939	1,526.8	213.3	3.9	947.1	712.2	.	10.0	30.4	121.9	61.4	7.6	0.2

Years	Denmark GR	Denmark FR	Finland GR	Finland FR	France GR	France FR	Germany GR	Germany FR	Greece GR	Greece FR
1920	36.0	7.7	12.8	.	.	.	.	.	.	.
1921	41.5	8.5	7.1	.	.	.	.	.	.	.
1922	47.9	2.7	7.2	17.2	.	.	.	.	.	.
1923	38.7	3.1	8.9	15.9	1,064.9	21.9	181.0	285.2	14.1	.
1924	35.1	8.2	8.3	13.9	954.1	18.1	287.6	241.9	17.0	17.3
1925	44.2	19.0	8.4	31.4	863.9	15.0	436.0	229.3	15.1	17.4
1926	54.9	7.1	8.3	27.2	585.4	13.5	436.0	229.3	13.1	18.0
1927	48.7	25.9	8.0	32.6	725.0	10.1	443.0	112.1	15.0	48.1
1928	46.3	30.2	7.7	18.8	1,224.5	1,263.3	651.3	126.0	7.2	32.1
1929	45.9	24.0	7.6	17.2	1,600.8	1,002.0	543.6	193.3	8.3	32.4
1930	46.1	26.5	7.6	23.8	2,142.5	1,048.2	528.9	182.3	6.6	12.7
1931	36.2	3.8	7.1	14.5	2,633.9	826.9	233.7	0.0	10.5	0.0
1932	25.2	0.0	4.8	11.5	3,325.2	179.3	191.4	0.0	15.0	0.0
1933	25.5	0.0	6.1	24.9	3,664.7	55.3	113.5	65.3	47.5	8.6
1934	30.0	0.0	7.2	32.1	5,541.5	64.1	31.5	35.5	34.2	5.2
1935	25.9	0.0	10.3	28.8	4,419.9	88.6	33.3	71.1	21.6	3.2
1936	26.3	0.0	18.0	32.8	7,453.9	86.0	26.6	44.8	25.8	.
1937	26.1	13.7	13.9	44.5	4,342.9	36.8	28.5	75.5	37.9	.
1938	25.6	18.4	24.4	49.7	2,937.6	23.4	28.5	79.1	41.4	.
1939	.	.	24.3	35.7	2,865.0	2.8	28.5	90.4	51.2	.

Table A.2.2
(continued)

B. Interwar

Years	Italy GR	Italy FR	Japan GR	Japan FR	Netherlands GR	Netherlands FR	Norway GR	Norway FR	Portugal GR	Portugal FR
1920	.	.	549.8	372.4	218.9	20.3	24.3	10.4	.	.
1921	.	.	588.9	316.8	203.9	19.9	22.4	7.2	.	.
1922	.	.	584.1	125.0	224.1	53.1	25.8	10.2	.	.
1923	190.5	32.0	589.3	107.8	227.6	20.7	24.6	5.3	8.7	3.5
1924	182.5	25.0	508.7	87.0	193.0	63.8	20.5	7.1	8.1	12.8
1925	167.7	27.7	473.4	55.3	177.9	80.7	26.3	12.5	10.2	14.7
1926	165.0	91.8	519.4	66.8	166.0	75.0	32.9	20.1	10.7	6.4
1927	230.7	383.5	515.2	61.1	160.4	67.4	38.3	15.6	9.4	3.9
1928	265.6	316.5	502.3	39.8	175.0	88.5	39.3	10.9	9.4	10.6
1929	271.9	269.8	503.2	.	179.5	88.4	39.2	17.6	9.4	12.5
1930	277.5	226.7	406.9	.	171.4	99.4	39.1	19.0	9.4	10.2
1931	293.6	113.3	197.5	.	356.8	34.6	38.9	5.5	12.7	22.8
1932	299.9	67.0	121.1	.	416.2	28.6	26.0	5.6	17.2	15.0
1933	454.9	19.6	109.5	.	476.9	0.5	30.7	1.1	29.8	4.5
1934	497.1	6.2	137.1	.	567.3	0.7	34.2	10.4	41.2	11.4
1935	249.8	30.3	143.2	.	435.4	1.4	45.6	11.3	40.4	13.4
1936	279.6	4.4	158.8	.	464.2	1.3	53.8	27.0	41.1	19.4
1937	210.3	1.7	231.5	.	751.9	2.8	44.8	58.0	41.1	20.4
1938	193.4	8.0	140.7	.	803.7	2.2	50.7	53.4	40.7	18.3

1939	142.4	20.4	126.8	.	540.8	1.1	48.2	23.1	37.2	18.8
	Spain		Sweden		Switzerland		UK		U.S.	
Years	GR	FR	GR	FR	GR	FR	GR	FR	GR	FR
1920	386.2	13.1	57.8	22.1	91.8	4.2	574.6	0.0	2,232.2	0.0
1921	339.3	5.7	63.1	31.0	95.4	10.2	603.9	0.0	3,044.3	0.0
1922	391.0	5.7	71.7	64.6	102.0	14.1	684.2	0.0	3,202.6	0.0
1923	364.0	4.3	72.2	38.0	97.0	17.0	709.1	0.0	3,249.7	0.0
1924	337.9	4.5	62.9	36.1	92.2	35.2	687.3	0.0	3,113.3	0.0
1925	364.0	4.3	61.7	54.2	90.3	42.9	698.2	0.0	2,872.3	0.0
1926	378.3	5.2	60.0	55.4	91.2	42.9	734.2	0.0	2,991.4	0.0
1927	444.0	6.3	61.7	70.5	99.6	38.1	740.9	0.0	2,903.3	0.0
1928	424.6	15.8	63.3	57.6	102.7	48.9	746.0	0.0	2,755.1	0.0
1929	375.7	14.8	65.6	71.0	114.7	68.1	709.6	0.0	3,020.3	0.0
1930	282.9	9.7	64.7	104.7	138.2	84.9	721.0	0.0	3,107.1	0.0
1931	213.9	26.6	52.0	12.4	455.3	20.0	550.1	0.0	3,174.5	0.0
1932	181.2	71.1	38.0	39.5	479.5	16.9	420.1	0.0	3,443.6	0.0
1933	239.6	97.8	81.5	98.3	496.2	4.2	808.1	0.0	4,859.4	0.0
1934	307.3	129.9	91.2	143.7	618.2	2.3	969.3	0.0	8,223.8	0.0
1935	297.9	128.0	103.1	159.0	451.4	2.3	980.9	0.0	10,125.1	0.0
1936	.	.	135.6	183.8	858.6	17.5	1,559.1	0.0	11,257.4	0.0
1937	.	.	137.4	250.8	645.0	117.7	1,613.4	0.0	12,760.3	0.0
1938	.	.	178.1	189.0	693.9	64.0	1,596.1	0.0	14,511.7	0.0
1939	.	.	162.9	72.2	534.7	81.5	.	0.0	17,643.5	0.0

Sources: See appendix 2.2. League of Nations 1930.
Note: Figures in millions of U.S. dollars.

Appendix 2.2   Data Sources

1880–1913: sixteen countries
Argentina, Australia, Belgium, Canada, Denmark, Finland, France,
Germany, Italy, Japan, The Netherlands, Norway, Sweden, Switzerland,
United Kingdom, United States.

1921–1939 and *1948–1996*: twenty-one countries
Argentina, Australia, Belgium, Brazil, Canada, Chile, Denmark,
Finland, France, Germany, Greece, Italy, Japan, The Netherlands,
Norway, Portugal, Spain, Sweden, Switzerland, United Kingdom,
United States.

1. Gold Reserves (data underlying appendix tables A.2.1 and A.2.2
and figures 2.1 and 2.2)

1880–1913

Australia, Canada, Denmark, Germany, Italy, Japan, The Netherlands,
Norway, Switzerland in Peter H. Lindert, (1967), *Key Currencies and
Gold Exchange Standard, 1900–1913*, Dissertation, Cornell University.

Belgium, Denmark, Finland, Sweden in Arthur I. Bloomfield, (1963),
Short-Term Capital Movements Under the Pre–1914 Gold Standard,
Princeton Studies in International Finance No. 11, Princeton University,
chart 2.

Argentina in Gerardo Della Paolera, (1988), "How the Argentine
Economy Performed during the International Gold Standard: A
Reexamination." Ph.D dissertation, University of Chicago, table 32.

Canada in C. A. Curtis, (1931), "Statistics of Banking," in *Statistical Contributions to Canadian Economic History*, Vol. I, eds. C. A. Curtis, and
K. W. Taylor.

France, Monetary Gold Stock in Michele Saint Marc, (1983), *Histoire
Monetaire de la France 1800–1980*, University of France Press, Paris.

United Kingdom, Monetary Gold Stock in David K. Sheppard, (1971),
The Growth and Role of UK Financial Institutions, 1880–1962, Methuen &
Co. Ltd, London, pp. 136–137, table (A) 1.12, col. 15.

United States, Gold Held in the Treasury and Federal Reserve Banks,
computed by NBER Historical Database from *Annual Reports of the
Secretary* and *Circulation Statements of U.S. Money*, U.S. Treasury
Department.

Sources for appendix 2.1. Alternative Measures of Reserves, figure 2.1 and table 2.1.

Series 2 (Aggregate Gold Reserves of thirty-five countries) interpolated between benchmarks in Peter H. Lindert, (1969), *Key Currencies and Gold, 1900–1913*, Princeton Studies in International Finance No. 24, Princeton University, p. 25.

1921–1939
League of Nations, *Statistical Yearbook*, Gold and Foreign Reserves, 1926, 1931, 1932, 1940 and 1941.

1948–1996
Gold (National Valuation) in International Monetary Fund (1997), *International Financial Statistics (IFS) CD-ROM.*

Sources for appendix 2.1. Alternative Measures of Reserves, figures 1 and 2 and table 1.

Series 3 (book value), world gold (book value) in *IFS CD-ROM* (1997).

Series 4 (market value), world gold (ounces) times price of gold in *IFS CD-ROM* (1997).

2. Foreign Exchange Reserves (data underlying figure 2.1 and appendix 2.1, tables A.2.1 and A.2.2 and figures 1 and 2)

1880–1913
Belgium, Denmark, Finland, France, Germany, Italy, Japan, The Netherlands, Norway, Sweden, Switzerland in Bloomfield (1963), appendix II.

Argentina, Australia, Canada in Lindert (1967), table 2-C.

Sources for appendix 2.1. Alternative Measures of Reserves, figure 1 and table 1.

Series 2 (Aggregate Foreign Exchange Reserves of 35 countries), Official Foreign Exchange Holdings computed from the data in Lindert (1967), table 2-C and table 5-4.

1921–1939
League of Nations, *Statistical Yearbook.*

1948–1996
Total Reserves minus Gold in *IFS CD-ROM* (1997).

Sources for appendix 2.1. Alternative Measures of Reserves, figures 1 and 2 and table 1.

Series 3 and Series 4, World Total International Reserves minus Gold in *IFS CD-ROM* (1997).

3. Statutory Gold Reserve Requirements (data underlying appendix 2.3, tables A.2.3, A.2.4, and A.2.5).

Sources:

1880–1914
Germany, Sweden, Italy in Michael D. Bordo and Anna J. Schwartz, eds.(1984), *A Retrospective on the Classical Gold Standard, 1821–1931*, Chicago: University of Chicago Press, chapters 7–9.

Other countries in Charles Conant (1924), *A History of Modern Banks of Issue Sixth Edition*. Reprinted by Augustus, M. Kelly Publishers, New York, 1969.

1925–1931
League of Nations (1930), *Legislation on Gold*, Geneva, table I–III.

1944–1972
Hans Aufricht (1961, 1967), *Central Banking Legislation*. 2 vols. Washington, D.C. International Monetary Fund.

Dummy for statutory gold reserve requirements = 1 if requirements are present, 0 otherwise.

4. Exchange Rate Regime

Sources:

1880–1939 and *1946–1960*
Michael D. Bordo and Anna J. Schwartz (1996), "The Operation of the Specie Standard: Evidence for Core and Peripheral Countries, 1880–1990," in *Currency Convertibility: The Gold Standard and Beyond*, eds. Jorge Braga de Macedo, Barry Eichengreen, and Jaime Reis, table 2.1 and table 2.2.

1961–1989
Atish R., Ghosh, Anne-Marie Gulde, Jonathan D. Ostry, and Holger C. Wolf (1995), "Does the Nominal Exchange Rate Regime Matter?" *IMF Working Paper*, appendix I and II, Exchange Rate Regime Classification.

1990–1996
International Monetary Fund (1996), *International Financial Statistics Yearbook*, p. 18, Exchange Rate Arrangement.

For *1880–1939*, exchange rate regime dummy = 0 if a country has a gold convertible regime, 1 otherwise. *After 1946*, exchange rate regime dummy = 0 if a country has a fixed exchange rate regime, 1 if a country has a floating exchange rate regime.

Note: Cooperative arrangements (European Monetary System) are classified as a fixed exchange rate regime.

5. Capital Controls

Sources:

1951–1995
Data are from elaborations on IMF *Annual Report on Exchange Rate Arrangements and Exchange Restrictions*, various issues.

Capital controls (current account) dummy = 1 if a country has restrictions on its current account, 0 otherwise. Capital controls (capital account) dummy = 1 if a country has restrictions on its capital account, 0 otherwise.

6. Nominal National Income

1880–1913 and *1921–1939*
Various Definitions in Bordo and Schwartz (1996).

1948–1996
GDP in *IFS CD-ROM* (1997).

7. Prices

1880–1913 and *1921–1939*
Various Definitions in Bordo and Schwartz (1996).

1948–1996
GDP deflator in *IFS CD-ROM* (1997).

8. Annual Exchange Rates

1880–1913 and *1921–1939*
Domestic Currency/U.S. Dollar in Bordo and Schwartz (1996).

1948–1996
Domestic Currency/U.S. Dollar (Average) in *IFS CD-ROM* (1997).

9. Monthly Exchange Rates

Exchange rate volatility = standard deviation of monthly exchange rates of major currencies.

1920–1939
U.S. Dollar/U.K. Pound in *Banking and Monetary Statistics*, Board of Governors of the Federal Reserve System, Washington, D.C., 1948, table 173.

1948–1996
Index of trade weighted Dollar in *IFS CD-ROM* (1997).

10. Monetary Base

1880–1913
Notes in Circulation in B. R. Mitchell, *International Historical Statistics: 1750–1988, Europe* (1992), *The Americas (1993), Africa, Asia, and Oceania* (1995), New York: Stockton Press.

1921–1939
Notes in Circulation in League of Nations, *Bulletin of Statistics.* Monthly, 1932–1939.

1948–1996
Reserve Money in *IFS CD-ROM* (1997).

11. Trade Volume

1880–1913 and *1921–1939*
Exports and Imports in Mitchell, *International Historical Statistics.*

1948–1996
Exports and Imports in *IFS CD-ROM* (1997).

Appendix 2.3 Central Bank Gold Reserve Statutes

Table A.2.3
Central bank statutory gold reserve requirements under the classical gold standard (1880–1914)

Country	Legal reserve requirements
Argentina	Currency Board (1899–1913).
Australia	25% in gold on bank notes up to £7,000,000, 100% above that (law of 1910). Before 1910 no government notes, no legal reserve requirements on commercial bank notes.
Belgium	33⅓% on notes and other demand liabilities.
Brazil	33⅓% in gold on note issue (act of 1890); 100% in gold and convertible securities: Currency Board (1906–1914).
Canada	25% on Dominion notes in excess of 20 million. No legal reserve requirements on chartered banks.
Chile	None.
Denmark	37.5% in gold coin or bullion on notes until 1907; thereafter 50%.
Finland	Maximum uncovered note issue of 40,000,000 marks, 100% cover in gold, foreign exchange above that.
France	None.
Germany	33⅓% in gold coin or bullion on note liabilities.
Greece	3⅓% in gold coin or bullion on notes.
Italy	40% in gold or silver on notes.
Japan	On note liability in gold coin or bullion in excess of fiduciary issue of 120,000,000 yen (1899).
Netherlands	40% in gold coin on notes and deposits.
Norway	On note liabilities, 100% in gold coin or bullion in excess of fiduciary issue of 35,000,000 crowns.
Portugal	33⅓% in gold coin or bullion on note circulation and demand liabilities.
Spain	33⅓% cash reserve on a maximum note issue of 1,500,000 pesetas, at least one half to be held in gold.
Sweden	40 million kroner in gold on notes.
Switzerland	40% in gold coin on notes.
United Kingdom	100% in gold coin or bullion on notes in excess of fiduciary issue (£14 million plus two-thirds of lapsed bank notes).
United States	As of 1900, Treasury minimum of 100 million in gold coin.

Sources: Germany, Sweden, Italy: Bordo and Schwartz 1984, chaps. 7–9. Other countries: Conant 1924/1969.

Table A.2.4
Central bank statutory gold reserve requirements under the gold exchange standard
(1925–1931)

Country	Legal reserve requirements
Argentina	None.
Australia	25% in gold coin or bullion on bank notes.
Belgium	On sight liabilities: 30% gold coin or bullion; 40% gold and gold exchange.
Brazil	None.
Canada	25% in gold or bullion on first 50 million Dominion notes; 100% on excess.
Chile	50% in gold and gold exchange on bank notes plus deposits.
Denmark	30% in gold coin or bullion on bank notes.
Finland	300 million marks in gold coin or bullion on all bank notes plus other sight liabilities up to 1,200 million mark.
France	35% in gold coin bullion on bank notes plus current credit accounts.
Germany	On note liabilities: 40% of which three-quarters (30%) in gold or day-to-day loans; on deposits: 40% in secondary names.
Greece	40% in gold and gold exchange on bank notes plus other sight liabilities.
Italy	40% in gold and gold exchange on notes and sight liabilities.
Japan	75% in gold coin or bullion on notes in excess of £260 million.
Netherlands	40% in gold coin or bullion on bank notes, bank assignations and demand deposits.
Norway	100% in gold coin or bullion on bank note circulation over 240 million Kroner.
Portugal	None.
Spain	40% in gold coin or bullion (in silver) on bank notes not exceeding 4,000 million pesatas; 50% (10% in silver) on bank notes exceeding 4,000 million pesetas but not exceeding 5,000 million pesetas unless increased to 6,000 million pesetas by special authorization.
Sweden	50% in gold coin or bullion on notes in excess of 250 million kroner; minimum gold reserve of 150 million kroner.
Switzerland	40% in gold or bullion on notes.
United Kingdom	100% in gold bullion on notes in excess of £260 million.
United States	40% in gold coin on Federal Reserve notes; 35% on Federal Reserve deposits.

Source: League of Nations 1930, tables I–III.

Table A.2.5
Central bank statutory gold reserve requirements under Bretton Woods (1944–1972)

Country	Legal reserve requirements
Argentina	NA.
Australia	None.
Belgium	$33^{1}/_{3}\%$ on sight liabilities in gold.
Brazil	NA.
Canada	25% in gold coin, bullion and foreign exchange on notes and deposit liabilities.
Chile	NA.
Denmark	25% in gold coin, gold bullion, gold exchange (maximum 5% of note circulation) or non-interest-bearing foreign exchange (maximum 5% of note circulation) *1936 Law*.
Finland	Not updated from *1925 Law*.
France	35% in bullion and gold coin on notes and current credit accounts.
Germany	None.
Greece	None.
Italy	None.
Japan	100% in gold and silver coin and bullion domestic assets and foreign exchange.
Netherlands	50% in gold and foreign exchange on bank notes, bank drafts, and credit balance on current accounts.
Norway	None.
Portugal	On notes in circulation and other sight liabilities in gold 25% in gold coin and bars; 25% in convertible foreign exchange.
Spain	None.
Sweden	On notes (in excess of 9,900 million kroner) equal to double the amount of gold reserve; the amount not covered by gold to consist of nongold assets; gold reserve minimum of 150 million kroner.
Switzerland	40% on notes; rest in nongold assets.
United Kingdom	100% in gold coin and bullion on note liabilities in excess of £1,575 million fiduciary issue.
United States	25% on notes and deposits (eliminated in 1965 and 1968).

Source: Aufricht 1961, 1967.

Appendix 2.4   The Ratio of Foreign Exchange Reserves to Gold Reserves

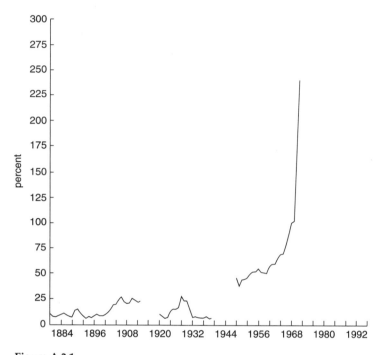

Figure A.2.1
Ratio of foreign exchange reserves to gold reserves
Note: Gold standard: thirty-five countries, gold reserves (interpolated between benchmarks); Lindert 1967, 1969.
Interwar: twenty-one countries, League of Nations.
Postwar: World, gold—book value, IFS.

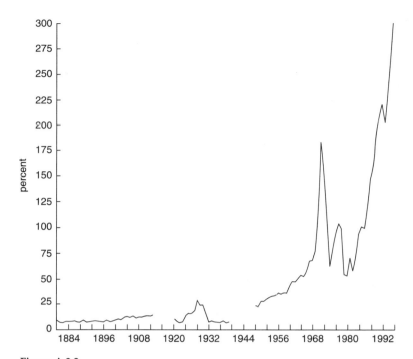

Figure A.2.2
Ratio of foreign exchange reserves to gold reserves
Note: Gold standard: sixteen countries, Bloomfield 1963 and Lindert 1967, 1969.
Interwar: twenty-one countries, League of Nations.
Postwar: twenty-one countries, gold—market value, IFS.

Notes

Prepared for the conference honoring Robert Mundell, co-sponsored by the IMF, the World Bank, the University of Maryland, MIT and UC Berkeley. Bordo is Professor of Economics and Director of the Center for Monetary and Financial History, Rutgers University. Eichengreen is George C. Pardee and Helen N. Pardee Professor of Economics and Political Science at the University of California, Berkeley. We thank Jongwoo Kim for capable research assistance, and Rex Ghosh, Gian Maria Milesi-Ferretti, and Peter Lindert for help with data. For helpful comments we thank Tam Bayoumi, Rich Clarida, Marc Flandreau, Peter Lindert, Robert Mundell, Jacques Polak, and Dick Ware.

1. Mundell refers to the Bretton Woods system as it operated through 1971 as "the gold-convertible dollar standard."

2. See, for example, Kenen and Yuden 1965 and Heller 1966.

3. Our emphasis on the fragility of the gold-exchange standard is consonant with theoretical work pointing to the inevitability in the long run of the collapse of any

commodity price support scheme in the face of unforeseen shocks. See Townsend 1977, Salant 1983, and Buiter 1989.

4. The problem with token coinage was that its face value exceeded the intrinsic value of its metallic content by definition, creating an incentive for counterfeiting and discouraging the authorities from issuing tokens. The constraint bound because the smallest practical gold coin was too valuable for day-to-day transactions. It was necessary to supplement gold with silver coinage (silver coins of comparable weight being worth only one-fifteenth as much). Issuing token coins and paper money was only practical once steam power permitted them to be stamped and printed with a precision that precluded easy counterfeiting. See Redish 1990.

5. Still, over much of the world, gold continued to circulate and provided the basis for day-to-day transactions. Things changed after World War I, as we explain below.

6. As emphasized by Bordo and Rockoff (1996).

7. On the transition from silver and bimetallism to gold and this convention of dating the emergence of a truly international gold standard around the first half of the 1880s, see Eichengreen and Flandreau 1996.

8. These estimates for the 1880–1913 period are for sixteen countries. For the interwar and post–World War II periods, we use a larger sample of twenty-one countries. Lindert (1967, 1969), by comparison, provides annual data on official foreign exchange reserves for thirty-five countries beginning in 1880 and a larger group of countries beginning somewhat later. He does not, however, provide annual data for individual countries' gold reserves over the 1880–1913 period, instead interpolating this series for the world between four benchmarks. In our work we have assembled annual estimates for a limited sample of countries rather than relying on interpolation. In addition, we limit our attention to countries for which the ancillary data used in the demand-for-reserves equations estimated below are consistently available. Notwithstanding these differences, Lindert's series and ours paint broadly the same picture (see figure A.2.1).

9. Gold reserves are valued at official prices throughout. Figure A.2.2 shows market values for gold reserves in the post-1973 period.

10. The principal countries holding foreign exchange reserves in 1880 were Austria, Belgium, Canada, Denmark, Finland, Germany, and Sweden (Lindert 1967, table 2-C).

11. Lindert's alternative series suggests an even more impressive rise, with the share of foreign exchange reserves in the total doubling between 1880 and 1913. If like Lindert one considers the foreign exchange assets of private as well as official financial institutions, then the relative rate of growth of foreign exchange claims is more impressive still.

12. Below, in the context of an econometric analysis of the demand for gold and foreign exchange, we find that the Chow statistic indicating a structural break in the determinants of the gold/total reserves ratio peaks in 1900–1901, consistent with this interpretation.

13. The role of income levels as a determinant of countries' reliance on gold versus foreign-exchange reserves is a theme of Eichengreen and Flandreau (1996).

14. The integration into this expanding international economy of Russia and India, two leading holders of foreign exchange reserves, epitomizes the process. Russia borrowed in Paris and held foreign balances there as collateral (Feis 1930). India went onto the gold standard at the end of the nineteenth century, when the British sovereign was

made legal tender there and the colonial government established a reserve in London (Keynes 1913).

15. Here we compress arguments made in Bordo and Kydland 1995 and Eichengreen 1996.

16. The United States, where universal male suffrage prevailed, provides proof by counterexample; the United States came within a hair's breadth of being driven off the gold standard by populist agitation in the 1890s. See below.

17. Evidence on the operation of these mechanisms is to be found in Hallwood, MacDonald, and Marsh 1996 and in Bordo and MacDonald 1997.

18. See Rockoff 1984 and Eichengreen and McLean 1994. A notable exception to this generalization is the cyanide process for extracting gold from impure ore; Rockoff shows that the rise in the real price of gold starting in the 1870s induced scientists in several countries to work simultaneously on its development.

19. An additional equilibrating mechanism was shifts of gold from nonmonetary to monetary uses. See Bordo 1981 and Cagan 1965 for evidence that this force and the response of gold production to changes in the real price worked with very long lags.

20. We refer to data for thirty-five countries. See Lindert 1967, table 5-4 and table 2-C.

21. The definitive treatment of these issues is De Cecco 1974. See also Triffin 1964.

22. In most cases this was done during the war itself, when gold was regarded as a national resource that could not be allowed to flow abroad and possibly fall into enemy hands.

23. A large literature debates the question of whether there was a significant decline in wage and price flexibility over the World War I watershed. Recent work suggests that the case is strongest for the United States, where the 1920s saw the rise of personnel departments and other institutionalized forms of labor relations, and in the United Kingdom, where union density rose sharply during the war and the government adopted an unemployment insurance scheme, sector-specific minimum wages (under the provisions of the Trade Boards Act), and other flexibility-reducing policies.

24. Mundell 1994, pp. 6, 8, 1995, p. 455.

25. League of Nations 1930, annex XIII, table III.

26. Depending on how much foreign exchange was also held by central banks authorized by statute to do so.

27. It then fell back to 37 percent in 1929 as financial instability loomed (Nurkse 1944, appendix I).

28. Cassel (1928) shared Mundell's worry about the adequacy of the world's stock of monetary gold now that the U.S. price level was so much higher (and the real price of gold was so much lower). But his preferred solution was not to change the real gold price, which would have created what we refer to now as time inconsistency problems. Starting with his contributions to the Expert Committee at the Genoa Conference in 1922 (of which he was a member), Cassel stressed the need to economize on monetary gold by withdrawing gold coin from circulation and encouraging central banks to supplement their gold reserves with convertible foreign exchange. Critical for encouraging this practice, he emphasized, was central bank cooperation, for a coordinated international

reduction in gold cover ratios would be less threatening than unilateral action to the credibility of monetary policy. In contrast, Charles Rist's solution in fact anticipated Mundell, arguing that the interwar "gold shortage" could have been alleviated by readjusting the price of gold in terms of the dollar and pound in 1924–1925 "to bring the purchasing power of gold nearer to what it would have been if the rise in prices had been due to an increase in the production of gold and not to monetized debt" (Cortney 1961, p. 8).

29. Cassel (1928) emphasized the progressive exhaustion of the South African mines on which the world depended so heavily for its incremental supplies of gold. While not questioning that new deposits would be discovered, he anticipated the picture of a relatively inelastic flow supply as described in the text. Bordo and Eichengreen (1997) demonstrate that had the Great Depression not terminated the gold exchange standard, the post–World War I deflation would have encouraged sufficient gold production and shifts of gold from nonmonetary to monetary uses to allow the principal countries to satisfy their legal gold reserve ratios. Their simulations are based on econometric estimates of relatively but not totally inelastic flow supplies of new gold.

30. In actual fact, new gold supplies rose significantly in the 1930s, following the collapse of commodity prices (and the consequent increase in real gold prices). But this price-level collapse was precisely the disaster that the progressive accumulation of foreign balances was meant to head off.

31. Mlynarski 1929, p. 89. Clearly, the "Triffin Dilemma" might equally well be labeled the "Mlynarski Dilemma."

32. See Eichengreen 1992 and Meltzer 1996.

33. As in the model of unstable target zones presented by Bertola and Caballero (1992). Eichengreen and Jeanne (1997) illustrate the applicability of this model to the interwar period.

34. Our view is thus different from Mundell's, as expressed for example in Mundell 1995, p. 458: "It is a mistake, though a common one, to blame the gold standard for the deflation and the great depression. The gold standard, however, is just a mechanism that worked well when it was managed well and worked badly when it was mismanaged." Our view emphasizes in contrast intrinsic instabilities in the system and their tendency to interact with policy problems.

35. As argued by Eichengreen and Sachs (1985) and Mundell (1995).

36. See Triffin 1947.

37. In fact Mundell advocated both raising the price of gold and the creation of Special Drawing Rights as ways of preserving the Bretton Woods dollar-gold standard (Mundell 1991, p. 223).

38. There was reason to expect that a country that revalued its gold reserves once might well do so again. This would have given other countries an incentive to shift out of foreign exchange and into gold in anticipation and only accelerated the eventual collapse of the gold-exchange standard. In his own writings, Mundell tends to minimize the importance of this time-inconsistency problem, suggesting that gold revaluation was a viable option for not only solving the problems of the Bretton Woods system but eliminating the excess demand for gold in the Great Depression as well. See Mundell 1995, p. 458. Some variants of this proposal (e.g., Rueff 1972) entailed using the profits from the increase in the dollar price of gold to liquidate the outstanding dollar balances. For this proposal to be effective it would have been necessary to proscribe central banks from

holding foreign exchange reserves in the future. And aside from the French, the major governments would have rejected this notion of returning to a pure gold standard. Indeed, Mundell (1973) was opposed to Rueff's solution for a return to a pure gold standard because of its deflationary consequences. We return to this issue below.

In addition, there was the problem that raising the dollar price of gold would reward two pariah nations, the Soviet Union and South Africa, that were major gold producers.

39. For other arguments against this solution, see Williamson 1977, pp. 33–34. For a contrary view see Meltzer 1991. Bordo and Eichengreen (1997) analyze the inevitability of the collapse of a hypothetical gold exchange standard constructed after World War II in a world where the Great Depression and the revaluation of gold to $35 per ounce by the United States had not occurred.

40. In recent writings, Mundell (1983, 1994, 1995) has advanced parallel proposals for the creation of an international reserve money, to be backed in whole or partially with gold, to regulate the global supply of international liquidity.

41. See Bordo, Simard, and White 1995.

42. See Bordo 1993 and Garber 1993.

43. A complementary explanation of the events leading to collapse is growing misalignment in real exchange rates between the United States and its principal competitors in the face of differential productivity trends. See Balassa 1964 and Marston 1987. In this view, expansionary U.S. monetary and fiscal policies exacerbated the misalignment by further overvaluing the dollar (Obstfeld 1993).

44. The recent definitive treatment of this history is James 1996.

45. Although both the United States and the IMF in fact sold some gold reserves in the 1970s.

46. In a sense, the problem is that we have many explanations and only one data point. But the fact that central banks are now liquidating what may be a substantial share of their gold reserves may help us to discriminate among these hypotheses. An adequate explanation for the phenomenon, in other words, must be capable of explaining both why the practice of holding gold reserves persisted for more than two decades after the breakdown of Bretton Woods and why it declined in the 1990s. In addition, some of these hypotheses can be tested using cross-country and time-series data on central bank portfolios.

47. These arguments suggest a continuous process in which gold reserves are drawn down as the hold of memory and habit gradually loosens. But experience suggests that the process develops discontinuously—that central banks as a group hold onto the bulk of their gold reserves until they reach a tipping point where they revalue and/or sell a substantial share of their gold. If so, memory and habit, though part of the story, are at best an incomplete explanation. A counterargument is that memory may be a strictly generational phenomenon. Thus, Lucchetti and Sesit (1997) cite a Bank of England official as saying that central banks are moving to a new generation of managers who don't carry the baggage of their predecessors.

48. What these dynamics cannot explain is why the process should proceed so discontinuously. And if this explanation is generally correct, it is paradoxical that the central banks of countries like Canada and Australia, where the gold-mining industry is disproportionately important, have been among the first to sell off their gold reserves.

49. Again, however, the explanation is at best partial, for it does not explain why central bankers feel a collective responsibility for the maintenance of the practice in the first place.

50. The problem is that the threat of Cold War conflict never deterred those countries that have taken the most dramatic steps to draw down their gold reserves (Canada, Australia, and Belgium among them), one presumes, from holding dollar-denominated assets. Those countries to which this argument most plausibly applies have not been in the vanguard of those drawing down their gold reserves.

51. We also included in some of our regressions short-term interest rates and the rate of change in the price of gold as opportunity cost variables. As in other studies, the opportunity cost variable was generally insignificant except in the recent managed float (Landell-Mills 1989). Hence these regressions are not reported.

52. Australia, Argentina, Belgium, Brazil, Canada, Chile, Denmark, Finland, France, United Kingdom, United States, Greece, Germany, Italy, Japan, The Netherlands, Norway, Portugal, Spain, Sweden, and Switzerland. For the 1880–1913 period because of data gaps we omitted Brazil, Chile, Greece, Portugal, and Spain.

53. For each regression, we used three dependent variables: (1) the level of total reserves, (2) the level of gold reserves, and (3) the ratio of gold to total reserves. To avoid redundancy, we report only those results related to our argument.

54. We used two methods to calculate the rolling Chow test: (1) floating the window size to exploit all the samples of each regime, and (2) fixing the window size as ten years (five years of samples are used before the break and another five years of samples are used after the break). For an example of the test for a break in 1890, the floating window size method uses the sample 1882–1890 (nine years) before the break and the sample 1891–1914 (twenty-four years) after the break. The fixed window size method uses the sample 1886–1890 (five years) before the break and the sample 1891–1895 (five years) after the break. There is a trade-off between the two methods: The floating method is exact (the test has high power) because of the large size of the sample used in estimation but has a bias to reject more toward the middle of the sample period; the fixed method is not biased but is not exact (the test has low power) because of the small size of the sample used in estimation. Fortunately, the estimated results are very similar using both methods. Hence, we report only the results of the floating window size method.

55. The relationship determining the demand for foreign exchange appears to shift earlier, in the late 1970s and early-to-mid 1980s, a phenomenon for which a myriad of explanations suggest themselves.

56. See, for example, Mundell 1983, p. 192, and Mundell 1994, p. 22.

57. Where there was more than one reserve-currency country, we used the three-year moving standard deviation of the log of the aggregate money supplies converted into dollars.

58. When we measure policy by changes in M2, however, this result evaporates.

59. For the interwar period we used the pound-dollar exchange rate; for the postwar period, the trade weighted dollar exchange rate.

60. See Mundell 1983, 1994, 1995. We used the weighted average of the G-5 inflation rate and, alternatively, the inflation rates of the same core countries as in the regressions with a measure of the volatility of monetary policy.

61. For direct evidence, see Alogoskoufis and Smith 1991.

62. Because the level of total reserves and the level of gold reserves are nonstationary variables, we used two stationary variables as dependent variables in sensitivity analysis: (1) the first log difference of total reserves, and (2) the first log difference of gold reserves. The results are very similar to those of the regressions which use the first lag of dependent variable as one of the explanatory variables. (See table 2.5.)

63. Furthermore, the combination of autocorrelated errors and lagged dependent variables introduces the possibility of biased coefficient estimates due to the correlation between the lagged variable and the error term.

64. Although those estimates will not be efficient if the adjustment has not dealt with the autocorrelation of the disturbance terms.

65. Unfortunately, we were unable to obtain this information for the post–Bretton Woods period. See appendix 2.3 for the individual country gold statutes for the three regimes ending with Bretton Woods.

66. After France abandoned the free coinage of silver in 1873, it adopted a limping gold standard in which silver remained legal tender although it was not freely coined. Bank of France notes were convertible into gold or silver coin by residents and foreigners only at the option of the authorities. The United States officially joined the gold standard in 1900, but it was only with the founding of the Federal Reserve in 1914 that statutory gold reserve requirements were instituted.

67. The exchange rate regime data were gathered mainly from IMF and League of Nations publications; for help with them we thank Rex Ghosh. For the data on capital controls we are grateful to Gian Maria Milesi-Ferretti.

68. Interestingly, the coefficient for floating-rate countries is positive and significant in the Bretton Woods years. This result is driven mainly by Canada, a gold mining country that held large reserves.

69. It should be noted that there is, however, evidence that the presence of capital account restrictions significantly *reduced* the demand for gold reserves in the Bretton Woods years. We examined also the effects of the presence of export-proceed-surrender requirements; the results for these were virtually identical to those for capital-account restrictions. In contrast, there was little evidence that the presence or absence of multiple exchange rates had much effect on reserve-holding behavior one way or another.

References

Alogoskoufis, G., and R. Smith. 1991. The Phillips curve, the persistence of inflation, and the Lucas critique: Evidence from exchange rate regimes. *American Economic Review* 81:1254–75.

Aufricht, Hans. 1961, 1967. *Central banking legislation*. 2 vols. Washington, D.C.: International Monetary Fund.

Balassa, B. 1964. The purchasing power parity doctrine: A reappraisal. *Journal of Political Economy* 72:584–96.

Bayoumi, T., and B. Eichengreen. 1996. The stability of the gold standard and the evolution of the international monetary system. In *Modern perspectives on the gold standard*, ed. T. Bayoumi, B. Eichengreen, and M. Taylor, 165–88. Cambridge: Cambridge University Press.

Bertola, G., and R. Caballero. 1992. Target zones and realignments. Centre for Economic Policy Discussion Paper no. 398, CEPR, London.

Bloomfield, A. I. 1963. Short-term capital movements under the pre-1914 gold standard. Princeton Studies in International Finance no. 11. International Finance Section, Department of Economics, Princeton University, Princeton, N.J.

Bordo, M. D. 1993. The Bretton Woods International Monetary System: A historical overview. In *A retrospective on the Bretton Woods system: Lessons for international monetary reform*, ed. M. D. Bordo and B. Eichengreen, 3–98. Chicago: University of Chicago Press.

Bordo, M. D. 1981. The classical gold standard: Some lessons for today. *Federal Reserve Bank of St. Louis Review* 63 (May):2–17.

Bordo, M. D., and B. Eichengreen. 1997. Implications of the Great Depression for the development of the international monetary system. Working paper no. 5883 (January). National Bureau of Economic Research, Cambridge, Mass.

Bordo, M. D., and F. Kydland. 1995. The gold standard as a rule: An essay in exploration. *Explorations in Economic History* 32:423–65.

Bordo, M. D., and R. MacDonald. 1997. Violations of the "rules of the game" and the credibility of the classical gold standard, 1880–1914. Working paper no. 6115 (July). National Bureau of Economic Research, Cambridge, Mass.

Bordo, M. D., and H. Rockoff. 1996. The gold standard as a "Good Housekeeping seal of approval." *Journal of Economic History* (June):389–428.

Bordo, M. D., and A. J. Schwartz. 1999. Monetary policy regimes and economic performance: The historical record. *Handbook of Macroeconomics*. Vol. I, ed. John B. Taylor and Michael Woodford, 149–234. New York: Elsevier Science Publishers.

Bordo, M. D., D. Simard, and E. White. 1995. France and the Bretton Woods International Monetary System 1960–1968. *The history of international monetary arrangements*, ed. J. Reis, 153–180. London: Macmillan.

Buiter, W. H. 1989. A viable gold standard requires flexible monetary and fiscal policy. *Review of Economic Studies* 56:101–18.

Cagan, P. 1965. *Determinants and effects of changes in the stock of money, 1875–1960*. New York: Columbia University Press.

Cassel, G. 1928. *Postwar monetary stabilization*. New York: Columbia University Press.

Cooper, R. N. 1993. Comment. In *A retrospective on the Bretton Woods system*, ed. M. D. Bordo and B. Eichengreen, 104–7. Chicago: University of Chicago Press.

Conant, C. 1924. *A history of modern banks of issue*. 6th ed. Reprint, New York: Augustus M. Kelly, 1969.

Cortney, P. 1961. Introduction. In C. Rist, *The triumph of gold*. New York: The Philosophical Library.

De Cecco, M. 1974. *Money and empire: The international gold standard*. Oxford: Blackwell.

Eichengreen, B. 1996. *Globalizing capital: A history of the international monetary system*. Princeton: Princeton University Press.

Eichengreen, B. 1992. *Golden fetters: The gold standard and the Great Depression, 1919–1939*. New York: Oxford University Press.

Eichengreen, B., and M. Flandreau. 1996. The geography of the gold standard. In *Currency convertibility: The gold standard and beyond*, ed. J. B. de Macedo, B. Eichengreen, and J. Reis, 113–43. London: Routledge.

Eichengreen, B., and O. Jeanne. 1997. Unemployment and currency crises: Sterling in 1931. Unpublished manuscript, University of California, Berkeley.

Eichengreen, B., and I. McLean. 1994. The supply of gold under the pre-1914 gold standard. *Economic History Review* new ser. 47:288–309.

Eichengreen, B., and J. Sachs. 1985. Exchange rates and economic recovery in the 1930s. *Journal of Economic History* 45:921–46.

Feis, H. 1930. *Europe, the world's banker*. New Haven: Yale University Press.

Garber, P. M. 1993. The collapse of the Bretton Woods fixed exchange rate system. In *A retrospective on the Bretton Woods system: Lessons for international monetary reform*, ed. M. D. Bordo and B. Eichengreen, 461–85. Chicago: University of Chicago Press.

Goodhart, C. 1995. The political economy of monetary union. In *Understanding Interdependence*, ed. P. B. Kenen, 448–506. Princeton: Princeton University Press.

Hallwood, P., R. MacDonald, and I. W. Marsh. 1996. Credibility and fundamentals: Were the classical and inter-war gold standards well-behaved target zones? In *Economic perspectives on the gold standard*, ed. T. Bayoumi, B. Eichengreen, and M. Taylor, 129–64. Cambridge: Cambridge University Press.

Heller, R. 1966. Optimal international reserves. *Economic Journal* 76:296–311.

Hume, D. [1752] 1952. On the balance of trade. In *Essays, moral, political, literary*, 330–45. London: Longmans, Green.

James, H. 1996. *International monetary cooperation since Bretton Woods*. New York: Oxford University Press.

Kenen, P. B., and E. Yudin. 1965. The demand for international reserves. *Review of Economics and Statistics* 47:242–50.

Keynes, J. M. 1913. *Indian currency and finance*. London: Macmillan.

Landell-Mills, J. M. 1989. The demand for international reserves and their opportunity cost. *IMF Staff Papers* 36:708–32.

League of Nations. 1930. *Interim report of the gold delegation*. Geneva: League of Nations.

Lindert, P. 1969. Key currencies and gold, 1900–1913. Princeton Studies in International Finance no. 24. International Finance Section, Department of Economics, Princeton University, Princeton, N.J.

Lindert, P. 1967. Key currencies and the gold exchange standard, 1900–1913. Ph.D. diss., Cornell University, Ithaca, N.Y.

Liviatan, N. 1963. Consistent estimation of distributed lags. *International Economic Review* 4:44–52.

Lucchetti, A., and M. Sesit. 1997. Bullion beef: Gold holds its luster with older investors despite forlorn price. *Wall Street Journal* (10 September), pp. 1, 15.

Marston, R. 1987. Real exchange rates and productivity growth in the United States and Japan. In *Real-Financial Linkages Among Open Economies*, ed. S. Arndt, 71–96. Cambridge: MIT Press.

Meltzer, A. H. 1996. A history of the Federal Reserve. Carnegie Mellon University. Mimeographed.

Meltzer, A. H. 1991. U.S. policy in the Bretton Woods era. *Federal Reserve Bank of St. Louis Review* 73 (May/June):54–83.

Mlynarski, F. 1929. *Gold and central banks*. London: Macmillan.

Mundell, R. 1995. The future of the exchange rate system. *Economic Notes of the Banca Monte dei Paschi di Sienna* 24:453–78.

Mundell, R. 1994. Prospects for the international monetary system. Research Study no. 8. World Gold Council, New York.

Mundell, R. 1991. The great exchange rate controversy: Trade balances and the international monetary system. In *International adjustment and financing: The lessons of 1988–1991*, ed. C. F. Bergsten. Washington, DC: Institute for International Economics.

Mundell, R. 1983. International monetary options. *Cato Journal* 3:189–210.

Mundell, R. 1973. The monetary consequences of Jacques Rueff. *Journal of Business* 46:384–95.

Mundell, R. 1971. *Monetary theory*. Pacific Palisades, Calif.: Goodyear.

Mundell, R. 1963. Capital mobility and stabilization policy under fixed and flexible exchange rates. *Canadian Journal of Economics* 29:475–85.

Nurkse, R. 1944. *International currency experience*. Geneva: League of Nations.

Obstfeld, M. 1993. The adjustment mechanism. In *A retrospective on the Bretton Woods system: Lessons for international monetary reform*, ed. M. D. Bordo and B. Eichengreen, 201–56. Chicago: University of Chicago Press.

Redish, A. 1990. The evolution of the gold standard in England. *Journal of Economic History* 50:789–805.

Rist, C. 1961. *The triumph of gold*. New York: The Philosophical Library.

Rockoff, H. 1984. Some evidence on the real price of gold, its costs of production, and commodity prices. In *A retrospective on the classical gold standard*, ed. M. D. Bordo and A. J. Schwartz, 613–14. Chicago: University of Chicago Press.

Rueff, J. 1972. *The monetary sin of the West*. New York: Macmillan.

Salant, S. W. 1983. The vulnerability of price stabilization schemes to speculation attack. *Journal of Political Economy* 91:1–38.

Svensson, L. 1994. Why Exchange Rate Bands? *Journal of Monetary Economics* 33:157–99.

Townsend, R. M. 1977. The eventual failure of price fixing schemes. *Journal of Economic Theory* 14:190–9.

Triffin, R. 1964. The evolution of the international monetary system: Historical reappraisal and future perspectives. Princeton Studies in International Finance no. 12. International Finance Section, Department of Economics, Princeton University, Princeton, N.J.

Triffin, R. 1947. National central banking and the international economy. *Postwar Economic Studies* 7:46–81.

Williamson, J. 1977. *The failure of monetary reform, 1971–74.* London: Thomas Nelson and Sons.

3

Fostering Financial Stability: A New Case for Flexible Exchange Rates

Roberto Chang and
Andrés Velasco

Introduction

Policy discussions on the choice of exchange rate arrangements are dominated by not one but two Mundells. Take the dozen "considerations in the choice of exchange rate regime" identified by the International Monetary Fund in the 1997 *World Economic Outlook*. Of those, six have to do with size of the economy, patterns of trade, extent of openness, degree of factor mobility—that is, with issues raised by the early Mundell in The theory of optimum currency areas (1961). Almost all remaining considerations—sources of shocks, adjustment under less-than-fully-flexible prices, consequences of capital movements—follow from the analysis of the somewhat less early Mundell of the classic (1963) paper containing what would become the Mundell-Fleming model.

Our chapter departs from this venerable tradition by studying one connection that, as far as we have been able to discover, neither the young Mundell nor the younger Mundell emphasized: the link between domestic financial fragility—in particular the instability of a banking system operating under fractional reserves—and the choice of exchange rate regime. Our starting point is the empirical observation that many of the recent *currency* crises in emerging markets have been linked to *financial sector* crises. The 1994 collapse of the Mexican peso and the 1997 Thai and Korean currency meltdowns were largely (though not exclusively) caused by quasi-bankrupt banking systems.[1] More formally, Kaminsky and Reinhart (1999) find that the occurrence of banking crises helps predict currency crises, while Sachs, Tornell, and Velasco (1996a) find that a weak banking system (proxied by a previous lending boom) is the best predictor of whether a country was hit by the "Tequila effect" in early 1995.

This evidence has given new urgency to the question of what exchange rate arrangements best deal with the dangers associated with financial fragility. It has been recognized by Calvo (1996) and others that weak banks may jeopardize the sustainability of a fixed exchange rate system. But, if fixed exchange rate systems are vulnerable, does adopting a currency board help? Or should countries move in the other direction and adopt flexible rates? Furthermore, for a given exchange rate regime, what are the proper complementary monetary or credit policies?

The objective of this paper is to address these issues in a rigorous way. Given that banking fragility is a core issue, we build upon the classic Diamond and Dybvig (1983) model of banks, which we embed into a general equilibrium macroeconomic model. The resulting framework departs in two fundamental ways from the Diamond and Dybvig benchmark. The first is the presence of foreign and domestic currencies, the latter introduced by means of a particular payments arrangement. The second is that the economy is open to international capital movements but, realistically, also faces a credit ceiling abroad.

In this context we consider currency boards, fixed exchange rates with central bank credit to commercial banks, and flexible exchange rates. In all cases we analyze the central bank's role as a lender of last resort and the possibility of equilibrium self-fulfilling runs on the bank and/or the currency. The main results are:

1. Under a currency board, currency crises are ruled out and the commercial banking system may implement a socially optimal allocation. However, this regime is vulnerable to self-fulfilling bank runs. Hence, fears that currency boards may leave banks at the mercy of "animal spirits" are justified.

2. If the central bank tries to fix the exchange rate but also acts as a lender of last resort, providing domestic credit to the banking system at times of trouble, it can preclude bank runs only at the cost of creating balance of payments crises. In fact, the central bank may be successfully attacked under exactly the same conditions that make bank runs possible in a currency board, and with the same real consequences.

Therefore, the possibility of a crisis (of either the banking or the balance of payments type) depends only on the central bank's attempt to fix the exchange rate. The reason is that implementing a socially optimal allocation may require, if the exchange rate is fixed, that the banking system as a whole be *internationally illiquid*, in the sense that its potential short-term liabilities (the total amount of demand deposits) may be larger than the amount of foreign currency available to the system in the short run.

3. The combination of flexible exchange rates and a lender of last resort dominates all other policy regimes, for it can implement the first best allocation while ruling out bank runs. Since the central bank is no longer compelled to sell all of the economy's assets, including the illiquid investments, this policy punishes those who run with a depreciation, while those who do not run know that there will still be dollars available for them to withdraw at a later date. As a consequence, running to the bank is no longer a best response to a run by others; pessimistic expectations are not self-fulfilling; and the depreciation does not happen in equilibrium.

In short, the chapter suggests that financial considerations have far-reaching consequences that deserve to be added to conventional "Mundellian" criteria for choosing among exchange rate regimes. And, financial factors add up to a new case for flexible exchange rates—one that is based primarily in the usefulness of exchange rate flexibility in preventing self-fulfilling financial crises.

The chapter is organized as follows: The next section describes the economic environment. Then a currency board is studied, followed by a study of a fixed exchange rate with a lender of last resort. Next, flexible exchange rates are analyzed. After a conclusion, some technical proofs are relegated to an appendix.

The Economic Environment

Consider a small open economy populated by a large number of ex ante identical agents. There are three periods indexed by $t = 0, 1, 2$. There is only one good, which can be consumed and invested. This good is freely traded in the world market at a fixed price, which we normalize at one unit of foreign currency (a "dollar").

Each agent is born at $t = 0$ endowed with access to a constant returns, long-term technology whose yield per dollar invested at $t = 0$ is either $r < 1$ dollars in period 1 or $R > 1$ dollars in period 2. That is to say, the long term technology is illiquid: it is very productive if the investment is held for two periods, but early liquidation causes a net loss of $(1 -$

r) > 0 per dollar invested. Only domestic residents have access to this technology.

In addition, there is a world capital market where each dollar invested at $t = 0$ yields one dollar in either period 1 or period 2. Domestic agents can invest as much as they want in this market, but can borrow a maximum of $e > 0$ dollars. We treat this credit ceiling as exogenous and motivate it no further, but it could be justified by recourse to the many theories of international borrowing under sovereign risk.

Because the domestic technology has a higher return than the world rate of interest, suitable borrowing/investment choices will enable domestic agents to consume nonzero amounts. For instance, if in period 0 an agent borrowed up to the full credit ceiling e, invested all of the loan proceeds in the domestic technology, and held the investment for two periods, her consumption in period 2 would be $(R - 1)$ $e > 0$ dollars.

Domestic agents face a nontrivial decision, however, because they may be forced to consume early. We will assume that at $t = 1$ each domestic agent discovers her "type." With probability λ she is "impatient" and derives utility only from period 1 consumption. With probability $(1 - \lambda)$ she turns out to be "patient" and derives utility only from period 2 consumption. We shall follow Diamond and Dybvig (1983) in assuming that the realization of each agent's type is private information to that agent, that the type realizations are identically and independently distributed across agents, and that there is no aggregate uncertainty, so λ is also the number of impatient agents as a fraction of the population.

Formally, let x denote the typical agent's consumption in period 1 if she turns out to be impatient, and y denote her consumption in period 2 if she turns out to be patient. Then the expected utility of the representative agent can be represented by

$$\lambda u(x) + (1 - \lambda)u(y). \tag{3.1}$$

The function u (.) is smooth, strictly increasing, strictly concave, and satisfies Inada conditions.

This setup is similar to the classic Diamond and Dybvig (1983) formulation in that there is uncertainty about the timing of consumption, and there is also a pattern of asset returns such that agents would prefer to invest in the world market if they knew they were impatient and in the illiquid technology if they knew they were patient. As in that paper, the private sector can be organized in various ways. One possibility is for each domestic agent to act in isolation from the others, interacting only with the central bank. Then each individual would be subject to idiosyncratic uncertainty; clearly, this can be improved upon if agents agree to pool their resources in some kind of insurance scheme. We shall assume that domestic agents in fact form a coalition, referred to as a *commercial bank*, whose objective is to maximize the welfare of its representative member (*depositor*). As we will see in more detail below, under such an arrangement residents will surrender their real resources to the bank (which in turn will invest them) in exchange for the right to make withdrawals at different points in time.

We introduce domestic money into this context in the simplest possible way: by law, bank deposits made with domestic residents must be denominated and payable in a domestic currency we call the *peso*. Pesos are freely created and destroyed by (and only by) a domestic central bank. Our assumptions ensure that the commercial bank will need to acquire pesos to honor its obligations against depositors, while depositors will need dollars to buy consumption. Hence the analysis of this model must include some assumption on the *exchange rate–monetary regime*, that is, a specification of the way pesos are issued and exchanged for dollars.

A Currency Board

This section analyzes regimes in which the central bank follows a very simple rule: it stands ready to exchange dollars for pesos at a fixed exchange rate and, in addition, it is committed not to create or destroy pesos in any other way. In other words, the central bank functions as a *currency board*.

We shall assume without loss of generality that the currency board guarantees that the exchange rate will be one peso for each dollar in both periods. If E_t is the exchange rate in period t, we have $E_1 = E_2 = 1$. To analyze the functioning of a bank in this context, we shall first characterize what the commercial bank can do in principle and then ask how it can be decentralized by means of demand deposits.

The Planning Problem and the Social Optimum

The bank must choose a contingent *allocation*, that is, a plan for borrowing, investing, and distributing the proceeds to depositors. This choice is restricted not only by resource feasibility constraints but also by the fact that type realizations are private information; the latter implies that the bank must restrict its choices to allocations that give no agent an incentive to misrepresent her type.[2] To formalize the related truth-telling or *incentive compatibility* constraints, it is necessary to make a more precise assumption about what the bank can and cannot observe. The simplest assumption, which will be maintained hereafter, is that the commercial bank can observe each agent's transactions with the domestic banking system, while transactions with others cannot be monitored.

The above discussion implies that the bank will choose an allocation that maximizes (3.1), subject to $E_1 = E_2 = 1$, and to

$$k + b \leq e, \tag{3.2}$$

$$\lambda x \leq b + rl, \tag{3.3}$$

$$(1 - \lambda)y \leq R(k - l) - (k + b), \tag{3.4}$$

$$l \leq k, \tag{3.5}$$

$$k, b, x, y, l \geq 0, \tag{3.6}$$

$$y \geq x. \tag{3.7}$$

Without loss of generality, the bank is assumed to borrow abroad k dollars in period 0 to invest in the domestic asset, and b additional dollars in period 1;[3] hence (3.2) is the credit ceiling. Equation (3.3) is the resource constraint in period 1. The bank must assign x units of consumption to each impatient; this can be financed with the b dollars borrowed abroad plus, possibly, the liquidation of some amount l of the domestic asset. Equation (3.4) is the period 2 resource constraint. Note that (3.3) and (3.4) incorporate the assumption that the bank can sell dollars to the central bank, and the depositors can acquire dollars from the central bank, both an at an exchange rate of one. Equations (3.5 and 3.6) are self-explanatory. Finally, equation (3.7) is the incentive compatibility constraint for patient agents. If a patient agent reports her type honestly she will consume y in period 2; if she lies she will only be given x dollars in period 1 with which, given our assumptions, she can purchase at most x units of consumption in period 2. Hence (3.7) ensures that she cannot gain from lying.

The above problem will be called the *planning problem*, and its solution denoted by tildes. In fact, the solution is this economy's *social optimum*, that is, the feasible allocation that maximizes the expected welfare of the representative depositor.

The analysis of the planning problem is straightforward and yields useful information on the social optimum. It can be shown that (3.2) holds with equality, so that the credit ceiling is binding. It can also be shown that $l = 0$—that is, there is no liquidation in period 1 of the domestic investment. This should be obvious, since the bank faces no aggregate uncertainty, and liquidating the domestic asset in period 1 is costly. Given this fact, it can be shown that the value of the planning problem is superior to the value of individual autarky.[4]

Optimal consumption is determined by two conditions, the first of which can be thought of as a *social transformation curve*:

$$R\lambda\tilde{x} + (1-\lambda)\tilde{y} = (R-1)e. \tag{3.8}$$

The second condition is that the *social indifference curve* be tangent to the above transformation curve:

$$u'(\tilde{x}) = Ru'(\tilde{y}). \tag{3.9}$$

Note that, since $R > 1$ and u (.) is concave, (3.9) guarantees that the incentive constraint (3.7) does not bind.

The feasibility constraint in period 1 now determines that $\tilde{b} = \lambda\tilde{x}$. This fact, together with (3.2) and (3.8), finally yields the optimal level of investment in the domestic asset:

$$\tilde{k} = \frac{\lambda\tilde{x} + (1-\lambda)\tilde{y}}{R-1}. \tag{3.10}$$

Demand Deposits and Bank Runs

Having identified the social optimum as the best the bank can do for its depositors, the next question is *how* that allocation will be implemented in practice and, more generally, how the banking system may try to accomplish any given objective. To answer such questions, we shall assume that the commercial bank and its depositors establish a particular contract. We shall also assume that the central bank and the commercial bank agree on procedures about how dollars and pesos will be exchanged and, possibly, a lending-borrowing relationship.

One natural way in which the bank can implement the social optimum is via *demand deposits*. Demand deposits are contracts that stipulate that in period 0 each agent must borrow an amount $\tilde{k}$ in the world market and turn it over to the bank, which invests it in the domestic technology. The bank also acquires the right to borrow up to

$\tilde{b}$ dollars on behalf of the depositor from the world market in period 1. In return, each depositor is given the right to withdraw either $\tilde{x}$ pesos in period 1 or $\tilde{y}$ pesos in period 2, depending on the report of her type. Finally, the bank promises to service all of the external debt.

Currency transactions are as follows. Whenever the bank obtains the dollar proceeds from its investments in either period 1 or period 2, it sells those dollars to the central bank in exchange for the pesos with which it can meet deposit withdrawals. After making withdrawals, depositors must visit the central bank and exchange their pesos for dollars at the prevailing exchange rate; then they can use the dollars to buy consumption.[5]

We assume that both the bank and the central bank must respect *sequential service constraints*. These constraints require, loosely speaking, that both the commercial bank and the central bank attend the requests of agents on a first-come, first-served basis.[6]

The demand deposit system implies that the bank will have obligations with both domestic agents and with foreigners. In order to isolate the analysis from issues related to international defaults, we shall focus on regimes for which external debts are always repaid. This requirement implies that, given domestic investment, there must be a maximum liquidation consistent with the bank's solvency. This limit, implied by (3.4) with $y = 0$ and assuming that borrowing in period 1 is as large as possible, can be written as

$$l^+ = \frac{R\tilde{k} - e}{R}. \tag{3.11}$$

We are now ready to complete the description of the demand deposit system. In period 1 depositors arrive to the bank in random order. Upon arrival, each depositor reports her type realization and withdraws either $\tilde{x}$ or 0 pesos, depending on her type. The commercial bank services requested withdrawals sequentially, as long as it is solvent, in which case it borrows from abroad or liquidates the domestic investment as needed to obtain dollars, which it exchanges for pesos at the central bank.

The bank becomes insolvent if withdrawals exceed the maximum amount of short term funds that the bank can use while ensuring that its external debt will be honored, which is given by

$$\tilde{s} = \tilde{b} + rl^+ = e\left(\frac{R-r}{R}\right) - (1-r)\tilde{k}. \tag{3.12}$$

If the bank becomes insolvent, it stops servicing further withdrawals and the nonliquidated portion of the domestic investment is earmarked to repay the external debt. Then the bank closes and disappears.

After all depositors have visited the bank and obtained pesos, the central bank starts selling dollars at an exchange rate of unity. We will assume that the central bank closes if it runs out of dollars (this cannot happen under a currency board, but will happen in other regimes).

If the bank did not close in period 1, in period 2 the bank liquidates all of its remaining investments, repays its external debt, and sells the remaining dollar proceeds to the central bank. It then pays $\tilde{y}$ pesos plus any profits to agents that reported patience in period 1.[7] These agents, finally, visit the central bank and exchange their pesos for dollars that they can use to buy consumption in the world market.

Given this regime, the depositors are engaged in an anonymous game whose *equilibria* naturally characterize the currency board's outcomes. An equilibrium is a description of the strategies of each depositor and aggregate outcomes such that the aggregate outcomes are implied by the depositors' strategies, and each depositor's strategy is optimal for her given the aggregate outcomes.[8]

The following can now be proven:[9]

PROPOSITION 1   There is an *honest* equilibrium. In this equilibrium, in period 1 impatient depositors retire $\tilde{x}$ pesos and patient ones retire nothing. The bank does not fail and pays $\tilde{y}$ to patient depositors in period 2.

This proposition clarifies the role of a banking system in a currency board regime (and also in other regimes). A banking system may implement an allocation that improves upon what agents can achieve in isolation.

However, the banking system may attain such improvement only by holding less internationally liquid assets than its implicit liabilities. Consequently, the banking system may be subject to a run. In particular, it can happen that all agents find it optimal to report impatience if they expect all others to do the same. In this case the bank runs out of resources and fails before it can meet all the claims made on it.

In particular, suppose that

$$\tilde{x} > \tilde{s}. \tag{3.13}$$

In such a case, a run emerges in equilibrium:

PROPOSITION 2   If (3.13) holds, there is an equilibrium in which all depositors claim to be impatient and the bank fails in period 1. If (3.13) does not hold, there cannot be equilibrium bank runs.

The proposition states that (3.13) is not only sufficient but also necessary for the existence of a bank run. Condition (3.13) is therefore crucial and corresponds to what we earlier called international illiquidity: a situation in which the potential short-run hard currency obligations of the financial system exceed the hard currency assets it can have access to, also in the short run.

While (3.13) expresses international illiquidity as a condition on the social optimum, it readily translates, using (3.10) and the definition of $\tilde{s}$, into an equivalent condition on the fundamental parameters of the economy:

$$\tilde{x} > \frac{er(R-1)}{R[1-\lambda(1-r)]} \equiv \tilde{x}^{run}. \tag{3.14}$$

Using this fact, it can be shown that a necessary and sufficient condition for the existence of a bank run is:

PROPOSITION 3   Let $\tilde{y}^{run} \equiv [(R-1)\,e - R\lambda\tilde{x}^{run}]/(1-\lambda)$. Then, a bank run is possible if and only if

$$u'(\tilde{x}^{run}) > Ru'(\tilde{y}^{run}). \tag{3.15}$$

Proof.   The conditions above ensure that (3.14) holds. ∎

Summary

Under a currency board, there can be no attacks on central bank reserves. A banking system operating with demand deposits can emerge and improve upon individual autarky. However, this arrangement may be prone to bank runs.

The situation is reminiscent to that in Argentina in 1995, where a sudden wave of deposit withdrawals threatened the integrity of the local banking system. The central bank could reduce bank reserve requirements, but beyond that had little room to intervene. What saved the day was an infusion of capital from abroad, mostly from the World Bank and the Inter-American Development Bank. The episode, nonetheless, underscored the potential fragility of banks under a currency board system.

Fixed Exchange Rates with a Lender of Last Resort

The rules of the currency board prevent the central bank from extending credit to the commercial bank even in the occurrence of a run. In other words, a currency board commits the central bank never to act as a lender of last resort. We shall now examine the consequences of dropping that commitment. However, we shall still assume that the central bank maintains a fixed exchange rate in the sense that it will defend the peso parity (at one-to-one to the dollar) until it is not feasible for the economy to obtain more dollars. We will see that the key implication of this regime is that, while the commercial bank may be insulated from crises, *balance of payments crises* become possible.

A regime of fixed exchange rates with a lender of last resort is best formalized as follows. The central bank offers to lend an unlimited quantity of pesos to the commercial bank in case more than λ customers claim to be impatient. If such emergency credit is used, though, we assume that the central bank obtains in period 1 control over the domestic asset $\tilde{k}$ and also assumes the debts that the commercial bank should have repaid in period 2. The central bank then liquidates the asset as needed to sell dollars to depositors who have claimed impatience, up to the maximum liquidation consistent with the repayment of the external debt. In period 1, the commercial bank meets withdrawals by borrowing $\tilde{b}$ on its remaining credit line abroad, and then drawing on the emergency credit from the central bank. Because the emergency credit is unlimited, the commercial bank does not close.

The central bank sells dollars at a unity exchange rate, using first the dollars obtained from the commercial bank, and then liquidating the domestic asset up to the limit l^+; this assumption implies that, just as under a currency board, the maximum quantity of dollars that the central bank can sell in period 1 is $\tilde{s}$. After the central bank sells this quantity of dollars, it stops selling further;[10] if this happens while there are still agents attempting to purchase dollars, we say that there is a balance of payments crisis.

Under these assumptions one can show that if all depositors act honestly, the social optimum is implemented:

PROPOSITION 4   The fixed exchange rate system with a lender of last resort has an *honest* equilibrium whose outcome is the social optimum.

The proof is similar to previous ones and left to the reader.

Now, the same conditions under which there was a bank run in the previous regime imply that there is a balance of payments crisis with a lender of last resort:

PROPOSITION 5   There is an equilibrium in which all depositors claim to be impatient and the central bank is unable to service all dollar demands in period 1 if and only if (3.13) holds.

The preceding proposition reveals that, if the central bank acts as a lender of last resort, the possibility of a crisis is the same as with a currency board. The difference is whether the crisis is expressed as a bank run or a balance of payments crisis, but this has no economic importance. The intuition is that, when (3.13) holds, implementing the socially optimal allocation under fixed rates requires that the financial system as a whole be internationally illiquid in the following sense: Given the commitment to fixed rates, the total amount of demandable debt of the system, $\tilde{x}$, is a dollar obligation that exceeds the amount of dollars that the system can tap in period 1. That this situation may cause a bank run under a currency board is not very surprising. What may be surprising is that the central bank cannot succeed as a lender of last resort. This happens because, although the central bank can print pesos, it cannot print the dollars that are effectively needed to back the whole amount of demand deposits.

Flexible Exchange Rates

The analysis of the previous section assumed that the central bank fights a devaluation "like a dog."[11] In particular, we assumed that the central bank stops selling dollars in period 1 only after the domestic asset has been liquidated to the maximum consistent with external debt being serviced. One may ask what would happen with a less committed central bank; for example, the central bank procedure may call for stopping the sale of dollars before using up the maximum amount of dollars available in the short run. Such a rule, in fact, would amount to a rule for when to devalue or let the peso float.

In this section we study such an alternative rule and construct a flexible rate system. Our main result is that flexible rates allow for the unique implementation of the social optimum. In particular, the possibility of a devaluation implies that equilibrium runs can be eliminated at no cost.

To prove the claims just stated, we shall retain all of the assumptions of the case of fixed rates with a lender of last resort, except that the central bank is no longer committed to fix the exchange rate at one. Instead, we will assume that the central bank allows exchange rates to change according to financial events.

Consider the following mechanism. The commercial bank and depositors agree on the same demand deposit contract as under fixed rates. When period 1 begins, depositors arrive to the commercial bank in sequence, and each has the option to withdraw $\tilde{x}$ pesos. The commercial bank services withdrawals first by borrowing abroad (up to $\tilde{b}$) and selling the dollar proceeds to the central bank at an exchange rate of one, and then by borrowing from the central bank. After all depositors have visited the commercial bank, the central bank sells dollars to them at an exchange rate equal to $E_1 = \text{Max}\{\lambda^r/\lambda, 1\}$ pesos per dollar, where λ^r denotes the fraction of agents who reported impatience. Hence, if $\lambda^r > \lambda$ there will be a devaluation.[12]

This devaluation rule can be interpreted in one of two equivalent ways. The first is that the central bank, after observing the actual pattern of withdrawals at the commercial bank, announces a devaluation. This rule is consistent with the existence of a sequential service constraint at the central bank since, as shown below, the devaluation is such that the central bank will not run out of dollars. A second interpretation, perhaps more appealing, is that there is no sequential service at the central bank but, instead, the exchange rate is determined by an auction. In the auction, the central bank offers the dollars sold to it by the commercial bank, and the λ^r depositors that reported impatience offer the $\tilde{x}$ pesos withdrawn from the commercial bank. The devaluation rule implies that reportedly impatient agents receive $\tilde{x}/E_1$ consumption units in the period 1.[13]

In period 2 the bank liquidates the domestic asset, repays its debts abroad, and sells the resulting $R\tilde{k} - e$ dollars to the central bank at an exchange rate of Q pesos per dollar. Here

$$Q = 1 + \frac{(\lambda^r - \lambda)\tilde{x}}{R\tilde{k} - e}$$

and, therefore, it may depend on what happened in period 1; the reason for this rule will be discussed shortly. The commercial bank then repays its debt (if any) with the central bank, and distributes its remaining pesos to the $(1 - \lambda^r)$ depositors that reported patience in period 1.

Finally, these depositors use their pesos to purchase dollars from the central bank at an exchange rate E_2 determined in an auction.

Given this procedure, it can be proven that the optimal allocation is an equilibrium:

PROPOSITION 6   There is an *honest* equilibrium that implements the social optimum. In this equilibrium the exchange rate is one at all times.

The proposition makes clear that, just like fixed rates systems, a flexible rates regime can implement the first best. But in spite of the equivalence of their honest outcomes, flexible rates and fixed rates are rather different. Under the proposed flexible rate regime, the possibility of a peso devaluation eliminates the incentives for any runs:

PROPOSITION 7   Runs cannot occur in equilibrium.

The intuition for this result is threefold. Since deposits are paid in pesos, the central bank can ensure that the commercial bank will always meet its promises by providing last resort lending. The devaluation that is triggered in a run punishes early withdrawals. At the same time, the central bank policy avoids premature liquidation of the domestic asset, which guarantees that patient agents will consume what they were promised by the bank. The consequence is that patient depositors cannot profit from joining a run.

Hence our analysis provides a case for the superiority of flexible exchange rates. At the same time, some qualifications to this result are in order. First, it should be apparent that, to be successful, a flexible rate system must be coupled with a carefully designed central bank policy. The central bank must be willing to serve as a lender of last resort. In addition, exchange rates must be guided judiciously.[14] Second, the beneficial effects of devaluation would not "work" if demand deposits were denominated in dollars instead of pesos. This can be seen as an argument to discourage "dollarization."

Final Remarks

The existence of vulnerable banks poses important constraints on the conduct of monetary policy and the feasibility of alternative exchange rate arrangements. We have developed a model in which these constraints become transparent and their implications precise. Fixed exchange rates imply that either the economy is subject to self-fulfilling crises or the first best cannot be obtained. Only a flexible rates regime is consistents with the unique implementation of the social optimum.

In trying to keep the analysis as simple as possible, we have neglected all the standard arguments for fixed rates. Credibility, visibility, the ease with which remonetization can be accomplished at the time of stabilization—all those alleged advantages of fixing are well understood, and could plausibly be incorporated into our model. Our intention is to stress a so-far ignored advantage of floating rates. Which regime is preferable in practice depends on specific country characteristics and remains an empirical matter.

Appendix

Proof of Proposition 1

Under the hypothesized behavior it is easy to check that the commercial bank does not fail, and that the central bank always has enough dollars to exchange for pesos. Only optimal behavior by depositors needs to be checked. But this is immediate: Impatient depositors consume $\tilde{x}$ if they withdraw honestly and nothing if they lie, and patient ones consume $\tilde{y}$ if honest and, as explained before, $\tilde{x} < \tilde{y}$ if dishonest.

Proof of Proposition 2

First we prove sufficiency. Suppose that every depositor claims to be impatient whatever her type. We saw above (by the argument preceding (3.12)) that the bank has at most $\tilde{s}$ dollars available to it. Then, (3.13) implies that the bank fails in period 1 after converting all available resources to pesos and handing them over to depositors. Depositors who get to the bank in time withdraw $\tilde{x}$. The central bank does not fail, but closes after selling $\tilde{s}$ dollars.

In the posited equilibrium, the bank closes in period 1, and hence no further payments will be given in period 2. Hence it is optimal for each depositor to withdraw $\tilde{x}$ early, regardless of her type.

To prove necessity, suppose that a number $\bar{\lambda}$ of depositors claim to be impatient in period 1. Clearly it is enough to restrict attention to the case in which $\bar{\lambda} > \lambda$. We shall argue by contradiction and show that if (3.13) does not hold the bank is able to pay at least $\tilde{y}$ pesos to honest patient types in period 2, which implies that it cannot be optimal for the patient to lie.

Let $\bar{l}$ denote the amount of liquidation of the domestic asset; it is defined by $\bar{\lambda}\tilde{x} = \tilde{b} + r\bar{l}$. Using this and $\lambda\tilde{x} = \tilde{b}$, one concludes that $r\bar{l} = (\bar{\lambda} - \lambda)\tilde{x}$. Now, it is easy to check that the bank will be able to pay $\tilde{y}$ to the $(1 - \bar{\lambda})$ reportedly patient depositors if $R(\tilde{k} - \bar{l}) - e \geq \tilde{y}(1 - \bar{\lambda})$. But this inequality is, from the definition of $\tilde{y}$ and the last equation for $\bar{l}$, equivalent to the failure of (3.13).

Proof of Proposition 6

First we prove the sufficiency of (3.13). If all depositors claim to be impatient, they withdraw their funds and arrive at the central bank with $\tilde{x}$ pesos in period 1. The central bank obtains $\tilde{b}$ dollars from the bank (which uses the remainder of its available international credit), and rl^+ from the liquidation of the domestic asset, for a total of $\tilde{s}$ dollars. Given (3.13), the central bank closes while there are still some agents trying to buy dollars.

Clearly, the bank does not close in period 1. Since all deposits are paid in period 1, the bank has no further liabilities vis-a-vis depositors in period 2.[15]

It remains to check that each depositor is acting optimally. This is easy and left to the reader.

The proof of necessity is almost identical to that in the currency board case and also left to the reader.

Proof of Proposition 7

Suppose all agents report their types honestly. Then $\lambda^r = \lambda$, and hence $E_1 = Q = 1$. It can be shown that in period 2 the commercial bank distributes exactly $R\tilde{k} - e$ pesos to the patient depositors. Since in period 2 the central bank sells the $R\tilde{k} - e$ dollars obtained from the bank, the exchange rate at which those dollars are sold must also be one.

The rest of the proof follows previous arguments and is left to the reader.

Proof of Proposition 8

Clearly, if a run is to occur, λ^r must be greater than λ. We will show that this implies that lying is not optimal for patient depositors.

Given the rules in this regime, neither the bank nor the central bank fails in any period. Now, Q has been defined so that E_2 is exactly one. To see this, note that in period 2 the debt of the commercial bank to the central bank is $(\lambda^r - \lambda)\tilde{x}$. Hence the commercial bank distributes $Q(R\hat{k} - e) - (\lambda^r - \lambda)\tilde{x}$ pesos to $(1 - \lambda^r)$ depositors. As a consequence, agents go to the central bank with a total of $Q(R\hat{k} - e) - (\lambda^r - \lambda)\tilde{x}$ pesos to buy $R\hat{k} - e$ dollars. The definition of Q ensures the these two quantities are equal, and hence $E_2 = 1$.

If a patient depositor lies, she gets $\tilde{x}/E_1 = \lambda\tilde{x}/\lambda^r < \tilde{x}$ units of consumption. But if she tells the truth, in period 2 her consumption will be at least $\tilde{y}$: she will receive $[Q(R\hat{k} - e) - (\lambda^r - \lambda)\tilde{x}]/(1 - \lambda^r)$ pesos from the bank, which is equal to $(R\hat{k} - e)/(1 - \lambda^r)$ dollars, given $E_2 = 1$ and the definition of Q. Since $\lambda^r > \lambda$, $(R\hat{k} - e)/(1 - \lambda^r) > (R\hat{k} - e)/(1 - \lambda) = \tilde{y}$. Since $\lambda\tilde{x}/\lambda^r < \tilde{x} < \tilde{y} < (R\hat{k} - e)/(1 - \lambda^r)$, a patient agent has no incentive to lie about her type.

Notes

The views expressed in this chapter are those of the authors and not necessarily those of the Federal Reserve Bank of Atlanta or the Federal Reserve System. Velasco acknowledges the financial support of the C.V. Starr Center for Applied Economics at NYU and of the Harvard Institute for International Development. E-mail addresses: Chang: roberto.chang@atl.frb.org. Velasco: velasco@fasecon.econ.nyu.edu.

1. In the case of Mexico, the difficulties posed by bank fragility for the proper defense of the fixed peso were recognized by the Banco de México itself in 1995. See Sachs, Tornell, and Velasco 1996b for further discussion.

2. This can be justified by the revelation principle, which, applied to the bank's problem, implies that the Bayesian Nash equilibria of any game that the depositors may play can be replicated by the truthful equilibria of a game in which each depositor is asked to report her type. See Myerson 1991 for an excellent introduction to the revelation principle.

3. One can assume instead that the bank borrows b in period 0 and invests it in the world market until period 1. This makes no difference in our context.

4. It is easy to show that any allocation that is feasible in autarky must be feasible for the commercial bank. This implies that the value of the planning problem must be at least as large as the value of autarky. The rest of the proof can be completed along the lines of Wallace 1996.

5. It may seem paradoxical that agents need dollars to "buy" domestically produced output. The matter becomes more sensible if one remembers that in this model, "dollars" and goods are the same thing. Hence, we could equivalently say that agents exchange their pesos for goods, which they then consume.

6. The existence of sequential service constraints can be justified by more primitive features of the environment, as suggested by Wallace 1996.

7. Profits are zero in equilibrium, but they can be nonzero off the equilibrium path.

8. This description is intentionally vague. This is because we have assumed a large number of depositors, each of whom has measure zero. Given this, the equilibrium definition must ensure that depositors assume that their impact on aggregate outcomes is negligible. In such case the appropriate equilibrium concept is that of Schmeidler (1973).

9. Unless explicitly stated, proofs are in the appendix.

10. And earmarks the nonliquidated domestic investment to service the external debt.

11. This famous phrase is attributed to Mexican President López Portillo in describing his commitment to defend the peso in 1982; he devalued a few weeks later.

12. There is some latitude in designing the devaluation policy to ensure the prevention of runs. The one described in this section is chosen for its simplicity: as shown in the appendix, it ensures that $E_2 = 1$ under all circumstances. However, there are other policies that accomplish the desired goals.

13. The auction interpretation has the advantage that the central bank does not need to know the number λ' of depositors who visited the commercial bank. It is enough for the monetary authority to put only $\tilde{x}$ dollars on the market, and the price λ'/λ will result whenever $\lambda' > \lambda$.

14. As in the fixed rate case, the central bank acts as a lender of last resort since it lends pesos to the commercial bank in a run. If that is not the case, there is an equilibrium in which the commercial bank fails. (We leave the details to the reader.)

15. The bank has no resources to repay its debt to the central bank in period 2, but this is not important, since by then the central bank has become bankrupt. Alternatively, one can assume that the debt is canceled when the central bank fails to return the long-term asset to the commercial bank.

References

Banco de México. 1995. Exposición sobre la política monetaria. Mexico City.

Calvo, G. 1996. Comment on Sachs, Tornell and Velasco. *Brookings Papers on Economic Activity*, 1:102–5.

Diamond, D., and P. Dybvig. 1983. Bank runs, deposit insurance, and liquidity. *Journal of Political Economy* 91:401–19.

International Monetary Fund. 1997. Exchange Rate Arrangements and Economic Performance in Developing Countries. *World Economic Outlook* (October).

Kaminsky, G., and C. Reinhart. 1999. The twin crises: The causes of banking and balance of payments problems. *American Economic Review* 89 (June):473–500.

Mundell, R. 1963. Capital mobility and stabilization policy under fixed and flexible exchange rates. *Canadian Journal of Economics and Political Science* 29:475–85.

Mundell, R. 1961. The theory of optimum currency areas. *American Economic Review* 51:657–65.

Myerson, R. 1991. *Game theory*. Cambridge: Harvard University Press.

Sachs, J., A. Tornell, and A. Velasco. 1996a. Financial crises in emerging markets: The lessons from 1995. *Brookings Papers on Economic Activity* 1:78–102.

Sachs, J., A. Tornell, and A. Velasco. 1996b. The collapse of the Mexican peso: What have we learned? *Economic Policy* 22:13–64.

Schmeidler, D. 1973. Equilibrium points of nonatomic games. *Journal of Statistical Physics* 4:295–300.

Wallace, N. 1996. Narrow banking meets the Diamond-Dybvig model. *Federal Reserve Bank of Minneapolis Quarterly Review* (Winter):3–13.

4

Curing a Monetary Overhang: Historical Lessons

Rudi Dornbusch and
Holger Wolf

Introduction

Maintaining macroeconomic balance in distorted economies becomes harder as wartime controls or outright political repression become less effective. This is especially the case in economies starting with a substantial overhang of liquid public debt or money. The European experience after the two wars and the adjustment of the transition economies over the last few years suggest that the combination of weakening control, large starting imbalances, a pervasive (and invasive) public sector, politicized wage setting, and an obedient central bank carries the seeds for endemic instability. Hyperinflations have been a common result in these instances. While the aftermath of World War I was largely characterized by open inflation, the post–World War II environment quite closely resembled the transition economies of eastern Europe. In the end, the central control—and the populations' willingness to succumb to the control—necessary to stabilize the fragile mixture of controlled prices, rations, and generous nominal wage growth crumbled at the end of hostilities.[1] That raised the question of how to deal with monetary overhang.

Appendix 4.1 shows a representative listing of inflation outcomes for these episodes, illustrating both the (at times) extreme outcomes and the wide disparity of policy experiences across countries. The table suggests an important lesson: inflationary doom can be avoided, no matter how desperate the initial conditions. Denmark, the Netherlands, and, to a large extent, war-ravaged France avoided the hyperinflationary turmoil of the post–WWI years. Denmark, Germany, and the Netherlands successfully restrained inflation following WWII. The Czech and Slovak Republics avoided hyperinflation following the collapse of socialism.

We will argue below that the initial successes in fending off hyperinflation in post–WWII Europe and in the transition economies reflected, for the most part, a courageous dissolution of the inherited *stock* imbalances. Initial triumph, however, did not uniformly translate into longer term real performance. For the latter, the resolution of the overhang had to complemented by restraint in the flow dimension of the fiscal deficit, along with structural reforms. The link between fiscal variables, inflation, and growth is itself the focus of a substantive literature; we will only parenthetically touch upon it here. The focus of the present paper is instead the first part of the story, the resolution of the stock problem of the monetary overhang itself.

Monetary Overhangs: Conceptual Issues

Stock monetary imbalances result from the combination of income growth in excess of desired consumption growth; binding constraints on equilibrating mechanisms, notably price controls; rationing; and an absence of assets with returns sufficient to induce optimal consumption postponement. Weakening central control softens these constraints, notably through the creation of pervasive black markets. Once authorities lose the ability to set both prices and quantities, the days of the monetary overhang are numbered. A resolution will come either through an elimination of the excess nominal money balances via a monetary reform—an outright cut or a forced conversion into debt or public sector assets—or through an upward revision of prices eliminating the excess demand.[2]

The fundamental disequilibrium is an excess of money supply over money demand. As a result, it would seem to make little difference a priori whether the overhang is eliminated by a downward adjustment in nominal money supply or an upward revision of prices. A core point of this chapter is that this equivalence is unlikely to hold in practice: to the extent that price and wage setting are staggered, it will be difficult to arrest the inflationary momentum once the overhang has been eliminated. If persistent inflation is even partly accommodated, the price liberalization route carries the danger of spawning persistent inflation rather than a one-time blip in the price level; with attendant negative consequence for real liquidity. The wide range of outcomes listed in appendix 4.1 illustrates that this danger is quite real.

The experiences of monetary adjustment after WWI, and in the transition economies, have been the subject of lively debate. Less attention has been devoted to the lessons of the post–WWII liberalization efforts of Western Europe. In the following sections we review this episode, with a particular focus on the German monetary reform of 1948.

Monetary Reforms in the 1940s

After 1939, war expenditures increased the outlays of the typical European country far beyond tax revenues. For reasons of morale, governments were reluctant to rely on extra taxation. Furthermore, debt sales, though generally successful, were rarely sufficient to cover the increased expenditure. Unfunded deficits prompted governments to relax regulations on the permissible degree of deficit monetization for the duration of the war, leading to substantial money supply growth, further aggravated in countries under occupation by the attempt of the occupying forces to extract support from the local economy (Klopstock 1946). To forestall the negative effect of inflation on morale, as well as on the military planning process, price controls soon followed. Coupled with the strictly enforced rationing of scarce consumption goods as resources were shifted toward the military sector, the stage was set for a substantial buildup of forced savings.[3]

At the end of the war, these accumulated funds—for the most part involuntarily postponed consumption rather than desired long-term savings—confronted an inadequate supply of consumption goods. Supply was low because of war destruction and the difficulty of converting factories back to the production of civilian goods. The implicit excess demand was kept in check by continued price controls and rationing. Yet these measures, accepted or at least endured during the war, became increasingly unpopular. More generally, they spawned extensive black markets and thus further reduced the supply of goods available at controlled prices.

The governments of Western Europe thus faced a problem: the restoration of a functioning market economy required flexible prices, yet price liberalization threatened to turn the monetary overhang into an inflationary avalanche. With the notable exception of Italy and the United Kingdom, governments were unwilling to risk inflation. Instead, a surgical removal of the monetary overhang prior to, or simultaneous with, price liberalization became the reform of choice.

Table 4.1 provides a summary overview of the reforms, illustrating the preference for nominal money supply reduction over inflation as a solution to the monetary overhang.[4] While the table reveals substantial

Table 4.1
Monetary reforms in the 1940s and 1950s

Country	Date	Registration	Blocking	Write-down	Levy
No reform					
Italy					
United Kingdom					
Reform					
Austria I	Jul. 1945		*		
Austria II	Nov. 1945		*		
Austria III	Nov. 1947			*	
Belgium	Oct. 1944		*		*
Bulgaria I	Mar. 1947		*		*
Bulgaria II	May 1952			*	
Czechoslovakia I	Oct. 1945		*		*
Czechoslovakia II	Jun. 1953			*	
Denmark	Jul. 1945	*	*		*
Finland	Dec. 1945		*		*
France I	Jun. 1945	*			
France II	Jan. 1948		*		*
Germany (East)	Jun. 1948		*	*	
Germany (West)	Jun. 1948		*	*	
Hungary I	Dec. 1945		*	*	
Netherlands	Sep. 1945				*
Norway	Sep. 1945	*		*	*
Poland I	Dec. 1944				*
Poland II	Oct. 1950			*	
Rumania I	Aug. 1947		*	*	
Rumania II	Jan. 1952			*	
USSR	Dec. 1947			*	
Yugoslavia	Apr. 1945		*	*	*
Hyperinflation					
Greece	Nov. 1944				
Hungary II	Aug. 1946				

Sources: Gurley 1953, Klopstock 1946, Pesek 1958, Dieterlen and Rist 1948, Snider 1948.

differences in the extent and severity of reforms, ranging from a temporary blocking to an outright forced levy, the reforms shared a number of common features, which we take up next before turning in more detail to what is probably the most famous postwar reform, the Tenenbaum/Erhardian miracle package of 1948.

Measuring the Overhang

The first challenge facing policymakers, and by no means a trivial one, was to assess the extent of the overhang, both in terms of absolute magnitude and in terms of its distribution across groups. The essential characteristic of a monetary overhang is an excess of the real money supply over the hypothetical real money demand if individuals could purchase assets or goods at given prices. The combination of price controls and rationing implies that the money will in fact be held, but the holding is involuntary. An opening of alternative spending opportunities in terms of assets or goods would result in an attempt to reduce real balances until, through a combination of goods and asset price adjustment, equilibrium is restored. Consider as a guide the quantity equation

$$V = PY/M, \tag{4.1}$$

where V denotes velocity, M the nominal money stock, and P and Y the levels of prices and of real income. During the war, the typical European country experienced a loss in output as a result of physical destruction and a substantial increase in money supply as a consequence of deficit monetization. At the same time, price levels remained fairly constant due to more or less extensive and effective controls. As a result, actual velocity declined substantially, and the monetary overhang is reflected in a fall of actual velocity relative to the equilibrium velocity in the absence of distortions. Following either price liberalization, relaxation of quantity constraints or an outright monetary reform, velocity returns to its (higher) equilibrium. Table 4.2 documents a few cases.

If it is assumed that the equilibrium velocity remained unchanged, an intuitive first measure of the overhang could be obtained by using the pre-war velocity together with an estimate of the change in nominal income to compute the implied equilibrium money stock and, by subtraction, the current excess. This procedure was, in fact, followed in the Netherlands as reported by Lieftinck (1973).[5] The approach has a few

Table 4.2
Velocity: Pre- and post-reform

Belgium		Czechoslovakia		Netherlands		Germany (West)	
Pre-reform							
1937	1.52	1937	0.74	1937	1.98	1937	3.73
1944	0.55	1945	0.32	1945	0.38	1948	0.18
Post-reform							
1944	1.58	1945	9.44	1945	1.01	1948	21.29
1949	1.59	1949	1.83	1949	1.95	1949	4.22

Source: Pesek 1958.

shortcomings. First, it stands to reason that frozen absolute and also relative prices, combined with pervasive rationing, pushes real output below potential output. As these restrictions are removed, income, and hence money demand, will rise, absorbing part of the overhang. This effect needs to be considered in the calculation.

Second, to the extent that some transactions are conducted unofficially prior to the reform, both the official price level and the official output figures understate the effective price and output level. A theoretically more appropriate approach to measuring the overhang starts—in the tradition of Barro and Grossman (1976)—with an explicit non-market clearing model endogenizing the effects of restrictions on goods and asset markets as well as of expectations about the likely future change in these restrictions on labor supply and the allocation of resources to official and unofficial markets, based on an appropriate specification of tastes and technology.

The intertemporal aspect is of particular significance: the expectation of an (eventually unavoidable) monetary reform might reduce the demand for real balances as money holders shift into black market goods, financial assets, or dollars, thereby increasing the monetary overhang. The German stock market, to take an example, experienced a substantial boom during the dismal years 1945 to 1948. As the likelihood of a confiscatory reform became more likely, the black market price of one favorite hard asset—cigarettes—increased tenfold from 5 to 50 RM while the price of dollar bills—hidden and hence exempted from the monetary cut—traded for up to 1,000 Marks (*Neue Zürcher Zeitung* 1948).[6]

In the end, there is no easy solution to the measurement problem, if only because the post-reform money demand needed to estimate the overhang crucially depends on post-reform expectations. They themselves are endogenous to the monetary reform—and hence to the estimated overhang. In short, the likelihood of obtaining an estimate with reasonably tight confidence intervals is illusionary. This creates a policy conundrum: should reforms be based on the upper or on the lower end of the estimated range of the overhang? In the latter case, the initial reform is less painful, but a second confiscatory helping might be needed later if initial reforms prove, ex post, to be insufficient. In the former case, the overhang is eliminated with near certainty, but at the risk of overkill and deflation.

In our view, the harsh reform option is preferable. An ex post, insufficiently soft reform either triggers inflation or necessitates further intervention, both of which would carry significant distortionary costs. If monetary reform is coupled with the introduction of a new money, difficult-to-reverse currency substitution might occur. In contrast, an overly hard reform has the drawback of keeping growth below potential, but it achieves the key objective of establishing market-based relative prices and turning attention from the obstacles of the past toward the opportunities of the future. Indeed, a scarcity of working balances might well have the additional desirable effect of forcing merchants to liquidate hoarded inventory, buttressing the reputation of the reform. In fact, this strategy was deliberately employed in the German monetary reform. Once the initial period of relative price adjustment has passed, a gradual remonetization—with the side benefit of seignorage revenues—can replenish lacking liquidity.

Dissolving the Overhang

Once a decision on the size of the overhang has been made, the next issue becomes the optimal method for its elimination. Five alternative mechanisms are available to restore monetary equilibrium:

1. An increase in the level of output, at the prevailing level of prices (but with an adjustment in relative prices, if necessary). To an extent, the end of hostilities enabled repairs to infrastructure and communication networks which in turn resulted in some output recovery. In general however, sluggish output and distorted relative prices are two sides of the same coin. A sustained growth rebound can thus not be expected before the monetary overhang is resolved. Growth will follow reform, not substitute for it.

2. A decrease in equilibrium velocity, at given prices, money, and output; for instance through an attempt to absorb some of the over-hang through higher rates on longer, fixed-term savings accounts. Two problems arise, however. First, it is questionable whether demand for longer-term nominal assets is sufficiently elastic with respect to the available policy instruments, in particular the interest rate, in an environment of extreme uncertainty to make this channel feasible for any but the smallest disequilibria. Second, any conversion into interest-bearing, long-term assets may further imperil the stability of the financial system. One option avoiding both problems is a forced conversion of short-term, liquid assets into long-term public sector real assets, either paying no interest or postponing interest payment through capitalization.[7]

3. The retirement of the overhang over time by budget surpluses.

4. A rise in the price level, by fiat or by market forces.

5. A blocking of nominal assets that immobilizes a portion of the monetary holdings.

6. A uniform or differentiated write-down of monetary assets including a forced conversion at above market clearing prices into public sector assets.

Neither of the easy options—an increase in output or a substantial fall in desired velocity—nor fiscal surpluses are likely to cure any but the mildest case of monetary overhang. The realistic choice faced by governments confronting a serious case of monetary overhang thus comes down to accepting a period, however brief, of rapid inflation or to opting for a reduction in the effective money supply. We now consider these options in turn.

Inflation

The only feasible alternative to reducing the effective nominal money supply is an increase in the price level. From a theoretical point of view, both policies are equivalent: whether the excess supply of real money balances is cured by a decrease in nominal money or by a one time increase in the price level is irrelevant.

In practice, economies with a monetary overhang face a dual problem. On the one hand, equilibrium in the money market requires an adjustment of the *absolute* price level. On the other hand, an alteration in the typically distorted *relative* price structure is necessary to restore goods market equilibrium. In the presence of indexation, implicit agreements and staggered price and wage setting, adjustment will not come as a blip in the price level but as a more or less protracted period of high inflation as relative prices slowly find their new equilibrium levels.[8]

High inflation, in turn, may feed upon itself. Two effects are of particular importance.[9] Inflation tends to reduce the real value of taxes. In the absence of additional revenue sources, the solution of the stock problem may thus give rise to a flow problem as the increased deficit is monetized. Furthermore, as inflation accelerates, economic institutions adjust to the new environment. In financial markets, the introduction of indexed assets combined with the gradual replacement of currency as a viable medium of exchange further increases desired velocity. In the goods and factor markets, payment arrangements shift toward more frequent adjustment, enhancing the economy's sensitivity to future inflationary shocks.

The importance of these factors will of course vary across economies. A resolution of the overhang based on price adjustment has the potential to turn the one-time stock adjustment problem into a protracted inflation problem. This situation confronts governments with the unenviable choice between causing a real contraction by refusing accommodation or spawning persistent inflation by accommodation. In the limit, in particular if fiscal policies are loose, the inflation may not even stop at moderate levels but deteriorate into high inflation, if not hyperinflation. The possibility is more than a theoretical curiosum: of the countries opting for the inflationary solution in preference to a reduction in effective money in the postwar period, Hungary and Greece still claim the top spots in the all-time record list of hyperinflation.[10] Italy and France, with more limited inflation, still experienced a vast rise in prices. In Italy, between 1945 and 1949 the price level doubled, and in France it increased fivefold.

Reducing Nominal Money

We can distinguish three basic types of monetary reform. The first is a mere change of numeraire: a new currency is issued with full conversion of the old currency into the new one for all nominal stocks and flows, including currency, bank accounts, debt, wages, and prices. The primary purpose of the conversion is convenience, the elimination of a number of zeros. It might also help determine the wealth distribution (with a view toward later taxation); eliminate illegally acquired currency hoards, for instance by requiring documentation of origin for large exchanges; or, if introduced jointly with other forms, buttress their signaling function. In essence, though, the reform per se has no real effects, except possibly as a signal that no further actions should be expected.

The second kind of reform immobilizes money holdings for a specified or for an unknown period by blocking bank accounts. Blocking temporarily deactivates the medium of exchange function, but retains the unit of account and—in a restricted way, subject to inflation—the store of value function. The measure is in essence a means to postpone a decision, since eventually blocked accounts must be either released, written off, or converted into other assets.

The third kind of monetary reform is confiscatory: currency and/or bank accounts are written off, either at a uniform conversion rate or on a differentiated basis. In this case the conversion is not merely nominal but real: stocks are converted at a less favorable rate than flows, such as wages or rents. A uniform conversion of all nominal assets held by the public is equivalent to a blip in the price level and thus has the same distribution effects. A more differentiated process can accommodate desired political features such as the special taxation of speculators (who hold large amounts of currency) or of affluent groups (who hold government debt and large deposits).

Blocking, forced conversion into non-monetary assets, and write-downs all achieve the desired objective of preventing the demand implicit in the excess *stock* of real balances to become realized in the goods markets, triggering inflation. A write-down avoids the spillover by directly reducing consumer's asset holdings to the desired level. Given current prices and income flows, total demand for goods will thus approximately equal new production, and inflation pressures will be subdued. Blocking and forced conversion into nonmonetary assets achieve the same objective by limiting the extent to which the desired substitution from monetary wealth to commodities can take place.

The two strategies differ however in the spending effect produced from an equal amount of unrestricted asset holdings. As long as consumers expect blocked accounts to be at least partly released, blocked balances (appropriately discounted) will be viewed as part of wealth, raising consumption demand. The same applies to monetary balances converted into nonmonetary assets perceived to be valuable. In consequence, the propensity to consume out of the free accounts will be higher in the case of blocking and conversion than in the case of a write-down. To achieve the same final consumption target, blocking and conversion ratios must thus exceed write-down ratios.

The choice between blocking and conversion is determined by a number of considerations. First, blocking assets in preference to outright conversion is politically attractive. It maintains the option of releasing funds later, without inflationary consequences, if economic conditions are revealed to be better than anticipated. At worst, it postpones the politically unpopular wealth tax. Second, conversion places holders of monetary wealth at a disadvantage vis-à-vis holders of real assets, though the resulting political conflict can, and has, been addressed by subsequent real wealth levies. Third, decisions about write-offs have to be considered in the context of the balance sheets of financial institutions. If the assets are non-performing, because of physical destruction of collateral, loss of territory or otherwise, there is simply no reasonable way of sustaining the liabilities. Of course, the government could guarantee the liabilities and place net worth certificates serviced out of general revenues in bank balance sheets, but this would evidently place a major burden on public finance unless there is a tie-in with other operations such as privatization or external loans.

Conversion and blocking are of course not mutually exclusive. Given a guesstimate of the size of the overhang and of the likely recovery of output, the combination of a generous conversion rate with a substantial blocking permits the government to adopt a wait-and-see attitude: If the initial guesses turn out to be correct ex post, the blocked funds can be released, maintaining the original generous conversion rate. If events take a less positive turn, a partial conversion of the blocked assets lowers the original conversion rate to a level more consistent with price level stability.

We now put some flesh on these bones by considering in more detail the West German case. It is an example of the buildup and eventual elimination of a monetary overhang and a case study of the relation between monetary reform and real performance.

Monetary Reform in Germany

The currency reform in the occupied German Tri-Zone on June 20, 1948, marked the beginning of the "Economic Miracle." In the five months directly following the reform, industrial output increased by more than

50 percent. Over the period 1947–1949 (reported) industrial production more than doubled. A ravaged, apparently moribund economy seemed to regain its health overnight. Furthermore, the strong growth performance was not restricted to an initial rebound of output to its potential. In fact, it continued well into the 1950s, suggesting continued expansion of potential output itself. The timing coincidence of currency reform and economic takeoff naturally raises the question of a causal link.

Background[11]

Fiscal and monetary policy since 1933 were completely subjugated to the "noiseless financing" of the military. To this effect, restrictions on the gold and foreign currency coverage of the note issue were lifted in 1933, leaving a formal coverage requirement in form of three month treasury bills and some forms of commercial paper (Klein 1956). The shift of resources from the civilian to the military sector resulted in increasing shortages of consumption goods, prompting the imposition of extensive rationing in 1939. Coupled with continued high employment and slightly increasing nominal wages, upward pressure on prices emerged as early as 1935–1936,[12] prompting the imposition of a virtually complete price freeze in 1936, followed by a wage freeze in 1938. The controls proved fairly effective, slowing the official inflation rate to an average of 1.5 percent over the period 1936 to 1944.[13]

With consumption limited to the rationed quantities of necessities being made available at the controlled prices, the difference between the fixed nominal incomes and the permitted consumption expenditures were accumulated as "forced savings." Lacking alternatives, these funds found their way to the commercial banks who in turn invested them in public debt instruments, allowing the government to cover part of its substantial primary deficit.[14] The larger part of the deficit was, however, financed by money creation, as table 4.3 illustrates. Debt and deficits grew year after year. As the Third Reich dissolved, claims on the government, and hence a major portion of the commercial bank assets, became non-performing, causing solvency though not liquidity problems.[15]

The military governments, faced with very limited supplies of consumption goods and the looming excess demand, maintained price and wage controls. The share of transactions conducted at these prices however declined as military governments had less success—and

Table 4.3
Money and debt in Germany, 1937–1944

	1937	1939	1944
Money	151	324	1,375
Debt	220	441	2,708
Prices	106	106	120

Sources: Veit. 1961, *Statistisches Handbuch fur Deutschland*, 1928, 1944.
Note: Values are for December 31 of the given years.

ultimately interest in—suppressing unofficial market transactions. Pervasive black markets for consumer goods developed, with prices frequently exceeding official prices by a factor of 100 and more. Similarly, firms finding themselves unable to acquire inputs with *Reichsmark* (RM) resorted to barter deals, spawning a new service industry of freelance or employed matchmakers specialized in securing needed inputs in barter transactions, thus reducing the informational inefficiencies of the nonmonetary exchange system. As wages reflected official prices, at which consumption choices were strictly limited, labor supply dwindled except in firms paying in kind. Leisure and black market activity became an increasingly popular alternative to paid work, further reducing the supply of goods available at controlled prices.[16]

When the belief in an eventual substantial cut in RM holdings became widespread, the proportion of transactions undertaken in RM dropped precipitously. The risk premia on all transactions except purchases of rationed goods and the repayment of debt skyrocketed, as illustrated in table 4.4. The deteriorating quality of the RM as a medium of exchange, store of value, and unit of account prompted the search for an alternative, which was found in the form of cigarettes.[17]

In the end, it proved easier to organize a non-monetary system of consumer goods markets than to replace money in the production system.[18] The breakdown of the monetary system thus affected industrial production more severely than consumption: after an initial rebound from the minimal levels reached in the final months of the war, (reported) industrial production essentially flattened out in mid 1947 at roughly 50 percent of the prewar level.[19] The steadily worsening situation placed a spotlight on resolving the monetary issue; between 1945 and 1948 more than 100 programs of currency reform were published. Experiences throughout Europe had already demonstrated how an overhang might be consolidated or at least immobilized. Finally it

Table 4.4
Ratio of black market to official prices: Germany, 1948

	Pre-reform		Post-reform				
	15.5	19.6	3.6	15.7	15.8	15.9	15.10
Rye bread	27.1	45.7	3.2	2.9	2.8	2.2	2.5
White sugar	33.9	135.5	5.1	4.6	4.2	4.4	4.7
Butter	133.3	195.3	4.3	4.6	4.4	4.6	5.8
Cigarettes							
American	20.0	133.3	1.0	1.3	1.3	1.3	1.3
German	12.5	93.8	1.3	1.3	1.3	1.1	1.8

Source: Mendershausen 1949.

Table 4.5
Initial allocation and conversion (stock of DM, billion)

	1948			1949	
	June	Sept.	Dec.	March	Dec.
Initial allocation					
Public authorities	2.5	3.45	3.45	3.45	3.45
Persons and firms	1.9	3.25	3.25	3.25	3.25
Conversion of deposits					
Free accounts	—	3.5	5.3	5.7	6.2
Blocked accounts	—	2.85	0.75	0.55	0.35

Note: 70 percent of blocked deposits were canceled in December 1948.

was the turn of Germany to undergo an already widely expected reform.

The Reform

The dismal economic situation, in conjunction with the developing strains between the Soviet Union and the Western Allies prompted the U.S. and the U.K. military government to abandon its prior objective of a monetary reform covering all four zones. Instead, in June 1948 a monetary reform was implemented in the American, British, and French occupied zones. Some of the most pertinent components of the reform are listed below.

Table 4.5 shows the resulting evolution of the initial allocations and the conversions. Just as the Rentenmark in the 1923 reform, the

Deutschemark (DM) found rapid acceptance. Hoarded inventories were offered for sale against DM starting the day after the reform, a willingness partly caused by a deliberately frugal initial cash allocation to firms and shops. The acceptance of the new currency, even before the sufficiency of the monetary cut could be assessed, stresses the prime importance of broad popular support for the reform. Such support derived on the one hand from the desire to return to a functioning monetary system and on the other from the decisiveness of the reform itself.

Main Provisions of the West German Currency Reform

1. Individuals and firms were issued in two installments a per capita allowance, DM60 per person and DM60 per worker for firms. The public sector also received an initial allowance.

2. Half of deposits were converted at the rate of 10:1 into deposits, the other half blocked. Subsequently, 70 percent of the blocked accounts were written off, and of the remainder, two-thirds were placed in free accounts and one-third into blocked investment accounts.

3. With few exceptions, all flow magnitudes, in particular wages, were converted at 1:1.

4. In contrast to holdings of the private sector, intra-bank RM claims, RM claims against the Third Reich (including public debt) and RM holdings of the public sector were canceled.

5. Commercial Banks were granted claims against the Laender, accepted at the Bank Deutscher Laender, to cover the shortfall of assets relative to liabilities due to the cancellation of government debt.

6. The DM was declared sole legal tender. The Bank Deutscher Laender, acting as central bank, was entitled to impose minimum reserve requirements. The total note issue was limited; the limit could only be raised with the consent of a qualified majority of the Laender.

7. Budget balance was prescribed by law.

Indeed, given the very uncertainties about the size of the overhang described above, for the purpose of establishing credibility the actual rate of conversion might matter less than the perceived determination of the authorities to carry the program through. This was recognized by Lt. Tenenbaum, the U.S. liaison officer with the German stabilization team, who stressed that a bold reform with an, ex post, incorrect conversion rate might well be preferable to a timid conversion at the, ex post, appropriate rate.[20] In Germany, the initial conversion took place at a rate of 10RM to 1DM, with half of the converted funds blocked and only released partially in the end. Ex post, the limited blocking turned out to be too generous: the half year following the reform was marred by some inflation. (See table 4.5.)

The availability of the blocked accounts provided the authorities with a means to fine-tune once the response of the economy to the initial reform became known. As continuing moderate inflation suggested an insufficiently harsh initial cut, 70 percent of the blocked accounts were canceled in a second step. Another 20 percent were released, and 10 percent continued to be blocked for later conversion into interest-bearing assets. The negative wealth effect of the second cut, combined with restrictive credit policy, dominated the liquidity effect from the additional released funds, and prices stabilized at year end. The success of the reform is mirrored in the decline of the black market premium documented in table 4.4. By 1950 the Bank Deutscher Laender (1950, p. 2) could appraise the gain in confidence:

Even the public, in spite of the heavy jolts which the Currency Reform gave to the holders of assets in monetary form for the second time in one generation, have to a large extent regained their confidence in money. Savings are increasing to a remarkable extent. Foreigners also have increasing confidence in the German currency, as is shown by the rise in the quotation of the DM on certain free markets abroad.

A number of factors buttressed the rapid establishment of the DM as a sound new monetary standard. First, the monetary reform initially made money scarce and subsequent credit policies remained tight. Second, the government, required in any case by the strict rules set by the occupation forces, and subsequently by the new constitution, to balance its books, in fact went beyond its obligations and maintained a fiscal surplus.[21] Third, the reestablishment of a hard monetary standard was buttressed by simultaneous and extensive liberalization measures. With the exception of controls and rationing for some basic materials and food, prices were freed, leading to a rapid decline in the black market premium even for rationed goods. The one exception to the liberalization trend came on the external side: while foreign trade transactions were progressively liberalized, current account convertibility came only a decade later.

On the real side, there is no shortage of stories about the immediate, dramatic effects on economic activity unleashed by the monetary reform and price liberalization. Rebounding confidence and changed incentives combined to unleash an initial spurt of dramatic growth.

This further buttressed expectations, boosted reconstruction investment and hence permitted further expansion once the initial "easy" recovery toward potential output had run its course. Labor input rebounded dramatically: while from December 1947 to May 1948 absenteeism averaged 14.7 percent of the workforce, the combination of wages paid in sound currency and increased consumption choices led to a decline in absenteeism to 9.6 percent in June 1948 and 6.3 percent in July 1948.[22] Industrial production and activity increased sharply. On the basis 1936 = 100, the index of production stood in June 1948 at 51. By the end of the year it had reached 79, and in April 1949 it had climbed to 89. Part of the increase undoubtedly merely reflected a shift from unofficial to official production, but even so there is little doubt that the liberalization measures decisively raised productivity.

While monetary reform and price decontrol are important as critical preconditions of the "economic miracle," continued growth beyond the initial rebound depended crucially on a combination of factors: fiscal balance to free resources for private and public investment, the radical "supply side" liberalization program undertaken by Ludwig Erhard with an emphasis on emphasizing competition, self help, low taxes and a tilting of incentives toward investment.[23] But there was also the inflow of some eight million largely skilled refugees providing ample labor supply while restraining wage growth, and of course the resources provided by the Marshall Plan.

Conclusion

In the period 1945–1959 European countries rebuilt their economies, gradually reestablished sound financial systems and liberalized, step by step, external trade and payments. Monetary reform was part, but only part, of the process. The stark differences in longer term performance—slow growth in Britain, fast growth in Austria, Italy, and Germany—primarily reflect differences in economic philosophy. There were early supply-side revolutions in Italy and Germany, a more interventionist approach in the United Kingdom. There were sharply different political constraints facing winners and losers: a desire to be compensated for sacrifices prompting demands for wage growth in the United Kingdom, general despondency suppressing wages in Italy and Germany.[24] Yet while not the dominant factor, monetary reform did set the stage for many of the subsequent reforms. What can be learned from the experience of postwar Europe?

First, monetary reform in the form of write-downs, by avoiding the burdening of an already difficult adjustment phase with additional unnecessary macroeconomic complications, provided a preferable alternative to the inflation solution to the overhang problem, provided the stock adjustment was buttressed by prudent fiscal policies.

Second, on balance tough reformers finished first. This suggests that what ultimately matters most is not so much the current loss but the certainty that, going forward, money will be sound among the countries undertaking monetary reforms. One critical component of the better performance of harsh reformers was a higher savings rate, crucial in a reconstruction environment. The postwar experience suggests that a write-down of the financial overhang is more conducive to enhancing private saving than continued large transfers associated with a consolidation of the overhang into interest-bearing debt. Lingering fiscal problems easily turn into inflation where the flight from money is the rule, even if in the aggregate it is self-defeating.

Third, it must be recognized that monetary reform, because it involves blocking or writing-down of assets, is thoroughly unpopular at the time of reform, and indeed, one finds remarkably few democracies in the sample of countries undertaking harsh reform. The short-term unpopularity must however be gauged relative to the expected longer-term gains: the alternatives to a write-down today are either higher taxes tomorrow to fund the necessary transfers to retire the overhang through fiscal surpluses or higher inflation to inflate the overhang away. Both presumably carry their own political cost.

In concluding, it is worth noting again that monetary reform may not be necessary and surely is not sufficient for success. Countries who did not have a monetary reform, for example Italy, did perform well after inflation had been brought under control. (Of course, the inflation did liquidate the government debt.) Other countries, notably Belgium, undertook monetary reforms but undermined their longer-term benefits by failing to follow through on the fiscal side, yet others—including all of eastern Europe—achieved at best mixed effects by failing to complement monetary reform with goods and factor market liberalization.

Policy makers must focus realistically on alternatives, and once that is done, monetary reform may appear the soundest option in quite a few situations. The popular argument that confiscatory reform weakens confidence just at a time where confidence is so essential must be rejected. Confidence depends on the future ability and willingness of a government to meet its commitments. Governments who have eliminated an overhang of money or debt will look better than governments who appear willing to honor their liabilities but are patently unable to do so. Against the illusion of easy solutions we hold the advice of W. Vocke, the first president of the postwar German central bank: "Soft measures don't create hard currencies."

Appendix 4.1 Overview of Monetary Reform

Austria 7/1945, 11/1945, 11/1947

New national currency (shilling). Sizable portion of currency and bank deposits blocked. Withdrawal for wage payments allowed. Account-to-account transfers allowed. Initial reform failed due to monetization of budget deficit. In 1947, conversion of currency at 1:3.

Belgium 10/1944

Blocking of currency and bank accounts. Withdrawal for wage payments allowed. Capital levy and war profit taxes imposed. Frozen accounts converted into forced loans. Anti inflationary intent failed as expenses for Allied army were monetized.

Bulgaria 3/1947 and 5/1952

Partial blocking of currency and deposits. In the conversion, holdings of private business treated unfavorably. Second reform closely modeled on Soviet example.

Czechoslovakia 10/1945 and 6/1953

New currency (Crown) introduced. Sizable part of money supply blocked. Withdrawal possible for wage payment. Progressive war gains tax and capital levy. No discernible effect on inflation. Second reform closely modeled on Soviet example and successful.

Denmark 7/1945

Partial blocking of currency and deposits for three months. Information gathering about asset distribution main objective of blocking.

Virtually all funds unblocked. Later imposition of war gains tax forced loan.

Finland 1/1946

No blocking of deposits. Banknotes above 100 Finmark cut into two halves, one serving as legal tender at one half the denomination, other as nonnegotiable government bond. Only 8 percent of money supply affected. Virtually all funds later unblocked. Little success in curbing inflation.

France 6/1945 and 1/1948

Partial blocking of large notes. Registration of money holdings; liberalization loan. Virtually all blocked funds returned. No restraining effect on inflation. Write-down and partial blocking. Price controls continued.

Germany (West) 6/1948

Write-down at 1:10 and blocking of deposits. Later further write-down. Prices and wages freed.

Greece 11/1944

Conversion at 50 billion-to-one in midst of hyperinflation. No budgetary adjustment. No success in halting inflation.

Hungary 12/1945 and 8/1946

Initial conversion of currency at 4 to 1 proved unsuccessful in light of continued deficit monetization. Introduction of parallel currency (tax pengo) resulted in temporary stability. After rekindling of inflation, a second conversion, covering both currency and deposits, at 400 octillion to one, succeeded in terminating the hyperinflation.

Netherlands 6/1945 and 9/1945

Notes above 100 Guilder ceased to be legal tender but could be deposited in bank accounts which were then blocked, except for tax and wage payments allowed. Account-to-account payments allowed. Inducement to convert blocked balances into 50-year bonds. Later partial blocking of remaining currency and all bank deposits. War profit taxes and capital levy.

Norway 9/1945

Partial blocking of money supply. Determination of asset distribution main objective. Later imposition of war profit tax and forced loan.

Poland 12/1944 and 10/1950

Occupation moneys exchanged into new currency (zloty). Excess currency holdings blocked. Second reform modeled on Soviet example.

Rumania 8/1947 and 1/1952

Modeled on the Soviet example. Bank deposits favored vis-à-vis currency. Price and wage structure revised and lowered.

Soviet Union 12/1947

Conversion rate depended upon amount exchanged. Deposits favored relative to currency. Formed the role model for the monetary reforms in Eastern Europe.

Yugoslavia 4/1945

Occupation moneys partially exchanged for dinars. Additional currency holdings and bank deposits blocked. Capital levy on monetary wealth.

Appendix 4.2   The Political Economy of Reform

Did the political institutions in place affect the decision whether to write off, to block, or to inflate? The choice of strategy to deal with the overhang differed widely across countries. It ranged from decisions to let inflation resolve the overhang, to temporary freezing of balances, to outright write-downs. It is therefore interesting to ask whether these choices were random or reflected particular characteristics of the countries and governments undertaking them. One hypothesis is that democracies, and in particular new democracies aiming to shore up widespread domestic support, might be less able to take drastic measures compared to less participatory forms of government.

Table A.4.1 sheds some light on this issue, reporting the correlation coefficients between political and economic characteristics and the type of reform chosen. The competition index jointly measures the effectiveness of the legislature; the competitiveness of the nominating process; the rivalry between parties; and the breadth of political representation. An increase in the index signifies a more competitive political process. The fractionalization index measures the distribution of parties in the legislature, ranging from zero for a monolithic, one-party state to one for a system of one-person parties. The power of parliament index refers to the dependence of the executive on the support of the legislature, ranging from (0) 1 for an independent executive (a nonexistent parliament) to 3 for a complete constitutional and effective dependence.

Qualitatively similar answers, not reported here, are obtained by examining the link between reform choice and the political and economic initial conditions more formally within a probit regression of the decision in favor of (1) or against (0) write-off, though, reflecting the small number of observations, individual coefficients are generally insignificant.

Table A.4.1
Political economy of reform choice: Correlations

	Full sample blocking	Full sample write-off	Full sample capital levy
Competition	0.22	−0.60	0.69
Fractionalization	0.06	−0.39	0.57
Power of parliament	0.08	−0.36	0.58
Socialist	−0.12	0.54	−0.35
	Non-socialist blocking	Non-socialist write-off	Non-socialist capital levy
Competition	−0.12	0.24	0.00
Fractionalization	0.01	−0.12	0.60
Power of parliament	−0.04	−0.08	0.58

Sources: Banks 1971, Series 10P, 10Q, and 1K.

The table provides some support for the conjecture. A highly competitive political system raises the penalty on politically unpopular steps, reducing the incentive to opt for the harsh write-off in preference to the temporary tranquilizer of blocking. The political cost of write-offs could be mitigated by the formation of national unity governments. The evidence suggests that in highly fractionalized political systems—hindering the accumulation of sufficiently broad based support—write-offs become less likely. Finally, executives which are highly dependent on the support of the legislative branch appear to be more reluctant to implement tough reforms than quasi-independent executives.

Notably, the socialist governments embarking on monetary reform, largely free of domestic political pressure, consistently choose the hard measures in preference to blocking. As expected, the imposition of a capital levy is highly correlated with the degree of democratic competition, reflecting the perception that the monetary reforms per se carried socially undesirable implications for income distribution. Capital levies, shifting part of the burden toward holders of real assets, provided a politically attractive rectification.

Notes

We would like to thank Stanley Fischer and the participants of seminars at MIT, the NBER, and the IMF for helpful comments and suggestions. Financial support was provided by a grant from the National Science Foundation.

1. See Dornbusch and Fischer 1986 and Dornbusch, Sturzenegger, and Wolf 1990 for the experience following World War I.

2. Below, we will review a number of additional mechanisms—slow retirement through fiscal surpluses, creation of long-term assets, etc. These alternative remedies are however unlikely to be appropriate for but the mildest case of overhang.

3. See Klein 1956 for a comparison between Germany, Italy, Great Britain, and the United States.

4. Details of the reforms are provided in appendix 4.1. We also refer to the various references that discuss the specifics of each reform. We note in particular that monetary reform goes beyond conversions of notes and deposits since it must deal with a wide variety of debts, including public debt, insurance, rent contracts etc.

We restrict our attention to Europe. Japan, for example, opted for a combination of conversion, blocking, and inflation. See Cohen 1949 and Goldsmith 1983.

5. See, too, Holtzman 1962 for the case of the Soviet Union.

6. Cigarettes were also used to satisfy the "precautionary" demand for money: In a situation of excess demand, large balances are advantageous to exploit rare purchasing

opportunities, yet such balances carried the risk of confiscatory monetary reform, spawning a second "cigarette currency." See Wirtschaftsspiegel 1948.

Some evidence on the anticipation of monetary reform in Germany, for example, is available. The exchange rate of the Swiss Franc (SF/100 RM) moved from 1.62 to 1.9 in the period January to May 1948 before declining to 1.25 in the final month before the reform. Interestingly, the rise falls far short of the actual write-off on German monetary assets.

7. A particularly interesting precedent is the Belgian reform in the 1920s. Facing funding crisis on an overhang of overly liquid debt, the government converted the debt claims into ownership certificates in the national railroad. Shepherd 1936 reports that the bond holders came out ahead.

8. From a policy point of view, a number of steps, in particular an adjustment of the relative price structure by decree prior to the unfreezing of prices and a mandatory renegotiating on long-term contracts at the time of the reform, can be undertaken to reduce if not eliminate the importance of factors leading to protracted inflation.

9. See Dornbusch, Sturzenegger, and Wolf 1990 for a detailed description of these feedback channels.

10. In the case of Greece, civil war was a decisive factor.

11. For a more detailed description, see Lutz 1949, and the references given therein.

12. Industrial production (1932 = 100) increased to 175 by 1936 and 203 by 1939. See Klein 1956.

13. See however Klein 1956, in which Klein argues that the official index was artificially low. Calculating an implicit price index, he finds the average annual inflation rate to be closer to 4.6 percent.

14. New capital issues were restricted in 1933. Part of the additional savings went into the stock market, generating a mini-boom from 1939 to 1941. After the imposition of a price freeze on stock markets in 1943, saving deposits formed the only remaining interest-bearing asset available to the public.

15. Paying taxes and the repayment of liabilities remained some of the few options available to holders of RM balances. As the eventual conversion of these holdings became more likely, the private sector used idle holdings to reduce outstanding debt. As a result, the claims of the commercial banking sector on the private sector declined significantly.

16. In 1947–1948, the average hourly wage amounted to 0.95 PM. At the same time, a single cigarette traded for 7 PM and a kilogram of butter for 900 RM on the black market.

17. See Neue Zurcher 1948 and Schmoelders n.d.

18. Concerned about nutrition (and the implied possible need for even larger food aid) the military authorities also took less pains to counteract black markets in consumption goods, notably staples, than in combating unofficial transactions between firms.

19. The statistics, based on reported output, place a large weight on the production of large enterprises. It is likely that some unreported production "for the shelves" in anticipation of a future return to normal monetary circumstances has taken place. Abelshauser (1977) argues on the basis of energy consumption statistics that output in fact continued to increase throughout 1947. See however Buchheim 1989 and Ritschl 1985 for a critical assessment of the revisionist view.

20. Few monetary reforms occur without decisive intervention and the driving force of a key personality, be it foreign or national. Razin played the role in Czechoslovakia, Schacht in Germany in 1923, Edwin Keimnerer throughout the world in the interwar period. In Germany's case, U.S. Lt. Tenenbaum may have been that key person, though his role remains unappreciated. See Bennett 1950 and Richter 1979.

21. See Reuss 1963, Hansen and Musgrave 1951, and Bank Deutscher Laender 1950.

22. See Guggenheim 1965, p. 37.

23. The occupation forces had raised marginal tax rates even beyond the extremely high rates of the war period. The tax rates were cut, in particular for middle-income workers, as part of the liberalization package. The average income in 1948 was about DM1,000. For the income bracket of DM1,200 to DM2,400, the marginal tax rate was cut from the 1946 level of 25 percent to 18 percent. In the next bracket (2,400–3,600) the rate was cut from 50 percent to 24 percent. But the upper rates remained extremely high, with the top marginal rate at 95 percent. For details see Heller 1949.

24. See Stolper and Roskamp 1979 and Denton, Forsyth, and Maclennan 1968 on these points. Growth performance was of course also boosted by the generous Marshall aid provided by the United States: see Moeller 1989, Milward 1984, and Kaplan and Schleiminger 1989.

References

Abelshauser, W. 1981. Wiederaufbau vor dem Marshall-Plan. *Vierteliahreshefte fuer Zeitgeschichte* 29:549–78.

Abelshauser, W. 1977. Die Rekonstruktion der westdeutschen Wirtschaft und die Rolle der Besatzungspolitik. In *Politische und oekonomische Stabilisierung Westdeutschlands 1945–1949*, ed. C. Schaff and H. Schroeder. Wiesbaden, Germany.

Ames, E. 1954. Soviet bloc currency conversions. *American Economic Review* 44(3):339–53.

Baffi, P. 1958. Monetary developments in Italy from the war economy to limited convertibility, 1935–1958. *Banca Nazionale del Lavoro Quarterly Review* (December):399–483.

Bank Deutscher Laender. 1950. *Report of the Bank Deutscher Laender for the years 1948 and 1949*. Frankfurt: Author.

Bank for International Settlements. Various years. *Annual report*.

Barro, R., and H. Grossman. 1976. *Money, employment and inflation*. Cambridge: Cambridge University Press.

Bennett, J. 1950. The German currency reform. *Annals of the American Academy of Political and Social Science* 267(1):41–54.

Brown, A. J. 1955. *The great inflation 1939–1951*. Oxford: Oxford University Press.

Buchheim, C. 1989. Zur Kontroverse ueber den Stellungswert der Waehrungsreform fuer die Wachstumsdynamik in der Bundesrepublik Deutschjand. In *Waehrunqsreform und Soziale Marktwirtschaft*, ed. P. Hampe. Munich.

Buchheim, C. 1988. Die Waehrungsreform 1948 in Westdeutschland. *Vierteliahreshefte fuer Zeitgeschichte* 36.

Casella, A., and B. Eichengreen. 1990. Halting inflation in Italy and France after World War II. University of California, Berkeley. Mimeographed.

Cohen, J. B. 1949. *Japan's economy in war and reconstruction*. Minneapolis: University of Minnesota Press.

Colm, G., J. M. Dodge, and R. Goldsmith. 1955. A plan for the liquidation of war finance and for the financial rehabilitation of germany. *Zeitschrift fuer die Gesamte Staatswissenschaft* 111:193–243.

Dieterlen, P., and C. Rist. 1948. *The monetary problem of france*. New York: King's Crown Press.

Denton, G., M. Forsyth, and M. Maclennan. 1968. *Economic planning and policies in Britain, France and Germany*. London: George Allen & Unwin.

Dornbusch, R., and S. Fischer. 1986. Stopping hyperinflations past and present. *Weltwirtschaftliches Archiv* 122(1):1–47.

Dornbusch, R., F. Sturzenegger, and H. Wolf. 1990. Extreme inflation: Dynamics and stabilization. *Brookings Papers on Economic Activity*.

Dupriez, L. 1947. *Monetary reconstruction in Belgium*. New York: King's Crown Press.

Foa, B. 1949. *Monetary reconstruction in Italy*. New York: King's Crown Press.

Goldsmith, R. 1983. *The financial development of Japan, 1868–1977*. New Haven: Yale University Press.

Guggenheim, T. 1965. *La reforme monetaire apres la deuxieme guerre mondiale*. Geneva: George & Cie.

Grotius, F. 1949a. Die Europaeischen Geldreformen Nach Dem Zweiten Weltkrieg. *Weltwirtschaftliches Archiv* 62(1):106–52.

Grotius, F. 1949b. Die Europaeischen Geldreformen Nach Dem Zweiten Weltkrieg II. *Weltwirtschaftliches Archiv* 63(2):276–325.

Gurley, J. 1953. Excess liquidity and European monetary reforms. *American Economic Review* 43(1):76–100.

Hansen, A., and R. Musgrave. 1951. *Fiscal problems of Germany*. Bonn: Minister of Finance of the Federal Republic of Germany.

Heller, W. 1949. Tax policy and monetary reform in occupied Germany. *National Tax Journal* 2(3):215–31.

Holtzman, F. 1962. *Soviet taxation*. Cambridge: Harvard University Press.

Kaplan, J., and G. Schleiminger. 1989. *The European payments union*. Oxford: Oxford University Press.

Klein, J. 1956. German money and prices, 1932–44. In *Studies in the quantity theory of money*, ed. M. Friedman. Chicago: University of Chicago Press.

Klemm, B., and G. Trittel. 1987. Vor dem "Wirtschaftswunder": Durchbruch zum Wachstum oder Laehmungskrise? *Viertellahreshefte fuer Zeitgeschichte* 35.

Klopstock, F. 1949. Monetary reform in western Germany. *Journal of Political Economy* 58(4).

Klopstock, F. 1946. Monetary reform in liberated Europe. *American Economic Review* 36(September):578–95.

Lieftinck, P. 1973. *The postwar financial rehabilitation of the Netherlands*. The Hague: Martinus Nijhoff.

Lutz, F. 1949. The German currency reform and the revival of the German economy. *Economica* 41(61):122–14.

Mendershausen, H. 1949. Prices, money and the distribution of goods in postwar Germany. *American Economic Review* 39(5):646–72.

Metzler, L. 1946. Experiences with monetary and financial reform. Reprinted in *Currency and economic reform: West Germany after World War II: A Symposium*, ed. R. Richter, in *Zeitschrift fuer die Gesamte Staatswissenschaft* 135 no. 3 (Spring 1979), 365–73.

Milward, A. 1984. *The reconstruction of western Europe 1945–51*. Berkeley: University of San Francisco Press.

Mitchell, B. R. 1978. *European historical statistics*. New York: Columbia University.

Moeller, H. 1989. Die Waehrungsreform von 1948 und die Wiederherstellung markt-wirtschaftlicher Verhaeltnisse. In *Waehrungsreform und Soziale Marktwirtschaft*, ed. P. Hampe. Munich.

Moeller, H. 1976. Die Westdeutsche Wahrungsreform von 1948. In *Waehrung und Wirtschaft in Deutschland 1876–1975*, ed. Deutsche Bundesbank. Frankfurt: Deutsche Bundesbank.

Moeller, H., ed. 1961. *Zur Vorgeschichte der Deutschen Mark*. Basel, Switzerland: Kyklos Verlag.

Montias, J. M. 1964. Inflation and growth: The experience of eastern Europe. In *Inflation and growth in Latin America*, ed. W. Baer and I. Kerstenetzky. New Haven: Yale University Press.

Pederson, J. 1949. An evaluation of postwar monetary reforms. *Weltwirtschaftliches Archiv* 62:198–213.

Pesek, B. 1958. Monetary reform and monetary equilibrium. *Journal of Political Economy* 66(5):375.

Reuss, F. 1963. *Fiscal policy for growth without inflation. The German experiment*. Baltimore: Johns Hopkins University Press.

Richter, R., ed. 1979. *Currency and economic reform: West Germany after World War II: A Symposium*, in *Zeitschrift fuer die Gesamte Staatswissenschaft* 135(3).

Ritschl, A. 1985. Die Waehrungsreform von 1948 und derWiederaufstieg der Westdeutschen Industrie. *Viertellahreshefte derZeitgeschichte* 33.

Sauermann, H. 1979. On the economic and financial rehabilitation of western germany. In *Currency and economic reform: West Germany after World War II: A Symposium*, ed. R. Richter, in *Zeitschrift fuer die Gesamte Staatswissenschaft* 135(3).

Sauermann, H. 1950. The consequences of the currency reform in western Germany. *Review of Politics* 12:175–96.

Schiller, K. 1989. Wirtschaftspolitische Konsequenzen der Waehrungsreform. In *Waehrungsreform und Soziale Marktwirtschaft*, ed. P. Hampe. Munich.

Schleiminger, G. 1949. Geldpolitische Erfahrungen. *Weltwirtschaftliches Archiv* 63(2):232–73.

Schlesinger, H. 1989. Vierzig Jahre Waehrungsreform. In *Waehrungsreform und Soziale Marktwirtschaft*, ed. P. Hampe. Munich.

Schmoelders, G. n.d. Die Zigarettenwaehrung. In *Sozialoekonomische Verhaltensforschung. Festschrift G. Schmoelders*. Berlin.

Shepherd, H. 1936. *The monetary experience of belgium*. Reprinted by Arno Press, New York.

Sherwin, S. 1956. *Monetary policy in continental western Europe 1944–52*. Madison: University of Wisconsin Press.

Snider, D. 1948. French monetary and fiscal policies since the Liberation. *American Economic Review* 38(3):309–27.

Stolper, W., and K. Roskamp. 1979. Planning a free economy: Germany 1945–1960. Mimeographed.

Veit, O. 1961. *Grundriss der Waehrungspolitik*. Frankfurt: Fritz Knapp Verlag.

Wallich, H. 1960. *The mainsprings of German revival*. New York: Harper.

Wandel, E. 1979. Historical developments prior to the currency reform of 1948. *Zeitschrift fuer die Gesamte Staatswissenschaft* 135(3):320–31.

Wirtschafts-Jahrbuch, Sueddeutsche Zeitung 1948, 1949, 1950.

5

Staying Afloat When the Wind Shifts: External Factors and Emerging-Market Banking Crises

Barry Eichengreen and
Andrew K. Rose

Introduction

Banking systems have emerged in the 1990s as the principal menace to financial stability in emerging markets, or as James Wolfensohn has referred to them, the Achilles' heel of developing economies. From Mexico and Argentina to Thailand and Korea, banking crises have threatened to derail policymakers' efforts to establish a stable macroeconomic and financial environment attractive to foreign capital and conducive to growth. Systemic banking problems are no new development, of course. They feature prominently in modern explanations for the Great Depression of the 1930s, for example.[1] The tight regulations placed on banks in response to this episode put a lid on the problem after World War II. But banking crises returned with a vengeance after 1970 as the pendulum swung back toward financial liberalization. Caprio and Klingebiel (1996) list forty-nine banking crises in the 1970s and 1980s. Even this number pales in comparison with that for the 1990s: the same authors count thirty-three banking crises over the first six years of the decade.

These problems have been anything but selective in their geographical incidence. Nearly every transition economy in Central/Eastern Europe experienced severe banking problems in the 1990s, reflecting nonperforming loans to state firms inherited from the pretransition era, continued pressure to extend credit to state and former-state enterprises, and an unstable macroeconomic environment. Banking crises reflecting the operation of many of these same factors have struck some two dozen African countries in the last decade. The problem is of longstanding in Latin America, where early examples include the exceptionally severe banking crisis that erupted in Chile starting in 1981–1982, an event which followed significant steps toward financial liberalization and then the sudden curtailment of capital inflows. More recently, the tradition was kept alive by the Mexican meltdown of 1994, where financial liberalization was again followed by a rise in the level of world interest rates and slowing capital inflows. Recently, East Asia has joined the crowd with the development of systemic banking problems in Thailand, insolvency among chaebol-linked financial institutions in Korea, and nascent banking problems in Malaysia, Indonesia, and the Philippines.[2]

By every measure, the cost of these episodes has been enormous. Published estimates put the budgetary cost of resolving financial crises and recapitalizing banking systems at some 10 percent of GDP in Malaysia (1985–1988), 15 percent of GDP in Mexico (1994–1997), 20 percent of GDP in Venezuela (1994–1997), 30 percent of GDP in Chile (1981–1986), and 50 percent of GDP in Kuwait (1990–1991). The macroeconomic cost has been significant as well. Most of the banking crises enumerated above were accompanied by major recessions.[3] The mechanisms are well illustrated by the recent Mexican episode, where banking problems boosted the level of interest rates, leading to disintermediation and causing problems of credit stringency for small firms; many of the latter blamed the interruption of their customary bank credit lines for forcing them to curtail production and lay off workers in Mexico's post–tequila crisis recession.[4]

Experiences such as these have prompted officials and others to seek to better understand the causes of banking crises and to draw lessons about how future crises might be averted (perhaps the most prominent recent report is by the Group of Ten 1997). A recent survey in *The Economist* is representative; it attributed banking crises in emerging markets to four factors: macroeconomic volatility, connected (or insider) lending, government involvement which distorts the incentives facing bank management, and the failure of prudential regulation to match the pace of financial liberalization.[5]

Still, it is fair to say the lessons drawn so far are based largely on intuition and informal observation. The role of these and other determinants of banking crises remains to be systematically documented. In particular, there is little consensus on the weight that should be attached to structural versus macroeconomic determinants of the incidence of crises, on the relative importance of domestic and international factors, and on whether the macroeconomic correlates of banking crises are properly seen as causes or consequences of financial problems.[6]

Previous studies of these questions can be counted on the fingers of one hand. Sundararajan and Balino (1991) conclude from the experience of seven (mainly) developing economies that banking crises occur after periods of rapid economic growth and mounting imbalances in the external accounts. The onset of crisis itself tends to be associated with a sharp deceleration in the growth rate or a decline in the level of output. This result is also found by Kaminsky and Reinhart (1996) in an analysis of twenty Asian, European, Latin American and Middle Eastern countries which experienced serious banking problems. Gavin and Hausmann (1995), in an analysis informed by Latin American experience, emphasize the development of unsustainable credit booms in the period leading up to crises. On the other hand, Caprio and Klingebiel (1997), upon broadening the analysis to a larger sample of industrial and developing countries, find no stable relationship between credit growth and banking problems.[7] These authors emphasize instead the dangers posed by the combination of shallow financial markets, which offer little insulation from shocks, and domestic macroeconomic volatility. Comparing economies experiencing banking crises with the Organization for Economic Cooperation and Development (OECD) countries in the 1960s (where the latter serve as a crisis-free control group), they find that crisis countries experienced significant greater GDP and terms-of-trade volatility in the period leading up to their crises (although they do not attempt formal statistical tests).[8] Kaminsky and Reinhart similarly report evidence of the importance of macroeconomic factors in banking crises: in their sample of twenty crisis countries, output, the stock market and the real exchange rate peak about a year before the onset of banking crises, with growth rates up to that point suggesting a boom in activity greater than that observed in tranquil periods; all three variables turn down subsequently. Real interest rates and bank deposits rise in the period leading up to the crisis, as if financial liberalization helps to set the stage for banking problems. In this connection, Caprio and Klingebiel suggest a role for poor supervision and regulation and for deficient bank management, although the weight that should be attached to these factors remains difficult to analyze systematically.[9]

Finally, in the work closest to our own, Demirgüç-Kunt and Detragiache (1997) consider the determinants of banking crises in a large sample of developed and developing countries between 1980 and 1994 using a multivariate logit model. They find that low growth and high inflation make crises more likely, that high real interest rates are associated with banking problems, and that deteriorating terms of trade may help set the stage for financial sector difficulties. They construct a dummy variable for the presence of an explicit deposit insurance scheme and an index of the quality of law enforcement and find that deposit insurance and lax law enforcement both heighten the probability of banking crises.[10]

In this chapter we build on this literature, providing a statistical analysis of the causes and consequences of banking crises in emerging markets. Our analysis departs from the work of the aforementioned authors in a number of important respects. In contrast to the Kaminsky-Reinhart, Caprio-Klingebiel and Demirgüç-Kunt–Detragiache studies, we confine our attention to developing countries on the grounds that their problems are distinctive and that it is within this group that we are most likely to find enough data variation to identify systematic effects. But unlike other authors, we do not limit the developing countries we consider to those experiencing banking problems. To avoid problems of sample selectivity we cast our net as widely as possible, including over one hundred developing countries for which the relevant data are available. As our control group of noncrisis cases we use not the OECD economies in the 1960s as in Caprio and Klingebeil, but rather all the developing country observations that do not qualify as crises.[11] We provide formal statistical tests for differences in the behavior of the relevant macroeconomic and structural variables at a variety of leads and lags and conduct multivariate as well as univariate tests of the significance of those variables. We utilize a considerably larger sample than previous authors. And finally, we draw our measures of banking crises from the work of other authors to protect against potential problems of selectivity.

The results paint a rather different picture from that suggested by other recent quantitative studies. We find that the stage is set for banking crises by the interaction of fragilities in domestic financial structure and unpropitious global economic conditions. Our central finding is a large, highly significant correlation between changes in industrial country interest rates and banking crises in emerging markets. We show that Northern interest rates rise sharply and significantly (relative to their level in noncrisis control-group cases) in the year preceding the onset of banking crises, before peaking in the crisis year and the year following. This result comes through strongly in univariate and multivariate analyses and is robust to changes in specification. It points strongly to the role played by external financial conditions—and in particular to the effect of rising interest rates in worsening the access of developing country banking systems to offshore funds, as well as in aggravating moral hazard problems—in heightening the vulnerability of emerging economies to banking problems. The "Argentine syndrome," in which that country experienced severe banking problems in 1995 as a result of events in world capital markets largely beyond its control, appears on the basis of our results to be quite general. There is also some evidence that the global business cycle, and OECD growth in particular, play a role in the incidence of banking crises, with slowing growth in the advanced industrial countries being associated with the onset of crisis.

This evidence is inconsistent with the notion that domestic macroeconomic problems provide the entire explanation for banking crises. While there are some signs that real overvaluation, tight fiscal policy, and slow economic growth help to set the stage for banking crises, this evidence is less robust.

Our finding of an important role for world interest rates in the onset of banking crises reinforces the conclusions of Calvo (1994), among others, who stresses the potential for capital inflows (whose availability is strongly correlated with the level of industrial-country interest rates) to reduce portfolio discipline in developing-country banking systems and for increases in world interest rates to precipitate banking problems.[12] It is consistent with the emphasis of Mishkin (1996) on changes in the level of interest rates in prompting banking crises. For developing countries, where the level of interest rates is heavily influenced by the state of international financial markets, this points to the need for special measures to protect domestic financial markets and institutions and the real economy from destabilization by external variables largely beyond their control.

Analytical Issues

A large literature has grown up around the causes and consequences of banking crises. In this section we review that work with an eye toward issues of relevance to emerging markets. We start with a discussion of what distinguishes banking from other sectors of the economy and motivates our concern with banking crises. We then turn to an enumeration of factors popularly identified as contributing to banking crises in emerging markets.

What Is Special about Banks?[13]

The financial services industry, and banking in particular, is different from other industries. The business of banks is providing liquidity-transformation services. Because they exploit economies of scale, they have a comparative advantage in the provision of such services—in other words, they are better able to make illiquid investments than the typical household or firm. Scale allows them to accept deposits from diverse households, all of which are unlikely to experience exceptional demands for liquidity simultaneously and force the banks' investments to be liquidated at a loss.[14] In addition, banks can exploit economies of scale and scope in assessing repayment capacity and monitoring the behavior of borrowers. Recent models demonstrate how savers may wish to delegate to banks responsibility for screening and monitoring.

From our perspective, that banks provide liquidity-transformation services in an environment of asymmetric information has three important implications.

First, banking crises have macroeconomic effects. If banks are relatively efficient at overcoming information asymmetries through monitoring or can reduce lending risks through portfolio diversification, disruptions to their operation will show up in the wedge between the return to lenders and the cost to borrowers. In turn, increases in that wedge will have an impact on the level of economic activity through what is known as the credit channel of monetary policy.[15]

Empirical studies of banking crises have documented that these events can have a significant impact on the real economy even after controlling for changes in the money multiplier and other sources of macroeconomic variability. Grossman (1993) and Eichengreen and Grossman (1997) document that bank failures contributed significantly to the American business cycle before 1913 even after controlling for their impact on money and interest rates. Bernanke (1983) and Bernanke and James (1991) provide evidence for the United States and other economies that the nonmonetary consequences of bank failures played a major role in the Great Depression.

The second implication of our framework is that banks are fragile. The fact that banks' assets are less liquid than their liabilities renders their financial condition delicate and confidence essential to their stability. If confidence wanes for any reason, the withdrawal of deposits can render banks unable to meet their obligations. And the sequential-service constraint under which banks operate (demands for funds are met on a first-come, first-served basis) gives creditors an incentive to liquidate their deposits at the first sign of trouble.[16] Insofar as bank portfolios are linked together by the interbank market, withdrawals from one bank can undermine the liquidity of others and lead to a generalized crisis.

Because banks operate in an environment of asymmetric information, their fragility is likely to be heightened by the operation of adverse selection. Under asymmetric information, borrowers with low-risk projects will be rationed out of the market by the price mechanism (since only those with high-risk projects will be prepared to pay high interest rates). By making it more likely that loans will be made to poor credit risks and to lenders whose own solvency is vulnerable to changing economic conditions, adverse selection can heighten banks' vulnerability to problems (Mishkin 1991). A further implication of asymmetric information is the scope it provides for moral hazard. One illustration, with obvious implications for banking crises, is gambling-for-redemption behavior, in which borrowers who see their financial condition worsening "double up their bets"—that is, engage in even riskier behavior in a desperate effort to generate cash.

The third implication is that owing to the opacity of their loan portfolios, banks will find it more difficult than nonfinancial firms to raise the liquidity needed to restructure (Simons and Cross 1991), increasing the likelihood that adverse shocks will result in failure.

Each of these characteristics of banks is likely to be particularly prevalent in emerging markets. In particular, the information and liquidity structure that makes banks distinctive is likely to be pronounced. Households on the margin of subsistence will attach particular value to the liquidity of their savings. Reluctant to fund long-term investments themselves, they will rely on the liquidity-transformation services of banks and other financial institutions. Financial disclosure and reporting standards being relatively primitive in developing economies, the information asymmetries that create a role for banks as delegated monitors and assemblers of information are likely to be particularly acute. Banks account for a larger share of the total assets of financial institutions in developing than advanced industrial countries. Correspondingly, a banking crisis which disrupts the supply of intermediation services can have a particularly devastating impact on economic activity.

Causes of Banking Crises in Emerging Markets[17]

The factors emphasized in earlier discussions of banking crises in emerging markets can be grouped under five headings: domestic macroeconomic policies, external macroeconomic conditions, the exchange rate regime, domestic financial structure, and problems of supervision and regulation.[18]

Domestic Macroeconomic Policies

Many accounts stress the role of macroeconomic policies in promoting rapid increases in bank lending which create trouble when they come to an end. The typical sequence runs as follows.[19] Expansionary monetary and fiscal policies fuel a lending boom which drives up equity and real estate prices as banks increase their commitments to securities brokers and the property market. Eventually it becomes necessary to tighten monetary policy to contain inflation, pricking the bubble. Individuals who borrowed from the banks to purchase and develop real estate or to speculate in securities find themselves unable to repay, saddling the banks with nonperforming loans that threaten their solvency.[20] Banks curtail their lending in response to the decline in the value of collateral caused by the collapse of equity and real estate prices, which further aggravates the problem of credit stringency depressing property and securities markets.

Thus, this school of thought points to the stance of monetary and fiscal policies (which typically swing from sharply expansionary to sharply contractionary) as the underlying determinant of financial booms and busts, to the expansion of bank credit as fuel for the flames, and to recession, credit stringency, and falling asset prices as the proximate factors precipitating the crisis. Insofar as banks provide a disproportionate share of intermediation services in developing countries and, historically, their monetary and fiscal policies have been relatively volatile, one would expect this constellation of factors to be particularly prominent in emerging markets.

External Economic Conditions

A distinct but related set of explanations emphasizes the role of external conditions. Shocks to the terms of trade can be of major importance to the profitability of domestic enterprise; a deterioration in export prices can render commodity exporters incapable of discharging their debts.[21] Small countries with low levels of export diversification are

particularly susceptible to terms-of-trade shocks capable of destabilizing the banking system. Unanticipated changes in the real exchange
rate (the relative price of traded and nontraded goods), whether caused
by shifts in domestic or foreign economic policies, can similarly leave
banks' customers unable to service their obligations.

A large literature (viz., Calvo, Leiderman, and Reinhart 1993) documents the sensitivity of capital flows to changes in the level of world
interest rates. Not only does a decline in industrial country interest
rates prod investors in money centers to search for higher yields
abroad, but it increases the creditworthiness of indebted countries
by reducing the cost of servicing short-term and variable-rate debts
(Eichengreen and Fishlow 1996). Thus, a sudden rise in the level of
interest rates can curtail the inflow of foreign funds and make trouble
for the banks. Banks in developing countries have a disproportionate
tendency to fund themselves offshore, offering relatively high returns
to attract foreign deposits. For them a rise in foreign interest rates
means a sudden fall in the level or growth of their funding. As the rise
in rates is passed through to domestic borrowers, the latter develop
problems repaying. Moreover, higher rates can aggravate agency problems by reducing franchise value (the present value of future profits).
They can reduce the average quality of bank liabilities by aggravating
adverse selection, thereby heightening failure risk.[22]

The Exchange Rate Regime
The exchange rate, being the relative price of different national currencies, does not fit neatly into either the domestic or external category.[23] One strand of thought highlights the association between
pegged rates and surges in capital inflows. An increasingly prevalent
view is that pegged rates are positively associated with banking crises
since the problems associated with dependence on foreign capital
emphasized in the preceding paragraph will be most pronounced in
countries operating a pegged-rate regime. Allowing the exchange rate
to fluctuate and thereby introducing an element of exchange risk will
tend to moderate capital inflows and minimize problems for the
banking system.

The opposing view is that pegged exchange rates are negatively associated with banking crises because they discipline erratic policymakers. If erratic aggregate demand policies at home are at the root of
problems in the banking system, then an exchange rate commitment
can constrain policymakers' erratic tendencies and share domestic

demand shocks with the rest of the world. The danger that the country's international reserves will be depleted and the currency peg will be jeopardized prevents policies conducive to the development of a domestic credit boom with the capacity to bring down the banking system from getting out of hand. The lending booms that are the ultimate source of banking problems should thereby be attenuated. And constraints on lender-of-last-resort activities ameliorate otherwise worrisome problems of moral hazard.

It will be evident that this debate is a particular instance of the general point that flexible exchange rates are preferable when disturbances are foreign, while pegged rates are preferred when shocks are domestic. Thus, when threats to the stability of the banking system take the form of changes in world interest rates that make it more difficult for banks to fund themselves offshore, there will be a case for exchange rate flexibility to discourage the banks from relying excessively on external sources of finance. Conversely, when the main threats to the stability of the banking system emanate from monetary and fiscal policies at home, there will be an argument for pegging the exchange rate to discipline domestic policies and vent domestic shocks via the external sector.

The other potential source of association between pegged exchange rates and banking crises derives from limits on the authorities' capacity to engage in lender-of-last-resort operations. Central banks can support troubled banks by injecting liquidity into the economy, making it easier for depository institutions to borrow on the interbank market or to discount with the central bank itself.

But supporting an exchange rate peg requires limiting the provision of liquidity to the economy. There may be one level of central bank credit consistent with exchange rate stability but another needed to prevent the collapse of distressed financial institutions. Injecting credit into the financial system may therefore undermine confidence in the currency peg and provoke a balance-of-payments crisis, deterring the central bank from aiding the banks.

Diamond and Dybvig (1984) show how the knowledge that the authorities stand ready to support distressed banks effectively removes the incentive for depositors to run on weak institutions. It follows that an exchange rate peg that prevents lender-of-last-resort operations can encourage bank runs and financial panics. Again, there is an opposing point of view, that the existence of a lender-of-last-resort encourages bankers to take additional risks since they know that the authorities stand ready to bail them out, a fact which only increases the likelihood that a crisis will eventuate.

Domestic Financial Structure

The structure of their balance sheets can influence the susceptibility of banks to both internal and external shocks. The implications of foreign funding for sensitivity to world interest rate shocks has already been noted.[24] In addition, devoting a disproportionate share of the loan portfolio to firms in the export sector can heighten vulnerability to terms-of-trade fluctuations, while carrying a disproportionate share of real estate loans can magnify real exchange rate risk. Currency mismatch, when banks borrow in foreign currency but denominate their loans in domestic currency, can create problems when the exchange rate depreciates, since a given stream of domestic-currency-denominated interest earnings will finance less foreign-currency-denominated debt service. Passing exchange risk through to the ultimate borrower may not help; insofar as the revenues of the latter still depend on the exchange rate, devaluation can precipitate loan default.

Maturity mismatch (when banks' assets are longer term than their liabilities) can pose problems when shocks precipitate a loss of confidence. Maturity transformation, as noted above, is the banking system's raison d'être. But the larger the shocks to the economy, the less the maturity mismatch will be consistent with financial stability. This suggests that banks in developing countries, where the economy is volatile, should match the maturity of their assets and liabilities relatively closely; in practice, however, the opposite tends to be true. Banks in emerging markets typically have poor access to long-term funding; compared to the advanced industrial countries, the average length of their liabilities is much shorter to maturity.[25]

Finally, a number of authors (viz., Calvo 1996; Sachs, Tornell, and Velasco 1995) have emphasized, with Mexican experience in mind, the connection between the structure of a country's external obligations and the stability of its banks. The crisis in Mexico, according to these authors, was aggravated by the fact that the authorities had issued large quantities of short-term, foreign-currency-indexed debt. The stock of such obligations greatly exceeded the central bank's reserves of foreign exchange. When investors refused to roll over these assets in 1994 and 1995, the government was forced to jack up interest rates to lure them back and defend its international reserves. The high interest rates, credit stringency, and recession that followed had predictably devastating effects on the banks. The implication is that countries with large amounts of short-term debt, variable-rate debt, foreign-currency-denominated debt, and foreign debt flowing through depository institutions are likely to be particularly prone to banking crises.

Problems of Supervision and Regulation

A final group of factors contributing to banking crises falls under the heading "problems of supervision and regulation." Often these problems arise in the aftermath of financial liberalization when banks are freed to enter new lines of business and make new, unfamiliar investments.[26] The removal of controls on lending and offshore borrowing may prompt a sudden expansion of business. If banks have inadequate trained personnel to evaluate the risks of the increase in their lending, the quality of their asset portfolios will decline. If they engage in connected lending (in which loans go mainly to influential insiders), more resources for the banks only add risk and worsen the allocation of funds. Financial liberalization thus places a premium on sound supervision and regulation while at the same time straining the capacity of regulators to carry out their tasks.

Flaws in the regulatory structure will be especially damaging where market discipline is weak. And market discipline will be least effective where there are defects in the accounting, disclosure, and legal frameworks for banking. Banks will be able to disguise loan losses, announcement of which typically requires management to take corrective action. They will overstate income and disguise the extent of their financial difficulties until it is too late. Thus, where accounting and disclosure are inadequate, neither regulators nor shareholders will be able to effectively discipline management.[27]

Finally, there is the possibility that government supervision and regulation are themselves a source of perverse incentives. Managers of state banks are unusually susceptible to political pressures to engage in directed lending; if supervisors see the allocation of loans as a device for furthering certain political objectives rather than maximizing the return on bank capital, problems of bank insolvency and illiquidity can result. A deposit insurance scheme in conjunction with a regulator who subscribes to the "too-big-to-fail" principle will encourage bank management to assume excessive risk and relieve customers and shareholders of all incentive to monitor its behavior.

Clearly, there is no shortage of potential explanations for banking crises in emerging markets. The issue is the generality and predictive power of these explanations. It is to this question that we now turn.

Data and Methodology

The most important methodological decision for any study of banking crises is dating the crises themselves. It is revealing of the difficulty of this task that a number of otherwise admirable studies avoid explicitly addressing this problem, analyzing banking crises without defining them. But a few previous studies have tackled the issue head on. Examples include Bordo 1985 and Bordo 1986, which define a banking crisis as a situation where actual or incipient bank runs or failures lead banks to suspend the internal convertibility of their liabilities. Caprio and Klingebiel 1996 define a systemic banking crisis as an instance in which bank failures or suspensions lead to the exhaustion of much or all of bank capital.[28]

Inevitably there is an element of judgement in any attempt to identify banking crises. To protect our analysis from the danger of picking crises consistent with our own prior intuitions concerning their correlation with macroeconomic and structural variables, we employ the list developed by Caprio and Klingebiel, which is the most comprehensive attempt to date to identify and date the incidence of banking problems. These authors identify crises of various degrees of intensity in sixty-nine countries, forming their judgement of the extent of the problem and the impact on net bank capital on the basis of both official published data and the opinion of country experts. We use only one observation for each banking crisis identified by Caprio and Klingebiel, namely the year that the crisis began.[29]

While Caprio and Klingebiel provide data on banking crises for both developing and advanced industrial countries, we limit our analysis to their developing country subsample. There may be good grounds for thinking that banking problems in developing and advanced industrial countries respond to some of the same determinants, but there are also reasons to anticipate differences between the two subsamples.[30] Banks account for a larger share of the total assets of financial institutions in developing than advanced industrial countries; developing countries also have systematically smaller financial systems than developed countries. The length of bank liabilities is typically shorter to maturity. Supervisory and regulatory structures are less articulated in developing countries. The susceptibility of banking systems to shocks to the terms of trade is likely to be greater in developing countries, where opportunities to hedge terms-of-trade risk are fewer. Less developed countries (LDCs), moreover, are exceptionally susceptible to changing international financial conditions.

We supplement this indicator of banking problems with the macro-economic and financial data set employed by Frankel and Rose (1996). This data set is extracted from the 1994 World Data CD-ROM, and consists of annual observations from 1975 through 1992 for one hundred and five countries.[31]

Our analysis focuses on nine key variables of interest. These are intended to capture the macroeconomic environment of the country in as comprehensive and succinct a fashion as possible.

Four of our variables are "international" in nature and measure the size of international reserves, external debt, the current account, and the degree of exchange rate overvaluation. Reserves are expressed as a percentage of monthly imports; external debt and the current account surplus (+) or deficit (−) are both expressed as percentages of GDP. We measure the real exchange rate by adjusting the nominal exchange rate for domestic and foreign GDP price levels and then nor-malizing the level of the resulting ratio over time on a country-by-country basis.

We also examine key "domestic" macroeconomic indicators, includ-ing broad measures of fiscal and monetary policy and the state of the business cycle. We measure these variables using the government budget surplus (+) or deficit (−) (again expressed as a percentage of GDP), domestic credit growth, and the growth rate of GDP per capita.

Finally, we include two "external" variables, the growth rate of real GDP in the OECD, and "Northern" interest rates. We construct the latter as the weighted average of short-term rates for the United States, Germany, Japan, France, the United Kingdom, and Switzerland; the weights are proportional to the fractions of the individual LDC's exter-nal debt denominated in the relevant currencies (so that they vary across countries for individual years).

Throughout, we rely on the "event study" methodology of Eichengreen, Rose, and Wyplosz (1996). We start by dividing the sample into country-year observations with banking crises, as identi-fied by Caprio and Klingebiel (using only the first year of a banking crisis if it is more than one year in length). We then construct two-sided, three-year "exclusion windows" around each crisis observation to avoid double counting. This is important given the observed persistence of banking crises. These procedures yield a total of thirty-nine banking crises. In addition, there are 1,600 observations which are not crises and do not fall into our exclusion window; we use these as our control sample of tranquil observations.

Results

We begin our analysis with a graphical examination of macroeconomic conditions in the periods surrounding the onset of banking crises. We then proceed to a multivariate analysis of these variables before focusing upon the roles of the exchange rate regime, external indebtedness, and the structure of the financial sector's balance sheet.

In the panels of figure 5.1, we plot the behavior of our nine macroeconomic and financial variables at the onset of thirty-nine developing country banking crises, as well as in the three years preceding and three years following these crises.[32] Consider the foreign interest rate, portrayed in the top-left panel. The vertical center bar marks the year when the banking crises began. The circled observation indicates that the average Northern interest rate for countries experiencing a banking crisis was around 12 percent; the lines above and below this indicate that the plus or minus two standard deviation confidence interval is approximately (11 percent, 13 percent). The average interest rate during periods of tranquility (i.e., for countries which did not suffer a banking crisis within a window of plus/minus three years) is marked with a horizontal line and lies below this confidence interval at the crisis onset. The behavior of foreign interest rates in the three years preceding the crisis is portrayed to the left of the vertical bar, the period after to the right. The other panels portray the eight other variables of interest to us. Note that the precise number of observations may differ across panels as a function of the availability of data.

By far the most striking variable is foreign interest rates. From essentially the same level as in tranquil periods three years before the onset of a banking crisis, foreign interest rates rise to significantly higher levels as the crisis approaches; the differential peaks in the year of the crisis and the year following, although it remains significantly higher for a second subsequent year before returning to noncrisis levels. There is a clear presumption, then, that global financial conditions play a role in developing country banking crises. Our other measure of external conditions, the OECD growth rate, also indicates adverse external conditions, but less dramatically so: Northern growth decelerates in the

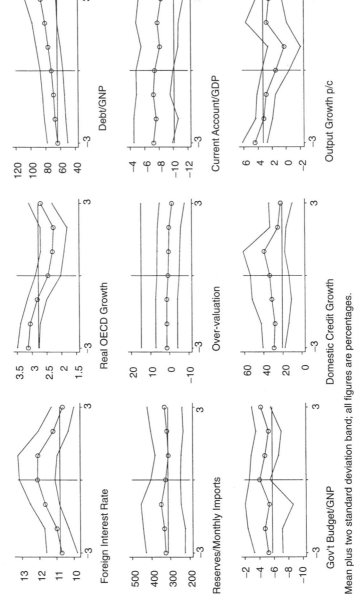

Figure 5.1
Macroeconomic characteristics of banking crises

periods leading up to banking crises but from a slightly above average level; it falls significantly below "normal" levels only in the periods after the onset of banking crises.

A second striking finding is the slight or perverse importance of our four "international" factors. While external debt rises throughout the periods surrounding banking crises, levels remain broadly similar to those in tranquil periods. The level of international reserves is also insignificantly different across crisis and non crisis periods. Even more surprisingly, exchange rates appear to be undervalued rather than overvalued, and (consistent with the former observation) current account deficits are actually smaller than in periods of tranquility. Thus, it is striking that a variety of high-profile indicators of the stance of international economic policies do not appear to matter in the expected way for the incidence of banking crises.

Nor do most standard measures of domestic macroeconomic conditions differ significantly (at the 95 percent confidence level) between crisis and noncrisis observations. Domestic output growth, while also decelerating over the period surrounding banking crises, does not differ significantly in the period leading up to the crisis relative to the control cases. There is, however, clear evidence of a recession one year following the event. More surprisingly, the typical post–banking crisis recession appears to be relatively short-lived; by the second post-crisis year, there is no longer evidence of a statistically significant recessionary effect. Finally, our measures of fiscal and monetary policy behave no differently in crisis and noncrisis cases. While the means of the variables are consistent with the hypotheses of relatively rapid domestic credit growth in the period leading up to banking crises, we cannot reject the hypothesis, at standard levels of statistical significance, that these variables behave the same as in noncrisis cases. Fiscal policy is, if anything, unusually tight at the time of banking crises.

All in all, our graphical analysis indicates that external factors are adverse during periods of Southern banking crises and significantly so. Northern interest rates tend to be high when banking crises break out in developing countries; the North tends also to be in recession. There is much less evidence that macroeconomic conditions in the South vary systematically between periods of tranquility and banking crises. Neither "international" factors (external debt, the current account, reserves, and the exchange rate level) nor "domestic" conditions (domestic growth, monetary and fiscal policy) appear to differ in easily identifiable ways between crisis and noncrisis periods.

These comparisons contrast the behavior of variables in crisis and noncrisis periods one at a time. A more demanding test involves estimating a multivariate model. We therefore turn to probit analysis, considering groups of variables and asking whether their joint behavior differs between crises and periods of tranquility. We estimate our models with maximum likelihood.

Various statistical measures suggest that goodness of fit is best when observations are weighted by GNP per capita; such weighting will also tend to minimize the influence of lower-quality data from poorer countries.[33] We refer to these GDP-weighted regressions as our baseline results, although we also report the unweighted regressions for completeness.[34]

Our benchmark regression is in the first column of table 5.1. As independent variables we include the nine variables portrayed in figure 5.1: the foreign interest rate, the change in OECD output, the change in domestic output, the change in domestic credit, the budget balance as a share of GDP, exchange rate overvaluation, the current account as a share of GDP, the ratio of reserves to imports, and the debt/GDP ratio. Since probit coefficients are not easily interpretable, we report the effects of changes in regressors on the probability of crisis (expressed in percentage points), evaluated at the mean of the variables. We also tabulate the associated z-statistics which test the null hypothesis of no effect. Diagnostics follow at the bottom of the table, including joint hypothesis tests for the significance of our four "international," three "domestic," and two "external" effects.

The majority of our variables enter with plausible signs and coefficients that differ from zero at standard levels of confidence. In particular, industrial country interest rates enter positively (confirming that higher world interest rates are associated with a higher probability of emerging-market banking crises).[35] OECD growth enters negatively, as if recession in the industrial world is also associated with banking problems in emerging markets. The two coefficients are jointly significant. Thus, the importance of global financial and economic conditions evident in the univariate results is affirmed and if anything strengthened by this multivariate analysis.

The negative coefficient on output growth indicates that slowing growth at home tends to be associated with banking crises, presumably reflecting the lesser ability of bank borrowers to service their loans. These results are thus consistent with the emphasis of Gavin and Hausmann, Gorton and others on slowing growth as a causal factor in

Table 5.1
Banking crises

	Default	Unweighted	Predictive	Without 1970s
External debt/GDP	0.002 (1.6)	0.025 (2.5)	0.001 (2.3)	0.001 (1.4)
Reserves/imports	0.000 (1.9)	0.001 (0.8)	0.000 (1.0)	0.000 (1.8)
Current account (% GDP)	−0.005 (1.0)	0.010 (0.2)	−0.002 (1.1)	−0.005 (1.1)
Overvaluation	0.005 (2.9)	0.018 (0.7)	0.003 (3.8)	0.005 (2.9)
Budget (% GDP)	0.025 (2.8)	0.239 (2.2)	0.014 (3.5)	0.018 (2.4)
Domestic credit growth	0.002 (1.4)	0.007 (0.5)	0.001 (1.7)	−0.000 (0.0)
Output growth	−0.015 (2.4)	−0.076 (0.9)	−0.004 (1.7)	−0.011 (2.1)
Northern interest rate	0.030 (2.4)	0.476 (2.3)	0.003 (5.3)	0.022 (2.2)
Northern output growth	−0.045 (2.2)	−0.075 (0.2)	0.001 (1.3)	−0.044 (2.4)
Observations	906	906	878	818
McFadden's R^2	0.37	0.06	0.50	0.42
Slopes [$\chi^2(9)$] (P-value)	60 (0.00)	16.4 (0.06)	80.3 (0.00)	75.5 (0.00)
International [$\chi^2(4)$] (P-value)	13.3 (0.01)	6.6 (0.16)	18.9 (0.00)	13.0 (0.01)
Domestic[$\chi^2(3)$] (P-value)	11.0 (0.01)	5.6 (0.13)	16.4 (0.00)	7.7 (0.05)
External [$\chi^2(2)$] (P-value)	17.8 (0.00)	8.4 (0.02)	29.7 (0.00)	15.4 (0.00)

Notes: Probit regressions estimated with maximum likelihood, weighted by GNP per capita. Derivatives (×100) reported for regressors; absolute z-statistics (for no significant effect) in parentheses.

banking crises, although as we shall see below this effect is not as robust as some other findings. Real overvaluation is significantly associated with the incidence of banking crises, perhaps reflecting a profitability squeeze on domestic borrowers or anticipating a subsequent step devaluation. Surprisingly, there is some evidence that, in this sample, larger government budget surpluses are associated with the probability of banking crises.[36]

The coefficients on the other variables are less robust or less plausible. Countries with higher ratios of external debt to output may be more prone to banking crises, since their banks are more dependent on foreign funding, but the coefficient on this variable falls short of significance at the 10 percent confidence level. The coefficients on the current account and domestic credit growth are insignificantly different from zero; this result for credit growth is striking given the emphasis placed by Gavin and Hausmann (1996) and Kaminsky and Reinhart (1996) on this variable. The ratio of international reserves to imports enters with a counterintuitive positive sign; one would anticipate a negative coefficient if additional reserves allow the authorities to engage in more extensive lender-of-last-resort operations.[37]

The remaining columns of table 5.1 report various exercises in sensitivity analysis. In the unweighted regression in the second column, the only effects that are statistically significant at standard confidence levels are the foreign interest rate, the domestic budget deficit, and the debt/GNP ratio. The third column is predictive in that the dependent variable is led by a year; the fourth column drops the observations for the 1970s. Neither of the last two perturbations substantially changes the impression from our baseline regressions. Throughout, the role of external factors—particularly Northern interest rates—remains economically important and statistically significant.

The Role of the Exchange Rate Regime

As noted above, considerable controversy surrounds the question of how the exchange rate regime affects the incidence of banking crises. To analyze this question we utilize data from *International Financial Statistics* (IFS) on countries' choice of exchange rate regime. Ghosh et al. (1995) have aggregated IFS's more detailed tabulation into three categories: "fixed" rate regimes (countries pegging to a single foreign currency, to a basket, or to the SDR), floating rate regimes, and "intermediate" exchange rate regimes (typically managed floaters). To check the robustness of our results, we also add a composite fourth category of "managed" exchange rate flexibility when a country is either "fixed" or "intermediate."

We first examine the simple correlation—the unconditional probability of a banking crisis under fixed and flexible exchange rates. The results are far from promising. When we split the banking crises and periods of tranquility into our three exchange rate regimes (fixed/intermediate/floating), there is only very weak evidence against the hypothesis that banking crises are randomly distributed across regimes. A formal chi-squared test of independence only rejects at the 4 percent significance level, as shown in the contingency table below.

	Fixed	Intermediate	Floating	Total
Tranquil	528	62	69	659
Banking crisis	15	4	6	25
Total	543	66	75	684

A careful test should account for other macroeconomic factors. We examined whether there is a partial correlation between pegged exchange rates and banking crises after controlling for macroeconomic variables included in our baseline regression—either the positive correlation predicted by those who associate pegged rates with constraints on the lender of last resort, or the negative correlation predicted by those who associate pegged rates with discipline and hence with a more stable expected future path for macroeconomic fundamentals. The results, in table 5.2, provide little ammunition for either view. The dummy variables for countries with pegged and intermediate exchange rate regimes enter with coefficients indistinguishable from zero whether they are entered separately or together. This negative result is insensitive to minor changes in the way that we estimate the equation. For instance, the second column reports results when we exclude the intermediate regime observations from the sample; and the third column is an analog with the managed regime composite in place of both fixed and intermediate dummies.[38]

To test the hypothesis (anticipated in "Analytical Issues," above) that pegged rates are preferable when disturbances are domestic, flexible rates when disturbances are external, we interacted our dummy variables for pegged and intermediate exchange rate regimes with our measures of external shocks (alternatively, foreign interest rates and the OECD growth rate).[39] In no case did any of the individual coefficients approach significance at standard confidence levels. And in no case did

Table 5.2
Banking crises and exchange rate regimes

External debt/GDP	−0.001 (0.3)	0.000 (0.1)	−0.000 (0.3)
Reserves/imports	0.0004 (1.8)	0.000 (0.1)	0.0003 (1.8)
Current account (% GDP)	−0.024 (1.8)	−0.011 (1.0)	−0.024 (2.0)
Overvaluation	0.001 (0.2)	0.003 (0.8)	0.000 (0.0)
Budget (% GDP)	0.026 (1.2)	0.013 (0.6)	0.025 (1.3)
Domestic credit growth	−0.007 (1.2)	−0.005 (1.1)	−0.007 (1.3)
Output growth	−0.009 (0.7)	−0.004 (0.3)	−0.009 (0.7)
Northern interest rate	0.011 (0.4)	0.022 (0.8)	0.009 (0.3)
Northern output growth	−0.065 (0.9)	−0.013 (0.2)	−0.056 (0.9)
Fixed peg	0.101 (0.4)	0.163 (0.8)	
Intermediate peg	0.015 (0.1)		
Managed peg			0.048 (0.2)
Observations	495	443	495
McFadden's R^2	0.38	0.40	0.37
Slopes [$\chi^2(11/10)$] (P-value)	16.4 (0.13)	11.5 (0.32)	16.2 (0.09)

Notes: Probit regressions estimated with maximum likelihood, weighted by GNP per capita. Derivatives (×100) reported for regressors; absolute z-statistics (for no significant effect) in parentheses.

the group of regime dummies and interaction terms achieve joint significance at even the 90 percent confidence level.

It could be that a country's declared exchange rate arrangement is a poor proxy for the actual stability of its exchange rate. Therefore, we also considered three measures of the actual stability or variability of the nominal rate. Results are reported in table 5.3. In the first column we include the measure of an exchange rate crash utilized in Frankel and Rose 1996: An exchange rate crash is a nominal depreciation of at least 25 percent that is also at least a 10 percent increase in the rate of depreciation over the previous period. Like the IFS measure of regime, the currency crash dummy has a statistically insignificant impact on the probability of a banking crisis.[40]

In addition, we constructed two alternative measures of the variability of the actual rate, one a dummy variable for cases where the exchange rate changed by less than 5 percent in the last year, the other an otherwise comparable dummy with a 10 percent variability cutoff. Both of these variables entered negatively and significantly, as if countries whose currencies were relatively stable were least prone to

Table 5.3
Banking crises and exchange rate stability

External debt/GDP	0.001 (1.6)	0.001 (1.3)	0.000 (1.6)
Reserves/imports	0.000 (1.8)	0.000 (1.7)	0.000 (1.8)
Current account (% GDP)	−0.003 (0.8)	−0.005 (1.2)	−0.004 (1.3)
Overvaluation	0.004 (3.1)	0.004 (3.3)	0.003 (3.1)
Budget (% GDP)	0.015 (2.4)	0.023 (3.2)	0.017 (3.6)
Domestic credit growth	0.001 (1.5)	0.002 (1.6)	0.000 (0.8)
Output growth	−0.012 (2.6)	−0.010 (2.2)	−0.005 (1.7)
Northern interest rate	0.020 (2.4)	0.028 (2.9)	0.014 (2.4)
Northern output growth	−0.027 (1.9)	−0.031 (2.0)	−0.028 (2.7)
Exchange rate crash	−0.043 (1.1)		
| Exchange rate change | < 5%		−0.079 (2.2)	
| Exchange rate change | < 10%			−0.215 (3.2)
Observations	906	906	906
McFadden's R^2	0.39	0.40	0.44
Slopes [$\chi^2(10)$] (P-value)	62.3 (0.00)	65.2 (0.00)	71.6 (0.00)

Notes: Probit regressions estimated with maximum likelihood, weighted by GNP per capita. Derivatives (×100) reported for regressors; absolute z-statistics (for no significant effect) in parentheses.

banking crises. These coefficients cannot reflect the effect of, say, faster domestic credit growth or larger budget deficits in such countries, since we are already controlling for these effects; rather, they presumably reflect the tendency for expectations about future policy to work in stabilizing directions where the authorities commit to stabilizing the exchange rate.

Thus, while the results are largely negative, they lend more support to the discipline than the lender-of-last-resort view.

The Role of External Debt

Sachs, Tornell and Velasco (1995) posit an association between the structure of the external debt and the stability of the financial system. Countries with large amounts of short-term, variable-rate, foreign-currency-denominated debt, are, in their view, especially prone to exchange rate crises. The fact or anticipation of a currency crisis can lead to an investor run as depositors scramble to get their money out of domestic banks and can force the government to jack up interest rates in order to lure back skittish investors, creating a problem of non-performing loans.

To test this hypothesis we extended our graphical analysis of macro-economic conditions in the periods surrounding the onset of banking crises. The nine panels of figure 5.2 show the evolution, in the periods surrounding banking crises (and the comparable control group cases), of the following measures of the structure of the external debt: the share of commercial bank debt in the total, the share of concessional debt in the total, the share of variable rate debt in the total, the share of public debt in the total, the share of short-term debt in the total, the share of multilateral rate debt in the total, the share of foreign direct investment (FDI) in the total, the overall debt/GDP ratio, and the interest payment/GDP ratio.

A number of these measures of debt structure behave differently in the periods surrounding banking crises. These include the debt flowing through the banking system, variable-rate debt, and short-term debt. All are significantly higher in periods leading up to banking crises than in control group cases, consistent with the motivating hypothesis.

When we add all of the aforementioned measures of debt structure to our baseline specification, as in the first column of table 5.4, they are highly significant as a group. The relevant χ^2 test rejects the null of zero coefficients for the group at better than the 95 percent confidence level. But only three of the individual debt structure variables enter with individual coefficients that differ from zero at the 95 percent confidence level: the share of multilateral debt, the share of concessional debt, and the share of short-term debt. Only the last of this trio is central to the "debt runs cause bank runs" hypothesis, and it enters with a negative coefficient inconsistent with that tale. The other variables central to the hypothesis—the share of debt flowing through the banks, which should render the banking system more fragile, ceteris paribus, or the share of DFI, which should be less volatile than other forms of external debt and hence less conducive to banking crises—enter with their anticipated signs but do not approach significance at standard confidence levels.

To be sure, the various measures of the structure of the external debt considered in this analysis are highly collinear, rendering individual point estimates and confidence intervals unreliable. Perhaps the best conclusion is a cautious one: there is evidence that the structure of the external debt matters for banking crises, even after controlling for a country's other macroeconomic fundamentals, but whether the chan-

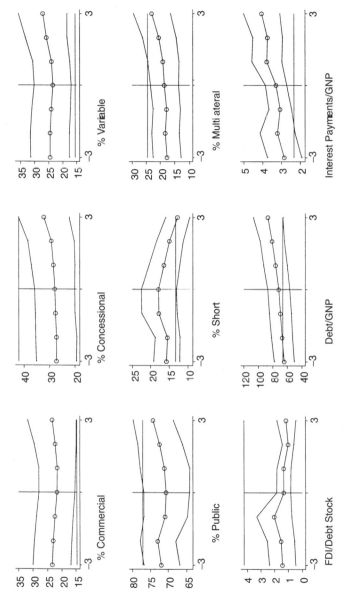

Figure 5.2
Characteristics of external debt around the time of banking crises

Table 5.4
Banking crises and external debt

External debt/GDP	−0.000 (0.0)
Reserves/imports	0.000 (1.0)
Current account (% GDP)	−0.006 (0.8)
Overvaluation	0.007 (2.9)
Budget (% GDP)	0.030 (3.0)
Domestic credit growth	0.000 (0.3)
Output growth	−0.011 (1.9)
Northern interest rate	0.022 (1.5)
Northern output growth	−0.053 (2.4)
% debt commercial	0.005 (0.7)
% debt concessional	−0.012 (3.0)
% debt variable rate	−0.010 (1.8)
% debt public	−0.008 (1.7)
% debt short	−0.014 (2.2)
% debt multilateral	0.009 (2.0)
FDI/debt	−0.016 (0.9)
Observations	824
McFadden's R^2	0.50
Slopes [$\chi^2(16)$] (P-value)	72 (0.00)
Debt slopes [$\chi^2(7)$] (P-value)	15.5 (0.03)

Notes: Probit regressions estimated with maximum likelihood, weighted by GNP per capita. Derivatives (×100) reported for regressors; absolute z-statistics (for no significant effect) in parentheses.

nels are those posited in the Sachs-Tornell-Velasco debt run story is less clear.

The Role of Domestic Financial Structure

A final possibility to be explored is that a fragile domestic financial structure is conducive to banking crises. While this hypothesis has intuitive appeal, there are difficulties in measuring financial fragility in ways that are internationally comparable. Countries do not report loan losses or loan loss provisioning systematically. The difficulty of obtaining data on such variables was an issue when the IMF sought to assemble a rescue package for Thailand in 1997, which led to U.S. government proposals that countries commit to releasing such information in a timely fashion.

We follow Demirgüç-Kunt and Detragiache in attempting to measure domestic financial fragility or vulnerability indirectly. We construct three measures: the ratio of broad money (M2) to reserves (an increase in which tends to follow financial liberalization, heightening financial fragility if bank supervision and regulation does not keep up with the growth of bank lending), a measure of the liquidity of the banking system (bank reserves as a share of bank assets), and the proportion of bank lending directed to the public sector (which may proxy for the extent of connected lending). All three variables are constructed from data in IFS.

When added to our default regression, none of the three variables enters with a coefficient significantly different from zero at standard confidence levels. M2 relative to reserves comes closest: it enters with a positive coefficient, as predicted, but differs from zero only at the 80 percent confidence level.

We interacted these three measures of domestic financial structure with the foreign interest rate in an effort to test more directly whether increases in world interest rates precipitate crises mainly when they are superimposed on a fragile financial structure. The interaction terms turned out to be insignificant individually and as a group.

Thus, we find little evidence that available measures of domestic financial fragility are useful for predicting banking crises. Admittedly, this may tell us more about the limitations of the data than about the validity of the underlying economic hypothesis.

Conclusions and Implications

The results of this chapter confirm that banking crises in emerging markets tend to occur in response to a conjuncture of unfavorable developments in domestic and international markets. Domestic imbalances play a role in crises; specifically, our results point to the importance of overvalued real exchange rates and slowing output growth. On the other hand, there is little evidence of an independent role for domestic credit booms of the sort emphasized by Gavin and Hausmann (1995) and Kaminsky and Reinhart (1996). But by far our strongest finding is of the role of changes in global financial conditions, and specifically of rising industrial country interest rates in precipitating banking crises. Insofar as our regressions have predictive implications, they suggest the following. Look first for countries with overvalued exchange rates and disappointing output growth, for their banks are most likely to be saddled with nonperforming loans. Look then for a rise in interest rates in the principal financial centers, for this will disrupt the availability of offshore funding for the banks and cause the smoldering crisis to burst into flames.

The ultimate test of any such model is its out-of-sample predictive power. For this purpose we can make use of the wave of banking crises that hit East Asia in the second half of 1997. In our estimation, this episode is consistent with our results, although the fit is not exceptionally good. Thailand, the first country to be so affected, did in fact develop a problem of significant real overvaluation in the period leading up to its crisis. The rate of growth of real GDP decelerated sharply after 1995. And in the first part of 1997, there was a tightening in global financial conditions resulting from a sudden rise in Japanese bond yields and the sharp rebound in the yen, which reduced the attractiveness of borrowing in Japan to finance investments in high-yielding markets elsewhere and signaled the possibility of more difficult financing conditions for emerging market borrowers.[41] But compared to the earlier experience we analyze, one would say that in Thailand the domestic imbalances were more pronounced, the tightening in global financial conditions less so.

Other cases like Indonesia and South Korea are more difficult to reconcile with our results. The evidence of real overvaluation and slower output growth is less impressive than in Thailand. And the evidence of an external funding shock is no greater. To be sure, there were a variety of subtler but nonetheless profound problems in the banking and corporate sectors of both countries, of a sort not easily captured by macroeconomic variables like those analyzed here. We suspect that there was a role in addition for the contagious spread of crises across countries. In previous work on foreign exchange crises (Eichengreen, Rose, and Wyplosz 1996), we established that a currency crisis in another country increased the probability that a neighboring country would experience a currency crisis of its own by fully 8 percent. We conjecture that similar spillovers operate in banking markets.

The policy implications are clear. Insofar as banking systems in emerging markets are unusually dependent on offshore funds and susceptible to destabilization by sudden changes in global credit conditions, standard levels of regulatory and macroeconomic prudence may not be enough to insulate them from banking crises. The prudential requirements used by high-income countries to protect their banking systems from domestic sources of instability may have to be supplemented in developing countries by an extra layer of insulation to protect their banking systems against externally generated or amplified disturbances. Examples of the kind of measures we have in mind include limiting the short-term, foreign-currency-denominated liabilities of banks, adjusting domestic reserve and liquidity requirements to prevent an elastic supply of foreign funds from encouraging an excessive expansion of cyclically sensitive loans, and requiring developing country banks to meet even more demanding capital standards than their industrial country counterparts.

More work will be needed to extend the sample to the advanced industrial countries and to determine whether the effects we have identified, notably the impact of global financial and economic conditions, have their largest impact on financial stability in emerging markets, independent of the domestic financial structures. But the evidence we have presented is at least consistent with this presumption. If borne out, this conclusion provides support for the increasingly widespread view that banking systems in emerging markets, owing to their special susceptibility to crisis, for reasons beyond those of their own making, need to be protected by prudential regulations and capital and liquidity requirements even more demanding than those of the advanced industrial countries.

Notes

We thank Maria Soledad Martinez-Peria for research assistance and the National Science Foundation (Economics Division) for financial support. The bulk of the analysis was conducted and a draft of the chapter was written while Eichengreen visited the Center for Advanced Study in the Behavioral Sciences and the IMF Research Department, and Rose visited the Federal Reserve Bank of San Francisco: we thank those institutions for hospitality and support. The STATA 5.0 data set used to generate our results is available at http://haas.berkeley.edu/~arose.

1. The locus classicus of this literature, Friedman and Schwartz (1963), is in fact on the United States, but subsequent work such as Bernanke and James 1991 extends it both analytically and geographically.

2. Of course, no list of East Asian financial crises would be complete without also mentioning the case of Japan. Although our focus here is on emerging markets, a comprehensive survey would include also systemic banking problems in the 1980s in the United States, the United Kingdom, and, toward the end of the decade, in the Nordic countries.

3. It is important to ask whether the banking crises caused the recessions in a meaningful economic sense, or whether recessionary forces set on foot for independent reasons themselves provoked the banking crises and persisted into the post-crisis period. Gorton

(1988) argues that the direction of causality throughout U.S. history has been mainly from recessions to bank failures rather than the other way around. We revisit this point below.

4. Rojas-Suarez and Weisbrod (1994), writing before the most recent Mexican crisis, emphasize the disproportionate importance of banking systems for small firm finance in Latin America and hence the scope for a banking crisis to give rise to a severe credit crunch.

5. *The Economist* 1997.

6. E.g., Caprio and Klingebiel 1997.

7. The same is true of the Kaminsky-Reinhart sample of twenty countries and of the Granger causality analysis for seven economies conducted by Sunderarajan and Balino.

8. Considering twenty-nine detailed country studies, they find a role for deteriorating terms of trade in twenty of them and of domestic recession in sixteen.

9. Kaminsky and Reinhart utilize changes in the level of real interest rates as a proxy for financial liberalization, although there are obviously also reasons why this might be regarded as a measure of macroeconomic conditions.

10. Demirgüç-Kunt and Detragiache (1997) simultaneously and independently of us use similar methods and data. They also use a panel approach, but combine developing and developed countries together using a logit model to analyze data for the 1980s and 1990s. Whereas we focus on the onset of banking crises using the Caprio-Klingebiel crisis dates, they study the incidence of banking crises (of whatever duration) using four different criteria. The studies share a set of macroeconomic regressors (e.g., both studies show that output growth is low during banking crises); we find an important role for external interest rates, while they find an important role for deposit insurance and law enforcement.

11. And that do not fall within an exclusion window we construct around our crisis observations.

12. See also Gavin and Hausmann 1995 and Eichengreen and Fishlow 1996.

13. Previous discussions of this issue, on which we build, include Mishkin 1996, which emphasizes the implications of asymmetric information for the structure and performance of the banking industry, and Gavin and Hausmann 1995, which is mainly concerned with the macroeconomic implications of banking crises.

14. Except in the event of doubts about the bank's own stability, as we describe below.

15. Bernanke and Blinder (1988, 1992) have provided formal models of the credit channel. Edwards and Vegh (1997) show that the mechanisms highlighted in these models are consistent with the assumption of optimizing behavior on the part of households and firms.

16. The existence of this incentive has given rise to a literature on random bank runs, in which depositors uncertain of a banks' solvency queue up to withdraw their deposits before the institution's limited liquidity is exhausted (Diamond and Dybvig 1983). Since a bank holding fractional reserves can satisfy only some of its depositors' demands for liquidity, such a run can be self-fulfilling. While the generality of these models have been questioned (viz., Schwartz 1996), the possibility they highlight serves to underscore the intrinsic fragility of banking systems.

17. Previous reviews of these issues, on which we build, include Goldstein and Turner 1996 and Demirgüç-Kunt and Detragiache 1997.

18. Inevitably these categories are overlapping, as will become apparent momentarily, but this five-part distinction is useful nonetheless.

19. And is emphasized by, inter alia, Gavin and Hausmann (1995), Kaminsky and Reinhart (1996), Demirgüç-Kunt and Detragiache (1997), Honohan (1997) and Kapur (1997). Caprio and Klingebiel (1997), on the other hand, question the generality of the association of lending booms with banking crises.

20. This is the typical sequence of events described by Kindleberger (1978) and emphasized by Gavin and Hausmann (1995) in the Latin American context.

21. Demirgüç-Kunt and Detragiache (1997) find weak evidence that terms of trade volatility is associated with banking crises.

22. Mishkin (1996) also argues that an increase in interest rates in the presence of adverse selection can precipitate banking crises by aggravating credit rationing and provoking a downturn in economic activity, augmenting the number of nonperforming loans.

23. The literature on this connection, along with historical evidence on its operation, may be found in Eichengreen 1997.

24. And is emphasized in the context of domestic financial structure by a number of authors; see for example Kapur 1997.

25. Goldstein and Turner (1996) note that in Germany nearly half of the liabilities of depository institutions are long-term, while the comparable figure for Japan is one-third; in developing countries, in contrast, banks have few sources of longer-term financing.

26. This regularity is emphasized by, among others, Goldstein and Turner (1996) and Honohan (1997).

27. See for example Smallhout 1997. Demirgüç-Kunt and Detragiache (1997) find that a measure of the strength of law enforcement is strongly associated with the incidence of banking crises.

28. Calomoris and Gorton (1991) define a banking panic, a closely allied concept, as a situation in which bank debt holders at all or many banks in the banking system suddenly demand that banks convert their debt claims into cash.

29. Slight judgment is sometimes involved, since not all banking crises are identified with individual years.

30. Eichengreen (1997) emphasizes parallels between industrial and developing country experiences.

31. However, numerous observations are missing for individual variables. The countries we include are: Algeria; Argentina; Bangladesh; Barbados; Belize; Benin; Bhutan; Bolivia; Botswana; Brazil; Burkina Faso; Burundi; Cameroon; Cape Verde; Central African Republic; Chad; Chile; China; Colombia; Comoros; Congo; Costa Rica; Cote d'Ivoire; Djibouti; Dominican Republic; Ecuador; Arab Republic of Egypt; El Salvador; Equatorial Guinea; Ethiopia; Fiji; Gabon; The Gambia; Ghana; Grenada; Guatemala; Guinea; Guinea-Bissau; Guyana; Haiti; Honduras; Hungary; India; Indonesia; Islamic Republic of Iran; Jamaica; Jordan; Kenya; Republic of Korea; Lao People's Democratic Republic; Lebanon; Lesotho; Liberia; Madagascar; Malawi; Malaysia; Maldives; Mali; Malta;

Mauritania; Mauritius; Mexico; Morocco; Myanmar; Nepal; Nicaragua; Niger; Nigeria; Oman; Pakistan; Panama; Papua New Guinea; Paraguay; Peru; Philippines; Portugal; Romania; Rwanda; St. Vincent and the Grenadines; Sao Tome and Principe; Senegal; Seychelles; Sierra Leone; Solomon Islands; Somalia; Sri Lanka; Sudan; Swaziland; Syrian Arab Republic; Tanzania; Thailand; Togo; Trinidad and Tobago; Tunisia; Turkey; Uganda; Uruguay; Vanuatu; Venezuela; Western Samoa; Republic of Yemen; Federal Republic of Yugoslavia; Zaire; Zambia; and Zimbabwe.

32. The actual list includes: Argentina 1980; Argentina 1989; Benin 1988; Burkina Faso 1988; Bangladesh 1988; Bolivia 1986; Brazil 1990; Central African Republic 1980; Chile 1976; Chile 1981; Cote d'Ivoire 1988; Cameroon 1987; Congo 1980; Colombia 1982; Costa Rica 1987; Ecuador 1980; Egypt 1980; Egypt 1990; Ghana 1982; Guinea 1985; Hungary 1991; Kenya 1985; Kenya 1992; Morocco 1980; Madagascar 1988; Mexico 1981; Mauritania 1984; Malaysia 1985; Nigeria 1990; Nepal 1988; Philippines 1981; Romania 1990; Senegal 1988; Thailand 1983; Turkey 1982; Tanzania 1987; Uruguay 1981; Venezuela 1980; and Zaire 1991. This tabulation shows that LDC banking crises were somewhat concentrated in the early 1980s, a period of high Northern interest rates and slow Northern growth. But the 1988 cluster of crises and the general distribution of crises across time is more difficult to explain with our Northern variables alone.

33. This suggests that the incidence of banking crises is easier to explain in terms of the systematic macroeconomic factors (both domestic and foreign) considered in the analysis in the relatively high-income developing countries, while crises in low-income developing countries are more heavily driven by idiosyncratic factors.

34. The baseline results should be interpreted therefore as attaching the most importance to relatively high-income developing countries.

35. Using the American interest rate instead of a weighted average of Northern rates does not change our results substantively.

36. We are unable to explain this result, which appears consistently throughout the analysis which follows.

37. An alternative explanation would emphasize the endogeneity of this variable: that countries vulnerable to banking crises build up an extra cushion of reserves precisely in order to protect against this contingency. This behavior is evident, for example, in the recent experience of Argentina.

38. We have also experimented by splitting the sample by regime with a similar lack of success.

39. In addition, in some regressions we also interacted these variables with the domestic growth rate, and we estimated our baseline regression separately for countries with pegged and floating rates. None of these specifications turned up evidence of an association between the exchange rate regime and the incidence of banking crises.

40. It could be that a currency crash destabilizes the banking system only with a lag (because, for example, it takes time for depreciation to translate into default by borrowers with foreign-currency-denominated debts but domestic-currency-denominated revenues, as in Mexico). We therefore substituted the lagged crash variable for its current value, but without success; the coefficient on the lagged crash variable is economically and statistically similar to that on the current value.

41. Japanese long rates ticked up from 2 to 2.5 percent when the outlook for the Japanese economy appeared to brighten after March, and short rates firmed with talk

that the Bank of Japan might raise rates by the end of the year. There were also small but significant increases in interest rates in the United Kingdom and Germany in the spring of 1997. A rise in U.S. rates may not have eventuated, but rumors that it was coming did nonetheless circulate. See IMF 1997.

References

Bernanke, B. 1983. Nonmonetary effects of the financial crisis in the propagation of the Great Depression. *American Economic Review* 73:257–76.

Bernanke, B., and A. Blinder. 1992. The federal funds rate and the channels of monetary transmission. *American Economic Review* 82:902–21.

Bernanke, B., and A. Blinder. 1988. Credit, money and aggregate demand. *American Economic Review* 78:435–9.

Bernanke, B., and H. James. 1991. The gold standard, deflation, and financial crisis in the Great Depression: An international comparison. In *Financial markets and financial crises*, ed. R. Glenn Hubbard, 33–68. Chicago: University of Chicago Press.

Bordo, M. D. 1986. Financial crises, banking crises, stock market crashes and the money supply: Some international evidence, 1870–1913. In *Financial crises and the world banking system*, ed. Forrest Capie and Geoffrey Wood, 190–248. London: Macmillan.

Bordo, M. D. 1985. The impact and international transmission of financial crises: Some historical evidence, 1870–1933. *Rivista di Storia Economica* (international issue) 2:41–78.

Calomiris, C., and G. Gorton. 1991. The origins of banking panics: Models, facts and bank regulation. In *Financial markets and financial crises*, ed. R. Glenn Hubbard, 109–74. Chicago: University of Chicago Press.

Calvo, G. 1994. Financial vulnerability and capital flows. Unpublished manuscript, University of Maryland, College Park.

Calvo, G. 1996. Capital flows and macroeconomic management: Tequila lessons. Unpublished manuscript, University of Maryland, College Park.

Calvo, G., L. Leiderman, and C. Reinhart. 1993. Capital inflows and real exchange rate appreciation in Latin America: The role of external factors. *IMF Staff Papers* 40:108–50.

Caprio, G., Jr., and D. Klingebiel. 1997. Bank insolvency: Bad luck, bad policy, or bad banking? In *Annual World Bank Conference on Development Economics, 1996*, 79–104. Washington, D.C.: World Bank.

Caprio, G., Jr., and D. Klingebiel. 1996. Bank insolvencies: Cross-country experience. Policy research working paper no. 1620, The World Bank, Washington, D.C.

Demirgüç-Kunt, A., and E. Detragiache. 1997. The determinants of banking crises: Evidence from developing and developed countries. Unpublished manuscript, International Monetary Fund, Washington, D.C.

Diamond, D., and P. Dybvig. 1983. Bank runs, liquidity and deposit insurance. *Journal of Political Economy* 91:401–19.

The Economist. 1997. A survey of banking in emerging markets. Supplement, 12 April, pp. 5–40.

Edwards, S., and C. A. Vegh. 1997. Banks and macroeconomic disturbances under predetermined exchange rates. Working paper no. 5977 (March), National Bureau of Economic Research, Cambridge, Mass.

Eichengreen, B. 1997. Exchange rate stability and financial stability. Unpublished manuscript, University of California, Berkeley.

Eichengreen, B., and A. Fishlow. 1996. Contending with capital flows: What is different about the 1990s? Occasional Paper, Council on Foreign Relations, New York.

Eichengreen, B., and R. S. Grossman. 1997. Debt deflation and financial instability: Two historical explorations. In *Asset prices and the real economy*, ed. F. Capie and G. Wood, 65–96. London: Macmillan.

Eichengreen, B., A. K. Rose, and C. Wyplosz. 1996. Exchange market mayhem: The antecedents and aftermath of speculative attacks. *Economic Policy* 21:249–312.

Frankel, J. A., and A. K. Rose. 1996. Currency crashes in emerging markets. *Journal of International Economics* 41 (3/4):351–66.

Friedman, M., and A. J. Schwartz. 1963. *A monetary history of the United States, 1863–1960*. Princeton: Princeton University Press.

Gavin, M., and R. Hausmann. 1995. The roots of banking crises: The macroeconomic context. In *Banking crises in Latin America*, ed. R. Hausmann and L. Rojas-Suarez, 27–63. Baltimore: Johns Hopkins University Press.

Ghosh, A., A.-M. Gulde, J. D. Ostry, and H. C. Wolf. 1995. Does the nominal exchange rate regime matter? Working paper no. 95/21 (November), International Monetary Fund, Washington, D.C.

Goldstein, M. 1997. *The case for an international banking standard*. Washington, D.C.: Institute for International Economics.

Goldstein, M., and P. Turner. 1996. Banking crises in emerging economies: Origins and policy options. Economic papers no. 46 (October), Bank for International Settlements, Basle, Switzerland.

Gorton, G. 1988. Banking panics and business cycles. *Oxford Economic Papers* 40:221–55.

Greenwald, B., and J. Stiglitz. 1988. Information, finance constraints, and business fluctuations. In *Expectations and Macroeconomics*, ed. M. Kohn. and S. C. Tsiang. Oxford: Oxford University Press.

Grossman, R. S. 1993. The macroeconomic consequences of bank failures under the national banking system. *Explorations in Economic History* 3:294–330.

Group of Ten Working Party on Financial Stability in Emerging Market Economies. 1997. Financial stability in emerging market economies. Unpublished report.

Honohan, P. 1997. Banking system failures in developing and transition countries: Diagnosis and prediction. Unpublished manuscript, University College, Dublin.

International Monetary Fund. 1997. *Interim assessment of the world economic outlook–Regional and global implications of the financial crisis in Southeast and East Asia*. Washington, D.C.: IMF.

Kaminsky, G., and C. Reinhart. 1996. The twin crises: The causes of banking and balance-of-payments problems. Unpublished manuscript, Federal Reserve Board and International Monetary Fund, Washington, D.C.

Kapur, A. 1997. "How to look for fundamental soundness in Asian banks." *Asian Wall Street Journal* 21 July, p. 12.

Kindleberger, C. P. 1978. *Manias, panics and crashes*. New York: Basic Books.

McKinnon, R., and H. Pill. 1995. Credible liberalization and international capital flows: The overborrowing syndrome. Unpublished manuscript, Stanford University, Stanford, Calif.

Mishkin, F. S. 1997. Asymmetric information and financial crises. A developing country perspective. *World Bank Annual Conference on Development Economics*, supplement to *World Bank Economic Review*, pp. 29–62.

Mishkin, F. S. 1996. Understanding financial crises: A developing country perspective. Working paper no. 5600 (May), National Bureau of Economic Research, Cambridge, Mass.

Mishkin, F. S. 1991. Anatomy of a financial crisis. Working paper no. 3934, National Bureau of Economic Research, Cambridge, Mass.

Rojas-Suarez, L., and S. R. Weisbrod. 1994. Financial market fragilities in Latin America: From banking crisis resolution to current policy challenges. Working paper no. 94/117, International Monetary Fund, Washington, D.C.

Sachs, J. 1995. Do we need an international lender of last resort? Unpublished manuscript, Harvard University.

Sachs, J. A., A. Tornell, and A. Velasco. 1995. The collapse of the Mexican peso: What have we learned? *Economic Policy* 22:15–56.

Schwartz, A. J. 1996. Comment on Jeffrey Sachs: "Do we need an international lender of last Resort?" Unpublished manuscript, National Bureau of Economic Research, Cambridge, Mass.

Simons, K., and S. Cross. 1991. Do capital markets predict problems in large commercial banks? *New England Economic Review* (May/June): 51–6.

Smallhout, J. 1997. How to contain banking crises. *Euromoney* (July): 10–12.

Sundararajan, V., and T. J. T. Balino. 1991. Issues in recent banking crises. In *Banking Crises: Cases and Issues*, ed. V. Sundararajan and T. J. T. Balino, 1–57. Washington, D.C.: International Monetary Fund.

6

Perspectives on the Recent Currency Crisis Literature

Robert P. Flood and
Nancy P. Marion

It is patently obvious that periodic balance-of-payments crises will remain an integral feature of the international economic system as long as fixed exchange rates and rigid wage and price levels prevent the terms of trade from fulfilling a natural role in the adjustment process.

—Robert A. Mundell, "A Theory of Optimum Currency Areas" (1961)

Introduction

In the 1990s, currency crises in Europe, Mexico, and Southeast Asia have drawn worldwide attention to speculative attacks on government-controlled exchange rates. To improve understanding of these events, research has proceeded on both theoretical and empirical fronts. The purpose of this chapter is to provide some perspective on this research and to relate it to earlier work in the area. The early work, now called *first-generation* research, responded to currency crises in developing countries such as Mexico (1973–1982) and Argentina (1978–1981). These crises were preceded by overly expansive domestic policies. First-generation models show how a fixed exchange rate policy combined with excessively expansionary precrisis fundamentals push the economy into crisis, with the private sector trying to profit from dismantling the inconsistent policies.

Newer models, the *second generation*, are designed to capture features of the speculative attacks in Europe and in Mexico in the 1990s. These attacks differ from the ones studied by the first generation in two important ways: (1) in the countries experiencing the attacks, the state of the business cycle and the banking system as well as borrowing constraints imposed by monetary policies in partner countries handcuffed authorities and prevented them from using traditional methods to support exchange rate parities; (2) the recent speculative attacks, particularly some of those in Europe, seemed unrelated to the economic fundamentals predicted by the first-generation models.

In this chapter we begin in the first section by presenting the first-generation attack model developed by Salant and Henderson (1978), Krugman (1979), and Flood and Garber (1984b).[1] This model has been extended widely, and a survey is provided by Agenor, Bhandari, and Flood (1992). We also discuss some recent extensions of the model designed to capture features of the crises in the 1990s. In the second section we present examples of second-generation models. In this section we also extend these models by deriving the optimal commitment to a fixed exchange rate. The section concludes with a proposal for a common cross-generational framework. In the third section we examine empirical work that seeks to identify determinants of currency crises. The fourth section concludes.

First-Generation Models

The canonical first-generation model is one of a small country that fixes the price of its currency in terms of the currency of a large foreign partner. Fixing the exchange rate is the responsibility of the domestic monetary authority, so the analysis revolves around private and government actions in the domestic money market.

Domestic money market equilibrium is given by

$$m - p = -\alpha(i), \alpha > 0, \tag{6.1}$$

where, in logs, m is the domestic supply of high-powered money, p is the domestic price level, and i is the domestic currency interest rate in levels. The domestic money supply is backed by two central bank assets: domestic credit, whose log is d; and international reserves, whose log is r. As an accounting identity, in levels, the high-powered money supply is equal to the sum of domestic credit and international reserves. We log-linearize this identity as[2]

$$m = d + r. \tag{6.2}$$

The domestic-currency interest rate and price level are subject to international arbitrage conditions. The price level is governed by purchasing power parity:

$$p = p^* + s, \tag{6.3}$$

where p^* is the log foreign price level, usually held constant by assumption, and s is the log exchange rate quoted as the domestic currency price of foreign exchange. The interest rate obeys uncovered interest rate parity:

$$i = i^* + \dot{s}, \tag{6.4}$$

where i^* is the foreign currency interest rate and $\dot{s}$ is the expected and actual rate of exchange rate change.

The standard exchange rate model outlined above is chosen for its simplicity rather than for its empirical performance. The basic ideas apply equally well to more complicated models. In the foregoing model, during a fixed exchange rate period, the domestic price level moves in lockstep with the foreign price level. The domestic currency interest rate is equal to the foreign currency interest rate and the quantity of international reserves adjusts to balance the money market. During a flexible exchange rate regime, the quantity of international reserves is normally held fixed, and the exchange rate is free to balance the money market. In applications of the model, or when using the model to discuss historical episodes, the money market is expanded to include such features as a money multiplier; a role for home-good prices; a scale variable such as income, consumption, or wealth; and a money market disturbance.[3]

In a world of certainty and with the exchange rate fixed at $s = \bar{s}$, it follows that $\dot{s} = 0$ and $i = i^*$. Suppose that deficit financing requires domestic credit to grow at a constant rate, μ, and that i^* and p^* are constant. Substituting from equations (6.2), (6.3), and (6.4) into equation (6.1) with $\dot{s} = 0$, it follows that

$$r + d - p^* - \bar{s} = -\alpha(i^*). \tag{6.5}$$

When the exchange rate, foreign price and foreign interest rate are fixed, d grows at the rate μ and r falls at the same rate, $\dot{r} = -\mu$. Clearly this country will run out of reserves eventually and the fixed rate will break down. To analyze the breakdown, we need to describe precisely what the government does when it runs out of reserves. Different plans for government behavior in the crisis turn out to influence the timing and size of the crisis.

In a crisis, most governments either allow the exchange rate to float, as did Mexico in 1994, or devalue the domestic currency from one fixed rate to another, as happened in most European countries in 1992–1993. Suppose that in a crisis speculators purchase the remaining government stock of foreign exchange reserves dedicated to defending the fixed rate, and then the government allows the exchange rate to float. We know that the fixed rate must break down eventually, but when? To find the time of the attack, we introduce the idea of the *shadow exchange rate*, which is defined to be the floating exchange rate that would prevail if speculators purchase the remaining government reserves committed to the fixed rate and the government refrained from foreign exchange market intervention thereafter. The shadow rate is crucial to assessing the profits available to speculators in a crisis since this is the price at which speculators can sell the international reserves that they buy from the government.

The shadow exchange rate, $\tilde{s}$, therefore is the exchange rate that balances the money market following an attack in which foreign exchange reserves are exhausted.[4] The exchange rate that solves the post-attack money market is consistent with[5]

$$d - \tilde{s} = -\alpha(\dot{\tilde{s}}).$$ (6.6)

That exchange rate is

$$\tilde{s} = \alpha\mu + d.$$ (6.7)

In figure 6.1 we plot equation (6.7) and the pre-attack fixed exchange rate. The two lines intersect at point A, where $d = d^A$.

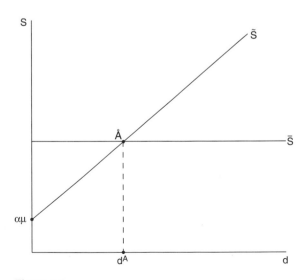

Figure 6.1
Attack time in a certainty model

Suppose that d is smaller than d^A. If speculators attack at such a level of d then post-attack the currency will appreciate and speculators will experience a capital loss on the reserves they purchase from the government. There will be no attack, therefore, when $d < d^A$. Suppose instead that speculators wait until $d > d^A$. Now $\tilde{s} > \bar{s}$, meaning that there is a capital gain to speculators for every unit of reserves purchased from the government. Speculators can foresee that capital gain and will compete against each other for the profit. The way they compete is to get a jump on each other and attack earlier. Such competition continues until the attack is driven back in time to the point where $d = d^A$. It follows that a foreseen attack must take place when $\bar{s} = \tilde{s}$. Exchange rate jumps are ruled out by speculative competition.

Let the size of the speculative attack be Δr, which is negative in an attack. From equation (6.7), the exchange rate will begin rising at the rate μ after the attack. Therefore, interest parity requires that the domestic currency interest rate jump up by μ. This point is key to the first-generation models—at the time of a foreseen speculative attack, the domestic currency interest rate must jump upward to reflect prospective currency depreciation.

Two things therefore adjust in the money market at the time of the attack: (1) the high-powered money supply drops by the size of the attack, and (2) the demand for domestic currency drops because the domestic currency interest rate increases to reflect prospective currency depreciation. Money market balance at the instant of the attack requires the drop in money supply to match exactly the drop in money demand, so $\Delta r = -\alpha\mu$. Since domestic credit follows $d_t = d_0 + \mu t$, international reserves follow $r_t = r_0 - \mu t$. At the time of attack, T, reserves fall to zero. The condition for the attack becomes $-\Delta r = r_0 - \mu T = \alpha\mu$. Rearranging terms, the attack time is[6]

$$T = \frac{r_0 - \alpha\mu}{\mu}. \tag{6.8}$$

Equation (6.8) shows that the higher the initial stock of reserves or the lower the rate of credit expansion, the longer it takes before the fixed exchange rate regime collapses.

Modified First-Generation Models

The first-generation model equates the attack-caused drop in the domestic money supply with the drop in money demand induced by higher domestic currency interest rates. The interest rate must rise to reflect post-attack currency depreciation. In the 1990s crises, the money supply effects of reserve losses were sterilized, allowing smooth money growth through the attack period.

What happens when sterilization policies are incorporated into the standard model? Let us return to the model above but now hold the money supply constant through the attack, so $m = \overline{m}$. While the exchange rate is fixed, money market equilibrium is

$$\overline{m} - p^* - \overline{s} = -\alpha(i^*). \tag{6.9}$$

Following an attack, international reserves are exhausted, the economy switches to a flexible exchange rate, and the money supply begins to grow at the rate $\mu > 0$. In that situation, the flexible exchange rate $\tilde{s}$ will rise also at the rate μ. Interest parity ensures that the domestic interest rate will be $i = i^* + \mu$. Just after an attack, therefore, domestic money market equilibrium will be

$$m - p^* - \tilde{s} = -\alpha(i^* + \mu). \tag{6.10}$$

Subtracting equation (6.10) from equation (6.9) reveals

$$\tilde{s} - \overline{s} = \alpha\mu > 0. \tag{6.11}$$

Equation (6.11) shows that $\tilde{s}$ is greater than $\overline{s}$ no matter how high the authorities set $\overline{s}$ or how great the quantity of international reserves held by the monetary authority. In other words, the simple model predicts that no fixed exchange rate regime can survive, even for a moment, if the monetary authority plans to sterilize an attack and those plans are understood by speculators.[7]

Complete sterilization evidently presents a problem for the simple model since it implies that fixed exchange rates are incompatible with complete sterilization. Yet fixing the exchange rate while sterilizing is common practice. This type of model can be (somewhat) rehabilitated, however, by recognizing that what sterilization does is remove the attack from the money market and push it off into another market. Sterilizing an attack on the country's foreign exchange reserves usually involves the monetary authority's expanding domestic credit and using it to purchase domestic government securities. The change in outstanding asset quantities is therefore shifted from the money market to the market for domestic bonds.

Flood, Garber, and Kramer (1996) pursue the speculative attack from the money market, where it resides in the standard model, into the bond markets, where it is driven by domestic sterilization operations. Monetary policy is the same as before except the attack itself is sterilized. Thus domestic credit still grows at the rate μ and is invariant to the speculative attack. Instead of the uncovered interest parity condition in equation (6.4), however, we now add a bond-based risk premium to the spread between domestic and foreign currency interest rates. The domestic currency interest rate is now[0]

$$i = i^* + \dot{s} + \beta(b - b^* - s), \tag{6.12}$$

where $\beta > 0$ is a constant, in logs b is the quantity of domestic government bonds in private hands and b^* is the quantity of foreign currency bonds in private hands.

Printing domestic credit at the rate μ creates incentives for private portfolio reallocation and ends up pushing international reserves out of government hands and into the private sector. Those reserves are interest-paying foreign currency securities, and as reserves decline, b^* rises. After accounting for private accumulation of reserves, the rate of change of reserves is now $\dot{r} = -\mu/(1 + \alpha\beta)$. Previously the attack was timed to avoid an exchange rate jump. The money supply jump exactly matched the money demand jump, so the exchange rate did not change at the moment of the attack. Now, since the money supply is unresponsive to the speculative attack, and since we still prohibit the exchange rate from jumping, the maintenance of money market equilibrium requires the additional condition that the domestic currency interest rate not jump at the time of a foreseen attack. It is evident from inspecting equation (6.12) that the speculative attack will therefore be timed so the upward jump in $\dot{s}$ exactly matches the downward jump in the risk premium.[9]

By adding a risk premium to the simple interest parity condition, we now have a model where sterilization is compatible with a fixed exchange rate. The risk premium adjusts to keep constant the demand for money while sterilization holds the money supply fixed. Yet the introduction of a risk premium into a perfect foresight model is an anomaly, to say the least.[10]

Attacks in Uncertainty

Thus far we have presented models of perfectly foreseen speculative attacks. This is not because attacks are foreseen perfectly, but to show in a simple setting the underlying economic structure of how the private sector responds to inconsistent economic policies. The important contribution of the first-generation models was to show that a large asset market event—an attack—need not be associated with a large shock. Indeed, in our examples so far there are no shocks. When using these models to interpret recent events, however, uncertainty becomes a crucial element. Market participants are never sure when an attack will take place, and they are never sure by how much the exchange rate will change if there is an attack. This uncertainty is reflected in data, in that domestic currency interest rates often rise in anticipation of a crisis.

In the certainty models, the process of fixing an exchange rate that is eventually attacked involves no transfer of wealth from the government to currency speculators. Yet in real-life crises, some people get rich, often at the expense of the government's price-fixing authority. The wealth transfer occurs when agents can buy international reserves from the government at the fixed exchange rate and resell those same reserves immediately at a higher post-crisis exchange rate. With uncertainty, the fixed rate system—with the possibility of attack—provides a free *call option* given by the exchange rate authority to speculators. Extending this analogy, the fixed exchange rate is the option's *strike price* and the quantity optioned is the amount of international reserves backing the fixed exchange rate. Of course, one important difference between an actual market-traded option and the option on the fixed exchange rate policy is that a clear set of property rights comes with the market-traded option but not with the policy option. In an attack, it is not clear how large the reserve commitment is nor how the commitment will be allocated. Will reserves be allocated on a first-come, first-served basis? Will they simply be given to favored insiders? Such pre-attack allocation uncertainty helps explain the crisis atmosphere surrounding actual attack episodes.

For current purposes, however, the important point is that the methods used in options pricing are relevant to understanding the behavior of speculators during a crisis period. In particular, when pricing an option on an asset, the mean and variance of that asset's price as well as other properties of the price distribution are relevant. For this reason, most of the literature on speculative attacks/crises in an uncertain environment relies on specific examples of the distribution function for underlying disturbances. As we shall see below, distribution shapes as well as the usual central moments (mean and variance) can affect policy conclusions.

In one paper where distribution shape matters, Flood and Marion (2000) construct a model with full sterilization and a risk premium in an explicitly stochastic environment. In their setup, the risk premium is derived from expected utility maximization, and the monetary base is held constant before, during, and after the crisis period. With these modifications, the interest parity relation becomes:

$$i = i^* + E_t \tilde{s}_{t+1} - \tilde{s}_t + \beta_t \left(b_t - b_t^* - \tilde{s}_t \right), \tag{6.13}$$

which differs from equation (6.12) in two respects. First, equation (6.13) embeds the risk premium in a discrete time, stochastic framework rather than in a continuous time, perfect foresight one. Second, the coefficient β is now subscripted by t, meaning it can change period by period. In particular, if agents maximize expected utility that is increasing in expected wealth and decreasing in the variance of wealth, then $\beta_t = z \text{Var}_t (\tilde{s}_{t+1})$, where z is a taste-determined constant and $\text{Var}_t(\tilde{S}_{t+1})$ is the conditional variance of the period-ahead shadow rate.

The model contains a nonlinearity in private behavior that admits multiple solutions. From equation (6.13) we see that if agents come to expect more currency variability in the future (a bigger $\text{Var}_t (\tilde{s}_{t+1})$), it affects the domestic interest rate through the uncovered interest parity relation and feeds into the demand for money, making the exchange rate more variable should the fixed rate be abandoned. The shift in expectations, therefore, alters the relevant shadow rate for determining whether an attack is profitable and changes the attack time. With a time-varying stochastic risk premium, currency crises can still be the outcome of inconsistent policies, an important message of the standard first-generation model, but crises can now arise also from self-fulfilling prophecies about exchange market risk for some range of fundamentals. Nonlinearities in private behavior can thus be an additional source of currency crises. Their existence suggests that an economy can jump suddenly from a no-attack equilibrium to an attack equilibrium.

Regime-Conditional Policy: An Introduction to Second-Generation Models

The standard first-generation model combines a linear behavior rule by the private sector (the money demand function) with linear government behavior (domestic credit growth). All of this linearity interacts with the condition that perfectly foreseen profit opportunities be absent in equilibrium to produce a unique time for a foreseen future

speculative attack. Second-generation models abandon the requirement of linear behavior, which often then leads to multiple solutions.
That nonlinear behavior rules by one or more agents can lead to multiple solutions in a model is no surprise to students of economics. An
attribute of second-generation models is that they take seriously one
or more nonlinearities ignored previously.

Second-generation models focus on potentially important nonlinearities in government behavior. They study what happens when
government policy reacts to changes in private behavior or when the
government faces an explicit trade-off between the fixed exchange rate
policy and other objectives. Some of the newer models show that even
when policies are consistent with the fixed exchange rate, attack-
conditional policy changes can *pull* the economy into an attack. In contrast, first-generation models generate an attack by having inconsistent
policies before the attack *push* the economy into a crisis. Other models
show that a shift in market expectations can alter the government's
trade-offs and bring about self-fulfilling crises. The newer models
admit the possibility that the economy can be at a no-attack equilibrium where speculators see but do not pursue available profit opportunities. In such a situation, anything that serves to coordinate the
expectations and actions of speculators can suddenly cause an attack.

Second-generation models emphasize multiple equilibria arising
from nonlinearities in government behavior. These nonlinearities have
been introduced in a variety ways in the literature. Our strategy in presenting this work is to illustrate in some detail two examples of these
nonlinearities.

Example 1
We begin by introducing a policy nonlinearity into the standard first-
generation model we have described already.[11] The policy nonlinearity
we consider is a conditional shift in the growth rate of domestic credit.
If there is no attack on the fixed exchange rate, domestic credit grows
at the rate μ_0; if there is an attack, domestic credit grows at the faster
rate μ_1.

Figure 6.2 duplicates figure 6.1, but now there are two shadow
exchange rate lines, one corresponding to a rate of credit expansion μ_0
and a higher one related to the higher rate of credit expansion μ_1. The
shadow rate line for μ_0 intersects the $\bar{s}$ line at point A and the shadow
rate line for μ_1 intersects at point B. For illustration purposes, suppose

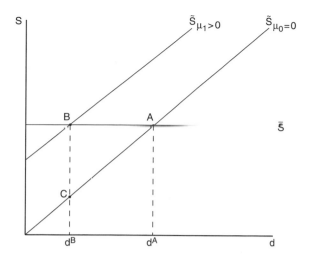

Figure 6.2
Attack times with attack-conditional policy shift

that $\mu_0 = 0$ so that for this policy setting the fixed rate would survive indefinitely for some amounts of domestic credit.

Suppose now that d lies in the range to the left of d^B. If there is no attack, the shadow rate is on the $s_{\mu 0}$ line. If speculators attack, the shadow rate jumps to the $s_{\mu 1}$ line, which is still below the fixed exchange rate. Since any attack leads to capital losses for speculators, there is no incentive to attack the fixed exchange rate if domestic credit is less than d^B. When domestic credit is not growing ($\mu_0 = 0$), the fixed exchange rate policy is compatible with domestic credit policy and the fixed rate survives indefinitely.

Now suppose that domestic credit is at the level d^B, where the $s_{\mu 1}$ shadow rate line intersects the $\bar{s}$ line. With $\mu = \mu_0$, the shadow rate is on the lower line at point C. If speculators attack the fixed rate, the shadow rate jumps from C to B. The attack is successful, but there is no profit for speculators since there is no immediate capital gain on the reserves purchased from the monetary authority. The economy can sit indefinitely at point C or it can move to point B in a speculative attack that ends the fixed exchange rate regime. Equilibrium can occur at either point B or C, but no unrealized profit opportunities drive the economy from point C to point B.

If domestic credit is in the range between d^A and d^B, then multiple equilibria may be possible if speculators are small and uncoordinated as a group or face costs in confronting the government. The economy could reside on the lower shadow rate line indefinitely if agents believe there is no chance that the market will mount an attack. At the other extreme, the economy could jump to the higher shadow rate line if agents are convinced there will be a run on the currency. Convinced of a run, no individual speculator will find it profitable to hold domestic currency since this would result in a sure capital loss when the run occurs. Consequently, all agents will participate in an attack, leading to a collapse of the fixed rate and more expansionary credit policy.

Do multiple equilibria exist when fundamentals range between d^A and d^B? If a large trader can take a massive position against the fixed exchange rate, as George Soros supposedly did against sterling in 1992, then there may be no multiple equilibria. The economy faces only the attack equilibrium since the well-financed speculator always moves to exploit available profit opportunities. But suppose there is no large trader in the foreign exchange market, only many small credit-constrained ones. Then without anything to coordinate their expectations and actions, they cannot mount an attack of sufficient size to move the economy from the no-attack equilibrium to the attack equilibrium. Then, as suggested in Obstfeld 1986b, there are multiple equilibria. The economy can maintain the fixed exchange rate indefinitely unless something coordinates expectations and actions to cause an attack.

The multiple equilibria story provides no explanation of the coordination mechanism—of what causes attacks to occur when they do. When individuals have common knowledge concerning the fundamentals—domestic credit policy in our example—then an explanation of the onset of an attack must appeal to an ad hoc shift in everyone's expectations to move the economy from the no-attack to the attack equilibrium. Ideally, we would like a rationale for the shift in expectations or an understanding of the mechanism for coordinating such a shift.

Morris and Shin (1995) show how some types of uncertainty can eliminate multiple equilibria and make the attack outcome the unique one. They describe a speculative game in which each economic agent obtains information about the state of the economy (domestic credit in our example), but with a small amount of error. Specifically, if the true state of the economy is $\bar{d}$, the agent observes a message that lies in the interval $[\bar{d} - \epsilon, \bar{d} + \epsilon]$, where ϵ is a small positive number and messages are independent across agents. With noisy differential information, it is never common knowledge that the fixed exchange rate is sustainable.

Consequently, each investor must consider the full range of possible beliefs held by others and must contemplate what to do if the parity is unsustainable. If there is a good chance other speculators believe the fixed exchange rate is unsustainable, and if it is not too costly to take a position against the currency, then it makes sense for the individual investor to speculate, even knowing the peg is otherwise viable. Holding onto the currency may yield a bigger gain if everyone else holds on as well, but it is a riskier course of action because it relies on everyone else behaving similarly. Consequently, the only equilibrium in the region bounded between d^A and d^B is the attack equilibrium.[12]

The 1992–1993 currency crisis in Europe has been cited as a case where extreme beliefs moved the market. While the Bundesbank's lukewarm support of some exchange rate mechanism (ERM) parities was well known in 1992, each new announcement by central bank officials caused commentators to debate anew the strength of the German commitment. In such a situation, even if an investor believes the fixed exchange rate to be sustainable, he has to worry about whether others interpret official announcements the same way. Therefore, a crisis can be caused by traders worried about the beliefs of others.

A related but separate explanation for the onset of a currency attack is information cascades. The cascades story, described in more detail in Banerjee 1992 and Bikhchandani, Hirshleifer, and Welch 1992, relies on actual observations of others' actions and, in contrast to Morris and Shin 1995, the lack of common knowledge about the state of fundamentals plays no important role. Although the information cascade phenomenon has not been formally applied to currency attacks, the argument might go as follows.[13] Suppose each investor has some information about the state of the economy (in our setup, about the range for domestic credit) and decides sequentially and publicly whether to hold the currency or sell it. If the first n investors happen to receive bad signals and sell, then the $(n + 1)$th investor may choose to ignore his own information—even if it is positive about the viability of the fixed exchange rate—and sell, based on the revealed information of those who came before him. This sequential decision rule results in "herd" behavior. People will be doing what others are doing rather than using their own information. Consequently, if some traders start selling the currency, others will join the herd, moving the economy from the no-attack to the attack equilibrium.

While there may be some elements of a cascades story in currency attacks, there are reasons to think that it is not the whole story. First, in an environment where traders can adjust their strategies continuously to new information, it is unlikely that individuals ignore their own information or new information. (Lee 1993 and Morris and Shin 1995). Second, if strategic interactions are important, it may be unsatisfactory to rely on a cascades story where the potential capital gain arising from the action of one agent does not depend on the actions chosen by others. (See Morris and Shin 1995).

Calvo and Mendoza (1995) depart from the sequential decision-making framework in Banerjee and consider instead a global market with many identical investors forming decisions simultaneously. They show that with informational frictions, herding behavior may become more prevalent as the world capital market grows. Globalization reduces the incentives to collect country-specific information to discredit rumors and increases the likelihood that fund managers who worry about their relative performance will each select the same portfolio. Consequently, small rumors can induce herding behavior and move the economy from the no-attack to the attack equilibrium.

Where does all this leave us? In the model described by figure 6.2, where policy responds to an attack, we can characterize four situations depending on the size of the state variable, d. In the first situation, $d < d^B$ and the post-attack policy shift offers no incentive to attack. In the second situation, $d = d^B$ and there is no profit in an attack but neither is there a loss. Points B and C are both viable equilibria. The economy can experience an attack or not depending on speculators' animal spirits rather than on profit opportunities. In the third situation, $d^B < d < d^A$, and multiple equilibria are possible if there are many small traders who must wait for some mechanism to coordinate their actions. The fourth situation occurs when $d \geq d^A$. Here, the fixed exchange rate is attacked.

Example 2

The second example of policy nonlinearity comes from Obstfeld (1994), who derived a closed-form solution for a monetary rule with an escape clause.[14] We present a simplified version of the Obstfeld model and use it as a vehicle to illustrate: (1) the role of an explicitly optimizing government, (2) the surprising policy implications present in many models that admit multiple solutions, (3) the optimal degree of commitment to a fixed exchange rate or, alternatively, the optimal attack frequency, and (4) a suggested reconciliation of first and second-generation approaches.

In the Obstfeld model, the government's optimizing behavior is at the center of the analysis and private behavior is kept in the background. Suppose that the government conducts exchange rate policy according to

$$\min L = \frac{\theta}{2}\delta^2 + \frac{(\delta - E\delta - u - k)^2}{2},$$ (6.14)

where L is the social loss function; δ is the rate of currency depreciation; $E\delta$ is the expected rate of currency depreciation; u is a zero-mean disturbance with variance σ^2; k is a measure of distortion; and θ is the relative weight attached to price changes.[15] All of the variables in this model are realized in the same period except the expectations operator, E, which is based on past information, so we drop the time dating. Two modes of policymaking are studied normally: (1) a rule and (2) discretion. The rule requires the government to set policy regardless of the current state of the economy (e.g., the disturbance u) and discretion allows the government to set policy after observing the state, including predetermined expectations.

Equation (6.14) is an adaptation of the Kydland and Prescott 1977, Barro and Gordon 1983 model of *time inconsistent* policymaking. Kydland and Prescott showed that policymaking is systematically inflationary when it is based on predetermined expectations in a distorted environment. The government is tempted each period to exploit predetermined private expectations to expand the economy and overcome the distortion. The private sector understands the nature of the temptation that the government faces, however. The private sector therefore expects inflation (devaluation in Obstfeld's model) and it turns out to be optimal for the government to validate that expectation.

We calculate the expected value of the loss function in (6.14) first for the rule, which we take to be a fixed exchange rate ($\delta = 0$), and then for discretion. Forming expectations in accord with the rule, the private sector sets $E\delta = 0$ so that

$$EL^R = \frac{\sigma^2 + k^2}{2},$$ (6.15)

where EL^R is the expected value of the loss function if the government follows the rule. If the government follows discretion, the private sector understands this policy and forms $E\delta^D = k/\theta$. Then (with $\theta = 1$ for simplicity) the expected value of the loss function becomes

$$EL^D = \frac{\sigma^2}{4} + k^2.$$ 　　　　　　　　　　　　　　　　　　　　　(6.16)

Equations (6.15) and (6.16) illustrate the Kydland and Prescott result: Absent shocks ($\sigma^2 = 0$), society is unambiguously worse off with discretion than with a rule, but when the rule cannot stipulate the course of action for every possible shock that could hit the economy, discretion may be superior. Clearly EL^D is better than EL^R for sufficiently high σ^2 relative to k.

More generally, the government should pursue a mixed strategy: follow the rule most of the time but invoke an escape clause from time to time when the disturbance turns out to be particularly disruptive. Of course, it must be made costly to the government to invoke the escape clause, otherwise discretion will always be followed. With an escape clause, the government follows the rule whenever:

$$L^R < L^D + C,$$ 　　　　　　　　　　　　　　　　　　　　　(6.17)

where C is a cost imposed whenever the escape clause is chosen. In Obstfeld's example, invoking the escape clause means devaluing the currency.

For a given value of C, the policymaker's problem is to decide the value of the disturbance that triggers the escape clause. That value is $\bar{u}$, where $\bar{u}$ solves

$$L^R(\bar{u}) = L^D(\bar{u}) + C.$$ 　　　　　　　　　　　　　　　　　(6.18)

Equation (6.18) is nonlinear in part because of the statistical problem individuals face at the beginning of the period when forming their expectations about the rate of currency depreciation. Before they see whether the rule or discretion is chosen, individuals set their expectation about the rate of currency depreciation by calculating a probability-weighted average of the expected rate to be chosen under the rule, $E\delta^R = 0$, and the expected rate to be chosen under discretion, $E\delta^R > 0$.

We portray in figure 6.3 the nonlinear problem as presented in Obstfeld 1994. In the figure, the curved line plots (a function of) $L^R - L^D$ and the horizontal line represents (a function of) an arbitrary level C.[16] The two lines intersect twice, once at a low value for the disturbance, $\bar{u}_L$, and again at higher one, $\bar{u}_H$. If the private sector adopts $\bar{u}_H$ as its belief about the level of the disturbance at which the government will abandon the rule, then the government finds that adopting this value

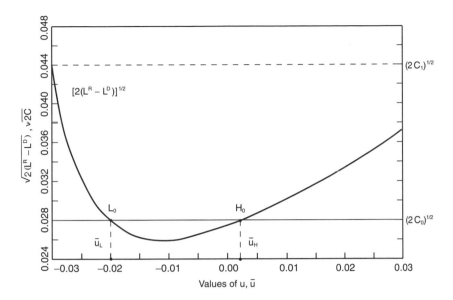

Figure 6.3
Multiple Solutions with Uniform Shock

solves the government's optimization problem as well. Consequently, this value of the disturbance is the one that triggers the escape clause. Similarly, if the private sector adopts $\bar{u}_L$ as its belief about the trip switch, then it is optimal for the government to adopt this value instead.[17]

Flood and Marion (1997b) study the policy implications of taking seriously both equilibria depicted in figure 6.3. They find that in an environment where the economy can jump from one equilibrium to another, increasing the cost of abandoning the fixed exchange rate may make a crisis more likely. This is clear from figure 6.3. If the economy regularly finds itself at equilibrium L_0, then raising C by a small amount lowers the value of the disturbance that triggers an attack and makes the crisis more likely.

C may be thought of as commitment staked on the fixed exchange rate. For example, convergence of the European Monetary System toward European Monetary Union is an increase in the cost of breaking the fixed exchange rate arrangement. According to this model, when multiple equilibria are a serious empirical possibility, tightening the commitment to the fixed rate may be exactly the wrong policy prescription. Raising the cost might make crises more frequent.[18]

Optimal Commitment to a Fixed Rate

Usually the cost of breaking the rule is interpreted as the loss to the government of reputation or credibility or the deadweight loss to society as a whole. Isard's (1995) work suggests another interpretation. The cost can be viewed, at least in part, as the capital gain foregone by the monetary authority—or the capital gain awarded to speculators— in the event the domestic currency is devalued. What is relevant to speculators is the size of the prospective devaluation multiplied by the reserve loss tolerated by the authority during a crisis. If this amount is small, the defense is half-hearted. If it is very large, then the currency peg may be nearly permanent.

Isard's (1995) interpretation is particularly nice in the present context for two reasons. First, it allows us to use economic incentives to distinguish among equilibria in Obstfeld's model. Suppose that a certain portion of the cost is distributed to speculators each time the fixed rate is attacked successfully. Other things equal, speculators prefer to settle on the solution where attacks are *most frequent*. This suggests that the economically relevant solution in these models is always at the lowest $\bar{u}$ solution. Second, interpreting this cost as (in part) the commitment to the fixed exchange rate leads naturally to thinking about the optimal commitment.

Viewed in this way, recent research on currency crises provides an interesting extension to Mundell's (1961) famous analysis of optimal currency areas. While Mundell's work directed attention toward forming permanent cross-country (or cross-area) currency arrangements, events have shown that all cross-country currency arrangements are ultimately temporary. Policymakers realize that they are faced with two important decisions. Not only do they have to select the appropriate exchange rate arrangement, they must worry also about how tightly to hold onto it. For countries adopting a fixed exchange rate, does research on currency crises provide any guidance about how strongly to defend a parity?

One answer to this question lies just below the surface in many second-generation models.[19] Suppose the cost imposed on the government when it breaks the fixed exchange rate rule is not a fixed parameter. While the cost must be exogenous from the monetary authority's perspective, it may be chosen by some higher entity ("society") to minimize expected social loss.[20] This optimal cost can be interpreted as the optimal level of support for the fixed rate. What is the size of this optimal cost? What does it imply for the optimal attack frequency?

We explore these questions in a pair of simulation models that differ only in their assumptions about the shape of the shock distribution hitting the economy. We consider two well-known distributions—uniform and normal—and find that the optimal level of support for the fixed exchange rate depends on the distribution of the shock.[21]

Again we use Obstfeld's model and his parameter values. In the first simulation, the shock is distributed uniformly and we calculate the expected social loss under the rule, discretion and the escape-clause policy. The loss under the escape clause is calculated for each level of $\bar{u}$, the threshold value of the disturbance that triggers an attack and a devaluation. The three expected social losses are plotted in figure 6.4.[22]

The vertical axis in figure 6.4 is obtained by scaling the expected social loss by $1/N$, where N is the amount society would be willing to pay for reducing the annual inflation/depreciation rate from 10 percent to 3 percent.[23] The various expected loss magnitudes can therefore be interpreted as the amount society would be willing to pay to defend the fixed exchange rate relative to the amount it would be willing to pay to reduce inflation from 10 to 3 percent. The horizontal axis in figure 6.4 is scaled to duplicate the numerical example in Obstfeld (1994), who worked with a uniform shock over the range [−0.03, 0.03]. For Obstfeld's uniform shock, figure 6.4 shows that the expected loss from discretion is always greater than the expected loss from permanently fixing the exchange rate. For a higher shock variance, the rankings can switch, however.

Inspecting figure 6.4, we also see that for very low $\bar{u}$, near −0.03, the expected loss from the mixed strategy is quite high—well above both the rule and discretion. As $\bar{u}$ rises, the expected loss from the mixed strategy falls. It eventually becomes less than the expected loss from discretion and finally approaches the expected loss from fixing permanently. Consequently in the Obstfeld model, using his parameter values and uniform shocks, the escape-clause policy is never optimal. By implication, the cost of abandoning the fixed exchange rate rule should be set so high that the currency is never devalued.[24]

How general is this result? From our simulations we know that it is specific to Obstfeld's parameters and to the variance of his shock. It is also specific to the uniform distribution. The uniform is special because its box shape cuts off its tails, and it is in the tails that discretion (devaluation) finds its advantage.

We next simulate the model for a normally distributed shock whose variance is equal to that in the uniform example and depict the results in figures 6.5 and 6.6. Figure 6.5 is the exact counterpart to figure 6.3,

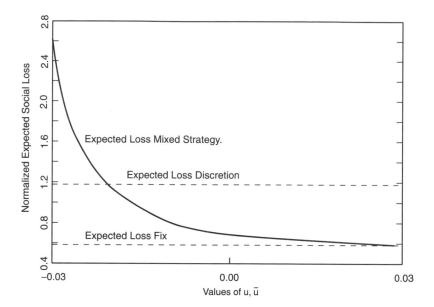

Figure 6.4
Expected social loss with uniform shock

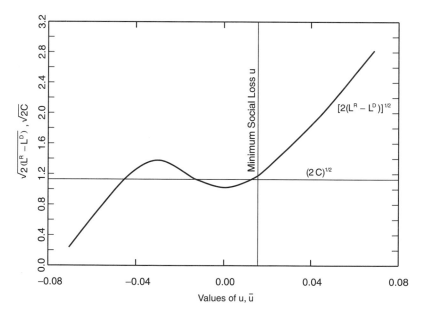

Figure 6.5
Multiple solutions with normal shock

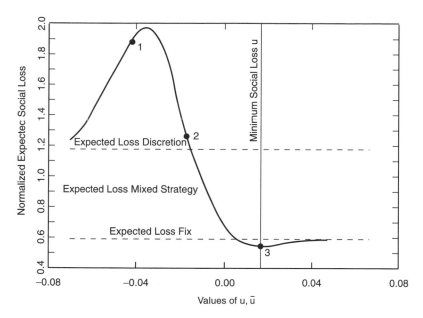

Figure 6.6
Expected social loss with normal shock

except constructed for normal shocks. From inspection of figure 6.5 multiple equilibria are clearly possible for an intermediate range of C. While possible, are the multiple equilibria relevant when C is set appropriately?

Figure 6.6 plots expected social losses for the three relevant strategies: the rule (fix irrevocably), discretion (devaluation period-by-period) and the mixed strategy (devalue when the shock exceeds a lower bound, $\bar{u}$). It is the counterpart to figure 6.4 but constructed for the normal distribution. What we see now is that the expected loss from the mixed strategy is no longer monotonic in $\bar{u}$. For low values of $\bar{u}$, it exceeds the loss from discretion. As $\bar{u}$ increases, the expected loss from the mixed strategy rises, reaches its maximum, and then falls to a minimum. Around the minimum, the expected social loss from the mixed strategy is smaller than the loss under the rule or discretion.

The value of C that produces the minimum expected loss for the mixed strategy shows that the resources devoted to maintaining the fixed rate should be no more than two-thirds the resource value of reducing inflation from 10 to 3 percent.[25] This value of C also produces multiple solutions for $\bar{u}$, the escape clause trigger. This result can be seen in figure 6.5, where the corresponding value of this C intersects the curved line $\sqrt{2(L^R - L^D)}$ three times. This solution multiplicity (three solutions here) is the counterpart to the two internal solutions that turned up in the example with a uniformly distributed shock.

The three solution values for $\bar{u}$ are mapped into figure 6.6 and give three possible expected losses for the mixed strategy at points 1, 2, and 3. The expected losses at points 1 and 2 are much greater than the loss at point 3. More important, if C is set to achieve the minimum expected loss, there is no guarantee that the economy will settle on the highest trigger value for the escape clause. Indeed, our earlier line of argument about relevant solutions suggests that the economically relevant solution—the one speculators would prefer—is the solution at point 1. Expected social loss at this solution is distinctly inferior to both the rule and discretion.

In order to avoid the solution multiplicity illustrated in figure 6.5, C could be set high enough to make the solution unique. This requires that C be at level where the resources supporting the fixed exchange rate are about 80 percent of the resources used to reduce inflation to from 10 to 3 percent. At this unique solution, the annual probability of speculative attack is about 10 percent, so that expected regime duration is around ten years. In other words, fixed exchange rate regimes will be attacked on average once every ten years. The "second-best" optimum gives an expected social loss above the loss at the (possibly unobtainable) social optimum, but the difference is small. The expected social loss of the second-best mixed strategy is less than the loss under discretion or under the irrevocably-fixed exchange rate rule, but it is not much less than the loss under the rule.

In the optimal currency area literature that followed Mundell, choosing the appropriate exchange rate regime often required knowing the mean and variance of the relevant shocks. The present analysis suggests that these central moments are relevant but they are not enough. In our simulations of the escape-clause model, the mean and variance of the shock are identical across the uniform and normal distributions, but the shapes of the two distributions give different policy guidance. With uniform shocks, having a speculative attack is never optimal; with the normal shocks, it is optimal to have an attack on occasion (about every ten years on average in our numerical example). The difference in optimal attack frequencies is due entirely to the shape of underlying shock distributions. The uniform distribution has short tails while the normal one has long tails. Extreme shock outcomes are thus more likely when shocks are distributed normally. While the escape clause should never be used for the uniform shocks, it should be invoked periodically if the economy typically faces normal shocks. After all, the whole reason for the escape clause is to have a contingency for extreme events.

Our example with one real shock and a simple rule suggests an intuitively pleasing addendum to Mundell's optimal currency area principle: holding shock variance constant, commitment to a fixed exchange rate should be inversely related to the likelihood of extreme shocks.

A Suggestion for a Common Cross-Generation Framework

The first- and second-generation models we have explored differ in a variety of ways, but most of the differences can be traced to one crucial assumption: first-generation models assume the commitment to a fixed exchange rate is state invariant whereas second-generation models allow it to be state-dependent.

The assumption of a state-invariant commitment does not square well with common observations or with careful empirical work. The government's commitment to the fixed exchange rate is often constrained by such factors as unemployment, the fragility of the banking system, the size of the public debt, or upcoming elections.[26] Recognizing that these factors affect the government's ultimate commitment to the fixed exchange rate is a major contribution of the second-generation work.

In many second-generation models, the constraints on government actions enter the social loss function as explicit policy objectives. Once we interpret the cost C as (in part) the optimal degree of reserve commitment to the fixed rate, then the state variables influence that commitment as well. For example, if the output distortion (k) in the Obstfeld model depends on lagged unemployment, n_{t-1}, then the optimal C is a function of n_{t-1}. As a linearization we can write

$$C_t = \lambda_0 + \lambda_1 \eta_{t-1}. \tag{6.19}$$

In the first-generation models, the government's commitment to the fixed exchange rate does not depend on such factors as the state of the business cycle. Instead, its commitment is modeled by setting post-attack international reserves, $\tilde{r}$, as a state-invariant constant, usually zero for simplicity.[27] As a result, the post-attack reserve level enters the shadow exchange rate equation as a constant or not at all.

Instead of having the post-attack reserve level be a fixed number, suppose it is chosen optimally period by period to minimize a government loss function that includes unemployment or other objectives. In the same way that state variables affect the cost in the escape clause model, we now have state variables affect the reserve commitment to the fixed rate

$$\tilde{r}_t = \gamma_0 + \gamma_1 \eta_{t-1}. \tag{6.20}$$

Where post-attack reserves were set at zero previously, they now depend on unemployment or any other state variable that influences the governments loss function.

Making $\tilde{r}_t$ endogenous implies having the government control part of the behavior of the shadow exchange rate period by period. A first-generation policy authority now has the same room to maneuver accorded in the second generation. In particular, in the basic model of the "First-Generation Models" Section, $r_t - \tilde{r}_t$ is now the maximum unsterilized intervention to be undertaken in defense of the fixed rate. The government can thus engineer the size of the attack-conditional exchange rate jump. For example, suppose that a first-generation government faces Obstfeld's trade-off between inflation and employment and that the government's only policy tool is to pick the maximum size of the commitment to unsterilized intervention—that is, to pick the reserve level at which the fixed rate is to be abandoned. This simply amounts to letting the jump to the shadow rate replace the depreciation rate in Obstfeld's problem. The reserve commitment enters the shadow rate equation and this is the tool the policymaker uses to control the shadow rate. The period-by-period optimal reserve commitment will be influenced by the state variables in the government's choice problem. While the potential profit opportunities for speculators are still crucial to the outcome, unemployment, the fragility of the banking system, and other state variables also influence the timing of currency crises.[28]

Making the commitment to the fixed exchange rate state-dependent in the first-generation model provides a potential reconciliation of first and second-generation models. This reconciliation is attractive for three reasons:

1. It gives policymakers in first-generation models the same degrees of freedom accorded them in second-generation models.

2. It keeps interactions between speculators and the government at center stage. This focus is especially important for presenting these

ideas to nonspecialist audiences. The degree of monetary policy commitment (unsterilized intervention) to the fixed rate versus other policy goals is the key for policymakers and speculators alike. It is very much in the spirit of Krugman's original probing speculators who had to guess at the reserve commitment to the fixed rate.

3. It allows the first-generation models to pick up what we think is the most important contribution of the second-generation models—state dependence of regime commitment—in a simple and intuitive way.

There are some drawbacks, however:

1. Without reconciliation, second-generation models seemed to avoid the chronic problem of relying on a tenuous foreign exchange market model to analyze currency crises. We think that this avoidance is an illusion, however. Speculators are an important part of speculative attacks. Modeling speculative profits seems essential to a complete story.

2. Without reconciliation, first-generation models with state-invariant reserve commitments were simple, depending only on parameters and fundamentals appearing in the money market. Adding a policy choice function adds several parameters to the shadow rate equation, but these are not literally free parameters. They should vary in predictable ways across policy choices.

Recent Empirical Work

The currency crises of the 1990s have raised questions about whether currency crises are predictable events with systematic early warning signals or whether they are essentially unpredictable, like stock market crashes.

To the extent that speculative attacks are predictable events, recent theoretical work has expanded the list of potential market fundamentals that can predict them. Indeed, any economic objective that is conceivably part of the government's social welfare function and whose attainment involves a trade-off with the fixity of the exchange rate is a potential fundamentals candidate. Focusing on a broader set of fundamentals, including unemployment and the state of the banking system, improves our ability to predict some currency crises, but it is hard to generalize these results since the relative importance of various fundamentals can vary over time for a single country and vary across countries during a single time period.

Prior to the events of the 1990s, currency crises were thought to have a significant predictable component, with the standard first-generation models identifying fundamentals useful for prediction. A fiscal deficit financed by domestic credit creation was considered to be the root cause of a speculative attack. As the monetary authority monetized the budget deficit, it caused a gradual decline in international reserves. Eventually, investors attacked the fixed exchange rate, depleting the government's reserve holdings used for a defense. Home goods prices began rising before the attack. These price increases led to a real exchange rate appreciation and a widening current account deficit prior to an attack. Empirical work on pre-1990s currency crises confirmed this pattern in the data.

For example, Blanco and Garber (1986) used a variant of the Krugman-Flood-Garber model to predict the timing of devaluations brought on by attacks on the Mexican peso over the 1973–1982 period. Using a structural model, they estimated the objective probability that the shadow rate would exceed the fixed rate in the next quarter. Their probability estimates were around 2–5 percent in tranquil times but rose above 20 percent before the 1976 and 1982 devaluations. The size of the probability estimates indicates that while the devaluations were not anticipated fully, neither were they a complete surprise. Further, the rate of domestic credit growth and the standard money demand variables were important determinants of the probability of devaluation. This work was extended by Goldberg (1994). Cumby and van Wijnbergen (1989) used a similar approach and found that the growth of domestic credit was the main factor behind the attack on the Argentine crawling peg of the early 1980s.

These studies used economic models to interpret data for particular countries in specific time periods, leaving open the question about the generality of the results. Later studies, using a nonstructural approach to analyze crisis episodes in a set of countries before the 1990s, confirmed the role of traditional fundamentals in predicting crises. For example, Edwards (1989) examined the evolution of a number of key variables during the three years preceding each of thirty-nine devaluation episodes in developing countries between 1962 and 1983. Comparing the outcomes with those from a control group that maintained a fixed exchange rate for at least ten years, he found that as the year of devaluation drew nearer, macroeconomic policies became increasingly expansive in the devaluing countries, the real exchange rate appreciated, the current account balance declined and there was an important rundown of international reserves. Klein and Marion (1997) used panel data for eighty devaluation episodes in Latin American countries during the 1957–1991 period and found the monthly probability of abandoning a pegged exchange rate increased with real overvaluation and declined with the level of foreign assets. Structural factors, such as the openness of the economy and its geographical trade concentration, political variables, such as changes in the executive, and time already spent on the peg also influenced the monthly probability of ending a fixed exchange rate.

The speculative attacks of the 1990s, particularly those in Europe, challenged the view that currency crises were due largely to the government's inability to achieve fiscal and monetary discipline. For many countries, these crises were not preceded by overly expansionary policies. In trying to understand the origins of these recent crises, a number of researchers have turned to exploratory empirical models that use a wide variety of information variables to distinguish between periods leading up to currency crises and tranquil periods. As examples of this type of work we shall review the studies of Eichengreen, Rose, and Wyplosz (1995); Sachs, Tornell, and Velasco (1996a); and Kaminsky, Lizando, and Reinhart (1997).[29]

Eichengreen, Rose, and Wyplosz (1995) (ERW) study a panel of twenty industrial countries over the 1959–1993 period. They depart from previous empirical work by constructing a definition of a currency crisis and then letting the data choose the episodes for study. ERW use the Girton and Roper (1977) idea of "speculative pressure," which is measured as a weighted average of exchange rate changes, interest rate changes and (the negative of) reserve changes. ERW then define speculative attacks as periods when this index of speculative pressure reaches extreme values.[30] In practice, ERW define extreme values to be those at least two standard deviations above the mean. They also conduct sensitivity analysis and discover that their results are "largely robust to [the] choice of weighting scheme." (ERW, 278, fn. 37)

In symbols, the ERW definition of crisis is as follows:

$$\text{Crisis if: } K_t = w_1 \Delta s_t + w_2(-\Delta r_t) + w_3 \Delta i_t > T, \tag{6.21}$$

where K_t is the ERW index of speculative pressure, the w_i are weights and T is the two-standard-deviation threshold.[31]

What do the attack models lead us to expect about the behavior of the pressure index, K_t? If the attack is anticipated perfectly and follows the pattern of the Krugman model literally, then at the moment of the attack international reserves drop by a discrete amount, the domestic currency interest rate jumps up by the size of the expected rate of depreciation, and there is no change in the exchange rate. Thus reserves and interest rates should both jump and the pressure index, K_t, will pick up the attack.

Now relax the Krugman assumptions that the opportunity cost of holding money is given by a zero-maturity domestic currency interest rate and that the crisis is foreseen perfectly. With a longer-term interest rate and uncertainty, the relevant interest rate will begin rising before the crisis, so reserves will leak out faster prior to the attack.[32] At the moment of attack, reserves still drop and the interest rate still jumps up, but the size of each jump is reduced to the extent the attack is anticipated. Since the crisis is only partly anticipated, the exchange rate will jump up also at the attack time. The important point is that the size of all these jumps is reduced at the attack time by the extent to which the attack is anticipated. Selecting only extreme values of K as a measure of crisis may reduce the share of predictable crises in the sample.

Next, depart from the Krugman scheme by allowing the crisis to end with a devaluation rather than with a float. Suppose further that the post-devaluation regime is expected to be stable, at least extending beyond the maturity of domestic currency interest rates used in money demand. Then in the period leading up to the devaluation, even if the crisis is only partially anticipated, domestic currency interest rates will rise to compensate domestic currency bond holders for the impending devaluation. Immediately following the devaluation, however, domestic currency interest rates will fall back to the level of foreign currency interest rates. Reserves, which flowed out of the domestic country before the crisis (because of expanding fundamentals and reduced money demand) will flow back into the domestic country to satisfy increased money demand.[33] Of course, in the event of the devaluation the exchange rate increases.

To the extent that the devaluation is anticipated, two of the three ERW indicators *point in the wrong direction* at the devaluation time. We emphasize that this analysis is not an impeachment of the ERW definition because the ERW definition does a good job at catching historical episodes that we would have classified as crises according to our prior beliefs. What it means is that if the Krugman model is correct, the ERW selection method of choosing extreme values of K predisposes the sample towards crises with significant unpredictable components.

How well does the ERW method predict crises? If crises have large unpredictable components, the pressure index K will more likely reach an extreme value, but the more unpredictable the crises, the less likely they are to be significantly correlated with the information variables selected as possible crisis determinants. Thus the empirical methods may not be able to predict these crises very well. Moreover, if the potential determinants of currency crises differ across countries and across time, panel regressions that look for consistent patterns may perform poorly.

ERW find that crises by their definition "tend to occur when unemployment is high and when political circumstances are unpropitious" (283) We interpret their findings to mean that data-defined crises are hard to predict using standard fundamentals and panel methods.[34]

ERW try to predict currency crises in industrial countries, the same low-inflation countries for which models of exchange rate determination perform poorly on fairly high frequency data.[35] Other empirical researchers have examined currency crises in developing countries, where larger variations in the data may help improve the predictive power of these models. Kaminsky, Lizando, and Reinhart (1998) (KLR), for example, apply a version of the ERW technique to a panel of fifteen developing and five developed countries.[36] They find that a number of variables, including traditional fundamentals, help predict crises.[37] Sachs, Tornell, and Velasco (1996a) (STV) compute an ERW-style pressure index variable for a sample of twenty developing countries over the 1994–1995 period. STV regress the actual monthly value of the index, which excludes interest rates, on nonlinear combinations of the real exchange rate, a measure of bank loan growth (an indicator of bank fragility) and the ratio of country M2 to reserves (an indicator of reserve adequacy). All three variables are found to be important predictors of movements in the pressure index.

The studies we have reviewed differ in sample selection methods and in the use of prior information. As is usual in international finance, developing countries (unfortunately) have much more data variance than industrial countries. Consequently, the empirical models do better at identifying variables that are significantly correlated with crises. While the empirical work on developing countries still finds an important role for traditional market fundamentals such as domestic credit growth, it goes a bit farther. In developing countries there is evidence that (1) the level of liquidity relative to reserves seems to be a good predictor of currency crises, and (2) a variety of indicators of economic conditions (e.g., recessions, the state of the banking system, monetary policy, and international interest rates) seem to matter for crises.

Conclusion

The currency crises of the 1990s have made us appreciate the fragility of fixed exchange rate regimes. Responsibility for these crises cannot be placed entirely on the shoulders of poorly behaved governments who pursue excessively expansionary policies. While some governments make policy mistakes and are disciplined eventually, others face hard policy choices not entirely of their own making. When speculators sense that a fixed parity is tightly constrained by other policy goals, that parity may be prone to attack.

Evidence to date reinforces the view that currency crises are not all alike (see Calvo 1995). Some crises, particularly those in developing countries, have a significant predictable component. Others may have a predictable component only in hindsight, once we broaden our notion of the fundamentals affecting the strategic interactions of governments and speculators. Still other crises are difficult to interpret exclusively on the basis of fundamentals and have led to new explanations based on informational frictions and herding behavior. We note, however, that the speculative attacks we understand least well occur in foreign exchange markets that we understand equally poorly.

Notes

This chapter is based on a paper that was presented at a Washington, D.C., conference honoring Robert Mundell on October 23–24, 1997. It is also reprinted with permission from *International Journal of Finance and Economics* 4 (1): 1–26 (John Wiley and Sons, publisher). We thank the 1997 Dartmouth College Summer Camp, Joshua Aizenman, Guillermo Calvo, Michael Connolly, Barry Eichengreen, Peter Garber, Michael Klein, Maurice Obstfeld, and Andrew Rose for helpful discussions.

1. The first-generation model was developed by economists working at the Board of Governors of the Federal Reserve System. Building on Hotelling 1931, Federal Reserve economists Steven Salant and Dale Henderson (1978) built a speculative attack model to study attacks on a government-controlled price of gold. Soon after the Salant-Henderson model was drafted, Paul Krugman visited the Federal Reserve and recognized that the Salant-Henderson analysis could be applied to fixed exchange rates. This led to Krugman 1979. While Robert Flood was an Economist at the Federal Reserve, he and Peter Garber constructed a linear model that simplified Krugman's account and extended the model to a stochastic environment. The result was Flood and Garber 1984b. While Peter Garber visited the Federal Reserve, he and Herminio Blanco developed the first structural test of the first-generation model, Blanco and Garber 1986.

2. For expositional purposes we adopt a simple linearization in equation (6.2). In empirical work, however, money might be log linearized as $m_t = a_o + a_1 d_t + a_2 r_t$, where $a_1 = D_t/M_t$ and $a_2 = (1 - a_1)$ at the point of linearization, usually the sample mean.

3. With the money market expanded appropriately, the model was applied to Mexican data in Blanco and Garber 1986 and to Argentine data in Cumby and van Wijnbergen 1989.

4. In general, the shadow rate is influenced by the amount of reserves the government continues to hold following its optimal defense of the fixed rate. For now, we set the log of reserves at zero after the attack. See section entitled "A Suggestion for a Common Cross-Generation Framework" for further discussion of this point.

5. For simplicity we set $i^* = p^* = 0$.

6. Similar timing equations are derived in Connolly and Taylor 1984 and Flood and Garber 1984b.

7. The importance of this point is hard to overemphasize. If the monetary authority is unwilling to allow monetary policy to play a secondary role to exchange rate policy—at least some of the time—then *any* fixed rate backed by *any* quantity of international reserves is at risk when capital is freely mobile. This conclusion contrasts strongly with much advice concerning "sufficient" reserve backing of currency pegs.

8. See Willman 1988.

9. After an attack the exchange rate reverts to its shadow value, $\tilde{s}$. For this portfolio-balance model of the exchange rate, the shadow rate is given by: $\tilde{s} = \kappa_0 + \kappa_1 d$, where $\kappa_1 = 1/(1 + \alpha\beta)$. At the instant of the attack, $\dot{s}$ jumps from zero to $\kappa_1\mu$ and the risk premium jumps down by $\beta 2\Delta r$, where Δr is the size of the attack. The "2" enters this expression because the attack is sterilized. The government uses domestic high-power money to buy domestic securities and compensate for the reserve loss, thereby decreasing the risk premium. In addition, the reserves held by the domestic central bank are now in private hands, reducing the risk premium again by the size of the attack.

When does this attack occur? The attack takes place when the interest rate will not jump and that happens when $\kappa_1\mu = -\beta 2\Delta r$. Therefore, the attack size is $\Delta r = -\kappa_1\mu/(2\beta)$. During the fixed-rate period reserves follow $r(t) = r(0) - (\mu t/(1 + \alpha\beta))$. Since the attack takes place precisely when $r = \Delta r$, it follows that the attack takes place when

$$T = \frac{r(0)(1+\alpha\beta)}{\mu} - \frac{1}{2\beta}.$$

As $b \rightarrow 0$ the attack is pushed toward the present.

10. It is tempting to dismiss sterilized intervention because of poor empirical performance (e.g., Frankel 1984), but that may be an overreaction. Recall that *no* exchange rate or other asset price model or any simple (nonarbitrage) parity condition works well for high-frequency, post–WWII industrial country data. Our asset market models serve, however, as intellectual organizing devices for discussions about foreign exchange and other asset markets.

11. This nonlinearity was suggested to Flood and Garber in private correspondence by Steven Salant. It first appeared in print in Flood and Garber 1984a, which was initiated in a set of briefing memos to the Federal Reserve governors serving on the Gold Commission. This nonlinearity was developed further by Obstfeld (1986b). Another early example is presented in Calvo 1988.

12. Morris and Shin (1995) show that multiple equilibria can exist for some departures from perfect information. For instance, if all investors observe a public signal about the true state of fundamentals, then the signal is common knowledge and the state of fundamentals is commonly known even if the signal does not give an accurate picture of the fundamentals. In such a situation, it is possible to have multiple equilibria.

13. The argument is presented in Morris and Shin 1995.

14. Rules with an escape clause were introduced by Flood and Isard (1989) and studied by Persson and Tabellini (1990) and Lohmann (1992).

15. Time-series variation in employment shocks may be embedded in k. Equation (6.14) is a simpler version of the loss function in Obstfeld 1994. It captures the government's attempt to minimize both actual price changes and a function of unexpected price changes. The government wants to minimize actual price changes for credibility reasons or to reduce distortions in cash balance holdings. The government wants to minimize a function of unexpected price changes to stabilize employment or business cycles.

16. The curved line is actually $\sqrt{2(L^R - L^D)}$ and the horizontal line is $\sqrt{2C}$. See Obstfeld 1994 for the specific functional forms for L^R and L^D.

17. As in Obstfeld 1994, we focus only on the interior solutions. The horizontal line at $\sqrt{2C}$ intersects the vertical axis. This left intersection is also an equilibrium of the model. This equilibrium will become an interior one in the normal distribution example in the next section.

18. If the private sector's expectations about future currency depreciation are dampened by increasing the opting-out cost, there may be less chance of the economy jumping to the lower equilibrium. But as long as there is the possibility of multiple equilibria, one equilibrium behaves perversely.

19. See e.g., Obstfeld 1997.

20. In a different context, Alexius (1997) also calculates the optimal cost in an escape clause model.

21. We use simulation models so we can check that our results will hold up for samples about as large as quarterly World War II data sets. They do. Figures 6.3–6.6 are plotted for much larger data sets.

22. The curve *Expected Loss, Mixed Strategy* in figures 6.4 and 6.6 is based on

$$E(L_{mixed}) = p(u < \bar{u})EL(u < \bar{u}) + [1 - p(u < \bar{u})][EL(u > \bar{u}) + C(\bar{u})],$$

where we treat C as part of the social loss. Note that for each level of $\bar{u}$ there is a uniquely associated cost. In general, a parameter may be attached to $C(\bar{u})$, reflecting that C may not be entirely social loss.

23. $N = (\theta/2)(0.10^2)(0.03^2)$, where the weight attached to reducing price variability in the loss function is $\theta = 0.15$, as in Obstfeld 1994. N is constant regardless of the distribution of the shock.

24. The cost should be set above the top horizontal line in figure 6.3. The normalized cost should be set above 1.356. Thus the resource cost of defending the fixed exchange rate should be at least 136 percent of the cost of reducing inflation from 10 to 3 percent. We state the resource cost as an inequality since C may include some deadweight loss elements in addition to the resources distributed to speculators.

25. The expected social loss from the mixed strategy reaches its minimum when $\bar{u} = 0.016$. The value of C for $\bar{u} = 0.016$ is 0.6639. The horizontal line in figure 6.5 is at $\sqrt{2C} = 1.152$, where $C = 0.6639$.

26. For example, see Obstfeld 1994 for a discussion of how unemployment or the cost of servicing the public debt can increase the pressure on the government to devalue. See Drazen and Masson 1994 for a model where persistent unemployment can increase the probability a government will devalue in the future if it chooses not to devalue when adverse shocks first hit the economy. See Calvo 1995 for a discussion of how the fragility of the banking sector constrained the decision of the Mexican government to support the peso.

27. The reserve constant need not be an arbitrary one. Blanco and Garber (1986) and Cumby and van Wijnbergen (1989) estimate the reserve level rather than impose it arbitrarily while Buiter (1987) sets the reserve constant optimally.

28. Buiter, Corsetti, and Pesenti (1996) suggest that the shift in attitude toward exchange rate and monetary policy coordination among European policymakers triggered the collapse of the ERM in 1992. In the present context, the policy stance of partner countries would influence the optimal reserve commitment to the fixed exchange rate, the shadow rate, and hence the attack time.

29. We focus on only one strand of empirical work. Jeanne (1997) initiated another strand that tests for multiple equilibria.

30. Speculative attacks are only one of the event types studied in ERW.

31. Versions of this definition have been used by Eichengreen, Rose, and Wyplosz (1996a, 1996b); Frankel and Rose (1996); Sachs, Tornell, and Velasco (1996a); Kaminsky and Reinhart (1996); and Kaminsky, Lizondo, and Reinhart (1997).

32. Assuming domestic and foreign bonds are perfect substitutes, domestic agents react to rising interest rates by exchanging some of their domestic currency for foreign currency denominated bonds, thereby depleting international reserves more rapidly. If domestic and foreign bonds are imperfect substitutes, then rising domestic interest rates may encourage agents to increase their holdings of domestic currency denominated bonds. In that case, reserves might not leak out faster prior to the attack.

33. These effects exist literally only in the Krugman model. In actual data, the analysis would be considerably clouded by time aggregation (especially for reserve flows) and by government pegging of (overnight) interest rates.

34. Otker and Pazarbasioglu (1994) (OP) estimate the one-month-ahead probabilities of speculative attacks in five European countries during the 1979–1993 period. They find that market fundamentals do quite well statistically (in terms of coefficient significance) for many of the countries and the fitted probabilities of crisis often rise to high levels (more than 50 percent) in the months immediately preceding crises. They also find that certain speculative proxies predict crises with reasonable accuracy. In addition, OP find that estimating their model as a panel gives quite poor predictions for the probability of devaluations. Consequently OP estimate probabilities on a country-by-country basis in the manner of the early structural models.

35. The classic reference is Meese and Rogoff 1983 . Of course, exchange rate models are not the only disappointing ones. All asset price models based on underlying fundamentals work poorly.

36. The panel includes the Mexican crises in 1976 and 1982 studied by Blanco and Garber (1986), the Argentine experience in the early 1980s studied by Cumby and van Wijnbergen (1989), and the 1994 Mexican crisis and the 1992 crises in Finland and Sweden. Since many developing countries did not have market-determined interest rates prior to the 1990s, the speculative pressure index for developing countries includes only reserve and exchange rate changes. If capital controls limit reserve leakages in the period leading up to a crisis, then the pressure index may register a big jump at the attack time even if a crisis has a significant predictable component. As a result, the sample of crises for developing countries is less likely to exclude crises with significant predictable components.

37. The KLR approach, which they term a *signals* approach, is more nonlinear than the ERW one, in that KLR determine signal thresholds for information variables as well as for crises, but it is in the same spirit. KLR find their crises to be predictable based on signals provided by exports, real exchange rates, broad money/international reserves, output, and equity prices.

References

Agenor, R. 1996. Models of currency crises: A brief overview. Working paper, International Monetary Fund, Washington, D.C.

Agenor, R. 1990. Exchange restrictions and balance of payments crises. Working paper, International Monetary Fund, Washington D.C.

Agenor, R., J. S. Bhandari, and R. P. Flood. 1992. Speculative attacks and models of balance of payments crises. Working paper no. 3919 (November), National Bureau of Economic Research, Cambridge, Mass. Condensed version published in *IMF Staff Papers* 39 (June):357–94.

Agenor, R., and B. Delbecque. 1991. Balance of payments crises in a dual exchange rate regime with leakages. Unpublished manuscript, International Monetary Fund, Washington, D.C. Mimeographed.

Agenor, R., and P. Masson. 1995. Credibility, reputation and the Mexican peso crisis. Unpublished manuscript, International Monetary Fund, Washington, D.C. Mimeographed.

Alexius, A. 1997. Inflation rules with consistent escape clauses. Unpublished manuscript, Stockholm School of Economics. Mimeographed.

Andersen, T. M. 1995. Shocks and the variability of a fixed exchange rate commitment. Economics Department, University of Aarhus, Aarhus, Denmark. Mimeographed.

Andersen, T. M., and O. Risager. 1991. The role of credibility for the effects of a change in the exchange-rate policy. *Oxford Economic Papers* 41 (January):85–98.

Atkeson, A., and J.-V. Ruis-Rull. 1996. The balance of payments and borrowing constraints: An alternative view of the Mexican crisis. *Journal of International Economics* 41 (3/4):331–50.

Bacchetta, P. 1990. Temporary capital controls in a balance-of-payments crisis. *Journal of International Money and Finance* 9 (March):246–57.

Banerjee, A. 1992. A simple model of herd behavior. *Quarterly Journal of Economics* 107:797–817.

Barro, R., and D. B. Gordon. 1983. A positive theory of monetary policy in a natural rate model. *Journal of Political Economy* 91 (August):589–610.

Bensaid, B., and O. Jeanne. 1997. The instability of fixed exchange rate systems when raising the nominal interest rate is costly. *European Economic Review* 41:1461–78.

Bertola, G., and R. Caballero. 1990. Reserves and realignments in a target zone. Unpublished manuscript, Princeton University, Princeton, N.J. Mimeographed.

Bikhchandani, S., D. Hirshleifer, and I. Welch. 1992. A theory of fads, fashion, custom, and cultural change as informational cascades. *Journal of Political Economy* 100:992–1026.

Bilson, J. F. O. 1979. Leading indicators of currency devaluations. *Columbia Journal of World Business* 14 (Winter):62–76.

Blackburn, K. 1988. Collapsing exchange rate regimes and exchange rate dynamics: Some further examples. *Journal of International Money and Finance* 7 (September):373–85.

Blackburn, K., and M. Sola. 1991. Speculative currency attacks and balance of payments crises: A survey. Discussion Paper No. 9204 (December), University of Southampton, Southampton, U.K.

Blanco, H., and P. M. Garber. 1986. Recurrent devaluation and speculative attacks on the Mexican peso. *Journal of Political Economy* 94 (February):148–66.

Bordo, M., and A. Schwartz. 1996. Why clashes between internal and external stability goals end in currency crises, 1797–1994. *Open Economies Review* 7:437–68.

Branson, W. 1968. *Financial capital flows in the U.S. balance-of-payments*. Amsterdam: North-Holland.

Buiter, W. H. 1987. Borrowing to defend the exchange rate and the timing of and magnitude of speculative attacks. *Journal of International Economics* 23 (November):221–39.

Buiter, W. H., G. Corsetti, and P. Pesenti. 1996. *Financial markets and international monetary cooperation: The lessons of the 92–93 ERM crisis*. Cambridge: Cambridge University Press.

Buiter, W. H., G. Corsetti, P. Pesenti, and V. Grilli. 1991a. The speculative attack paradox and its resolution. Unpublished manuscript, Yale University, New Haven, Conn. Mimeographed.

Buiter, W. H., G. Corsetti, P. Pesenti, and V. Grilli. 1991b. Anomalous speculative attacks on fixed exchange rate regimes. In *Exchange rate targets and currency bands*, ed. P. Krugman and M. Miller, 140–76. Cambridge: Cambridge University Press.

Bullard, J. 1991. Collapsing exchange rate regimes: A reinterpretation. Unpublished manuscript, Federal Reserve Bank of St. Louis. Mimeographed.

Burki, S., and S. Edwards. 1995. Latin America after Mexico: Quickening the pace. Unpublished manuscript, The World Bank, Washington, D.C. Mimeographed.

Calvo, G. A. 1997. Rational herd behavior and the globalization of securities markets. Unpublished manuscript, University of Maryland, College Park.

Calvo, G. A. 1996. Capital flows and macroeconomic management: Tequila lessons. Unpublished manuscript, University of Maryland, College Park.

Calvo, G. A., and E. Mendoza. 1995. Mexico's balance-of-payments crisis: A chronicle of a death foretold. *Journal of International Economics* 41 (3/4):235–64.

Calvo, G. A. 1995. Varieties of capital-market crises. Working paper, University of Maryland, College Park.

Calvo, G. A. 1988. Servicing the public debt: The role of expectations. *American Economic Review* 78:1411–28.

Calvo, G. A. 1987. Balance of payments crises in a cash-in-advance economy. *Journal of Money, Credit and Banking* 19 (February):19–32.

Calvo, G. A. 1983. Staggered contracts and exchange rate policy. In *Exchange rates and international macroeconomics*, ed. J. A. Frenkel, 235–52. Chicago: University of Chicago Press.

Calvo, S., and C. M. Reinhart. 1996. Capital flows to Latin America: Is there evidence of contagion effects? In *Private capital flows to emerging markets after the Mexican crisis*, ed. G. Calvo, M. Goldstein, and E. Hochreiter, 151–71. Washington, D.C.: Institute for International Economics.

Cavalleri, L., and G. Corsetti. 1996. Policymaking and speculative attacks in models of exchange rate crises: A synthesis. Unpublished manuscript, University of Rome. Mimeographed.

Chen, Z. 1995. Speculative market structure and the collapse of an exchange rate mechanism. Discussion paper no. 1164, Center for Economic Policy Research, London.

Claessens, S. 1991. Balance of payments crises in an optimal portfolio model. *European Economic Review* 35 (January):81–101.

Claessens, S. 1988. Balance-of-payments crises in a perfect foresight optimizing Model. *Journal of International Money and Finance* 7 (September):363–72.

Cole, H., and P. Kehoe. 1996. A self-fulfilling model of Mexico's 1994–1995 debt crisis. *Journal of International Economics* 41 (3/4):309–30.

Connolly, M. B. 1986. The speculative attack on the peso and the real exchange rate: Argentina, 1979–81. *Journal of International Money and Finance* 5 (March):117–30.

Connolly, M. B., and D. Taylor. 1984. The exact timing of the collapse of an exchange rate regime and its impact on the relative price of traded goods. *Journal of Money, Credit and Banking* 16 (May):194–207.

Connolly, M. B., D. Taylor, and A. Fernandéz. 1987. Speculation against the pre-announced exchange rate in Mexico: January 1983 to June 1985. In *Economic reform and stabilization in Latin America*, ed. M. Connolly and C. Gonzaléz-Vega, 161–74. New York: Praeger Publishers.

Cumby, R. E., and S. van Wijnbergen. 1989. Financial policy and speculative runs with A crawling peg: Argentina 1979–1981. *Journal of International Economics* 27 (August):111–27.

Daniel, B. 1997a. Seignorage, fiscal constraints and the viability of a fixed exchange rate. Unpublished manuscript, State University of New York at Albany. Mimeographed.

Daniel, B. 1997b. Fiscal policy and the predictability of exchange rate collapse. Unpublished manuscript, State University of New York at Albany. Mimeographed.

Davies, G., and D. Vines. 1995. Equilibrium currency crises: Are multiple equilibria self-fulfilling or history dependent? Working paper no. 1239, Center for Economic Policy Research, London.

Delbecque, B. 1993. Dual exchange rates under pegged interest rate and balance of payments crisis. *Journal of International Money and Finance* 12:170–81.

Dellas, H., and A. Stockman. 1988. Self-fulfilling expectations, speculative attacks, and capital controls. Working paper no. 138 (June), University of Rochester, Rochester, N.Y.

de Valle, Alejandro. 1995. Sustainability of the exchange rate policy. Unpublished manuscript, Banco de Mexico, Mexico City, Mexico.

Dornbusch, R. 1987. Collapsing exchange rate regimes. *Journal of Development Economics* 27 (October):71–83.

Dornbusch, R. 1976. Expectations and exchange rate dynamics. *Journal of Political Economy* 84 (December):1161–76.

Dornbusch, R., I. Goldfajn, and R. Valdes. 1995. Currency crises and collapses. *Brookings Papers on Economic Activity* (no. 2):219–95.

Drazen, A., and E. Helpman. 1998. Stabilization with exchange rate management under uncertainty. In *Economic effects of the government Budget*, ed. E. Helpman, A. Razin, and E. Sadka. Cambridge: MIT Press.

Drazen, A., and P. Masson. 1994. Credibility of policies versus credibility of policymakers. *Quarterly Journal of Economics* 109 (3):735–54.

Edlin, P.-A., and A. Vredin. 1993. Devaluation risk in target zones: Evidence from the Nordic countries. *Economic Journal* 103 (January):161–75.

Edwards, S. 1996. Exchange-rate anchors, credibility, and inertia: A tale of two crises, Chile and Mexico. *American Economic Review Papers and Proceedings* 86:176–80.

Edwards, S. 1989. *Real exchange rates, devaluation and adjustment: Exchange rate policy in developing countries* Cambridge: MIT Press.

Edwards, S., and P. J. Montiel. 1989. Devaluation crises and the macroeconomic consequences of postponed adjustment in developing countries. *IMF Staff Papers* 36 (December):875–903.

Edwards, S., and J. Santella. 1993. Devaluation controversies in the developing countries: Lessons from the Bretton Woods era. In: *A retrospective on the Bretton Woods system: Lessons for international monetary reform*, ed. M. D. Bordo and B. Eichengreen, 405–55. Chicago: University of Chicago Press.

Eichengreen, B., A. Rose, and C. Wyplosz. 1996a. Contagious currency crises. Working Paper No. 5681 (July), National Bureau of Economic Research, Cambridge, Mass.

Eichengreen, B., A. Rose, and C. Wyplosz. 1996b. Speculative attacks on pegged exchange rates: An empirical exploration with special reference to the European monetary system. In *Transatlantic economic issues*, ed. M. Canzoneri, P. Masson, and V. Grilli, Cambridge: Cambridge University Press.

Eichengreen, B., A. Rose, and C. Wyplosz. 1995. Exchange market mayhem: The antecedents and aftermath of speculative attacks. *Economic Policy* (October):251–96.

Eichengreen, B., and C. Wyplosz. 1993. The unstable EMS. *Brookings Papers on Economic Activity* 1:51–143.

Flood, R. 1996. Discussion. In *Transatlantic economic issues*, ed. M. Canzoneri, P. Masson, and V. Grilli. Cambridge: Cambridge University Press.

Flood, R., and P. Garber. 1991. Linkages between speculative attack and target zone models of exchange rates. *Quarterly Journal of Economics* 106:1367–72.

Flood, R., and P. Garber. 1984a. Gold monetization and gold discipline. *Journal of Political Economy* 92 (1):90–107.

Flood, R., and P. Garber. 1984b. Collapsing exchange-rate regimes: Some linear examples. *Journal of International Economics* 17:1–13.

Flood, R., P. Garber, and C. Kramer. 1996. Collapsing exchange rate regimes: Another linear Example. *Journal of International Economics* 41 (3/4):223–34.

Flood, R., and R. J. Hodrick. 1986. Real aspects of exchange rate regime choice with collapsing fixed rates. *Journal of International Economics* 21 (November):215–32.

Flood, R., and P. Isard. 1989. Monetary policy strategies. *IMF Staff Papers* 36:612–32.

Flood, R., and C. Kramer. 1996. Economic models of speculative attacks and the drachma crisis of May 1994. *Open Economies Review* (no. 7):583–92.

Flood, R., and N. P. Marion. 2000. Self-fulfilling risk predictions: An application to speculative attacks. *Journal of International Economics* 50:245–68.

Flood, R., and N. P. Marion. 1997a. The size and timing of devaluations in capital-controlled countries. *Journal of Development Economics* 54:123–47.

Flood, R., and N. P. Marion. 1997b. Policy implications of second-generation crisis models. *IMF Staff Papers* 44:10–17.

Frankel, J. 1984. Tests of monetary and portfolio-balance models of exchange-rate determination. In *Exchange rate theory and practice*, ed. J. Bilson and R. Marsten, 239–60. Chicago: University of Chicago Press.

Frankel, J., and A. Rose. 1996. Currency crashes in emerging markets: An empirical treatment. International finance discussion paper no. 534 (January), Board of Governors of the Federal Reserve, Washington, D.C.

Frenkel, M., and M. Klein. 1991. Balance of payments crises and fiscal adjustment measures. *Journal of Macroeconomics* 13 (Winter):657–73.

Froot, K., and M. Obstfeld. 1991. Stochastic process switching: Some simple solutions. *Econometrica* 59 (January):241–50.

Garber, P. M., and V. U. Grilli. 1989. Bank runs in open economies and the international transmission of panics. *Journal of International Economics* 27:165–75.

Garber, P. M., and L. Svensson. 1994. The operation and collapse of fixed exchange rate regimes. Working Paper No. 4971 (December). National Bureau of Economic Research, Cambridge, Mass.

Gerlach, S., and F. Smets. 1994. Contagious speculative attacks. Discussion paper no. 1055 (November), Center for Economic Policy Research, London.

Gil-Diaz, F. 1995. A comparison of economic crises in Chile 1982, Mexico in 1995. Unpublished manuscript, Banco de Mexico, Mexico City. Mimeographed.

Girton, L., and D. Roper. 1977. A monetary model of exchange market pressure applied to postwar Canadian experience. *American Economic Review* (no. 76):537–48.

Goldberg, L. S. 1994. Predicting exchange rate crises: Mexico revisited. *Journal of International Economics* 36:413–30.

Goldberg, L. S. 1988. Collapsing exchange rate regimes: Shocks and Biases. Working paper no. 2702, National Bureau of Economic Research, Cambridge, Mass.

Goldfajn, I., and R. Valdes. 1995. Balance of payments crises and capital flows: The role of liquidity. Unpublished manuscript, Massachusetts Institute of Technology, Cambridge, Mass.

Goldstein, M. 1996. Presumptive indicators/early warning signals of vulnerability to financial crises in emerging markets. Unpublished manuscript, Institute for International Economics, Washington, D.C. Mimeographed.

Grilli, V. 1990. Managing exchange rate crises: Evidence from the 1890's. *Journal of International Money and Finance* 9 (September):135–82.

Grilli, V. 1986. Buying and selling attacks on fixed exchange rate systems. *Journal of International Economics* 20 (February):143–56.

Gros, D. 1992. Capital controls and foreign exchange market crises in the EMS. *European Economic Review* 36 (December):1533–44.

Gupta, P. 1996. Currency crises, banking crises and twin crises: A comprehensive review of the literature. Unpublished manuscript, International Monetary Fund, Washington, D.C.

Hernandez, D. Alejandro, and F. Zapatero. 1996. Exchange rate determination and the collapse of a target zone with stochastic capital flows. Unpublished manuscript, Centro de Investigation Economica, Mexico City, Mexico.

Hotelling, H. 1931. The economics of exhaustable resources. *Journal of Political Economy* 39 (April):137–75.

International Monetary Fund. 1993–1997. *International capital markets: Developments, prospects, and policy issues.* Washington, D.C.: World Economic and Financial Surveys.

Isard, P. 1995. *Exchange rate economics.* Cambridge: Cambridge University Press.

Ize, A., and G. Ortiz. 1987. Fiscal rigidities, public debt, and capital flight. *IMF Staff Papers* 34 (June):311–32.

Jeanne, O. 1997. Are currency crises self-fulfilling speculation? A test. *Journal of International Economics* 43:263–86.

Jeanne, O. 1994. Models of currency crises: A tentative synthesis with special reference to the 1992–3 EMS crisis. Unpublished manuscript, Ecole Nationale des Ponts et Chaussees (CERAS), Paris. Mimeographed.

Kamin, S., and J. Rogers. 1996. Monetary policy in the endgame to exchange rate based stabilizations: The case of Mexico. *Journal of International Economics* 41 (3/4):285–308.

Kaminsky, G., and L. Leiderman. 1995. High real interest rates in the aftermath of disinflation: Credit crunch or credibility crisis? Unpublished manuscript, Board of Governors of the Federal Reserve System, Washington, D.C.

Kaminsky, G., S. Lizando, and C. M. Reinhart. 1998. Leading indicators of currency crises. *IMF Staff Papers* 45:1–48.

Kaminsky, G., and C. Reinhart. 1999. The twin crises: The causes of banking and balance-of-payments problems. *American Economic Review* 89:473–500.

Kenen, P. 1996. Analyzing and managing exchange-rate crises. *Open Economies Review* 7:469–92.

Klein, M., and N. P. Marion. 1997. Explaining the duration of exchange-rate pegs. *Journal of Development Economics* 54:387–404.

Krasker, W. 1980. The "peso" problem in testing efficiency of forward exchange markets. *Journal of Monetary Economics* 6 (March):269–76.

Krugman, P. 1996. Are currency crises self-fulfilling? In *NBER Macroeconomics Annual*, eds. B. Bernanke and J. Rotemberg, 345–78. Cambridge: MIT Press.

Krugman, P. 1991a. Target zones and exchange rate dynamics. *Quarterly Journal of Economics* 106 (August):669–82.

Krugman, P. 1991b. International aspects of financial crises. In *The risk of economic crisis*, ed. Martin Feldstein, 85–108. Chicago: University of Chicago Press.

Krugman, P. 1979. A model of balance-of-payments crises. *Journal of Money, Credit, and Banking* 11:311–25.

Krugman, P., and J. Rotemberg. 1990. Target zones with limited reserves. Working paper no. 3418 (August), National Bureau of Economic Research, Cambridge, Mass.

Kydland, F., and E. Prescott. 1977. Rules rather than discretion: The inconsistency of optimal plans. *Journal of Political Economy* 85 (June):473–91.

Lee, I. H. 1993. On the convergence of informational cascades. *Journal of Economic Theory* 61:395–411.

Leiderman, L., and A. Thornw. 1995. Mexico's 1994 crisis and its aftermath: Is the worst over? Unpublished manuscript, Tel Aviv University, Tel Aviv, Israel.

Lohmann, S. 1992. The optimal degree of commitment: Credibility versus flexibility. *American Economic Review* 82:273–86.

Lustig, N. 1995. The Mexican peso crisis: The forseeable and the surprise. Discussion Papers in International Economics no. 114, Brookings Institute, Washington, D.C.

Masson, P. 1995. Gaining and losing ERM credibility: The case of the United Kingdom. *Economic Journal* 105:571–82.

Masson, P., and R. Agenor. 1996. The Mexican peso crisis: Overview and analysis of credibility factors. Working paper no. 96/6, International Monetary Fund, Washington, D.C.

Melick, W. 1996. Estimation of speculative attack models: Mexico yet again. Working paper no. 36, Bank for International Settlements, Basle, Switzerland.

Mendoza, E., and M. Uribe. 1996. The syndrome of exchange-rate-based stabilization and the uncertain duration of currency pegs. Working paper, Board of Governors of the Federal Reserve, Washington, D.C.

Meese, R., and K. Rogoff. 1983. The out-of-sample failure of empirical exchange rate models: Sampling error or misspecification? In *Exchange rates and international macroeconomics*, ed. Jacob Frenkel, 67–105. Chicago: University of Chicago Press.

Milesi-Ferretti, G. M., and A. Razin. 1995. Current account sustainability. Unpublished manuscript, International Monetary Fund, Washington, D.C.

Miller, M. H., and P. Weller. 1991. Exchange rate bands with price inertia. *Economic Journal* 101:1380–99.

Miller, V. 1996a. Speculative currency attacks with endogenously induced commercial bank crises. *Journal of International Finance and Money* 15:383–404.

Miller, V. 1996b. Exchange rate crises with domestic bank runs. Evidence from the 1890s. *Journal of International Money and Finance* 15:637–56.

Miller, V. 1995. Domestic bank runs and speculative attacks on foreign currencies. Unpublished manuscript. University of Quebec at Montreal. Mimeographed.

Mizen, P. 1996a. The behavior of foreign currency holdings during currency crises: Causes and consequences. *Open Economies Review* 7 (suppl. 1):651–73.

Mizen, P. 1996b. Can foreign currency deposits prop up a collapsing exchange rate regime? Unpublished manuscript, University of Nottingham, Nottingham, U.K. Mimeographed.

Moreno, R. 1995. Macroeconomic behavior during periods of speculative pressure or realignment: Evidence from Pacific Basin countries. *Economic Review* (Federal Reserve Bank of San Francisco) (no. 3):3–16.

Morris, S., and H. S. Shin. 1995. Informational events that trigger currency attacks. Working paper no. 95–24, Federal Reserve Bank of Philadelphia.

Mundell, R. 1961. A theory of optimum currency areas. *American Economic Review* 51 (September):657–65.

Obstfeld, M. 1997. Destabilizing effects of exchange rate escape clauses. *Journal of International Economics* 43:61–78.

Obstfeld, M. 1996. Models of currency crises with self-fulfilling features. *European Economic Review* 40:1037–47.

Obstfeld, M. 1995. International currency experience: New lessons and lessons relearned. *Brookings Papers on Economic Activity* 1:119–220.

Obstfeld, M. 1994. The logic of currency crises. *Cahiers Economiques et Monetaires* (Bank of France) 43:189–213.

Obstfeld, M. 1986a. Speculative attacks and the external constraint in a maximizing model of the balance of payments. *Canadian Journal of Economics* 19 (March):1–22.

Obstfeld, M. 1986b. Rational and self-fulfilling balance of payments crises. *American Economic Review* 76 (March):72–81.

Obstfeld, M. 1984. Balance of payments crises and devaluation. *Journal of Money, Credit and Banking* 16 (May):208–17.

Obstfeld, M., and K. Rogoff. 1995. The mirage of fixed exchange rates. *Journal of Economic Perspectives* 9 (no. 4):73–96.

Otani, K. 1989. The collapse of a fixed rate regime with a discrete realignment of the exchange rate. *Journal of the Japanese and International Economies* 3 (September):250–69.

Otker, I., and C. Pazarbasioglu. 1997a. Likelihood versus timing of speculative attacks: A case study of Mexico. *European Economic Review* 41:837–45.

Otker, I., and C. Pazarbasioglu. 1997b. Speculative attacks and macroeconomic fundamentals: Evidence from some European currencies. *European Economic Review* 41:847–60.

Otker, I., and C. Pazarbasioglu. 1996. Speculative attacks and currency crises: The Mexican experience. *Open Economies Review* 7:535–52.

Otker, I., and C. Pazarbasioglu. 1994. Exchange market pressures and speculative capital flows in selected european countries. Working paper no. 94/21 (November), International Monetary Fund, Washington, D.C.

Ozkan, F. G., and A. Sutherland. 1998. A currency crisis model with an optimizing policymaker. *Journal of International Economics* 44:339–64.

Ozkan, F. G., and A. Sutherland. 1995. Policy measures to avoid a currency crisis. *Economic Journal* 105 (March):510–19.

Penati, A., and G. Pennacchi. 1989. Optimal portfolio choice and the collapse of a fixed-exchange rate regime. *Journal of International Economics* 27 (August):1–24.

Persson, T., and G. Tabellini. 1990. *Macroeconomic policy, credibility and politics*. Chur, Switzerland: Harwood Academic.

Rodriguez, C. 1978. A stylized model of the devaluation-inflation spiral. *IMF Staff Papers* 25 (March):76–89.

Rogoff, K. 1985. The optimal degree of commitment to an intermediate monetary target. *Quarterly Journal of Economics* 100 (November):1169–89.

Sachs, J., A. Tornell, and A. Velasco. 1996a. Financial crises in emerging markets: The lessons from 1995. *Brookings Papers on Economic Activity* (no. 16):147–215.

Sachs, J., A. Tornell, and A. Velasco. 1996b. The collapse of the Mexican peso: What have we learned? *Economic Policy* 22:15–63.

Salant, S. 1983. The vulnerability of price stabilization schemes to speculative attack. *Journal of Political Economy* 91 (February):1–38.

Salant, S., and D. Henderson. 1978. Market anticipation of government policy and the price of gold. *Journal of Political Economy* 86:627–48.

Savastano, M. 1992. Collapse of a crawling peg regime in the presence of a government budget constraint. *IMF Staff Papers* 39 (1):79–100.

Schmulker, S., and J. Frankel. 1996. Crisis, contagion and country funds. Unpublished manuscript, University of California, Berkeley.

Shiller, R. 1995. Conversation, information and herd behavior. *American Economic Review Papers and Proceedings* 85:181–5.

Steiner, R. 1995. The Mexican crisis: Why did it happen and what did we learn? Unpublished manuscript, The World Bank. Washington, D.C. Mimeographed.

Sutherland, A. 1992. State contingent and time dependent switches of exchange rate regime. Unpublished manuscript, University of York. Mimeographed.

Tobin, J. 1969. A general equilibrium approach to monetary theory. *Journal of Money, Credit and Banking* 1 (1):15–29.

Townsend, R. 1977. The eventual failure of price fixing schemes. *Journal of Economic Theory* 14:190–9.

Valdes, R. O. 1996. Emerging market contagion: Evidence and theory. Unpublished manuscript, Massachusetts Institute of Technology, Cambridge, Mass.

van Wijnbergen, S. 1996. When are fixed exchange rates really fixed? Working paper no. 5842 (November), National Bureau of Economic Research, Cambridge, Mass.

van Wijnbergen, S. 1991. Fiscal deficits, exchange rate crises, and inflation. *Review of Economic Studies* 58 (January):81–92.

van Wijnbergen, S. 1988. Inflation, balance of payments crises, and public sector deficits. In *Economic effects of the government budget*, ed. E. Helpman, A. Razin, and E. Sadka. Cambridge: MIT Press.

Velasco, A. 1987a. Financial crises and balance of payments crises. *Journal of Development Economics* 27 (October):263–83.

Velasco, A. 1987b. Financial and balance of payments crises: A simple model of the Southern Cone experience. *Journal of Development Economics* 27 (October):263–83.

Willman, A. 1987. Speculative attacks on the currency with uncertain monetary policy reactions. *Economics Letters* 25 (January):75–8.

Willman, A. 1988. The collapse of the fixed exchange rate regime with sticky wages and imperfect substitutability between domestic and foreign Bonds. *European Economic Review* 32 (November):1817–38.

Willman, A. 1989. Devaluation expectations and speculative attacks on the currency. *Scandinavian Journal of Economics* 91 (March):97–116.

Willman, A. 1991. Why there is a lower bound on the central bank's foreign reserves. *Finnish Economic Papers* 4 (Autumn):113–29.

Wood, P. R. 1991. Balance-of-payments crises with an optimizing central bank. Unpublished manuscript, Board of Governors of the Federal Reserve System, Washington, D.C.

Wyplosz, C. 1986. Capital controls and balance of payments crises. *Journal of International Money and Finance* 5 (June):167–79.

7 Progress in the Theory of Economic Policy

Francesco Giavazzi and
Alberto Giovannini

Introduction

By providing governments with simple models that capture the essence of macroeconomic interactions in an open economy, Robert Mundell has greatly contributed to shaping successful economic policies. He has disseminated ideas on the appropriate use of monetary and fiscal policies in the open economy that have proved to be not only resilient over the years, but robust to very different national environments, including industrial and developing countries. In this chapter we examine, from the perspective of Mundell's contributions, the state of the theory of economic policy and ask what might be the areas of progress in this field.

Our (limited) experience with the government of a large industrial country—we are aware that the experience in developing countries and in transition economies might be quite different—suggests that while the influence of economists in shaping stabilization policies is often critical, their success at bringing forward the need for structural reform based on economic principles has been more limited. The fruitful collaboration that so often develops between economists and governments in the design of appropriate macroeconomic policies—but also in thinking about how to structure new institutions, as has been the case in Europe with the single currency project—is seldom reproduced in the area of market reform or in addressing the distortions caused by special interest groups.

We are aware that labor market reform, a sound financial system, action on property rights and corruption, an efficient judicial system, and effective public administrations are all nonstarters when inflation and the budget deficit are out of control. Macro stabilization is the precondition for structural reform. But when this is achieved and the time comes to address structural reform, the lively interaction between academics and policymakers which is often instrumental at adopting a stabilization program—the Israeli stabilization of 1985 is one of the best examples of such a fruitful interaction—seems to come to an end.[1]

This is not because the normative analysis that lies behind structural reforms is too technical or obscure to have an impact on policymakers. Rather, we believe that this is because a government and the institutions (both nonphysical institutions, such as rules and regulations, and physical ones, such as roads and railways) that affect economic interactions in an advanced society are not the product of tabula rasa design: they are inherited from the past. Adaptation to new circumstances is much more difficult in the government than in the rest of society—for example because special interest groups can lobby more effectively than a dispersed group of consumers.[2]

One example is the different speed in the response of governments and markets to a financial crisis. It takes little time for speculators to form a view on the sustainability of a currency peg. But it may take months for a government to convince parliament to adopt the legislation that is necessary to change economic policies in a way that would convince markets that the peg is sustainable.

In the first two sections of this chapter we review the areas of success in the theory of macroeconomic policy and identify a few problem areas as well. In a nutshell, we find that economists are most influential when countries are in deep trouble, either because they entered a financial or foreign exchange crisis or because they are following an unsustainable path, in domestic public finances or in foreign accounts, and need some form of stabilization. These are situations where the problems a country faces are too big for an interest group, no matter how powerful, to be able to influence policies. Therefore, the advice economists give is not only valuable, but also effective. By contrast, in the drudgery of the day-to-day work of governments, when the pressure of special interests often wins the day over the best analytical arguments, economists are much less effective.

Economists, however, are not only ineffective in situations where interest groups are powerful. Often their advice is ineffective simply because they ignore the distortions which affect the economic environment. Policy economists have GDP statistics, interest rates, the rate of unemployment, and the exchange rate at their finger tips: little do they know, for example, about the time it takes to settle a civil lawsuit and the extent to which such delays affect the cost of borrowing.

This lack of knowledge undermines the effectiveness of their analyses. How many policy economists would be able to answer the following question with reference to a specific country: Which are the five most glaring distortions that prevent a proper functioning of the economy?

We argue that the simplest set of ideas which justify the role and scope of government in market economies have been largely excluded from the process of policymaking (at least in the country we know best, but we suspect that this is the case in the world as a whole). We offer our own explanation for this exclusion: the combination of small interest groups generating large distortions, with the absence of proper incentives on governments to adapt to technological progress and other changes in circumstances, is such that public policies are almost doomed to be inefficient. We survey three areas where, in Europe at least, these problems appear to be more serious: property rights, the labor market, and capital markets. Our illustration of the problems in Europe is hopefully suggestive of a pattern that appears to be more general and involve a large number of countries. We conclude discussing possible initiatives.

The "Mundell Tradition" in the Theory of Economic Policy

Robert Mundell's research has inspired generations of economists as a model for the analysis of economic policy in open economies. Much of Mundell's work has three distinguishing features: it discusses problems of significance for economic policymakers, it employs simple and elegant mathematical models, and it explicitly accounts for the openness of the economy, and for the role of international capital markets.

Mundell's research reflects and adds to the strong intellectual traditions of Chicago and Cambridge. Like many of his colleagues and precursors (among them Harberger, Machlup, Meade, Alexander, Tsiang, Cooper, and Metzler) Mundell contributed to the refinement of the Keynesian analysis of an open economy with the inclusion of a consistent monetary analysis. Like many of his followers, he paid keen attention to the connections between financial markets and the macroeconomy.

The successful integration of money—through the so-called neoclassical synthesis—into the Keynesian model, the emphasis on financial markets through the international interest rate and exchange rate linkages and the resulting attention to the formation of expectations, and in particular expectations on economic policies, set the stage for the developments of the following thirty years.[3]

Tobin and Buiter extended the model to recognize the intertemporal aspects of fiscal policy. Bruno, Kouri, Mussa, Dornbusch and Fischer, and Sachs incorporated the dynamics of the current account and analyzed the link between the exchange rate and the current account, which had been weakened by the assumption of perfect substitutability among financial assets—an issue first investigated by Branson and by Frenkel and Rodriguez. The analysis of expectations was pioneered by Dornbusch. Hamada extended the two-country model to allow for strategic interactions among monetary authorities, an avenue subsequently pursued by Rogoff, who showed the open economy implications of the Barro-Gordon "games" between the private sector and the monetary authorities. Krugman initiated the study of why fixed exchange rate regimes may collapse, and Dornbusch first addressed the role of the exchange rate regime in a disinflation. These contributions, and many more, have advanced our understanding of important issues, in particular in the areas of: optimal monetary policy and the design of monetary institutions; monetary and fiscal policy interactions; monetary and fiscal policy rules; and gradualism versus "cold turkey" economic policies.

Much of this literature has taken inspiration from the rational expectations results, which had sharpened the analysis of the interactions between authorities and markets.[4] The Mundell/Chicago/rational expectations approach, by emphasizing budget constraints, the link between inflation and monetary policy, the role of financial markets in triggering crises, and the limits of economic policymaking, has underlain many of the stability-oriented policies undertaken in a large number of countries, industrial and developing.

This phenomenon, no doubt, has also a generational aspect. After the 1960s the number of foreign students enrolled in U.S. economics departments has increased very significantly.[5] Many of these students, after obtaining their doctorates have become deeply involved in economic policies in their own countries, either directly or through international institutions like the International Monetary Fund (IMF) and the World Bank. Their cultural influence in the economic policies pursued by a wide array of countries, including former communist countries, is all too evident.

Central banks have been among most powerful supporters of the Mundell/Chicago/rational expectations approach. Indeed, many refinements of the models of macroeconomic policy have been triggered by the questions posed by central banks—examples are the work of the International Finance Division of the Board of Governors of the Fed and, in Europe, the ongoing collaboration between the Centre for Economic Policy Research (CEPR) and E.U. central banks. The interaction between academics and central bankers has had the very positive effect of furthering research and making it more relevant, as well as sharpening the actions of monetary authorities. In addition, the close relation of academics and central bankers has been central to important developments in institutional reform, like for example the process of monetary union in Europe.

Thus a happy situation was established. The model was intellectually kept alive by ongoing research, and at the same time, constant use of the model as an analytical framework for policymaking made sure that the ideas would not go out of fashion.

The Mundell Tradition and the Reality of Policymaking

The cultural influence of the Mundell/Chicago/rational expectations approach has done a lot to help policymakers build a stable macro environment. But when this is achieved, why is the lively interaction between academics and policymakers which is often instrumental at adopting a stabilization program, so rarely reproduced in discussing structural reform?

The two most respected, policy-oriented economic research groups, the National Bureau of Economic Research (NBER) in the United States and the CEPR in Europe, show a clear bias towards the analysis of macro issues. Out of 528 working papers published by NBER between January 1996 and August 1997, only forty-one address issues such as regulation and liberalization of markets, in particular credit markets, privatization of pension funds, health reform, firms' access to the capital market, training, competition policies, and banking reform—although many more address traditional public finance issues. At CEPR discussion papers on similar subjects were 27 out of 306 published over the same period. *Economic Policy*, Europe's leading journal specializing in the analysis of policy-relevant issues, has done slightly better: since its beginning in 1985, the journal has published 120 articles: among

them, no more than one out of three addresses issues such as those indicated above. The apparent lack of interest in the working of markets
reflected in the NBER papers could be a U.S. bias, the product of an
economy in which, by and large, markets work relatively well; this
however does not apply to continental Europe where most markets are
quite far from efficiency.

In his 1984 "Mais Lecture" Nigel Lawson, Chancellor of the Exche-
quer in Mrs. Thatcher's second government, clearly stated the limits of
macroeconomic policy: "The conventional post war wisdom was that
unemployment is a consequence of inadequate economic growth, and
economic growth is to be secured by macroeconomic policy. . . . The
conclusion on which the present government's economic policy is
based is that there is indeed a proper distinction between the objectives
of macroeconomic and microeconomic policy, and a need to be concerned with both of them. It is the conquest of inflation, and not the
pursuit of growth and employment, which is or should be the objective of macroeconomic policy. And it is the creation of conditions conducive to growth and employment, and not the suppression of price
rises, which is or should be the objective of microeconomic policy."

Lawson's views were echoed in Jacob Frenkel's remarks during the
roundtable discussion at the 1997 IMF Conference on EMU: "Economic
policy should no longer be concerned with countercyclical actions.
Rather it should simply provide the framework within which markets
can operate efficiently." (Frenkel 1997). Of course Robert Mundell
himself has recognized the importance of efficiency in our economies.
His policy advice to the so-called supply-siders of the early 1980s is
inspired by the awareness of the issues that we want to discuss here.[6]

The World Bank and the IMF have recently put new emphasis on
structural reform. The IMF has been advocating a "second generation"
of reforms: "Argentina has been successful largely because sound
macroeconomic policies have remained firmly in place for a number of
years, and considerable progress has been made on what might be
described as the 'first generation' of structural reform. . . . But clearly a
situation where unemployment is high and not all are sharing fully in
the benefit of stronger growth, calls for further action. . . . The crux of
the 'second generation' of reforms concerns completing the transformation of the state's role in the economy" (Camdessus 1997). For a discussion of the reform process in Latin America see also Naim 1995).
The IMF identifies a number of issues on which a government should
focus its action: establishing a simple and transparent regulatory

system that ensures equal access to markets and encourages competition; upholding the independence and the efficiency of the judicial system; improving the quality of public expenditure; and reducing unproductive expenditure to make room for investment in human capital and basic infrastructure. In the words of Michel Camdessus: "The second generation of reforms requires good governance in all its dimensions, including, in particular, effective and reliable public institutions" (Camdessus 1997).

Which areas should economic policy, in particular, target? Financial markets: "increasing the flow of timely, comprehensive, and accurate information between banks and supervisory authorities, between borrowers and lenders, between financial institutions and their shareholders to encourage better governance." Fiscal reform: "improving tax administration and tax compliance, thus creating room to reduce tax rates, especially payroll taxes that discourage job creation". Labor market reform, understanding that "the key to preserving and expanding employment, particularly among the less skilled, is a flexible labor market that encourages mobility and keeps labor costs in line with labor productivity" (Camdessus 1997).

The World Bank, in the 1996 and 1997 editions of the *World Development Report*, has attracted our attention to the importance of the state, asking what should governments do, how should they do it, and how they can do it given the situation from which they start. The reports suggest that

• countries should focus the state's activities to match its capabilities. Many states try to do too much with few resources and little capability. Governments should enhance the state's effectiveness by concentrating on core public activities;

• a state can improve its capability by reinvigorating public institutions, in particular looking for mechanisms that give public officials the incentive to do their jobs better and to be more flexible, but which also provide restraints to check arbitrary and corrupt behavior.

One recent European example that parallels Camdessus' discussion of Argentina can be found in Italy. After a failed exchange rate–based stabilization—which failed essentially because it was not accompanied by a consistent fiscal policy—the Italian government opted, in 1993–96, for flexible exchange rates, and a combination of a monetary anchor and sharp fiscal consolidation: Mundell's assignment problem in action. The policy mix worked: inflation, the fiscal deficit, and the current account imbalance, all soon disappeared. However, none of the country's deep-seated problems were addressed. Fiscal consolidation occurred thanks to a large increase in tax rates, including on labor, and, especially, to the fall in interest rates, but without addressing the spending side of the budget. Lack of competition, suffocating regulation, tax distortions, corruption, an underdeveloped financial market: none of these issues was seriously addressed. As a result, rampant, regionally concentrated unemployment was unaffected by the stabilization.

Throughout the Italian stabilization, economists (both from Italy and elsewhere) have contributed to, and sometimes influenced, a lively debate on the appropriate macroeconomic framework. Their success at bringing forward the micro issues, however, has been much more limited—a surprising outcome considering that some of the best known Italian contributions to economics are precisely in the public finance field: from Francesco Ferrara, Matteo Pantaleoni, and Antonio De Viti de Marco in the 1880s, to Amilcare Puviani who in 1903 first criticized the view that governments set taxes according to optimal taxation theorems, suggesting that politicians may be driven by self-interest.

The Maastricht Treaty offers a remarkable example of the consequences of fiscal rules that are not supported by consistent analysis of the role of the state in an economy. By the end of 1997 most E.U. countries had satisfied the 3 percent deficit rule, but few of them had addressed the reasons that underlie the increasing share of government spending in GDP, nor the efficiency of such expenditure. Fiscal retrenchment occurred mostly as a result of increases in tax revenue, reclassifications of public expenditure and by releasing Treasury funds in accordance to incoming revenues rather than spending commitments. In some cases this has produced the accumulation of arrears that impose high social costs and breed cynicism about the ability of the government to stand up to its commitments—a problem well know in transition economies (see World Bank 1996, chap. 7).

The inability of economists to get across to policymakers the importance of well-functioning markets and of a scientific approach to government spending is a common feature in continental Europe. In Germany, the documents regularly produced by the "5 Wisemen" (the government's economic advisers), which command a lot of attention throughout the country, typically concentrate on monetary and fiscal policy, rarely addressing the operation of markets. Policymakers keep relying on economists whose advice was very valuable when their primary concerns were macroeconomic stability, or the choice of an international exchange rate system, but who are not very perceptive to the "second generation of reforms" and thus are unable to convince policy makers of their importance.[7]

We find the initiatives at the World Bank and at the IMF extremely promising: they correctly identify a major area of initiatives for policy reformers; as institutions, they are also ideally suited, being the most independent government bodies that exist and having a large accumulated knowledge both across countries and time. Yet, we feel uneasy about the "laundry list" character of many of the problems identified and about the lack of analysis underlying many of the common sensical prescriptions. These initiatives may also come too late: financial crises of the late 1990s are also a result of the lack of progress on structural reform in the areas of bankruptcy procedures, corporate governance, regulation and supervision of financial intermediaries.

The Roles of Government in the Economy

A logically consistent and reliable set of principles to guide economic policy making should be based on an analysis of the economic role of government in a country and in the world economy. The theories of general equilibrium, welfare economics, and public finance have all provided a wealth of propositions based on which an active role of government in the economy is justified. More importantly, economic theory has also provided guidelines on the nature of the appropriate intervention of government in the economy.

In our discussion on the state of the science of economic policy we find it natural to start from the best known and most general theorems justifying government intervention as the fundamental elements from which to both build a critique of current policy practice and suggest some proposals for improvement. Such theorems are so well known that they are taught in introductory economics or public finance courses in undergraduate programs. Thus, we use a standard textbook catalog of justifications of government intervention (Stiglitz 1986):

1. *Failure of competition*: Natural monopolies need to be regulated to ensure marginal cost pricing. Governments should sanction anticompetitive behavior, or collusion. Failure of competition justifies granting regulatory powers to governments. This is an area of tremendous importance in countries such as Italy, where a plethora of services are offered under government-sponsored cartel agreements.

2. *Public goods/services*: Public goods/services (goods/services that can be enjoyed by individuals at zero marginal cost and goods/services whose consumption cannot be rationed by the government) are usually not supplied efficiently by the private sector, since the private sector cannot ensure the revenue it needs to cover costs. Notice that the criteria for the definition of a "public" good or service are quite stringent: in particular, they are often not satisfied by what usually are referred to as "public services" like electricity, garbage collection, etc., which can perfectly well be provided by the private sector.

3. *Externalities:* Pollution, congestion, and overexploitation of natural resources are all examples where optimizing private behavior cannot achieve the first best. In these examples the role of government is one of providing either regulatory constraints or tax/subsidy incentives to offset the externalities. One good example is the case of multiple equilibria in the banking industry, where runs can occur due to the relative illiquidity of banks' assets compared to their liabilities. Deposit insurance (which does not have to be provided by the government but which the government can make mandatory) is one solution to this problem.

4. *Incomplete markets*: Financial markets are usually cited as examples where private individuals find it difficult or unprofitable to run businesses that are good for the community as a whole. Insurance is an example of a business where a government could very efficiently pool risks which the private sector might find it more difficult to bear at a fair price. Many of the examples of incomplete markets, however, are taken from an era of widespread financial regulation, which provided a number of constraints to the private sector, thus making it difficult, if not impossible to enter into businesses that were both good for the community and profitable. The removal of many regulations affecting financial institutions has opened up new markets in areas where private activity was difficult to conceive in the past (catastrophe insurance is one good example).

5. *Information failures*: Information has sometimes the features of a public good: it is difficult to restrict its dissemination, and the private sector does not have the incentives to provide the adequate amount of it. Thus, just as in the case of public goods, there is a role for government either in the direct supply of information that has public good qualities, or in the enforcement of information supply by private market participants.

6. *Redistribution*: The five preceding arguments for government intervention are based on the premise that, if the economy were left to itself, it would not reach a Pareto-optimal allocation of resources. There are, however, other reasons, based on ethical arguments, for government intervention in the economy. These are usually cast together under the label of redistribution. The idea is that some individuals in the population live in conditions that grant support from the rest of society. Their support, inevitably, comes from the better-off classes.

Notice the important difference between principles 1 to 5 and the sixth principle. Government intervention under 1 to 5 is directed at correcting market failures: it does not entail, necessarily, redistribution of resources. The provision of public goods could be financed by estimating the normal rate of consumption of public goods by different classes of citizens, and imposing taxes on them such as to cover their respective estimated consumption rates.

It is difficult a priori to determine what should be the relative weight of redistribution versus correction of market failures in government activities. What we observe in most countries is that redistribuion[8] takes up the lion's share although we suspect that the amount of resources actually redistributed is very seldom if ever know or publicized, both in the aggregate and in per capita terms. We suspect that this is not the result of optimal design and is produced by the working of interest groups in a democratic system.

The importance of the principles 1 to 6 cannot be overemphasized, especially by economists. They are, unarguably, a very powerful set of ideas on which to base economic analysis of government. Indeed, we know of no other set of ideas on which to base policymaking.

It is thus rather surprising that, in the actual practice of government, economic policymaking issues are not systematically argued with reference to principles 1 to 6. It cannot be that these propositions are difficult to understand by noneconomists. The superiority of free trade over protectionism is as difficult to understand, if not more difficult, and yet it has had tremendous influence on policy choices during the past two centuries.

There are two possible explanations for this disregard of our principles. The first is the knowledge gap: macro-inspired economic policies are typically not based on micro foundations, hence they are difficult to rationalize on the basis the above principles. The second is what we regard as a failure of the democratic process: spelling out the rationale for government intervention and quantifying the effects of redistributive policies would make the job of special interest groups much more transparent, hence much more difficult. We turn to these issues in the next sections.

Why Economic Principles so Rarely Make it to Policymaking

Two explanations can be offered for the fact that the economic principles discussed in the previous section are so seldom applied in the design of government policies and/or institutions. One is that these ideas are too technical and obscure, and they are only devices used by organizations like the World Bank in part to justify their own existence. We object to this explanation, because we think that, with the obvious complexities, these ideas are as powerful and effective as any other economic ideas which are routinely applied in the conduct of business and government.

Another explanation, which we subscribe to, is that two classes of distortions account for the very large gap between the ideal world spelled out in the previous section and reality. The first is the problem of small interest groups causing large distortions. The second, related, is the problem of inertia in the economic functions of government. These are powerful ideas that help us to understand why, in the case of government, adaptation to new circumstances is much more difficult and slow than in the rest of society. History matters. Government in industrial countries and elsewhere is not the product of tabula rasa design. It is what is inherited from the past.

A very superficial survey of the history of governments in industrial countries shows that many of them experienced socialization of means of production and regimes of command economy during the two world wars. The Great Depression fueled the views that markets are inefficient, and government intervention is desirable. These ideas were still powerful in the early postwar period and underpinned the creation of the welfare state and of mixed economies, characterized by a deep and pervasive presence of government in economic activity. It thus comes as no surprise that the general economic principles we listed above find no significant role in government institutions and seldom provide guidance in economic policymaking.[9]

One should, however, recognize that there are institutions where policymaking is guided by a "scientific" approach: international organizations like the World Bank systematically use cost-benefit analysis, a method of evaluation of government-sponsored development projects solidly grounded on microeconomic analysis. The IMF, as discussed above, has recently put new emphasis on structural reform. The Fund has traveled a long way since the days of financial programming, when the working of financial institutions was never perceived as an important issue; it has promoted new research on financial markets and banking supervision, and it has increasingly drawn the attention of its members to the importance of sound financial institutions.

Examples of national governments that customarily apply a scientific approach to government are however less frequent. One exception from the 1970s was the Regulatory Analysis Review Group created and chaired in the Carter White House by Charles Schultze, then Chairman of the Council of Economic Advisers (Eizenstat 1992): the Group submitted to the President proposals on ways to reduce the cost of regulations, while adhering to the requirements of the law. In Europe the U.K. Treasury is the exception. As far as we know it is the only government agency in the European Union which bases fiscal policy decisions on a microeconomic analysis of public expenditure.

The European Commission constantly attempts to base its decisions on economic principles, in particular in its efforts to promote competition and the efficiency of markets. The elimination of capital controls, the first steps towards the liberalization of the telecom market, and the gradual reduction of state aid to industry, all came mostly as a result of action from Brussels. It is interesting to note that in the areas where the commission has executive powers, and can thus take decisions by issuing directives and regulations, progress has been relatively fast. Where instead, as in the area of tax competition, it can only submit proposals to the Council of E.U. Ministers, progress has been much slower. The explanation for why the commission is more interested in promoting markets than national governments is likely to rest with the incentives of the Brussels bureaucracy. The power of a national bureaucracy often depends on the extent to which is can control economic activities, either through direct state ownership of firms or through a system of regulations and authorizations. The Brussels bureaucracy does try to impose its own regulations, but in order to do that it must first dismantle national ones. Capturing the Brussels bureaucracy is also more difficult: interest groups must first coordinate among themselves across national borders. The outcome is a net increase in competition. More fundamentally, the raison d'etre of the European Commission is the single European market: if this market failed, the

Commission itself would fade away. With these qualifications we now turn to the role of interest groups and inertia.

Interest Groups

The phenomenon of interest groups, even small ones, causing large distortions is well known from the international trade literature. Political economy models of trade and tariffs often use the following parable. Trade liberalization is a reform that benefits "the economy as a whole." By increasing the purchasing power of earnings, it improves the consumption possibilities of all consumers. At the same time, however, trade liberalization tends to shrink the import-competing industry and causes a loss of income to those who own the factors of production that are used relatively more intensely in the import-competing industry.

The question, in a democracy, is how to efficiently trade-off the interest of the entirety of consumers with those of the much smaller group of owners of the factors used intensely in the import-competing industry. What complicates the question is that, in most cases, the per capita gains to the population of consumers are a tiny fraction of the per capita losses of the owners of the factors of production in the import-competing industry. What incentives do consumers have to get organized and lobby for the efficient solution?

The political economy of distortions from international trade barriers is one of the most popular models among economists, and the problem of incomplete participation in lobbying is well known in the literature. The parable described above has nothing to do with international trade per se, and can be applied in any situation where special interest groups can make themselves heard by those who set laws and regulations.[10]

The distortions that special interest groups (that is groups which have gained special privileges for their members) bring to a country depend on their number, on the pattern of their activities, and on the magnitude of the distortions they cause. The World Bank's 1997 *World Development Report* (see table 9.1 thereof and the references quoted thereabout) lists many examples of interest groups and discusses the distortions to which they give rise.

Contrary to the often dispersed constituencies that would benefit from change, interest groups have strong incentives to organize in order to resist fiercely any change in government policies which might decrease their privileges. Special interests might cause, initially, only small distortions; however, with economic progress, the distortions become enormous.

An illuminating analysis of the distortions associated with interest groups is provided by Hernando de Soto (1989). His research with the Instituto Libertad y Democracia (ILD) has systematically studied the features of the Peruvian legal system that represent hindrances to efficient economic activities. De Soto's study should not be dismissed by scholars of advanced industrial democracies as one that raises problems which are special to developing countries like Peru: many of the general pathologies that De Soto identifies are also present in industrial countries.

For example, the ILD has considered in detail legislative production in the economic field by the Peruvian lawmakers and concluded that the near entirety of it is redistributive in nature. The prevalence of rules whose effects are redistributive raises a number of distortions in a democracy, caused by the proliferation of pressure groups aimed at affecting such redistribution to their own favor. The result is overspending by the government, a manifestation of the "common pool" problem well known in the economic literature (see, for example, Persson 1998).

The problem is not redistribution per se, which is a legitimate role of government. Rather, it is redistribution induced by lobbying that takes place without full awareness by citizens, and often even by government and parliament.

Inertia

A second class of distortions, related to the problem of interest groups, pertains to the dynamics of government. Consider the following problem: Assume that a government in a democracy is able to achieve a Pareto-efficient allocation of resources through the appropriate combination of taxes, subsidies, and regulations. Suppose that the economy is subject to a shock that makes the current allocation Pareto-inefficient. What takes the government to the new Pareto-efficient allocation? The answer is: nothing that we know.

This state of affairs is in striking contrast with the dynamics of responses to shocks by the private sector (see Giovannini 1997). In a competitive private economy, Pareto-efficient allocations are reached through the working of the market mechanism. In other words, individuals have an incentive to recontract, and their recontracting leads to a new Pareto-efficient allocation. By contrast, the response of governments to changes in economic circumstances has to come from the initiative of governments themselves. In addition, governments, unlike the private sector in competitive economies, have to see the full picture of the new allocation of resources, and they have to know how to get there: a very big task indeed.[11] In the private sector, when conditions change, individuals have an economic incentive to trade again, and the combined effect of these trades will be an efficient response to the new circumstances. Thus, individuals do not need to know the grand scheme that will bring about the optimal allocation: they just need to follow their own interests. A government, instead, can only adapt by sheer enlightenment, that is, only by seeing the problems and tackling them in the most appropriate way.

This observation should now be combined with the discussion at the beginning of this section to explain the dynamic evolution of governments. Not only do governments not have incentives to adapt to changes in economic conditions, and not only might they have problems in determining what the most appropriate changes should be: a number of powerful forces might actually militate against such changes. These forces are the special interests that have been successful in securing economic privileges to their own members.

Box 7.1
A Partial and Imbalanced List of Distortions Affecting European Economies

> One illuminating example of the power of small interest groups is the peculiar institution of notary publics in Spain, France, Germany, and Italy. Created in the Middle Ages to enforce property rights in a technologically backward society that lacked proper civil law procedures, notary publics have resisted change and developed into a powerful impediment to efficient transactions. But the damage produced by this small interest group may be even bigger. In Italy, for instance, by providing a formal certification of property rights, notary publics have relieved the pressure for the reform of civil law procedures which remain slow and unreliable, and substantially weaken the enforcement of property rights.
>
> One of Europe's objectives, written in 1958 in the Treaty of Rome, is to preserve its agriculture, in particular individual farmers. There are two ways to do this: with direct subsidies to farmers, or through a tariff. It is well known that direct subsidies (as used for example in the United Kingdom before it joined the European Commission) are less distortionary. However, they are also more visible, because anyone who looks

at the government budget can immediately see how much of her taxes are spent on farmers. Mainly for this reason the European Union runs a complicated, and much more distortionary, system of agricultural tariffs, and has so far been unable to change it: farmers have blocked any reform of the system.

Reform in the area of the fiscal treatment of income from financial assets is another example. There are two countries in the E.U. where non-residents can avoid tax on such income: Austria and Luxembourg. Because any change of E.U. legislation in the fiscal area requires unanimity, reform has so far been impossible. A shift to decisions through qualified majority, as opposed to unanimity, was proposed in the drafting of the Amsterdam Treaty but blocked by the two small European Union members. Reform could still happen if a way is found to compensate Austria and Luxembourg, but apparently other E.U. governments believe that such compensations would be politically unacceptable in their own countries.

The labor market is perhaps the example best know to economists. The idea that unions are controlled by "insiders" who give limited consideration to the impact of labor contracts on the "outsiders" has been formalized by Lindbeck and Snower (1989). The decisions of the French and Italian governments to give in to the request to introduce a thirty-five–hour work week at unchanged pay, when both countries experience unemployment rates in excess of 12 percent, is just a recent example of the power of "insiders."

The debate on labor market inefficiencies has been paralleled by a similar debate on the inefficiencies of capital markets. The history of capital markets in Europe and elsewhere is one of pervasive controls and regulations lasting well into the 1980s, and often designed to protect individual groups in the market. One set of issues involve the rules affecting corporate control and shareholders' rights. Influential observers have argued that the current set of rules are, in the case of Italy in particular, strikingly at odds with the objectives of shareholders' value, management incentives, and contestability of corporate control (see Bragantini 1996 and Marchetti 1996). As these authors argue, the Italian stock market is characterized by a number of rules that allow very efficient control of large corporations by (economically) small shareholders. Such control is efficient (from the viewpoint of the controllers) also because it prevents external bids. A by-product of this system is that the universe of "minority" shareholders often receive abnormally low returns on their investments without being able to affect the decisions of management.

Lack of contestability of corporate control induces distorted incentives and suboptimal investment decisions. However, as in the examples discussed in the previous section, reform has long been postponed largely because of the effective lobbying of organized interest groups. Privatizations are one area where this problem can produce large distortions. Privatizations have been hailed by policy economists, who saw them as a way to eliminate inefficient government control of economic activities, when it is not justified by the criteria listed above in the section entitled "The Roles of Government in the Economy." However, in the presence of capital markets that are distorted by the mechanisms described above, privatizations provide only a limited Pareto improvement. This applies in particular to the effectiveness of corporate governance procedures: weak boards offer no guarantee that the transfer of property rights from the state to the private sector will result in improved management and more efficiently run companies.

At least in Italy, the role of economists as "advocates" of reform (see, e.g., Associazione Disiano Preite 1997) has recently been influential in building the consensus that made possible a first reform of corporate governance rules.

An Agenda for Initiatives

In this chapter we have argued that a reliable and effective theory of economic policy should be firmly based on the economic analysis of distortions. To paraphrase, we advocate more microfoundations to economic policy. In principle, our position is not very different from that of macro theorists who in the past advocated more microfoundations to the field of macroeconomics. In practice, however, the research agenda we propose differs markedly from that pursued by some macroeconomic theorists.

The microfoundations approach to macroeconomics has spawned a family of computable general equilibrium models, which generate dynamic fluctuations in model economies where individuals and firms consistently optimize over their planning horizons.

What we would like to propose here is a very different and probably more ambitious research program. Such program should be first and foremost empirical: information and hard data on the main inefficiencies in modern, complex industrial economies is largely unavailable. Collecting such data and information is likely to be extremely expensive, and governments should spearhead this effort. We suggest a way to induce governments to undertake such a program: to insert a requirement that every law or act of government contain an explanation of its economic rationale based on an analysis of how principles 1 to 5 apply. In addition, there should be a requirement that every law or act of government clearly explain and quantify the envisaged redistributive effects, both in the aggregate and in per capita terms.

This simple reform would have two effects. On the one hand, it would force more transparency in economic policymaking and render the job of special interest groups harder. On the other hand, it would spawn an economic culture of lawmaking, which would trigger large efforts at collecting the data and information that are the necessary conditions for such "technological" progress in economic policymaking to take place.

Our approach complements the current wave of political-economic models. These seek to explain the origin of observed distortions by explaining the interactions among interest groups that caused them; they also suggest institutional arrangements that would make it easier to avoid these problems. We think that economists can and should do more. Governments need all the good advice they can use, and academic economists are ideally equipped to provide it, but such advice need to be based on a detailed knowledge of the facts.

Dixit (1997) has pointed to two different roles that economists can play as policy advisers: "They can limit themselves to quantify the gains and losses that are at stake in a particular policy decision. Alternatively they can directly participate in the debate using strategic moves of their own." In the first case economists provide politicians with a basis for evaluating the tradeoffs they face; thus they help them to strike a deal among opposing interests. The second role is more active: in the free trade debate, for instance, they could "stake out a pure position in favor of free trade and try to align public opinion on their side by creating a status quo favorable to free trade."

We would like to go beyond the observation made by Dixit, and suggest that the two roles are not equivalent. In the battle to get rid of the distortions caused by the presence of special interests, economists can be instrumental in tilting the balance in favor of the removal of the distortions. This requires an active role as "advocates," trying to enlist the support of the public in favor of policies that benefit the majority of the population. In other words, they can do a lot to remove the inefficiency caused by the free rider problem that prevents the majority from carrying the day and thus allows interest groups to prevail. But this, as noted by Dixit, requires "direct participation in the debate using strategic moves of their own."

Parallel to their role as advocates, economists can help improve the working of existing institutions by introducing a more "scientific" approach" to policymaking. We have proposed what we believe would be a powerful innovation of the current set of rules, in many countries:

a requirement that new legislation be justified on the basis of the principles we have laid out and which represent the state of our knowledge on what governments should do. Such a requirement would provide the best guide of public (parliamentary) debate on new proposals in the area of economic policy.

These proposals, of course, do not in any way renege the importance of sound macro stabilization policies in the Mundell tradition. But both to make those policies more effective, and to move further, we believe in progress in the theory of economic policymaking.

Notes

A first version of this chapter was presented as a paper at the Festschrift Conference in honor of Robert A. Mundell, held in Washington on October 23–24, 1997. We thank Rudi Dornbusch, Mario Draghi, Luigi Spaventa, Guido Tabellini, and an anonymous referee for their comments on an earlier draft.

1. Elhanan Helpman has often made this point in connection with economic policy in Israel after the 1985 stabilization.

2. Recent research (see, e.g., Persson 1998; Persson, Roland, and Tabellini forthcoming, 1998) has advanced our understanding of the reasons why, for instance, public policy is often shaped by special interest groups. This work points to institutional arrangements that could correct such distortions, making a "scientific approach" to government policy possible.

3. For a review of these developments see, for example, Dornbusch and Giovannini 1990, where all the references cited in this section can be found.

4. The rational expectations literature has been influential in changing policymakers' attitude toward markets: "The relationship between the policymaker and the market is not what it used to be. In the old days, policymakers thought that to be effective, they had better surprise the market. Announcements should be made when the markets were closed. Everyone had to be surprised. The markets were adversaries to the policymakers. However, it is a new world now. Now, the role of policies is a dialogue with the markets; but in order to have a dialogue, your actions must be transparent, clear, accountable, and predictable. You must have an open way of policymaking" (Frenkel 1997).

5. At MIT, for instance, the number of foreign students who received a Ph.D. in economics has increased from 22 percent of all economic students in the 1950s, to 25 percent in the 1960s and 1970s, to 36 percent in the past fifteen years. Moreover, while in the earlier period many of the foreign students were Canadians, in time their countries of origin have spread over the entire world.

6. See, e.g., Mundell 1995 and the discussion of taxation and growth in Mundell 1971.

7. Recent work on "transition economies" is an important exception. The challenge posed by the need rebuild a market economy from scratch has forced macroeconomists to think about institutions; property rights; the legal framework and the enforcement of laws; budget procedures; the design of regulatory agencies; etc. Examples are the NBER volumes on Eastern Europe. See Blanchard, Froot, and Sachs 1994. On budget procedures and budget institutions, see Alesina 1996.

8. In most G-7 countries redistribution is largely across generations.

9. Even free trade had a hard time being accepted as the guiding principle of economic policy in the early postwar period. During the negotiations leading to the Mutual Aid Agreement between the U.S. administration and the British government, Keynes "shocked American officials by making a strong statement about Britain's postwar economic policies. He declared that the British government would find itself beset by such grave economic difficulties at the end of the war that it would be forced to resort to bilateral arrangements and other forms of outright discrimination against the US." Only at the insistence of the State Department, the final text of the Atlantic Charter expresses the desire of the two countries "with due respect for their existing obligations, to further . . . access, on equal terms, to the trade and raw materials of the world" (Gardner 1980).

10. Persson 1998 provides an extensive discussion and a transparent analysis of the role of special interest politics in modern democracies.

11. See the debates on central planning during the 1930s and 1940s: e.g., Lange and Taylor 1938, and Lerner 1946.

References

Alesina, A. 1996. Politics, procedures, and budget deficits. Unpublished manuscript, Harvard University.

Associazione Disiano Preite. 1997. *Rapporto sulla Societá Aperta*. Bologna: Il Mulino.

Blanchard, O. J., K. A. Froot, and J. D. Sachs. 1994. *The transition in Eastern Europe*. Chicago: University of Chicago Press.

Bragantini, S. 1996. *Capitalismo all'Italiana*. Milan: Baldini & Castoldi.

Camdessus, M. 1997. Toward a second generation of structural reform in Latin America. Unpublished address at the 1997 National Banks Convention, Buenos Aires, May 21. Washington: International Monetary Fund.

De Soto, H. 1989. *The other path*. New York: Harper & Row.

Dixit, A. K. 1997. *The making of economic policy*. Cambridge: MIT Press.

Dornbusch, R., and A. Giovannini. 1990. Monetary policy in the open Economy. In *Handbook of monetary economics*, vol. 2, ed. B. M. Friedman and F. H. Hahn, Amsterdam: North-Holland.

Eizenstat, S. E. 1992. Economists and White House decisions. *Journal of Economic Perspectives* 6(3).

Frenkel, J. A. 1997. Comments. In *EMU and the international monetary system*, ed. Masson, Krueger, and Turtleboon. Washington, D.C.: International Monetary Fund.

Gardner, R. N. 1980. *Sterling-dollar diplomacy in current perspective*. New York: Columbia University Press.

Giovannini, A. 1997. Comments on Joseph Stiglitz's "Role of government in the contemporary world." In *Role of government in the contemporary world*, ed. Vito Tanzi. Cambridge: MIT Press.

Lange, O., and F. M. Taylor. 1938. *On the economic theory of socialism*. Minneapolis: University of Minnesota Press.

Lerner, A. P. 1946. *The economics of control.* New York: Macmillan Co.

Lindbeck, A., and D. Snower. 1989. *The insider-outsider theory.* Cambridge: MIT Press.

Marchetti, P. 1996. Corporate Governance e Disciplina Societaria Vigente. *Rivista delle Società* 41(2–3):1547–64.

Mundell, R. A. 1995. Unemployment, competitiveness, and the welfare state. In *Rivista di Politica Economica*, 130–93.

Mundell, R. A. 1971. The dollar and the policy mix: 1971. *Essays in International Finance* (International Finance Section, Princeton University) (no. 85):3–28.

Naim, M. 1995. Latin America's journey to the market: From macroeconomic shocks to institutional therapy. Occasional paper no. 62, International Center for Economic Growth. San Francisco: Institute for Contemporary Studies Press.

Persson, T. 1998. Economic policy and special interest politics. *Economic Journal* 108:310–27.

Persson, T., G. Roland, and G. Tabellini. 1998. Toward micropolitical foundations of public finance. *European Economic Review* (no. 42):685–94.

Persson, T., G. Roland, and G. Tabellini. Forthcoming. Comparative politics and public finance. *Journal of Political Economy.*

Puviani, A. 1903. *Teoria dell'Illusione Finanziaria.* Palermo: R. Sandrom.

Stiglitz, J. 1986. *The economics of the public sector.* New York: Norton.

World Bank. 1997. *The state in a changing world—World Development Report 1997.* Oxford: Oxford University Press.

World Bank. 1996. *From market to plan—World Development Report 1996.* Oxford: Oxford University Press.

8 International Trade and Factor Mobility: An Empirical Investigation

Linda S. Goldberg and
Michael W. Klein

Introduction

It is a notable achievement to develop an economic model that provides a framework for understanding and analyzing important economic issues of the day. It is an even more striking achievement to develop an economic model that addresses an issue that will be of central importance in the future. In the 1950s, a time when cross-border capital movements were largely stymied by government regulations, Robert Mundell published a series of papers studying the implications of capital mobility. Today's central paradigms for studying events in a world characterized by vast flows of capital across national boundaries draw on Mundell's analysis that foresaw such a world. An examination of the linkages between international capital movements, domestic production, and international trade is especially timely today, given the massive and volatile capital flows to emerging markets observed through the 1990s.

Mundell studied capital mobility in a variety of frameworks. He is best known for the Mundell-Fleming model (Mundell 1968), which analyzes the effect of portfolio capital movements on the efficacy of monetary and fiscal policy. Monetary authorities today are intimately aware of the central lessons of this model. Less well known, but increasingly relevant, are issues considered in Mundell's work on the implications of physical capital mobility for international trade. In a world of significant growth of both international direct investment and international trade, this work raises important considerations for policy makers who are concerned with understanding trade and direct investment linkages among countries.

In "International Trade and Factor Mobility" (1957), Mundell demonstrates the substitutability of international trade and factor mobility. In the context of the Heckscher-Ohlin-Samuelson (HOS) model, perfect factor mobility across sectors within an economy provides a tendency for commodity-price equalization, even in the absence of international trade in goods. This result complements the Stolper-Samuelson theorem (1941), which demonstrates the tendency for factor-price equalization as a consequence of goods trade, even in the absence of international trade in factors. International factor mobility also serves as a substitute for trade in another sense in the HOS model, since an increase in the volume of factor movements can decrease the volume of trade.

Subsequent theoretical work has demonstrated that models which diverge from the standard HOS assumptions can result in complementarity, rather than substitutability, between factor trade and goods trade (Wong 1986). There are a variety of ways this subsequent work differs from Mundell's original contribution, including allowances for differences in technologies across countries (Kemp 1966, Jones 1967, Purvis 1972, Svensson 1984, and Markusen and Svensson 1985), introduction of production taxes, monopoly market structure, external economies of scale or factor market distortions (Markusen 1983), and permitting foreign capital to promote domestic development (Schmitz and Helmberger 1970). In all of these cases, an increase in international direct investment may promote greater international trade.

Understanding the relationship between trade in goods and trade in factors is important for obtaining a complete picture of international linkages. For example, it is often the case that the amount of international trade undertaken by a country serves as a proxy for its level of "openness" or, in a bilateral context, as a measure of the international linkages between two countries. Mundell's analysis implies that focusing on trade as a proxy for openness may be misleading when international capital flows are significant. Empirically, it is important to consider whether this bias is significant and systematic in a particular direction.

Another key reason for understanding these linkages arises in the aftermath of the currency and financial crises of the 1990s. If capital inflows to a country are large, but also can abruptly change course, important real consequences can ensue. In Latin America, in Asia, or elsewhere, even exogenous reversals in foreign capital availability can lead to a redistribution of productive factors within a country. The availability of investment funds and new physical capital can have important consequences for the future structure of a country's trade and the welfare of its citizens.

The broad challenge posed by the theoretical and policy arguments can only be resolved through careful analytical and empirical studies. Recent empirical research in this area includes work by Collins, O'Rourke, and Williamson (1997), who studied the historical link between labor mobility and trade, and our own work on the response of exports and imports of selected Latin American and Southeast Asian countries to direct investment from the United States and Japan (Goldberg and Klein 1998). Collins, O'Rourke, and Williamson found little evidence of substitutability between labor movement and trade. We found some evidence of complementarity between capital flows and bilateral trade, especially in the Asian region: direct investment from Japan to Southeast Asian countries significantly increased the bilateral exports and imports of those countries with Japan. We found no evidence of significant links between capital flows and bilateral trade, however, between Latin American countries and either Japan or the United States, or between the United States and Southeast Asian countries.

In this chapter we provide a motivating theoretical model, followed by a detailed empirical study of the effects of direct investment flows on levels of international trade. We present the first empirical analysis, to our knowledge, of this relationship at a sectoral level. Specifically, we study how the net exports of specific manufacturing sectors of eight Latin American countries (Argentina, Brazil, Chile, Colombia, Ecuador, Mexico, Peru, and Venezuela) respond to direct investment from the United States into those specific sectors, as well as into other manufacturing and nonmanufacturing sectors of their economies. We demonstrate empirically the varied direction and levels of response of sectoral trade volumes to direct investment across manufacturing sectors and across countries.

Based on this detailed empirical evidence, we conclude that the theoretical debate is justified. In Argentina, where investments into manufacturing industries have been concentrated in food-related industries or chemical industries, the net exports of these industries have expanded (despite these industries remaining net importers overall), without significant detriment to other manufacturing industries. In Brazil and Venezuela, FDI into particular manufacturing industries— flows that have been concentrated in chemicals, machinery, and transportation equipment—have been associated with expanded net import positions by these industries. Foreign investment into wholesale and retail trade worsened the net export positions of manufacturing industries in Mexico and Columbia (suggesting that this FDI facilitated Latin

imports) but improved the net export positions in Brazilian manufacturing industries. Our detailed examination of the experience of individual industries, using cross-country and time-series data, does not
suggest strong or systematic linkages between sectoral trade and FDI
in Latin America.

Direct Investment in Sector-Specific Capital and Trade

Overview

To set the stage for our empirical analysis, in this section we review the
main distinctions between general equilibrium models that find that
factor mobility and trade are substitutes, versus those models that find
that they are complements. We then present a simple version of the
Rybczynski theorem to highlight the role of sector-specific capital. Our
objective is use the theoretical exposition to motivate our empirical
tests for sectoral trade volumes and foreign direct investment linkages,
allowing *both* for direct effects on trade of foreign capital inflows into
a sector and for spillovers effects from inflows into other sectors.

In these general equilibrium models, the relative returns to factors and
the level of production and trade are jointly determined. Typically,
models differ in their predictions about the relationship between factor
movements and trade volumes because of differences in assumptions
about production, which lead to differences in the relative returns to
factors. Across models, however, the manner in which the change in a
factor endowment affects the production of each good in the economy
is similar. The basis of this relationship is the Rybczynski theorem, which
then drives the association between factor flows and trade volumes.

We illustrate the Rybczynski-based association between capital flows
and trade volumes in the context of two types of models: in the first,
countries differ in their endowments of factors but have identical production technologies (an HOS-style model). In the second, production technologies are different in the two countries (a Ricardian-style
model). Basic forms of these models include two goods and two
factors—labor and capital. In this setting, the Rybczynski theorem
states that, given the prices of goods, an inflow of capital leads to an
increase in the level of production of the good which uses capital relatively intensively and a decrease in the level of production of the good
which uses labor relatively intensively. These changes in production
have direct implications for trade volumes and, in fact, will be the sole

source of changes in trade volumes under the assumption of homo-thetic and identical preferences in each country.

Mundell studied the relationship between factor flows and trade in an HOS model. He considered a situation where a prohibitively high tariff on imports shuts off trade and raises the return to capital in the country where it is the relatively scarce factor. This leads to a capital inflow to that country and, through the Rybczynski effect, an increase in the production of the capital-intensive good (which had been the imported good before the tariff was put in place) and a decrease in the production of the labor-intensive good (which had been the export). Capital inflows continue until relative factor endowments in the two countries are identical.

If the tariff were then removed, there would be no trade in goods. The reason is that the initial basis for trade in this model, autarky dif-ferences in relative factor endowments and the accompanying differ-ences in relative goods prices, has been eliminated through factor flows. Factor flows can give rise to commodity price equalization, much as in the standard HOS model goods trade gives rise to factor price equalization. More broadly, in a model of this nature, an increase in the volume of factor flows causes a decrease in the volume of trade. Factor flows substitute for trade flows.

An alternative result can arise in a Ricardian model in which coun-tries have different technologies. For example, suppose each of two countries has the same labor productivity but one country enjoys higher capital productivity. The country with the higher capital pro-ductivity will export the capital-intensive good. When capital is inter-nationally mobile, it will seek its highest returns and thus flow to the high capital-productivity country. Through the Rybczynski effect, these capital inflows increase the production of the capital-intensive good (that country's export) and decrease the production of the labor-intensive good (that country's import). In this simple example, factor flows complement trade flows.

A Basic Specific Factors Model

A basic model provides a context for our empirical exploration of the way in which foreign direct investment to a particular sector affects the volume of exports and imports of that sector as well as of other sectors. There are two goods, *A* and *B*. The factors of production include domestic and foreign capital used solely in the production of good *A*,

K_A, and F_A, respectively, domestic and foreign capital used solely in the production of good B, K_B, and F_B, respectively, and labor, L. Labor, unlike capital, costlessly shifts from one sector to another in response to an incipient wage differential. The amount of labor used in the production of good A is denoted as L_A and the amount used in the production of good B is denoted as L_B.

There are two other key assumptions in this partial-equilibrium analysis. First, domestic and foreign capital are completely sector-specific. The assumption that foreign capital is sector-specific reflects the prevalent view that direct investment typically involves some active management of an asset. (This treatment contrasts with a view of portfolio investment as only requiring the bearer to passively hold the asset.) The direct management of foreign investment requires some sector-specific knowledge that makes an investor focus on a sector within which she has particular expertise.

The second key assumption is that foreign direct investment is exogenous, an assumption which makes this a partial-equilibrium exercise. This clearly runs counter to the standard modeling assumption of perfect capital mobility since it does not allow for arbitraging rates of return across sectors.[1] The implication of this second assumption is that we do not endogenously determine the equalization of returns to investments across borders, or the equilibrium volume of international capital flows.[2] A general equilibrium approach could accomplish this goal, but it would likely still give rise to similar qualitative results as those shown using the simple partial equilibrium setting.

Assume that production functions take the form

$$A = f(K_A + F_A, L_A) \quad B = g(K_B + F_B, L_B),$$

(8.1)

where the partial derivatives with respect to labor, (f_L, g_L), and capital, (f_k, g_k), are positive. The cross-partial derivatives with respect to labor and capital from either foreign or domestic sources, (f_{LK}, g_{LK}), also are positive. All second partial derivatives, $(f_{LL}, f_{KK}, g_{LL}, g_{KK})$, are negative.

With labor perfectly mobile across sectors and the labor market competitive, the wage paid to labor in sector A, w, is the same as the wage paid to labor in sector B. The first-order conditions for profit maximization require that firms in each sector hire labor to the point where the product wage equals the marginal product of labor,

$$\frac{w}{p_A} = f_L \quad \frac{w}{p_B} = g_L.$$

(8.2)

Totally differentiating each of these relationships, and dividing through by the product wage or the marginal product of labor, we obtain

$$\frac{dw}{w} - \frac{dp_A}{p_A} = \left(\frac{f_{LL}}{f_L}\right)dL_A + \left(\frac{f_{LK}}{f_L}\right)dF_A$$

$$\frac{dw}{w} - \frac{dp_B}{p_B} = \left(\frac{g_{LL}}{g_L}\right)dL_B + \left(\frac{g_{LK}}{g_L}\right)dF_B,$$

(8.3)

where dL_i represents the change in employment in sector i and dF_i represents foreign direct investment to sector i. Setting dK_i equal to zero reflects our assumption of sector-specific domestic capital and our interest in considering the effects of FDI rather than changes in domestic capital.[3] Full employment of labor ensures that $L = L_A + L_B$, where L is the total amount of labor in the economy. With a constant labor force,[4] we have

$$dL_A = -dL_B.$$

(8.4)

Wages are continuously equated across the two sectors, and, therefore, the proportionate change in wages across sectors is equal. Solving the sets of equations for the change in labor in each sector yields

$$dL_A = \left(\frac{f_{LK}g_L}{Z}\right)dF_A - \left(\frac{g_{LK}f_L}{Z}\right)dF_B + \left(\frac{f_Lg_L}{Z}\right)\left[\frac{dp_A}{p_A} - \frac{dp_B}{p_B}\right]$$

$$dL_B = \left(\frac{f_Lg_{LK}}{Z}\right)dF_B - \left(\frac{f_{LK}g_L}{Z}\right)dF_A + \left(\frac{f_Lg_L}{Z}\right)\left[\frac{dp_B}{p_B} - \frac{dp_A}{p_A}\right],$$

(8.5)

where $Z = -(f_{LL}g_L + g_{LL}f_L) > 0$.

These equations show that foreign direct investment to sector A ($dF_A > 0$) pulls labor into that sector, reducing the labor employment in sector B, all else equal. The implication is that a collapse of (foreign) capital in a sector leads that sector to contract employment, leaving labor to flow to the other sector. The marginal products of labor and the degree of complementarities between labor and capital in production determine the magnitudes of the worker reallocation.

There are straightforward output implications of these labor and capital adjustments. From the production functions,

$$dA = f_K dF_A + f_L dL_A$$

$$dB = g_K dF_B + g_L dL_B.$$

(8.6)

Substituting in the results from above, we obtain

$$dA = \frac{f_L^2 g_L}{Z}\left[\frac{dp_A}{p_A} - \frac{dp_B}{p_B}\right] + \left(f_K + \frac{f_{LK}g_L f_L}{Z}\right)dF_A - \frac{f_L^2 g_{LK}}{Z}dF_B$$

$$dB = \frac{g_L^2 f_L}{Z}\left[\frac{dp_B}{p_B} - \frac{dp_A}{p_A}\right] + \left(g_K + \frac{g_{LK}g_L f_L}{Z}\right)dF_B - \frac{g_L^2 f_{LK}}{Z}dF_A.$$

(8.7)

These equations show that sectoral output is stimulated by an increase in its relative price or by FDI into that sector; its output is decreased by FDI into the other sector. The basic intuition is that an inflow of foreign capital into a sector increases sectoral output directly, by providing more capital, and indirectly, by raising the marginal product of its labor and drawing workers away from the other sector. Overall, investment to one sector increases production in that sector and decreases production in the other sector, all else equal.

Returning to the issue originally considered by Mundell and others, the implication of these results is that the effects of FDI on trade volumes depend upon whether a sector was initially a net exporter or a net importer. Assuming no demand-side effects (as would be consistent with the assumption of homothetic demand), and that relative price effects are second order, an increase in production in sector A causes international trade by that sector to increase if that sector was initially a net exporter, or to decrease if that sector was initially a net importer. The converse also holds. In all these cases, direct investment into a sector should cause an increase in the net exports of that sector and a decrease in the net exports of other sectors, all else equal.

Capital and Trade Flows with Latin America

Data

In this section we explore the relationship between trade and FDI using detailed sectoral data on FDI inflows and trade between the United States and eight Latin American countries: Argentina, Brazil, Chile, Colombia, Ecuador, Mexico, Peru, and Venezuela[5] (sources: United States Bureau of Economic Analysis Statistics on U.S. Direct Investment Abroad and the Feenstra NBER Trade Database). The data on FDI span both manufacturing and nonmanufacturing industries; the bilateral trade data spans only the manufacturing industries. The sample period for which both trade and FDI data are available is 1972 through 1994. Trade, investment, and U.S. income series are converted into real dollar values using the U.S. producer price series. The GDP series for individual Latin American countries enters in the regressions as millions of real local currency units.

The series on FDI into Latin America from the United States, broken down by recipient country and by sector, are a construction based on the U.S. Direct Investment Position Abroad series generated by the Bureau of Economic Analysis (BEA). This BEA stock series measures the year-end value of U.S. parent's equity (including retained earnings) in, and outstanding loans to, their foreign affiliates. Our FDI proxy is the change in this stock series, deflated by an annual dollar producer price index. This proxy combines direct investment capital flows plus valuation adjustments, so that FDI can be positive or negative in any period. As described by the BEA, valuation adjustments result from price changes, exchange rate changes, and other factors. Although our proxy for FDI clearly is not a perfect measure, it is the closest series we have (and most comparable across countries) for indicating annual FDI by sector.

Latin American countries have been regular recipients of erratic U.S. outward investment flows over the past decades. As shown in figure 8.1, U.S. FDI flows to various regions, including Latin America and the Asia-Pacific area, have been growing following a period of decline and stagnation in the early to mid-1980s. In general, FDI flows to Latin America account for about 13 percent of U.S. FDI to the three major FDI recipient regions (Europe, Latin America, and Asia-Pacific). Within Latin America, the main recipient countries have been Brazil, Mexico, and Argentina, respectively accounting for approximately 45, 30 and 10 percent of the region's inflows from the United States over the two decades we examine. Figure 8.2 shows the considerable volatility of these flows across countries and over time.[6]

For our purposes, it also is informative to consider the sectoral composition of these flows. Table 8.1 shows that, across Latin America, chemical and allied products; transportation equipment; and other manufacturing have been regular recipients of investment capital owned by the United States. Recent years have been marked by an explosion of funds into food and kindred products and banking and finance sectors. This latter phenomenon is driven by flows into Chile, where banking and finance[7] sectors are the entry point for most foreign capital. We do not know the extent to which this capital is channeled to local manufacturing or nonmanufacturing industries.

The pattern of exports, imports, and capital flows for the individual sectors of each country is shown in detail in the panels of table 8.2. In Argentina, the favored sectors for FDI have been food and kindred products; wholesale trade; and banking and finance. In Brazil, foreign

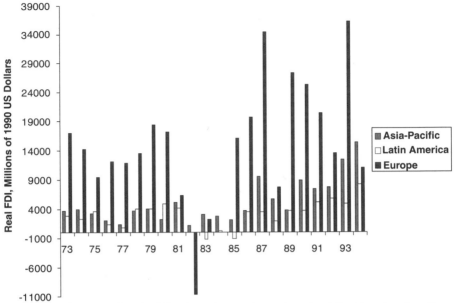

*Constructed as the deflated year-to-year change in regional direct investment position for all industries covered by the BEA statistics on direct investment position abroad.

Figure 8.1
U.S. FDI by region

Table 8.1
Sectoral composition of U.S. FDI in Latin America over selected intervals (millions of 1990 $U.S.)

	1973–1977	1978–1982	1983–1988	1989–1994
Food and kindred products	635.13	1,124.66	20.17	3,974.41
Primary and fabricated metals	731.62	700.22	421.33	−351.34
Chemical and allied products	1,895.85	1,523.33	926.00	2,138.16
Machinery, except electrical	421.75	1,068.73	705.54	−544.61
Electric and electronic equipment	.	399.96	129.08	729.99
Transportation equipment	591.59	1,350.41	1,028.49	1,573.77
Other manufacturing	2,042.42	1,895.85	1,077.82	1,349.30
Wholesale trade	941.52	599.76	−220.04	1,854.25
Banking and other finance	1,377.24	1,729.70	1,005.22	3,701.49
Services	.	.	800.40	699.44
Other nonmanufacturing	319.41	115.44	−262.33	2,937.35

Note: FDI numbers were obtained by summing the deflated year-to-year changes in BEA direct-investment-position-abroad data across for all eight countries in the sample.

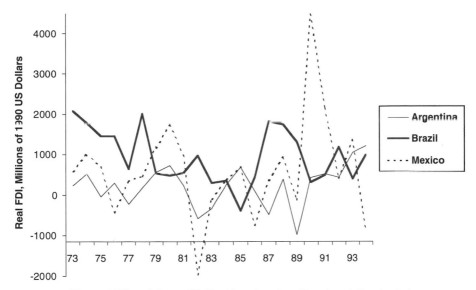

*Source: BEA statistics on US direct investment position abroad. Constructed as the sum over all manufacturing and nonmanufacturing industries in the sample of the the deflated year-to-year change in direct investment position.

Figure 8.2
Annual FDI from the United States

capital inflows have been directed toward a broad range of industries, a substantial portion of which fall into chemicals, transportation, and the other manufacturing (residual) categories. In Mexico, the food, chemicals, and transportation sectors have been important attractors of foreign capital. In Chile it is less transparent which sectors ultimately receive FDI from the United States: capital inflows land in finance, banking and "other" nonmanufacturing industries. These sectors presumably reinvest some significant resources across manufacturing, but the data do not provide specifics on the ultimate sectoral beneficiaries of these foreign long-term investments.

Table 8.2 also presents evidence on the sectoral pattern of exports and imports of the manufacturing sectors of each Latin American country. Nonelectrical machinery shipments make up a significant portion of Latin American exports to the United States, even though all countries in the sample are net importers in this sector. The chemical sectors have been important, and transportation has grown considerably in importance over the past decade. In Ecuador and Venezuela, manufacturing products are a small share of the overall export revenues. Table 8.2 also

Table 8.2
Sectoral composition of trade and FDI by country, 1972–1994

Country	Manufacturing				
	Food and kindred products	Chemicals and allied products	Primary and fabricated metals	Machinery, except electrical	Electric and electronic equipment
Sectoral FDI from the United States as a fraction of total FDI from the United States, by recipient country					
Argentina	0.16	0.10	−0.01	0.05	0.00
Brazil	0.08	0.12	0.05	0.07	0.03
Chile	0.02	0.07	0.00	0.00	0.00
Colombia	0.25	0.30	0.02	−0.06	0.01
Ecuador	0.23	0.08	−0.05	0.00	0.07
Mexico	0.20	0.18	0.03	0.01	0.04
Peru	−0.13	0.08	0.01	−0.01	0.02
Venezuela	0.20	0.19	0.03	−0.05	0.00
Sectoral exports to the United States as a fraction of total manufacturing exports to the United States, by source country					
Argentina	0.01	0.23	0.06	0.30	0.12
Brazil	0.02	0.26	0.06	0.26	0.12
Chile	0.04	0.19	0.05	0.33	0.09
Colombia	0.05	0.24	0.05	0.27	0.08
Ecuador	0.06	0.18	0.06	0.29	0.09
Mexico	0.05	0.10	0.11	0.19	0.20
Peru	0.11	0.19	0.07	0.32	0.07
Venezuela	0.07	0.14	0.07	0.32	0.10
Sectoral imports from the United States as a fraction of total manufacturing imports from the United States, by destination country					
Argentina	0.40	0.07	0.18	0.03	0.01
Brazil	0.21	0.04	0.16	0.08	0.05
Chile	0.11	0.07	0.70	0.00	0.00
Colombia	0.22	0.04	0.05	0.00	0.01
Ecuador	0.76	0.01	0.04	0.00	0.00
Mexico	0.05	0.03	0.10	0.08	0.34
Peru	0.23	0.01	0.55	0.00	0.00
Venezuela	0.05	0.11	0.57	0.03	0.01

	Nonmanufacturing				
Transportation equipment	Other manufacturing	Wholesale trade	Banking and finance	Services	Other non-manufacturing industries
0.05	0.10	0.13	0.30	0.03	0.06
0.10	0.20	0.03	0.18	0.05	0.02
0.00	0.00	0.10	0.77	0.00	0.14
−0.01	0.07	0.21	0.14	0.03	0.00
0.01	0.01	0.12	0.02	−0.01	0.00
0.15	0.10	0.10	0.13	0.03	0.15
−0.02	−0.07	0.14	0.09	0.00	−0.11
0.15	0.16	0.04	−0.01	−0.05	0.03
		Manufacturing exports to the United States as a fraction of total exports to the United States			
0.13	0.14	0.75			
0.18	0.10	0.72			
0.13	0.16	0.54			
0.16	0.15	0.23			
0.12	0.19	0.09			
0.14	0.21	0.86			
0.13	0.10	0.50			
0.16	0.15	0.04			
		Manufacturing imports from the United States as a fraction of total imports from the United States			
0.02	0.29	0.89			
0.11	0.34	0.78			
0.00	0.11	0.83			
0.00	0.67	0.85			
0.00	0.19	0.91			
0.17	0.23	0.92			
0.00	0.21	0.81			
0.06	0.16	0.81			

makes evident the varied the importance of manufacturing trade relative to total trade across the Latin American countries.

Since our theoretical section emphasized that sectoral net trade positions, that is, whether a sector is a net importer or net exporter, are relevant for understanding the implications of FDI, it is useful to consider this directly for the sectors of the Latin American economies. Table 8.3 provides a very general overview of sectoral net export position by country. For Venezuela and for Mexico, the "other" nonmanufacturing sector contains a significant fraction of the economy's exports because of heavy reliance on the petroleum sector. Most of the remaining manufacturing sectors are net importers. The remaining Latin American countries are large net exporters of food and kindred products. All countries in the sample except Colombia, Ecuador, and Venezuela also are large net exporters of primary and fabricated metals.

Testing for FDI Effects on Trade

The two-factor model presented in the second section demonstrates that direct investment into a particular sector raises its level of output. The overall volume of trade in goods produced by that sector will increase if that sector was initially a net exporter and it will decrease if that sector was initially a net importer. Conversely, direct investment to one sector is expected to draw labor away from other sectors and cause output in those sectors to contract. In this case, the volume of trade in goods produced by the contracting sector decreases if that sector initially had a trade surplus and increases if that sector initially had a trade deficit. Direct investment to a sector is predicted to increase its net export balance, ceteris paribus, and to decrease the net export balance of other sectors, by drawing resources away from these other sectors. We test these predictions of the theory using sectoral trade and investment data from seven Latin American countries.[8]

The basic time-series cross-section regression equation for a particular Latin American country takes the form

$$\Delta netX_t^i = \alpha_0^i + \alpha_1 \Delta USrealGDP_{t,t-1} + \alpha_2 \Delta OwnrealGDP_{t,t-1}$$
$$+ \alpha_3 \Delta RER_{t,t-1} + \alpha_4 OwnFDI_{t-1,t-2}^i \qquad (8.8)$$
$$+ \alpha_5 OtherFDI_{t-1,t-2}^i + u_t^i + v_t$$

where $\Delta netX_t^i$ represents the change in net exports of sector i; $\Delta USrealGDP$ represents the change in real GDP of the United States;

Table 8.3
Net export position for the entire sample period (1972–1994) (millions of 1990 $U.S.)

	Food and kindred products	Primary and fabricated metals	Chemicals and allied products	Machinery, except electrical	Electric and electronic equipment	Transportation equipment	Other manufacturing
Argentina	6,781	1,101	-6,806	-9,851	-4,193	-4,295	369
Brazil	19,998	10,706	-19,191	-15,426	-5,834	-4,977	24,296
Chile	479	7,598	-3,559	-7,842	-2,218	-3,198	-2,489
Colombia	142	-1,321	-8,595	-9,875	-2,881	-6,120	643
Ecuador	1,066	-880	-2,769	-4,554	-1,331	-1,923	-2,504
Mexico	-5,645	-12,019	-26,726	-46,452	20,830	-2,833	-11,861
Peru	672	5,033	-3,369	-5,924	-1,278	-2,382	581
Venezuela	-5,526	-2,489	-11,618	-27,139	-8,204	-13,128	-11,750

Note: Numbers were obtained by summing over all years (for each industry) the value of U.S. imports from a given country minus the value of U.S. exports to that country.

$\Delta OwnrealGDP$ represents the change in the real GDP of the Latin American country; ΔRER represents the change in the real exchange rate of that country (with a positive value representing a dollar appreciation); $OwnFDI^i$ represents the direct investment flow from the United States into sector i; $OtherFDI^i$ represents the direct investment flow to all manufacturing sectors other than sector i; α_0^i is a fixed-effects dummy variable on levels of net exports for manufacturing sector i; and subscripts on these variables refer to time periods.

The subscript $t, t-1$ reflects the inclusion in the regressions of both a current and a lagged term, while the subscript $t-1, t-2$ reflects the inclusion of both a one-period and a two-period lag. Thus the coefficients α_i represent two coefficients, one on the contemporaneous variable and one on the lagged variable or, in the case of the FDI variables, one on the variable lagged one period and one on the variable lagged two periods. The model presented above suggests that the sum of coefficients represented by the coefficient α_4 is positive while the sum of the coefficients represented by the coefficient α_5 is negative. Standard trade models suggest that the sum of coefficients represented by each of the coefficient α_1, α_2 and α_3 are positive.[9]

The results from the regression analysis can be combined with information on net trade flows to address the question of whether direct investment promotes or diminishes trade. A positive and significant coefficient on the change in own-sector direct investment α_4 indicates that direct investment promotes trade if the country's bilateral trade balance with the United States is negative. This case, corresponding to Mundell's analysis, is one in which direct investment decreases overall trade by reducing exports from the United States to the particular country (assuming that the negative overall trade statistic does not mask a shift from a long-standing negative position to a larger positive position which has only occurred for a few years in the sample period). Conversely, the combination of a positive and significant value of α_4 with a positive trade balance for a country indicates that direct investment to that country promotes trade by expanding an already-existing trade surplus. This corresponds to the situation in the Ricardian model discussed above. A negative and significant value of the coefficient on other-sector direct investment, α_5, bined with a national bilateral trade deficit with the United States suggests that direct investment promotes the volume of trade, all else equal, by increasing trade flows from the United States. Conversely, when a country has a bilateral trade surplus with the United States, direct investment to one sector which diminishes net exports of other sectors serves to reduce the overall volume of trade, all else equal.

The error term in the regression equation (8.8) consists of an error specific to the particular industry for the particular year, u_t^i, and an error common to all industries in the country for that year, v_t. The presence of the common error term, v_t, can typically be addressed using a fixed-effects dummy variable or, equivalently, subtracting the year-specific mean value from all the variables in the regression. In this case, however, we have regressors common to all industries in any particular year, such as the change in the real exchange rate, the change in domestic income and the change in United States income. Thus we cannot subtract out the year-specific mean value since these aggregate regressors are common across all cross-sectional units. Instead, we use an iterative procedure which estimates the variance of v_t and then adjusts the variance-covariance matrix in an appropriate manner (see Kloeck 1981 for a discussion of this problem and its resolution).

Empirical Results

Summary results for regressions using the specification in equation (8.8) are presented in the two panels of table 8.4. Each of these panels represents sets of regressions, where the sets are differentiated by the amount of information included in the other-sector FDI variable. In regressions summarized in panel A, each country's regression contains terms for own industry FDI and for FDI elsewhere in manufacturing.[10]

Panel A results suggest that a significant role is played by own-sector FDI in promoting net exports in Argentina. Own-sector direct investment promotes net exports in Mexico with a one-year lag, as shown in the complete results presented in table A.8.1. By summing across the rows for Argentina and Mexico in table 8.3, we observe that both countries have a bilateral trade deficit with the United States with respect to manufactured goods. Thus for these countries, which represent two of the three largest United States trading partners in Latin America, there is evidence that own-sector direct investment has the marginal effect of reducing the volume of bilateral trade in a way consistent with Mundell's analysis.

The results in panel A also suggest that other-sector direct investment tends to reduce net exports in Mexico and increase net exports in Columbia. This mitigates, but does not reverse, the conclusion that direct investment to Mexico tends to reduce the volume of trade since

Table 8.4
Regression results for direct investment coefficients: summed two-period effects

	Argentina	Brazil	Chile	Colombia	Mexico	Peru	Venezuela
Panel A							
Own industry FDI	0.591**	-0.193	0.217	0.679	0.358	-0.611	-0.151
	(0.272)	(0.138)	(0.876)	(0.485)	(0.299)	(1.56)	(0.309)
FDI to other manufacturing industries	-0.023	0.045	-0.076	0.24**	-0.222**	-0.406	-0.179
	(0.044)	(0.046)	(0.28)	(0.113)	(0.095)	(0.709)	(0.153)
Number of observations	96	133	66	90	125	83	110
Panel B							
Own industry FDI	0.533	-0.242*	0.546	-0.072	0.519	-0.859	-0.716*
	(0.363)	(0.138)	(1.083)	(0.778)	(0.4)	(1.657)	(0.378)
FDI to other manufacturing industries	0.01	0.027	-0.225	0.129	0.29	-0.326	-0.487**
	(0.057)	(0.041)	(0.412)	(0.228)	(0.232)	(0.758)	(0.242)
FDI to wholesale and retail trade	-0.424	0.803***	0.178	-13.36**	-1.49**	0.592	3.438
	(0.332)	(0.234)	(0.933)	(5.538)	(0.716)	(1.515)	(2.138)
FDI to banking, finance, insurance, and real estate	0.153	-0.043	0.068	0.934	-1.151	-0.131	1.259*
	(0.256)	(0.071)	(0.178)	(0.937)	(0.818)	(1.468)	(0.666)
Number of observations	76	133	66	69	110	83	91

Note: Standard errors in parentheses. *, **, and *** indicate significance at the 10, 5, and 1 percent levels, respectively.

the sum of the coefficients on own-sector direct investment, 0.358, is greater, in absolute value, than the sum of the coefficients on other-sector direct investment, −0.222. For Colombia, the marginal effect of direct investment is to promote exports and, therefore, reduce the volume of bilateral trade in manufacturing goods since both the own-sector and other-sector coefficients are positive.

In panel D, we allow for direct investment into nonmanufacturing sectors to also affect the output and, therefore, the trade of manufacturing sectors. There are two possible channels through which these implications may arise. The first channel is that associated with labor reallocation across sectors, as emphasized in the model presented above. The second channel recognizes the role of the output of one sector as an input to the production of other sectors. In this way, direct investment to, for instance, the financial sector may serve to increase output in manufacturing sectors, as the expanded finance sector serves the needs of the manufacturing sectors. Likewise, expansion of the wholesale trade sector may enable manufacturing sectors to expand output for domestic sales, or it may lead to expanded opportunities for imports. Given the tendency toward manufacturing sector trade deficits with the United States, a positive coefficient on nonmanufacturing direct investment implies that this type of direct investment causes a decline in the volume of bilateral trade with the United States, whereas a negative coefficient means that this type of direct investment serves to increase the volume of bilateral trade, all else equal.

Table 8.4, panel B, presents summed two-year net export effects derived from regressions which include both own-sector and other-manufacturing–sector direct investment, plus two other sectoral direct investment measures: direct investment in the finance, banking, and real estate sectors; and direct investment in the wholesale and retail trade sector. These results show that foreign direct investment into the banking, finance, and real estate sectors, as well as to the wholesale and retail trade sector, have a significant effect on cross-sectional sectoral trade in a number of countries although the direction of this effect differs across countries. Direct investment to the wholesale and retail trade sector has a positive and significant effect on trade by manufacturing sectors in Brazil and, with a one-period lag only, in Venezuela. Conversely, direct investment to this sector has a negative and significant effect on trade by manufacturing sectors in Colombia and Mexico. The effect of direct investment into the banking, finance, and real estate sectors on trade by manufacturing sectors is significant for Argentina, Mexico, and Venezuela. In Argentina and Mexico, the initial effect is to promote trade while the effect after one year is to diminish trade. In Venezuela, direct investment to the finance, banking, and real estate sectors also significantly increases trade at the 90 percent level of confidence, with a significant coefficient on the two-year lag at the 95 percent level of confidence.

A comparison of the results in panel A and panel B shows that the inclusion of direct investment from these nonmanufacturing sectors also affects the pattern of significance on the own-sector and other-manufacturing sector direct investment variables. But some of these differences arise due to differences in the samples available when including the nonmanufacturing direct investment measures. The sample sizes for the results in panel B are smaller than those in panel A. Using the restricted samples employed in panel B, but running regressions of the form presented in panel A, coefficients on direct investment variables which are reported as significant in panel A for Argentina, Mexico (on own-sector direct investment), and Venezuela are no longer significant.

Our second and final group of regressions were run on data grouped by industry instead of by country. The regression specification employed is analogous to the one used in the country regressions and incorporates appropriate modifications. Specifically, since the industry regressions include as the left-hand-side variable the net export data for one industry and several countries, the industry dummies are discarded in favor of country dummies. These regressions do not require the type of correction to the variance-covariance matrix discussed above since regressors such as the real exchange rate and income are not common to all cross-sectional units in a particular year.

Table 8.5 displays regression results for the cumulative effects of lagged independent variables. The results for own industry FDI are less illuminating for these regressions than those obtained in the country runs; own industry FDI affects trade significantly only in the case of the "other manufacturing" (residual) category, where FDI flows stifle net exports after one year while stimulating them after two, the cumulative effect being a decrease in net exports.

Stronger evidence is provided for the role of FDI into other industries in drawing resources away from primary and fabricated metals. In addition, FDI to industries other than electric and electronic equipment sector had a significant negative effect on trade in that industry after one year; the same coefficient was negative but insignificant after two years, causing the cumulative effect of both coefficients to be insignificant. The regression results for the electric and electronic

Table 8.5
Regression results for direct investment coefficients: Summed two-period effects

	Food and kindred products	Primary and fabricated metals	Chemicals and allied products	Machinery, except electrical	Electric and electronic equipment	Transportation equipment	Other manufacturing
Panel A							
Own industry FDI	-0.333 (0.206)	0.471 (0.457)	-0.238 (0.17)	0.140 (0.262)	-0.373 (0.796)	0.113 (0.317)	-0.63* (0.333)
FDI to other manufacturing industries	0.026 (0.047)	-0.158** (0.079)	0.026 (0.043)	-0.077 (0.085)	-0.031 (0.121)	-0.108 (0.117)	0.037 (0.107)
Number of observations	143	107	148	135	77	91	73
Panel B							
Own industry FDI	-0.202 (0.371)	0.155 (0.531)	-0.385 (0.242)	0.371 (0.285)	1.051 (0.776)	0.057 (0.459)	-0.808* (0.426)
FDI to other manufacturing industries	0.06 (0.062)	0.025 (0.122)	0.071 (0.062)	0.07 (0.12)	-0.239* (0.139)	-0.247 (0.177)	0.107 (0.15)
FDI to wholesale and retail trade	0.205 (0.239)	0.008 (0.402)	0.242 (0.24)	-0.403 (0.469)	0.644 (0.413)	0.898 (0.638)	0.016 (0.357)
FDI to banking, finance, insurance, and real estate	0.039 (0.167)	0.198 (0.271)	0.164 (0.132)	0.039 (0.30)	0.567*** (0.197)	0.524 (0.0426)	0.048 (0.21)
Number of observations	121	89	124	114	72	75	68

Note: Standard errors in parentheses. * , ** , and *** indicate significance at the 10, 5, and 1 percent levels, respectively.

equipment sector also provides evidence that banking and other types of financial FDI inflows stimulate net exports.

Concluding Remarks

The increasing importance of foreign direct investment in the world economy calls for theoretical and empirical investigations into the manner in which FDI affects the linkages among countries. A central question concerning FDI is whether it increases or decreases the volume of trade. Mundell's early contribution showed a channel through which investment substitutes for trade, while later theoretical research presents cases where trade and investment may serve as substitutes or complements.

Our theoretical model highlights some basic aspects of the different channels through which foreign direct investment can alter the sectoral composition of capital and labor in an economy. We provide the results of a detailed examination of the linkages between FDI into particular sectors of Latin American economies and the net exports of those and other manufacturing sectors. Our analysis indicates that some FDI tends to expand manufacturing trade, while other FDI clearly reduces the volumes of manufacturing trade. In Latin American countries, FDI from the United States can lead to significant and varied shifts in the composition of activity in many countries across many manufacturing sectors.

Given the mixed pattern linkages, it is reasonable to ask whether the Latin American results are expected to generalize to other partnering relationships among countries around the world. We conjecture that bilateral sectoral investment and trade flows—other than those between the United States and Latin America—may reveal stronger relationships than the mixed picture presented here. For example, in our earlier work (Goldberg and Klein 1998) we present evidence of relatively strong and significant effects of overall bilateral direct investment from Japan on the overall bilateral trade of Southeast Asian countries. The weakest results in that earlier paper were for the effects of United States direct investment on the trade of Latin American countries. Those results did not use data disaggregated by sectors and, unfortunately, data availability precluded us from studying the effects of sectoral direct investment from Japan. While the Latin American results that we have presented do not provide strong evidence that capital flows systematically and generally expand or contract trade flows, the experiences of other important regions around the world could also provide important lessons.

Appendix

Table A.8.1
Regression results for direct investment coefficients (Panel A)

	Argentina	Brazil	Chile	Colombia	Mexico	Peru	Venezuela
Own industry FDI, one-period lag	0.193 (0.180)	0.031 (0.096)	-0.614 (0.583)	0.271 (0.331)	-0.191 (0.164)	-1.134 (1.045)	-0.122 (0.225)
Own industry FDI, two-period lag	0.398* (0.203)	-0.224** (0.097)	0.831 (0.670)	0.408 (0.340)	0.548** (0.249)	0.524 (0.971)	-0.289 (0.178)
FDI to all other manufacturing industries, one-period lag	-0.025 (0.034)	0.047 (0.040)	-0.168 (0.187)	0.078 (0.06)	-0.152** (0.062)	-0.271 (0.428)	-0.232* (0.127)
FDI to all other manufacturing industries, two-period lag	0.002 (0.035)	-0.002 (0.039)	0.092 (0.27)	0.162** (0.078)	-0.07 (0.056)	-0.135 (0.416)	0.053 (0.091)
Real exchange rate	0.746** (0.311)	2.202* (1.179)	-4.37*** (1.289)	5.182*** (1.658)	16.9*** (3.814)	0.236 (0.306)	-2.979 (1.95)
Real exchange rate, one-period lag	0.099 (0.433)	4.896*** (1.284)	0.871 (0.976)	-2.793 (2.002)	-1.451 (4.148)	0.122 (0.322)	0.223 (2.058)
U.S. real GDP	$1.82e-4$ ($1.13e-4$)	$6.0e-4$*** ($2.0e-4$)	$1.75e-4$ ($2.07e-4$)	$2.05e-4$** ($8.94e-5$)	$1.5e-4$ ($5.8e-4$)	$5.78e-5$ ($1.43e-4$)	$6.11e-5$ ($1.44e-4$)
U.S. real GDP, one-period lag	$-1.64e-4$ ($1.07e-4$)	$1.41e-5$ ($2.32e-4$)	$7.36e-5$ ($1.29e-4$)	$1.05e-4$ ($9.77e-5$)	$-5.52e-4$ ($5.2e-4$)	$4.12e-5$ ($1.36e-4$)	$-7.97e-5$ ($1.54e-4$)
Local real GDP[a]	-0.012*** (0.003)	-157.1** (65.6)	$-1.3e-4$** ($5.13e-5$)	$-8.6e-5$*** ($3.15e-5$)	-0.004 (0.003)	-0.034 (0.027)	-0.001*** ($1.84e-4$)
Local real GDP[a], one-period lag	-0.003 (0.003)	4.2 (51.8)	$6.4e-5$ ($4.4e-5$)	$7.7e-5$ ($4.34e-5$)	-0.001 (0.003)	-0.011 (0.033)	$2.7e-4$ ($2.61e-4$)
Number of observations	96	133	66	90	125	83	110

Note: Standard errors in parentheses. *, **, and *** indicate significance at the 10, 5, and 1 percent levels, respectively.
[a] Millions of local currency units.

Table A.8.2
Regression results for direct investment coefficients (Panel B)

	Argentina	Brazil	Chile	Colombia	Mexico	Peru	Venezuela
Own industry FDI, one-period lag	0.079 (0.251)	-0.001 (0.095)	-1.241* (0.738)	0.29 (0.49)	-0.183 (0.196)	-1.217 (1.092)	-0.351 (0.259)
Own industry FDI, two-period lag	0.455* (0.274)	-0.242** (0.096)	1.997** (0.864)	-0.14 (0.571)	0.702** (0.316)	0.358 (1.055)	-0.365 (0.287)
FDI to all other manufacturing industries, one-period lag	-0.001 (0.034)	0.02 (0.035)	-0.717** (0.325)	0.061 (0.103)	-0.162 (0.115)	-0.269 (0.465)	-0.244 (0.163)
FDI to all other manufacturing industries, two-period lag	0.012 (0.049)	0.007 (0.032)	0.597* (0.336)	0.133 (0.171)	0.453*** (0.171)	-0.057 (0.457)	-0.243 (0.248)
FDI to wholesale trade industries, one-period lag	-0.278 (0.216)	0.387*** (0.132)	-0.36 (0.458)	-8.76** (3.988)	-0.105 (0.414)	0.437 (1.247)	2.301*** (0.764)
FDI to wholesale trade industries, two-period lag	-0.147 (0.172)	0.415*** (0.132)	0.803 (0.642)	-3.25* (1.868)	-1.343*** (0.474)	0.156 (1.054)	1.148 (1.632)

FDI to banking and FIRE, one-period lag	0.972** (0.396)	0.05 (0.06)	-0.104 (0.169)	0.696 (0.442)	0.617*** (0.225)	-0.415 (0.942)	-0.46 (0.581)
FDI to banking and FIRE, two-period lag	-0.819** (0.410)	-0.934 (0.061)	0.152 (0.104)	-0.016 (0.648)	-1.768* (0.937)	0.234 (1.157)	1.719** (0.792)
Real exchange rate	-1.368 (0.928)	2.776*** (0.952)	-7.1*** (1.545)	8.452*** (1.882)	20.118*** (4.66)	0.191 (0.339)	7.716 (5.092)
Real exchange rate, one-period lag	1.111 (0.897)	4.003*** (1.027)	0.575 (0.888)	-31.50** (12.693)	-5.602 (5.976)	0.139 (0.354)	7.511 (6.889)
U.S. real GDP	$3.29e-4**$ $(1.29e-4)$	$0.001***$ $(1.94e-4)$	$5.4e-4***$ $(2.1e-4)$	$-3.84e-5$ $(2.04e-4)$	$7.61e-5$ $(5.65e-4)$	$8.65e-5$ $(1.62e-4)$	$8.64e-4$ $(6.44e-4)$
U.S. real GDP, one-period lag	$-4.6e-4***$ $(1.21e-4)$	$4.31e-4*$ $(2.34e-4)$	$1.41e-4$ $(1.37e-4)$	$-4.43e-4$ $(3.72e-4)$	$7.76e-6$ $(5.18e-4)$	$4.19e-5$ $(1.72e-4)$	$-1.03e-4$ $(3.93e-4)$
Local real GDP[a]	$-0.028***$ (0.007)	$-274.0***$ (65.3)	$-2.5e-4***$ $(6.28e-5)$	$-2.48e-5$ $(3.67e-5)$	$-0.005*$ (0.003)	-0.032 (0.036)	$-0.002***$ $(5.85e-4)$
Local real GDP[a], one-period lag	-0.003 (0.005)	-81.3 (50.6)	$1.34e-4**$ $(5.52e-5)$	$3.11e-4**$ $(1.35e-4)$	-0.004 (0.003)	-0.019 (0.044)	$-5.04e-4$ $(9.94e-4)$
Number of observations	76	133	66	69	110	83	91

Note: Standard errors in parentheses. *, **, and *** indicate significance at the 10, 5, and 1 percent levels, respectively.
[a]Millions of local currency units.

Table A.8.3
Regression results for sectoral direct investment coefficients (Panel A)

	Food and kindred products	Primary and fabricated metals	Chemicals and allied products	Machinery, except electrical	Electric and electronic equipment	Transportation equipment	Other manufacturing
Own industry FDI, one-period lag	-0.117 (0.12)	-0.228 (0.295)	-0.055 (0.115)	-0.068 (0.188)	-0.692 (0.507)	-0.153 (0.181)	-0.339 (0.225)
Own industry FDI, two-period lag	-0.216 (0.196)	0.699** (0.327)	-0.183 (0.124)	0.208 (0.186)	0.319 (0.511)	0.266 (0.243)	-0.290 (0.225)
FDI to all other manufacturing industries, one-period lag	-0.039 (0.031)	-0.197*** (0.0567)	0.006 (0.03)	-0.185 (0.061)	-0.074 (0.086)	-0.118 (0.081)	-0.142* (0.073)
FDI to all other manufacturing industries, two-period lag	0.065 (0.034)	0.039 (0.053)	0.02 (0.029)	0.108 (0.062)	0.043 (0.083)	0.01 (0.085)	0.179** (0.078)
Real exchange rate	0.56 (0.675)	3.721*** (1.321)	0.931* (0.502)	2.99*** (1.09)	0.951 (1.055)	3.049* (1.769)	5.685*** (1.454)
Real exchange rate, one-period lag	0.202 (0.702)	0.723 (1.395)	0.794 (0.525)	1.255 (1.934)	-0.069 (1.081)	2.321 (1.867)	1.19 (1.416)
U.S. real GDP	$1.89e-4$* $(1.13e-4)$	$4.98e-4$* $(2.57e-4)$	$8.94e-5$ $(1.52e-4)$	$7.08e-7$ $(3.28e-4)$	$1.46e-4$ $(2.43e-4)$	$-1.07e-4$ $(4.28e-4)$	$5.38e-4$** $(2.73e-4)$
U.S. real GDP, one-period lag	$1.32e-4$ $(1.08e-4)$	$-3.49e-4$ $(2.52e-4)$	$3.3e-4$ $(1.47e-4)$	$-1.51e-4$ $(3.15e-4)$	$-1.62e-4$ $(2.51e-4)$	$3.23e-4$ $(4.32e-4)$	$-2.85e-4$ $(2.43e-4)$
Local real GDP[a]	$-4.44e-5$ $(6.74e-5)$	$8.35e-6$ $(1.15e-4)$	$(4e-5)$ $(5.07e-5)$	$-7.1e-5$ $(1.11e-4)$	$-8.77e-5$ $(1.73e-4)$	$-4.01e-4$ $(3.64e-4)$	$-2.78e-5$ $(1.54e-4)$
Local real GDP[a], one-period lag	$7.11e-6$ $(6.77e-5)$	$9.23e-5$ $(1.3e-4)$	$6.05e-5$ $(5.68e-5)$	$3.11e-5$ $(1.16e-4)$	$1.52e-5$ $(1.98e-4)$	$-1.33e-4$ $(3.66e-4)$	$5.04e-6$ $(1.84e-4)$
Number of observations	143	107	148	135	77	91	73

Note: Standard errors in parentheses. *, **, and *** indicate significance at the 10, 5, and 1 percent levels, respectively.
[a] Millions of local currency units.

Table A.8.4
Regression results for sectoral direct investment coefficients (Panel B)

	Food and kindred products	Primary and fabricated metals	Chemicals and allied products	Machinery, except electrical	Electric and electronic equipment	Transportation equipment	Other manufacturing
Own industry FDI, one-period lag	-0.276 (0.202)	-0.229 (0.353)	-0.096 (0.162)	0.351* (0.204)	0.207 (0.492)	-0.083 (0.298)	-0.463* (0.272)
Own industry FDI, two-period lag	0.074 (0.277)	0.384 (0.409)	-0.289* (0.171)	0.019 (0.201)	0.845* (0.479)	0.141 (0.291)	-0.3445 (0.270)
FDI to all other manufacturing industries, one-period lag	0.021 (0.046)	-0.16* (0.09)	0.043 (0.046)	-0.193 (0.089)	-0.178** (0.09)	-0.256* (0.136)	-0.094 (0.091)
FDI to all other manufacturing industries, two-period lag	0.039 (0.053)	0.185** (0.087)	0.028 (0.047)	0.263*** (0.092)	-0.06 (0.092)	0.009 (0.149)	0.201* (0.107)
FDI to wholesale trade industries, one-period lag	0.023 (0.157)	-0.058 (0.27)	0.082 (0.154)	-1.008*** (0.303)	0.115 (0.253)	0.166* (0.404)	-0.091 (0.229)
FDI to wholesale trade industries, two-period lag	0.181 (0.153)	0.066 (0.26)	0.159 (0.157)	0.605** (0.305)	0.528** (0.261)	0.732 (0.416)	0.107 (0.225)

Table A.8.4
(continued)

	Food and kindred products	Primary and fabricated metals	Chemicals and allied products	Machinery, except electrical	Electric and electronic equipment	Transportation equipment	Other manufacturing
FDI to banking and FIRE, one-period lag	0.141 (0.126)	0.059 (0.232)	−0.004 (0.09)	0.056 (0.23)	0.602*** (0.135)	0.303 (0.371)	0.138 (0.145)
FDI to banking and FIRE, two-period lag	−0.103 (0.138)	0.14 (0.245)	−0.16 (0.124)	−0.018 (0.245)	−0.035 (0.196)	0.221 (0.396)	−0.09 (0.184)
Real exchange rate	0.489 (0.8)	2.999** (1.444)	0.867 (0.572)	2.34** (1.095)	0.514 (0.903)	3.173 (2.066)	5.249*** (1.756)
Real exchange rate, one-period lag	0.394 (0.867)	0.236 (1.589)	1.03 (0.61)	0.436 (1.216)	0.396 (0.928)	1.834 (2.266)	0.922 (1.667)
U.S. real GDP	$3.1e-4$** $(1.57e-4)$	$6.4e-4$** $(3.11e-4)$	$-7.96e-5$ $(1.76e-4)$	$6.98e-5$ $(3.37e-4)$	$1.14e-4$ $(2.28e-4)$	$2.13e-4$ $(5.39e-4)$	$5.21e-4$ $(3.42-4)$
U.S. real GDP, one-period lag	$1.04e-4$ $(1.25e-4)$	$-3.55e-4$ $(2.81e-4)$	$-3.46e-4$** $(1.63e-4)$	$6.61e-5$ $(2.99e-4)$	$-2.43e-5$ $(2.32e-4)$	$3.89e-4$ $(5.06e-4)$	$-2.83e-4$ $(2.92e-4)$
Local real GDP[a]	$-5.01e-5$ $(7.49e-5)$	$-5.42e-6$ $(1.28e-4)$	$-2.41e-5$ $(5.73e-5)$	$-8.85e-5$ $(1.11e-4)$	$-1.57e-4$ $(1.53e-4)$	$-3.66e-4$ $(4.44e-4)$	$1.11e-5$ $(1.73e-4)$
Local real GDP[a], one-period lag	$-1.5e-5$ $(7.45e-5)$	$1.01e-4$ $(1.43e-4)$	$5.11e-5$ $(6.39e-5)$	$4.37e-6$ $(1.13e-4)$	$-6.72e-5$ $(1.74e-4)$	$-2.01e-4$ $(4.54e-4)$	$-4.02e-5$ $(2.14e-4)$
Number of observations	121	89	124	114	72	75	68

Note: Standard errors in parentheses. *, **, and *** indicate significance at the 10, 5, and 1 percent levels respectively.
[a] Millions of local currency units.

Notes

This chapter was prepared for the Festschrift in Honor of Robert Mundell. The views expressed are those of the individual authors and do not necessarily reflect the position of the Federal Reserve Bank of New York or the Federal Reserve System. We thank Alan Winters for comments on an earlier draft. Jenessa Gunther and Kevin Caves provided excellent research assistance. Address correspondences to Linda S. Goldberg, Federal Reserve Bank of NY, Research Department, 33 Liberty St., NY, NY 10045. Tel:212-720-2836; fax:212-720-6831; email: Linda.Goldberg@ny.frb.org.

1. Recent research questions the assumption of the equalization of rates of return for a variety of types of capital. Most relevant in this context is the work of Froot and Stein (1991), who model foreign direct investment with imperfect capital markets. Empirical results in their paper, as well as in research by Klein and Rosengren (1994), suggest that there is a lack of perfect capital mobility for direct investment.

2. Markusen (1995) argues that there is little evidence that direct foreign investment is related to differences in factor endowments across countries or to differences in the general return to capital.

3. The structure of production given in equation (8.1) implies that domestic and foreign capital are perfect substitutes within a sector.

4. We could easily assume a growing labor force, an assumption which would not change our results.

5. In order to make to sector definitions consistent across the trade and the FDI series, we use the manufacturing decomposition delineated by the FDI numbers, that is, with a breakdown into food and kindred products; chemicals and allied products; primary and fabricated metals; industrial machinery and equipment; electronic and other electric machinery; transportation; and other manufacturing. Data also are available for FDI into nonmanufacturing sectors, which are comprised of wholesale trade, banking, finance, services, and other industries. These later series are somewhat less complete, since observations are sometimes not disclosed if the scale of specific investments can be traced to individual investors from the United States.

6. Despite the apparent volatility of these flows, Lipsey (1999) still finds that foreign direct investment is the most stable source of international capital for emerging market economies.

7. "Finance" is used here in place of the FIRE acronym, representing Finance, Insurance, and Real Estate.

8. Because of missing data, we exclude Ecuador from this part of our empirical analysis.

9. The change in the real exchange rate, the change in domestic income and the change in U.S. income are aggregate regressors in that they have the same value across all sectors in any particular year. Aggregate regressors of this type preclude the use of time dummy variables and require the adjustment of the standard errors, as shown by Kloeck (1981).

10. Tables A.8.1 and A.8.2 provide estimates of the individual regression coefficients that form the basis of the numbers reported in table 8.4, panels A and B, respectively tables A.8.3. and A.8.4. report estimates used in table 8.5, panels A and B, respectively.

References

Collins, W. J., K. H. O'Rourke. and J. G. Williamson. 1997. Were trade and factor mobility substitutes in history? Working Paper no. 6059 (June), National Bureau of Economic Research, Cambridge, Mass.

Froot, K., and J. Stein. 1991. Exchange rates and foreign direct investment: An imperfect capital markets approach. *Quarterly Journal of Economics* 106:1191–1217.

Goldberg, L. S., and M. W. Klein. 1998. Foreign direct investment, trade and real exchange rate linkages in developing countries. In *Managing capital flows and exchange rates: Lessons from the Pacific Basin* ed. Reuven Glick, 73–100. Cambridge: Cambridge University Press.

Jones, R. W. 1967. International capital movements and the theory of tariffs and trade. *Quarterly Journal of Economics* 81 (February):1–38.

Kemp, M. C. 1966. The gain from international trade and investment: A neo-Heckscher-Ohlin approach. *American Economic Review* 61 (September):788–809.

Klein, M. W., and E. Rosengren. 1994. The real exchange rate and foreign direct investment in the United States: Relative wealth vs. relative wage effects. *Journal of International Economics* 36:373–89.

Kloeke, T. 1981. OLS estimation in a model where a microvariable is explained by aggregates and contemporaneous disturbances are equicorrelated. *Econometrica* 49(1):205–07.

Lipsey, R. E. 1999. The role of foreign direct investment in international capital flows. Working paper no. 7094 (April), National Bureau of Economic Research, Cambridge, Mass.

Markusen, J. R. 1995. The boundaries of multinational enterprises and the theory of international trade. *Journal of Economic Perspectives* 9(2):169–89.

Markusen, J. R. 1983. Factor movements and commodity trade as complements. *Journal of International Economics* 13:341–56.

Markusen, J. R., and L. E. O. Svensson. 1985. Trade in goods and factors with international differences in technology. *International Economic Review* 26:175–92.

Mundell, R. 1957. International trade and factor mobility. *American Economic Review* 47 (June):321–35.

Mundell, R. 1968. *International Economics*. New York: The Macmillan Co.

Purvis, D. D. 1972. Technology, trade and factor mobility. *Economic Journal* 82:991–99.

Schmitz, A., and P. Helmberger. 1970. Factor mobility and international trade: The case of complementarity. *American Economic Review* 60:761–67.

Stolper, W., and P. Samuelson. 1941. Protection and Real Wages. *Review of Economic Studies* 9:58–73.

Svensson, L. E. O. 1984. Factor trade and goods trade. *Journal of International Economics* 16:365–78.

Wong, K.-y. 1986. Are international trade and factor mobility substitutes? *Journal of International Economics* 21(1/2):25–44.

9 Saving, Investment, and Gold: A Reassessment of Historical Current Account Data

Matthew T. Jones and
Maurice Obstfeld

Introduction

This chapter revises pre–World War II current account data for thirteen countries by taking explicit account of the distinction between monetary and nonmonetary international flows of gold. The new data are used to examine the historical cross-sectional correlation between national saving and domestic investment rates. Our statistical analysis is based on an econometric specification that is appropriate for a world in which gold serves as both domestic and international money.

In a seminal paper, Feldstein and Horioka (1980) demonstrated that industrial countries with high saving rates also tend to have high investment rates in post-1960 data. The interpretation of this finding has proven controversial, and has spawned a vast literature. Feldstein and Horioka interpreted their result as indicating a long-term international immobility of capital: national savings, rather than seeking out the most productive uses anywhere in the world, remain in their country of origin. Current account imbalances thus do not allow countries to finance long-run capital needs with foreign savings. Many subsequent authors have been reluctant to embrace this vision, because it contradicts other evidence pointing to a high degree of capital mobility within the modern industrial world.[1]

A natural question to consider, therefore, is whether the Feldstein-Horioka regularity persists in data from the classical gold standard, a period of presumed high capital mobility. An affirmative answer would tend to support the critics of Feldstein and Horioka who have argued that common determinants of saving and investment rates, not capital immobility per se, generate the high post-war saving-investment correlations. Bayoumi (1990) and Eichengreen (1992a) both examined gold standard data, but reached different conclusions. Bayoumi, who worked with data from 1880–1913 for eight countries, found no significant cross-sectional correlation for any sub-period of the gold standard. In contrast, using different data for a sample of nine countries (the additional country being the United States), Eichengreen found much higher and marginally significant coefficients in cross-sectional regressions of investment on saving.

Both Bayoumi and Eichengreen relied heavily on standard data sources such as Mitchell (1981, 1983, 1988, 1992). While these data are often useful for the purposes of historical comparison, they have at least two shortcomings. One shortcoming that is particularly worrisome for an analysis of current accounts during the gold standard era is the treatment of gold in trade statistics. For many countries in the available sample, official balance of payments statistics confound net exports of commodity gold with monetary gold flows. Some countries exclude all gold flows, while others attempt to make a distinction between nonmonetary and monetary gold trade. Nonmonetary gold exports are a valid current account credit, while exports of monetary bullion and coin should be treated as a capital account credit, and not a current account credit. This misclassification can introduce substantial errors into saving rates, which in the absence of direct observations must be estimated residually as the sum of investment and the current account. As we shall see, however, it is often impossible to classify particular gold transactions as either monetary or nonmonetary.

A further shortcoming of Mitchell's data is their omission of inventory changes from many countries' investment data. When data are available, estimates of gross capital formation should include changes in stocks or inventories as well as gross fixed capital formation. Overlooking inventory accumulation may give an upward bias to estimates of the correlation between saving and investment.[2]

Our yearly data on saving and investment rates from the late nineteenth century through World War II expands the sample of countries examined in previous work.[3] The data we report include inventories for a larger number of countries and treat international flows of gold on a more consistent basis. Our basic finding is that the cross-sectional correlation between gold-standard-era saving and investment rates is somewhat lower, and less significant, than Eichengreen's (1992a) estimates suggest, but it is still greater than the correlation Bayoumi (1990) reports. The explanatory power of these regressions is uniformly much lower under the gold standard than in post–World War II data.

Although we present a specific application of these data, they obviously have many other uses. Researchers interested in studying long-run saving behavior or economic growth, for example, should find the data we present useful.

The Treatment of Gold Flows in Current Account Data

Under the classical gold standard (ca. 1870–1914), gold was the predominant means of official international settlement, as well as being the lodestar of monetary policy in most market economies.

Prior to 1914 the major nations had alternated between gold and silver and bimetallic standards, but by 1870 gold ruled the roost. Gold was the anonymous monarch in a world of creative nationalism, and it counted for more than a mere medium of exchange and contract; it symbolized internationalism and the rule of international law. (Mundell 1968, 288)

In addition to its monetary role, however, gold was also a traded commodity, the product of mineral exploitation. Indeed, the growth of world monetary gold reserves depended on new production and discovery. For gold producing countries, official statistics on gold exports and imports usually did not attempt to distinguish between exports of nonmonetary gold (such as exports of newly produced unrefined gold) and shipments of preexisting monetary stocks. Exports of newly produced gold, for example, represent a current account credit, just like any other merchandise or service export; ceteris paribus they add to national saving. Net shipments to foreigners of monetary gold, however, are a capital account credit.

Why worry at all about distinguishing monetary from nonmonetary gold flows in the balance of payments? After all, exports of monetary gold and newly produced gold alike serve the purpose of allowing an economy to consume more of other commodities, now or in the future. Our motive for pursuing the distinction is to preserve the traditional conceptual separation that balance of payments statistics make between current and capital transactions, or between transactions on goods and asset account. In the traditional framework, an economy's current account balance measures its accumulation of negotiable foreign claims—of which gold was the example par excellence during the period we study here. It is especially important to maintain the identity of the current account as net foreign asset accumulation when we are obliged to measure saving indirectly, as the sum of the current account and investment. Thus, despite the manifest imperfections in the period's data, some attempt at an appropriate adjustment of the standard current account figures seems warranted.

Of course, the preceding rationale for hoping to distinguish monetary from nonmonetary gold flows leads to well-known ambiguities. Why not consider silver to be an international asset and separate monetary from nonmonetary silver flows as well? Why not do the same with diamonds, or other precious items often hoarded as part of wealth? While there is a coherent conceptual case for proceeding in this manner, especially as regards silver, in practice we must draw the line somewhere, and in this study we have chosen—arbitrarily, some will conclude—to draw the line at gold. Our basic reason is that over our sample period as a whole, gold stood without peer as a universally acceptable reserve asset, and as the clear leader in quantitative importance.[4]

Historians have dealt with the problem of classifying gold flows by using several different methodologies. One practice (Feinstein 1972, 115 n. 1) has been to classify all gold movements as monetary in nature, and to subtract them from measured export balances in calculating the current account. A second procedure is to leave all gold shipments in the current account (Viner 1924). A third approach, theoretically preferable to the first two, is to attempt to distinguish monetary from nonmonetary gold movements. Doing so is not always straightforward, however, as we shall see. The next section describes the assumptions that underlie proper application of this third approach.

Gold Flows in the Balance of Payments

It might appear feasible to adjust official current account data simply by subtracting some measure of the net shipments of monetary gold. Typically, countries classified gold flows into three different categories: specie (coin), bullion, and unrefined gold. Unfortunately, these three categories do not correspond directly to monetary and nonmonetary flows of gold. For example, circulating coins may be melted down to bullion and exported to finance the balance of payments. This would imply that monetary gold flows were not fully captured by the data on specie exports. As Morgenstern (1955, 5) observes:

The separation of monetary and non-monetary gold is neither simple nor conclusive. Gold can move from one category into the other within one country and domestic gold production can affect the stocks of both. During the classical gold standard period it was impossible to know, in the vast majority of cases, whether gold leaving and arriving came from one or the other of these sources and whether it was going—or in which proportions—to industrial or monetary use.

Figure 9.1 illustrates the problem by showing two equivalent international transactions.[5] In the first, indicated in the upper half, an ounce of newly mined gold ore is shipped directly from an Australian mine to an industrial user in the United Kingdom. This transaction raises Australia's official current account surplus (in terms of gold) by one ounce. Since the transaction clearly is not a monetary gold shipment, any reasonable measure of the current account surplus would rise by one ounce.

The lower half of figure 9.1 shows what happens when the U.K. industrial user satisfies his or her demand by purchasing an ounce of monetary gold in Australia, instead of relying on a direct shipment of ore. In this version of the transaction, the gold ore enters the Australian monetary gold stock in the form of bullion but is then immediately shipped abroad for industrial end use (so that Australia's monetary gold stock is not affected within the accounting period).[6] Is the gold shipment to be considered monetary or nonmonetary? If it were labeled as "monetary" and subtracted from Australia's exports to the United Kingdom, then, arguably, Australia's current account deficit would be overstated by one ounce of gold and Britain's surplus correspondingly overstated.

To avoid such problems, it is standard practice in balance of payments accounting to classify all movements of gold from domestic nonmonetary sources into the domestic money supply as nonmonetary gold exports. To offset this current account credit in the balance of payments, an equal capital account debit is added. The debit reflects the

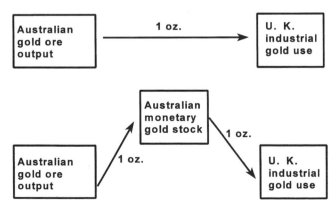

Figure 9.1
Equivalence of different gold transactions

acquisition of foreign assets and is a monetary gold import.[7] The rationale for this practice is that any increase in the monetary gold stock is an increase in national foreign exchange reserves. As Gardner (1953, 159) writes:

Gold is peculiar . . . in the way it affects international monetary reserves. Sales of ordinary merchandise increase those reserves only if the sale is to foreigners. Domestic sales of newly mined gold . . . to the Central Bank or Treasury of the producing country effect the same additions to the country's international reserves as if the gold has been exported and sold abroad. Foreign exchange or its equivalent is created in the hands of the monetary authorities by either process. Hence newly mined gold is regarded as an export of the country whether sold abroad or directly to the local monetary authorities.

Similarly, domestic consumption out of the monetary gold stock is regarded as a simultaneous import of nonmonetary gold and export of monetary gold (the latter being a capital inflow). A key implication is that *any* increase in the domestic monetary gold stock is deemed a monetary gold import (and an "international" capital outflow).

Under this convention, it becomes straightforward to separate monetary from nonmonetary gold flows. Let ΔMG be the change in the monetary gold stock. Since ΔMG also equals net monetary gold imports, net nonmonetary gold exports can be calculated as total net gold shipments to foreigners, SG, less net monetary gold exports, $-\Delta MG$:

$$\text{Net nonmonetary gold exports} = SG - (-\Delta MG) = SG + \Delta MG. \qquad (9.1)$$

On this definition, the true current account, CA, is the sum of the current account excluding all gold flows, CA^{NG}, and net nonmonetary gold exports from equation (9.1):

$$CA = CA^{NG} + SG + \Delta MG. \qquad (9.2)$$

Notice that any monetary gold shipments in SG are canceled by the corresponding decrease in the monetary gold stock MG and thus do not affect the true current account. Equation (9.2) also has the following interpretation: under a gold standard, the current account equals total net foreign asset accumulation including all net accumulation of monetary gold.

Returning to the examples in figure 9.1, neither transaction sequence changes Australia's monetary gold stock, so both of the gold shipments shown raise Australia's current account balance as measured in equation (9.2) by one ounce of gold.

Application

We now describe the standard historical data and the adjustments that we have made to them. Our adjustments amount to adding the change in the domestic monetary gold stock to the current account inclusive of all international gold shipments.[8] Given the unrivaled universality of gold as an international reserve asset in our sample period, this adjustment is appropriate even when a country is not formally on the gold standard; we therefore apply it in every year for which we have data. We treat Australia and Canada individually and then discuss more briefly the treatment of other countries.[9]

Australia

The standard historical data on the Australian current account are those compiled by N. G. Butlin (1962). He adjusts the Australian current account figures by using data on gold production instead of net exports:

$$CA^{BUTLIN} = CA^{NG} + YU = CA^{O} - SG + YU, \tag{9.3}$$

where CA^{O} is the current account inclusive of all gold shipments SG, and YU is Australia's total output of unrefined gold. Butlin argued that gold production was the appropriate current account credit for a gold producing country. Boehm (1965) criticized N. G. Butlin's treatment of gold, and argued that this procedure overstates the extent of gold exports, and consequently understates the current account deficit. We can see that the approach adopted by Butlin omits some of the terms that appear in equation (9.2), and is, therefore, a less accurate correction of official statistics. No doubt Butlin proposed this approximation because the problem of identifying monetary gold flows is particularly acute for a gold producing country such as Australia. For instance, one might hope to identify monetary gold movements with gold shipped by banks and then adjust the trade figures accordingly. Unfortunately, it is not clear from the data that banks were always shipping gold to reduce desired domestic monetary gold holdings. To get the appropriate current account figure for Australia, we can modify equation (9.3) to get

$$CA = CA^{BUTLIN} + SG - YU + \Delta MG. \tag{9.4}$$

We applied this procedure to Australia to calculate a new current account series. Estimates of the change in the monetary gold stock were derived as follows. Specie flows into and out of New South Wales,

Victoria, and Western Australia (as reported in Annual Report of United Kingdom, Deputy Master of the Mint) were added to the change in the total bullion holdings of Australian trading banks. The mint reports document the flow of gold specie into and out of the three colonies only. However, this measure of the change in Australia's monetary gold stock appears to be the best available. For data after 1900, we use the estimates of the gold coin and bullion stock compiled by S. J. Butlin et al. (1971).

Canada
Viner's (1924) classic study assembled balance of payments data for Canada between 1900 and 1913. Viner's current account estimates, however, included all international gold shipments (monetary as well as nonmonetary). Thus, Viner's empirical measure of the current account corresponded to CA^O. Hartland (1954) extended Viner's methodology to cover the years 1868–1899.

In a meticulous analysis, Rich (1988) adjusted the Canadian data to account properly for monetary gold flows. Rich's current account estimates for Canada, however, omit net interest and dividend flows, despite his recognition that they constituted "a sizeable item in the Canadian balance of payments" (Rich 1988, 248). His motive in this omission was the unreliability of available estimates of net foreign asset income.

We calculate Canada's current account for the years 1870–1926 as follows. We take the current account including all gold shipments from Urquhart 1986. As in equation (9.2), we add the change in the total domestic monetary gold stock, as calculated by Rich (1988) for 1872 through 1913, supplemented by our own estimates for 1869–1871 and 1914–1926. Thus our approach corresponds to Rich's, except that Urquhart's data include superior estimates of net dividend and interest payments.[10] For 1927 onward, we use the Dominion Bureau of Statistics estimates presented in Urquhart and Buckley 1965, which appropriately separate monetary from nonmonetary gold flows.

Other Countries
Given the predominance of gold as an international reserve asset for the entire period, we perform the gold adjustment for all countries in every year of our sample.

For Denmark, France, Germany, Italy, Japan, Norway, Russia, Sweden, and the United Kingdom, the standard current account data exclude all gold flows. The Finnish data on the current account include all gold shipments. The standard data for the United States current account include all gold shipments prior to 1874; thereafter they include nonmonetary gold exports (calculated appropriately as the sum of total net gold shipments and the change in the monetary gold stock).

For Denmark, Norway, and Finland, data limitations lead us to proxy the monetary gold stock by the stock of gold at the central bank. Data on net shipments of gold for Denmark and Norway are derived by taking the change in the monetary gold stock, supplemented by League of Nations data and trade statistics. For Sweden the gold holdings of the central bank were used to calculate changes in the monetary gold stock for several periods, supplemented by data on gold in banks. Data on net gold shipments and the monetary gold stock for Germany are reported by the Bundesbank.

For France, the data on net shipments of gold include silver until 1870, then subsequently include gold only.[11] Up until 1913, estimates of the French monetary gold stock are based on the work of Flandreau (1995) and Sicsic (1989); later data come from the *Annuaire Statistique* (France, Ministère des Finances et des Affaires Économiques 1966). For Italy and Japan, the specie component of the monetary gold stock is estimated in a manner similar to the Australian calculations: taking the sum of inflows and outflows of coin from the mints and trade statistics.[12] The Italian data relating to monetary bullion are fragmentary and difficult to interpret, so we make no use of them. For Japan, the change in the monetary gold stock is calculated as the change in the estimated stock of specie in the country, less net exports of bullion. Use of bullion exports is problematic, as we have discussed, but should induce less serious errors than in the case of a gold producer like Australia. For Russia, the monetary gold stock is proxied by the sum of gold holdings in the treasury and state bank until 1891; thereafter gold in circulation is included.

For the United Kingdom, estimates of the monetary gold stock outside the Bank of England are provided by Capie and Webber (1985) up to 1921. We add to their numbers data on Bank of England gold holdings. After 1921 data limitations lead us to proxy the U.K. monetary gold stock essentially by the gold holdings of the Bank of England. Trade statistics provide the estimates of net gold shipments from the United Kingdom. For the United States prior to 1874, the treasury figures on the monetary gold stock are used throughout: we add changes in the monetary gold stock to the official pre–1874 current account numbers, which include all gold flows across United States borders.

From the preceding discussion it is obvious that the data on monetary gold flows and net shipments of gold are far from perfect. Our reliance (in some cases) on central bank gold holdings for estimates of changes in the monetary gold stock overlooks the important role often played by changes in private hoards. The gaps in the trade data for some countries also force us to rely on central bank gold stocks to proxy gold trade figures, a procedure that effectively ignores industrial consumption of gold. Thus we are often left with imprecise measures of gold flows.

However, it is difficult even today to obtain accurate estimates of currency in the hands of the public, because of unrecorded flows into and out of a country. The object of this chapter is to obtain estimates of gold flows for a wide group of countries and then ensure the consistent treatment of gold in the current account statistics. The inaccuracies of the data must be considered in light of that objective. Bearing in mind these caveats, the data we have compiled should provide a superior estimate of the current account and savings flows, one that is less distorted by the conflicting national treatments of gold in the balance of payments.

The end result of the estimation of gold flows is presented in figure 9.2, which shows average current account-to-GDP ratios over 1885–1913 for the countries in our sample.[13] The figure presents the original current account figures given in the standard historical sources, along with the gold-adjusted figure, as per equation (9.2). We can see from this figure that correcting for gold flows can make a substantial difference to the measured current account, even when averaged over relatively long periods of time.

Adjusting for gold flows has the biggest impact on the averaged original data for Australia, Canada, France, Japan, Russia, and the United Kingdom. We would expect Australia, Canada, and Russia, as major gold producers, to be prime candidates for current account mismeasurement. The standard current account figures for both France and Japan exclude all gold flows. Therefore, the differences between the original current accounts and the gold-adjusted figures represent nonmonetary gold flows, which seemingly were substantial for these two countries.[14] Both of these instances should be treated with caution, since they may reflect mismeasurement of the change in the monetary gold

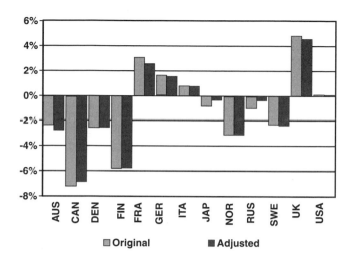

Figure 9.2
Current account with original and gold-adjusted data, 1885–1913, period averages (percentage of GDP)

stock. For example, French gold imports that did not find their way into the measured stock of monetary gold may well have entered private hoards rather than industrial use, and in that form could have been highly substitutable for monetary gold. Our skepticism regarding the adjusted Japanese numbers led us to check all the econometric results reported below for their sensitivity to our adjustment of Japan's customary current account data. That adjustment made no discernible difference to our results.

Table 9.1 shows the effect of adjusting the current account statistics for gold flows for each country. We can see from this table that our treatment of gold provides current account estimates that diverge from the standard historical measures. The mean absolute deviation (MAD) measure presented in the table suggests that for some countries the absolute divergence is frequently large, especially for Denmark, France, Japan, and Russia.

Inventories Data

An analysis of saving and investment flows requires a measure of total gross investment. Gross investment consists of the sum of fixed investment plus changes in stocks or inventories. As Eichengreen (1992a) points out, previous compilations of historical statistics have often

Table 9.1
Effect of gold adjustment on current accounts: Means and standard deviations of original data, gold-adjusted data, and mean absolute difference (expressed as a percentage of GDP)

Country	Full sample period					1885 to 1913				
	Original CA		Adjusted CA		MAD	Original CA		Adjusted CA		MAD
	Mean	Std. dev.	Mean	Std. dev.		Mean	Std. dev.	Mean	Std. dev.	
Australia	-3.9	6.2	-4.2	6.1	0.5	-2.4	6.0	-2.8	6.0	0.5
Canada	-3.5	5.7	-3.4	5.7	0.3	-7.2	3.7	-6.9	3.6	0.4
Denmark	-0.2	4.6	-1.2	2.1	1.2	-2.6	1.5	-2.6	1.4	0.2
Finland	-5.2	5.5	-5.1	5.6	0.2	-5.8	2.5	-5.8	2.5	0.1
France	2.6	3.9	2.6	3.9	0.9	3.1	1.1	2.6	1.2	0.6
Germany	1.2	1.3	1.2	1.3	0.1	1.6	0.7	1.6	0.7	0.1
Italy	-1.3	4.5	-1.3	4.5	0.1	0.8	2.3	0.8	2.3	0.0
Japan	-0.2	3.2	0.1	3.2	0.3	-0.8	3.0	-0.3	2.9	0.5
Norway	-1.7	4.0	-1.7	4.0	0.2	-3.2	2.8	-3.1	2.9	0.2
Russia	-1.0	1.5	-0.4	2.5	1.4	-1.0	1.5	-0.4	2.5	1.4
Sweden	-0.8	3.3	-0.8	3.5	0.3	-2.3	2.1	-2.4	2.1	0.1
U.K.	2.3	3.8	2.3	3.7	0.5	4.8	2.5	4.6	2.6	0.3
U.S.	0.5	1.6	0.5	1.6	0.0	0.1	1.2	0.1	1.2	0.0

Note: The full sample period consists of Australia: 1861–1945; Canada: 1870–1945; Denmark: 1874–1914, 1921–1945; France: 1851–1913, 1919–1938; Germany: 1877–1913, 1925–1938; Italy: 1861–1936; Japan: 1885–1944; Norway: 1865–1939; Russia: 1885–1913; Sweden: 1875–1945; United Kingdom: 1869–1945; United States: 1870–1945.

Table 9.2
Estimates of changes in stocks/inventories (as a percentage of GDP), period averages

Country	Sample period	Stocks ratio	Country	Sample period	Stocks ratio
Australia	1861–1945	1.00	Japan	1885–1944	2.79
Canada	1926–1945	0.57	Norway	1900–1939	–0.04
Denmark	—	—	Russia	1885–1913	1.69
Finland	1860–1945	3.74	Sweden	1861–1945	0.03
France[1]	1850–1938	2.08	United Kingdom	1850–1945	0.48
Germany[2]	1872–1938	0.97	United States	1869–1945	2.05
Italy	1861–1945	0.12			

[1] No data for 1914 to 1918.
[2] No data for 1914 to 1924.

ignored the role of inventories in gross investment. We have gathered additional data on inventories, so that the investment numbers for Australia, Canada, Finland, France, Germany, Italy, Japan, Norway, Russia, Sweden, the United Kingdom, and the United States now include estimates of changes in stocks or inventories. The details are discussed in appendix 9.2.[15]

The omission of inventories introduces a source of bias into regression estimates of saving-investment correlations. Table 9.2 shows the magnitude of changes in stocks and inventories for countries with available data. It is evident from the magnitude of the numbers in this table that adjusting for inventory changes may have potentially large effects.[16]

Empirical Analysis

In a world on the gold standard, the two principal outside financial assets are capital and monetary gold. In a closed economy, all saving must flow into one of these two assets. Thus,

$$I = S - \Delta MG. \tag{9.5}$$

Under a gold standard, the Feldstein-Horioka capital immobility hypothesis (in its most extreme form) is that all trade imbalances are financed by international gold flows, rather than by private capital flows (which could involve repayment or political risk). This implies that equation (9.5), which was derived as a closed-economy identity, also applies to open economies when international borrowing and lending are impossible. For example, a country's investment can increase above its saving only if it exports monetary gold abroad or transforms some of its monetary gold into plant and equipment.

Because of the imprecise or inadequate nature of historical national accounts data, historical estimates of saving must be calculated residually as the sum of investment and the current account:

$$S = I + CA. \tag{9.6}$$

Under a gold standard, the appropriate definition of saving recognizes that the current account is equal to net foreign asset accumulation, including monetary gold acquisitions. The typical (post–gold standard) implementation of the Feldstein-Horioka test is a cross-sectional regression of I on S, with both variables defined as ratios to Gross Domestic Product (GDP) or Net National Product (NNP). The more appropriate test under the gold standard is a regression of I on $S - \Delta MG$, according to equation (9.5).

There are thus two ways to implement the Feldstein-Horioka test in a world where gold plays an important monetary role. The first is to run the cross-section regression

$$\frac{I}{Y} = \alpha + \beta \frac{S}{Y} + \gamma \frac{\Delta MG}{Y} + u. \tag{9.7}$$

The Feldstein-Horioka hypothesis is that $\beta = 1$ and $\gamma = -1$. Alternatively, one could impose the constraint that saving and the change in the monetary gold stock have coefficients equal in absolute magnitude but of opposite sign. This procedure leads to the specification

$$\frac{I}{Y} = \alpha + \beta \frac{(S - \Delta MG)}{Y} + u. \tag{9.8}$$

The Feldstein-Horioka hypothesis implies that $\beta = 1$.

Notice that $S - \Delta MG$ is the saving measure one derives by adding to investment the current account inclusive of *all* gold shipments, CA^O, as per Viner's (1924) current account estimates for Canada, described above. Why is Viner's concept, rather than the one used to construct true saving, S, the appropriate one to use on the right hand side of equation (9.8)? Suppose a country imports gold coin to add to its money stock ($\Delta MG > 0$) with true saving, S, unchanged. If investment does not fall by an equal amount, then the country would necessarily be borrowing abroad to maintain an unchanged path of national wealth. If international borrowing and lending are ruled out (as implied by the Feldstein-Horioka hypothesis), however, it follows that increases in national saving (given ΔMG) and decreases in monetary gold holdings (given S) both feed through fully to increased investment.[17]

Our empirical analysis is based on data from thirteen countries: Australia (1861–1945), Canada (1870–1945), Denmark (1874–1914, 1921–1945), Finland (1872–1945), France (1851–1913, 1919–1938), Germany (1877–1913, 1925–1938), Italy (1861–1936), Japan (1885–1944), Norway (1865–1939), Russia (1885–1913), Sweden (1875–1945), the United Kingdom (1869–1945), and the United States (1870–1945). The data sources are described in appendix 9.2. Figure 9.3 presents scatter plots of the average saving and investment rate data for two sub-periods, 1885–1913 and 1919–1936. (Rather than giving true saving, S, the horizontal axes in figure 9.3 give the independent variable in equation (9.8).)

Table 9.3 presents the basic Feldstein and Horioka (1980) cross-sectional regression of average investment rates on average saving rates, using the specification of equation (9.8).[18] The estimates of the slope parameter range from just under 0.5 to close to 1. The later samples (after World War I) tend to have stronger correlations and, after 1931, much more explanatory power. (After 1931, the R^2 statistics are above 0.90.) Prior to 1914 the R^2 statistics are much lower than those

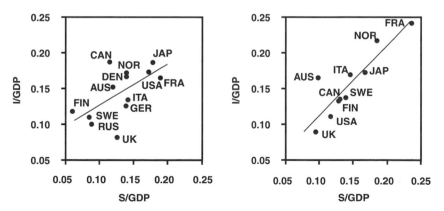

Figure 9.3
Saving and investment rates (expressed as ratios to GDP): 1885–1913 and 1919–1936

Table 9.3
Parameter estimates from regression of investment on savings ($S \equiv I + CA^{NG} + SG - \Delta MG$)

Sample period	Number of countries	Coefficient on S	Standard error	Adj. R^2
1880–1913	11	0.45	0.26	0.16
1885–1913	13	0.55**	0.22	0.30
1880–1890	11	0.44	0.28	0.13
1891–1901	13	0.62***	0.16	0.54
1902–1913	13	0.60**	0.27	0.25
1919–1924	10	1.00**	0.36	0.43
1925–1930	12	0.70***	0.15	0.66
1931–1936	12	0.91***	0.09	0.90
1937–1939	9	0.92***	0.09	0.92

Notes: The estimates for 1880–1913 and 1880–1890 exclude Japan and Russia; for 1919–1924 they exclude Denmark, Germany, and Russia; for 1925–1930 and 1931–1936 they exclude Russia; and for 1937–1939 they exclude France, Germany, Italy, and Russia. *, **, *** indicate significance at the 10 percent, 5 percent, and 1 percent level, respectively.

found for industrial countries in the 1960s (usually around 0.90) and even lower than those found for the 1980s (usually around 0.5 to 0.7, depending on the period of estimation).[19]

The results presented in the table suggest that the saving-investment correlation has been lower in periods when the gold standard prevailed. The immediate post–World War I period (1919–1924) and later samples (1931–1936, 1937–1939), periods when many countries were not on strict gold standards, both have higher correlations. These periods also saw rather widespread use of capital controls. Because these controls became much more stringent in the 1930s, they probably are the major explanation for the very high R^2 statistics reported in table 9.3 post 1931.[20]

Even though the R^2 statistics tend to be low before the 1930s, and especially before World War I, the 1891–1901 decade is an exception, with an R^2 not far from those one finds in Organization for Economic Cooperation and Development (OECD) data from the 1980s and 1990s. In addition, the slope coefficient is sometimes significant under the classical gold standard, notably after 1891, when its magnitude is comparable to the estimates from recent OECD data. The results for the late nineteenth century seem even more comparable with those in recent data when one observes that several of the countries in the gold-standard sample could be classified as developing then. Even in post–World War II samples that include the developing countries, the empirical saving-investment link appears weaker prior to the 1982 debt crisis; see Dooley, Frankel, and Mathieson 1987 and Summers 1988.

Having estimated the regression equation, we now turn to tests of some hypotheses. The first question to consider is whether there is sufficient evidence to believe that the coefficient on saving is equal to 1, that is, that saving and investment are perfectly correlated in cross-section. We see from figure 9.4 that the 95 percent confidence intervals for most of the slope estimates are quite wide. Because most of the point estimates are clustered around 0.5, we perform a t test of the hypothesis $\beta = 0.5$ against the alternative $\beta \neq 0.5$. We also perform the one-tailed test of the restriction that $\beta = 1$ against the alternative hypothesis that $\beta < 1$. We present the results of these hypothesis tests in table 9.4. The column labeled p *Value of Test* $\beta = 0.5$ gives the result of the hypothesis test that the coefficient on savings, β, is equal to one-half, against the alternative that β differs from one-half. The p value is the probability of incorrectly rejecting the null hypothesis when it is true, so a low p value implies strong evidence against the null hypothesis that $\beta = 0.5$. We see from this column that we can reject the hypothesis $\beta = 0.5$ only for the last two sub-samples in our data set: 1931–1936 and 1937–1939. The column labeled p *Value of Test* $\beta = 1$ shows we can reject that hypothesis for all sample periods except 1919–1924 and 1931–1939.

To summarize the results of the previous two tables, we do not find strong evidence against the coefficient on saving being equal to 0.5. We have evidence that the coefficient is less than 1 for most periods examined. There is some evidence of a positive relationship between saving

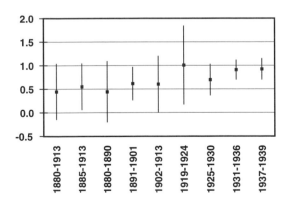

Figure 9.4
Slope estimates (β) and 95-percent confidence intervals

Table 9.4
Hypothesis tests from regression of investment on savings ($S \equiv I + CA^{NG} + SG - \Delta MG$)

Sample period	Coefficient on S	p value of test, $\beta = 0.5$	p value of test, $\beta = 1$
1880–1913	0.45	0.84	0.03
1885–1913	0.55**	0.82	0.03
1880–1890	0.44	0.85	0.04
1891–1901	0.62***	0.48	0.02
1902–1913	0.60**	0.71	0.08
1919–1924	1.00**	0.20	0.50
1925–1930	0.70***	0.21	0.03
1931–1936	0.91***	0.00	0.17
1937–1939	0.92***	0.00	0.22

Notes: The estimates for 1880–1913 and 1880–1890 exclude Japan and Russia; for 1919–1924 they exclude Denmark, Germany, and Russia; for 1925–1930 and 1931–1936 they exclude Russia; and for 1937–1939 they exclude France, Germany, Italy, and Russia. *, **, *** indicate significance at the 10 percent, 5 percent, and 1 percent level, respectively.

and investment rates even under the classical gold standard. This last result stands in contrast to Bayoumi (1990), who found no significant cross-sectional relationship between saving and investment for any period from 1880–1913. However, Eichengreen (1992a) reported relatively high estimates of the β coefficient over some sub-samples.[21] The results in tables 9.3 and 9.4 indicate slope coefficients generally lower than those found by Eichengreen but higher and more significant than the ones Bayoumi estimated.

Table 9.5 presents the parameter estimates of Bayoumi (1990) and Eichengreen (1992a) for comparison. Using the same countries and time periods, we estimated the correlations using our gold-adjusted data. For instance, the third column, labeled *Adjusted Bayoumi*, shows the results of the regression using our gold-adjusted data, but with only the eight countries that Bayoumi included in his sample. Similarly, the column labeled *Adjusted Eichengreen* shows the results of the regression using our gold-adjusted data for the nine countries in Eichengreen's sample. The column labeled *Full-Sample Estimates* shows the results from table 9.3, that is, the slope coefficient estimates using the gold adjusted data for all available countries. Bayoumi's conclusions appear to stem mainly from the use of a small sample of countries. Eichengreen's addition of the United States raises the slope coefficients and increases the statistical power available. But our addition of more countries to Eichengreen's sample moderates his findings somewhat.

Table 9.5
Comparison of parameter estimates from Bayoumi, Eichengreen, and gold-adjusted data

Sample period	Bayoumi estimates	Adjusted Bayoumi	Eichengreen estimates	Adjusted Eichengreen	Full-sample estimates
1880–1913	0.29	0.43	0.63*	0.57	0.45
1880–1890	0.48	0.14	0.59*	0.50	0.44
1891–1901	0.69	0.63	0.71***	0.68*	0.62***
1902–1913	−0.10	0.89	0.72	0.86	0.60**
1924–1936	—	0.70**	1.06***	0.76**	0.80***
1925–1930	—	0.56	1.22***	0.55	0.70***

Notes: Bayoumi's sample of countries consisted of Australia, Canada, Denmark, Germany, Italy, Norway, Sweden, and the United Kingdom. Eichengreen added the United States. Our data set adds Finland, France, Japan, and Russia and adjusts for gold flows. The full sample estimates for 1880–1913 and 1880–1890 exclude Japan and Russia; for 1924–1936 they exclude Germany and Russia; for 1925–1930 they exclude Russia.
*, **, *** indicate significance at the 10 percent, 5 percent, and 1 percent level, respectively.

Table 9.5 suggests that the selection of countries in the cross-sectional average is of key importance. Indeed, this appears to matter as much as the gold adjustment we perform. As we show in appendix 9.1, the parameter estimates are sensitive to the choice of countries in the cross-sectional average. Changing the countries in the sample can alter the estimated slopes by as much as 0.3, and the explanatory power of the investment-on-saving regression can vary by as much as 40 percent. Despite these caveats, the significance of parameter estimates seems fairly robust in the face of single deletions from the sample of countries. Thus, despite the sensitivity of the estimates to outliers, the broad thrust of the full-sample results suggested by the preceding two tables remains valid.

A sample period of particular interest is 1925–1930, during which Britain adhered to the interwar gold standard, and most market economies in the world likewise rejoined the gold standard. Eichengreen (1992a) estimates a highly significant slope coefficient of 1.22 under the resuscitated gold standard that prevailed during the years 1925–1930 (see table 9.5), much higher than those found for the classical, pre-1914 gold standard. On that basis he disputes the theory, advanced by the *Economist* magazine among others (*Economist* 1989), that the greater nominal exchange rate certainty prevailing under gold-standard regimes necessarily leads to greater international capital mobility and thereby to lower saving-investment coefficients.

Table 9.5 shows, however, that for Eichengreen's original sample of nine countries, our adjusted data lead to a statistically insignificant slope coefficient of only 0.55, which is quite comparable to those one finds for pre-1914 data.[22] In our fully-sized sample the estimated slope is somewhat higher, at 0.70, and is significantly different from zero at the 1 percent level. Nonetheless, our estimated slope for 1925–1930 seems markedly lower than those we estimate for any other subperiod of the interwar span (see table 9.4).

Thus, there is indeed some evidence that the interwar gold standard made a difference for the cross-country saving-investment relationship. Exchange rate volatility could be only a minimal part of the reason, however. The restored interwar gold standard was accompanied by a general relaxation of exchange controls, which may well have had a much greater impact on capital mobility than the nominal exchange rate regime.

If the cross-sectional averages used in the saving-investment regression correspond to the years when each country was on the gold standard, then the estimated correlations actually are higher.[23] However one cannot conclude from this result that gold standard adherence resulted in a tighter saving-investment link. Countries may have been more likely to be on gold in periods when their current accounts were near balance.

Conclusions

In this chapter we have presented revised estimates of saving and investment for thirteen countries over the period from 1850 to 1945. We have constructed a measure of the current account that treats gold flows on a consistent basis across countries, and also adjusted investment data to account for changes in inventories.

Our methodology for removing monetary gold flows from current account data led naturally to a gold standard version of the Feldstein-Horioka (1980) hypothesis on capital mobility. Our regression results are in broad agreement with Eichengreen (1992a), who found a significantly positive cross-sectional correlation between saving and investment even during some periods when the gold standard prevailed. Despite the high level of capital mobility that prevailed under the gold standard, it seems that average national saving and domestic investment rates were cross-sectionally correlated, contrary to the Feldstein-Horioka hypothesis. Nonetheless, the explanatory power of the pre-1914 regressions is usually much lower than in the corresponding post-1960 regressions.

Despite reaching broadly similar conclusions, we estimate correlations between saving and investment that are somewhat lower than those Eichengreen (1992a) found. In particular, we find that in comparison to other interwar subsamples, the saving-investment correlation is markedly low during the fleeting years of a revived world gold standard, 1925–1930. The proportions in which this phenomenon should be ascribed to greater exchange rate predictability as opposed to relaxed capital controls is a topic for future research.

Appendix 9.1   Omitted Variables Bias, Alternative Specification, and Parameter Sensitivity

This appendix deals with the sensitivity of the parameter estimates in the paper to the inclusion of gold flows and inventory data, and to the set of countries included in the cross-sectional average.

Gold Flows

We argued in the text that in regressions of investment on saving, figures for the current account should include all data on gold flows. This choice leads to the specification in equation (9.8). Omitting data on total net gold shipments introduces an omitted variables bias into the estimates.

We denoted the true variable of interest, the current account including all gold (expressed as a fraction of GDP or NNP), by CA^O. It is defined as the sum of the nongold current account, CA^{NG}, and net shipments of gold to foreigners, SG:

$$CA^O = CA^{NG} + SG. \tag{A.9.1}$$

The true relation we are interested in estimating is

$$I = \alpha + \beta(I + CA^O) + u. \tag{A.9.2}$$

This expression can be rewritten using equation (A.9.1):

$$\begin{aligned} I &= \alpha + \beta(I + CA^{NG} + SG) + u \\ &= \alpha + \beta(I + CA^{NG}) + \beta SG + u. \end{aligned} \tag{A.9.3}$$

Table A.9.1
Comparison of parameter estimates from regression of I on $(I + CA^{NG} + SG)$ with regression of I on $(I + CA^{NG})$

Sample period	Estimated parameter	With SG	Without SG	Percentage bias†
1885 to 1913	Slope: β	0.55**	0.44*	−19.78
All countries	Adj. R^2	0.30	0.20	−33.56
1919 to 1936	Slope: β	0.95***	0.89***	−7.00
Excl. Den, Fra, Ger, Rus	Adj. R^2	0.74	0.66	−9.98

†Percentage bias is calculated by taking the difference in parameter estimates as a proportion of the correctly specified parameter.
*, **, *** indicate significance at the 10 percent, 5 percent, and 1 percent level, respectively.

Excluding gold flows from the measured value of the current account introduces a source of bias into the estimation procedure, as regressing I on $I + CA^{NG}$ (and a constant) only omits the third term on the right hand side of equation (A.9.3). The extent of the omitted variables bias is illustrated in the following table.

The table illustrates that the slope coefficient is underestimated by almost 20 percent when the 1885 to 1913 data are used. When data from the interwar period are used, the extent of the understatement of the slope coefficient is reduced, but it still remains important. In both cases the explanatory power of the regression is reduced. These results are in accord with our intuition of the likely impact of including gold flows, as nongold current account balances tend to be negatively correlated in cross-section with net outward shipments of gold.[24] Adding gold flows to the estimated equation thus has the effect of raising the measured correlation between saving and investment, as the table demonstrates.

Inventories

We pointed out in the paper that figures for gross investment should include the value of changes in inventories or stocks. Omitting data on stocks will introduce another source of bias into the estimates.

Suppose that the true variable of interest is total gross investment, I, which is defined as the sum of gross fixed investment, I^F, and changes in inventories or stocks:[25]

$$I = I^F + \Delta Stocks. \tag{A.9.4}$$

Saving is defined residually, as the sum of the current account and gross investment

$$S = CA + I. \tag{A.9.5}$$

Let the level of *fixed* saving, S^F, be defined as the current account plus gross *fixed* investment,

$$S^F = CA + I^F, \tag{A.9.6}$$

such that $S = S^F + \Delta Stocks$. Now suppose that the true relation we are interested in estimating is given by the expression

$$I = \alpha + \beta S + u. \tag{A.9.7}$$

This expression can be rewritten by using equations (A.9.5) and (A.9.6):

$$I^F = \alpha + \beta S^F + (\beta - 1)\Delta Stocks + u. \tag{A.9.8}$$

Excluding inventory data from the measured value of investment introduces a potential source of bias into the estimation procedure, as regressing fixed investment on fixed saving omits the third term on the right-hand side of equation (A.9.8). The extent of the resulting omitted variables bias is illustrated in table A.9.2.

There is a large effect for the 1885–1913 sample. When inventories data are excluded, the slope coefficient is overstated, as is the explanatory power of the regression.

Alternative Regression Specification

An alternative specification, given in equation (9.7), allows for possibly different coefficients on saving and the change in the monetary gold stock. Results from this specification are presented in table A.9.3.

Table A.9.2
Comparison of parameter estimates from regression of I on $(S^F + \Delta Stocks)$ with regression of I^F on S^F

Sample period	Estimated parameter	With $\Delta Stocks$	Without $\Delta Stocks$	Percentage bias†
1885 to 1913	Slope: β	0.55**	0.67***	20.92
All countries	Adj. R^2	0.30	0.60	96.41
1919 to 1936	Slope: β	0.95***	0.93***	−2.47
Excl. Den, Fra, Ger, Rus	Adj. R^2	0.74	0.55	−25.19

†Percentage bias is calculated by taking the difference in parameter estimates as a proportion of the correctly specified parameter.
*, **, *** indicate significance at the 10 percent, 5 percent, and 1 percent level, respectively.

Table A.9.3
Parameter estimates from regression of I on S and ΔMG ($S \equiv I + CA^{NG} + SG + \Delta MG$)

Sample period	Sample size	Coefficient on S: β	Standard error	Coefficient on ΔMG: γ	Standard error	Wald test $\beta = 1$, $\gamma = -1$	Adj. R^2
1880–1913	11	0.42	0.25	8.33	7.48	3.07	0.20
1885–1913	13	0.55**	0.23	0.03	3.78	1.90	0.24
1880–1890	11	0.37	0.23	11.27**	4.66	6.23**	0.45
1891–1901	13	0.61***	0.17	−0.68	1.76	2.72	0.50
1902–1913	13	0.55*	0.27	5.10	5.71	1.59	0.25
1919–1924	10	1.13**	0.44	−4.37	5.55	0.18	0.38
1925–1930	12	0.75**	0.24	−1.37	2.46	1.96	0.63
1931–1936	12	0.94***	0.09	0.34	0.79	1.85	0.91
1937–1939	9	0.94***	0.10	−0.67	0.70	0.36	0.91

Notes: The estimates for 1880–1913 and 1880–1890 exclude Japan and Russia; for 1925–1930 and 1931–1936 they exclude Russia; for 1937–1939 they exclude France, Germany, Italy, and Russia. for 1919–1924 they exclude Denmark, Germany, and Russia; for 1885–1913 they exclude Russia; for 1937–1939 they exclude France, Germany, Italy, and Russia.

*, **, ***indicate significance at the 10 percent, 5 percent, and 1 percent level, respectively.

We can see from the results in this table that including the monetary gold stock adds little to the previous results. The explanatory power does not change by much, because the coefficient estimates on the change in the monetary gold stock are mostly insignificant, even at the 10 percent level. We can reject the hypothesis that the coefficient on saving equals 1 and the coefficient on changes in the monetary gold stock equals −1 for a single period only: 1880–1890.

Outlier Sensitivity

This section deals with the question of how sensitive the parameter estimates are to outliers. Table A.9.4 presents the results of the regressions for different time periods when one country is dropped from the sample at a time. Using this procedure, the highest and lowest parameter estimates were obtained. For comparison, the full sample estimates of the slope are presented in the final column.

We can see from this table that the parameter estimates are quite sensitive to the sample of countries in the cross-sectional average. The estimated slope coefficient can change by as much as 0.3, and the explanatory power can change by more than 60 percent. For the pre–World War I period, the inclusion of the United States tends to raise the parameter estimates, while Finland tends to lower the estimates. For the post–World War I period, the inclusion of Germany tends to raise the saving-investment correlations, while Australia tends to lower them.[26]

Parameter Estimates: On or Off Gold Standard

Another interesting question to consider is whether being on the gold standard makes a difference to the estimated saving-investment correlation. This question can be addressed by estimating the parameters only for countries that were on the gold standard for the entire sample period, or by using data for the years that a country was on the gold standard.[27] We adopt both approaches here. Table A.9.5 shows the results of estimating the parameters for countries that were on the gold standard, and it shows country averages based on the period for which the country was on the gold standard. For comparison, we include in the final two columns the parameter estimates based on all available data.

We can see from the results presented in this table that including only countries on the gold standard for the entire sample period tends to

Table A.9.4
Maximum and minimum slope estimates from regression of investment on savings

Sample period	Min β parameter	Adj. R^2	Missing country	Max β parameter	Adj. R^2	Missing country	Full sample β
1880–1913	0.38	0.07	SWE	0.50	0.09	FIN	0.45
1885–1913	0.49*	0.23	RUS	0.63**	0.28	FIN	0.55**
1880–1890	0.23	−0.06	USA	0.49	0.18	CAN	0.44
1891–1901	0.53**	0.37	JAP	0.68***	0.57	FIN	0.62***
1902–1913	0.54*	0.18	RUS	0.74*	0.22	FIN	0.60**
1919–1924	0.80**	0.37	NOR	1.14**	0.55	AUS	1.00**
1925–1930	0.55*	0.27	FRA	0.89***	0.94	AUS	0.70***
1931–1936	0.86***	0.87	GER	0.97***	0.92	UK	0.91***
1937–1939	0.87***	0.92	JAP	0.96***	0.95	AUS	0.92***

Notes: The full sample estimate for 1880–1913 and 1880–1890 excludes Japan and Russia; for 1919–1924 it excludes Denmark, Germany, and Russia; for 1925–1930 it excludes Russia; for 1931–1936 it excludes Russia; for 1937–1939 it excludes France, Germany, Italy, and Russia.
*, **, *** indicate significance at the 10 percent, 5 percent, and 1 percent level, respectively.

Table A.9.5
Slope estimates from regression of investment on savings for countries on the gold standard and for years on the gold standard

Sample period	Including countries on gold standard		Including years on gold standard		All available data	
	β	Adj. R^2	β	Adj. R^2	β	Adj. R^2
1880–1913	0.46	0.17	0.58**	0.33	0.45	0.16
1885–1913	0.44	0.14	0.57**	0.31	0.55**	0.30
1880–1890	0.44	0.12	0.44	0.13	0.44	0.13
1891–1901	0.52**	0.37	0.66***	0.54	0.62***	0.54
1902–1913	0.63*	0.25	0.63*	0.25	0.60**	0.25
1919–1924	—	—	—	—	1.00**	0.43
1925–1930	0.78**	0.87	0.79***	0.71	0.70***	0.66

Notes: The estimates for countries on the gold standard for 1880–1913, 1885–1913, 1880–1890, and 1891–1901 exclude Italy, Japan, and Russia; the estimates for 1902–1913 exclude Italy; the estimates for 1925–1930 include only Germany, Sweden, the United Kingdom, and the United States. The full sample estimates for 1880–1913 and 1880–1890 exclude Japan and Russia; for 1919–1924 they exclude Denmark, Germany, and Russia; for 1925–1930 they exclude Russia.
*, **, *** indicate significance at the 10 percent, 5 percent, and 1 percent level, respectively.

lower the estimated saving-investment correlation. However, taking the country average for years that a country was on the gold standard tends to raise the estimated correlation as well as the explanatory power of the regression. As noted in the text, this result is difficult to interpret because the timing of gold standard adherence was endogenous for many countries.

Appendix 9.2   Data Sources and Methods

The investment ratios estimated in the paper were calculated by taking current price estimates of gross domestic capital formation (gross fixed investment plus changes in stocks/inventories) as a percentage of gross domestic product at market prices.[28] The estimates of stocks may include changes in the value of livestock.[29] The saving ratio was estimated by adding the investment ratio to the current account to GDP or NNP ratio, measured in current prices. The saving ratio is thus defined residually, and hence incorporates all measurement error from both investment and the current account.

Australia

GDP
GDP data from 1861–1900 are from N. G. Butlin 1962, 6, table 1, col. 2, market prices, calendar years, millions of pounds. GDP data from 1900 to 1944 are from M. W. Butlin 1977, 78–79, table IV.1, col. 11, current prices, millions of (Australian) dollars. Data are for financial years (July 1 to June 30), 1900/1901 to 1944/1945.

Capital Formation
Capital formation data for 1861–1900 are from N. G. Butlin 1962, 16, table 4, total public and private gross domestic capital formation, market prices, calendar years, thousands of pounds. Capital formation data include changes in stocks. Changes in stocks data for 1861–1900 are from N. G. Butlin 1962, 22, table 7, livestock accumulation, market prices, calendar years, thousands of pounds. N. G. Butlin (1962, 21) argues that "Livestock assets form a large part of the total private Australian assets, and changes in livestock assets are very large in relation to total private gross capital formation." N. G. Butlin proposed a measure of domestic capital accumulation equal to capital formation plus changes in livestock. This procedure is used for Australian data prior to 1901.

This inclusion of livestock accumulation estimates in capital formation data is controversial, however. As Boehm (1965, 211) argues, "The alternative sequence warrants close attention in income and growth analyses because the general effects on output and expenditure of changes in livestock are not necessarily comparable with the effects of changes in fixed assets." For Australia, increases in livestock average around 1.07 percent of GDP from 1861 to 1900, and then 0.94 percent from 1900/1901 to 1944/1945.

From the perspective of national accounts classification, the System of National Accounts advocates the classification of livestock accumulation into estimates of changes in stocks. According to the United Nations Statistical Office (1952, 80), the value of the increase in stocks should be classified in the same way as fixed capital formation in the national accounts. The System of National Accounts was adopted by many countries in our dataset and applied retrospectively to historical data. Thus, for the purposes of this chapter, we will follow this procedure and include livestock accumulation in estimates of changes in stocks.

Capital formation data from 1900 to 1944 are from M. W. Butlin 1977, 78–79, table IV.1, private plus public fixed capital formation, current prices, millions of dollars. Data are for financial years (July 1 to June 30), 1900/1901 to 1944/1945. Capital formation data include changes in stocks. Data for changes in stocks from 1900 to 1944 are from M. W. Butlin 1977, 78–79, table IV.1, current prices, millions of dollars. Data are for financial years (July 1 to June 30), 1900/1901 to 1944/1945.

Current Account
Current account data for 1861–1900 are from N. G. Butlin 1962, 444, table 265 for current account balance, in millions of pounds. (The number in Butlin's table is defined as an excess of debits, so that number with its sign reversed is used for the current account balance— that is, a positive number implies surplus.) Current account data for 1900–1944 are from M. W. Butlin 1977, 108–109, table IV.17 for data on exports, imports, and net property income paid overseas (cols. 1, 2, and 4 respectively). Data are in current prices, millions of dollars. Data are for financial years (July 1 to June 30), 1900/1901 to 1944/1945. The value of exports less imports less net property income paid overseas gives the current account balance. For the current account data prior to 1901, N. G. Butlin excluded net exports of gold and included gold production, "treating gold production as the proper current account credit of a gold producing country" (Butlin 1962, 435). M. W. Butlin also followed this procedure for data from 1900/1901 to 1944/1945. To arrive at figures for the current account excluding all gold flows, we subtracted gold production from the Butlin current account figures.

Gold
Data on the gross value of gold production from 1861 to 1900 are from N. G. Butlin 1962, 115, table 55. Data on gold production from 1900 to 1945 are from McLean 1968, 83–86, row 2, gold production, millions of pounds. Data from 1901 to 1913 are for calendar years, data from 1914 are for financial years (July to June). Data on net exports of gold coin and bullion from 1861 to 1900 are from N. G. Butlin 1962, data on current account credits for gold and specie exports from 410–411, table 247, line 12, and gold and specie imports are from 413–414, table 248, line 11. Data on net exports of gold coin and bullion from 1901 to 1945 are from the *Official Yearbook of the Commonwealth of Australia* (Australia, Commonwealth Bureau of Census and Statistics, various years), exports of gold bullion and specie less imports of gold bullion and

specie. The *Yearbook* data from 1901 to 1913 are for calendar years, data from 1914 are for financial years. Data from 1901 to 1914 are converted to financial years by averaging with the data from the previous year.

The monetary gold stock includes coin and bullion held by the treasury, mints, banks, and the public. According to the *Statistical Register* of New South Wales (Colony of New South Wales 1876, 255, and 1890, 255), data on gold coin and bullion held by the New South Wales Treasury and mint for 1867–1876 and 1881–1890 suggest that mint holdings of coin are negligible (maximum value of £804). Bullion held at the mint reaches a maximum of £136,904 in 1874. Treasury holdings of bullion and coin are listed as being negligible. Data on bullion in the hands of the public (outside of banks) are not available. The bullion component of the monetary gold stock held by the public and official agencies is therefore ignored in these calculations.

For data on the monetary gold stock of Australia, the flows of gold reported by the three mints (Sydney, Melbourne, and Perth) can be added to provide an estimate of changes in the total coin stock of the country. For New South Wales, data on gold coin in banks of issue and private hands from 1855 to 1890 are taken from the *Statistical Register* of New South Wales (Colony of New South Wales 1890, 234). Data for 1891 to 1899 are taken from the *Annual Report* of the United Kingdom (United Kingdom, Deputy Master of the Mint, various issues). Data for 1900 and 1901 are estimated by adding gold coin issued by the mint less gold coin withdrawn, plus coin imported less coin exported by the Colony of New South Wales, using data from the *Annual Report* (United Kingdom, Deputy Master of the Mint 1901, 138).

For Victoria, there is little data available on the stock of gold coin in banks and private hands. However, the *Annual Report* (United Kingdom, Deputy Master of the Mint 1893, 123; 1899, 123; 1901, 138) gives data on gold coin flows for the colony of Victoria from the opening of the Melbourne mint in 1872. The sum of the data on gold coin issued less coin withdrawn, plus gold coin imported less coin exported from the colony of Victoria gives the change in gold coin in the colony.

For Western Australia, the *Annual Report* (United Kingdom, Deputy Master of the Mint 1901, 138) gives data on gold coin flows for the colony of Western Australia from the opening of the Perth mint in 1899. The sum of the data on gold coin issued less coin withdrawn, plus gold coin imported less coin exported from the colony gives the change in gold coin in Western Australia.

Data on the stock of gold bullion held by the banks is taken from S. J. Butlin et al. 1971, 113, table 1, average of weekly figures for December quarter until 1900, then average of weekly figures for June quarter. The data are for total bullion, but according to the notes on page 77, bank bullion holdings are mainly gold bullion.

For the years 1861–1900, changes in the monetary gold stock for Australia are then estimated as the sum of changes in the stock of gold coin in banks of issue and private hands in New South Wales, plus the sum of changes in the gold coin stock in the colonies of Victoria and Western Australia, plus the change in bullion held by Australian Trading Banks. Data from 1861 to 1900 are for calendar years. Data on the monetary gold stock for 1901 to 1944 are taken from S. J. Butlin et al. 1971, 453–457, table 42, total gold coin held by banks and the public, and bullion held by Australian Trading Banks from S. J. Butlin et al. 1971, 115, table 1, end of financial year (June quarter averages). An estimate of the gold stock for the financial year 1899 was calculated as the average of the gold stock in 1899 and 1900. The estimated gold stock at the end of 1899 and 1900 was calculated by taking the cumulative sum of net additions to coin in the colonies of Victoria and Western Australia from 1872 to 1899 and 1900 (i.e. the sum of gold coin issued less coin withdrawn, plus gold coin imported less coin exported), plus the stock of gold coin in banks of issue and private hands in New South Wales in 1899 and 1900, plus the gold bullion holdings of Australian Trading Banks. Data on changes in the monetary gold stock from 1900/1901 onwards are calculated as the first difference of the sum of coin stock held by banks and the public plus bullion held by trading banks, listed in S. J. Butlin et al. 1971.

The main drawback with estimating the monetary gold stock using this method is that it tends to overstate the actual gold stock. As S. J. Butlin et al. (1971, 92) caution: "Because of inadequacies in the gold production figures and the freedom until 1914 with which coins in circulation in Australia were imported and exported and the probable statistical significance thereafter of unrecorded imports and exports of coins, it is not possible to produce satisfactory estimates of coinage in use in the nineteenth century, or to be more exact, it would not be possible to do so without conducting much more detailed research." Another relevant comment on the accuracy of the statistics is made in the *Annual Report* (United Kingdom, Deputy Master of the Mint 1902, 138): "The above return shows that only 13.73 percent of the gold coined at the Melbourne, Sydney, and Perth Mints during the last 29

years has been retained in the States coining it. The amount actually
retained is probably much less than this, for considerable quantities are
taken away by passengers for Europe which do not appear in the
Customs House Returns, and which probably are not counterbalanced
by sums brought in by incoming passengers. . . ." Since reliable data
are not available on funds taken overseas and inbound by passengers,
there is little that can be done to the estimated figures for the monetary
gold stock to adjust for this source of error.

Canada

GDP

GDP data from 1870 to 1926 are calculated by subtracting net interest
and dividend payments from abroad from the figures for GNP. Data
for GNP are from from Urquhart (1986, 11–15, table 2.1, row 25), market
prices, thousands of (Canadian) dollars. GNP data from 1927 to 1944
are from Urquhart and Buckley (1965, 131, series E27), gross national
expenditure at market prices, millions of dollars. Data for net interest
and dividend payments from 1870 to 1926 are from Urquhart (1986,
11–15, table 2.1, row 8 less row 21), interest and dividends credits less
interest and dividends debits, market prices, thousands of dollars. Data
from 1927 to 1944 are from Urquhart and Buckley (1965, 160, series F60
less F66), current receipts of interest and dividends less current payments of interest and dividends, millions of dollars.

Capital Formation

Capital formation data for 1870 to 1926 are from Urquhart (1986, 16–17,
table 2.2, col. 8), grand total, gross fixed capital formation, current
dollars, millions. Data from 1927 to 1944 are from Urquhart and
Buckley (1965, 131, series E17), total business gross fixed capital
formation, millions of dollars. Capital formation data for 1927–1944,
unlike pre-1927 data, include changes in stocks. Changes in stocks data
for 1927–1944 from Urquhart and Buckley (1965, 131, series E21), total
value of the physical change in inventories, millions of dollars.

Current Account

Current account data from 1870 to 1926 are from Urquhart (1986, 20–25,
table 2.4, rows 9 and 22), total current credits and total current debits,
thousands of dollars. These data include net exports of gold coin and
bullion. Data from 1927 to 1944 are from Urquhart and Buckley (1965,

160, series F71), net balance, all countries, millions of dollars. Data include net exports of nonmonetary gold. Data for the current account excluding all gold flows from 1870 to 1926 are calculated by subtracting net exports of gold coin and bullion from the current account. Data on the current account excluding gold from 1927 to 1944 are calculated by subtracting net exports of nonmonetary gold from the current account.

Gold

Data on net exports of gold coin and bullion for 1870 to 1926 are from Urquhart (1986, 20–25, table 2.4, rows 2 and 16), exports of gold coin and bullion, less imports of gold coin and bullion, thousands of dollars. Data on net exports of nonmonetary gold for 1868 to 1899 are from Rich (1988, 245–246, table A-3, col. 3), millions of dollars. Data on net exports of nonmonetary gold for 1900 to 1913 are calculated by taking the sum of net gold exports and the change in the monetary gold stock. Data on net gold exports are from Urquhart (1986) as listed above. Data on the change in the monetary gold stock are from Rich (1988) as listed below. Data on net exports of nonmonetary gold from 1927 to 1944 are from Urquhart and Buckley (1965, 160, series F58), current receipts, net exports of nonmonetary gold, millions of dollars, all countries. Data on net exports of monetary gold from 1927 to 1937 are from Urquhart and Buckley (1965, 164, series F99), monetary gold movement (net). Data for 1938–1939 are calculated as the change in the gold holdings of the Bank of Canada, from *The Canada Yearbook* (Canada, Dominion Bureau of Statistics 1939, 934 and 1941, 805). Data for 1940–1945 are from Canada, Dominion Bureau of Statistics 1949, 57, statement 8—Canada's holdings of gold and U.S. dollars converted to Canadian dollars at the official exchange rate of US$0.909090 = C$1. Net exports of gold from 1927 to 1944 are calculated as net exports of nonmonetary gold minus the change in the monetary gold stock.

Data on the monetary gold stock from 1869 to 1871 are calculated as the sum of bank gold and subsidiary coin plus the stock of gold held against Dominion notes. Data on bank gold and subsidiary coin are from Curtis 1931, 36, current gold and subsidiary coin, thousands of dollars, December figures. Data on gold held against Dominion notes are from Curtis 1931, 92, thousands of dollars, December figures. Data on the monetary gold stock from 1872 to 1913 come from Rich 1988, 239–242, table A1, Dominion government gold holdings plus the gold holdings of chartered banks, end of year. Data on the monetary gold stock from 1914 to 1926 are calculated as the sum of official Canadian gold reserves, plus bank gold and subsidiary coin holdings, plus bank gold held in the central reserves of the banking system (a private gold reserve managed by trustees from the Ministry of Finance and the Canadian Bankers Association). Data on the offical gold reserves are from *The Canada Yearbook* (Canada, Dominion Bureau of Statistics 1927–1928, 857, table 3), total Canadian gold reserves, end of year figure. Data on bank gold and subsidiary coin are from Curtis (1931, 36) current gold and subsidiary coin, thousands of dollars, December figures. Data on bank gold held in the central gold reserves are from Curtis (1931, 35), gold coin, thousands of dollars, December figures.

Denmark

GDP
GDP data from 1850 to 1944 are from Hansen 1977, 261–263, table 5, gross factor incomes (*bruttofaktorindkomst*) plus net import of goods and services (*netto import af varer og tjenester*) plus indirect taxes less subsidies (*indirekte afgifter—pristilskud*), equaling disposal of merchandise and services (*varer og tjenester til radighed*), current market prices (*lobende markedspriser*), millions of kroner.

Capital Formation
Capital formation data from 1850 to 1944 are from Hansen 1977, 264–266, table 6, col. 2, gross investment (*brutto-investering*), current prices, millions of kroner. Data do not include stocks.

Current Account
Current account data from 1874 to 1944 are from Bjerke and Ussing 1958, 152–153, table VI, col. 4, net imports of goods and services, millions of kroner. According to the League of Nations 1927, 85, Danish trade statistics exclude gold bullion and all specie. Silver bullion is included in merchandise trade. Thus the current account data should not include gold trade.

Gold
Data on the monetary gold stock from 1874 to 1906 are from the United States, Bureau of the Mint 1876–1920. Data on the gold stock for 1875 and 1894 are calculated by adding net exports data for the following year to gold stock figures for the previous year. Data on the gold stock for 1877 and 1886–1888 are calculated by subtracting net exports data

for the year from the gold stock figures for the previous year. Data on the gold stock for 1874 and 1878 are calculated as the average of the preceding and following years. U.S. dollar values are converted to kroner at the exchange rate of 0.268 U.S. dollars per kroner. Data on the gold holdings of the central bank (*Danmarks Nationalbank*) from 1907 to 1944 are from Denmark, *Danmarks Statistik 1897–1947*. The change in the monetary gold stock is assumed to equal the change in the gold holdings of the central bank.

Data on gold exports and imports for 1874 to 1906 are from the United States, Bureau of the Mint 1876–1920. Data on gold imports and exports from 1910 to 1930 are from the League of Nations 1924, 1927, 1931, 1932, bullion and specie import, bullion and specie export, then gold import and export. The figures for bullion and specie import include some non-gold coin. However, there is a close correspondence between gold bullion and specie trade and total bullion and specie trade from the League of Nations figures for the years with overlapping data (1922–1930), suggesting that the non-gold element of bullion and specie trade was small. On this basis, the figures for total bullion and specie trade were used from 1910 to 1921, then gold bullion and gold specie trade figures were used from 1922 to 1930. Net exports of gold from 1907 to 1909 and from 1931 to 1934 are assumed to equal minus the change in the monetary gold stock (i.e., an increase in the monetary gold stock implies and equal amount of gold imports). Data on monetary gold exports for 1935 to 1944 are from Denmark, *Danmarks Statistik 1897–1947*. Again due to lack of data, total net exports of gold for 1935 to 1944 are assumed to equal monetary gold exports.

Finland

Finland became an autonomous Grand Duchy connected with Russia in 1809, and declared independence from Russia on December 6, 1917. Finland had its own monetary system from 1860 and was on the gold standard from 1877 to 1914. The unit of currency was the Finnmark (*Finnish markka*, FIM), equivalent to one French gold franc. Finland returned to the gold standard on January 1, 1926 and remained on the gold standard until October 1931.

GDP
GDP data from 1860 to 1944 from Hjerppe 1989, 201–203, table 3A1, col. 1, market prices, thousands of FIM.

Capital Formation

Capital formation data from 1860 to 1938 from Hjerppe 1989, 201–203, table 3A1, col. 5, gross fixed capital expenditure, market prices, thousands of FIM. Changes in stocks data from 1860 to 1938 from Hjerppe 1989, 201–203, table 3A1, col. 7, increase in stocks plus statistical discrepancy, market prices, thousands of FIM.

Current Account

Current account data from 1860 to 1938 from Hjerppe 1989, 201–203, table 3A1, cols. 2 and 6, imports of goods and exports of goods, market prices, thousands of FIM. The statistical discrepancy includes data on net exports of services. Since these are not reported separately by Hjerppe, we exclude them from our current account data for Finland. According to the League of Nations (1927, 104), Finnish merchandise trade statistics include gold specie and bullion movements in the data for manufactured gold and unwrought gold, respectively.

Gold

Net exports of gold from 1860 to 1909 from Pihkala 1970, 80–91, table 2, value of exports [43: *Raha* (coinage)] less Pihkala 1970, 112–123, table 7, value of imports [1252: *Hopea, kulta, platina* (silver, gold, platinum)]. These data include some silver and platinum trade. Net exports of gold from 1910 to 1930 are from the League of Nations 1924, 1927, 1931, 1932, gold bullion and specie export less gold bullion and specie import. Net exports of gold from 1931 to 1944 are from Finland, *Suomen Virallinen Tilasto* 1929–1947, item numbers 951–953, precious metal imports: *Kultaa: valmistamatonta ja jatteita, lankaa ja levya, teoksia muunlaisia, rahaa, muita* (gold, manufactured and unmanufactured, coin), then from 1939 items 61-005, 61-102 to 61-014, and 62-001. Exports data are given in series 61-002 (*Kultaa: valmistamaton seka jatteet ja romu*) and 62-001 (*Kultaraha* or gold coin).

Data on the monetary gold stock from 1871 to 1944 are taken from Finland, *Tilastollinen Paatoimisto* 1907–1951, gold assets of the Bank of Finland. The change in the monetary gold stock is calculated as the first difference of the gold assets of the Bank of Finland. Data on the current account excluding gold are calculated by subtracting net gold exports (which include some silver and platinum) from the current account data.

France

GDP

GDP data from 1850 to 1900 are from Lévy-Leboyer and Bourguignon 1985, 329–332, table A-III, series 1, *produit interieur brut, millions de francs courants*. Data from 1901 to 1944 are from Villa 1993, 459, series PIBQ, *production interieure brute en valeur–en gros francs courants*.

Capital Formation

Capital formation data from 1850 to 1900 are equal to gross fixed capital formation plus changes in stocks. Capital formation data are from Lévy-Leboyer and Bourguignon 1985, 329–332, table A-III, series 4, *investissements, bruts* (gross fixed capital formation), *millions de francs courants*. Changes in stocks data from 1850 to 1900 are from Lévy-Leboyer and Bourguignon 1985, 329–332, table A-III, series 8, *variations des stocks* (change in stocks), *millions de francs courants*. Capital formation data from 1901 to 1944 are equal to gross fixed capital formation plus changes in stocks. Capital formation data are from Villa 1993, 439, series IE, IG, IM, *investissement des entreprises, investissement des administrations, investissement des menages, en valeur, en gros francs courants* (sum of investment by businesses, government, households). Changes in stocks data are from Villa 1993, 457, series DS, *variations de stocks en valeur–en gros francs courants* (changes in stocks).

Current Account

Current account data from 1850 to 1900 are from Lévy-Leboyer and Bourguignon 1985, 329–332, table A-III, series 5, 6, and 7, *exportations* (exports) *plus gains invisibles* (invisible earnings) minus *importations* (imports), *millions de francs courants*. Current account data from 1901 to 1923 are from Villa 1993, 435–448 series EXPORT, plus series SUS, plus series IDVX, plus series DREX, series DOMX, minus series IMPORT minus series ODRX, *exportations en valeur* (exports), plus *solde des utilisations de services* (balance of services), plus *interets et dividendes verses par l'exterieur* (interest and dividends), plus *depenses et recettes exterieurs* (external expenditures and revenues), plus *dommages de guerre verses par l'exterieur* (war reparations), minus *importations en valeur* (imports), minus *operations diverses de rapartitions exterieur* (sundry external transactions), all *en gros francs courants*. Current account data from 1924 to 1944 are from Villa 1993, 436, series EBX, *epargne brute de l'exterieur–en gros francs courants*.

According to France, Ministère des Finances et des Affaires Économiques 1952, 195, external trade data exclude gold, silver, and copper coin, raw gold and silver, gold and silver in bars, ingots, and powder. On this basis, the current account data excluding gold were assumed to equal the original current account data.

Gold

Data on net exports of gold and silver for 1850 to 1875 are from the United States, Bureau of the Mint 1900, 424–425. U.S. dollar values are converted to French francs at the par exchange rate of 0.193 U.S. dollars per franc.

Data on net exports of gold from 1876 to 1914 are from the National Bureau of Economic Research series 14114, excess of gold exports over imports, sum of 12 months data. Data for 1915 to 1930 are from the League of Nations 1924, 1927, 1931, 1932, gold bullion and specie exports less gold bullion and specie imports. Data from 1931 to 1944 are from France, Ministère des Finances et des Affaires Économiques 1966, 365, table I, *mouvements d'or, million de francs* 1928. The figures for net exports of gold include gold and silver from 1850 to 1870.

Estimates of the French monetary gold stock for 1850 to 1878 are reported by Flandreau 1995, 308. (Indeed, his estimates reach back to 1840.) According to him (see his footnote 54), the figures includes gold holdings of the Bank of France. Data from 1879 to 1913 are estimated using data from Sicsic 1989, 728, table 4, and 732, table 11. Sicsic provides revised estimates of the monetary gold stock, apparently including Bank of France holdings, in 1878, 1885, 1891, 1897, 1903, and 1909. These estimates are regressed on a constant and the annual monetary gold stock data for the corresponding years as calculated by J. Denuc (method of M. Pupin), which Sicsic reports in his table 4. The coefficients from this regression are then used together with the Denuc-Pupin annual data to arrive at predicted figures for the monetary gold stock from 1878 to 1913. To avoid a discontinuity in 1879 from changing over from Flandreau's data to Sicsic's, the change in the monetary gold stock for 1879 is calculated as the difference between our predicted 1879 value based in the Denuc-Pupin data Sicsic reports and Sicsic's own estimate for 1878.

Data on the monetary gold stock from 1913 to 1927 are from France, Ministère des Finances et des Affaires Économiques 1966, 517, table III, *Banque de France encaisse d'or* (Bank of France gold holdings, annual average). Data from 1928 to 1945 are from France, Ministère des

Finances et des Affaires Économiques 1966, 562, table II, *Banque de France encaisse d'or* (Bank of France gold holdings, year end), multiplied by the price of gold from France, Ministère des Finances et des Affaires Économiques 1966, 562, table II, *cours de l'or à Paris, cours d'achat par la Banque de France*. Price data from 1938 to 1945 are from France, Ministère des Finances et des Affaires Économiques 1952, 503, *cours de l'or à Paris et à Londres depuis 1938*, end of December figures.

Germany

GDP

GDP data from 1850 to 1939 are from Hoffman 1965, 825–826, table 248, col. 5, *Nettosozialprodukt zu Markt-preisen* (NNP at market prices), raised 8.4 percent to approximate GDP following the procedure in Maddison 1991.

Capital Formation

Capital formation data from 1850 to 1939 from Hoffman et al. 1965, 825–826, table 248, col. 2, *Nettoinvestitionen* (net investment). Data include stocks. Hoffman et al. 1965 report separate inventory figures only for the years 1924–1939 and 1950–1959; see Hoffman et al. 1965, 237, table 32, col. 4, *Investitionen der Landwirtschaft, Vorrate* (investment in agriculture, stocks), plus 247, table 36, col. 3, *Investitionen im Gewerbe, Vorrate*, (investment in trade/industry, stocks). Our pre-1913 numbers on stocks in trade and industry (used only for illustrative purposes in appendix 9.1) are estimated by calculating the average of stocks to the sum of fixed investment and stocks for the years 1924–1939, 1950–1959, and multiplying that average by the annual sum data on total investment.

Current Account

Current account data from 1860 to 1938 are from Hoffman et al. 1965, 825–826, col. 4, *Saldo der Leistungsbilanz*. The current account data exclude net exports of precious metals. The current account excluding gold is calculated by adding net exports of precious metal to the current account and subtracting net exports of gold.

Gold

Exports data from 1872 to 1942 from Germany, Deutsche Bundesbank 1976, 324, table J 1.03, col. 11, *Ausfuhr, darunter gold* (exports of gold) and col. 13, *Einfuhr, darunter gold* (imports of gold). Exports data for 1872 to 1879 are estimated by taking the average of gold exports to total exports of precious metal for the period 1880 to 1913 and multiplying by the corresponding figure for total precious metal exports. Imports data for 1872 to 1875 are estimated by taking the average of gold imports to total imports of precious metal for the period 1876 to 1913 and multiplying by the figure for corresponding figure for total precious metal imports.

Gold holdings of the Reichsbank for 1876–1945 from Germany, Deutsche Bundesbank 1976, 36, table C 1.01, col. 2, *Aktiva: Gold in Barren and Munzen* (gold in bars and coin). Data for 1878, 1879, 1883, 1887, 1888, 1890 are not shown separately, but data are given for sum of *Gold in Barren und Munzen* and *Deutsche Scheidemunzen* (total gold in bars and coin and German subsidiary coin). Data for 1878, 1879, 1883, 1887, 1888, 1890 are estimated by taking the ratio for the previous year of gold in bars and coin to the sum of gold in bars and coin plus subsidiary coin, and multiplying by the corresponding sum for the missing year. Gold coin in circulation from 1876 to 1913 from Germany, Deutsche Bundesbank 1976, 14, table B 1.01, col. 7, *Munzen, Goldmunzen* (coin, gold coin). The monetary gold stock is calculated as the sum of gold coin in circulation plus the gold holdings of the Reichsbank.

Italy

GDP

GDP data are calculated by taking the figures for GNP and subtracting net factor incomes and current transfers received from the rest of the world. GNP data from 1861 to 1925 are from Italy, Instituto Centrak di Statistica (ISTAT) 1957, 249–250, table 36, col. 6, *reddito nazionale lordo ai prezzi di mercato* (gross national product at market prices), *milioni di lire*. Net factor incomes from abroad are from Italy, ISTAT 1957, 249–250, table 36, col. 3, *esterno redditi netti dall'estero, milioni di lire*. Current transfers are from Italy, ISTAT 1957, 255, table 39, col. 4, *trasferimenti correnti, saldo, milioni di lire*. GNP data for 1926 to 1945 are from Italy, ISTAT 1986, 143, table 8.1, col. 1, *reddito nazionale netto* (net national income), plus col. 2, *ammortamenti* (depreciation). Net factor incomes from abroad are from Italy, ISTAT 1986, 151, table 8.11, cols. 2, 7, *exportazione redditi dei fattori* less *importazione redditi dei fattori* (exports of factor income less imports of factor income).

Capital Formation

Data from 1861 to 1925 are from Italy, ISTAT 1957, 264–265, table 44, col. 6, *investimenti lordi* (gross investment), current prices. Data includes stocks. Data for 1926 to 1945 are from Italy, ISTAT 1986, 143, table 8.1, col. 6, *investimenti lordi* (gross investment). Data on changes in stocks from 1861 to 1925 are from Italy, ISTAT 1957, 264–265, table 44, col. 5, *variazioni scorte* (change in stocks). Data on changes in stocks for 1926 to 1945 are from Italy, ISTAT 1986, 166, table 8.28, col. 5), *variazione delle scorte* (change in stocks).

Current Account

Data from 1861 to 1925 are from Italy, ISTAT 1957, 255, table 39, col. 5, *bilancia dei pagamenti correnti, conto transazioni e trasferimenti correnti* (balance of current payments, including current transfers) Data for 1926 to 1945 are from Italy, ISTAT 1986, 151, table 8.11, col. 11, *saldi, transazioni correnti* (settlement of current transactions), equal to the sum of net exports of goods, services, factor income, and transfers. Merchandise trade figures include silver bullion, but exclude gold bullion and silver coin of the Latin Union. The current account excluding gold is therefore taken to be the the same as the original current account figure.

Gold

Data for 1861 to 1936 are from Di Mattia 1967. Data for gold and silver coin withdrawn from 473–474, table 8, cols. 1 and 2 (withdrawn coins, gold and silver). Data for gold and silver coined and recoined from 477–478, table 9, col. 1 (coinage and recoinage, gold and silver). Imports and exports data from 481–482, table 10, cols. 1, 2, 5, 6 (exports unrefined gold, exports gold coin, imports unrefined gold, imports gold coin).

Since gold and silver flows are not shown separately prior to 1878, our 1861–1877 data for gold specie exports are calculated by taking the average of gold specie to total specie exports for the years 1878–1936 and multiplying by the annual figure for total specie exports. Similarly, 1861–1877 data for unrefined gold exports are calculated by taking the average of gold specie to total specie exports for the years 1878–1936, and multiplying by the annual figure for total unrefined gold and silver exports. The data for gold imports are calculated similarly.

The change in the monetary gold stock is calculated as the sum of specie imports less specie exports plus coinage and recoinage less withdrawn coin. Data on official reserves of gold from Italy, ISTAT 1968, 105, table 83, col. 11.

Japan

The New Coinage Act of 1871 declared the gold yen as the standard unit of value and legal tender for transactions of any value. Silver coins were relegated to subsidiary money, legal tender up to 10 yen. However, the Act also declared the silver Yen Trade Dollar as legal tender within the confines of treaty ports. An amendment in May 1878 made the silver Trade Dollar legal tender throughout the Empire of Japan. Thus both gold and silver were legal tender within Japan and for all foreign transactions from 1878 to 1897. It was not until the Coinage Act of 1897 declared the gold yen as the standard unit of value and legal tender that Japan officially adopted the gold standard. The coinage of the Yen Trade Dollar ceased, and they were gradually withdrawn from circulation.

GDP
GDP calculated by subtracting net factor incomes and transfers received from the rest of the world from GNP. Gross national expenditure (GNE) data from 1885 to 1929 are from Ohkawa et al. 1979, 251–253, table A1, col. 7, gross national expenditure at market prices, millions of yen, current prices. GNE data from 1930 to 1944 are from Ohkawa et al. 1979, 254, table A2, col. 7, gross national expenditure at market prices, millions of yen, current prices. GNP figures are calculated as GNE plus the current account balance, as calculated below. Data on net factor incomes received from the rest of the world are from Ohkawa et al. 1979, 332–335, table A31, cols. 3, 6, exports: income from abroad less imports: income from abroad. Data on net transfers from abroad are from Ohkawa et al. 1979, 332–335, table A31, col. 8, net transfers from abroad.

Capital Formation
Capital formation data equal gross domestic fixed capital formation plus changes in stocks. Data from 1885 to 1929 from Ohkawa et al. 1979, 251–253, table A1, col. 3, gross domestic fixed capital formation. Data from 1930 to 1944 from Ohkawa et al. 1979, 254, table A2, col. 3, gross domestic fixed capital formation. Change in stocks data from 1885 to 1929 are calculated by taking inventory change as percent of GNE from

Ohkawa et al. 1979, 63, quoting from Fujino and Akiyama 1973, and multiplying by GNE. Inventories data from 1930 to 1944 are from Ohkawa et al. 1979, 254, table A2, col. 4, increase in stocks.

Current Account

Data for 1868 to 1940 from Ohkawa et al. 1979, 332–335, table A31, col. 9, surplus on current account (excluding reparations). Data do not include nonmonetary or monetary gold shipments. Data from 1940 to 1944 from Ohkawa et al. 1979, 336, table A32, col. 9 surplus on current account (excluding reparations).

Gold

Gold coinage data for 1871 to 1897 are from Matsukata 1899, 13, table II, amount of gold coins issued, and 14, table III, amount of silver coins issued. Data for 1900 to 1939 are from Japan, Ministry of Finance 1901, 1910, 1916, 1926, 1940, coins turned out by the mint. Data for 1913 to 1936 on coinage withdrawn are from Japan, Bank of Japan 1932, 1937, 2, amount of coin melted by the mint.

Data on gold exports and imports for 1872–1933 on exports and imports of gold from Ishibashi 1935, 431–433, 436–437, details of coin and bullion exported, details of coin and bullion imported, gold bullion and total of gold coin and bullion. Data are for Japan Proper (ie excludes Korea and Taiwan after annexation). Data for 1934–1936 on net exports of gold coin and bullion from Japan, Prime Minister's Office 1949, 520–521, table 280, col. 7–8, domestic (Japan Proper) exports and imports of gold coin and bullion. Silver exports and imports data for 1872–1933 are from Ishibashi 1935, 433–435, 437–439, details of coin and bullion exported, details of coin and bullion imported, silver bullion and total of silver coin and bullion. Data are for Japan Proper (i.e., excludes Korea and Taiwan). Data for 1934–1936 on net exports of silver coin and bullion from Japan, Prime Minister's Office 1949, 520–521, table 280, col. 7–8, domestic (Japan Proper) exports and imports of silver coin and bullion. Data on gold coin and bullion imports and exports and silver coin and bullion imports and exports for 1937 to 1945 are from Japan, Bank of Japan Statistics Department 1966, 157, 561.

Data on coins existing in the country from 1868 to 1900 from Japan, Ministry of Finance 1901. Data on coins existing in the country from 1901 to 1914 from Shinjo 1962, 101, table XXB. Data on the estimated stock of specie in the country from 1872 to 1914 is derived from the data on coins existing in the country. Data after 1914 take the previous years' estimate of specie existing in the country, plus coins turned out by the mint, less coin melted by the mint, less net exports of specie. Changes in the monetary stock take the change in estimated stock of specie, less net exports of bullion. Data after 1934 are based on coinage less recoinage less net exports of gold coin and bullion.

Norway

GDP
GDP data from 1865 to 1938 are from Norway, Statistisk Sentralbyrå 1965, 340–343, table 49, row 11, current prices, millions of kroner.

Capital Formation
Capital formation data from 1865 to 1938 are from Norway, Statistisk Sentralbyrå 1965, 340–343, table 49, row 5, current prices, millions of kroner. Data include increase in stocks from 1909. Data on increase in stocks for 1900–1908 are from Norway, Statistisk Sentralbyrå 1953, 107, table 2, col. 9, *lagerendring* (change in stocks). Data for 1909–1939 are from Norway, Statistisk Sentralbyrå 1965, 340–343, table 49, row 7. Increase in stocks not estimated for the years 1865–1899. For 1900–1913 and 1921–1929 only net increase in standing forests and in livestock are included. From 1930 increase in standing forests is regarded as fixed capital investment.

Current Account
Current account data from 1865 to 1899 are from Mitchell 1993, 922, 927, table J3, current prices, millions of kroner. Current account data for 1900–1929 are from Norway, Statistisk Sentralbyrå 1953, 126, table 12, col. 5, *netto oking eller nedgang i Norges netto fordringer pa utlandet* (net increase or decrease in Norway's foreign assets). Data for 1930–1939 from Norway, Statistisk Sentralbyrå 1965, 184–185, table 25, row 16. The current account data exclude crude gold and silver and coins.

Gold
Data on gold and silver holdings from 1865–1913 are (the two metals are not reporated separately) from Norway, Statistisk Sentralbyrå 1978, 484, table 257, col. 1&6, *metallfondene* (gold and silver) at bank of Norway. Data from 1914–1939 from Norway, Statistiske Oversikter 1948, 300–303, table 159, rows 1 & 4, *gullbeholdning* (gold stock), and *midlertidig anbrakt i gull* (temporarily invested in gold). The change in

the monetary gold stock is calculated as the first difference of the gold stock at the Bank of Norway (gold and silver stock until 1914). According to United States, Bureau of the Mint 1886, 222, "the amount of gold in banks, other than the Bank of Norway, or in circulation, has probably not been considerable."

Data on gold exports and imports for 1865 to 1896 are calculated as the first difference of the gold and silver holdings of the Bank of Norway (the negative of the change in the monetary stock equals the net exports—i.e., an increase in the monetary stock corresponds to an import). Data on gold exports and imports from 1895 to 1909 and for 1931 to 1944 are from Norway, Statistisk Sentralbyå 1897–1947, unwrought platinum, gold and silver and coins and medals. Missing trade returns data for 1897 and 1899 are interpolated linearly from the previous and subsequent years. Data on net exports of gold from 1910 to 1930 are from the League of Nations 1927, 1931, 1932, exports of bullion and specie less imports of bullion and specie (including silver and platinum, as per the trade returns).

Russia

GDP

Data on net national product are from Gregory 1982, table 3.2, net national product, Russian Empire, millions of credit roubles.

Capital Formation

Data on capital formation are from Gregory 1982, table 3.2, net investment, Russian Empire, millions of credit roubles. Data include inventories. Data on inventories are from Gregory 1982, table 3.2, inventories, total, Russian Empire, millions of credit roubles.

Current Account

Data on the current account are from Gregory 1982, table 3.2, net foreign investment, Russian Empire, millions of credit roubles. The current account data include net exports of silver.

Gold

Data on the monetary gold stock are from United States, Bureau of the Mint 1876–1920. Data for 1880–1891 are calculated as the sum of bullion and gold coin of the treasury at the Bank of Russia plus gold specie on hand at the Bank of Russia (belonging especially to the Bank of Russia).

Data on the monetary gold stock from 1891 to 1914 are the sum of gold coin in circulation plus gold coin and bullion in the treasuries and the state bank.

Data on net exports of gold from 1885 to 1913 are from United States, Bureau of the Mint 1876–1920. Missing data for 1900, 1901, and 1912 are estimated using a regression of net exports on net national product and changes in the monetary gold stock for all other years of available data (1885–1899, 1902–1911, 1913). Predicted values from this regression are used to proxy the missing net gold exports data.

United States dollar values are converted to roubles at the exchange rate of 0.7718 roubles per U.S. dollar until the end of 1897, then 0.514556. Data on monetary gold and net exports of gold are converted from roubles to credit roubles by multiplying by a factor of 1.5.

Sweden

GDP
Data on gross domestic product at factor cost data for 1861 to 1945 are from Krantz and Nilsson 1975, 154–155, table 1:2, col. 4. Indirect taxes and customs duties from Krantz and Nilsson 1975, 154–155, table 1:2, col. 3. GDP at market prices calculated as sum of GDP at factor cost plus indirect taxes and customs duties.

Capital Formation
Data on capital formation for 1861 to 1945 are from Krantz and Nilsson 1975, 150–152, table 1.1, col. 6, domestic investment. Data do not include stocks. Data on stocks for 1861 to 1945 are from Johansson 1967, 38–39, table 1, col. 3, changes in livestock. Our data on capital formation are calculated by adding domestic investment to changes in livestock.

Current Account
Data on the current account from 1861 to 1930 from Lindahl et al. 1937, 598–599, table 174, col. 8, net balance on goods and services. Data do not include shipments of gold and silver. Data for 1931 to 1935 from Ohlsson 1969, 123, table B:1., col. 6, *bytesbalansens saldo*. Data do not include net exports of gold and silver. Data for 1936 to 1945 from Sweden, Statistiska Centralbyran 1960, 64, table 33, row 6. Data do not include net exports of gold and silver. Net exports of silver are added to the current account balance. Data on net silver exports, 1861–1910,

are from Lindahl et al. 1937; 1911–1945 data are from Sweden, Statistiska Centralbyran 1960.

Gold
Data on net exports of gold from 1861 to 1874 from Lindahl et al. 1937, 604–605, table 175, col. 1, net imports of gold according to trade statistics. Data on gold and specie flows from 1861 to 1871 included both gold and silver. According to Lindahl et al. 1937, 610, the figures included only insignificant quantities of gold, so the net export of gold is assumed to be zero from 1861–1871. Data from 1875 to 1913 from Lindahl et al. 1937, 604–605, table 175, col. 4, change in bank holdings plus gold absorbed by industry. Lindahl et al. argue that the trade statistics data suffer from several shortcomings with regards to the net exports of gold, so they use the estimated change in the stock of gold held by banks and the value of gold absorbed by industry as the measure of net gold exports. Data from 1914 to 1945 are from Sweden, Statistiska Centralbyran 1960, 62, table 30, cols. 2, 5, 9, 12, imports of unmanufactured gold and gold coins and exports of unmanufactured gold and gold coins. Data on changes in the monetary gold stock for 1875 from Lindahl et al. 1937, 604, table 175, col. 2, increase in bank holdings of gold. Data on the monetary gold stock from 1876 to 1945 from Sweden, Statistiska Centralbyran 1960, 97, table 76 and 98, table 77, gold holdings of banks (including *Riksbank*). Change in the monetary gold stock is calcuated as the change in the gold holdings of banks.

United Kingdom

GDP
From 1850 to 1869 from Mitchell 1988, 831–832, chap. 16, table 5, Gross domestic product at market prices. Data from 1870 to 1944 from Feinstein 1972, T10–T11, table 3, gross domestic product at market prices.

Capital Formation
Data from 1850 to 1869 from Mitchell 1988, 831–832, chap. 16, table 5, gross domestic fixed capital formation plus value of physical increase in stocks. Data from 1870 to 1920 from Feinstein 1988, 462–463, table 17, gross domestic fixed capital formation plus value of physical increase in stocks and works in progress. Data from 1921 to 1944 from Feinstein 1972, T8–T9, table 2, gross domestic fixed capital formation plus value of physical increase in stocks and works in progress.

Current Account

Data from 1850 to 1869 from Imlah 1958, 70–72, table 4, balance on current account. Imlah's data include net exports of gold and silver bullion and specie. Data from 1870 to 1920 from Feinstein 1988, 462–463, table 17, net investment abroad. Feinstein's (1988) current account data are calculated as the balance of current account transactions not involving gold or silver *plus* the net increase in the U.K. stock of monetary gold and silver. Data from 1921 to 1944 are from Feinstein 1972, T38–T39, table 15, net investment abroad. The data from Feinstein (1972) include silver trade after 1913, but, as noted in the body of this paper, exclude all gold flows. Our own data for the current account CA^{NG} excluding all gold flows (but including all silver flows) are calculated as follows. For 1850 to 1869 we take the current account data from Imlah 1958, less net exports of gold and silver, plus net exports of silver (with net exports of the precious metals as calculated below). For 1870 to 1920 we take the current account numbers of Feinstein 1988, less the change in the total gold and silver money stock (as calculated below), plus net exports of silver. For 1921 to 1944 we simply take the Feinstein 1972 series on net investment abroad, which includes all silver trade and excludes all gold trade.

Gold

Imlah (1958, 70–72, table 4), reports data on net shipments of gold and silver for the years 1850–1870. Imlah's data do not separate net gold from silver shipments, but instead aggregate the numbers for both metals. Separate gold and silver net exports data for 1858–1916 and 1920–1945 are from United Kingdom, Board of Trade 1870–1938, exports of (gold, silver) bullion and specie less imports of (gold, silver) bullion and specie. (This source also provides data on the separate levels of gold and silver imports and exports for 1858–1916 and 1920–1945.) Gold net exports data for 1917–1919 are from Morgan 1952, 335, table 52, net exports of gold coin and bullion. Silver net exports data for 1917–1919 from Morgan 1952, 341, table 53, net exports of gold and silver, less net exports of gold from 335, table 52. Although separate silver and gold *exports* data are reported by the board of trade for 1850–1857, separate silver and gold *imports* data are not reported prior to 1858. To calculate net gold shipments for 1850–1857, we therefore must estimate gold imports separately for those years. We do this in three steps as follows. First, we use the 1858–1916, 1920–1945 board of trade data to measure the average ratio k of silver imports to silver imports plus silver exports. (This ratio is much more stable over time than the corresponding ratio for gold trade, which is why we take this rather roundabout route to estimating 1850–1857 gold imports.) Because we do have yearly silver exports data, X_S, for 1850–1857, we then estimate silver imports in any year as $M_S = kX_S/(1 - k)$. That is the second step in our procedure. The third and final step is to estimate gold imports for 1850–1857 as the sum of gold and silver exports (from Board of Trade) less our estimated silver imports less the Imlah 1958, 70–72, table 4, figures for net shipments of gold and silver together.

Data on changes in the monetary gold stock from 1868 to 1921 are calculated as the change in the estimated stock of gold coin outstanding, plus the change in the stock of gold in the Bank of England. Data on gold in the Bank of England (issue and banking departments) are taken from the *Economist* 1850–1932 (various issues, last week of December). Data on the change in the monetary stock of gold coin are from Capie and Webber 1985, 198–200, table 7.3. Mid-year data from 1868 to 1904 were converted to year-end data by adding data from the following year and dividing by two (this procedure assumes an even distribution across years). Data on the gold coin stock from 1915 to 1920 are calculated by taking the average of the gold coin stock to the total coin stock for the years 1868 to 1914 and multiplying by the figure for the total coin stock. The silver coin stock from 1905 to 1920 is calculated by taking the average of the silver coin stock to the total coin stock for the years 1868 to 1905 and multiplying by the figure for the total coin stock.

After 1921, our estimates assume that the only sources of change in the monetary gold stock are changes in the gold holdings of the Bank of England or the Exchange Equalisation Account. This procedure was adopted because of the lack of available data on holdings of gold coin outside the Bank of England after 1921. For 1922–1932 we use the *Economist* 1850–1932 data on Bank of England gold holdings. Data from 1933 to 1945 are from United Kingdom, Financial Secretary of the Treasury 1951, gold reserves in the Bank of England Issue Department and the Exchange Equalisation Account until 1939, then gold and dollar reserves from 1940 to 1945 (which were not reported separately).

United States

GDP
Data for 1869 to 1888 from Kuznets 1961, 561–562, table R-25, col. 3, GNP, Variant III, five-year centered moving average and 557–558, table

R-23, col. 1, B. Variant III, billions of dollars. Using annual data from 1889–1892, the five-year moving average number for 1890 is used to deduce the level of GNP in 1888 as five times the five-year centered moving average for 1890 less the actual levels for 1889–1892. Using a similar procedure, the annual data for 1869–1888 are derived by dis-aggregating the five-year moving averages. Data for 1889 to 1928 are from Kendrick 1961, 296–297, table A-IIb, col. 11, GNP, Commerce concept, millions of dollars. Data from 1929 to 1945 are from United States, Bureau of the Census 1975, 229, series F47, GNP, current prices. GDP data are calculated by subtracting net income from investments abroad and net unilateral transfers from abroad from the figures for GNP. The data on income on investments abroad are from United States, Bureau of the Census 1975, 865, series U13, then 864, series U5, U6, U13, income on investments abroad, private and public (U5 + U6) less income on foreign investments in United States (U13). The data on unilateral transfers are from United States, Bureau of the Census 1975, 866–867, series U16 and U17, unilateral transfers, net private (U16) plus unilateral transfers, net public (U17).

Capital Formation
Data for 1869 to 1888 from Kuznets 1961. Kuznets' figures on capital formation include net changes in claims against foreign countries, so we subtract changes in those claims to get our own figure for gross capital formation. Thus, our capital formation figures are calculated as Kuznets 1961, 572–574, table R-29, col. 1, gross capital formation, five-year centered moving average, less 599–660, table R-34, col. 3, net changes in claims against foreign countries, five-year centered moving average. Annual data are derived from the five-year centred moving average using the same procedure that was applied to the GNP series. Data from 1889 to 1928 are from Kendrick 1961, 296–297, table AIIb, col. 7, gross private domestic investment, commerce basis, millions of dollars. Data from 1929 to 1945 are from United States, Bureau of the Census 1975, 229, series F52, gross private domestic investment, current prices. Data on stocks for 1869 to 1888 from Kuznets 1961, 599–600, table R-34, col. 1, net changes in inventories, current prices, five-year centered moving average, and 490, table R-4, col. 3, net changes in inventories, billions of dollars. Annual data are derived from the five-year centered moving average using the same procedure that was applied to the GNP series, except the data are unscrambled from 1920 backwards. Data from 1889 to 1928 are from Kendrick 1961, 296–297,

table AIIb, col. 8, change in business inventories, millions of dollars. Data from 1929 to 1945 are from United States, Bureau of the Census 1975, 230, series F60, total net change in business inventories, current prices.

Current Account

Data for 1869 to 1945 from United States, Bureau of the Census 1975, 866–868, series U15, balance on goods and services, plus series U16 and U17, net private and government unilateral transfers. Data from 1869 to 1899 are for fiscal year ended June. Data are converted to calendar year basis by adding each year to subsequent year and dividing by two. For instance, fiscal year data for 1869 are added to fiscal year data for 1870 and divided by two, yielding data for calendar year 1869. Data from 1900 are for calendar year. Data to 1873 include exports and imports of gold. Data from 1874–1945 include nonmonetary gold exports. Data for nongold current account for 1869–1873 are calculated by taking the current account balance less net exports of gold. Data for nongold current account for 1874–1945 are calculated by taking the current account balance less net exports of gold less change in the monetary gold stock (equivalent to subtracting nonmonetary gold exports).

Gold

Exports: Data for 1869 to 1914 are from the National Bureau of Economic Research, series 14112, net gold exports, thousands of dollars, monthly data. Annual data are derived by adding the sum of monthly net exports for each year (fiscal or calendar). Data from 1915 to 1945 from United States, Bureau of the Census 1975, 884–885, series U197 less U198, gold exports less imports, calendar year, millions of dollars.

Monetary gold stock data for 1869 to 1878 are from United States, Bureau of the Census 1975, 993, series X417, billions of dollars, annual average. Monthly data from 1879 to 1945 are supplied by the National Bureau of Economic Research, series 14076, billions of dollars. To construct our own annual data we select the December level of the monetary gold stock.

Notes

We are grateful to Tamim Bayoumi, Walter Beckert, Galina Borisova Hale, Lisa Cook, Marc Flandreau, Lars Jonung, Jan Tore Klovland, Ian McLean, Marinella Moscheni, Christine Nagorski, Stefan Palmqvist, Giovanni Peri, David Pope, Pierre Sicsic, and Giuseppe Tattara for assistance with data and sources. We have benefited from helpful suggestions from Tamim Bayoumi, Michael Bordo, Barry Eichengreen, Marc Flandreau, Steve Golub, Kevin O'Rourke, and Alan M. Taylor. Jay Shambaugh provided excellent research assistance. All errors, omissions, and interpretations are our own. Research support from a National Science Foundation grant to the National Bureau of Economic Research (NBER) and from the Center for German and European Studies at the University of California, Berkeley, is gratefully acknowledged. The authors can be reached via e-mail at hcmtj@ibm.net and obstfeld@econ.berkeley.edu. The data from this paper, along with the spreadsheets for constructing it, are available in electronic format at http://www.nber.org/jones-obstfeld.html.

1. See Obstfeld 1995 for a survey.

2. See appendix 9.1 for a discussion of this point.

3. The thirteen countries in our sample are Australia, Canada, Denmark, Finland, France, Germany, Italy, Japan, Norway, Russia, Sweden, the United Kingdom, and the United States. Finland was a province of Russia until 1917, when it declared independence. Even before independence, however, Finland had a high degree of economic autonomy, having its own currency and central bank. For further details on sources and methods, see appendix 9.2. Our study is very much in the spirit of Bloomfield (1968), who assembled the available data on net capital movements for a sample of countries that partially overlaps our sample.

4. France, a leading bimetallic power, suspended specie payments in 1870, then ended the free coinage of silver in September 1873 by limiting the daily coinage. Silver coinage was fully suspended in 1876. In January 1878, gold specie payments resumed. See Flandreau 1996 for details. For the United States, we do not consider the period from 1873 to 1878 when the Coinage act of 1873 was in force to be a true bimetallic standard. The act did not allow for unlimited coinage of silver, and excluded the standard silver dollar from the definition of acceptable coinage. Furthermore, no silver coin was to be legal tender beyond the limit of five dollars. According to Friedman (1990, 1165), "The omission of any mention of the standard silver dollar in the Coinage Act of 1873 ended the legal status of bimetallism in the United States." Notwithstanding our own decision to adjust only for gold flows, our data appendix (appendix 9.2) in several cases describes sources for relevant silver data we have encountered, in case other researchers should wish to attempt a full correction of historical current account figures for silver as well as gold flows. These data are available on the NBER website mentioned in the introductory footnote. Where the standard national current account data exclude silver flows, we make no systematic attempt in this paper to reintroduce data on silver shipments into the current account.

5. This example draws on Gardner 1953.

6. Clearly, we are abstracting from costs of turning an ounce of gold ore into an ounce of bullion.

7. This accounting convention is the one recommended by the International Monetary Fund. For further details, see Inter-Secretariat Working Group on National Accounts 1993.

8. Morgenstern (1955) argued forcefully that monthly and quarterly historical data on bilateral gold flows are too inaccurate to be useful. Thus it might seem pointless (and at worst harmful) to adjust the standard series using data on international gold flows. Goodhart (1969), after examining 1900–1912 data on bilateral flows between the United States and United Kingdom, concludes that Morgenstern overstated the case. We use

annual data on each country's total gold flows, which presumably are less subject to error than bilateral monthly data.

9. See appendix 9.2 For a detailed description of the data sources and methods used in this paper. We have attempted to assemble estimated data for all of the components of equation (9.2) for each country, even when not all of them are strictly necessary to adjust the standard current account numbers. The extended data set allows an assessment of the bias that results from alternative current account definitions.

10. See Sinclair 1993 for details. Urquhart's estimates of net dividends and interest payments are based on direct estimates of asset and liability stocks. In contrast, Viner and Hartland used cumulated current account balances to estimate net foreign asset income.

11. We are forced to include data on silver shipments for France before 1870 because of the lack of information that would allow us to separate silver from gold movements.

12. Italy adopted the use of gold and silver as legal tender throughout the country on March 23, 1862. Legislation dated August 24, 1862 gave silver limited legal tender. As Fratianni and Spinelli (1997, 65–66) argue, this had the effect of making gold the only metal of exchange in international dealings, and "introduced a gold-based mono-metallism in disguise." A government decree of May 1, 1866 proclaimed banknotes no longer convertible into gold or silver, effective May 2, 1866. Inconvertible banknotes circulated until 1884, when gold convertibility was restored, but Italy remained on the gold standard only until 1894. For Japan, the New Coinage Act of 1871 declared the gold yen as the standard unit of value and legal tender for transactions of any value. Silver coins were relegated to subsidiary money, legal tender up to 10 yen. However, the act also declared the silver Yen Trade Dollar as legal tender within the confines of treaty ports. An amendment in May 1878 made the silver Trade Dollar legal tender throughout the Empire of Japan. Thus both gold and silver were legal tender within Japan and for all foreign transactions from 1878 to 1897. It wasn't until the Coinage Act of 1897 declared the gold yen as the standard unit of value and legal tender that Japan officially adopted the gold standard. The coinage of the Yen Trade Dollar ceased, and they were gradually withdrawn from circulation.

13. Net national product is used in place of GDP for Germany and Russia.

14. Nonmonetary gold exports can be calculated as the sum of net gold shipments, SG, plus the change in the monetary gold stock, ΔMG. The ratio of nonmonetary gold exports to GDP for 1885–1913 is Australia: 4.2%, Canada: 0.7%, Denmark: 0.0%, Finland: −0.0%, France: −0.5%, Germany: −0.0% (of NNP), Italy: 0.0%, Japan: 0.5%, Norway: 0.0%, Russia: 0.6% (of NNP), Sweden: −0.1%, the U.K.: −0.1%, the U.S.: 0.2%.

15. Eichengreen (1992a) added inventory data for Canada and the United Kingdom to the countries for which Mitchell (1983) reports inventory changes. Our coverage expands Eichengreen's by adding inventory data for Australia, Finland, France, Japan, Russia, and Sweden.

16. In our 1885 to 1913 sample, omitting data on inventories raises the estimated slope coefficient in the Feldstein-Horioka regression by more than 20 percent, and lowers the standard deviation of the slope coefficient by more than 30 percent. Thus it appears that including estimates of changes in stocks or inventories is an important consideration in any analysis of saving-investment correlations. See appendix 9.1 for a full discussion of the effect of removing stocks/inventories data. For Finland, inventory data are not reported separately but are summed with the statistical discrepancy. We use that total as a proxy for inventories.

17. The regression thus tests the hypothesis that an increase in national saving, net of the increase in monetary gold holdings, flows completely into domestic investment. To see this another way, observe from equations (9.1) and (9.3) that $CA^O = CA^{NG} + SG = CA - \Delta MG$. Thus CA^O equals the difference between an economy's total outward shipments of goods, services, and gold and its total inward shipments, which must equal its net accumulation of nongold foreign claims. This follows from the balance of payments identity that the true current account surplus plus the nongold capital account surplus equals monetary gold acquisitions. Therefore, the Feldstein-Horioka hypothesis implies that $CA^O = S - \Delta MG - I = 0$.

18. Regression estimates of the specification in equation (9.7) are presented in appendix 9.1, third section.

19. See Obstfeld 1995 for a discussion of recent data. Taylor 1996 reviews the behavior of the saving-investment correlation over time since the nineteenth century.

20. On interwar capital controls, see Obstfeld and Taylor 1998.

21. Bayoumi's sample of countries consisted of Australia, Canada, Denmark, Germany, Italy, Norway, Sweden, and the United Kingdom. Eichengreen added the United States. Our data set adds Finland, France, Japan, and Russia.

22. In recomputing Eichengreens's (1992a) estimates using the Mitchell 1992 data (with our Australian, Canadian, and U.S. data, without gold adjustments) and Eichengreen's specification, we found a slope coefficient of 0.656 for 1880–1913, 0.529 for 1880–1890, 0.778** for 1891–1901, 0.749 for 1902–1913, 0.873*** for 1924–1936, and 0.853*** for 1925–1930. When Eichengreen uses alternative data for the United States compiled by Roger Ransom and Richard Sutch, he finds a slope coefficient of 0.58* for 1925–1930. (The asterisks denote alternative significance levels of estimates. See note to table 9.3 for definitions.)

23. See appendix 9.1, fifth section, for more details.

24. For the full sample period, the time-series correlation between net gold shipments and the current account exclusive of all gold flows was negative for Australia, Finland, France, Italy, Japan, Norway, the United Kingdom, and the United States (eight out of our thirteen countries). For the 1885–1913 sub-period, the correlation was negative for Denmark, France, Germany, Italy, Japan, Norway, Sweden, the United Kingdom, and the United States (nine out of our thirteen countries).

25. Expressed as a percentage of gross domestic or net national product.

26. An alternative method to test the sensitivity of the parameter estimates to the sample of countries is to perform bootstrap regressions. Bayoumi (1990) calculates bootstrap estimates for his sample of eight countries and finds parameter estimates quite similar to his least squares calculations.

27. The dates we use for gold standard adherence are as follows. Australia: 1852–1915, 1925–1929; Canada: 1853–1914, 1926–1931; Denmark: 1873–1914, 1927–1931; Finland: 1877–1914, 1926–1931; France: 1878–1914, 1928–1936; Germany: 1871–1914, 1924–1931; Italy: 1862–1866, 1884–1894, 1927–1936; Japan: 1897–1917, 1930–1931; Norway: 1875–1914, 1928–1931; Russia: 1897–1914; Sweden: 1873–1914, 1924–1931; United Kingdom: 1821–1914, 1925–1931; United States: 1879–1933. See Bordo and Kydland 1995, Bordo and Schwartz 1996, and Eichengreen 1992b for surveys of gold standard participation.

28. Net national product if GDP is unavailable.

29. See the notes on capital formation in Australia for a discussion of this point.

References

Australia, Commonwealth Bureau of Census and Statistics. 1908–1949. *Official yearbook of the Commonwealth of Australia.* Canberra: Commonwealth Government Printer.

Baba, M., and M. Tatemoto. 1968. Foreign trade and economic growth in Japan: 1858–1937. In *Economic growth: The Japanese experience since the Meiji era*, ed. L. Klein and K. Ohkawa. Homewood, IL: Richard D. Irwin.

Bayoumi, T. 1990. Saving-investment correlations. *IMF Staff Papers* 37 (June):360–87.

Bjerke, K., and N. Ussing. 1958. *Studier over Danmarks Nationalprodukt 1870–1950.* Copenhagen: G. E. C. Gad.

Bloomfield, A. I. 1968. Patterns of fluctuation in international investment before 1914. Princeton Studies in International Finance, no. 21. International Finance Section, Department of Economics, Princeton University, Princeton, N.J.

Boehm, E. A. 1965. Measuring Australian economic growth, 1861 to 1938–39. *Economic Record* 41 (94):207–39.

Bordo, M. D., and F. E. Kydland. 1995. The gold standard as a rule: An essay in exploration. *Explorations in Economic History* 32(4):423–64.

Bordo, M. D., and A. J. Schwartz. 1996. The operation of the specie standard— Evidence for core and peripheral countries, 1880–1990. In *Currency convertibility: The gold standard and beyond*, ed. J. Braga de Macedo, B. Eichengreen, and J. Reis. London: Routledge.

Butlin, M. W. 1977. A preliminary annual database 1900/01 to 1973/74. Research Discussion Paper no. 7701 (May), Reserve Bank of Australia, Sydney.

Butlin, N. G. 1962. *Australian domestic product, investment and foreign borrowing 1861–1938/39.* Cambridge: Cambridge University Press.

Butlin, S. J. 1986. *The Australian monetary system, 1851 to 1914.* Sydney: Ambassador Press.

Butlin, S. J., A. R., Hall, and R. C. White. 1971. Australian banking and monetary statistics 1817–1945. Occasional Paper No. 4A, Reserve Bank of Australia, Sydney.

Canada, Dominion Bureau of Statistics. 1928, 1936, 1939, 1941. *The Canada yearbook.* Ottawa: General Statistics Branch, King's Printer and Controller of Stationery.

Canada, Dominion Bureau of Statistics. 1949. *The Canadian balance of international payments 1926 to 1948.* Ottawa: International Payments Section, Department of Trade and Commerce, King's Printer and Controller of Stationery.

Capie, F., and A. Webber. 1985. *A monetary history of the United Kingdom, 1870–1982. Vol 1: Data, sources, methods.* London: George Allen and Unwin.

Colony of New South Wales [Australia]. 1876–1902. *Statistical register.* Compiled from official returns in the Registar General's Office, presented to both Houses of Parliament, by Command. Sydney: Government Printer.

Colony of Victoria [Australia]. 1896–1898. *Statistical register*. Compiled from official records in the Department of Trade and Customs and Office of the Government Statist, presented to both Houses of Parliament by His Excellency's Command. Melbourne: Government Printer.

Curtis, C. A. 1931. *Statistical contributions to Canadian history, Vol. 1, Statistics on banking*. Toronto: Macmillan Company of Canada.

Denmark, Danmarks Statistik. 1897–1947. *Statistisk Arbog Danmark*. Copenghagen: Det Statistiske Departement.

Di Mattia, R. 1967. *I bilanci degli istituti di emissione italiani dal 1845 al 1936*. Altre serie storiche di interesse monetario e fonti. Rome: Banca D'Italia.

Dooley, M. P., J. A. Frankel, and D. J. Mathieson. 1987. International capital mobility: What do saving-investment correlations tell us? *IMF Staff Papers* 34 (September):503–30.

The Economist. 1850–1932. Various issues.

The Economist. 1989. A capital mystery, 7 October, p. 83.

Eichengreen, B. 1992a. Trends and cycles in foreign lending. In *Capital flows in the world economy*, ed. H. Siebert. Institut für Weltwirtschaft an der Universität Kiel. Tübingen, Germany: J. C. B. Mohr.

Eichengreen, B. 1992b. *Golden fetters*. New York: Oxford University Press.

Feinstein, C. H. 1988. Stocks and works in progress, overseas assets, and land. In *Studies in capital formation in the United Kingdom 1750–1920*, ed. C. H. Feinstein and S. Pollard. Oxford: Clarendon Press.

Feinstein, C. H. 1972. *National income, expenditure and output of the United Kingdom 1855–1965*. Cambridge: Cambridge University Press.

Feldstein, M., and C. Horioka. 1980. Domestic saving and international capital flows. *Economic Journal* 90 (June):314–29.

Finland, Suomen Virallinen Tilasto. 1929–1947. *Ulkomaankauppa Vuosijulkaisu*. Helsinki.

Finland, Tilastollinen Paatoimisto. 1907–1951. *Suomen Tilastollinen Vuosikirja*. Helsinki.

Flandreau, M. 1996. The French crime of 1873: An essay on the emergence of the international gold standard, 1870–1880. *Journal of Economic History* 56(4):862–97.

Flandreau, M. 1995. Coin memories: Estimates of the French metallic currency 1840–1878. *Journal of European Economic History* 24(2):271–310.

Fleetwood, E. E. 1947. *Sweden's capital imports and exports*. Stockholm: Natur och Kultur.

France, Ministère des Finances et des Affaires Économiques. 1952, 1966. *Annuaire Statistique*. Institut National de la Statistique et des Études Économiques. Paris: Imprimerie Nationale.

Fratianni, M., and F. Spinelli. 1997. *A monetary history of Italy*. Cambridge: Cambridge University Press.

Friedman, M. 1990. The crime of 1873. *Journal of Political Economy* 98(6):1159–94.

Friedman, M., and A. J. Schwartz. 1963. *A monetary history of the United States, 1867–1960*. Princeton: Princeton University Press.

Fujino, S., and R. Akiyama. 1973. *Zaiko to Zaiko Toshi, 1880–1940*. Hitotsubashi Daigaku, Keizai Kenkyujo.

Gardner, W. R. 1953. Merchandise trade in the balance of payments. In *International trade statistics*, ed. R. G. D. Allen and J. E. Ely, 155–85. New York: John Wiley and Sons.

Germany, Deutsche Bundesbank. 1976. *Deutsches Geld- und Bankwesen in Zahlen 1876–1975*. Herausgeber: Deutsche Bundesbank, Frankfurt am Main, Verlag Fritz Knapp GmbH, Frankfurt.

Goodhart, C. A. E. 1969. *The New York money market and the finance of trade, 1900–1913*. Cambridge: Harvard University Press.

Gregory, P. R. 1982. *Russian national income 1885–1913*. Cambridge: Cambridge University Press.

Hansen, S. A. 1977. *Økonomisk vækst i Danmark*. Bind II: 1914–1975. Københavns Universitet Institut for Økonomisk Historie, Publikation no. 6, Akademisk Forlag, Copenhagen.

Hartland (Thunberg), P. 1954. *The Canadian balance of payments since 1868*. Unpublished working paper, National Bureau of Economic Research, New York.

Henriksen, I., and N. Kægård. 1995. The Scandinavian currency union 1875–1914. In *International monetary systems in historical perspective*, ed. J. Reis. London: Macmillan Press.

Hjerppe, R. 1989. *The Finnish economy 1860–1985: Growth and structural change*. Bank of Finland Publications, Studies on Finland's Economic Growth XIII. Helsinki: Bank of Finland Government Printing Centre.

Hoffman, W. G., F. Grumbach, and H. Hesse. 1965. *Das Wachstum Der Deutschen Wirtschaft Seit Der Mitte Des 19. Jahrhunderts*. Berlin: Springer Verlag.

Imlah, A. H. 1958. *Economic elements in the Pax Britannica: Studies in British foreign trade in the nineteenth century*. Cambridge: Harvard University Press.

Inter-Secretariat Working Group on National Accounts. 1993. *System of national accounts 1993*. Washington, D.C.: World Bank.

Ishibashi, T., ed. 1935. The foreign trade of Japan: A statistical review. *Oriental Economist* (Tokyo).

Italy, Istituto Centrale di Statistica (ISTAT). 1986. *Sommario di Statistiche Storiche 1926–1985*. Rom: Author.

Italy, Istituto Centrale di Statistica (ISTAT). 1957. Indagine Statistica sullo Sviluppo del Reddito Nazionale dell'italia dal 1861 al 1956. *Annali di Statistica*, Anno 86, Serie VIII, vol. 9. Rome: Author.

Japan, Bank of Japan. 1932, 1937. *Economic statistics of Japan*. Tokyo.

Japan, Bank of Japan Statistics Department. 1966. *Hundred year statistics of the Japanese economy*. Tokyo: Author.

Japan, Ministry of Finance. 1901, 1910, 1916, 1926, 1940. *Financial annual of Japan*. Tokyo.

Japan, Prime Minister's Office. 1949. *Japan statistical yearbook* 1949. ed. Executive Office of the Statistics Commission and the Statistics Bureau of the Prime Minister's Office. Tokyo: National Statistical Association.

Johansson, O. 1967. *The gross domestic product of Sweden and its composition 1861–1955*. Stockholm: Almqvist and Wiksell.

Kendrick, J. W. 1961. *Productivity trends in the United States*. National Bureau of Economic Research No. 71, General Series. Princeton: Princeton University Press.

Kennard, H. P., ed. 1914. *The Russian yearbook for 1914*. London: Eyre and Spottiswoode.

Kennett, J. A. 1972. *The Australian commercial-bank-managed-gold-exchange standard: 1880–1913*. Undergraduate Thesis, Economic History IV, Sydney University.

Krantz, O., and Nilsson, C.-A. 1975. *Swedish national product 1861–1970: New aspects on methods and measurement*. Lund, Sweden: CWK Gleerup.

Kuznets, S. 1961. *Capital in the American economy: Its formation and financing*. National Bureau of Economic Research, Studies in Capital Formation and Financing, vol. 9. Princeton: Princeton University Press.

League of Nations. 1931a. *Memorandum on international trade and balance of payments 1927–1929. Vol. 3: Trade statistics of sixty-four countries*. Geneva.

League of Nations. 1931b. *Memorandum on trade and balance of payments 1927–1929. Vol. 3: International trade statistics*. Geneva.

League of Nations. 1927. *Memorandum on balance of payments and foreign trade balances 1911–1925. Vol. 2: Trade statistics of sixty-three countries*. Geneva.

League of Nations. 1924. *Memorandum on balance of payments and foreign trade balances 1910–1923. Vol. 2: Trade statistics of forty-two countries*. Geneva.

Lévy-Leboyer, M., and Bourguignon, F. 1985. *L'Économie Française au XIXe Siècle: Analyse Macro-économique*. Paris: Economica.

Lindahl, E., E. Dahlgren, and K. Koch. 1937. *Wages, cost of living and national income in Sweden 1860–1930. Vol. 3: National income of Sweden 1861–1930*. Stockholm: Institute for Social Sciences, University of Stockholm.

Maddison, A. 1991. A long run perspective on saving. Research memorandum no. 443 (October), Institute of Economic Research, Faculty of Economics, University of Groningen, Groningen, The Netherlands.

Matsukata, M. 1899. *Report on the adoption of the gold standard in Japan*. Tokyo: Government Press.

McLean, I. W. 1994. Saving in settler economies: Australian and North American comparisons. *Explorations in Economic History* 31:432–52.

McLean, I. W. 1991. Australian saving since 1861. In *Saving and policy: Proceedings of a conference*, ed. P. J. Stemp. Canberra: Centre for Economic Policy Research, Australian National University.

McLean, I. W. 1968. The Australian balance of payments on current account 1901 to 1964–65. *Australian Economic Papers* 7 (10):77–90.

Mitchell, B. R. 1992. *International historical statistics: Europe 1750–1988*. 3d ed. New York: Stockton Press.

Mitchell, B. R. 1988. *British historical statistics*. Cambridge: Cambridge University Press.

Mitchell, B. R. 1983. *International historical statistics: The Americas and Australasia.* Detroit: Gale Research Company.

Mitchell, B. R. 1981. *European historical statistics 1750–1975.* 2d ed. New York: Facts on File.

Morgan, E. V. 1952. *Studies in British financial policy, 1914–25.* London: MacMillan & Company.

Morgenstern, O. 1955. The validity of international gold movement statistics. Special Papers in International Economics no. 2, International Finance Section, Department of Economics and Sociology, Princeton University, Princeton, N.J.

Mundell, R. A. 1968. *International economics.* New York: Macmillan.

National Bureau of Economic Research. *NBER macrohistory database* [electronic database] [http://www.nber.org/databases/macrohistory/contents/index.html].

Norway, Statistisk Sentralbyrå. 1948. *Statistiske Oversikter*, Norges Offisielle Statistikk. Oslo.

Norway, Statistisk Sentralbyrå. 1978. *Historisk Statistikk 1978.* Norges Offisielle Statistikk, vol. 12, no. 291. Oslo.

Norway, Statistisk Sentralbyrå. 1965. *Nasjonalregnskap 1865–1960.* Norges Offisielle Statistikk, vol. 12, no. 163, Oslo.

Norway, Statistisk Sentralbyrå. 1953. *Nasjonalregnskap 1900–1929.* Norges Offisielle Statistikk vol. 12, no. 143. Oslo.

Norway, Statistisk Sentralbyrå. 1897–1947. *Norges handel.* Oslo.

Obstfeld, M. 1995. International capital mobility in the 1990s. In *Understanding interdependence: The macroeconomics of the open economy*, ed. P. B. Kenen, 201–61. Princeton: Princeton University Press.

Obstfeld, M., and A. M. Taylor. 1998. The Great Depression as a watershed: International capital mobility over the long run. In *The defining moment: The Great Depression and the American economy in the twentieth century* ed. M. D. Bordo, C. Goldin, and E. N. White, 353–402. Chicago: University of Chicago Press.

Ohkawa, K., M. Shinohara, and L. Meissner. 1979. *Patterns of Japanese economic development: A quantitative appraisal.* Economic Growth Center and Council on East Asian Studies, Yale University. New Haven: Yale University Press.

Ohlsson, L. 1969. *Utrikeshandeln Och Den Ekonomiska Tillvaxten I Sverige 1871–1966.* Stockholm: Almqvist and Wiksell.

Oksanen, H., and E. Pihkala. 1975. *Suomen Ulkomaankauppa 1917–1949.* Helsinki: Suomen Pankki Julkaisuja, Kasvututkimuksia VI.

Pihkala, E. 1970. *Suomen Ulkomaankauppa 1860–1917.* Helsinki: Suomen Pankin Taloustieteellisen Tutkimuslaitoksen Julkaisuja, Kasvututkimuksia II.

Rich, G. 1988. *The cross of gold: Money and the Canadian business cycle, 1867–1913.* Ottawa: Carleton University Press.

Rossi, N., A. Sorgato, and G. Toniolo. 1992. Italian historical statistics: 1890–1990. Dipartimento di Scienze Economiche, Universita degli Studi de Venezia, *Nota di Lavoro*, no. 92.18 (November).

Shinjo, H. 1962. History of the yen—100 years of Japanese money-economy. Research Institute for Economics and Business Administration, Kobe University, Kobe, Japan.

Sicsic, P. 1989. Estimation du stock de monnaie métallique en France à la fin du XIXe siecle. *Revue Économique* 40(4):709–36.

Sinclair, A. M. 1993. Balance of international payments, 1870–1925. In ed. M. C. Urquhart, *Gross national product, Canada, 1870–1926: The derivation of the estimates.* Kingston and Montreal: McGill–Queen's University Press.

Summers, L. H. 1988. Tax policy and international competitiveness. In *International aspects of fiscal policies,* ed. J. Frenkel. Chicago: University of Chicago Press.

Sweden, Statistiska Centralbyran. 1960. *Historisk Statistik for Sverige.* Stockholm: Statistiska Oversiktstabeller.

Taylor, A. M. 1996. International capital mobility in history: The saving-investment relationship. Working paper no. 5743, National Bureau of Economic Research, Cambridge, Mass.

Toutain, J. C. 1987. Le produit interieur brut de la France de 1789 à 1982. *Economie et Societes* 21. Quoted in B. R. Mitchell, *International historical statistics Europe 1750–1988.* 3d ed. New York: Stockton Press, 1987.

United Kingdom, Board of Trade. 1870–1938. *Statistical abstract for the United Kingdom.* London: His Majesty's Stationery Office.

United Kingdom, Central Statistical Office. 1948. *Annual abstract of statistics.* London: His Majesty's Stationery Office.

United Kingdom, Deputy Master of the Mint. 1870–1944. *Annual report.* Presented to both Houses of Parliament by command of Her Majesty. London: Her Majesty's Stationery Office.

United Kingdom, Financial Secretary of the Treasury. 1951. *Reserves and liabilities 1931 to 1945.* Presented by the Financial Secretary to the Treasury to Parliament by Command. (Cmd. 8354). London: His Majesty's Stationery Office.

United Nations, Statistical Office. 1952. *A system of national accounts and supporting tables.* New York: Author.

United States, Bureau of the Census. 1975. *Historical statistics of the United States, colonial times to 1970.* Bicentennial ed. Washington, D.C.: U.S. Government Printing Office.

United States, Bureau of the Mint. 1876–1920. *Annual report of the director of the Mint to the Secretary of the Treasury.* Washington, D.C.: Government Printing Office.

Urquhart, M. C. 1993. *Gross national product, Canada, 1870–1926: The derivation of the estimates,* Kingston and Montreal: McGill–Queen's University Press.

Urquhart, M. C. 1986. New estimates of gross national product, Canada 1870–1926: Some implications for Canadian development. In *Long term factors in American economic growth,* ed. S. L. Engerman and R. E. Gallman. National Bureau of Economic Research Studies in Income and Wealth, vol. 51. Chicago: University of Chicago Press.

Urquhart, M. C., and K. A. H. Buckley, eds. 1965. *Historical statistics of Canada.* Cambridge: Cambridge University Press.

Villa, P. 1993. *Une Analyse Macroéconomique de la France au XXe Siècle*. Monographies D'Économétrie. Paris: CNRS Editions.

Viner, J. 1924. *Canada's balance of international indebtedness 1900–1913*. Cambridge: Harvard University Press.

Yamamoto, Y. 1975. *Japanese balance of payments 1868–1967: Data and findings*. Working paper no. 24 (August), Institute of Economic Research, Kobe University of Commerce, Kobe, Japan

Yamazawa, I., and Y. Yamamoto. 1979. Trade and balance of payments. In *Patterns of Japanese economic development: A quantative appraisal*, ed. K. Ohkawa, M. Shinohara, and L. Meissner. Economic Growth Center and Council on East Asian Studies, Yale University. New Haven: Yale University Press.

10   Globalization and the Consequences of International Fragmentation

Ronald W. Jones and
Henryk Kierzkowski

Introduction

The dominant paradigm in the pure theory of international trade envisaged trade taking place in final consumer goods (augmented, on occasion, by trade in natural resources). More than forty years ago Robert Mundell (1957) challenged this scenario in the American Economic Review by considering a trading world in which real factor mobility provided an alternative to goods trade, one that could be activated by policies such as tariffs which interfere with trade in final commodities. This article opened up the floodgates to a more intensive study of the positive and normative consequences of allowing trade in productive factors and intermediate goods. The present chapter fits into this literature by considering the process whereby improvements in transportation, communication, knowledge, and technology allow a finer division of labor and a fragmentation of the production process so that previously integrated productive activities can be segmented and spread over an international network. This segmentation may involve the creation of multinational enterprises or, instead, be carried out in arm's-length transactions where the costs of coordination have been sufficiently reduced to allow a spillover of productive activity abroad. In the past it was international capital mobility which created occasional public fears in exporting and importing countries alike. In the former, concerns were expressed that domestic employment and wages would be adversely affected if local producers invest abroad. In the latter an inflow of investment from abroad was sometimes described as selling the country out to foreigners. Today, globalization often provokes similar reactions.

The term "globalization" has entered everyday usage. It is employed frequently by professionals and the general public but rarely given a precise meaning. At a very basic level, one speaks of globalization of the world economy when the intensity of trade relations between national economies has reached a certain threshold, such as indicated by a high trade-to-income ratio. If globalization were only that, then it was already achieved in the nineteenth century. But globalization means more than the intensification of trade relations. In fact it connotes several different phenomena: While for some countries the trade volume already looked impressive in relation to GNP a century ago, many fruits of human labor could not and would not enter international commerce. The subset of nontradeables was filled with many goods and services, particularly the latter. By contrast, today it would be difficult to find a good that could not in principle be traded. More significantly, services—once a perennial example of nontradedness—have increasingly become a subject of international commerce.

It could be argued that what sets apart current globalization from that which occurred in the aftermath of the Industrial Revolution is the widening of the spectrum of goods and services entering international trade. This process has been a consequence of trade liberalization, increased freedom of establishment, and technical innovations allowing long-distance delivery of services. When more goods and services become tradeable, one can speak of *extensive* growth of international trade. We argue in this chapter and elsewhere (Jones and Kierzkowski 1990) that the world economy has also been experiencing *intensive* growth of international trade. The driving force behind the intensification of international trade is fragmentation of the production process. Integrated technology requiring production of a good to occur in one place and in "one go" is replaced by fragmented technology that breaks down the manufacturing process into separate production blocks. These production blocks need not be produced by one firm, at the same time, in one place. They need not even be produced in the same country.

It can be readily seen how an increased fragmentation of production leads to a finer and finer division of labor. Services—ranging from transportation and insurance to telecommunications and banking—play a crucial role in the fragmention process since they connect various production blocks.[1] Fragmentation may well be initially confined to national boundaries of a country, since international service links are likely to be more expensive than the domestic ones, and since coordination of production and quality control is more difficult to achieve internationally than domestically. Over time, however, fragmentation is bound to spill over into international markets in response to lowering prices of services, increased tradedness of services, and a whole range of technical improvements and innovations that allow geographic deconcentration of production.

New patterns of production and trade may emerge in response to such fragmentation. In a multicommodity world it takes just one good to capture the benefits of trade. Similarly, having a comparative advantage in a single production stage may suffice to allow a country to branch into international markets without any need at all to be an efficient producer of the entire product. However, the aggregate welfare gains that may arise from globalization (e.g., Arndt 1997) could well coincide with some factors becoming worse off. As we show in this chapter, naming the winners and losers is not a trivial task. The effects of globalization on wages have attracted a lot of attention and provoked fears, and it is on this issue we focus in the chapter. We ask as well about the impact of fragmentation on inter and intrasectoral resource allocation. Finally, it may be the case that a country as a whole loses as a consequence of international fragmentation.

The Framework

The present chapter builds on a framework developed in Jones and Kierzkowski 1990. The main motivation behind that effort, undertaken during the period of the Uruguay Round, was to expand the traditional production structure used in trade theory in order to analyze the role of producer services. As a result, new questions could be posed, such as: What impact can liberalization of trade in services be expected to have on trade in manufactured goods? Are less developed countries, often not the most efficient producers of services, justified in their fears of being further marginalized in international trade? Can the international economy become more interdependent as a consequence of liberalization of the rights of establishment and freedom of exchange of services?

The essential element of the framework presented in Jones and Kierzkowski 1990 is the distinction between integrated and fragmented technologies. In the former the process of manufacturing of a good takes place within a single production block. Factors of production and raw materials are brought together, and a final good is created through the process described by a production function. Services have some role to play in the process of production based on integrated technology, but their role is rather limited. Economies of scale of the type envisaged as early as Adam Smith may eventually allow the production process to be broken down into two or more stages. Under fragmented technology individual production blocks are arranged in a more or less complicated production sequence, coordinated by a series of producer services. Some of the production blocks may find uses in more than one good or in different models of the same good. Some may even be utilized in a number of industries. Fragmented technology is more complex than an integrated production process in that it requires that individual production blocks be connected by service links. These links can be best thought of as consisting of bundles of activities—coordination, transportation, telecommunication, administration, insurance, financial services, and so on. Efficient production requires that production moves smoothly from one stage to another. For example, the so-called just-in-time technology can be seen as a natural outcome of fragmentation of production.

In this chapter we put aside issues of increasing returns and focus attention instead on a case in which one final productive activity gets segmented into two (or more) components as a consequence of a reduction in the cost of international service links. This sets the stage for differences in technology or factor skills between countries to realign the location of production according to comparative advantage, with differences in factor proportions and the technology and prices of other goods helping to determine the subsequent trading patterns. Thus both Ricardian and Heckscher-Ohlin characteristics (with the potential in the background for increasing returns to foster the fragmention process) enter into determining the consequences of international fragmentation. Specifically, a country might gain by such a process even if it loses out, say, in producing the labor-intensive segment of a previously integrated process in which it had a comparative advantage. A fear frequently expressed in relatively capital-abundant countries is that such a loss of a labor-intensive activity creates difficulty for unskilled labor. We show that this need not be the case—especially for well-to-do countries. Alternatively, international fragmentation may destroy a previous position of comparative advantage in an integrated activity which is based on technical prowess that is relatively high in both (or more) segments, but not high enough to survive a finer application of Ricardian-type specialization. By contrast, a less developed country which was initially frozen out of producing a commodity may, with fragmentation, find that it can now compete successfully in a labor-intensive component. Such fragmentation could improve that country's overall level of income while, at the same time, reducing the wage rate for unskilled workers. Furthermore, just as fragmentation may result in a country's loss of all segments in a process, it is possible that a country might end up specialized in all segments of the fragmented process, whereas previously it was producing completely different commodities. A multicommodity framework is utilized to capture these issues for finite changes in production patterns.

In what follows we consider two productive inputs, capital and labor. But "capital" could just as well refer to the human variety so that the consequences of fragmentation for the skilled/unskilled wage differential would provide the focus of attention. The labels are chosen for both analytical and semantic simplification.

International Fragmentation

Our focus is on the consequences for the pattern of production, the pattern of trade, aggregate country welfare, and the array of factor prices of a technological improvement (e.g., in transportation or communication) that allows components of a production process to be traded on the international market. Prior to the innovation, any country wishing to produce the product in question would have to do so in a vertically integrated process, whereas after the innovation two (or more) components can be separately produced and can enter individually into international trade.

Figure 10.i illustrates the situation in which the process of producing commodity 3 in an integrated manner involves inputs of two factors of production, say capital and labor in the amounts shown by 3_I ("3 Integrated") to produce \$1 worth of this commodity at the given world price. Points A and B indicate input bundles which would be required to produce \$1 worth of the integrated commodity 3. Before international fragmentation these components cannot be traded internationally, so that no trade prices are quoted. Instead, points 3_K and 3_L indicate capital and labor inputs which would be required to produce \$1 worth of the component assuming it is valued at local factor costs. (Thus the slope of the chord connecting 3_K and 3_L reflects initial factor prices.) These costs, in turn, depend on the local technology and world prices for other goods which this economy may produce in the pre-fragmentation equilibrium. The factor requirements to produce \$1 of final good 3 in the integrated process is a weighted average of points

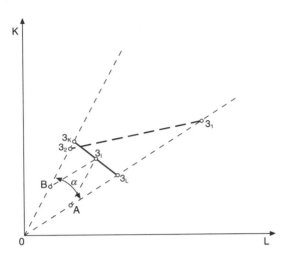

Figure 10.1
Fragmentation and new prices in sector 3

3_K and 3_L, with weights showing the distributive value shares of each segment in the integrated technology.

To simplify, we assume throughout that all technology exhibits rigid input-output coefficients (including the quantity of each segment required to produce a unit of final commodity 3). The α-cone in figure 10.1 displays the cone of diversification spanned by the technologies for the components.

After improvements in transportation or communication costs allow a decoupling of these components for commodity 3, world prices for the separate segments emerge. Countries are assumed to differ in their technologies and factor skills, so that a finer division of activities typically allows efficiency gains according to the Ricardian concept of comparative advantage. In figure 10.1 this is captured by new combinations of capital and labor to produce $1 worth of each segment at new world prices. Point 3_I for the formerly integrated process is replaced by points 3_1 and 3_2 for the separate labor-intensive and capital-intensive segments. If this country were to attempt to produce both segments (and no separate assembly costs are assumed),[2] it would take a greater quantity of capital and labor than previously to produce the integrated product. That is, even though prices for all other commodities are assumed to remain the same, fragmentation would typically allow a reduction in the final price for commodity 3.

Figure 10.1 also assumes that the labor-intensive segment, 3_1, is *dominated* by the capital-intensive segment, 3_2, in the sense that less capital and less labor are required to earn \$1 at new world prices, producing segment 3_2 as opposed to segment 3_1. Thus segment 3_1 would no longer be produced at home. Point 3_2 has arbitrarily been drawn a bit closer to the origin than is 3_K. This placement reveals that the country is in a strong position to be an exporter of the capital-intensive segment since its world price is higher than the imputed initial cost (shown by 3_K). The post-trade alignment of prices for fragments, relative to initial imputed costs, reveals much about the Ricardian comparison of productivities among countries. As the next section reveals, the production and trade pattern depends as well on a Heckscher-Ohlin comparison of factor proportions.

International Trade with Fragmentation

The potential impact of international fragmentation on the pattern of production and factor prices can be traced through on a diagram showing, for a small price-taking country, the Hicksian composite unit-value isoquant in figure 10.2 the kind of fragmentation for commodity 3 shown in figure 10.1 is illustrated together with unit value isoquants with fixed-coefficient technology for activities 1, 2, 4, and 5. The

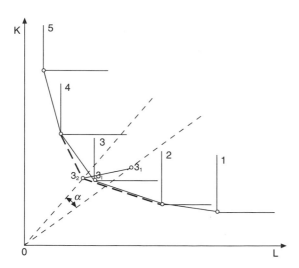

Figure 10.2
The Hicksian composite isoquant with loss of labor-intensive fragment

original Hicksian convex hull, shown by the broken solid line, is enhanced by fragmentation and the emergence of activity 3_2 instead of 3_1 as the point on the new Hicksian composite unit-value isoquant. The labor-intensive segment, 3_1, would not be produced with trade; nor, for that matter, would any of this segment be imported since we have assumed away a separate process for integrating the components.

Figure 10.2 suggests that the country is not competitive in producing the labor-intensive component of commodity 3. This lack of competitiveness is not a question of factor endowments. Rather, the technology and/or skills of local factors do not measure up to those found somewhere else in the world economy. However, the *consequences* of this lack for factor prices and the pattern of production *do* depend upon the economy's factor endowment proportions. If the endowment capital/labor ratio lies within the cone of diversification (α) for commodity 3, the wage/rental ratio must fall. Furthermore, this is the fate awaiting labor if originally the country was more labor-abundant and produced commodities 2 and 3. Figure 10.2 also reveals that if the country did not originally produce integrated 3_1, fragmentation of this activity does not disturb production patterns or factor prices. As will be explained with reference to figure 10.3, this result is not robust—technical progress which allows fragmentation of an activity not originally produced may nonetheless allow some segment of this activity to start production, with attendant changes in the distribution of income.

The country's loss of production of more labor-intensive segment 3_1 may suggest that the resulting fall in the wage/rental ratio is a natural consequence of an increase in the relative supply of labor which cancellation of 3_1 represents.[3] This, however, is not the logic embedded in Heckscher-Ohlin theory in this two-factor setting. Instead, note that if the country is originally producing integrated activities 3 and 2, fragmentation is akin to experiencing technical progress in the activity which is capital-intensive. Activity 3_1 has been replaced by the segment 3_2, which, at initial factor prices (shown by the slope of the segment connecting activities 3_1 and 2), represents a more highly valued productive activity. But *must* relative wages fall? Not if the economy's endowment proportions are sufficiently capital-abundant that after fragmentation it produces activities 4 and 3_2. In such a case, fragmentation works like an improvement in technology in the economy's *labor-intensive* commodity—represented by the move from 3_1 to 3_2—resulting in a *rise* in the wage/rental ratio.

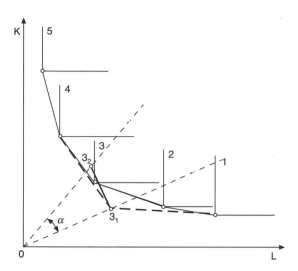

Figure 10.3
The Hicksian isoquant with loss of capital-intensive fragment

This latter possibility is important. Referring again to figure 10.2, consider an economy whose factor proportions lie between the ratios illustrated by activities 4 and 3_2—a country that is capital-abundant relative even to the capital-intensive segment of newly fragmented sector 3. Fragmentation leads to the country's loss of labor-intensive component 3_1, and yet the wage/rental ratio rises. Thus the charge that if international trade causes a country to lose a production activity which is intensive in its use of labor, it will cause the wage rate to fall, need not be true—especially for relatively capital-abundant countries. And yet these are the very countries which often express this fear. Furthermore, although the diagrams easily identify what happens to the *wage/rental ratio*, the effect on the *real wage* is in the same direction. The reason for this similarity is the magnification effect, whereby factor price changes contain commodity price changes (plus technical progress changes). When segment 3_2 replaces integrated 3_1 and the relatively capital-abundant country also produces commodity 4, the change in the wage rate must be positive since the price of commodity 4 is unchanged—and the rental on capital must fall.

Figure 10.3 serves to confirm that if an originally integrated activity becomes fragmented by trade, laborers in relatively capital-abundant countries which are engaged in this activity gain and those in relatively labor-abundant countries lose, even if it is the more capital-intensive segment that gets discarded because it is inefficient by world standards. There are important differences, however, between the situations shown in figures 10.2 and 10.3.[4] Suppose a country's endowment proportion lies within the cone of diversification (α) of the fragmented segments of commodity 3. The case in which it is the labor-intensive component (3_1) which is lost through inefficiency (figure 10.2) is the case in which the real wage declines, whereas the real wage rises if the labor-intensive component is the one which survives world competition. This different outcome is analogous to the remark that with technical progress in a Heckscher-Ohlin setting, the *bias* (i.e., whether labor-saving or capital-saving) may matter in the effect on factor prices for changes of finite size even though, for infinitesimally small changes, bias is unimportant for this question.

One possible consequence of fragmentation with international trade is that a relatively labor-abundant country which proves uncompetitive in the production of an integrated activity may, after fragmentation, be able to produce some labor-intensive segment. This ability is illustrated in figure 10.3 for an economy whose endowment proportions lie between the intensities required to produce commodities 1 and 2. Fragmentation leads such an economy to switch from activity 2 to the more capital-intensive activity 3_1. Nonetheless, such a move reduces the real wage since it is like experiencing technical progress at the capital-intensive end of the productive spectrum.

Fragmentation with international trade has been shown in figures 10.2 and 10.3 to have profound effects on the allocation of resources *within* the fragmented sector of the economy. But what can be said about resource allocation between the fragmented sector and the other productive sector? In figure 10.2 suppose the endowments allowed an initial production of commodities 2 and 3_I. Trade in fragments knocks out labor-intensive component 3_1, thus replacing the integrated activity with capital-intensive 3_2. Employment in sector 3 (all in 3_2) falls as a consequence.[5] On the other hand, a more capital-abundant economy producing commodity 4 and segment 3_2 after fragmentation will actually employ *more* labor in producing 3_2 than it originally employed in the integrated activity 3_I.

Fragmentation with Both Segments Surviving

Fragmentation need not condemn one of the segments to succumb to international competition. Figures 10.4 and 10.5 illustrate a pair of cases

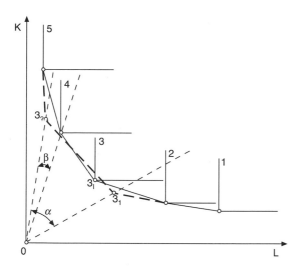

Figure 10.4
Both segments survive fragmentation

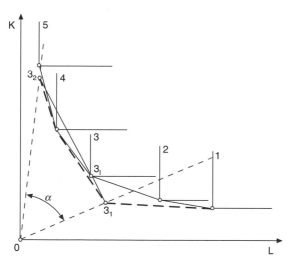

Figure 10.5
Both segments survive, but only one can be produced

in which the post-fragmentation Hicksian composite unit-value iso-quant contains both 3_1 and 3_2. These figures are drawn to illustrate a case in which the share of the capital-intensive segment is relatively small. This segment might represent "headquarter services," which, with the presumed lowered cost of service links, could be located in one country while still allowing the production block 3_1 to be located in another.

When both segments of fragmented sector 3 appear in the convex hull, more attention must be paid to a situation in which the economy's endowment proportions are located within the cone spanned by individual segments 3_1 and 3_2. In figure 10.4 for endowments within cone α production is concentrated on the two components, but international trade allows them to be produced in proportions different from that of the integrated technology. Our earlier general results for endowment proportions lying *outside* cone α remain as before: Capital-abundant countries could see an improvement in real wages, and labor-abundant countries would experience a wage fall. But within diversification cone α these results are completely reversed: Relatively capital-abundant countries suffer a fall in wages and labor-abundant countries experience a wage increase.

To understand this reversal consider, first, an economy which is capital-abundant relative to integrated activity 3_I, but not so capital-abundant as to lie in cone β in figure 10.4. For such an economy fragmentation is like experiencing technical progress in its capital-intensive activity as production of 3_2 replaces activity 4 and technical *regress* in its labor activity as 3_1 replaces integrated activity 3_I. Hence rents rise and wages fall. However, the situation for an economy whose endowment proportions place it in the β cone is different. Note that it originally produces commodities 5 and 4, and replaces both of these activities with the two segments of commodity 3. At the capital-intensive end it replaces activity 5 with activity 3_2, which, at original factor prices, is like experiencing technical progress in the capital-intensive good, thus encouraging a fall in wages. At the labor-intensive end it replaces activity 4 with activity 3_1, which at its initial factor prices (shown by the slope of segment connecting the isoquant corners for commodities 4 and 5) is like technical regress, which would also serve to depress the wage rate. At the other end of cone α, labor-intensive activity 2 is replaced by the superior activity (at initial factor prices) 3_1, and capital-intensive 3_I is replaced by 3_2 which, at initial factor prices, is like technical regress, hence causing wage rates to rise. In figures 10.4 and 10.5 note that if the endowment ray lies within the cone of diversification of sector 3, the new fragmented activity lies at the capital-intensive end of competitive activities for relatively capital-abundant endowments in the cone and at the labor-intensive end of the range for relatively labor-abundant countries. This reverses the ordering for economies whose endowment proportions lie outside the cone, and is the basis for the turnabout in results alluded to above: Outside the cone it is relatively capital-abundant countries whose labor has nothing to fear from fragmentation, while inside the cone relatively capital-abundant countries experience declines in real wages.

Figure 10.5 also illustrates a situation in which both the capital-intensive and labor-intensive segments of the production process for commodity 3 survive the fragmentation process and are potentially competitive on world markets. However, the line segment connecting them is no longer part of the Hicksian convex hull. As a result, an economy whose endowment proportions lie within diversification cone α will produce one segment or the other, but not both. Economies with a capital/labor endowment ratio higher than that used in commodity 4 suffer a loss in wages, while more labor abundant economies within cone α experience a wage increase. Indeed, consider such an economy which originally produces integrated 3_I along with more labor-intensive commodity 2. At initial factor prices the switch from producing integrated 3_I to commodity 4 is akin to technical *regress* at the capital-intensive end coupled with a switch from activity 2 to segment 3_1 (like technical progress) at the labor-intensive end. Once again, for economies whose endowments lie outside diversification cone α, if wages are affected they rise for relatively capital-abundant countries and fall for relatively labor-abundant countries.

Fragmentation with No Segment Surviving

An economy which would successfully compete in producing an integrated activity in a world market might find that fragmentation of this activity drives it completely out of that sector. Figure 10.6 illustrates this case. Initially if the economy's factor endowments allowed production of integrated activity 3_1 it might have been the case that potential rivals in other countries could have had poor skills in one segment even if superior skills in the other. By contrast, the home country might have been "second best" in both, so that its *average* cost of producing 3 made it competitive. The decoupling process accompanying fragmentation gives finer possibilities for countries to specialize in those

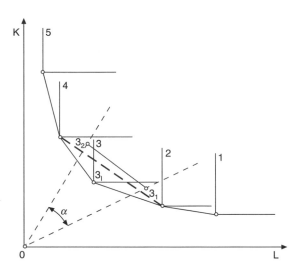

Figure 10.6
Fragmentation and the loss of both segments

segments in which productivity is high without being dragged down by home production in the other segment. The resulting price drops for segments 3_1 and 3_2 could lead to both activities lying *within* the new convex hull in figure 10.6. An analogy can be helpful here. Suppose that the Olympic games consisted of only one discipline—the decathlon—and that one champion dominated the discipline completely. Imagine now that the rules have been changed and the decathlon has been replaced by ten independent disciplines. Can the old champion expect to win a large number of gold medals? In fact, he or she may not win even a single medal.

If this country produced commodity 3 before fragmentation, it now has to spend more capital and labor to earn $1 on world markets. The new Hicksian convex hull is inferior—containing the dashed line segment connecting activities 2 and 4. Two further remarks are worth noting in this case. First, although the convex hull is made less attractive by fragmentation, the country's net real income might be improved. Suppose the country initially even exported commodity 3, whose price has deteriorated. Nonetheless, if this price falls sufficiently, the gain to home consumers might result in a net gain to the community. Secondly, the behavior of the wage/rent ratio outside cone α is just the opposite from figures 10.2 and 10.3 where the country retains a productive segment after fragmentation: Relatively capital abundant countries suffer a drop in wage rates since fragmentation is like technical regress at the labor-intensive end.[6]

Fragmentation with Specific Factors

A standard characteristic of international trade models is that the effects of technical progress or price changes on the distribution of income are quite sensitive to the specification of the production structure. In particular, in the Heckscher-Ohlin framework of the past sections two productive factors were mobile amongst all sectors. By contrast, some factors may be less mobile and there may be more factors than commodities produced. Such is the case with the specific factors model. Suppose that in each sector there is a type of capital used only in that sector, whereas labor is mobile and homogeneous in all activities. If all commodities are traded with commodity prices given on world markets, in each sector there would generally be complete specialization to a single commodity or, alternatively, there could be one sector in which two traded commodities are produced.[7] Assume the former case. The first remark that comes to mind is that we must abandon the assumption that technology is rigid and allow for factor substitutability in each sector. Nonetheless, begin the analysis at an initial free-trade equilibrium in which only final goods enter trade, and once again let a single commodity 3 now be fragmented into two segments, with trade permissible in each.

We focus on the situation shown in figure 10.2, in which it is the capital-intensive component in industry 3 that will survive international fragmentation. Whereas little room exists in the Heckscher-Ohlin model for the importance of factor *bias* in technical progress (except for finite changes), this is a feature that comes into its own in models with more factors than goods, such as the specific factors model. Thus fragmentation that knocks out the labor-intensive segment in producing commodity 3 will, at initial factor prices, create an excess supply of labor and, when markets clear, bring about a fall in the wage rate relative to returns on all types of specific capital. By contrast, fragmentation in which it is the capital-intensive segment of producing commodity 3 that gets ruled out in competition would serve to raise the wage rate relative to all rentals. These results correspond more closely to the widely held view that labor in advanced countries loses out when increases in the extent of world trade lead to losses of labor-intensive sectors.

Although this argument reveals the effects of fragmentation on the *ratio* of wages to rentals, it does not necessarily expose the effect on the *real* wage. The analogy to technical progress is once again useful. Technical progress in any sector has two types of effects on wages. To the extent that it saves on the use of labor, the wage rate is depressed. But the wage rate is positively affected by technical progress in *any* sector. And if the degree of factor substitutability is sufficiently high, the latter effect prevails over the former. For example, in Jones 1996 it is shown that for pure Hicksian labor-saving technical progress of the same extent in each industry, real wages for mobile labor nonetheless rise if on average the elasticity of substitution between labor and capital exceeds the ratio of capital to labor shares (which ratio is usually taken to be around one-half).

Concluding Remarks

One of the often-referenced facts of economic life is that the volume and value of international trade is increasing, even relative to national incomes. Furthermore, a greater fraction of such trade is taking place in intermediate goods, raw materials, producer goods, and other non-final consumer goods. Aiding and abetting this phenomenon is the decreased cost of the international fragmentation of the production process due to technological advances in transportation and communication, greater knowledge of legal systems in other countries and attendant lowering of risks in coordinating production of various segments at locales around the globe, whether within a multinational firm or making use of arms-length transactions. In this chapter we concentrate on the consequences of this process for aggregate country national income, the array of factor prices and the inter and intrasectoral allocation of employment.[8]

Perhaps the most normal-sounding result of such fragmentation is one that flows from the specific factors setting of the preceding section, whereby losses of labor-intensive segments of production to international competition increase the relative supply of labor to other sectors and, assuming commodity prices remain constant, lower the wage rate relative to returns to various types of capital. But even here the prognosis for a nation's labor supply need not be gloomy, since such fragmentation tends as well to work like technical progress in raising the returns to all factors. If factor substitution possibilities are sufficiently large, the real wage can rise even if the return to capital increases by more.

It is in a setting in which all factors of production are internally mobile and trade focuses productive activities to the same number of commodities as factors that a richer variety of outcomes, some rather surprising, can emerge. Here we have severely limited the analysis in two ways—we have considered only the two-factor case and assumed technology allows no factor substitution. Furthermore, we have abstracted from the important costs involved in the act of providing service links to bring together various segments or intermediate goods into a separate assembly operation. Thus a formerly integrated process involving two segments can, as a consequence of background improvements in costs of transport or coordination, appear separately in international trade. Both Ricardian and Heckscher-Ohlin elements help to determine new production networks. Inadequate factor skills and/or technology may render one of the segments uncompetitive in that it is dominated by the other segment (as in figures 10.1 and 10.2). Alternatively, the use of different factor intensities may result in one segment lying within, instead of on, the Hicksian convex hull of production possibilities at given world prices (as in figure 10.3). The consequences of such fragmentation then depend on the country's factor endowment proportions. Specifically, is the capital/labor ratio greater than either segment of the fragmented process, less than either segment, or does it lie within the cone of diversification of the fragmented process? If a country loses the labor-intensive segment, the wage rate need not fall. The analogy with the way in which technical progress affects factor prices in a Heckscher-Ohlin world provides the clue to explaining the possibilities. Thus if fragmentation takes place in a sector which is capital-intensive relative to the other sector's production requirements, the real wage (as well as the wage/rental ratio) must decline, whether it is the relatively labor-intensive fragment or the capital-intensive fragment in the sector which is lost to competition. However, for a relatively capital-abundant country fragmentation may take place at the labor-intensive end, and this serves to increase the real wage, even if it is the labor-intensive segment of the fragmented process that gets lost to international competition.

Our entire discussion took place in a setting in which factor prices change in order to clear factor markets so that problems of aggregate unemployment are set aside. Nonetheless, it is possible to inquire about changes in employment levels within and between sectors. Clearly fragmentation can have severe effects on the locale of employment within the fragmented sector—the entire segment can be lost to trade. But intersectoral employment flows may more than make up the difference. An example was provided in figure 10.2, in which a country could lose the labor-intensive segment of a fragmented process, but end up with a net transfer from its capital-intensive sector 4 so that the now-tradeable capital-intensive segment in the fragmented sector hires more labor than did the entire previous integrated sector. And the wage rate would rise.

It bears repeating that many questions central to the phenomenon of globalization have not been addressed in this chapter. This omission is deliberate, since the potential consequences of international fragmentation for national resource allocation and income distribution are sufficiently complex as to merit separate attention. It is certainly not the case that the loss to international competition of a labor-intensive process must be harmful to the interests of labor.

Notes

Early versions of this chapter have benefited from comments provided at presentations at Claremont University, the Chinese University of Hong Kong, and Tor Vergata University in Rome.

1. Innovations in communications have been singled out by some authors as a principal cause of globalization. See for instance Harris (1993, 1995).

2. This represents a polar stance to that of the "middle-products" approach (Sanyal and Jones 1982), in which all final goods are nontradeables, produced by combining local factors (labor) with components (or raw materials) available at given prices on world markets.

3. If the endowment ray is flatter than 03_1, cancellation of segment 3_1 increases the relative supply of *capital* to the rest of the economy (i.e., to 3_2 as well as 2). Nonetheless, the wage rate falls (and allocation of allocation of labor to labor-intensive commodity 2 increases).

4. Note that in figure 10.2 the labor-intensive segment of commodity 3 is dominated by the capital-intensive segment at world prices. By contrast, in figure 10.3 the labor-intensive segment does not dominate; the capital-intensive segment is nonetheless not competitive because a combination of 3_1 and activity 4 proves superior—a reflection in part of the local technology of producing 4 and its world price.

5. Suppose the endowment ray allows initial production of commodities 2 and 3 in figure 10.2, and let k, k_2, and k_3 indicate capital/labor ratios in the economy, in sector 2, and in sector 3 respectively. k is the weighted average, $\lambda_{L2} k_2 + \lambda_{L3} k_3$ where λ_{Lj} is the fraction of the labor force employed in sector j. The move from integrated 3_1 to capital-intensive 3_2

represents an increase in k_3, which must (since k_3 exceeds k_2) be balanced by a matching reduction in λ_{L3}.

6. To be more precise, wages fall if the country originally produced commodity 4 and integrated activity 3.

7. Details of such a model are provided in Jones and Marjit 1992. There the setting begins with autarky equilibrium in which commodity prices adjust to local demand conditions and in each sector there may be a number of commodities produced using capital specific to that sector. The move to free trade in all commodities then requires that in each sector only one commodity survives competition at given world prices (the small country case), which would correspond with the $(n + 1) \times n$ specific factors framework, or in one sector two commodities survive in a "nugget," which corresponds to a form of the Heckscher-Ohlin model made popular in the 3×3 version of Gruen and Corden (1970).

8. Globalization can also affect the *internal* geographic location of industrial activity. For an interesting analysis of this issue for Mexican production see Hanson 1996.

References

Arndt, S. 1997. Globalization and the gains from trade. In *Trade, Growth, and Economic Policy in Open Economies*, ed. K. Jaeger and K. Koch (New York: Springer-Verlag).

Gruen, F., and W. M. Corden. 1970. A tariff that worsens the terms of trade. In *Studies in international economics*, ed. I. McDougall and R. Snape, 55–8. Amsterdam: North-Holland.

Hanson, G. 1996. Localization economies, vertical organization, and trade. *American Economic Review* 86(5):1266–78.

Harris, R. G. 1995. Trade and communications costs. *Canadian Journal of Economics* 28 (special issue):S46–S75.

Harris, R. G. 1993. Globalization, trade and income. *Canadian Journal of Economics* 26(4):755–76.

Jones, R. W. 1996. International trade, real wages and technical progress: The specific factors model. *International Review of Economics and Finance* 5(2):113–24.

Jones, R. W., and H. Kierzkowski. 1990. The role of services in production and international trade: A theoretical framework. In *The political economy of international trade*, ed. R. Jones and A. Krueger, 31–48 (Cambridge, MA Blackwell).

Jones, R. W., and S. Marjit. 1992. International trade and endogenous production structures. In *Economic Theory and International Trade: Essays in Memoriam J. Trout Rader* (Springer-Verlag). ed. W. Neuefeind and R. Riezman, 173–96.

Mundell, R. A. 1957. International Trade and Factor Mobility. *American Economic Review* 47:321–35.

Sanyal, K., and R. W. Jones. 1982. The theory of trade in middle products. *American Economic Review* 72:16–31.

11   Money Shocks and the Current Account

Philip R. Lane

Introduction

In his famous 1963 paper "Capital Mobility and Stabilization Policy under Fixed and Flexible Exchange Rates," Bob Mundell showed how international capital mobility, in the presence of sticky prices, can strikingly alter the macroeconomic effects of monetary and fiscal policy in an open economy, since the capability to run current account imbalances delinks absorption and production in the short run. During the 1980s, this account of short-run current account determination was complemented by a literature that emphasized the intertemporal, dynamic aspects of current account behavior.[1] Central to this literature was an emphasis on a country's intertemporal budget constraint: a current account deficit today implies trade surpluses in the future. For technical reasons, this literature focused on flexible-price economies.

In recent years, a synthesis of these two approaches has been developed.[2] In this theoretical literature, fully dynamic economies that exhibit short-run price or wage rigidity have been analyzed. In these new models, it is possible to analyze the impact and dynamic effects of monetary shocks in the presence of sticky prices and international capital mobility. In this way, the short-run account of Mundell (1963) can be integrated into a more general dynamic model that respects the intertemporal constraints that are at the heart of current account determination.

In this chapter, we ask whether monetary shocks empirically matter in explaining fluctuations in the U.S. current account. One reason to explore this question is to evaluate whether the new class of sticky-price intertemporal open economy macroeconomic models is empirically relevant. If the data indicate that money shocks are important for the determination of real variables, such as the current account, this provides legitimacy for this line of research, since the existence of nominal rigidities provides a candidate explanation for the real effects of monetary shocks.[3]

A second justification is in terms of understanding current account determination. In previous empirical analysis of the intertemporal approach to the current account, the focus has been on flexible-price economies. Accordingly, it has been natural for researchers to focus on random fluctuations in endowments, technology, and government consumption as the sources of movements in the current account.[4] In that literature, a major puzzle has been an inability to explain the high volatility in actual current account data (Baxter 1995). This has led one researcher to speculate that there is actually excessive capital mobility in the world (Ghosh 1995)! Allowing a role for monetary shocks may help in explaining such volatility in external balances.

Third, if monetary shocks are shown to matter for current account determination, this may lead to a reinterpretation of some of the previous empirical current account literature. Many of these papers derive a tight empirical specification from an underlying flexible-price theoretical model. If the flexible-price model is an inappropriate characterization of the world, the theoretical interpretation of the empirical work in these papers must be altered. Indeed, Glick and Rogoff (1995) acknowledge that their investigation into the effects of productivity shocks on the current account is potentially fragile to an alternative specification that allows a role for aggregate demand.

Finally, empirical evidence on this question can be helpful in distinguishing between those sticky-price intertemporal models that predict a current account surplus in response to a monetary shock, as in Mundell (1963) or Obstfeld and Rogoff (1995), and those in which a current account deficit occurs (Chari et al. 1997, Kollman 1996, Betts and Devereux 1997, Bergin 1995).

In some recent papers, versions of a sticky-price intertemporal model have been explored via numerical calibrations (see Betts and Devereux 1997, Kollman 1996, and Chari et al. 1997). The focus in these papers has been on the behavior of nominal and real exchange rates rather than on the current account. While providing important insights, such exercises are limited for many purposes since the models are calibrated in order to match unconditional moments of the model to the measured unconditional moments in the data. This can be misleading if we are interested in the responses of macroeconomic variables conditional on the occurrence of a given structural shock. Econometric work that asks such conditional questions is a complementary approach to empirical evaluation of this class of models. My econometric approach is inspired by the efforts of Clarida and Gali (1994) and Eichenbaum and Evans (1995) to identify the impact of monetary shocks on the behavior of real and nominal exchange rates.[5]

To illustrate the potentially ambiguous relationship between monetary shocks and the current account, I outline a small open economy version of a sticky-price intertemporal model in the next section. Depending on the relative magnitudes of two key parameters, this model is capable of generating either a current account surplus or a deficit in response to a monetary shock. This captures the important theoretical ambiguity in the literature outlined above. In subsequent sections I move on to the actual empirical work, discuss the econometric results, and offer some conclusions.

An Illustrative Model

We develop a two-sector model. The nontraded sector is monopolistically competitive, with an elastic labor supply and prices set one period in advance. Production of the homogeneous traded good, in contrast, is viewed as exogenous and the price of traded goods is covered by the law of one price.[6] This asymmetric treatment of the nontraded and traded sectors is intended to capture the idea that domestic aggregate demand conditions matter much more for the nontraded sector than for the traded sector and that traded producers have much less latitude in setting prices.[7]

The notion is that, within this framework, an aggregate demand shock primarily affects the nontraded sector. However, it can spill over into the traded sector and the current account by the effects of a shift in consumption of nontradables on optimal consumption of tradables. For instance, in the case that tradables consumption rises in line with nontradables consumption, a boom in the nontraded sector is associated with an increase in demand for imports and a current account deficit. Alternatively, if traded and nontraded goods are sufficiently good substitutes, a rise in nontraded output and consumption may be associated with a fall in tradables consumption and a current account surplus.

In the model developed below, utility is modeled as having a constant relative risk aversion form in aggregate consumption. In turn, aggregate consumption is taken to be a constant elasticity of substitution index over consumption of traded and nontraded goods. As will be made clear below, this general specification is capable of generating different kinds of current account responses to a monetary shock, depending on the relative strengths of the intertemporal elasticity of aggregate consumption and the intratemporal elasticity of consumption between tradables and nontradables. Only the special case when these two elasticities have the same value is analyzed in the model developed in the appendix to Obstfeld and Rogoff 1995b and chapter 10 of Obstfeld and Rogoff 1996: in this case, a monetary shock has a zero impact on the current account.

Consider an economy populated by a continuum of yeoman-farmers along the unit interval [0,1]. Agent j has the objective function

$$V_j = \sum_{s=t}^{\infty} \beta^{s-t} \left[\frac{\sigma}{\sigma-1} C_s^{(\sigma-1)/\sigma} + \frac{\chi}{1-\varepsilon} \left(\frac{M_s}{P_s} \right)^{1-\varepsilon} - \frac{\kappa}{2} y_{Ns}^2 \right], \tag{11.1}$$

where σ, ε and $\kappa > 0$. The consumption index C aggregates consumption of traded and nontraded goods

$$C = \left[\gamma^{1/\theta} C_T^{(\theta-1)/\theta} + (1-\gamma)^{1/\theta} C_N^{(\theta-1)/\theta} \right]^{\theta/(\theta-1)}, \tag{11.2}$$

where θ is the constant elasticity of substitution between traded and nontraded goods. The second term in the objective function V_j reflects the utility derived from holding real balances, for instance in facilitating transactions. The third term captures the disutility of work effort.

The flow budget constraint faced by agent j is given by

$$P_{Tt} B_{t+1} + M_t = P_{Tt}(1+r)B_t + M_{t-1} + P_{Nt}(j)y_{Nt}(j) + P_{Tt}y_T - P_t C_t - P_{Tt}\tau_t. \tag{11.3}$$

B_t denotes the number of real bonds (in units of the tradable good) that pay off a real return r, which is given exogenously. The consumption price index is given by

$$P = \left[\gamma P_T^{1-\theta} + (1-\gamma)P_N^{1-\theta} \right]^{1/(1-\theta)}. \tag{11.4}$$

Agent j is the monopoly producer of variety j of the nontraded good and faces the demand function

$$y_N^d(j) = \left[\frac{p_N(j)}{P_N} \right]^{-\mu} C_N^A, \quad \mu > 1, \tag{11.5}$$

where C_N^A is aggregate consumption of nontraded goods and the index functions for nontraded consumption and prices are respectively

$$C_N = \left[\int_0^1 c_N(z)^{(\mu-1)/\mu} \, dz \right]^{\mu/(\mu-1)}, \tag{11.6}$$

$$P_N = \left[\int_0^1 p_N(z)^{1-\mu} \, dz \right]^{1/(1-\mu)}. \tag{11.7}$$

Each agent also receives an exogenous endowment y_T of the traded good each period. Finally, we assume zero government expenditure so that all seigniorage revenues are returned to the population in the form of lump-sum transfers

$$\tau_t = -\left(\frac{M_t - M_{t-1}}{P_{Tt}} \right). \tag{11.8}$$

First-Order Conditions

For simplicity, we assume $\beta(1 + r) = 1$, which rules out the desire to borrow and lend in the steady state. Maximization of (11.1) subject to (11.3), (11.5), and a no-Ponzi-Game condition generates the relationships

$$\frac{C_{Tt+1}}{C_{Tt}} = \left[\frac{\left(\dfrac{P_t}{P_{Tt}} \right)}{\left(\dfrac{P_{t+1}}{P_{Tt+1}} \right)} \right]^{\sigma-\theta}, \tag{11.9}$$

$$\frac{C_{Nt}}{C_{Tt}} = \frac{1-\gamma}{\gamma} \left(\frac{P_{Nt}}{P_{Tt}} \right)^{-\theta}, \tag{11.10}$$

$$\frac{M_t}{P_t} = \left[\frac{\chi C_t^{1/\sigma}}{1 - \dfrac{\beta P_{Tt}}{P_{Tt+1}}} \right]^{1/\varepsilon}, \tag{11.11}$$

$$y_{Nt}^{(\mu+1)/\mu} = \left(\frac{\mu-1}{\mu} \right) (C_{Nt}^A)^{1/\mu} C_t^{-1/\sigma} \left(\frac{P_{Nt}}{P_t} \right). \tag{11.12}$$

Equation (11.9) is the Euler equation governing the dynamic evolution of consumption. The dependence of consumption growth on the sequence of relative prices is the "consumption-based real interest rate" effect, first emphasized by Dornbusch (1983). If the aggregate price level relative to the price of traded goods is currently low relative to its future value, this encourages present over future consumption, since the consumption-based real interest rate is lower. However, it also encourages substitution from traded to nontraded goods. The former effect dominates if the intertemporal elasticity of substitution is greater that the intratemporal elasticity of substitution ($\sigma > \theta$), and conversely.[8]

Equation (11.10) links consumption of nontraded and traded goods. The elasticity of substitution is parameterized by θ; if the relative price is unity, the relative consumption of nontraded goods is larger the smaller is the parameter γ. Demand for real balances is captured by equation (11.11): real money demand is increasing in the level of consumption and declining in the nominal interest rate. Finally, equilibrium supply of nontraded goods is given by equation (11.12): the higher is the consumption index C, the lower is the level of production, as agents increase leisure in line with consumption of other goods.

Steady-State Equilibrium

We first consider the case when all prices are fully flexible and all exogenous variables, including the money stock, are constant. We assume the initial stock of net foreign assets is zero ($B_0 = 0$). We normalize the endowment of the traded good so that the relative price of nontraded goods in terms of traded goods is unity in this steady state $P_N/P_T = 1$.[9] In this symmetric equilibrium, $C_{Nt}^A = y_{Nt} = (1 - \gamma) C_t$ and the steady-state production and consumption of nontraded goods is given by

$$y_N = C_N = \left[\frac{\mu - 1}{\mu \kappa} \right]^{\sigma/(\sigma+1)} (1 - \gamma)^{1/(1+\sigma)}. \tag{11.13}$$

From this expression, production of the nontraded good will be larger when the nontraded goods sector is more competitive (the larger is μ), work effort is less taxing (the smaller is κ), and the weight placed on consumption of nontraded goods in the utility function is larger (the larger is $(1 - \gamma)$). The initial equilibrium price level P_0 can be found using the constancy of the price level in the steady state (from the no-bubbles condition) and the initial value for the money stock M_0.

An Unanticipated Money Shock

There exists a nominal price rigidity in the economy: prices in the nontraded sector are set one period in advance. In the event of an unanticipated monetary shock, this means that agents can only adjust prices with a one-period delay. This permits a monetary shock to have real effects, given the initial period in which prices do not immediately respond to the disturbance. We want to distinguish between the short-run and long-run effects of the monetary shock. For any variable X, let $\tilde{X} \equiv (X_1 - \overline{X}_0)/\overline{X}_0$ denote the short-run percentage deviation in X from $\overline{X}_0$ the initial steady-state value of X, and $\hat{X} = (\overline{X} - \overline{X}_0)/\overline{X}_0$ denote the long-run (steady-state) percentage deviation. Given the structure of the nominal rigidity, the new steady state is attained after one period.

We consider a surprise permanent expansion in the money stock $\tilde{M} = \hat{M} > 0$. The short-run stickiness of nontraded prices means that $\tilde{P}_N = 0$. From equation 11.9, $\tilde{C}_T$ and $\hat{C}_T$ are linked by

$$\hat{C}_T - \tilde{C}_T = (\sigma - \theta)\left(\tilde{P} - \tilde{P}_T\right) - (\sigma - \theta)\left(\hat{P} - \hat{P}_T\right). \tag{11.14}$$

We also know that steady-state consumption of traded goods, given a constant endowment of traded goods, can only be increased by the income earned from the accumulation of foreign assets

$$\hat{C}_T = r\frac{dB}{C_0}. \tag{11.15}$$

In turn, the accumulation of foreign assets dB is generated by the short-run current account surplus

$$\frac{dB}{C_0} = -\tilde{C}_T, \tag{11.16}$$

which implies the relationship between $\hat{C}_T$ and $\tilde{C}_T$

$$\hat{C}_T = -r\tilde{C}_T. \tag{11.17}$$

That is to say, the price of increasing consumption of tradables by Δ in the short run is to reduce steady-state consumption of tradables by $-r\Delta$.[10]

From (11.10), we can link the steady-state changes in the consumption of nontraded and traded goods

$$\hat{C}_N - \hat{C}_T = -\theta\left(\hat{P}_N - \hat{P}_T\right). \tag{11.18}$$

We know that the steady-state change in nontraded consumption is just equal to the steady-state change in nontraded production. From the supply condition (11.12) and the optimized relationship between C_N and C,

$$\hat{C}_N = \hat{y}_N = \frac{(\sigma - \theta)\gamma}{1 + \sigma}\left(\hat{P}_N - \hat{P}_T\right). \tag{11.19}$$

Combining (11.18) and (11.19), we can express the steady-state change in tradables consumption as a function of the steady-state change in the relative price of nontraded goods in terms of traded goods:

$$\hat{C}_T = \left[\theta + \frac{(\sigma-\theta)\gamma}{1+\theta} \right] \left(\hat{P}_N - \hat{P}_T \right). \tag{11.20}$$

In the short run, sticky prices ($\tilde{P}_N = 0$) mean that the nontraded production is driven by the level of demand, which is given by (11.10)

$$\tilde{y}_N = \tilde{C}_N = \theta \tilde{P}_T + \tilde{C}_T. \tag{11.21}$$

Finally, from (11.11), the short-run and steady-state monetary equilibrium equations are given by

$$\varepsilon\left(\tilde{M} - \tilde{P}\right) = \frac{\theta}{\sigma}\left[\tilde{P}_T - \tilde{P}\right] + \frac{1}{\sigma}\tilde{C}_T - \frac{1}{r}\left[\hat{P}_T - \tilde{P}_T\right], \tag{11.22}$$

$$\varepsilon\left(\hat{M} - \hat{P}\right) = \frac{\theta}{\sigma}\left[\hat{P}_T - \hat{P}\right] + \frac{1}{\sigma}\hat{C}_T. \tag{11.23}$$

Equations (11.14) to (11.23) permit us to solve for the short-run and steady-state effects of an unanticipated permanent monetary disturbance.

The solution has the form

$$\tilde{P}_T = c_1 \hat{M}, \tag{11.24}$$

$$\tilde{y}_N = \tilde{C}_N = c_2 \hat{M}, \tag{11.25}$$

$$\tilde{C}_T = c_3(\sigma - \theta)\hat{M}, \tag{11.26}$$

$$\hat{P}_T = c_4 \hat{M}, \tag{11.27}$$

$$\tilde{C}_T = -\frac{c_3(\sigma - \theta)}{r}\hat{M}, \tag{11.28}$$

$$\hat{P}_N - \hat{P}_T = -c_5(\sigma - \theta)\hat{M}, \tag{11.29}$$

$$\hat{y}_N = \hat{C}_N = -c_6(\sigma - \theta)\hat{M}, \tag{11.30}$$

where $c_1, c_2, c_3, c_4, c_5, c_6 > 0$ are functions of the parameters σ, θ, r, γ. There are three cases to consider: (1) $\sigma = \theta$; (2) $\sigma > \theta$; and (3) $\sigma < \theta$. In case (i), the monetary shock causes a short-run boom in the nontraded sector and causes the price of traded goods to rise (the nominal exchange rate to depreciate) in both the short run and the long run. However, intertemporal and intratemporal substitution effects cancel out so that there is no spillover effect on consumption in the traded sector. Accordingly, the current account remains in balance and there are no long-run real effects from the monetary shock. An example of case (1) is the model written in the appendix to Obstfeld and Rogoff (1995b) and developed in Obstfeld and Rogoff 1996, chap. 10, in which utility is log-separable in traded and nontraded goods ($\sigma = \theta = 1$).[11]

In case (2), a surprise monetary expansion stimulates extra demand, and hence production, of the nontraded good and causes an immediate depreciation of the exchange rate (the price of traded goods rises). Increased consumption of nontradables also stimulates consumption of tradables, since the elasticity of substitution between consumption of nontradables and tradables is low (relative to the intertemporal elasticity of substitution). Accordingly, the current account goes into deficit. In the long run, the current account is in balance, so long-run consumption of tradables must fall to permit the trade surplus that is required to finance interest payments on the external debt that was incurred. In equilibrium, a decline in long-run tradables consumption requires a long-run real depreciation.

Notice that in this case, the model generates a current account deficit in response to a monetary shock without relying on an investment channel. This stands in contrast to the claim of Chari et al. (1997) that models without capital are incapable of matching the unconditional correlation in the data that the current account is countercyclical.[12]

In case (3), the spillover between nontraded and traded consumption is negative, as the intratemporal substitution effect of the short-run real depreciation dominates the intertemporal substitution effect of a temporarily low price level. Accordingly, a short-run current account surplus is generated. This permits an increase in the long-run level of tradables consumption. In equilibrium, the long-run real exchange rate must appreciate (the relative price of nontradables in terms of tradables must rise).

This case corresponds to the traditional Mundell-Fleming model in the sense that a monetary shock generates a current account surplus. However, in this generalized model, this outcome is not the only possibility, since we have seen that a monetary shock can also potentially have a negative or zero effect on the current account, depending on the balance of $\sigma - \theta$. As such, empirical investigation is of much interest, since theory does not firmly tie down the current account response to a monetary shock.[13]

An interesting result is that production and consumption of the non-traded good falls in the new steady state in both cases (2) and (3), as can be seen in equation (11.30).[14] In both cases, the level of consumption of the traded good changes in the new steady state, due to the accumulation (decumulation) of net external assets. This has a wealth effect on the level of desired consumption of the nontraded good and also on the optimal supply of labor to the nontraded sector. The strength of the former effect inversely depends on the intratemporal elasticity of substitution θ and the strength of the latter effect inversely depends on the intertemporal elasticity of substitution σ, with the former effect dominating if $\sigma > \theta$ and conversely. When $\sigma > \theta$, the decline in long-run consumption of tradables on net leads to a decline in the consumption and production of nontradables, as the desired decline in the long-run consumption of nontradables exerts a stronger effect than the desired increase in labor supply when consumption falls. Asymmetrically, when $\sigma < \theta$, the increase in long-run consumption of tradables on net again leads to a decline in consumption and production of nontradables as the desired increase in consumption of nontradables is a weaker effect than the desired contraction in labor supply when consumption of tradables rises.

This model captures the spirit of the recent intertemporal sticky-price literature by explicitly deriving the short- and long-term effects of a monetary shock in a fully dynamic model with utility-maximizing agents. Moreover, it illustrates the theoretical ambiguity concerning the sign of the current account response to a monetary disturbance. However, it is clearly a highly stylized model, with a simplistic account of the sources and duration of price stickiness and lacking an explicit description of the monetary transmission mechanism's role for capital accumulation. For this reason, we do not attempt to derive a structural econometric model from this foundation. Rather, following Sims (1980), our econometric approach is a broader one that employs theory in a less restrictive way in identifying the role of monetary shocks in external account fluctuations. The results from a flexible approach to econometric identification have the further advantage of possibly showing the direction future research efforts should take in order to reconcile differences between the theoretical predictions and the empirical evidence.

Empirics

Data

The source for most of the data is the International Monetary Fund's *International Financial Statistics* on CD-ROM. The rest of the world

(RoW) is proxied by the non-U.S. G-7 countries, and the RoW variables are constructed as a GDP-weighted average of national variables for these countries.[15] The series for the stock of nonborrowed reserves, which is used below as a measure of the monetary policy stance in the United States, was downloaded from the St. Louis Fed website. The real exchange rate is the ratio of CPI indexes, adjusted by the nominal exchange rate. The ratio of the current account to GDP is in nominal prices and seasonally adjusted. When using monthly data, the trade balance is measured as the ratio of exports to imports, in constant prices. The RoW interest rates are the treasury bill rates for the United Kingdom, Canada, and France and the call money rate for Japan, Germany, and Italy.

The External Account and the Real Exchange Rate

In figure 11.1, we plot the time series for the U.S. current account and real exchange rate over 1974.1–1996.3. The graph displays a striking regularity in the data: real appreciation is associated with deterioration in the current account, with the real exchange movement leading the change in the current account by about a year. (The contemporaneous correlaton between the two series is 0.5; the cross correlation is maxi-

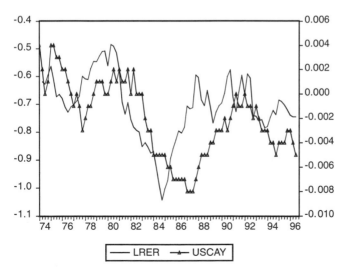

Figure 11.1
USCAY is ratio of U.S. current account to GDP; LRER is the log real exchange rate, as described in the text (1974.1–1996.3)

mized at a lag of six quarters at 0.76.) This pattern of comovements—exchange rate depreciation associated with improvement in the current account—is consistent with a role for monetary shocks leading to current account improvements. However, it is insufficient to just consider such unconditional correlations if we want to adequately address the conditional question: what is the response of the current account to a monetary shock? Accordingly, we now turn to the VAR econometric methodology that is expressly designed to allow us to ask such questions. We consider two alternative approaches to identification of VARs.

Long-Run Restrictions

Blanchard and Quah (1989) proposed an identification scheme for VARs that proceeds by imposing long-run restrictions on the behavior of the variables in the system. Ideally, these long-run restrictions are derived from the underlying intertemporal economic theory. Here, we apply this approach to identifying the effects of a monetary shock on the current account. We consider a three-variable system $z = [Y/Y^*,$ $(CA/Y), P/P^*]$ where Y/Y^* is the log ratio of home to foreign output, (CA/Y) is the home country's current account to GDP ratio and P/P^* is the log ratio of home to foreign price levels (consumer price indexes). This is an adaptation of the system studied by Clarida and Gali (1994), with the exception that we focus on the current account rather than the real exchange rate. In fact, a bivariate system in $[(CA/Y), P/P^*]$ would be sufficient to identify the impact of monetary shocks on the current account. However, the trivariate system allows us to additionally distinguish between "supply" and "absorption" shocks and provides greater comparability with the Clarida-Gali real exchange rate study.

   I assume that the trivariate system is driven by the sequence of orthogonal structural shocks $\varepsilon_s = [\varepsilon_{1s}, \varepsilon_{2s}, \varepsilon_{3s}]$, with the moving average representation

$$z_t = C_0\varepsilon_t + C_1\varepsilon_{t-1} + C_2\varepsilon_{t-2} + \dots. \tag{11.31}$$

   The reduced-form VAR representation for z_t is

$$z_t = \sum_{i=1}^{p} A_i z_{t-1} + u_t, \tag{11.32}$$

which allows us to write z_t as a moving average of the reduced-form residuals u_t:

$$z_t = u_t + B_1 u_{t-1} + B_2 u_{t-2} + \ldots .$$ (11.33)

Let $C(1) = C_0 + C_1 + C_2 + \ldots$ denote the matrix of long-run coefficients. If $C(1)$ is restricted to be lower triangular, than C_0 can be identified.[16] $C(1)$ lower-triangular means that only the ε_1 shocks affect output in the long run; ε_1 and ε_2 shocks may affect the current account in the long run, but ε_3 shocks do not; and all three kinds of shocks ε_1, ε_2, and ε_3 may affect the price level in the long run. In light of these identification assumptions, it makes sense to label the ε_1 disturbance a "supply" shock, ε_2 an "absorption" shock, and ε_3 a "monetary" shock.

Otherwise, no other restriction is imposed on the VAR. The restriction that the long-run current account response to a nominal shock is zero is an equilibrium property of models such as that in the second section.[17] The identification scheme does not require any restrictions on the process for the relative price level.

The data are quarterly over 1974.1–1996.3. The home country is the United States and the rest of the world is proxied by a GDP-weighted average of the other G-7 nations.

The system is estimated in first differences, with eight lags.[18] Figure 11.2 shows the impulse response function detailing the behavior of the current account in the wake of a positive one standard deviation mon-

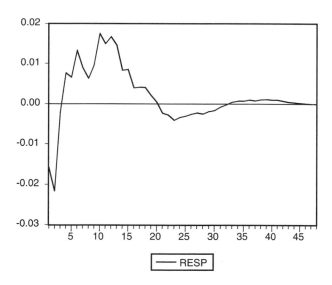

Figure 11.2
Response to USCAY to money shock, long-run identification (1974.2–1996.3)

etary shock. The current account initially deteriorates but quickly starts to improve and moves into surplus after about a year. This surplus is quite persistent and is maximized only after ten quarters before dying out. The maximal impact on the current account is an improvement of 0.016 percentage points in the ratio of the current account to GDP, which is 5.2 percent of its standard deviation. In figure 11.3, plus or minus two standard deviation bands for the impulse response function are included. The narrowness of these bands indicates that the estimated current account response is statistically significant.[19]

The pattern of an initial deficit followed by a move into surplus describes a J-curve. One explanation for this pattern is that the monetary shock generates a significant investment response, as in the models of Betts and Devereux (1997) and Chari et al. (1997), that initially causes the current account to go into deficit. However, this is an unlikely explanation if there are "time to build" lags in the investment process. A second interpretation, which is the traditional explanation of the J-curve effect, is that sales contracts are predetermined in the very short term, and so the impact effect of exchange rate depreciation is just to increase the value of imports and widen the trade deficit. A third interpretation is that the estimated initial response is just noise and that lags

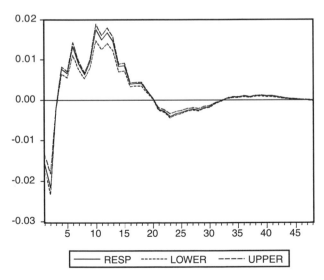

Figure 11.3
Response to USCAY to money shock, long-run identification; bands are +/– two standard errors (1974.2–1996.3)

in the monetary transmission channel explain the delayed occurrence of the current account surplus.

To illustrate the quantitative contribution of monetary shocks to current account volatility, we present in table 11.1 the variance decomposition for the current account generated by this system. According to theses estimates, monetary shocks account for about half of the variation in the current account at horizons even up to twenty quarters.

A similar proportion is also estimated by Kumar and Prasad (1997) under a different set of identifying assumptions (in their results, however, the relative contributions of supply and absorption shocks are reversed). They consider a three-variable system consisting of relative output levels, the real exchange rate, and the trade balance. Their identification scheme labels shocks that have no long-run effect on the the real exchange rate but that may have a long-run effect on the trade balance as monetary in nature. However, in the sticky-price intertem-

Table 11.1
Variance decomposition of current account I: Long-run model

Step	Standard error	Supply	Absorption	Money
1	0.067	43.50	6.87	49.63
2	0.074	36.62	6.43	56.94
3	0.075	38.17	6.28	55.55
4	0.083	35.92	14.90	49.18
5	0.084	35.88	14.70	49.42
6	0.086	36.27	15.95	47.78
7	0.086	36.31	15.88	47.81
8	0.086	36.23	15.86	47.91
9	0.087	36.39	16.35	47.26
10	0.087	36.12	16.77	47.11
11	0.088	36.00	16.61	47.39
12	0.088	36.00	16.59	47.40
13	0.088	36.00	16.60	47.41
14	0.088	35.96	16.63	47.41
15	0.088	35.81	16.66	47.54
16	0.088	35.78	16.75	47.47
17	0.088	35.70	16.73	47.57
18	0.088	35.72	16.74	47.54
19	0.089	35.72	16.81	47.47
20	0.089	35.70	16.81	47.49

Note: Quarterly horizons.

poral models discussed in the second section, if monetary shocks have a long-run effect on the trade balance, they will also have a long-run effect on the real exchange rate and so the Kumar-Prasad identification scheme is difficult to interpret within the context of this class of theoretical models. (At an empirical level, Gagnon (1996) shows that real exchange rates are heavily influenced at long horizons by accumulated net foreign asset positions.)

Ahmed and Park (1994) include the trade balance in a four-variable VAR model for a set of small open economies, where the four variables are U.S. output, domestic output, the trade balance, and the domestic price level. A crucial long-run identification restriction in their work is that the cumulative trade balance effect of a monetary shock is zero. This is not an assumption that is warranted by the sticky-price intertemporal models described in the second section: if a monetary shock causes a temporary current account imbalance, it has a permanent effect on the trade balance, since the accumulation (decumulation) of net external assets generates international investment income flows that permits the coexistence of a zero current account balance and a permanent trade imbalance.

Similarly, Lee and Chinn (1998) study a bivariate VAR system containing the real exchange rate and the current account. Their identifying assumption is that temporary (monetary) shocks have no permanent impact on the real exchange rate. Again, this restriction is not warranted in the context of intertemporal sticky-price models: for instance, in the model laid out in the second section, if a monetary shock induces a current account imbalance, there is a permanent impact on the real exchange rate.

Finally, it is worth remarking that the size of the contribution of monetary shocks in current account fluctuations is quite similar to that estimated by Clarida and Gali (1994) for the role of monetary shocks in explaining bilateral real exchange rate fluctuations, using the United States/Germany and the United States/Japan country pairs. This is consistent with the underlying theory, which models the current account and the real exchange rate as jointly determined by the same set of underlying structural disturbances.

Recursive Ordering

An alternative approach to identification is to impose a set of exclusion restrictions on the contemporaneous relationships between the variables in the VAR system.[20] Consider a vector x_s where x_s includes both the current account and a monetary policy instrument and may also include extra economic variables. The VAR system has the representation

$$x_t = A_0 x_t + \sum_{i=1}^{p} A_i x_{t-i} + u_t.$$

For identification, the elements of x_t are ordered so that A_0 is lower-triangular. This imposes a recursive structure on the relationships among the variables. A shock to the first variable in the system transmits only with a lag to the other variables in the system; in contrast, the last variable in the system is allowed to be contemporaneously affected by shocks to all the variables in the system.

Consider the system $\{Y/Y^*, P/P^*, MPI, R^{RoW} - R^{US}, RER, TB\}$, where Y/Y^* is the log ratio of home to foreign industrial production, P/P^* is the log ratio of home to foreign consumer price indexes, MPI is the monetary policy instrument employed by the domestic monetary authority, $R^{RoW} - R^{US}$ is the short-term interest rate differential, RER is the log real exchange rate, and TB is the log ratio of domestic exports to domestic imports.[21] The recursive identification scheme implied by the ordering of the variables in this system allows monetary policy to contemporaneously respond to shocks to relative output and price levels, and it allows the interest rate differential, the exchange rate, and the trade balance to contemporaneously respond to monetary shocks. The trade balance is ordered last in the system to allow for contemporaneous effects of all shocks on the trade balance. Although these ordering restrictions are somewhat arbitrary, it turns out our main results are robust to alternative orderings of the variables in the system.

Data are monthly over 1974.1–1996.12. (It is important to use monthly data given the use of timing restrictions in the identification scheme.) The VAR includes six lags of each variable, plus a time trend. We consider two alternative measures of the U.S. monetary policy instrument: the Federal Funds Rate (FFR) and the level of nonborrowed reserves (NBR).

Figure 11.4 gives the impulse response function of the trade balance with respect to a monetary shock, as proxied by a negative shock to the FFR (i.e., a monetary expansion). Initially, the estimated trade balance response is choppy, but it moves into a sustained surplus position after a period of about a year. The maximum trade balance response is only after forty-three months, which is somewhat longer than the estimate

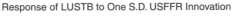

Response of LUSTB to One S.D. USFFR Innovation

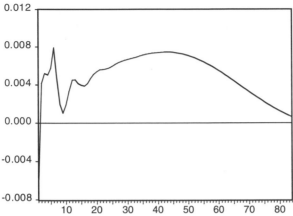

Figure 11.4
Response of log(EXP/IMP) to money shock, recursive identification (1974.1–1996.12)

of ten quarters that was obtained above using long-run restrictions for identification. The maximum impact on the trade balance measure is an improvement of only 5 percent of its standard deviation. Eichenbaum and Evans (1995) found the maximum exchange rate response to a monetary shock to occur with almost as long a lag (twenty-two to thirty-two months in bilateral VARs).[22] The longer lag for the trade balance is consistent with the timing pattern in the raw data shown in figure 11.1, by which changes in the real exchange rate lead changes in the current account. Figure 11.5 duplicates figure 11.4, but with the inclusion of plus or minus two standard error bands.

Table 11.2 shows the associated variance decomposition of the trade balance. Shocks to the FFR account for only a small fraction of the variance in the trade balance at short horizons but climbs above 10 percent at around forty months and reaches 14.4 percent at a sixty-month horizon. The smaller role played by monetary shocks in this identification scheme relative to the long-run system in the third section can be attributed to the greater noise in monthly data and the narrower definition of a monetary shock under this approach to identification: disturbances to the monetary policy instrument that are orthogonal in a six-variable VAR system. Put differently, in the recursive approach, money shocks are identified by disturbances to a monetary policy intrument whereas, under long-run identification, shocks are identified by the pattern of macroeconomic outcomes.

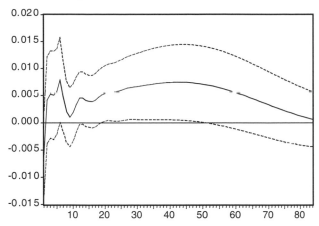

Figure 11.5
Response of log(EXP/IMP) to FFR shock, recursive identification; bands are +/− two standard errors (1974.1–1996.12)

Table 11.2
Variance decomposition of current account II: FFR shocks

Period	Standard error	DLIND	DLPL	USFFR	DINT	LRER	LUSTB
1	0.009	1.10	0.03	0.90	0.23	0.23	97.51
5	0.019	8.42	0.57	2.43	2.52	2.01	84.05
9	0.022	9.35	0.87	3.59	2.46	5.54	78.19
13	0.024	8.42	1.10	3.97	2.90	13.28	70.33
17	0.025	7.42	2.30	4.39	3.11	20.75	62.13
21	0.025	6.67	3.73	5.01	3.06	26.05	55.48
25	0.025	6.15	5.21	5.84	2.78	29.92	50.10
29	0.026	5.67	6.30	6.82	2.58	32.87	45.76
33	0.026	5.25	7.01	7.84	2.55	35.09	42.26
37	0.027	4.90	7.38	8.92	2.67	36.63	39.50
41	0.027	4.63	7.51	10.04	2.89	37.52	37.41
45	0.027	4.44	7.50	11.16	3.18	37.88	35.86
49	0.027	4.33	7.40	12.21	3.49	37.83	34.74
53	0.027	4.31	7.27	13.16	3.79	37.52	33.96
57	0.027	4.37	7.14	13.93	4.06	37.07	33.43
60	0.027	4.47	7.06	14.39	4.22	36.72	33.14

Notes: Monthly horizons. DLIND is log of relative industrial production; DLPL is log of relative CPIs; USFFR is Federal Funds rate; DINT is interest rate differential; LRER is log of real exchange rate; and LUSTB is log (EXP/IMP).

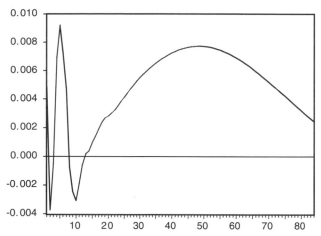

Figure 11.6
Response of log(EXP/IMP) to NBR shock, recursive identification (1974.1–1996.12)

A similar pattern is generated when the monetary shock is proxied
by a shock to NBR in figure 11.6: after an initial turbulent period of
about nine months, a sustained trade balance surplus is generated by
the monetary shock. The maximum response occurs after forty-eight
months: the magnitude is again small, corresponding to 5.2 percent of
its standard deviation. (It is noteworthy that each of our three experiments delivers a similar estimate in this regard.) Figure 11.7 includes
plus or minus two standard error bands around the estimated impulse-
response function. Table 11.3 shows the associated variance decomposition of the trade balance, which attributes a slightly smaller role to
money shocks in current account fluctuations relative to the results
from the FFR experiment. The pattern of a sustained trade surplus
(after an initial one year lag) in the wake of a positive monetary shock
tallies well with the findings for bilateral trade balances between the
United States and other G-7 countries that are produced by Betts and
Devereux (1997), who adopt a similar VAR specification and consider
NBR as the monetary policy instrument.

Discussion and Conclusions

In this chapter, I have explored the role played by monetary shocks in
U.S. external account fluctuations. Taken together, the alternative iden-

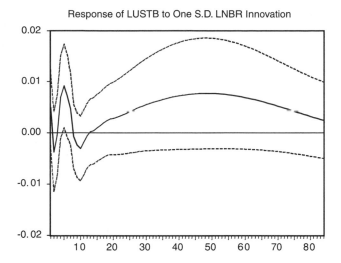

Figure 11.7
Response of log (EXP/IMP) to NBR shock, recursive identification; ban ds are +/− two
standard errors (1974.1–1996.12)

Table 11.3
Variance decomposition of current account III: NBR shocks

Period	Standard error	DLIND	DLPL	LNBR	DINT	LRER	LUSTB
1	0.061	0.60	0.00	0.64	0.85	0.17	97.73
5	0.073	8.28	1.59	3.18	0.97	1.92	84.05
9	0.079	9.28	1.64	4.03	2.56	8.46	74.03
13	0.086	7.95	2.31	3.59	5.12	17.95	63.08
17	0.093	7.07	3.16	3.14	5.84	26.79	53.99
21	0.10	6.80	3.81	3.04	6.10	33.11	47.14
25	0.106	6.79	4.42	3.19	6.15	37.53	41.92
29	0.111	6.87	4.90	3.65	6.20	40.48	37.90
33	0.116	6.92	5.26	4.36	6.28	42.33	34.85
37	0.12	6.86	5.50	5.27	6.43	43.37	32.56
41	0.124	6.70	5.66	6.33	6.64	43.81	30.87
45	0.127	6.48	5.74	7.47	6.87	43.80	29.64
49	0.129	6.26	5.76	8.64	7.10	43.48	28.77
53	0.131	6.11	5.75	9.76	7.30	42.94	28.15
57	0.132	6.09	5.71	10.78	7.44	42.28	27.70
60	0.133	6.19	5.67	11.45	7.51	41.74	27.44

Note: Monthly horizons. LNBR is log of stock of nonborrowed reserves. See note to table
11.2 for key to remaining abbreviations.

tification schemes indicate a reasonably clear pattern in the data. I found that monetary shocks are a significant source of variation in the external account and can help explain its high volatility, which has been a puzzle in the empirical current account literature. A surprise monetary expansion generates a persistent external account surplus, albeit after a one year initial lag, but there is also some evidence (in the long-run identification scheme) that the direct impact effect is initially negative. In broad terms, this is in line with the early contribution of Mundell (1963) and some of the recent intertemporal sticky-price models of the open economy. That said, the different identification schemes do produce quite different estimates of the quantitative contribution of monetary shocks in current account fluctuations, so that considerable uncertainty remains along this dimension. The finding that the conditional correlation between monetary expansions and the current account is positive can be reconciled with the stylized fact of a countercyclical current account surplus by recognizing that monetary shocks are not the only, indeed not the dominant, source of macroeconomic disturbances.

An item for future empirical research is to apply the VAR methodology employed in this chapter to examine the current accounts of other countries. At least for the VAR identification scheme that relies on contemporaneous exclusion restrictions, this is not straightforward, since it appears that foreign monetary authorities respond very quickly to changes in U.S. monetary policy and U.S. macroeconomic conditions, requiring modifications to the identification scheme (Grilli and Roubini 1996, Furman and Leahy 1996, Cushman and Zha 1997).

Another item on the research agenda is to empirically analyze the transmission of technology, fiscal, and consumption shocks in the presence of nominal rigidities. One reason this is important is that monetary shocks alone cannot adequately explain current account dynamics. A second is that the transmission mechanism is likely to be significantly different under sticky prices or wages than in the case of full flexibility (Basu et al. 1998, Gali 1998).

The delayed movement of the external account into surplus, plus the persistence of the effects of the monetary shock, are dimensions that are not easily explained within the framework of the simplest intertemporal sticky-price models. Allowing for staggered pricing or other mechanisms that generate slow adjustment would better match the theory to the data. For instance, a potentially fruitful avenue for future research is to extend aspects of the work that has been done on the balance sheet and bank lending channels of the monetary transmission mechanism to an open-economy environment (Bernanke and Gertler 1995), in order to build a more realistic account of the role played by monetary disturbances in macroeconomic fluctuations.

Finally, it is useful to recognize that the true role of monetary policy in current account determination is larger than is measured by my "money shocks" approach. Activist monetary policy that stabilizes output and prices in the face of productivity or absorption shocks is ignored within this framework. Accordingly, another potentially interesting route for future research is to examine whether there is a feedback channel from current account imbalances to monetary policy choices (see Clarida, Gali, and Gertler 1997).

Notes

Part of the work on this project was done during a visit to the IMF's Research Department. I thank Mick Devereux, Jordi Gali, Eswar Prasad, an anonymous referee, and participants in the 1997 Castor Workshop at the University of Washington, the Dublin Economics Workshop, the 1998 North American Winter Meetings of the Econometric Society (Chicago), and seminars at Berkeley, Stanford, and York for helpful suggestions. Eswar Prasad generously provided some RATS program code.

1. See Sachs 1982, Svensson and Razin 1983, Matsuyama 1987 and the survey by Obstfeld and Rogoff (1995a).

2. See Obstfeld and Rogoff 1995b, 1996; Svensson and van Wijnbergen 1989; Bergin 1995; Hau 1996; Betts and Devereux 1996, 1997; Kollman 1996; and Chari et al. 1997. Lane (1999) provides a survey.

3. Of course, nominal rigidities also affect the transmission of other types of disturbances, such as technology or fiscal shocks. It follows that incorporating nominal rigidities into theoretical models may be important even if monetary shocks are not a major source of economic fluctuations. See Basu et al. 1998 and Gali 1998.

4. See Sheffrin and Woo 1990, Otto 1992, Ghosh 1995, Glick and Rogoff 1995, and Elliott and Fatas 1996. Obstfeld and Rogoff (1995a) survey this literature.

5. Obstfeld (1995) has earlier pointed out the potential role for the VAR methodology in analyzing the response of the current account to macroeconomic shocks.

6. In what follows, I normalize the foreign currency price of the traded good to unity and consider a flexible exchange rate regime so that the domestic currency price of the traded good and the nominal exchange rate are coterminous: $P_T = E$, where E is the nominal exchange rate, defined as the number of domestic currency units per unit of foreign currency.

7. Of course, some traded producers may have international market power, as the pricing to market literature has emphasized.

8. See Obstfeld and Rogoff 1996, chap. 4 for a discussion of this result. Calvo and Vegh (1994) employ a similar framework in analyzing the effects of a permanent change in the

rate of money growth in the presence of backward indexation of wages. They describe the supply side of their model only by a partial adjustment price equation and do not deal with explicit labor supply decisions, imperfect competition, or welfare.

9. The normalization is that the endowment is such that $y_T = (\gamma/1 - \gamma) y_N$ in the steady state.

10. For instance, if $r = 0.05$, a 1 percent increase in short-run consumption of tradables implies a 0.05 percent decline in steady-state consumption of tradables in the new steady state.

11. Lane (1997) also uses this version of the model for analysis of monetary policy.

12. McCallum and Nelson (1997) advocate the use of models without capital for business cycle and monetary policy analysis.

13. Tesar (1993) estimates a value for θ of 0.44, which lies inside the range of values estimated for σ. Ostry and Reinhart (1992) jointly estimate the two elasticities for a set of thirteen developing countries and estimate θ to be significantly larger than σ, which would generate the current account surplus scenario. The rudimentary nature of direct estimation of these elasticity parameters provides another motivation for the more indirect econometric approach we follow below.

14. This result illustrates that there is no structural correlation between changes in the relative price of nontradables to tradables and the level of consumption of the nontraded good.

15. The weights are constructed using average GDP in international prices from the Penn World Tables v5.6. The weights are 0.34 (Japan); 0.18 (Germany); 0.15 (France); 0.14 (Italy); 0.12 (the United Kingdom); and 0.07 (Canada).

16. See Blanchard and Quah 1989, Clarida and Gali 1994, and Hamilton 1994 for proofs of this statement.

17. Admittedly, it is true that long-run output may be affected by even temporary absorption or nominal shocks via the operation of wealth effects on labor supply, but this effect is likely to be minor, and Blanchard and Quah (1989) show that "small" violations of an identification restriction are relatively unimportant.

18. Augmented Dickey-Fuller tests could not reject that each of the variables was nonstationary. A Johansen cointegration test did not indicate the presence of any cointegrating relationships among the variables. Accordingly, a first-difference specification is appropriate.

19. The standard errors are calculated by Monte Carlo simulations with 500 replications.

20. See Sims 1980. Eichenbaum and Evans 1995 followed this approach in identifying the effects of monetary shocks on exchange rates.

21. This is an extension of the system examined by Eichenbaum and Evans (1995) to include the trade balance. I study the trade balance rather than the current account in this case in order to employ data at a monthly frequency.

22. The behavior of the real exchange rate in our system is similar to that reported by Eichenbaum and Evans (1995).

References

Ahmed, S., and J. H. Park. 1994. Sources of macroeconomic fluctuations in small open economies. *Journal of Macroeconomics* 16(1):1–36.

Baxtes, Marianne. 1995. International trade and business Cycles. In eds. G. Grossman and K. Rogoff, 1801–1864. *Handbook of International Economics*, vol. 3. Amsterdam: North-Holland.

Basu, S., J. Fernald, and M. Kimball. 1998. Are Technology Improvements Contractionary? International Finance Discussion Paper no. 625, Board of Governors of the Federal Reserve System, Washington, D.C.

Bergin, P. 1995. Mundell-Fleming revisited: Monetary and fiscal policies in a two-country dynamic general equilibrium model with wage contracts. Unpublished manuscript, Yale University, New Haven, Conn.

Bernanke, B., and M. Gertler. 1995. Inside the black box: The credit channel of monetary policy transmission. *Journal of Economic Perspectives* 9:27–48.

Betts, C., and M. Devereux. 1997. The international monetary transmission mechanism: A model of real exchange rate adjustment under pricing to market. Unpublished manuscript, University of British Columbia, Vancouver. Mimeographed.

Betts, C., and M. Devereux. 1996. Exchange rate dynamics in a model of pricing to market. Unpublished manuscript, University of British Columbia, Vancouver Mimeographed.

Blanchard, O., and D. Quah. 1989. The dynamic effects of aggregate demand and supply disturbances. *American Economic Review* 79:655–73.

Calvo, G., and C. Vegh. 1994. Stabilization dynamics and backward-looking contracts. *Journal of Development Economics* 43:59–84.

Chari, V. V., P. Kehoe, and E. McGrattan. 1997. Monetary shocks and real exchange rates in sticky price models of international business cycles. Working paper no. 5876, National Bureau of Economic Research, Cambridge, Mass.

Clarida, R., and J. Gali. 1994. Sources of real exchange rate fluctuations: How important are nominal shocks? *Carnegie-Rochester Conference Series on Public Policy* 41:1–56.

Clarida, R., J. Gali, and M. Gertler. 1997. Monetary policy rules in practice: Some international evidence. Working paper, Columbia University and New York University, New York.

Cushman, D., and T. Zha. 1997. Identifying monetary policy in a small open economy under flexible exchange rates. *Journal of Monetary Economics* 39:433–48.

Dornbusch, R. 1983. Real interest rates, home goods and optimal external borrowing. *Journal of Political Economy* 91:141–53.

Eichenbaum, M., and C. Evans. 1995. Some empirical evidence on the effects of shocks to monetary policy on exchange rates. *Quarterly Journal of Economics* 110:975–1010.

Elliott, G., and A. Fatas. 1996. International business cycles and the dynamics of the current account. *European Economic Review* 40:361–87.

Furman, J., and J. Leahy. 1996. The international transmission of monetary policy: Evidence from the United States and Canada. Harvard Discussion paper no. 1764, Harvard Institute of Economic Research, Cambridge, Mass.

Gagnon, J. 1996. Net foreign assets and equilibrium exchange rates: Panel evidence. Unpublished manuscript, International Finance Division, Board of Governors of the Federal Reserve System, Washington, D.C.

Gali, J. 1999. Technology, employment, and the business cycle: Do technology shocks explain aggregate fluctuations? *American Economic Review*, 89(1):249–71.

Ghosh, A. 1995. Capital mobility amongst the major industrialized countries: Too little or too much? *Economic Journal* 105:107–28.

Glick, R., and K. Rogoff. 1995. Global versus country-specific productivity shocks and the current account. *Journal of Monetary Economics* 35:159–92.

Grilli, V., and N. Roubini. 1996. Liquidity models in open economies: Theory and empirical evidence. *European Economic Review* 40:847–59.

Hamilton, J. 1994. *Time series analysis*. Princeton: Princeton University Press.

Hau, H. 1996. Exchange rate determination: The role of factor price rigidities and market segmentation. Unpublished manuscript, École Supérieure des Sciences Economiques et Commerciales, Paris. Mimeographed.

Kollman, R. 1996. The exchange rate in a dynamic optimizing current account model with nominal rigidities: A quantitative analysis. Unpublished manuscript, University of Montreal. Mimeographed.

Kumar, M., and E. Prasad. 1997. International trade and the business cycle. Unpublished manuscript, International Monetary Fund, Washington, D.C. Mimeographed.

Lane, P. R. 1999. The new open-economy macroeconomics: A survey. Unpublished manuscript, Trinity College, Dublin. Mimeographed.

Lane, P. R. 1997. Inflation in open economies. *Journal of International Economics* 42:327–47.

Lee, J., and M. Chinn. 1998. The current account and the real exchange rate: A structural VAR analysis of major currencies. Working paper no. 6495, National Bureau of Economic Research, Cambridge, Mass.

Matsuyama, Kiminori. 1987. Current account dynamics in a finite horizon model. *Journal of International Economics* 23:299–313.

McCallum, B., and E. Nelson. 1997. An optimizing IS-LM specification for monetary policy and business cycle analysis. Working paper no. 5875, National Bureau of Economic Research, Cambridge, Mass.

Mundell, R. 1963. Capital mobility and stabilization policy under fixed and flexible exchange rates. *Canadian Journal of Economics and Political Science* 29:475–85.

Obstfeld, M. 1995. International currency experience: New lessons and lessons relearned. *Brookings Papers on Economic Activity* 1:119–220.

Obstfeld, M., and K. Rogoff. 1996. *Foundations of international macroeconomics*. Cambridge: MIT Press.

Obstfeld, M., and K. Rogoff. 1995a. The intertemporal approach to the current account. In *Handbook of International Economics*, ed. G. Grossman and K. Rogoff, 1731–99. vol. 3. Amsterdam: North-Holland.

Obstfeld, M., and K. Rogoff. 1995b. Exchange rate dynamics redux. *Journal of Political Economy* 103:624–60.

Ostry, J., and C. Reinhart. 1992. Private saving and terms of trade shocks: Evidence from developing countries. *IMF Staff Papers* 39:495–517.

Otto, G. 1992. Testing a present-value model of the current account: Evidence from U.S. and Canadian time series. *Journal of International Money and Finance* 11:414–30.

Sachs, J. 1982. The current account in the macroeconomic adjustment process. *Scandinavian Journal of Economics* 84:147–59.

Sheffrin, S., and W. T. Woo. 1990. Present value tests of an intertemporal model of the current account. *Journal of International Economics* 29:237–53.

Sims, C. 1980. Macroeconomics and reality. *Econometrica* 48:1–48.

Svensson, L., and A. Razin. 1983. The terms of trade and the current account: The Harberger-Laursen-Metzler effect. *Journal of Political Economy* 91:97–125.

Svensson, L., and S. van Wijnbergen. 1989. Excess capacity, monopolistic competition, and international transmission of monetary disturbances. *Economic Journal* 99:785–805.

Tesar, L. 1993. International risk-sharing and non-traded goods. *Journal of International Economics* 35:69–89.

12

Euroland and East Asia in a Dollar-Based International Monetary System: Mundell Revisited

Ronald I. McKinnon

Robert Mundell's longstanding enthusiasm for European monetary unification was vindicated by the formal advent of the euro on January 1, 1999. For almost thirty years, he has seen clearly the advantages of a common European currency would swamp any disadvantages.

But therein lies a paradox. The fierce scholarly debate for more than a decade before EMU's advent on whether a one-size-fits-all monetary policy was appropriate for Europe pitted politicians, who on the continent were mainly in favor, against economists, who generally were much more doubtful. And the doubters who opposed EMU used arguments drawn from Mundell's own work! Specifically, his classic article, "A Theory of Optimum Currency Areas" (1961) comes down against a one-size-fits-all monetary policy—and seems to argue in favor of making currency areas smaller rather than larger.

In this chapter, I will first present some doctrinal history to resolve the paradox and better explain Mundell's position today. Second, I will look at how the new euro and the dollar can best coexist, given the latter's traditional role as international money. Third, in the absence of an "Asian euro," I will argue for a common monetary standard in East Asia based on the dollar.

Some Doctrinal History

At the conference on Optimum Currency Areas held in Madrid on March 16–19, 1970, Robert Mundell presented two prescient papers on the advantages of common currencies. Perhaps in part because the conference proceedings themselves were not published until several years later, in 1973, these papers were overshadowed by his earlier technical masterpieces on optimum currency areas, the redundancy problem, the assignment problem, the Mundell-Fleming model, the international disequilibrium system, and so on (Mundell 1968)—all of which assumed more or less stationary expectations.

The first of these little-known Madrid papers, "Uncommon Arguments for Common Currencies," is of great intrinsic interest because very early it emphasized the forward-looking nature of the foreign exchange market. As such, it counters today's received academic wisdom that asymmetric shocks—that is those where an unexpected disturbance to national output affects one country differently from another—undermine the case for a common monetary standard. Instead, Mundell showed how having a common currency across countries can mitigate such shocks. Under a common currency, a series of asymmetric shocks can be better smoothed because of reserve pooling and more efficient forward contracting.

Otherwise, if the exchange rate between the two countries were left flexible, currency risk would inhibit proper risk pooling in the international capital market in the present because agents would worry that unpredictable shocks could move the exchange rate in the future. A country devaluing in the face of an adverse shock finds that its domestic-currency assets buy less on world markets. The cost of the shock is now more bottled up in the country where the shock originated. As Mundell in 1970 put it,

A harvest failure, strikes, or war, in one of the countries causes a loss of real income, but the use of a common currency (or foreign exchange reserves) allows the country to run down its currency holdings and cushion the impact of the loss, drawing on the resources of the other country until the cost of the adjustment has been efficiency spread over the future. If, on the other hand, the two countries use separate monies with flexible exchange rates, the whole loss has to be borne alone; the common currency cannot serve as a shock absorber for the nation as a whole except insofar as the dumping of inconvertible currencies on foreign markets attracts a speculative capital inflow in favor of the depreciating currency. (Mundell 1973a, 115)

But this view of the advantages of international risk sharing through better portfolio diversification under a common currency is very different from the thrust of what Mundell had written earlier. Mundell's most famous article, "The Theory of Optimum Currency Areas," was published in 1961 in *The American Economic Review*, about nine years before "Uncommon Arguments," with its forward-looking analytical outlook, was written. Because at that time Mundell still assumed stationary expectations in the postwar Keynesian mode, he looked more favorably on flexible exchange rates to give regional governments autonomy to fine-tune their monetary and fiscal policies should macro-economic shocks hit them asymmetrically when factors of production were not mobile across regional boundaries. And "Optimum Currency Areas" became enormously influential as the analytical basis for much of open-economy macroeconomics in the 1990s, and for scholarly skepticism as to whether Western Europe really was an optimum currency area.

The outstanding scholarly skeptic, Barry Eichengreen—whose many articles (with several coauthors) were consolidated in his book *European Monetary Unification* (1997)—acknowledged Mundell's influence thus:

> The theory of optimum currency areas, initiated by Robert Mundell (1961), is the organizing framework for the analysis. In Mundell's paradigm, policy-makers balance the saving in transactions costs from the creation of a single money against the consequences of diminished policy autonomy. The diminution of autonomy follows from the loss of the exchange rate and of an independent monetary policy as instruments of adjustment. That loss will be more costly when macroeconomic shocks are more "asymmetric" (for present purposes, more region- or country-specific), when monetary policy is a more powerful instrument for offsetting them, and when other adjustment mechanisms like relative wages and labor mobility are less effective. (Eichengreen 1997, 1–2)

But this poses a paradox. How can the analysis of eminent scholars like Eichengreen—who, based on a Mundellian analytical framework, have been skeptical of a common European currency—be reconciled with Mundell's own almost three decades of unalloyed enthusiasm for European monetary unification?

One answer is that there are two Mundell models. The first is the static, but highly persuasive, 1961 model of Optimum Currency Areas—which was published in a prestigious journal and became the bread and butter of textbooks on open-economy macroeconomics. The second is contained in his forward-looking Madrid papers of 1970, which were buried in an obscure conference volume that took three years to get published. But his overriding concern that leaving exchange rates free to fluctuate would impart great volatility to, and hopelessly undermine the efficiency of, the intra-European capital market did not become evident until the Madrid conference. Indeed, it took another decade before two of Mundell's students, Jacob Frenkel and Michael Mussa (1980), succeeded in projecting the forward-looking asset market approach to the exchange rate into the academic domain.

Mundell's second Madrid paper, "A Plan for a European Currency," makes clear his enthusiastic promotion of a common currency for Europe. Until 1970, European countries had achieved a degree of mutual exchange rate stability by all pegging to the same outside currency: the U.S. dollar. But the commitment to firm dollar parities was eroding—in large measure because the monetary anchor provided by the center country was beginning to slip. So Mundell stated:

The only way to establish a unified money market is to kill the sporadic and unsettling speculation over currency prices that ravaged the European markets between 1967 and 1969, and permitted discounts and premia to develop on currency futures. The exchange rate should be taken out of both national and international politics within Europe.

Rather than moving toward more flexibility in exchange rates within Europe the economic arguments suggest less flexibility and a closer integration of capital markets. These economic arguments are supported by social arguments as well. On every occasion when a social disturbance leads to the threat of a strike, and the strike to an increase in wages unjustified by increases in productivity and thence to devaluation, the national currency becomes threatened. Long-run costs for the nation as a whole are bartered away by governments for what they presume to be short-run political benefits. If instead, the European currencies were bound together disturbances in the country would be cushioned, with the shock weakened by capital movements. (Mundell 1973b, 147, 150)

Interestingly, in 1970, Mundell's plan for weaning Europe away from dollar dependence began by selecting one European country's currency to provide a new numéraire to which the others, by mutual agreement, would fix their exchange rates. But all European countries party to the new exchange rate agreement would send representatives to sit on the numéraire country's monetary board. Although any sizable European country's currency would do in Mundell's view, he suggested that the pound sterling was the best choice for numéraire because "Britain is the largest financial power and the pound is still a world currency (p. 158)." Clearly, he wanted Britain to be in on European monetary unification right from the start!

We now know that the relatively more stable German monetary policy, with the deutsche mark (DM) as the numéraire currency, became the focal point to rebuild first exchange rate stability and then monetary unity in Europe—while Britain continues to dither. And over 30 years, there were many slips twixt cup and lip before the formal advent of the euro on January 1, 1999. The forward-looking Mundell of the Madrid papers "triumphed" over his earlier Keynesian incarnation as the originator of the theory of optimum currency areas.

Updating Mundell

From the intellectual vantage point so nicely provided by Mundell's Madrid papers, what can we say about proper exchange rate policies in the new millenium among what have now become the three major industrialized blocs: the United State, Europe, and East Asia?

The traditional role of the U.S. dollar as the world's central currency—as the invoice currency for world commodity trade, as the dominant vehicle currency in the world's spot and forward foreign exchange markets, and as the official exchange reserve asset of choice—remains, and will remain, much as it was in 1970. But America's benign neglect of fluctuations in the dollar/euro exchange rate needs to be differentiated from a more purposeful policy toward East Asia—where much greater exchange rate stability is required.

Because the euro now establishes a large zone of monetary stability in continental western Europe and its periphery, the best near-term strategy is a hands-off, laissez-faire policy over a wide range of values for the dollar/euro exchange rate. The dollar is no longer needed as the common monetary anchor as it was in the 1960s. Indeed, the euro's fall from $1.18 in January 1999 to about $0.97 in March 2000 is not out of line with similar fluctuations in the "synthetic euro"—weighted by the importance of its constituent currencies—from 1980 through 1998 as shown in figure 12.1. (In the longer run, more active cooperation by the U.S. Federal Reserve and the European Central Bank to narrow the range of fluctuations in the dollar/euro exchange rate may well become appropriate—with a more precisely defined set of rules for doing so (McKinnon 1996).) In the euro's shakedown phase, however, the two central banks need intervene only if obvious panic develops, as for example, if the euro started plunging instead of just drifting down.

However, economic recovery in East Asia requires different and stronger medicine. Because no region-wide "Asian euro" exists or is in prospect, the dollar is the only plausible anchor for creating an East Asian zone of monetary stability in price levels and exchange rates. In order to prevent competitive devaluations and inflationary upheavals in the future, this zone would cover both the smaller East Asian countries that fell victim to the great 1997 currency crisis and China, which did not.

The advantage to Japan of being part of the dollar zone is somewhat different. Prolonged stability in the yen/dollar exchange rate is the key to quashing the *deflationary* expectations that have gripped the Japanese economy for almost a decade. But let us consider Euroland first.

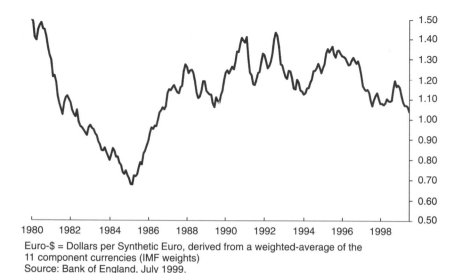

Euro-$ = Dollars per Synthetic Euro, derived from a weighted-average of the
11 component currencies (IMF weights)
Source: Bank of England, July 1999.

Figure 12.1
Euro–$ (January 1980–July 1999)

The Dollar versus the Euro

In judging the euro's impact on the dollar, consider two competing economic interpretations of the euro's potential future role in the world
economy.

The first focuses on economic integration in goods and factor
markets within Europe and with surrounding countries: an extended
optimum currency area. Because of the European Union's huge economic size and far-reaching trade connections, this interpretation suggests a wider influence for the euro well beyond the current political
boarders of the European Union.

The EU countries will constitute an economic mass nearly as large
as that of the United States itself, and European exports to the rest
of the world (net of what are currently counted as intra-European
exports) will be similar in magnitude to American exports. Many
eastern European countries will opt to peg to the euro because they are
so open to EU trade—as are many former European colonies in Africa.
For both types of countries, the new euro could well dominate as an
intervention and reserve currency.

The second interpretation focuses on the need for international
money *beyond* that associated with unusually close trade linkages. The

world economy itself needs a unit of account, means of payment, and store of value for both governments and private firms. In the absence of a generally accepted metallic money such as gold or even a dominant country like the United States, one of the national currencies would still be selected by habit or custom. Once selected, however, this national currency's role as international money becomes a natural monopoly. That is, the scope for more than one national currency to serve in a dual role as international and domestic money is limited.

In the aftermath of World War II, the United States provided the essential funding for the International Monetary Fund, the Marshall Plan, and the Dodge Plan, which jointly restored exchange and price-level stability among the industrial countries while replenishing official exchange reserves (McKinnon 1996). The world's only capital market without exchange controls was the American. Thus, the U.S. dollar became the dominant international vehicle currency for private transacting, and the reserve currency for official interventions.

Even when the American money manager, the Federal Reserve System, was doing quite badly—as from the inflationary 1970s into the early 1980s—the dollar-based system proved surprisingly resilient. Although many other countries had by then opened their financial markets, the dollar was not significantly displaced as international money. Now that American monetary policy has been quite stable for more a decade, could the momentous advent of the euro—with an open European capital market—displace the dollar?

The Role of an International Vehicle Currency

Consider first a world of N national currencies without official interventions or foreign exchange targeting by governments. In organizing private interbank markets for foreign exchange, great savings in transactions costs can be had if just one national currency, the Nth, is chosen as the vehicle currency. Then all foreign exchange quotations—bids and offers—at all terms to maturity can take place against this one vehicle currency. The number of active markets can be reduced from $N(N - 1)/2$ to just $N - 1$. In a world of more than 150 national currencies, this is a tremendous economy of markets for the large commercial banks that make the foreign exchange market. The dollar's interbank predominance (being on one side of almost 90 percent of interbank transactions) allows banks to cover both their forward exchange and options exposures much more efficiently.

Trade in primary commodities shows a similar pattern of using one national money as the main currency of invoice. Exports of homogeneous primary products such as oil, wheat, copper, and so on, all tend to be invoiced in dollars with worldwide price formation in a centralized exchange. Spot trading, but particularly forward contracting, is concentrated at these centralized exchanges—which are usually in American cities such as Chicago and New York, although dollar-denominated commodity exchanges do exist in London and elsewhere. In periods of reasonable confidence in American monetary policy, these *dollar* commodity prices are relatively invariant to fluctuations in the dollar's exchange rate. In contrast, if any other country allows its exchange rate to fluctuate against the dollar, its domestic currency prices of primary commodities will vary in proportion—unless its trade is restricted.

Invoicing patterns for exports of manufactured goods are more complex. Major industrial countries with strong currencies tend to invoice their exports in their home currencies. More than 75 percent of German exports were invoiced in marks, more than 50 percent of French exports were invoiced in francs, and so on. With the advent of EMU, continental European countries will begin invoicing their net exports outside the European Union mainly in euros.

However, Japan only invoices about 36 percent of its exports in its own currency—which is low by the standards of other large industrial countries, in part because the United States is its main export market. On the import side, about 70 percent of goods coming into Japan are invoiced in dollars, in part because Japan is such a heavy importer of primary products and manufactures from the United States. Thus, Japan suffers high variation in domestic yen prices, i.e., "pass-through" is high, when the yen/dollar exchange rate fluctuates.

At the other extreme, the U.S. price level is fairly immune to fluctuations in the dollar's exchange rate against other currencies because *both* its exports and imports are largely invoiced in dollars: 98 percent of American exports of primary products and manufactures are dollar invoiced, and an amazing 88 percent or so of American imports are as well. (For example, almost all of Japan's exports to the United States are dollar invoiced.) In addition, for trade not directly involving the United States, the dollar is heavily used as an invoice currency for manufactured (and of course primary) exports from developing and transitional economies—in Asia, Latin America, and elsewhere.

Here then lies an important distinction between Euroland and East Asia. Euroland is naturally more insular in a monetary sense. It is a large integrated economy that uses its own currency for invoicing much of its foreign trade. Fluctuations in the euro/dollar exchange rate have little impact on Europe-wide price indexes, and thus, over moderate ranges, they can be more or less ignored. In contrast, the price levels of all the East Asian countries—including Japan's—are much more affected by fluctuations in their separate exchange rates against the region's dominant trading currency, the U.S. dollar.

Once private interbank foreign exchange and commodity markets are set up with the dollar as the vehicle and invoice currency, official interventions follow the same pattern. Governments pursue their exchange rate objectives more conveniently by intervening only in dollars (at different terms to maturity) against their domestic monies. Using only one currency for intervention prevents inconsistency in the setting of cross rates with other foreign monies.

This pattern of official intervention determines the pattern of official holdings of foreign exchange. Apart from gold, about 70 percent of official reserves held outside Europe are dollar denominated. True, the desire for safety through portfolio diversification is important. But this cuts against the convenience of holding reserves in the intervention currency, with its relative stability in real purchasing power measured against internationally traded goods. Thus governments outside Europe have preferred to hold dollars—mainly U.S. treasury bonds. Certainly, most of these governments will want to hold euros to replace their DM, franc, and sterling assets as these national European currencies eventually disappear. But it seems unlikely that any *official* demand to hold euro assets will be much greater than the former demand for reserve holdings in Europe's legacy currencies.

There is the further problem of what the benchmark euro asset will be. The EU central government itself does not have significant debt outstanding like the huge stock of U.S. treasuries. In Europe, government debt is lodged with the old national, now middle-level, governments who no longer control their own central banks. Now, default risk is not insignificant. In comparison to U.S. treasuries, a position in euro-denominated bonds will involve some (possibly minor) default risk which differs by country. Although both U.S. treasuries and European government bonds now denominated in euros will be subject to (differing) currency risk—i.e., concern for inflation and devaluation—

the European bonds will probably remain marginally less attractive to foreign governments as official reserve assets.

But in Euroland private euro-denominated bond issues are now growing explosively. For the first half of 1999, table 12.1 shows overall euro bond issues growing by 80 percent compared with bond issues in the old legacy currencies during the first six months of 1998. Most strikingly, issues of euro-denominated *corporate* bonds are running at a rate almost four times as high in 1999 compared to 1998. Why the startling difference?

Table 12.1
European bond issues: 1999 versus 1998

Volume of euro-denominated international bonds, by issuer type, January 1 through June 30, 1999

	Total		
	Amount in millions (U.S.$)	Percent	Issues
Banks/finance	240,209.117	66.15	597
Corporate	79,012.498	21.76	166
Utilities	16,771.171	4.62	33
Sovereign	16,130.135	4.44	38
Supranational	7,012.887	1.93	31
Others	4,005.959	1.10	30
Local authority	4,005.959	1.10	30
Total	363,141.767	100.00	895

Volume of international bonds issued in legacy currencies (including ecu and euro), by issuer type, January 1 through June 30, 1998

	Total		
	Amount in millions (U.S.$)	Percent	Issues
Banks/finance	131,561.740	65.85	548
Sovereign	28,462.517	14.25	49
Corporate	20,263.587	10.14	97
Supranational	11,595.437	5.80	56
Utilities	6,889.331	3.45	16
Others	1,023.143	0.51	6
Local authority	1,023.143	0.51	6
Total	199,779.755	100.00	772

Source: Capital Data, Aldwych House, London.

In the pre-euro regime when the DM was king, corporations in European countries on the German periphery—such as Italy, Portugal, and Spain—suffered currency risk relative to German issuers of mark-denominated bonds because of the existence of the lire, escudo, and peseta. The resulting risk premia, that is, higher interest rates particularly at longer term, kept finance short term and largely bank based. In 1999, the extinction of these risky currencies has allowed previously hobbled Italian, Portuguese, and Spanish (and even French?) firms to lengthen the term structure of their debts by issuing euro-denominated bonds at lower interest rates while escaping from the clutches of their bankers. European banks, in turn, are madly consolidating—although unfortunately only at the national level. Thus is the term structure of corporate finance in Europe being lengthened and made more secure. Because the elimination of currency risk makes intra European Portfolio diversification more attractive, this great improvement in the European capital market is precisely what the forward-looking Mundell of the Madrid papers (1973a,b) had in mind.

Nevertheless, on the broader global stage, the dollar's continued vehicle-currency role is unlikely to be displaced by the extended currency-area role for the new euro. However, the euro is now the world's most important regional currency, and it is making possible the lengthening of the term structure of finance within Europe—particularly in those countries which had been "peripheral." Even if the dollar's role as an international vehicle currency is largely unaltered by the euro's advent, eliminating currency risk within the greater European economy is a remarkable benefit—as Mundell correctly foresaw.

Currency Crises and the Nascent EMU

Although the explosive growth in private eurobond issues is recent, *preparation* for EMU had already insulated the western European economy from the currency crises that swept through much of the rest of the world in the two years before the euro's official birth on January 1, 1999. After the attack on the Thai baht in July 1997, the contagious flight into dollars spread to Indonesia, Korea, and Malaysia into 1998. Similar, if less acute, foreign exchange pressure on most Latin American economies developed in 1998, most notably or Brazil, which required a multibillion dollar assistance program finalized in November 1998. And then, of course, there was the spectacular Russian collapse and outright default on August 17, 1998. But throughout all of this turmoil, no western European country, i.e., an actual or putative member of EMU, experienced a currency attack.

Western Europe's not-so-distant past is a different story. In the currency crises of 1992–1993, the great flight into German marks is still fresh in people's minds. Britain, Italy, Spain, and Sweden all had to devalue, and other members of the old European monetary system (EMS) were attacked to lesser degrees. Before 1987, precarious exchange rate stability in Europe was only sustained with the aid of capital controls in the balance of payments. However, by 1997–1998 with capital controls removed, western Europe had become much less vulnerable. Why?

By 1997, remarkable economic convergence—of inflation rates toward zero, of exchange rates toward purchasing power parity, and then of interest rates to within a half a percentage point of Germany's—had occurred. This convergence, together with the fiscal constraints imposed by the Masstricht agreement, and then the Growth and Stability pact, led markets to expect that future exchange rates among various European currencies would be close to what they were in 1997 and 1998. (This of course is also the key to the emergence of a long-term, Europe-wide bond market.) Because macroeconomic convergence had created a common monetary standard *before* EMU, speculators saw little point in attacking the regime of fixed exchange rates leading up to EMU.

After the currency attacks of 1997–1998, East Asia now faces a monetary rebuilding problem similar to what the western Europeans faced after the attacks of 1970–1971 and again of 1992–1993—together with the further problem of recapitalizing and properly regulating banks and other financial institutions. Although introducing a common currency into East Asia in the European mode is politically out of the question, a common monetary standard that anchors the common price level and secures exchange rates among national monies could again coalesce.

The East Asian Dollar Standard

With the important exception of Japan, a common East Asian monetary standard existed before the crises of 1997. By keying on the dollar, Indonesia, Korea, Malaysia, Philippines, and Thailand tied their macroeconomic policies to each other—and to those of the noncrisis economies of Hong Kong, Singapore, and Taiwan. Their dollar exchange rates had been fairly stable for more than a decade and, by the purchasing power parity criterion, were more or less correctly aligned with each other and with the American (McKinnon 2000). Besides insulating each country from beggar-thy-neighbor devaluations, these informal dollar pegs had successfully anchored their domestic (wholesale) price levels during their rapid economic growth from the 1980s through 1996. (Similarly, a credible peg of 360 yen to the dollar was the monetary anchor in Japan's own great high-growth era of the 1950s and 1960s.) However, before the 1997 crises, the East Asian dollar standard had two major problems.

First, in the five crisis economies, banks and other financial institutions were poorly regulated but nevertheless insured against bankruptcy by their national governments. Moral hazard was responsible for the excessive buildup of short-term foreign currency indebtedness throughout the region, and was exacerbated by the absence of capital controls in the balance of payments. (In the case of Korea, controls had been removed three years before as a condition for joining the OECD!) If prudential regulations requiring banks and corporations to cover their foreign currency and term-structure risks are ineffective, then capital controls can break the buildup of short-term indebtedness in foreign currencies. Indeed, it had been textbook wisdom that, in the optimum order of economic liberalization, capital controls should be removed only after macroeconomic and regulatory control had been secured (McKinnon 1993).

Second, the yen/dollar exchange rate was a "loose cannon." Before the 1997 crisis, cyclical variations in the real yen/dollar rate continually upset the competitive positions of the dollar-bloc countries and destablized inflows of direct investment from Japan. For example, the yen came down from its high of 80 to the dollar in April 1995 to 114 to the dollar in June 1997. The East Asian Five's bilateral real exchange rates against the dollar, and against each other, had been quite stable. But when the yen fell, their *effective* real exchange rates appreciated just before the currency attacks began in July 1997. This loss of competitiveness was compounded by Japanese corporations' reducing direct investment in, and outsourcing from, the East Asian Five. Thus, before the crash, East Asian economic growth had already slowed.

But the untethered yen/dollar exchange rate had a further, more subtle, impact on the smaller Asian economies. Since 1971, the long-term upward drift in the nominal dollar value of the yen eventually became built into market expectations—which exist to the present day. This expectation of an ever higher yen drove (and still drives in the new millenium) nominal interest rates on yen assets far below those prevailing in other industrial countries and other parts of Asia. This unnatural interest rate disparity aggravates hot money flows in the region.

In the Asian Five debtor economies before the 1997 crises, low interest rates in Japan tempted banks with moral hazard to overborrow by accepting cheap yen deposits without covering the foreign exchange risk. In Japan, banks and other financial institutions were tempted to overlend by purchasing foreign currency assets with higher nominal yields. American and European hedge funds got involved in the so-called Japan carry trade: they borrowed cheaply in Tokyo or Osaka at short-term to lend almost anywhere else—Russia, Brazil, and to the East Asian debtor economies without capital controls. (China prudently prevented overborrowing by keeping capital controls in place.)

Japan's Problem

But the economy hurt worst of all by not being securely tethered to the East Asian dollar standard was, and still is, Japan itself. The breakdown of the Bretton Woods system of fixed exchange rate parities in 1971 left Japan vulnerable to American mercantile pressure to allow, or encourage, yen appreciation (McKinnon and Ohno 1997).

The resulting anticipation of an ever-higher yen against the dollar is coupled with the expectation of domestic (WPI) deflation. This expectation depresses the Japanese economy. Potential homeowners are reluctant to buy because they feel that property values will continue to slide. Similarly, Japanese businesses are reluctant to invest in plant and equipment today because the yen might jump once more, and again make their products uncompetitive in world markets. Caught by this exchange rate-imposed, low-interest-rate trap, the Bank of Japan cannot combat this slump in aggregate demand by easing monetary policy. Nominal interest rates cannot be reduced below zero (people would simply hold cash balances rather than bonds with a negative yield), even though real interest rates in Japan remain high because of anticipated deflation. Nor can the exchange rate be effectively depreciated much below its currency PPP rate—about 120 yen to the dollar in 1999. (McKinnon 1999, McKinnon and Ohno forthcoming)

In 1999 into 2000, as the Bank of Japan tried to hold the rate below 107 yen per dollar, the fear of a higher yen returned. Despite short-term interest rates on yen assets being effectively zero and long rates 4 percentage points less than those on dollar bonds, upward pressure on the yen from March 1999 to March 2000 caused Japan's exchange reserves to jump by over 70 billion dollars. The market seemed to be projecting a return of American pressure for the yen to appreciate.

To quash this expectation of an ever higher yen, the Japanese and American governments need to go to the root of the problem. To spring the low-interest-rate trap and revive aggregate demand in Japan, today's expectation that dollar value of the yen will be higher ten, twenty, or thirty years from now must end. But to be credible, *both* the American and Japanese governments must agree on a benchmark forward parity for the yen/dollar exchange rate—at say, 120 yen to the dollar. The precise number is less important than the existence of an unchanging benchmark around which long-term exchange rate expectations can coalesce (McKinnon and Ohno 1997). Then Japanese nominal interest rates can rise to more normal world levels. The so-called Asian carry trade will end, and "hot" money flows in the region should diminish correspondingly.

A Common Monetary Standard for East Asia in the Twenty-first Century?

Clearly, if Japan and the United States succeed in stabilizing the yen/dollar rate and so ending ongoing deflation in Japan, the smaller east Asian economies will quickly come around to restoring their own, formal or informal, dollar parities. China could be the model. The renminbi has been successfully pegged at about 8.3 yuan to the dollar for almost five years. But to hold this rate, China needs the recovery of the other East Asian economies, and needs the assurance that other competitor economies—such as Korea, Thailand, or Taiwan—will not gain allow their currencies to depreciate and undermine China's competitiveness.

With proper bank regulation or capital controls in place, a restored dollar-based exchange rate regime in which Japan participates would better protect the smaller East Asian economies from exchange rate shocks and from borrowing too much at short-term because interest rates will be better aligned. But the collective advantages are mutual. By being formally part of such an arrangement, Japan could be better protected politically against future American demands to appreciate the yen—and such protection is necessary for Japan's economy to recover from its deflationary slump of the 1990s.

However, even if a common East Asian monetary standard was successfully reestablished by mutual fixes on the dollar, Robert Mundell would worry about dollar hegemony in the event that the U.S. economy becomes unstable. The Europeans are now significantly insulated from this uncomfortable possibility—as he wanted them to be. But the East Asians have little choice but to go along with a dollar-based system in the foreseeable future. The political conditions for establishing an independent East Asian "euro" are stringent and less likely to be realized than what Mundell in 1970 projected for Europe.

The case for a European money is . . . tied up with the case for integration. Since the case for integration rests on social, political, military, cultural and intellectual grounds our arguments for a European money based on economic grounds alone is as if we had just examined the tip of the iceberg and left untouched the seven-eighths of the true case lying underneath. (Mundell 1973b, 167)

Note

The author is William D. Eberle Professor of International Economics, Stanford University, Stanford, California 94305; tel. 650 723-3721, e-mail: mckinnon@leland.stanford.edu. This chapter was completed while the author was a Houblon-Norman fellow at the Bank of England.

References

Eichengreen, B. 1997. *European monetary unification: Theory, practice, and analysis.* Cambridge: MIT Press.

Frenkel, J., and M. Mussa. 1980. The efficiency of the foreign exchange market and measures of turbulence. *American Economic Review* 70(2):374–81.

McKinnon, R. I. 2000. The East Asian dollar standard: Life after death? Paper presented at World Bank conference on Rethinking the East Asian Miracle, Washington, D.C, published in *Economic Notes* 29(1):31–82.

McKinnon, R. I. 1999. Wading in the yen trap. *The Economist* (July 24):83–86.

McKinnon, R. I. 1996. *The rules of the game: International money and exchange rates.* Cambridge: MIT Press.

McKinnon, R. I. 1993. *The order of economic liberalization: Financial control in the transition to a market economy.* 2nd ed. Baltimore: Johns Hopkins University Press.

McKinnon, R. I., and K. Ohno. Forthcoming. The foreign exchange origins of Japan's economic slump and low-interest liquidity trap. *World Economy.*

McKinnon, R. I., and K. Ohno. 1997. *Dollar and yen: Resolving economic conflict between the United States and Japan*. Cambridge: MIT Press. Japanese translation, Nihon Keizai, 1998.

Mundell, R. 1973a. Uncommon arguments for common currencies. In *The economics of common currencies*, ed. H. G. Johnson and A. K. Swoboda, 114–32. London: Allen and Unwin.

Mundell, R. 1973b. A plan for a European currency. In *The economics of common currencies*, ed. H. G. Johnson and A. K. Swoboda, 143–72. London: Allen and Unwin.

Mundell, R. 1968. *International economics*. New York: Macmillan.

Mundell, R. 1961. A Theory of Optimum Currency Areas. *American Economic Review* 51 (November): 509–17.

13

The Business Cycles of Balance-of-Payments Crises: A Revision of a Mundellian Framework

Enrique G. Mendoza and
Martín Uribe

The confidence that once prevailed in the permanence of the existing exchange parity no longer exists. . . . Fear of inconvertibility or devaluation often swamps the effects of small differences in rates of interest between money markets, and encourages capital outflows. But confidence is generally linked to the level of exchange reserves. Other things the same, confidence is higher the larger the central bank holdings of foreign exchange.

—Robert A. Mundell, "The Monetary Dynamics of International Adjustment under Fixed and Flexible Exchange Rates"

Introduction

In a path-breaking paper that originated in his doctoral dissertation, "The Monetary Dynamics of International Adjustment under Fixed and Flexible Exchange Rates" (1960), Robert A. Mundell proposed an innovative framework that was the first to attempt an explicit treatment of macroeconomic dynamics under fixed and flexible exchange rates. Using the tools from Samuelson's *Foundations of Economic Analysis*, Mundell established a result that is now a classic principle: a fixed exchange rate may dominate a flexible exchange rate, in the sense of exhibiting better stabilizing properties in the face of exogenous shocks, if there is a high degree of international capital mobility. The apparatus he developed to derive this result was the backbone of the Mundell-Fleming model, which remained the dominant paradigm in international macroeconomics for the next twenty-five years.[1]

We argue in this chapter that, in the light of the globalized economy we live in today, Mundell's article contains another pioneering contribution: the first formal dynamic analysis of balance-of-payments crises. His analysis included some of the key ingredients of the classic models of balance-of-payments crises developed much later by Krugman (1979) and Obstfeld (1986). He explicitly asked the same question that models of this kind continue to raise today: "to what extent can off-setting central bank action stabilize a system which is inherently unstable because of speculative capital movements?" (Mundell 1960, 228). Mundell examined this question in the context of a fixed-exchange-rate economy where the investors' confidence in the currency is positively related to the central bank's holdings of foreign reserves, and he studied how this affected the equilibrium determination of the interest rate and the price level. His key finding was that the dynamics of adjustment could be stable or unstable, cyclical or asymptotic depending on the relative size of two "response" parameters: (a) the parameter governing the offsetting response of economic policy to a surge in private capital outflows and (b) the parameter that determines the magnitude of a surge in these outflows in response to an observed decline in foreign reserves. An economy where the second parameter is sufficiently larger than the first would exhibit unstable or cyclical dynamics, whereas an economy with the opposite feature would exhibit stable, asymptotic dynamics.

In the environment of highly restricted capital flows of the 1960s, Mundell's exploration of balance-of-payments crises seemed of little relevance compared to his findings regarding the stabilizing properties of fixed exchange rates. Hence, his analysis of speculative capital flows was largely ignored in the large literature that followed the Mundell-Fleming model. Today, however, the situation is the opposite. The case of limited capital mobility is at best a teaching tool, and perfect or near-perfect capital mobility is the framework from which academic and policy discussions start. Recurrent episodes like the collapse of the exchange rate mechanism (ERM) in Europe, the Mexican crisis of 1994, the Southeast Asian crises of 1997, the collapse of the Russian ruble in 1998, and the recent collapse of the Brazilian real illustrate the key relevance of the analysis of speculative attacks in an environment of highly integrated capital markets.

This chapter reformulates Mundell's analysis from the perspective of modern international macroeconomics. Like Mundell, we study the dynamics of an economy where the likelihood that a currency peg will be maintained depends on the stock of foreign reserves. In contrast with his analysis, however, we examine a framework in which private agents formulate rational expectations of the possibility of abandonment of the peg. In equilibrium, these expectations will be consistent with the policy reaction function of the central bank. The latter is modeled to conform to a commitment to let the nominal interest rate be determined by uncovered interest parity, with a currency risk premium that evolves as a decreasing function of the stock of foreign exchange reserves. Hence, in equilibrium the rational expectations of devaluation of the private sector will also be a decreasing function of foreign reserves. Since changes in reserves are determined by the optimal plans of private agents, both the probability of devaluation and the currency risk premium will be endogenous outcomes of the model.

We borrow from Mundell's analysis the assumption that the central bank faces a borrowing constraint that imposes a minimum level of reserves below which the currency can no longer be pegged. Hence, balance-of-payments crises (i.e., situations in which reserves hit their critical level and force a devaluation) can emerge endogenously in this framework.

Our analysis also updates Mundell's in that the implications of the monetary dynamics of a fixed exchange rate for the real sector of the economy are derived as features of the general equilibrium interaction of profit-maximizing firms and utility-maximizing households in an environment with uncertainty. Thus, the dynamics that lead to the collapse of a currency peg are accompanied by a "real business cycle." This monetary nonneutrality results from specifying a transmission mechanism in which the state-contingent distortions on the nominal interest rate that result from a time-varying currency risk premium create tax-like distortions on saving, investment, and the supply of labor. Our aim in proceeding in this way is to capture the spirit of Mundell's framework, in which the dynamics of currency speculation are accompanied by output and price fluctuations. This approach also resembles that of real business cycle models driven by exogenous shocks, but it differs in that the underlying shock driving business cycles is monetary in origin, and the stochastic process that describes it is endogenous.

The business cycle transmission mechanism that we study also features a state-contingent, fiscal-induced wealth effect similar to that identified by Calvo and Drazen (1993) in their study of uncertain duration of policy reforms.[2] This wealth effect is produced by the combination of two key assumptions: First, the government wastes seigniorage revenue in unproductive expenditures. A devaluation, therefore, entails the risk of a sudden fiscal expansion at the expense of private absorption. Second, markets of contingent claims are incomplete, so that private agents are unable to insure away the adverse wealth effect resulting from this sudden fiscal expansion.

It is important to note that, although considering intertemporal decision making under uncertainty adds important elements that were missing from Mundell's analysis, intertemporal microfoundations are already commonplace in the modern literature on currency crises (see, for example, Calvo 1987, Drazen and Helpman 1988, and Obstfeld 1995). For the most part, however, this literature has focused on the *qualitative* implications of the theory, seeking to establish whether these implications were in line with basic qualitative features of the data. Our aim is to build on this literature to explore the *quantitative* predictions of a model of currency crises under uncertainty and general equilibrium, exploring the extent to which the model can account for both the monetary dynamics of balance-of-payments crises and the business cycle facts associated with currency pegs.

The quantitative emphasis of our analysis is justified partly by necessity, since models with the features we described tend to be analytically intractable, forcing researchers to explore them with numerical methods. However, the main justification for the quantitative approach is not theoretical but empirical, and it relates to two major challenges faced by current research on the dynamics of currency pegs. These challenges are (a) to develop models that can explain the business cycle regularities of fixed-exchange-rate regimes in high-inflation countries (as documented by Helpman and Razin (1987), Kiguel and Liviatan (1992), and Végh (1992)) and (b) to rationalize recent findings on the robustness of leading indicators or predictors of the collapse of fixed exchange rates (see, for example, Kaminsky and Reinhart 1999).

Exchange rate–based stabilizations are characterized by three key stylized facts: the real exchange rate appreciates sharply, external deficits widen considerably, and output and domestic absorption boom. In addition, most plans end up failing with recessions predating currency collapses, periods of stability of the real exchange rate in between periods of sharp, rapid appreciation, and a high degree of correlation between private expenditures and the real exchange rate. Despite significant progress in developing models that can account for some of these observations from a qualitative standpoint, Rebelo and Végh (1996), Mendoza and Uribe (2000), and Uribe (1997) have shown that the same models confront serious difficulties in explaining the quantitative features of the data. In particular, the models produce negligible consumption booms and real appreciations compared to actual observations, and the observed coexistence of a gradual real appreciation with a gradual consumption boom is a theoretical impossibility for most of the models that exist in the literature—this is the *price-consumption puzzle* identified by Uribe (1998a).[3]

A series of recent empirical studies provide growing evidence indicating that a few key macroeconomic indicators are robust predictors of currency crises, in the sense of statistical causality. Studies like Kaminsky and Reinhart 1999, Klein and Marion 1997, or Frankel and Rose 1996 find that the real exchange rate, foreign reserves, and the current account deficit systematically predate the occurrence of devaluations. Thus, a framework that may account for the business cycle regularities of exchange rate–based disinflations must also try to rationalize the evidence on the predictive power of leading indicators of currency crashes. In this chapter, we study whether a model of business cycles driven by endogenous exchange rate uncertainty can help us to rationalize both sets of stylized facts.

The focus on explaining simultaneously the dynamic monetary process that leads to a devaluation and the business cycle facts of exchange rate–based stabilizations is aimed at developing a framework in which the two phenomena are joint equilibrium outcomes. This is done in an effort to connect two literatures that in general have approached each issue separately. For example, the large literature on "credibility" models initiated by Calvo (1986) explains the real effects of stabilization plans by studying optimal household behavior assuming a given date in which there is an exogenous and fully anticipated collapse of the currency. Similarly, most models of speculative attacks inspired in the work of Krugman (1979) and Obstfeld (1986) study dynamics of reserve losses and devaluations without explaining the process that leads to exchange rate vulnerability reflected in large external deficits or overvalued real exchange rates. Paradoxically, Mundell's (1960) model was again unique in that it was explicitly aimed at studying the overall macroeconomic effects of currency speculation. Calvo 1987 and Drazen and Helpman 1988 are also exceptions that aimed to study both the real effects of exchange rate–based stabilizations and the collapse of fixed exchange rates.

The results of our analysis suggest that the model we study can explain some of the empirical regularities of exchange rate–based stabilizations. In particular, the model can produce an endogenous time path of devaluation probabilities roughly consistent with the J-shaped path estimated in several empirical studies (see in particular Blanco and Garber 1986 and Klein and Marion 1997). These devaluation probabilities are consistent in equilibrium with a pattern of macroeconomic dynamics that is roughly in line with basic business cycle features of the data, including the aforementioned price-consumption puzzle. Moreover, our model also produces results that resemble the findings of Mundell's work. In particular, the time path of devaluation probabilities and the characteristics of equilibrium dynamics depend heavily on the relative values of (a) the parameter that captures the response of capital outflows to changes in foreign reserves and (b) the parameter that captures the stance of fiscal policy. Economies where the former is sufficiently large relative to the latter exhibit an endogenous balance-of-payments crisis, and the crisis occurs sooner as the difference grows larger.

The remainder of the chapter describes the model, follows with a characterization of the equilibrium and a discussion of the numerical solution method, then moves to an examination of the simulations of the model, and closes with conclusions and policy implications.

A Model of Business Cycles and Balance-of-Payments Crises

The model we propose represents a two-sector small open economy in which competitive firms produce traded and nontraded goods using capital and labor, and capital is an accumulable, tradable factor of production. Factors of production are modeled as in the specific factors framework of the trade literature, so as to simplify the analysis by preventing labor and capital from moving across sectors. Money balances are used to economize transactions costs. Households and firms have unrestricted access to a perfectly competitive world capital market, but markets of contingent claims are incomplete.

The Private Sector

Households are infinitely lived and maximize the following expected utility function:

$$E_0 \sum_{t=0}^{\infty} \beta^t \frac{\left[C_t(1 - L_t^N - L^T)^\rho\right]^{1-\sigma}}{1-\sigma},$$ (13.1)

$$C_t = \left[\omega(C_t^T)^{-\mu} + (1-\omega)(C_t^N)^{-\mu}\right]^{-1/\mu}.$$ (13.2)

Private consumption C_t is represented by the isoelastic aggregator of consumption of traded goods, C_t^T, and nontraded goods, C_t^N, defined in equation (13.2), with $1/1 + \mu$ denoting the elasticity of substitution between traded and nontraded goods. Households supply labor to industries producing both goods. Labor is specific to each industry and is supplied inelastically to the industry that produces traded goods, in an amount equivalent to L^T units of "raw time." Labor supplied to the nontraded goods industry, L_t^N, and leisure are perfect substitutes, so that, normalizing the time constraint, leisure is simply defined as $1 - L_t^N - L^T$. Leisure enters in multiplicative form in utility, with ρ governing the steady-state leisure-to-consumption ratio. Utility from consumption and leisure is represented by a constant relative risk aversion function, with σ measuring both the coefficient of relative risk aversion and the inverse of the intertemporal elasticity of substitution in consumption. The parameter $\beta \in (0, 1)$ is the subjective discount factor.

Households maximize (13.1) subject to the following two constraints:

$$B_{t+1} - (1+r^*)B_t + \left(C_t^T + p_t^N C_t^N\right) + I_t = A_t^T (K_t^T)^{1-\alpha T} (L^T)^{\alpha T}$$

$$+ p_t^N A_t^N (K^N)^{1-\alpha N} (L_t^N)^{\alpha N}$$

$$- \frac{\varphi}{2} (K_{t+1}^T - K_t^T)^2 - m_t V_t S(V_t) \tag{13.3}$$

$$+ \frac{m_{t-1}}{1+e_t} - m_t + T_t,$$

$$I_t = K_{t+1}^T - (1-\delta)K_t^T. \tag{13.4}$$

In addition, agents are assumed to be subject to a no-Ponzi-game constraint. World asset trading is limited to one-period bonds B paying the time-invariant real interest rate r^* in units of the traded good. The uses of household income on the left-hand side of (13.3) are purchases of traded and nontraded goods for consumption and investment, I, and changes in bond holdings net of interest. The relative price of non-tradables is defined as p^N, and, since purchasing power parity (PPP) with respect to tradables holds, it also represents the real exchange rate. The sources of household income on the right-hand side of (13.3) are factor incomes from industries producing traded and nontraded goods (net of capital adjustment costs, transaction costs, and changes in real money balances) and government transfers.

Production functions are Cobb-Douglas. Capital is specific to each industry and is inelastically supplied to the nontraded sector in the amount K^N, facing a zero depreciation rate. Capital in the traded sector, K_t^T, is a traded good and depreciates at rate δ. Capital adjustment costs distinguish financial from physical assets to prevent excessive investment variability as in Mendoza 1995. Real money balances, m, are measured in terms of traded goods and enter the model as a means to

economize transaction costs (as in Greenwood 1983, 1984 and Kimbrough 1986). Transactions costs per unit of private absorption are
given by S, which is a convex function of expenditure velocity $V =$
$(C^T + p^N C^N + I)/m$. Given PPP in tradables and constant foreign prices,
e represents both the inflation rate of tradables and the depreciation
rate. T is a lump-sum transfer from the government.

Government Policy

A key feature of equilibrium models of currency crises is the explicit
link between fiscal and exchange rate policies established by the government budget constraint. In our case, the probabilistic setting with
incomplete markets implies that we must be explicit about the stance
of both policies during the states of nature in which the currency
remains fixed as well as in those that a devaluation occurs. The policy
regime in our model is described as follows.

Exchange Rate Policy
The Central Bank's Policy Reaction Function
The exchange rate policy we study is an exchange rate–based stabilization program of uncertain duration. Specifically, we assume that
before period 0 the economy was in a "sustainable" exchange rate
regime with a constant rate of depreciation equal to $e^h > 0$. This regime
was "sustainable" in the sense that e^h is consistent with a stationary
equilibrium of the model, as described in the next section. At $t = 0$, the
government announces and implements a currency peg, so that $e_0 = 0$.
As long as the peg lasts, the policy reaction function of the central bank
is represented by a logistic stochastic process according to which the
conditional probability of devaluation (or hazard rate), $z_t \equiv \text{Prob}[e_{t+1} >$
$0 | e_t = 0]$ for $t \geq 0$, is given by

$$z_t = \frac{\exp\left[\Gamma + \dfrac{B}{\left(\dfrac{R_{t-1}}{Y_{t-1}}\right) - \left(\dfrac{R}{Y}\right)^{\text{crit}}}\right]}{1 + \exp\left[\Gamma + \dfrac{B}{\left(\dfrac{R_{t-1}}{Y_{t-1}}\right) - \left(\dfrac{R}{Y}\right)^{\text{crit}}}\right]} \quad \text{for} \quad 0 \leq t < J-1, \qquad (13.5)$$

and $z_t = 1$ for $t \geq J-1$.

Devaluation is assumed to be an absorbent state, so $\text{Prob}[e_{t+1} > 0 | e_t > 0]$ = 1. In addition, it is assumed that there exists a date $J > 0$ which exchange rate uncertainty ends and there is a devaluation with probability 1.[4] In equation (13.5), R represents central bank holdings of interest-bearing foreign reserves, Y is the economy's total output in units of tradables, and B and Γ are exogenous parameters.

Equation (13.5) sets the probability of devaluation as a decreasing function of the observed gap between the lagged reserves-to-GDP ratio and a minimum critical value of this ratio. By conditioning the probability of devaluation on foreign reserves we aim to capture the crucial feature of Mundell's (1960) analysis, in which a decline in reserves triggers speculative capital outflows.[5] The parameter B is intended to reflect the sensitiveness of these outflows to changes in reserves. We also specified (13.5) to make the model consistent with Krugman-style models of speculative attacks: if at any date t between 0 and $J - 1$ the ratio R/Y hits the critical level, a balance-of-payments crisis occurs with probability 1 in period $t + 1$. Note, however, that the policy reaction function also allows implicitly for the possibility of "surprise" devaluations between dates 0 and $J - 1$ triggered by exogenous shocks, even if reserves have not been depleted to the critical level.

The last element of exchange rate policy is the response to a currency crisis. When the currency peg collapses, there is a switch to a deterministic environment in which the exchange rate depreciates at a constant rate. We follow the typical assumption of the credibility literature based on Calvo 1986 that collapse implies a return to the same high rate of inflation and depreciation that reigned before the stabilization plan was implemented, e^h. Hence, the postcollapse depreciation rate is fixed for all devaluation states of nature at any date t. Since the depreciation rate will be shown to act like a distortionary tax in our model, this assumption plays a key role in ensuring that distortions affecting private sector behavior are limited only to those related to the uncertainty regarding the duration of the peg, and not to the postcollapse realization of the depreciation rate. Moreover, since the postcollapse depreciation rate must be "sustainable" and identical across all states of nature, the collapse of the peg must be accompanied by a state-contingent adjustment in fiscal policy that makes that outcome consistent with intertemporal fiscal solvency, as we clarify later.

Given this structure of exchange rate policy, the logistic reaction function setting z_t can be interpreted alternatively as a reaction function determining the expected rate of currency depreciation under a fixed exchange rate (note that $E(e_{t+1}|e_t = 0) = z_t e^h + (1 - z_t)0 = z_t e^h$). Moreover, interest parity, assuming a constant world interest rate, implies that the reaction function can also be interpreted approximately as a reaction function for the nominal interest rate. In fact, if households were risk-neutral, the reaction function we specified is equivalent to a reaction function for the nominal interest rate (in this case, interest parity implies that the domestic interest rate equals the constant world interest rate plus expected depreciation).

Fiscal Policy

The linkage between exchange rate policy and fiscal policy is captured by the following government budget constraint:

$$G_t + T_t + R_{t+1} = m_t - \frac{m_{t-1}}{1+e_t} + m_t V_t S(V_t) + (1+r^*)R_t. \tag{13.6}$$

The government undertakes unproductive expenditures G, holds foreign reserves, issues money, and makes transfer payments to households, all in units of traded goods. Both seigniorage and transactions costs are assumed to be part of government revenue.[6] During the currency peg, G and T are fiscal policy choices governed by the rules defined below, and the dynamics of m and V reflect optimal plans of the private sector that are fully accommodated by the central bank. It follows, therefore, that while the peg is in place (13.6) determines the evolution of foreign reserves (i.e., the balance of payments) so as to satisfy the government budget constraint.

Fiscal policy is assumed to follow three rules. First, the government sets unproductive expenditures to match exactly current revenue from seigniorage and transactions costs:[7]

$$G_t = m_t - \frac{m_{t-1}}{1+e_t} + m_t V_t S(V_t). \tag{13.7}$$

This rule, in conjunction with the assumption of incomplete insurance markets, implies that the model features the same state-contingent, fiscal-induced wealth effects as in Calvo and Drazen 1993 and Mendoza and Uribe 2000. A currency collapse leads to a surge in seigniorage and an increase in velocity, thereby inducing an expansion of unproductive government purchases. This simple rule allows us to develop a tractable extension of the solution method we proposed in our previous work to the case of endogenous probabilities studied here.

The second fiscal rule dictates that, while the currency peg is in place, total government outlays are constant and equal to a fraction κ of their prestabilization level:

$$e_t = 0 \Rightarrow G_t + T_t = \kappa(G_{-1} + T_{-1}). \tag{13.8}$$

Hence, (13.7) and (13.8) combined imply that while the exchange rate remains fixed, changes in G_t induce an offsetting adjustment in T_t so as to ensure that total outlays remain constant. This rule is required to ensure that the time path of reserves during a currency peg reflects only adjustments in private optimal plans regarding the velocity of circulation of money and money demand, and is not driven by arbitrary changes in the time path of government outlays. A similar assumption is a typical feature of models of currency crises. In Krugman 1979 or Calvo 1987, for example, government outlays are kept constant at the level they had before the peg began, and the focus is on determining the endogenous date in which reserves are depleted down to the critical level triggering a currency collapse. This scenario is included in our model (since $\kappa = 1$ is not ruled out), but we also allow for the option that some fiscal adjustment may accompany the introduction of the peg. The size of this initial fiscal adjustment will be a key determinant of the duration of a fixed-exchange-rate regime, resembling results in Helpman and Razin 1987 and Drazen and Helpman 1988.

The third fiscal rule establishes that the collapse of the peg must be followed by adjustments in lump-sum transfers, so that, given the previous two rules and the assumption that e^h is "sustainable" regardless of the date on which collapse occurs, the government's intertemporal budget constraint holds. In particular, we allow for adjustments in lump-sum transfers after the state-contingent date of a currency crash that ensure that $\lim_{t \to \infty} (1 + r^*)^{-t} R_t = 0$. This in turn ensures that, as long as (13.6) and (13.7) hold, the present value of transfers as of $t = 0$ equals $(1 + r^*)R_0$.

It is instructive to compare our fiscal and exchange rate policy regime with the one assumed in Calvo's (1987) perfect-foresight equilibrium model of balance-of-payment crises. In Calvo's regime, government outlays take the same value before and after the collapse of the peg, and fiscal solvency is maintained through an endogenous increase in the depreciation rate at the time the peg is abandoned.[8] In contrast, in our regime the abandonment of the peg is accompanied by an exogenous increase in the depreciation rate that is constant across states of nature, and fiscal solvency is maintained via endogenous, state-contingent adjustments of government outlays. Under perfect foresight, both regimes are closely related. In fact, they induce identical dynamics if we consider a deterministic, endowment economy version of our model in which the postcollapse depreciation rate is set at a value such that no postcollapse fiscal adjustment is required. However, under uncertainty the two regimes are quite different. The reason is that our regime uses nondistorting, state-contingent lump-sum transfers to make the postcollapse depreciation rate independent of the date in which the program is abandoned. In Calvo's regime, on the other hand, uncertainty would imply that the rate of depreciation after the collapse varies with the duration of the program, which would create an extra distortion affecting the nominal interest rate and through it all endogenous real variables of the model.[9]

Equilibrium and Numerical Solution

The Model's Monetary Transmission Mechanism

The first-order conditions that characterize the households' optimal choices in this model are identical to those obtained in Mendoza and Uribe 1997. Hence, we limit the discussion here to a brief description of their implications for macroeconomic dynamics. The model embodies three atemporal and three intertemporal optimality conditions. The three atemporal conditions equate (a) the marginal utility of consumption of the numéraire good C^T with the marginal utility of wealth multiplied by the marginal cost of transactions (with the latter at equilibrium as an increasing function of the nominal interest rate, as shown below), (b) the marginal rate of substitution between C^T and C^N with the corresponding relative price, and (c) the marginal disutility of labor in the nontradables sector to its marginal benefit, which is equal to the real wage adjusted by the marginal cost of transactions. The three intertemporal conditions are Euler equations that equate the marginal costs and benefits of sacrificing a unit of tradables consumption and investing it in each of the three assets available in the economy: foreign bonds, real balances, and physical capital.

To study how exchange rate uncertainty distorts the real economy, it is useful to examine the Euler equation for accumulation of real money balances, which can be written as follows:

$$S'(V_t^L)(V_t^L)^2 = \frac{r^*}{(1+r^*)} + \left[\frac{\lambda_{t+1}^H}{E_t[\lambda_{t+1}|e_t=0]}\right]\left(\frac{z_t e^h}{(1+e^h)(1+r^*)}\right). \tag{13.9}$$

This equilibrium condition describes the behavior of velocity from the perspective of any date t in which the stabilization plan is in place, and hence the depreciation rate is at its low state $e_t^l = 0$, with the corresponding state-contingent choice for velocity denoted V^L. Condition (13.9) reflects the fact that optimal money holdings are determined so that the marginal benefit of holding an extra unit of real balances, in the left-hand side of (13.9), equals the opportunity cost of holding money in the right-hand side—which is also equal to the nominal interest rate factor: $i_t/(1 + i_t)$. Moreover, equation (13.9) and the assumptions that S is convex and continuously differentiable imply that in equilibrium V is an increasing function of i. This implies in turn that the marginal cost of transactions $h(i)$ (where $h(i_t) \equiv 1 + S[V(i_t)] + V(i_t)S'[V(i_t)]$) is also increasing in i.

Equation (13.9) shows that this model features a differential between the domestic and world nominal interest rates (recall that world inflation is zero, so r^* is also the world nominal interest rate) that reflects a risk-adjusted uncovered interest parity condition. The time path of the interest differential is determined by two effects: (1) changes in the expected rate of depreciation of the currency $z_t e^h$ and (2) changes in the marginal utility of wealth in the high-depreciation-rate state λ_{t+1}^H relative to its conditional mean $E_t[\lambda_{t+1} \mid e_t = 0]$. The first effect reflects the standard expected-depreciation premium under risk neutrality. The second effect magnifies that premium by incorporating a wealth effect that reflects the combined influence of risk aversion and incomplete markets. We infer that the wealth effect magnifies the interest premium—that is, $\lambda_{t+1}^H/E_t[\lambda_{t+1} \mid e_t = 0] > 1$—because a return to high inflation increases seigniorage and unproductive government purchases and thus reduces wealth and increases the marginal utility of wealth.

The time-variant interest rate premium leads to changes in velocity and the marginal cost of transactions that distort saving, investment, and labor supply decisions. These distortions affect the margins of optimal decision making in a manner analogous to stochastic taxes on factor incomes and the return on saving. As Mendoza and Uribe (2000) showed, the model's consumption Euler equation can be simplified to show that the ratio of marginal transaction costs between two contiguous periods (i.e., $h(i_t)/h(i_{t+1})$) is equivalent to a stochastic tax on the intertemporal relative price of consumption of tradables. Similarly, $h(i_t)$ can be shown to act as a tax on current labor income and $h(i_{t+1})$ can be shown to act as a random tax on capital income (specifically, on the marginal product of capital at $t + 1$).

In addition to the taxlike distortions, devaluation risk introduces state-contingent wealth effects because of the unproductive use of government revenue and the assumption of incomplete insurance markets. These wealth effects affect both consumption and the supply of labor. Moreover, the random taxes on factor income distort the accumulation of capital and the time path of factor payments, and hence introduce state-contingent wealth effects that remain in place even when government revenue is fully rebated to households.

The fiscal-induced wealth effect at work in this model is similar to the one that drives the analysis of Calvo and Drazen (1993), but the distortions on the intertemporal consumption margin differ in a significant way. The wealth effect is produced by the fact that, given the incompleteness of insurance markets, each period that the currency peg continues results in an increase in permanent income by the amount of the foregone unproductive expenditures that would have been financed by the collapse of the peg and the switch to the high inflation regime. This wealth effect will be stronger, favoring an upward-sloping consumption path, the lower the elasticity of intertemporal substitution in consumption (as Calvo and Drazen proved).

If government revenue were fully rebated, the devaluation would not induce an adverse wealth effect, but the distortion affecting the intertemporal relative price of tradables via state-contingent changes in the ratio $h(i_t)/h(i_{t+1})$ would still be present. This intertemporal distortion has two important features that differ from the one at work in the Calvo and Drazen setting: First, it can favor either current or future consumption depending on the time path of devaluation probabilities. Calvo and Drazen deal instead with a tariff elimination of uncertain duration such that current observed prices (if the trade reform is in place) are always lower than expected future prices, and hence the intertemporal distortion always favors current consumption. Second, in our setting the value of the intertemporal distortion depends on the probability of policy reversal (since i_t while the peg is place depends on the probability of devaluation), whereas in Calvo and Drazen the tariff is always zero while the trade reform is in place.

The real effects we described in the previous paragraphs differ significantly from the effects at work in perfect-foresight models and stochastic models with complete insurance markets examined in the literature on exchange rate–based stabilizations. In the perfect-foresight models, there is no interest differential between the domestic economy and the rest of the world while the currency remains pegged, and hence there are no distortions on relative prices within the fixed-exchange-rate period. In complete-markets models the valuation of wealth is not contingent on the state of nature, and thus the surge in seigniorage after a devaluation becomes a source of insurable, country-specific risk.

Rational Expectations Equilibrium

In order to define a rational expectations equilibrium, note that the time path of devaluation probabilities specified in (13.5) is endogenous and must be determined simultaneously with the equilibrium allocations and prices. Given a time path of devaluation probabilities between dates 0 and J, the model can be solved to yield particular paths for optimal state-contingent plans of the private sector. Taking the optimal plans for m and V, and the fiscal policy rules, one can compute the dynamics of reserves via equation (13.6). However, the given path of devaluation probabilities will only be consistent with a rational expectations equilibrium if the optimal plans that they support yield dynamics of reserves via (13.6) that produce an identical time path of devaluation probabilities when those dynamics of reserves are passed through (13.5).

A rational expectations equilibrium for this model consists therefore of intertemporal sequences of allocations and prices, and a time path of devaluation probabilities, satisfying the following conditions: (1) the optimality conditions of households and firms, (2) the market-clearing conditions for traded and nontraded goods, (3) the intertemporal government budget constraint, and (4) the consistency condition that equilibrium dynamics of reserves resulting from (13.6), for a given sequence of devaluation probabilities $Z \equiv \{z_0, \ldots, z_{J-1}\}$, must produce the same sequence Z when used to compute the time path of devaluation probabilities via (13.5). This last condition ensures that, in equilibrium, the devaluation probabilities that reflect the central bank's policy reaction function are consistent with the rational expectations of currency collapse formulated by the private sector.

The nature of the policy experiment we posed implies that in the long run the equilibrium always converges to the stationary state of a deterministic setting with a constant rate of depreciation e^h. Hence, our experiment begins and ends in well-defined, deterministic stationary equilibria compatible with e^h. The steady-state equilibrium conditions that characterize this outcome, and the corresponding implicit connection between e^h and the stance of fiscal policy, can be illustrated clearly in a one-good version of the model in which labor supply is inelastic. In this case, the following conditions characterize a stationary equilibrium:

$$A\gamma\left(\frac{C/Y}{m/Y}\right)^{1+\gamma} = \frac{(a+e^h)(1+r^*)-1}{(1+e^h)(1+r^*)},$$

(13.10)

$$\frac{C}{Y} = 1+r^*\left(\frac{R}{Y}+\frac{B}{Y}\right)-\frac{G}{Y},$$

(13.11)

$$\frac{G}{Y} = \left(\frac{m/Y}{C/Y}\right)\frac{C}{Y}\left(\frac{e^h}{1+e^h}\right)+\frac{C}{Y}\left[A\left(\frac{C/Y}{m/Y}\right)^\gamma\right],$$

(13.12)

$$(1-\alpha)A\left(\frac{K}{L}\right)^{-\alpha} = (r^*+\delta)h((1+e^h)(1+r^*)).$$

(13.13)

Notice that this system is expressed in terms of output shares to be consistent with the calibration exercise of the next section. We also adopted from the next section the exponential transactions cost technology $S = AV^\gamma$.

The steady-state system (13.10)–(13.13) features the common problem of open economy models with standard preferences and trade in one-period bonds that the steady-state foreign asset position depends on initial conditions (see Mendoza and Tesar 1998). Given an initial prestabilization asset position and the fact that e^h is exogenous, it follows that in the prestabilization equilibrium (13.10)–(13.12) is a block-recursive, three-equation system in the variables (C/Y), (m/Y), and (G/Y), and (13.13) determines the steady-state capital/output ratio (and hence the level of output given the Cobb-Douglas technology). It also follows from (13.12) and the steady-state government budget constraint that in the prestabilization steady state, transfers must be set to rebate the interest income on foreign reserves: $T = r^*R$. Note that, given the functional forms we chose, the steady-state output shares of reserves and foreign assets, and the value of e^h, there are generally unique solutions for the deterministic steady-state system.[10]

The introduction of the peg sets the model's dynamics in motion since at $e = 0$ the steady-state conditions will no longer hold. Every period during the peg there is some chance that the rate of depreciation is reset to e^h and the economy becomes deterministic. However, each date that this can happen the "initial conditions" of the corresponding deterministic postcollapse regime (i.e., the values of B, R, and K at the date of collapse) would differ, and hence since the steady state depends on initial conditions, the deterministic long-run equilibrium to which the model converges from each possible date of collapse will generally differ. The fact that the same e^h is maintained across states of nature simplifies the analysis by ensuring that the long-run capital/output ratio and money velocity, as well as the steady-state levels of Y and K, are independent of the date of the currency collapse (as follows from (13.10) and (13.13)), but the stationary equilibria of consumption, real money balances, and government purchases will still vary depending on the overall net foreign asset position (i.e., $R + B$) to which the economy converges from each possible devaluation date. The same holds in the steady-state system of the richer model that incorporates the nontradables sector and the endogenous labor supply, with the caveat that in this case the steady-state output and capital stock would also depend on initial conditions.

Numerical Solution Method

The algorithm that solves the model extends the one we developed for a setting with exogenous devaluation probabilities in Mendoza and Uribe 1997 to the case in which these probabilities are endogenous. The algorithm of that paper can be thought of as a subprogram that yields equilibrium dynamics for a given Z.

We solve the model using the following iterative procedure:

1. Fix the values of parameters for preferences, technology, the hazard rate function, the maximum duration of exchange rate uncertainty, J, the postcollapse constant depreciation rate, e^h, the initial and critical reserve-to-GDP ratios, R_0/Y_0 and $(R/Y)^{\mathrm{crit}}$, and the fiscal adjustment parameter κ.

2. Start with a guess for the hazard function, Z^0, and use the subprogram from Mendoza and Uribe 1997 to compute equilibrium dynamics as if the hazard function were exogenous.

3. Use the sequence of reserve-to-GDP ratios implied by step 2 to construct a new hazard function, Z^1, using equation (13.5). If this hazard function coincides with Z^0, then a rational expectations equilibrium has been found, else perform step 2 using Z^1 as the new guess.

The subprogram that computes equilibrium dynamics for a given Z takes advantage of the fact that at any date $t > 0$ there are only two possible realizations of e_t: 0 or $e^h > 0$. Since the state $e_t = e^h$ is absorbent, in each date macroeconomic aggregates can either (a) follow the optimal state-contingent path corresponding to the state in which $e_t = 0$, or (b) switch to the perfect-foresight path corresponding to the constant rate of depreciation e^h and the initial conditions pinned down by the values of the state variables on that date. The subprogram follows an iterative, backward-recursion strategy. Given Z and J, and an assumed post-collapse stationary equilibrium for the state variables K and B, the model features well-defined state transition probabilities and terminal conditions, so that paths (a) and (b) can be solved by backward recursion. If these paths yield initial values for the state variables that are not the same as those compatible with the values set in the calibration, the terminal conditions are updated and the solution repeated until it converges (see the appendix to Mendoza and Uribe 1997 for details).

Note that, although the maximum duration of the currency peg J is exogenous, this does not imply that the date of a speculative attack is necessarily exogenous. Nothing rules out a situation in which reserves reach the critical level before period J, triggering a speculative attack at a date that is endogenous to the model's dynamics. Similarly, the value of J can be set very high to examine the implications of a long horizon for currency risk.

Calibration and Numerical Simulations

Calibration

The model is calibrated to mimic some key aspects of Mexico's exchange rate–based stabilization plan of 1987–1994, following the review of the stylized facts in Mendoza and Uribe 2000.

Financial Sector
The transaction costs technology adopts the form $S(V_t) = AV_t^\gamma$, so that the equilibrium condition for accumulation of money balances implies an implicit money demand function $V_t = (i_t/1 + i_t)^{1/(1+\gamma)}(\gamma A)^{-1/(1+\gamma)}$, where i is the nominal interest rate. This function is calibrated to M2 money demand in Mexico, given strong empirical evidence in favor of a log-linear relationship between m and $i/1 + i$.[11] The coefficient $-1/(1 + \gamma)$ is the elasticity of money demand with respect to $i/(1 + i)$, estimated at -0.15, so $\gamma = 5.66$. The scale parameter A is set so that the high-inflation, prestabilization steady state mimics Mexico's M2/GDP ratio

(31.8 percent on an annual basis) and nominal interest rate (177 percent annually) at the end of 1987. These two figures are inserted in the expression for equilibrium velocity $V_t = (i_t/1 + i_t)^{1/(1+\eta)}(\gamma A)^{-1/(1+\eta)}$, and the expression is then solved for A (the result is $A = 0.19$).

Preferences and Technology
The risk aversion coefficient is set at $\sigma = 5$, which is the lower bound of the GMM estimates obtained for Mexico by Reinhart and Végh (1995) using quarterly data for the period 1981–1991. Other preference and technology parameters are taken from the developing country model calibrated in Mendoza 1995 and are set as follows: $\rho = 0.786$, $\omega = 0.5$, $\mu = -0.218$, $\alpha T = 0.42$, $\alpha N = 0.34$, and $\delta = 0.1$. $\phi = 0.06$ is set to mimic the standard deviation of Mexican investment using also Mendoza 1995. Finally, we assume $\beta = (1 + r^*)^{-1}$ with r^* set at 6.5 percent per annum, which corresponds to the average real rate of return on equity in the United States in the period 1948–1981 reported by King, Plosser, and Rebelo (1988).

Balance of Payments and Fiscal Policy
The initial and critical values of the ratio of foreign reserves to gross domestic product are calibrated to mimic, respectively, the values observed at the beginning and at the end of the Mexican stabilization plan. The initial ratio (which uses gross reserves as of the end of February 1988, when the exchange rate was initially fixed) was 7.1 percent in annual terms. The final ratio, which uses gross reserves in November 1994, was 2.8 percent also in annual terms. Notice that this final ratio corresponds to reserves in the period just before the devaluation. The prestabilization and postcollapse depreciation rates are both set to $e^h = 27$ percent at a quarterly frequency, to reflect Mexico's inflation rate at the end of 1987 (which was 160 percent on a twelve-month basis). We also set $J = 24$ to reflect the fact that Mexico has suffered currency collapses at the end of the six-year presidential terms in 1976, 1982, and 1994.

Given the above parameter values and functional forms, a system analogous to (13.10)–(13.13), expanded to reintroduce nontraded goods and endogenous labor supply, is used to solve for the prestabilization steady state. The solution includes the prestabilization steady-state values of seigniorage and transactions cost revenue, government purchases and transfers, so that the prestabilization amount of government outlays $(G_{-1} + T_{-1})$ can be determined.

The parameter κ, which measures the magnitude of fiscal adjustment during the peg as a fraction of $(G_{-1} + T_{-1})$, is calibrated by requiring that the reserve-to-GDP ratio (R/Y) hits its critical level at date $J - 2$ if the peg is in place at that point. Thus, we adopt the view that in the benchmark case, agents in period $J - 1$ expect a peg that has survived until then to collapse in period J with probability 1 both because J is the assumed maximum duration of the program and because reserves just hit their critical level one period earlier.[12] The implied value of κ is 0.133, which means that when the stabilization program is announced the government tightens fiscal policy sharply to reduce total outlays by 87.7 percent.

Determining the value of κ that satisfies the above conditions requires a slight extension of the solution method. In particular, we use the following iterative procedure:

1. Start with an initial guess, Z^0.

2. Obtain a rational expectations equilibrium given Z^0 using the subprogram described in Mendoza and Uribe 1997.

3. Compute κ^0 as the solution to the difference equation $R_{t+1} = (1 + r^*)R_t + SR_t + TC_t - \kappa^0(T_{-1} + G_{-1})$, with initial condition $R_0 = (R_0/Y_0)Y_0$ and terminal condition $R_{J-2} = (R/Y)^{\text{crit}}Y_{J-2}$, where SR_t and TC_t are short for seignorage revenue and transaction costs, respectively. This equation results from combining equations (13.7) and (13.8). The solution takes the form[13]

$$\kappa^0 = r * \left[\frac{\left(\dfrac{R_0}{Y_0}\right)Y_0(1+r^*)^{J-2} + \displaystyle\sum_{j=0}^{J-3}(1+r^*)^{J-3-j}\left(SR_j + TC_j - \left(\dfrac{R}{Y}\right)^{\text{crit}}Y_{J-2}\right)}{(G_{-1}+T_{-1})\left((1+r^*)^{J-2} - 1\right)} \right].$$

(13.4)

Note that all the terms on the right-hand side of (13.14) are provided either in step 2 or by the solution of the prestabilization steady state. Once κ^0 has been obtained, a series for foreign reserves can be constructed using the above difference equation.

4. Construct a new hazard function, Z^1, by passing the time path of reserves from step 3 through equation (13.5). If Z^1 equals Z^0, then a rational expectations equilibrium has been found; otherwise, perform steps 2 and 3 using Z^1 as the guess. Continue this procedure until the

hazard function converges. The value of κ resulting from step 3 in the last iteration is the one used in the benchmark calibration of the model.

Parameters of the Hazard Rate Function

We parameterize the hazard rate function starting from the premise that the model ought to mimic devaluation probabilities that have been estimated in the empirical literature. Recent empirical evidence yields one robust prediction in this regard: devaluation probabilities under fixed-exchange-rate regimes evolve as J-shaped curves over time. The devaluation probability is decreasing after a peg is introduced, and eventually becomes increasing and higher than when the peg started.

Ample evidence in favor of J-shaped devaluation probabilities has been found both in country-specific studies based on models of speculative attacks and in cross-country studies of the determinants of exchange rate vulnerability as well. For example, Blanco and Garber (1986) estimated devaluation probabilities for the Mexican peso in the six years before the devaluations of 1976 and 1982 based on a Krugman-style model of balance-of-payment crises and an econometric model of Mexican money demand. These authors estimated a probability of collapse of 0.2 early in 1977, declining to near zero in about a year, rising slowly in 1978–1979, and rising rapidly to about 0.3 before the collapse. These results are qualitatively consistent with the findings of Goldberg (1994), who also studied Mexico but extended the sample to include the 1980–1986 period. Klein and Marion (1997) use a logit method to identify factors that influence the duration of currency pegs in a panel of monthly data for seventeen countries over the 1957–1991 period. They find strong evidence showing that sharp real appreciations and losses of foreign reserves predate devaluations and that devaluation probabilities are J-shaped. Probabilities of collapse one month before a devaluation are as high as 0.89, with 10 percent of the estimates higher than 0.55. Frankel and Rose (1996) and Kaminsky and Reinhart (1999) provide further support for the finding that real appreciation and reserve losses are key predictors of currency crises.

In view of the fact that most of the empirical literature (except Klein and Marion) does not yield direct estimates of the parameters of hazard rate functions like (13.5), we opted for setting the values of these parameters following a "curve-fitting" procedure: First, we set a smooth J curve to represent a "target" hazard function consistent with the empirical evidence of J-shaped devaluation probabilities—this target function is the same exogenous hazard rate function used in Mendoza and

Uribe 2000, which featured an initial devaluation probability at about 0.4, falling to zero in about twelve quarters and rising to 0.8 prior to the collapse. Second, we set the algorithm that solves the equilibrium of the model to search for values of B and Γ that yield the closest approximation, in the Euclidean sense, to the target hazard rate function. This approach yields the following parameter structure: $B = 0.17$ and $\Gamma = -2.9$. Note that this procedure does not impose any specific restrictions on the two parameters. Still, the solution yields $B > 0$, which is consistent with the view that the probability of devaluation increases as reserves fall. The value of Γ reflects the initial odds of a devaluation at the time the currency peg is introduced, given the initial gap between observed lagged reserves and their critical level.

Benchmark Simulation and Mexico's Stylized Facts

The solutions for state-contingent macroeconomic dynamics and the endogenous devaluation probabilities produced by the benchmark calibration are plotted in figure 13.1. The equilibrium dynamics plotted in this figure correspond to state-contingent allocations measured as percentage deviations from the deterministic prestabilization steady state. The continuous lines represent the dynamic equilibrium paths in the event that the currency peg continues, and the dotted lines indicate the allocations to which the variables shift on impact when a devaluation occurs.

Since the model was calibrated to capture roughly the policy stance of Mexico's 1987–1994 exchange rate–based stabilization, it is instructive to review briefly the cyclical dynamics of the Mexican economy during that period following the discussion in Mendoza and Uribe 2000. From the first quarter of 1988 to the last quarter of 1994, Mexico's real exchange rate appreciated by 35.4 percent—the Mexican plan was announced in December of 1987 but the exchange rate was fixed two months later. The deviations from trend in investment, GDP, and private consumption widened considerably during 1988–1992, but in 1993 all three fell below trend, in line with the common feature of exchange rate–based stabilizations that recessions often predate currency collapses. The fluctuations in real variables were also very large. At the peak of the cycle in 1992, the deviations from trend in GDP and consumption were about six percentage points higher, and the one for investment was fifteen percentage points higher, than at the cyclical minimum reached just before the beginning of the program in early

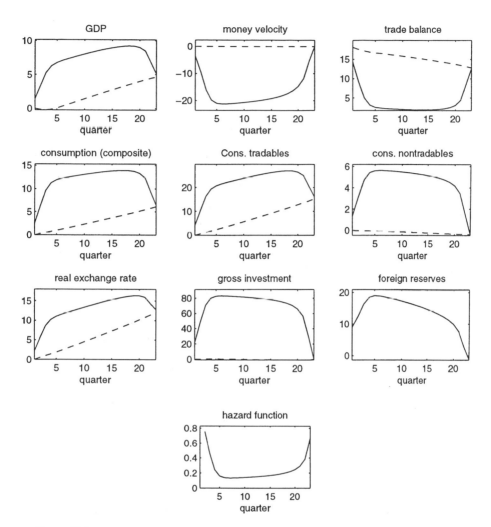

Figure 13.1
Macroeconomic dynamics of an exchange rate–based stabilization with endogenous devaluation probabilities. All variables, except the trade balance and the hazard function, are percentage deviations from the prestabilization steady state. The trade balance is expressed as the ratio of net exports to GDP. Key: solid line, values of the variables in the state of nature in which the stabilization plan continues; dashed line, values to which the variables jump when the currency collapses

1987. The boom in private consumption and the appreciation of the real exchange rate were nearly perfectly positively correlated until 1993, when consumption began to slow down but the real appreciation continued. Mexico's external imbalances worsened at a steady rate until the current account deficit reached 8 percent of GDP just before the devaluation at the end of 1994.

The results of the benchmark simulation show that the model is roughly consistent with these stylized facts. In particular, the model recreates boom-recession cycles in GDP, consumption, and investment with recessions that predate the devaluations. Aggregate and sectoral consumption move together with the real exchange rate for most of the duration of the stabilization plan, suggesting that the model can explain the high correlation between the real exchange rate and consumption that lies behind the price consumption puzzle. The trade balance worsens markedly on the early stages of the peg and then remains stable until it improves in a sudden jump that coincides with the collapse of the currency.

The endogenous monetary dynamics of the model are in line with the predictions typical of a model of balance-of-payments crises. Central bank foreign reserves increase initially, as the decline in the velocity of circulation that occurs in the early stages of the peg reflects the remonetization of the economy in response to the reduction in the nominal interest rate and the boom in real economic activity.[14] This remonetization plays a key role in allowing the model to mimic the initial declining path observed in empirical estimates of devaluation probabilities. After this initial stage, reserves decline gradually and then rapidly until they are finally depleted in a sudden jump to their critical level just before the collapse of the peg. This pattern in turn produces an endogenous time path of devaluation probabilities that, after the initial declining stage, begins to increase gradually and then rapidly, thus approximating the J shape of devaluation probabilities identified in empirical research.

The model does share an important empirical drawback of most existing models of balance-of-payments crises in that it requires a collapse of money balances at the time of the currency crash. Mexico's monetary aggregates did not collapse as the December 1994 devaluation took place. This resilience of the quantity of money followed several months of massive sterilized intervention by the central bank and large-scale swapping of public debt from peso-denominated public bonds to dollar-linked bonds (see Calvo and Mendoza 1996). In line with this evidence, some recent studies have examined models in which a balance-of-payments crisis may occur without a collapse in the demand for money (see Kumhof 1999).

In comparing the model's predictions to Mexican data, we acknowledge that Mexico's business cycles are caused by several factors in addition to the distortions resulting from currency risk, which is the only driving force of business cycles in the model we proposed. In Mendoza and Uribe 2000, we addressed this issue by trying to isolate the potential contribution of exchange rate uncertainty from the effects of other sources of business cycles using a VAR model proposed by Calvo and Mendoza (1996). We used the interest rate differential between Mexican and U.S. treasury bills as a measure of the probability of devaluation and default, and found that this differential explains about 40 percent of the variability of macroeconomic aggregates and the real exchange rate over twenty-four quarters.[15] Taking into account the total magnitude of the observed fluctuations, this suggests that an ideal simulation of our model should not be able to account for real appreciation in excess of 18 percent, consumption and GDP booms in excess of 2 percent, or investment booms in excess of 5 percent. Hence, the 14 percent real appreciation produced by this model is less than one-half the full real appreciation observed in Mexico during 1988–1994, but it is close to the 18 percent appreciation measured using the VAR.

We also acknowledge that in our effort to follow Mundell's analysis, we specified a functional form for the central bank's reaction function that may be too restrictive in the light of existing empirical evidence. Klein and Marion (1997), Frankel and Rose (1996), and Kaminsky and Reinhart (1999) all show that the appreciation of the real exchange rate is a robust predictor of the collapse of fixed exchange rates even when the information provided by foreign reserves is taken into account. Moreover, Klein and Marion show that even if both reserves and the real exchange rate are used as predictors, the duration of the peg per se is also a robust predictor of currency crashes. In line with this finding, we found that simulations of the model in which a linear term t is introduced into the functional form of z_t produce a closer fit to the J-curves estimated in the data than the basic specification set in equation (13.5). Thus, we did not expect our basic specification to mimic closely the Mexican data, but were still surprised by its ability to approximate some of their key features.

Policy Determinants of Currency Crashes: Revisiting Mundell's Findings

The last set of numerical exercises examines the implications of altering the responsiveness of the policy reaction function to observed changes in reserves (i.e., altering the value of B) with the aim of exploring the predictions of the model for an experiment analogous to the one conducted by Mundell (1960). We conduct this analysis in two stages. First, we simulate the model under alternative values of B, keeping the values of all other parameters constant, and compare the results to those of the benchmark model. Second, we allow B to vary as in the first case, but we also allow fiscal policy to vary so as to "put up a fight" for the central bank's foreign reserves. This is done by computing for each value of B the fiscal adjustment (i.e. the required changed in κ) that is necessary for the currency peg to have a chance to continue to last a maximum of J periods—the same as is the benchmark case.

The first experiment, in which B is changed while maintaining unaltered the rest of the structure of the model, sheds some light on the model's predictions regarding the occurrence of endogenous speculative attacks that lead to a currency collapse before date J. Figure 13.2 plots the hazard function, the reserves-to-GDP ratio, GDP, and the real exchange rate for the benchmark case and for cases in which the value of B is 10, 20, and 40 percent larger than in the benchmark parameterization. The horizontal dotted lines in the plots of the reserves-to-GDP ratio indicate the values of R_0/Y_0 and $(R/Y)^{\text{crit}}$, both of which are constant across the simulations.

The plots in figure 13.2 show that as the speculative capital outflows indirectly captured in B strengthen, the same stance of fiscal and exchange rate policies results in currency collapses that occur sooner than in the benchmark case. This is the case despite the fact that the domestic nominal interest rate will also increase more and faster than in the benchmark case (as implied by the interest parity condition implicit in equation (13.9)). When B is 40 percent higher than in the benchmark case (panel (d) of the figure), the devaluation probability remains very high throughout the duration of the peg, and the peg itself cannot last more than four quarters. Foreign reserves decline very rapidly and the cyclical increases in real output and the real exchange rate are smaller than in the benchmark simulation. Naturally, the opposite results would obtain if we tried reducing B instead of increasing

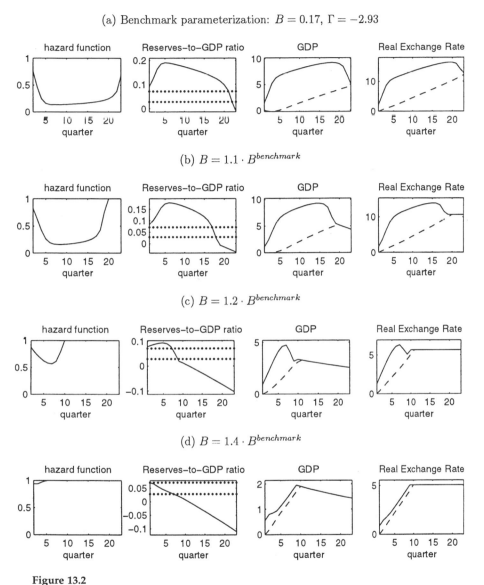

Figure 13.2
Sensitivity analysis: Varying the sensitivity of the hazard function to changes in foreign reserves. GDP and the real exchange rate are percentage deviations from the prestabilization steady state. Key: solid line, values of the variables in the state of nature in which the stabilization plan continues; dashed line, values to which the variables jump when the currency collapses. Dotted lines in the charts of the Reserves-to-GDP Ratio denote initial (R_0/Y_0) and critical $(R/Y)^{crit}$ levels of this ratio, with $(R_0/Y_0) > (R/Y)^{crit}$

it—as speculation becomes weaker, the same stance of fiscal policy would result in currency pegs that could be maintained for more than J periods (if we relaxed the assumption that at J the currency must collapse with probability 1).

A higher value of B brings forward the date of a speculative attack in part simply because changing this exogenous parameter implies a higher probability for the collapse of the currency for any given fall in the reserves-to-GDP ratio. There is in addition an endogenous channel that accelerates the collapse by altering the dynamics of reserves. As z_t rises, the premium on the domestic interest rate rises, the velocity of circulation of money rises and the demand for money falls, thereby altering the time path of reserves. The plots in figure 13.2 show that, as a result, an increase in B leads to a smaller initial surge in reserves— or even no increase at all as in the case of panel (d)—and a more rapid depletion of reserves after the initial surge.

The results for the second experiment, where B and κ are allowed to vary, are plotted in figure 13.3. Note that κ is falling in each case so that larger cuts in government outlays during the stabilization plan ensure that the ratio of reserves to GDP does not reach the critical level until the same date as in the benchmark scenario. Clearly, this response of the government neutralizes the effects of modest variations in B and yields results roughly similar to the benchmark case. However, if B is too large (as in panel (d)), the logistic functional form of z_t produces probabilities of devaluation that are virtually equal to 1 despite the dynamics of reserves. Hence, even tough foreign reserves reach the critical level at $t = J - 1$, the results are similar to the case in which government policy is not tightened and reserves reach the critical level much earlier.

Figures 13.2 and 13.3 can now be examined jointly to study the implications of an experiment similar to the one in Mundell 1960, in which the government tightens policy in an effort to defend the peg as speculation grows stronger. There is a nontrivial difference because Mundell focused on the case in which this is done by the central bank adopting measures to increase the nominal interest rate under conditions of imperfect capital mobility. This is ruled out by the assumption of perfect capital mobility in our model, and hence we consider instead the adjustment to fiscal policy as the closest approximation. As mentioned in the introduction, Mundell showed that macroeconomic dynamics would vary widely depending on the particular static parameters that measured the "speeds of response" of speculators and

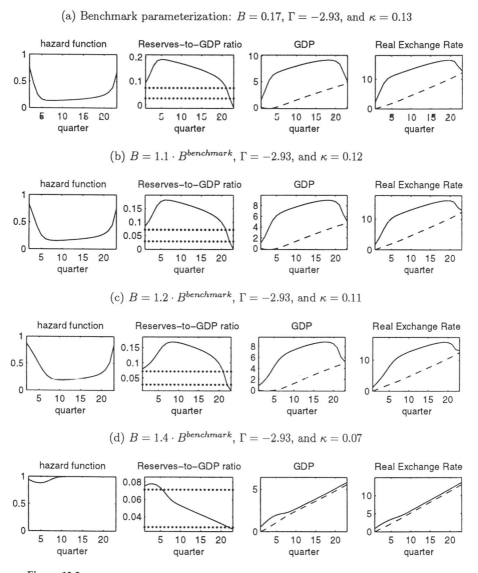

Figure 13.3
Sensitivity analysis: Varying the sensitivity of the hazard function to changes in foreign reserves and the degree of fiscal adjustment. The adjustment of κ in each row ensures that, if the currency peg survives until date $J - 2$, then the Reserves-to-GDP Ratio hits its critical level on that date. For key to the charts is as in figure 13.2

policy makers, and that dynamics could turn from stable to unstable, or from cyclical to asymptotic.

Comparing figures 13.2 and 13.3, we find that in our model, just as in Mundell's, the relative responses of speculative capital outflows and fiscal policy tightening are critical for determining macroeconomic dynamics. These figures represent two extreme cases of the government's response. Figure 13.2 illustrates cases in which the government does not respond and simply keeps κ at the benchmark level of 13.3 percent, whereas figure 13.3 reports cases in which the government responds fully and hence reduces κ to protect its foreign reserves. Comparing panels (b) and (c) of the two figures we note that the cyclical dynamics of GDP and the real appreciation differ sharply between these two extreme cases. While none of these experiments show the oscillatory dynamics that Mundell argued could exist for some combinations of speed-of-response parameters, we did find other rare examples in which equilibrium dynamics could display oscillations (for instance in the case in which $\Gamma = 0$, $B = -0.17$, and $\kappa = 0.234$). Hence, we conclude that Mundell's findings are roughly consistent with the quantitative predictions of our model.

Conclusion

This chapter reexamined Mundell's (1960) model of balance-of-payments crises in the light of modern international macroeconomics. In particular, the chapter derived the quantitative predictions of an intertemporal, general equilibrium model in which the probability of devaluation is endogenous and depends on the observed evolution of foreign reserves. The model represents a two-sector small open economy with perfect capital mobility, but with incomplete contingent claims markets. In this model, exchange rate uncertainty introduces a time-variant premium on the domestic interest rate that induces stochastic distortions affecting the relative prices determining saving, investment, and the supply of labor. In addition, market incompleteness implies that these distortions also introduce state-contingent wealth effects resulting from the unproductive use of government revenue and suboptimal investment decisions.

The economic fluctuations that result from the distortions on relative prices and wealth reproduce some basic features of exchange rate–based stabilizations. In particular, the model is consistent with large real appreciations, large external deficits, booms in output and absorption followed by recessions that predate currency collapses, and a high positive correlation between the real exchange rate and domestic absorption for the duration of currency pegs. The model is also relatively successful in producing endogenous devaluation probabilities that capture the J-shaped nature of devaluation probabilities that have been identified in actual data. These results also imply that the model can be useful for providing an economic interpretation to the findings of several recent studies that identify foreign reserves, and other key macroeconomic variables, as robust predictors of currency crashes.

Our analysis suggests that, for a given policy setting, endogenous speculative attacks occur earlier in economies where devaluation probabilities are more sensitive to observed changes in foreign reserves. This is in part because in such a case investors simply grow more anxious about the sustainability of a currency peg for a given change in reserves, but also because in equilibrium their increased sensitiveness results in a higher premium on the domestic interest rate that magnifies the distortions of the model and accelerates the depletion of reserves. The simulations also produce results consistent with Mundell's (1960) analysis of speculators and policy makers engaged in a "fight" over foreign reserves. Mundell showed that, depending on the sensitiveness of investors to changes in reserves relative to the policy response of the government, the dynamics of adjustment could be stable or unstable, oscillatory or asymptotic. In our model equilibrium dynamics are also very sensitive to increases in the sensitiveness of speculators that are matched by a tightening of fiscal policy intended to protect foreign reserves.

The policy lessons that can be drawn from this exercise are interesting. First, we note that in this model losses of foreign reserves, real appreciation and external deficits are *not* exogenous triggers of balance-of-payments crises. What lies behind these crises is the lack of confidence of the private sector, which is implicitly modeled here via a central bank policy reaction function that sets the probability of devaluation as a decreasing function of the stock of foreign reserves. Second, the cyclical dynamics of exchange rate–based stabilizations and the collapse of fixed exchange rates do not need to result from sudden changes in fiscal or monetary policies. We showed that a model calibrated to reflect Mexico's tight and sustained policies between 1987 and 1993 still yields large real appreciation and large trade deficits, and that the currency crises may occur sooner or later depending on the stance of fiscal policy and the sensitiveness of speculative capital outflows to observed changes in foreign reserves. Third, since crises in our model can be produced by lack of confidence and confidence is linked to foreign reserves, Mundell's key policy recommendation remains valid today: "an effective system of international payments based on fixed exchange rates must be one which provides a reasonably high degree of international liquidity" (1960, 246). As Calvo and Mendoza (1996) noted, however, this "reasonable high degree of international liquidity" can be a very large figure in today's global economy.

Notes

Comments and suggestions by Guillermo Calvo, Hal Cole, Allan Drazen, Tim Kehoe, Kent Kimbrough, Juan Pablo Nicolini, Carmen Reinhart, Stephanie Schmitt-Grohe, Carlos Vegh, and seminar participants at the University of Washington, the University of Maryland, and Di Tella University are gratefully acknowledged.

1. It is worth noting that Mundell's (1960) setup assumed flexible prices, in contrast with the sticky-price assumption of the classic Mundell-Fleming model. Mundell noted that price stickiness was not required by the arguments of his 1960 article.

2. Mendoza and Uribe (1997) and (2000) examined models with this feature, but taking devaluation probabilities as exogenous and ignoring foreign reserves, so currency collapse is also exogenous.

3. Models in this class include perfect-foresight models with time-separable preferences and no borrowing constraints. Some models that can resolve the puzzle have been developed recently by using preferences displaying habit formation (Uribe 1998a) or by introducing uncertainty regarding the duration of the peg (Mendoza and Uribe 2000).

4. We show in Mendoza and Uribe 2000 that this assumption could be changed with little effect on the numerical results for the assumption that at J there is a devaluation with positive probability, and after that date there is no currency uncertainty.

5. Note that this framework can be easily extended to condition z_t on other key predictors of currency collapses identified in the recent empirical literature such as the real exchange rate. Uribe (1998b) shows that real exchange targeting, that is, exchange rate policies whereby the rate of depreciation is set as an increasing function of the relative price of nontradables in terms of tradables, can produce endogenous aggregate instability.

6. The term $m_t V_t S(V_t)$ in (13.6) can be interpreted as profits of government-owned banks. However, since they will be used only for unproductive government purchases, we could also assume that transaction costs are simply a deadweight loss.

7. Mendoza and Uribe (2000) showed that a model in which seigniorage and transaction costs are rebated to households as lump-sum transfers fails to account for key features of the data. Moreover, the analytical work of Calvo and Drazen (1993) and Helpman and Razin (1987), as well as our review of Mexican fiscal policy during the 1987–1994 exchange rate–based stabilization (which is the benchmark for the calibration of the model), suggests that the case without rebates is perhaps more realistic.

8. There are three other important differences between our model and Calvo's: (a) in Calvo's model government outlays are only lump-sum transfers, which rules out the fiscal-induced wealth effects of our model; (b) in Calvo's model money velocity is constant, whereas in our model it is a decreasing function of the nominal interest rate; and (c) our model allows for changes in the depreciation rate to affect labor supply and capital accumulation, whereas in Calvo's endowment-economy model these changes can affect only consumption.

9. Note that this key difference between the two approaches would still be present even if we altered our model to bring it closer to Calvo's by considering an endowment economy in which seigniorage and transaction cost revenue are fully rebated to households.

10. Calvo (1987) suggested that there is a risk of obtaining multiple solutions for long-run monetary equilibria using interest-elastic money demand. However, we have ample numerical evidence showing that this is generally not the case with the functional form $S = AV^\gamma$.

11. See Calvo and Mendoza 1996 and Kamin and Rogers 1996.

12. We show in the simulation results that under alternative parameter configurations, particularly as κ and B change, the peg may endogenously terminate before period J.

13. Note that the necessary fiscal adjustment is higher (i.e., κ^0 is smaller) the higher the prestabilization level of government outlays, the higher the critical level of foreign reserves, the lower the initial level of reserves, and the lower the level of seigniorage revenue and transaction costs.

14. Typically, models of currency crises do not focus on this initial buildup of reserves because they start from an existing fixed exchange rate, whereas our policy experiment starts with a switch from a floating exchange rate to a fixed exchange rate.

15. Note, however, that the interest differential is almost perfectly correlated with the Mexican interest rate, and the latter was influenced by sterilized intervention of large capital flows during 1990–1994. Thus, the differential is at best a noisy measure of the "market" expectations of the sustainability of the peg.

References

Blanco, H., and P. M. Garber. 1986. Recurrent devaluation and speculative attacks on the Mexican peso. *Journal of Political Economy* 94:148–66.

Calvo, G. A. 1987. Balance of payments crises in a cash in advance economy. *Journal of Money, Credit and Banking* 19:19–32.

Calvo, G. A. 1986. Temporary stabilization: Predetermined exchange rates. *Journal of Political Economy* 94:1319–29.

Calvo, G. A., and A. Drazen. 1993. Uncertain duration of reform: Dynamic implications. Working Papers in International Economics no. WP 4, Center for International Economics, University of Maryland, College Park.

Calvo, G. A., and E. G. Mendoza. 1996. Mexico's balance-of-payments crisis: A chronicle of a death foretold. *Journal of International Economics* 41(3–4):235–64.

Drazen, A., and E. Helpman. 1988. Stabilization with exchange rate management under uncertainty. In *Economic Effects of the Government Budget*, ed. E. Helpman, A. Razin, and E. Sadka, 310–327. Cambridge: MIT Press.

Frankel, J. A., and A. K. Rose. 1996. Currency crashes in emerging markets: An empirical treatment. *Journal of International Economics* 41(3–4):351–67.

Goldberg, L. S. 1994. Predicting exchange rate crises: México revisited. *Journal of International Economics* 36:413–30.

Greenwood, J. 1984. Non-traded goods, the trade balance, and the balance of payments. *Canadian Journal of Economics* 17:806–23.

Greenwood, J. 1983. Expectations, the exchange rate and the current account. *Journal of Monetary Economics* 12:543–69.

Helpman, E., and A. Razin. 1987. Exchange rate management: Intertemporal tradeoffs. *American Economic Review* 77:107–23.

Kamin, S., and J. H. Rogers. 1996. Monetary policy in the end-game to exchange-rate-based stabilizations: The case of México. *Journal of International Economics* 41:285–307.

Kaminsky, G., and C. M. Reinhart. 1999. Twin crises: The causes of banking and balance of payments crises. *American Economic Review* 89:473–500. forthcoming.

Kiguel, M., and N. Liviatan. 1992. The business cycle associated with exchange rate based stabilization. *World Bank Economic Review* 6:279–305.

Kimbrough, K. P. 1986. The optimum quantity of money rule in the theory of Public Finance. *Journal of Monetary Economics* 18(3):277–84.

King, R. G., C. I. Plosser, and S. T. Rebelo. 1988. Production, growth, and business cycles. *Journal of Monetary Economics* 21:s126–s150.

Klein, M. W., and N. P. Marion. 1997. Explaining the duration of exchange-rate pegs. *Journal of Development Economics* 54:387–404.

Krugman, P. 1979. A model of balance-of-payments crises. *Journal of Money, Credit, and Banking* 11:311–25.

Kumhof, M. 1999. Lower inflation through lower interest rates—Capital inflow sterilization in small open economies. Unpublished manuscript, Department of Economics, Stanford University. Mimeographed.

Mendoza, E. G. 1995. The terms of trade, the real exchange rate and economic fluctuations. *International Economic Review* 36:101–37.

Mendoza, E. G., and L. L. Tesar. 1998. The international ramifications of tax reforms: Supply side economics in a global economy. *American Economic Review* 88(1):226–45.

Mendoza, E. G., and M. Uribe. 2000. Devaluation risk and the syndrome of exchange-rate-based-stabilizations. Caruegie Rochester Conference Series on Public Policy, forthcoming.

Mendoza, E. G., and M. Uribe. 1997. The syndrome of exchange-rate-based stabilizations and the uncertain duration of currency pegs. Discussion paper no. 121, Institute for Empirical Macroeconomics, Federal Reserve Bank of Minneapolis.

Mundell, R. A. 1960. The monetary dynamics of international adjustment under dixed and flexible exchange rates. *Quarterly Journal of Economics* 74(2):227–57.

Obstfeld, M. 1995. International currency experience: New lessons and lessons relearned. *Brookings Papers on Economics Activity* no. 1:119–215.

Obstfeld, M. 1986. Rational and self-fulfilling balance-of-payments crises. *American Economic Review* 76:72–81.

Robolo, S. T., and C. A. Végh. 1995. Real effects of exchange-rate-based stabilization: An analysis of competing theories. In *NBER Macro economics Annual, 1995*, ed. B. Bernanke and J. Rotemberg, 125–174. Cambridge, Mass.: MIT Press.

Reinhart, C. M., and C. A. Végh. 1995. Nominal interest rates, consumption booms, and lack of credibility: A quantitative examination. *Journal of Development Economics* 46:357–78.

Uribe, M. 1998a. Habit formation and the dynamics of currency pegs. Department of Economics, University of Pennsylvania. Mimeographed.

Uribe, M. 1998b. Real exchange rate targeting and aggregate instability. Department of Economics, University of Pennsylvania. Mimeographed.

Uribe, M. 1997. Exchange-rate-based inflation stabilization: The initial real effects of credible plans. *Journal of Monetary Economics* 39(2):197–221.

Végh, C. A. 1992. Stopping high inflation: An analytical overview. *IMF Staff Papers* 39:626–95.

14

Tariffs, Unemployment, and the Current Account: An Intertemporal Equilibrium Model

Shouyong Shi

Introduction

Tariffs protect jobs, at least in the short run. This idea was sometimes proposed as a policy prescription for reducing unemployment (Cripps and Godley 1978) and has been rationalized by models with sticky prices or wages. By creating a gap between the real wage and the marginal product of labor, the nominal rigidities generate unemployment and leave output to be determined by aggregate demand. If nominal prices are sticky, as in the celebrated framework of Mundell (1968) and Fleming (1962), tariffs shift demand from imports to domestic goods, a shift which is absorbed by increased labor demand and output. This mechanism continues to work in modern versions of sticky prices models, including the intertemporal model by Obstfeld and Rogoff (1995). If nominal wages are sticky, the shift in demand toward domestic goods improves the country's terms of trade and so reduces the wage measured in domestic goods—the product wage. Again, labor demand and output increase.

The assumption of nominal rigidities is controversial, and the positive employment effect of tariffs may be rejected on this ground alone.[1] However, this rejection is a weak one, because central to the argument for a positive employment of tariffs is not the nominal rigidity per se but the existence of unemployment created by the deviation of the real wage from the marginal product of labor. The nominal rigidity is only a convenient way to generate such deviation. To have a stronger rejection to the positive employment effect of tariffs, one must then show that tariffs reduce employment even when persistent unemployment exists for reasons other than nominal rigidities.

This chapter does exactly that. To achieve this objective, I must first construct a model that has two necessary ingredients. One is a real friction rather than a nominal one that generates unemployment in the long run, for reasons discussed above. The second is a dynamic general equilibrium framework that permits the distinction between short-run and long-run effects of tariffs. This is necessary because optimal wealth accumulation places restrictions on the long-run product wage and has direct implications on the effects of tariffs. For example, with time-additive preferences, optimal wealth accumulation implies that the long-run capital/labor ratio is determined by the equality between the long-run marginal product of capital and the exogenous subjective discount rate. If the labor market is frictionless, then the long-run product wage must also be exogenous, irrespective of the tariff.[2]

A model that has the above ingredients is rare in international economics, since dynamic general equilibrium models have typically ignored the issue of unemployment and models of unemployment have typically employed nominal rigidities. Fortunately, a recently developed model in macroeconomics meets the criteria (Merz 1995; Andolfatto 1996; and Shi and Wen 1997, 1999). It is the intertemporal version of the search unemployment theory by Mortensen (1982) and Pissarides (1990). In this theory unemployment persists because firms must maintain costly vacancies in order to hire workers and unemployed workers must search in order to find a job. The marginal product of labor is strictly higher than the product wage so as to compensate for the firm's hiring (vacancy) cost. This gap allows tariffs to affect employment without wage rigidity: Permanent increases in tariffs can permanently affect the product wage and employment without affecting the marginal product of labor.

The product wage, determined by Nash bargaining between firms and workers, is a weighted sum of the marginal product of labor and a reservation wage.[3] With an intertemporal setting, the reservation wage equals the marginal rate of substitution between consumption and leisure. There are two ways in which a tariff affects the reservation wage in the current model, depicted in figure 14.1. The first is the *direct product wage* effect: A tariff increases the price of the domestic good and so reduces the product wage. The second is the *consumption bundle* effect: A tariff increases the price of the goods bundle, both directly through the import price and indirectly through the terms-of-trade improvement, which reduces the marginal value of wealth measured in the import and raises the marginal rate of substitution between leisure and consumption.

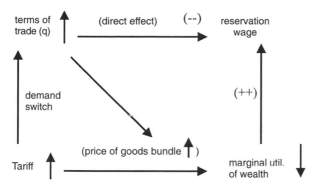

Figure 14.1

The two effects of the tariff are opposite to each other, and their relative strength depends on the elasticity of intertemporal substitution. The consumption bundle effect dominates the direct product wage effect when the elasticity of intertemporal substitution is small, in which case consumption varies very little in response to the higher price, leaving the marginal value of wealth to fall significantly and the product wage to rise. With realistic values of the elasticity of intertemporal substitution, the overall effect of the tariff is to raise the product wage and reduce employment in both the long run and short run. Thus, the presence of the search friction and unemployment is insufficient for generating a predominant, positive employment effect for the tariff.

The tariff may also change utility. In the special case where the country has no influence on the terms of trade, the tariff reduces steady state consumption, increases leisure, and increases steady state utility. But the steady state utility gain is completely wiped out by the cost of transition, so the tariff has no effect on intertemporal utility. When the country has some limited influence on the terms of trade, the welfare effect of the tariff is analytically ambiguous.

The model constructed in this chapter enhances the dynamic general equilibrium paradigm that has been extensively used in international economics since the late 1970s. The paradigm has often been criticized for lacking some realistic features such as unemployment. By allowing for persistent unemployment and yet maintaining flexible prices and wages, the current framework provides a viable alternative to models with nominal rigidities for addressing international policy issues related to unemployment. The search approach to unemployment is chosen here because it matches the statistical definition of unemployment and is tractable in a dynamic optimization environment that involves a long horizon.

To emphasize the importance of the search friction, a small open economy is adopted so that the product wage effect of the tariff would be absent in the long run if the friction were eliminated, as in Sen and Turnovsky 1989. The intertemporal analysis is related to the voluminous literature on the Laursen-Metzler effect (see Obstfeld 1982 and Persson and Svensson 1985). The presence of unemployment links the analysis to some trade models, such as Matusz 1986, Fernandez 1992, Brecher 1992, and Neary 1982, but the current work differs in two aspects. First, the current chapter focuses on the macroeconomic effects of tariffs rather than the sectorial effects in the trade models. Second, the current chapter employs an intertemporal structure, while those trade models are typically either static or very restrictive on agent's intertemporal decisions.

The remainder of this chapter is organized as follows. The second section constructs an intertemporal maximization model with labor market search. The third section isolates the consumption bundle effect by assuming that the economy faces exogenous terms of trade. The fourth section examines the case of endogenous terms of trade. The fifth section discusses the welfare effect of the tariff. The sixth section concludes the chapter, and the appendices provide necessary proofs.

Labor Market Search in a Small Open Economy

Goods and Assets

Consider a small open country that imports a good whose price in the world market is normalized to one. The country imposes a tariff rate τ on imports, and the country's residents face an import price $(1 + \tau)$. The country produces a single good, called the domestic good, which can be consumed or exported. The relative price of the domestic good to the import in the world market is q, which is the country's terms of trade. The assumption of complete specialization in production places the focus of this chapter on the aggregate effect of the tariff rather than its sectorial effects. As in Sen and Turnovsky 1989, the country may be able to influence the terms of trade, and so tariffs can affect employment through the terms of trade. This influence is captured by an export function, $x(q)$, which satisfies

$$x'(q) \leq -x(q)/q \leq 0. \tag{14.1}$$

These properties ensure that the foreign demand for the country's good is a decreasing function of the good's price and has an elasticity greater than unity. The latter reflects the fact that a small country's influence on the terms of trade is limited. A special case is $x'(q) = -\infty$, in which case the country faces exogenous terms of trade.

The country consists of many identical households whose size is normalized to one. Households have an unrestricted access to the world good and asset markets. In particular, capital is perfectly mobile across countries, so households can borrow and lend at a constant world interest rate $\rho > 0$. A household's portfolio consists of domestic capital K, measured in terms of domestic goods, and foreign assets F, measured in terms of the import before the tariff. The rental rate of capital is r. Because the terms of trade can vary over time, holding domestic capital yields a capital gain (or loss) $\dot{q}/q$ relative to holding foreign assets. Therefore, the arbitrage between domestic capital and foreign assets yields

$$r + \frac{\dot{q}}{q} = \rho. \tag{14.2}$$

In contrast to capital mobility, labor is immobile across countries.

For the demand for goods, denote a representative household's consumption of the domestic good by d and the consumption of the import by f. To simplify analysis, assume that d and f enter the household's utility function through a linearly homogeneous aggregator $H(d, f)$ that is increasing and concave in each argument.[4] In this case, a household's optimal consumption can be chosen in two stages. First, for any given $c > 0$, it is optimal to choose the bundle (d, f) to solve

$$c \cdot p(q, \tau) \equiv \min_{(d,f)} \{qd + (1+\tau)f : H(d, f) \geq c\}.$$

The function $p(q, \tau)$ defined above is the unit cost (or expenditure) function dual to H, which will be referred to as the *price index* of the consumption bundle. In the second stage of the consumption choice, c is chosen to maximize intertemporal utility, as described in the next subsection. I will refer to c as consumption of the goods bundle.

It is well known that $p(q, \tau)$ is increasing and concave in each argument and is linearly homogeneous in $(q, 1 + \tau)$. For given c, the demand functions for goods are

$$d = c \cdot p_1(q, \tau), \quad f = c \cdot p_2(q, \tau). \tag{14.3}$$

It is reasonable to require that the share of consumption on the domestic good, qp_1/p, be a nondecreasing function of the tariff and a nonincreasing function of the terms of trade. That is, $pp_{12} \geq p_1 p_2$ and $pp_1 \leq q(p_1^2 - pp_{11})$. These requirements can be easily satisfied if, for example, H is a Cobb-Douglas aggregator.

Households

Each household consists of many infinitely lived agents, each endowed with a fixed flow of time, T. At any given point in time, an agent can choose only one of the following activities: working for wages, searching for a job, or enjoying leisure. Agents who are searching for jobs are called unemployed agents. Unemployed agents are randomly matched with job vacancies according to a matching function described later. Since the timing of a match is random, agents face idiosyncratic risks in income and leisure. This randomness can complicate the analysis by generating distributions of wealth and consumption across agents. To focus on the aggregate behavior, I will assume that each household consists of a continuum of agents with measure T and that all members care only about the household's utility. In this case, individual risks in consumption and leisure are completely smoothed within each household. A similar approach is adopted in the literature on indivisible labor, where employment lotteries are used to smooth the risk across states of employment (see Hansen 1985 and Rogerson 1988).[5]

The utility function of a household is

$$\int_0^\infty \{u(c) - \beta[n + l(s)]\}e^{-\rho t}dt, \quad \beta > 0, \tag{14.4}$$

where $c = H(d, f)$ is the household's consumption of the bundle, n is the size of household members in work, and s is the size of unemployed members. The labor force participation rate is $(n + s)/T$ and the unemployment rate is $s/(n + s)$. The function $l(s)$ measures the efficiency units of time in search relative to working. Note that the utility function is linear in the hours of work, as implied by the above-cited literature on indivisible labor with employment lotteries. Also, the rate of time preference equals the international interest rate, which is necessary for consumption to converge to a steady state in a small open economy with a constant rate of time preference.

The function $u(.)$ is assumed to be increasing and concave, with an intertemporal elasticity of substitution $\sigma \equiv -u'(c)/[cu''(c)]$. Hall (1988) and Epstein and Zin (1991) have found that the intertemporal elasticity of substitution is empirically small and below unity. I thus assume $\sigma \leq 1$. I also assume that the search effort is inelastically supplied, so s is fixed at a level $s_0 = 1$. This assumption is made for analytical tractability: Without it the model cannot be analytically solved. It should be interpreted as an extreme approximation for the reality that the search effort is much less elastic than vacancy (Layard et al. 1991). Accordingly, the qualitative results obtained herein should hold more generally for such economies. Note that fixing s fixes the level of unemployment but leaves the rate of unemployment to be determined endogenously.[6]

As in other search models, employment in the current model is predetermined at each given time; it changes only gradually as workers quit or unemployed agents find jobs:

$$\dot{n} = ms_0 - \theta n. \tag{14.5}$$

The constant θ is the rate of job separation, and m is the rate at which each unemployed agent finds a job. As discussed later, m depends on the ratio of aggregate vacancy to unemployment. However, an individual household takes m as given.

A representative household's maximization problem is

$$(PH) \max_{(c,F)} U,$$

subject to

$$\dot{F} = \rho F + q(wn + \pi) - pc + L; \quad F(0) = F_0 \text{ given.} \tag{14.6}$$

Here π is the dividend to capital (defined later), measured in terms of the domestic good; w is the wage measured in terms of the domestic good (i.e., the product wage); and L is the lump-sum rebate of the tariff revenue. The household takes (m, w, π, q, p, L) as given in the maximization. Note that n is not in the list of the household's choice variables. This is because, with the assumed inelastic search effort, employment dynamics described by (14.5) are exogenous to the household. Employment is demand-driven, determined by the firm's hiring decision and a wage equation described later.

Let ϕ be the current-value shadow price of wealth measured in terms of import before tariffs. Standard dynamic optimization techniques generate

$$\dot{\phi} = 0, \tag{14.7}$$

$$u'(c) = p\phi. \tag{14.8}$$

Since the world interest rate always equals the rate of time preference, the shadow value of wealth must be constant over time along any continuous path, as is typical in a small open economy. That is, any changes in ϕ must be once-and-for-all and occur immediately after shocks hit the economy. Equation (14.8) states the familiar relation that the marginal utility of consumption of the goods bundle is equal to the marginal value of wealth, evaluated with the price index p. Once c is determined, the demand for each good is given by (14.3).

Firms

There are many identical firms in the economy. The production function is $G(K, n)$, which is increasing and concave in each argument and linearly homogeneous. Each firm maintains vacancies in order to hire workers. The cost of maintaining a number v of vacancies is $B(v)$ in terms of the domestic good. This cost function is increasing and convex, with a vacancy elasticity $\varepsilon = B'(v)/[vB''(v)]$. Let μ be the rate at which a vacancy finds a match. Like m, the rate μ depends on aggregate vacancy and unemployment, but an individual firm takes μ as given. A firm's employment evolves as follows:

$$\dot{n} = \mu v - \theta n. \tag{14.9}$$

Adjustments in physical capital are also costly, as in Hayashi 1982. That is, to increase physical capital by an amount i, the firm must invest a total amount $Q(i)$. The function Q has the following properties:

$$Q'(i) > 0, Q''(i) > 0, Q(0) = 0, Q'(0) = 1.$$

An individual firm takes as given the wage rate w offered by other firms. The firm also takes (μ, q, r) as given and maximizes the present value:

$$(PF) \max_{(v,i,n,k)} \int_0^\infty \pi(t) e^{-\int_0^t r(z)dz} dt$$

subject to (14.9) and the following constraints:

$$\pi = G(K, n) - wn - B(v) - Q(i);$$

$$\dot{K} = i; \tag{14.10}$$

$$n(0) = n_0, K(0) = K_0 \text{ given.}$$

Let 'I' be the current-value shadow price of an additional worker to the firm and Ω the marginal value of capital. The optimal conditions for (PF) are

$$\Psi = B'(v)/\mu; \tag{14.11}$$

$$\dot{\Psi} = (\theta + r)\Psi - (G_2 - w); \tag{14.12}$$

$$\Omega = Q'(i); \tag{14.13}$$

$$\dot{\Omega} = r\Omega - G_1. \tag{14.14}$$

Equation (14.11) characterizes the firm's optimal decision for vacancy—the investment in employment. It requires the marginal cost of a vacancy, $B'(v)$, to be equal to the marginal benefit, $\mu\Psi$. Equation (14.12) requires the "return" to employment, $(\theta + r)\Psi$, to be equal to the sum of the "dividend" from hiring, $(G_2 - w)$, and the capital gain, $\dot{\Psi}$. Equations (14.13) and (14.14) are similar conditions for the investment in physical capital.

I will refer to the difference $(G_2 - w)$ as the firm's surplus from hiring. In contrast to a typical neoclassical model, the marginal product of labor here must exceed the wage rate in order to give firms a positive surplus from hiring that compensates for the hiring cost. If $G_2 = w$, the shadow price of an additional worker to the firm would be zero in the steady state and so vacancies and employment would be zero in the steady state (see (14.12)).

Matching and Wage Determination

The matching for each vacancy and unemployed agent is random, but the aggregate number of job matches is deterministic and given by a matching function. Let $\bar{v}$ and $\bar{s}_0$ be the aggregate number of vacancies and unemployed agents, respectively. The flow of job matches is

$$M(\bar{v}, \bar{s}_0) = M_0\bar{v}^\alpha \bar{s}_0^{1-\alpha}, \quad \alpha \in (0, 1), \tag{14.15}$$

where M_0 is a positive constant. The matching technology exhibits constant returns-to-scale, as is empirically supported (see Blanchard and Diamond 1989). The Cobb-Douglas form is adopted for analytical simplicity. With the normalization $\bar{s}_0 = 1$, we have

$$m(\bar{v}) \equiv M/\bar{s}_0 = M_0\bar{v}^\alpha, \quad \mu(\bar{v}) \equiv M/\bar{v} = m(\bar{v})/\bar{v}. \tag{14.16}$$

Note that the matching rate for vacancy, μ, is a decreasing function of $\bar{v}$. Also, $\mu\bar{v} = m$, so the two laws of motion for n, (14.5) and (14.9), coincide in any symmetric equilibrium. (I will hereafter suppress the bar in $\bar{v}$ and $\bar{s}_0$.)

Once an unemployed agent is matched with a vacancy, the agent and the firm negotiate the agent's current and future wage rates. The outcome is determined by Nash bargaining, which maximizes the weighted surpluses of the household and the firm. To be precise, let $t0$ be the time when a match is created. Denote by $\{\hat{w}(t)\}_{t \geq t0}$ the path of wage rates to be determined for the new worker, conditional on the continuation of the agent's employment. Wage rates are measured in terms of the domestic good. Hiring an additional worker of size dn with the wages increases the firm's current-value surplus at each time $t \geq t0$ by $[G_2(t) - \hat{w}(t)]dn$. Having an additional member working at the wages increases the household's income (in terms of imports) at each time $t \geq t0$ by $\hat{w}(t)q(t)dn$. The utility value of such increased income is $\phi(t)\hat{w}(t)q(t)dn$, since $\phi(t)$ is the marginal utility of time-t income (wealth).[7] The associated leisure cost is βdn, so the household's surplus is $[\hat{w}(t)q(t)\phi(t) - \beta]dn$ at each time $t \geq t0$. With normalization, the Nash bargaining solution solves

$$\max_{\hat{w}}[G_2 - \hat{w}(t)]^{1-\lambda}\left[\hat{w}(t) - \frac{\beta}{q\phi}\right]^\lambda, \quad \text{for } t \geq t0.$$

The parameter $\lambda \in (0, 1)$ can be interpreted as the worker's bargaining weight.[8] Solving this bargaining problem yields

$$\hat{w}(t) = \lambda G_2(t) + (1 - \lambda)\frac{\beta}{q(t)\phi(t)}. \tag{14.17}$$

Since all firms are identical, they must offer the same wage in any symmetric equilibrium. Since the wage formula is independent of when the match is formed (i.e., independent of $t0$), two workers who are hired by the same firm at different times must be paid the same wage at any given time. Thus, $\hat{w}(t) = w(t)$ for all t, and hereafter the hat is suppressed.

The product wage rate is a weighted sum of the marginal product of labor, G_2, and the reservation wage, $\beta/(q\phi)$, with the weights being the bargaining weights of the worker and the firm. Since $G_2 > w$, as argued before, $G_2 > \beta/(q\phi)$. The product wage lies between the marginal rate of substitution $\beta/(q\phi)$ and the marginal product of labor, in contrast to a standard neoclassical model where $w = \beta/(q\phi) = G_2$. Even if the marginal product of labor is constant, a tariff can still affect the product wage through the terms of trade and the marginal value of wealth. These induced responses of q and ϕ will be the two channels through which a tariff affects employment, as analyzed later.

Equilibrium Definition

For a finitely elastic export function, $x(q)$, the terms of trade are determined by the market clearing condition for the domestic good:

$$d + x(q) + B(v) + Q(i) = G. \tag{14.18}$$

An equilibrium can be defined as follows:

DEFINITION 14.1.   A search equilibrium is a converging sequence of $\{c(t), d(t), f(t), n(t), F(t), K(t), v(t), i(t)\}_{t\geq0}$, goods prices $\{q(t)\}_{t\geq0}$, factor returns $\{r(t), w(t)\}_{t\geq0}$, dividends $\{\pi(t)\}_{t\geq0}$, matching rates $\{m(t), \mu(t)\}_{t\geq0}$, and rebates $\{L(t)\}_{t\geq0}$ such that

1. Given $\{q, r, w, \pi, m, \mu, L\}$, $\{c, F\}$ solve (PH) and $\{d, f\}$ satisfy (14.3);

2. Given $\{q, r, w, m, \mu, L\}$, $\{n, K, v, i\}$ solve the firm's problem (PF);

3. $\{r, \pi, w\}$ satisfy (14.2), (14.10) and (14.17);

4. $\{m, \mu\}$ are given by (14.16);

5. $L = \tau f$ and q satisfies (14.18).

Central to this equilibrium is the feature that employment is driven by the firm's decision on vacancy. The dynamics of vacancy can be obtained from (14.11) and (14.12) by eliminating Ψ and substituting the wage equation (14.17):

$$\dot{v} = \gamma\left[(\theta+r)v - \frac{(1-\lambda)m(v)}{B'(v)}\left(G_2 - \frac{\beta}{q\phi}\right)\right], \tag{14.19}$$

where $\gamma = \varepsilon/[1 + (1 - \alpha)\varepsilon] > 0$. Vacancy increases if and only if the return to vacancy, $(\theta + r)vB'/m$, exceeds the firm's surplus from hiring. In the steady state, the two are equal to each other and so steady state vacancy, denoted v^*, is given by

$$(\theta + \rho)\frac{v^* B'(v^*)}{m(v^*)} = (1 - \lambda)\left(G_2 - \frac{B}{q^* \phi}\right). \tag{14.20}$$

I have used the fact that $r = \rho$ in the steady state.

The marginal product of labor in the steady state is exogenous, as the steady state capital/labor ratio is pinned down by the exogenous rate of time preference through $G_1 = \rho$. Therefore, a tariff can affect steady state job vacancy and employment only through the reservation wage $\beta/(q^* \phi)$. This effect can be channeled either through a change in the terms of trade (the direct product wage effect of tariffs), or through a change in the marginal value of wealth (the consumption bundle effect of tariffs).

Equation (14.20) implicitly characterizes the long-run supply of the goods market. It gives a positive relation between steady state vacancy (and hence output) and the marginal utility of wealth ϕ, depicted by the upward sloping curve VV in figure 14.2. The VV curve will be

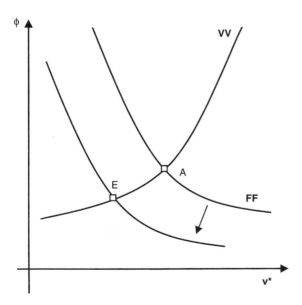

Figure 14.2

termed the long-run "aggregate supply curve," with the marginal utility of wealth being the "price." A high marginal utility of wealth lowers the reservation wage, increases the firm's surplus from hiring, and so stimulates hiring and output.

The Case of Exogenous Terms of Trade

In this section I isolate the consumption bundle effect of the tariff. This is achieved in a special case where the country faces an infinitely elastic foreign demand for its good, that is, $x'(q) = -\infty$. In this case the terms of trade are constant, eliminating the direct product wage effect of the tariff. With constant terms of trade, the rental rate of capital must be equal to the world interest rate at each point of time, that is, $r(t) = \rho$ for all $t \geq 0$. To ease exposition in this section, I also assume that the marginal adjustment cost in physical investment is flat, that is, $Q'' = 0$. In this case the marginal value of capital is unity and $G_1 = \rho$ for all $t \geq 0$. Therefore, the capital/labor ratio is constant, denoted $\kappa = K/n$. The variable K can be replaced by κn and $\dot{K}$ by $\kappa \dot{n}$.

The Dynamic System and the Solution

The dynamic system for this special case consists of differential equations for (v, n, F). The dynamic equation for v is given by (14.19) with $r = \rho$. The dynamic equation for n is given by (14.5). To obtain the dynamic equation for F, substitute π from (14.10) and $L = \tau f$ into the dynamic equation for F in (14.6) to obtain

$$\dot{F} = \rho F + q[G - B - \kappa(m - \theta n)] - (p - \tau p_2)c. \tag{14.21}$$

The initial conditions for the dynamic system of (v, n, F) are $n(0) = n_0$ and $F(0) = F_0$.

Vacancy is constant along the transition path in this special case. To see this, notice that (q, r, G_2, ϕ) are all constant along the transition path, so (14.19) is an autonomous equation for vacancy. Since the right-hand side of (14.19) is an increasing function of vacancy, the return to vacancy exceeds the firm's surplus from hiring if and only if vacancy exceeds its steady state level v^* defined by (14.20). Thus, vacancy increases over time if and only if vacancy exceeds its steady state level. The steady state level can be reached only when $v(t) = v^*$ for all t. More precisely, when responding to disturbances like the tariff, vacancy jumps immediately to the steady state level and stays there afterward.

With constant vacancy, the dynamic equations for n and F are linear differential equations that can be solved to generate the following proposition (see appendix 14.1).

PROPOSITION 14.1.   When the terms of trade are constant, the stable paths of (n, F) are characterized as follows for any given (n_0, F_0):

$$n(t) = \frac{m(v^*)}{\theta} + \left[n_0 - \frac{m(v^*)}{\theta}\right]e^{-\theta t},$$
(14.22)

$$F(t) = F^* - \frac{q^*}{\theta + \rho}\left(\frac{G}{n} + \theta \kappa\right)\left[n(t) - \frac{m(v^*)}{\theta}\right],$$
(14.23)

where F^* is the steady state value of F and is given by

$$F^* = \frac{1}{\rho}\{(p - \tau p_2)c - q^*[G - B(v^*)]\}.$$
(14.24)

Proposition 14.1 states that claims on foreign assets are negatively related to employment and hence to output along the stable path. This is because an increase in employment raises the marginal product of capital, which in turn induces agents to switch investment from foreign assets to domestic capital. As a result, the current account, F, is negatively related to changes in employment.

Proposition 14.1 also implies that the steady state depends on the initial conditions (n_0, F_0), as is typical in a small open economy model with a constant rate of time preference. Equation (14.23) at $t = 0$ helps to determine the marginal utility of wealth, ϕ. Substituting (14.24) into (14.23), setting $t = 0$, and noticing $c = u'^{-1}(p\phi)$ yields

$$\frac{G_2}{\theta + \rho}m(v^*) - B(v^*) + \rho\left(\kappa + \frac{G_2}{\theta + \rho}\right)n_0 = \frac{1}{q^*}[(p - \tau p_2)u'^{-1}(p\phi) - \rho F_0].$$
(14.25)

This steady state equation gives a negative relationship between steady state vacancy and the marginal utility of wealth, depicted by the curve FF in figure 14.2. The left-hand side of (14.25) is an increasing function of v^*, measuring the amount of goods available for consumption and export.[9] The right-hand side of the equation is a decreasing function of ϕ, measuring the expenditure on goods and foreign debt service. The FF curve will be termed the long-run "aggregate demand curve."

The intersection between the two curves VV and FF in figure 14.2 determines steady state vacancy and the marginal utility of wealth.

Once (v^*, ϕ) are determined, other steady state values (n^*, K^*, F^*, c) can be determined accordingly.

A Permanent Increase in the Tariff

Suppose that the economy is in a steady state at time 0, with $\tau = 0$ and $(n(0), K(0), \Gamma(0)) - (n_0, \kappa n_0, F_0)$. Then the tariff rate has a once-and-for-all, unexpected increase to a new level $d\tau > 0$, which is sufficiently small.[10] Since the terms of trade are fixed, the tariff affects the product wage only through its effect on the marginal value of wealth, ϕ. This consumption bundle effect arises from the fact that the tariff makes the consumption bundle more expensive, that is, increases p. The marginal value of wealth, $\phi = u'(c)/p$, falls, and the reservation wage rises. The product wage rises, which reduces the firm's surplus from hiring and reduces vacancy. Depicted in figure 14.2, the long-run aggregate demand curve FF shifts to the left, as consumers now can only afford to buy a smaller quantity of the consumption bundle than before for any given ϕ. The VV curve does not shift, and so job vacancy is lower in the new steady state (point E) than in the original steady state (point A). Consequently, steady state employment and capital stock are lower in the new steady state.

The employment response to the tariff clearly relies on the reservation wage being endogenous. It also depends critically on the non-Walrasian feature of the labor market. In particular, the bargaining power of the firm in the wage determination, $(1 - \lambda)$, plays an important role. If the firm has a very low bargaining power, for example, changes in the product wage induced by the tariff will have only a small effect on the firm's surplus from hiring, in which case the responses of vacancy and employment to the tariff will be small. In terms of figure 14.2, a lower bargaining power of the firm corresponds to a steeper long-run aggregate supply curve VV, in which case the shift in the FF curve generates a large change in ϕ but only a small change in v.

The importance of the labor market friction sets the current analysis apart from the Sen and Turnovsky 1989 model, where the labor market is Walrasian. In a Walrasian labor market, the marginal product of labor equals the marginal rate of substitution between consumption and leisure. In this case the VV curve is horizontal and an increase in the tariff generates the largest (negative) consumption bundle effect. Thus, the search friction in the labor market attenuates the consumption bundle effect that a tariff has on employment.

The transitional dynamics after the tariff increase can be analyzed as follows. Since $(n^*, K^*) < (n_0, K_0)$, (14.22) implies that employment and the capital stock monotonically decrease along the stable path. Thus, raising the tariff reduces employment and output, both in the long run and in the short run—there is no trade-off between the short run and the long run effects of a tariff in this special case. The tariff raises the long-run level of claims on foreign assets, which can be verified from (14.24). The country experiences current account surpluses along the entire transition path (see (14.23)), as investors switch investments from domestic capital to foreign assets.

The dynamic adjustments in the labor market can be illustrated by figure 14.3 in the subspace of the vacancy rate $vv = v/n + 1$ and the unemployment rate $ss = 1/n + 1$, where $n + 1$ is the size of the labor force. The long-run relationship between these two variables is given by $\dot{n} = 0$, that is, by $m(v^*) = \theta n^*$, which is depicted by the downward sloping Beveridge curve, BEV. The increase in the tariff moves the economy from one steady state (point A) to another (point E). The transition of (vv, ss) traces a stylized counterclockwise trajectory around the Beveridge curve (see Layard et al. 1991), as depicted by the path ABE. At the instant when the tariff increases, the unemployment rate ss does not change, since n is predetermined. In contrast, vacancy immediately falls to the new long run level, inducing an overadjustment in the vacancy rate vv relative to its long-run adjustment. This is the discontinuous drop from point A to point B in figure 14.3. After this instantaneous change, the vacancy rate and the unemployment rate both rise gradually to reach the new steady state (point E) as employment falls to the new long-run level.

The results of this subsection can be summarized as follows:

PROPOSITION 14.2.   When the country faces exogenous terms of trade, the tariff reduces employment, capital and output in both the long run and short run. The transition features a current account surplus and an overadjustment (a fall) in the vacancy rate followed by increases in both the vacancy rate and the unemployment rate.

A Permanent Improvement in the Terms of Trade

In this subsection I examine the effect of an exogenous improvement in the terms of trade, which generates an exogenous direct product wage effect. The purpose of doing so is to highlight the conflict between

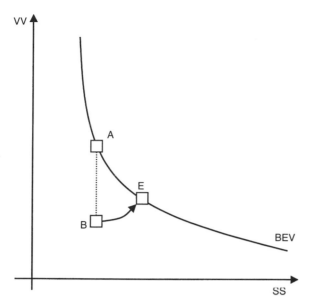

Figure 14.3

the consumption bundle effect illustrated in the last subsection and the direct product wage effect.

Suppose that the economy is in a steady state at time 0, with $q = q_0$ and $(n(0), K(0), F(0)) = (n_0, \kappa n_0, F_0)$. The terms of trade then have an unanticipated, once-and-for-all (marginal) increase to q^*. Like the tariff in the last subsection, the terms-of-trade improvement makes the consumption bundle more expensive. This generates the consumption bundle effect, which increases the product wage for any given q. The terms-of-trade improvement also directly reduces the product wage for any given ϕ. This direct product wage effect increases vacancy. Overall, the product wage falls if and only if the direct wage effect outweighs the consumption bundle effect.

The conflict between the two effects can be illustrated with figure 14.2 (where the corresponding shifts of the curves for the current case are not drawn). The direct product wage effect shifts the aggregate supply curve VV down to the right. That is, for any given marginal value of the wealth ϕ, a higher value of q increases the firm's surplus from hiring and increases vacancy. The consumption bundle effect corresponds to a downward shift of the aggregate demand curve FF to the left. That is, for any given ϕ, an increase in q increases the price of the goods bundle and reduces the amount agents can consume; to maintain the equilibrium, vacancy must fall to reduce the supply accordingly.[11] Overall, the marginal value of wealth is unambiguously lower in the new steady state than in the old one, but vacancy can be either higher or lower in the new steady state. Vacancy increases only if the aggregate supply curve VV shifts downward by more than the aggregate demand curve FF does.

Whether the direct product wage effect dominates the consumption bundle effect depends on the elasticity of intertemporal substitution, σ. The larger the elasticity of intertemporal substitution, the weaker the consumption bundle effect, and the more likely that the direct product wage effect dominates the consumption bundle effect. The explanation is as follows. When the elasticity of intertemporal substitution is large, the consumption smoothing motive is weak. In this case consumption of the goods bundle falls a lot in response to the increase in the goods price. The resulted increase in the marginal utility of consumption mitigates the rise in price and so the marginal utility of wealth $\phi = u'(c)/p$ falls very little, leading to a small consumption bundle effect. In contrast, when the elasticity of intertemporal substitution is small, consumption on the goods bundle falls very little in response to the price increase, leaving the marginal utility of wealth to fall significantly.

The above explanation can be supported by showing that the terms-of-trade improvement raises vacancy if and only if

$$\sigma > qx/f. \tag{14.26}$$

Whether this condition is satisfied clearly depends on the nature of the economy. There are realistic economies that satisfy (14.26). For example, if the value of the export is 70 percent of the import, (14.26) would require the elasticity of intertemporal substitution to exceed 0.7, which is possible with some of the estimates in Epstein and Zin 1991. Despite this possibility, I will show in the next section that the terms-of-trade improvement induced by a tariff is not sufficient to produce a dominant, direct product wage effect.

The dynamic responses of (n, F) to the terms-of-trade improvement can be analyzed using figure 14.4. The lines STP and STP' depict the stable path, given by (14.23), before and after the terms-of-trade improvement. Since the slope of the stable path depends positively on q^*, the terms-of-trade improvement increases the slope of the stable path. The initial steady state is at point A. The dynamics depend on whether (14.26) is satisfied. If (14.26) is satisfied, the new steady state

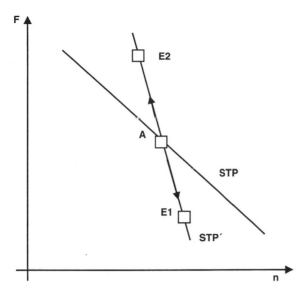

Figure 14.4

is at point *E1*, in which case employment increases and the current account is in a deficit along the adjustment path. If (14.26) is violated, the new steady state is at point *E2*, in which case employment falls and the current account is in a surplus along the adjustment path.

The Case of Endogenous Terms of Trade

I now examine the dynamic effects of a tariff when the terms of trade are endogenous. A global dynamic analysis like the one in the last section is no longer possible, hence only local dynamics are considered. As in the last section, let the tariff change be a marginal, permanent, and unanticipated increase from the initial level 0. The economy is in a steady state prior to the tariff change, with $(n(0), K(0), F(0)) = (n_0, \kappa n_0, F_0)$.

Characterization of the Stable Dynamic Path

With endogenous terms of trade, the dynamic system consists of seven variables, $(r, \Omega, q, v, n, K, F)$. Solving for equilibrium dynamics is analytically possible only when $\alpha = 1 - \lambda$, which will be assumed hereafter as in Merz 1995 and Andolfatto 1996. This condition requires that the firm's power in wage bargaining, $1 - \lambda$, exactly compensates for the contribution of the vacancy to the match formation, measured by α (see Hosios 1990). Without losing the essence of the analysis, I will also restrict the marginal adjustment cost of investment to be sufficiently flat around the steady state, that is, $Q''(0) \approx 0$ and so $Q(i) \approx i$. In this case the marginal value of capital, Ω, is close to 1 and so the rental rate of capital is close to the marginal product of capital. The dynamics of the other five variables (q, v, n, K, F) can be approximated by the following system:[12]

$$(E)\begin{cases} \dot{q} = q(\rho - G_1) \\ \dot{v} = \gamma\left[(\theta + G_1)v - \dfrac{(1-\lambda)m(v)}{B'(v)}\left(G_2 - \dfrac{\beta}{q\phi}\right)\right] \\ \dot{n} = m(v) - \theta n \\ \dot{K} = G - [d + x(q)] - B(v) \\ \dot{F} = \rho F + qx(q) - f. \end{cases}$$

The initial conditions are $(n(0), K(0), F(0)) = (n_0, \kappa n_0, F_0)$, where κ is the steady state capital labor ratio, given by $G_1(\kappa) = \rho$. The conditions for $\dot{q}$ and $\dot{v}$ are derived from (14.2) and (14.19) by replacing r with its proxy G_1. The condition for n is a copy of (14.5). The condition for K comes from the goods market clearing condition (14.18) using the approximation $Q(i) \approx i$. The condition for F is derived from substituting $(L, \pi, \dot{K})$ into (14.6). Since the variables (d, f) are function of (q, τ, ϕ) (see (14.3)), the system (E) is a complete dynamic system of the five variables (q, v, n, K, F) once ϕ is determined. According to (14.7), ϕ is constant along the equilibrium dynamic path. Its value is determined through a stability requirement described later.

Denote worldwide consumption of the country's good by $D(q, \phi, \tau) = d + x(q)$, where $d = p_1 u'^{-1}(p\phi)$. The earlier assumption on x and p imply $D_1 < 0$. Appendix 14.2 shows that the dynamic system is saddle-path stable if the demand for the domestic good is sufficiently elastic (i.e., if D_1 is sufficiently negative). This result is not surprising since the dynamic system is stable when $D_1 = -\infty$, as demonstrated in the previous section. In particular, the dynamic system has two real, negative roots, $\omega_2 < \omega_1 < 0$. Denote $Y = (q, v, n, K)^T$ and Y^* the steady state value of Y. The stable path is characterized as follows (see appendix 14.2).

PROPOSITION 14.3. The stable path of (E) is

$$Y(t) - Y^* = (Z_1, Z_2) \begin{pmatrix} b_1 e^{\omega_1 t} \\ b_2 e^{\omega_2 t} \end{pmatrix}, \tag{14.27}$$

$$F(t) - F^* = (n_0 - n^*)(\Gamma_2 e^{\omega_2 t} - \Gamma_1 e^{\omega_1 t}), \tag{14.28}$$

where Z_1 and Z_2 are 4×1 vectors and (b, Γ) are constants, both given in appendix 14.2, with $\Gamma_1 > \Gamma_2 > 0$ and $\omega_1 \Gamma_1 < \omega_2 \Gamma_2$.

Long-Run Effects of the Tariff

Let us determine the steady state. Since the capital/labor ratio is κ in both steady states before and after the tariff, steady state capital stock and employment always respond to the tariff in the same direction:

$$K^* - K_0 = \kappa(n^* - n_0). \tag{14.29}$$

Steady state employment is $n^* = m(v^*)/\theta$, which depends on steady state vacancy. Steady state vacancy in turn depends on the terms of trade and the marginal value of wealth. In particular, (14.20) holds in the steady state, which can be used to solve for v^* as an increasing function of (ϕ, q^*). Denote this function as $v(\phi, q^*)$. Steady state terms of trade and the marginal utility of consumption are determined by the market clearing conditions for the domestic good and the condition for the country's balance of payment.

The domestic good market clearing condition is given by the K equation in (E). Setting $\dot{K} = 0$ and substituting the function $v(\phi, q^*)$ yields the following equation for (ϕ, q^*):

$$\frac{G}{n} \cdot \frac{m(v(\phi, q^*))}{\theta} - B(v(\phi, q^*)) - p_1 u'^{-1}(p\phi) - x(q^*) = 0. \tag{14.30}$$

The left-hand side of this equation is the excess supply of the domestic good. Note that G/n is an exogenous constant in the steady state. Equation (14.30) gives a negative relation between steady state terms of trade and the marginal utility of wealth, depicted by the HH curve in figure 14.5. A higher marginal utility ϕ decreases the reservation wage, increases vacancy, and increases the supply of the domestic good. To clear the market for the domestic good, the price of the domestic good must fall.

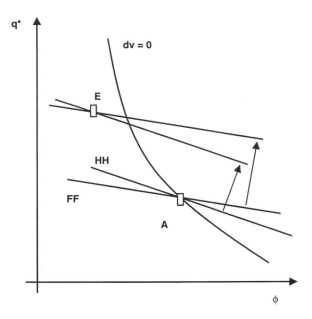

Figure 14.5

The condition for the country's balance of payment is given by the F equation in the system (E). Setting $\dot{F} = 0$ and substituting F^* from the version of (14.28) at $t = 0$ gives the following equation for (ϕ, q^*):

$$p_2 u'^{-1}(p\phi) - q^* x(q^*) - \rho\left\{F_0 - \delta\left[\frac{1}{\theta}m(v(\phi, q^*)) - n_0\right]\right\} = 0. \tag{14.31}$$

where $\delta \equiv \Gamma_1 - \Gamma_2 > 0$. The left-hand side of this equation is the country's current account deficit in the steady state. The net of the first two terms is the net import. The last term is the interest receipts from foreign asset claims, where the change in the asset position is accounted for by the term $\delta[.]$.

Equation (14.31) gives an ambiguous relationship between steady state terms of trade and the marginal utility of consumption. To see the ambiguity, note first that a higher ϕ increases the supply of the country's export through increased vacancy and output, which must be absorbed by a fall in the relative price of the country's good—the terms of trade. However, since the demand for the import is $f = p_2 u'^{-1}(p\phi)$, a higher ϕ also reduces the demand for the foreign good and its relative price $1/q^*$. When the intertemporal elasticity of substitution σ is small, the second effect is small and dominated by the first effect and so (14.31) gives a positive relationship between q^* and ϕ. Otherwise the relationship is negative, as depicted in figure 14.5 by the FF curve.

Regardless of the nature of the slope of the FF curve, there is a unique solution for (ϕ, q^*). In particular, when the FF curve is negatively sloped, appendix 14.3 shows that the HH curve is steeper than the FF curve, as depicted by figure 14.5. Since the analysis with a positively sloped FF curve is similar to that with a negatively sloped FF curve, I will analyze only the case of a negatively sloped FF curve. Figure 14.5 also draws a reference curve $dv = 0$, along which the reservation wage is fixed at the level of the original steady state. That is, $q\phi$ is constant in the steady state along the curve $dv = 0$. Steady state values of (q, ϕ) before the increase in the tariff are given by point A. Points above the $dv = 0$ curve have more vacancies and higher employment than in the initial steady state and points below the $dv = 0$ curve have fewer vacancies and lower employment.

The long-run effect of a tariff on employment is summarized below (see appendix 14.3 for a proof):

PROPOSITION 14.4.   Under the assumption that the foreign demand for the country's good is sufficiently elastic in the sense that (A.14.2) holds, a permanent increase in the tariff reduces steady state vacancy, employment, and output.

The negative employment effect of the tariff can be illustrated with figure 14.5. The increase in the tariff shifts the FF curve up because, for any given ϕ, the tariff reduces the demand for the import. The resulted current account surplus must be eliminated in the steady state by a terms-of-trade improvement, which increases the demand for the import and reduces the export. The tariff also shifts the HH curve up because, for any given ϕ, the tariff increases the demand for the domestic good. The resulting excess demand for the domestic good must be eliminated in the steady state by a terms-of-trade improvement, which stimulates domestic production and curtails the country's demand for the domestic good. The new levels of (q^*, ϕ) are given by point E. Appendix 14.3 shows that the upward shift of the FF curve is more than the upward shift of the HH curve, and the new steady state is below the curve $dv = 0$. Thus although the terms of trade improve as a result of the tariff, the improvement is proportionally less than the fall in the marginal utility of wealth. The consumption bundle effect of the tariff on the product wage through the marginal utility of wealth dominates the direct product wage effect through the terms of trade. The product wage rises, so the tariff reduces steady state vacancy and employment.

An explanation for why the consumption bundle effect dominates the direct product effect is that the improvement in the terms of trade induced by the increase in the tariff is proportionally less than the increase in the tariff itself. As a result, the price index increases by more proportionally than do the terms of trade. When the consumption smoothing motive is strong (i.e., $\sigma < 1$), most of the increase in the price index must be absorbed by the reduction in the marginal value of wealth (since $\phi = u'(c)/p$) and so the latter falls by more proportionally than the improvement in the terms of trade. Therefore, $q\phi$ falls, and the product wage rises.

A more elaborate explanation relies on the following corollary (the omitted proof is a direct computation using (A.14.8):

COROLLARY 14.5. For any given marginal utility of wealth ϕ, the following inequalities hold:

$$0 < \partial(f^* - q^*x^* - \rho F^*)/\partial q^* < q^*\partial(G^* - d^* - x^* - B^*)/\partial q^*, \tag{14.32}$$

$$\frac{-\partial(f^* - q^*x^* - \rho F^*)/\partial \tau}{\partial(f^* - q^*x^* - \rho F^*)/\partial q^*} > \frac{-\partial(G^* - d^* - x^* - B^*)/\partial \tau}{\partial(G^* - d^* - x^* - B^*)/\partial q^*} > 0. \tag{14.33}$$

Equation (14.32) states that, in response to a terms-of-trade improvement, the current account deficit increases by less than does the excess supply of the domestic good. This is because, for fixed ϕ, the excess supply of the domestic good increases in response to an improvement in the terms of trade not only through the reduction in the demand for the domestic good, as does the current account deficit, but also through an increase in the supply when hiring increases (since wage falls for fixed ϕ). Equation (14.33) states, as a consequence of (14.32), that to eliminate the current account surplus generated by the tariff requires a larger terms-of-trade improvement than to eliminate the excess demand for the domestic good. In figure 14.5, this means that the upward shift in the FF curve must be larger than that of the HH curve. Thus, the steady state moves below the locus $dv = 0$, and employment falls.

Dynamic Effects of the Tariff

The dynamic effects of the tariff on employment and capital can be obtained by differentiating with respect to time the stable path in

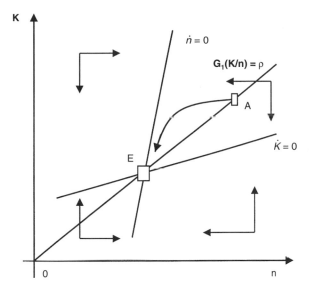

Figure 14.6

(14.27) for these variables. The dynamics are illustrated in figure 14.6, where the long-run capital/labor ratio lies along the line $G_1 = \rho$. The explicit expressions for the $\dot{n} = 0$ and the $\dot{K} = 0$ schedules are provided in appendix 14.3, which establishes the following features: (1) Both the $\dot{n} = 0$ and the $\dot{K} = 0$ schedules are positively sloped; (2) the $\dot{n} = 0$ schedule is steeper than the line $G_1 = \rho$ and steeper than the $\dot{K} = 0$ schedule; (3) and the $\dot{K} = 0$ schedule can be either steeper or flatter than the line $G_1 = \rho$. To avoid repetition, I discuss only the case where the $\dot{K} = 0$ schedule is flatter than the line $G_1 = \rho$.

The initial steady state is point A and the new steady state is point E, both lying on the line $G_1 = \rho$. The tariff induces the capital stock and employment to fall monotonically toward the steady state E. Output also falls monotonically in this case. The dynamics of the vacancy rate and unemployment rate can be analyzed using figure 14.3, but such an analysis is omitted here. It is clear that the unemployment rate increases monotonically along the transition path, so the tariff has qualitatively the same effect on the unemployment rate in both the short run and the long run.

Since the domestic capital stock monotonically falls, investment is redirected toward foreign assets during the transition. That is, the current account is in surplus along the transitional path and reaches zero in the new steady state. This can be verified by differentiating

(14.28) with respect to time to obtain the following expression for the current account:

$$\dot{F}(t) = (n_0 - n^*)(\Gamma_2 \omega_2 e^{\omega_2 t} - \Gamma_1 \omega_1 e^{\omega_1 t}). \tag{14.34}$$

Since $\omega_2 < \omega_1 < 0$, $\omega_1 \Gamma_1 < \omega_2 \Gamma_2 < 0$ and $n^* < n_0$, we have $\dot{F} > 0$ for all t.

An interesting feature of the dynamics is that the terms of trade respond to the tariff in a nonmonotonic fashion. To see this non-monotonic adjustment, notice first that $q(0) < q^*$ (see appendix 14.3). That is, the immediate improvement in the terms of trade after the increase in the tariff is less than in the long run. After this immediate improvement, the terms of trade continue to improve in order to main-tain the arbitrage condition (14.2), since the rising capital/labor ratio in the earlier stage of the transition (see figure 14.6) pushes down the domestic interest rate. In this process the terms of trade overshoot the new long-run level. In the middle of the transition, the capital/labor ratio begins to fall, which pushes up the domestic interest rate and induces the terms of trade to deteriorate toward the new long-run level. The complete adjustment of the terms of trade is characterized by an immediate jump, which is followed by a hump-shaped path.

This particular adjustment path of the terms of trade implies over-shooting product wage and vacancy. Since the terms of trade rise immediately by less than in the long run, and the marginal value of wealth ϕ falls immediately to the new long-run level, the reservation wage, $\beta/(q\phi)$, must immediately overshoot its new steady state level. Since both the capital stock and employment are predetermined, the marginal product of labor is predetermined, so the product wage must immediately overshoot its new steady state level. After this over-shooting, the product wage rate falls toward its new steady state level. As the product wage overshoots, vacancy immediately falls below its long-run level.

Welfare Effects of the Tariff

Let us first examine the welfare effects of the tariff employing a com-monly used welfare criterion—the steady state utility level. The tariff affects steady state utility in two ways. First, by reducing long-run employment, the tariff increases leisure and hence utility in the steady state. Second, the tariff changes steady state consumption of the goods bundle. The second effect is ambiguous, depending on the elasticity of the foreign demand for the country's export. For any finitely elastic export function, the response of steady-state consumption to the tariff is

$$c_\tau^* = \frac{\sigma cq/p}{(-DT)}[p_2(x+qx')E_1 - p_2x'E_2 + cpp_{12}x],$$

where the subscript τ denotes the change of the variable with respect to the tariff and $DT < 0$, $E_1 > 0$, and $E_2 > 0$ are given in appendix 14.3. Thus, if the export function has a unit elasticity $(x + qx' \to 0)$, then $c_\tau^* > 0$. In contrast, if the export function is infinitely elastic as in the third section, then differentiating (14.25) yields

$$c_\tau^* = \frac{q}{p}\left(\frac{G_2}{\theta+\rho}m' - B'\right)v_\tau^* = \frac{\beta\theta}{(\theta+\rho)u'}n_\tau^* < 0, \tag{14.35}$$

where the second equality comes from substituting G_2 from (14.20).

Surprisingly, in both cases the increase in leisure is strong enough to increase steady state utility. The increase in utility is obvious when the export function has a unit elasticity, since both steady state consumption and leisure increase with the tariff there. When the export function is infinitely elastic, the discounted present value of steady state utility responds to the tariff as follows:

$$U_\tau^* = \frac{1}{\rho}\left(u'c_\tau^* - \beta n_\tau^*\right) = -\frac{\beta}{\theta+\rho}n_\tau^* > 0. \tag{14.36}$$

It is tempting to draw a similarity between this positive steady state welfare gain and the optimal tariff literature (e.g., Johnson 1951–1952), where increasing tariffs from the level zero can improve welfare by improving the terms of trade. Such a similarity is superficial and misleading for two reasons. First, the tariff increases steady state welfare in the above cases primarily by increasing consumption of the non-traded good, that is, leisure, which is not essential in the traditional optimal tariff argument. Second, unlike any static trade models, here capital can freely flow between countries, and it is the intertemporal wealth accumulation decision that ultimately determines the long-run consumption level. Thus even though the terms of trade remain unchanged in the case where the export function is infinitely elastic, the tariff reduces steady state consumption of the (traded) goods bundle here but has no such effect in the optimal tariff literature.

Now let us employ the correct measure of welfare—intertemporal utility. The steady state utility is a misleading criterion of welfare because it ignores the cost of adjusting toward the steady state. In the current context, the steady state utility measure gives tariffs an upward bias on the welfare effect. To see this, linearizing (14.4) around the steady state, we have

$$U_\tau^* - U_\tau = \sigma c \phi p_1 \int_0^\infty \left[q_\tau(t) - q_\tau^*\right] e^{-\rho t} dt + \beta \int_0^\infty \left[n_\tau(t) - n_\tau^*\right] e^{-\rho t} dt,$$

where the relation $u'(c) = p\phi$ is used to express $c_\tau - c_\tau^*$ as a function of $q_\tau - q_\tau^*$. The right-hand side above measures the dynamic welfare cost associated with the transition. To calculate the two integrals, the differences $q_\tau - q_\tau^*$ and $n_\tau - n_\tau^*$ can be calculated using (14.27) if $-x' < \infty$ and using (14.22) if $-x' = \infty$. Since employment monotonically decreases along the transition path, $n_\tau > n_\tau^*$ for all $t \geq 0$, and so the second integral is positive. The first integral is also likely to be positive. This is because, as discussed above, the terms of trade overshoot the steady state level in the transition, so $q_\tau > q_\tau^*$ in a large part of the transition. Thus, $U_\tau < U_\tau^*$, so the welfare effect of the tariff is less than the steady state effect.

It is possible that the cost of transition can completely eliminate the steady state welfare gain. Consider the case $-x' = \infty$, for example. In this case the terms of trade do not change and so the first integral is zero. For changes in employment, we can use (14.22) to compute

$$n_\tau(t) - n_\tau^* = -n_\tau^* e^{-\theta t}.$$

Then the cost associated with employment transition can be calculated as $-\beta n_\tau^*/(\theta + \rho)$, which exactly equals the steady state utility gain, U_τ^* (see (14.36)). Thus, when the export function is infinitely elastic, there is no welfare gain from increasing the tariff from the level zero, despite that the tariff increases the consumption of the nontraded good. It would be nice if this type of calculation could be carried out for the general case where the country has some, but limited, influence on the terms of trade. Unfortunately, the analytical result is not revealing, so the welfare effect of the tariff remains ambiguous in this case.

Conclusion

This chapter integrates labor market search into a dynamic general equilibrium model to analyze the macroeconomic effects of a tariff. The search friction creates a wedge between the marginal product of labor and the product wage. With perfectly flexible prices and wages, the model captures the intuitive effect that a permanent increase in the tariff improves the country's terms of trade, which tends to reduce the product wage directly through the reservation wage and stimulates labor demand. However, the tariff also increases the price of the consumption goods bundle, reduces the marginal utility of wealth, and increases the product wage through the reservation wage. With a realistically strong consumption smoothing motive, this consumption bundle effect of the tariff dominates the direct product wage effect, causing vacancy and employment to fall both in the long run and short run. Thus, even with persistent unemployment, raising tariffs is not the means by which a government in a small open economy can succeed in increasing employment, short run or long run. International finance theorists who argue for a predominantly positive employment role for tariffs must look for other labor market frictions to support their arguments.

There might be ad hoc rationales for a government to increase tariffs (in practice). This chapter indicates two. One is redistributional: The government might want to boost the product wage. An increase in the tariff achieves this purpose and does so in a larger scale in the short run than in the long run. The second reason might be current account management: An increase in the tariff produces a current account surplus along the entire transition path. However, neither rationale has a sound justification. In particular, even though a tariff increases the product wage, it is unlikely to raise workers' standard of living, because the wage measured in terms of the goods bundle is likely to fall.

For tractability, the chapter has abstracted from the possible strategic responses by the rest of the world to the increase in the tariff. This omission is not as serious as it appears. Although the tariff deteriorates the terms of trade of the rest of the world, it also increases the capital flow into the rest of the world. Since it is not clear whether the rest of the world stands to lose or gain from the tariff, it is not clear whether it has the incentive to retaliate. Addressing the strategic interaction requires a two-country model and may be worth pursuing in future research. As far as the small country is concerned, a possible shortcut to modeling the response of the rest of the world would be to assume that the export function, $x(q)$, depends on the tariff. In particular, one can view that a tariff may trigger responses that make the export function more elastic. This will exacerbate the negative effect of the tariff on the country's employment.

Appendix 14.1.   Proof of Proposition 14.1

Since v is constant along the transition path, $n(t)$ can be solved directly by integrating the equation for n. The result is given by (14.22). Substitute this solution in (14.21) and notice that G/n depends only on the capital/labor ratio and hence is constant along the transition path. Integrating (14.21) generates

$$F(t) = F^* - \frac{q}{\theta + \rho}\left(\frac{G}{n} + \theta\kappa\right)\left(n(t) - \frac{m}{\theta}\right)$$

$$+ \left[F_0 - F^* + \frac{q}{\theta + \rho}\left(\frac{G}{n} + \theta\kappa\right)\left(n_0 - \frac{m}{\theta}\right)\right]e^{\rho t}.$$

For F to converge to a steady state, it is necessary and sufficient that the second term is always zero and this holds when

$$F_0 - F^* = -\frac{q}{\theta + \rho}\left(\frac{G}{n} + \theta\kappa\right)\left(n_0 - \frac{m}{\theta}\right).$$

Under this condition, the solution for $F(t)$ given above becomes (14.23). QED.

Appendix 14.2   Proof of Proposition 14.3

Since the dynamics of $Y = (q, v, n, K)^T$ are autonomous for any given ϕ, let us examine them first. Linearizing the dynamic equations for Y in (E) yields

$$\dot{Y} = J(Y - Y^*),\tag{A.14.1}$$

where Y^* is the steady state value of Y and J is the following matrix:

$$J = \begin{bmatrix} 0 & 0 & -qG_{12} & -qG_{11} \\ -\dfrac{\gamma A\beta}{\phi q^2} & \theta + \rho & \gamma G_{12}(v + A\kappa) & \gamma G_{11}(v + A\kappa) \\ 0 & m' & -\theta & 0 \\ -D_1 & -B' & G_2 & \rho \end{bmatrix}.$$

Here $A = \alpha m/B' > 0$ and all elements of the matrix are evaluated at the steady state with $\tau = 0$.

Denote a typical eigenvalue of matrix J by ω and let $\xi = \omega(\omega - \rho)$. The determinant of matrix J can be expressed as the following quadratic function of ξ:

$$g(\xi) \equiv \xi^2 - [\theta(\theta + \rho) + qD_1G_{11} - \gamma G_{11}(v + A\kappa)(B' + \kappa m')]\xi$$

$$+ \theta(\theta + \rho)qD_1G_{11} - \gamma G_{11}\frac{A\beta}{4\psi}[m'(G_2 + \rho\kappa) - \theta B'].$$

Denote the two solutions to the equation $g(\xi) = 0$ by ξ_1 and ξ_2. These roots are real numbers if and only if

$$0 < [\theta(\theta + \rho) + qD_1G_{11} - \gamma G_{11}(v + A\kappa)(B' + \kappa m')]^2$$

$$- 4\theta(\theta + \rho)qD_1G_{11} - 4\gamma G_{11}\frac{A\beta}{q\phi}[m'(G_2 + \rho\kappa) - \theta B']$$

The right-hand side of the above inequality can be equivalently written as

$$[\theta(\theta + \rho) - qD_1G_{11} - \gamma G_{11}(v + A\kappa)(B' + \kappa m')]^2$$

$$- 4\gamma G_{11}\left[qD_1G_{11}(v + A\kappa)(B' + \kappa m') - \frac{A\beta}{q\phi}(m'(G_2 + \rho\kappa) - \theta B')\right],$$

and so a sufficient condition for the inequality to hold is

$$qD_1G_{11} > \frac{A\beta}{q\phi} \cdot \frac{m'(G_2 + \rho\kappa) - \theta B'}{(v + A\kappa)(B' + \kappa m')}. \tag{A.14.2}$$

This condition requires the export function to be sufficiently elastic, as $-D_1$ increases with $-x'$. The condition (A.14.2) is maintained throughout. Then (ξ_1, ξ_2) are positive and distinct. Let $\xi_1 < \xi_2$. It can be shown that $g(qD_1G_{11}) < 0$ and so $qD_1G_{11} \in (\xi_1, \xi_2)$.

Since ξ_1 and ξ_2 are positive, matrix J has two positive real eigenvalues and two negative real eigenvalues, calculated through the equations $\omega(\omega - \rho) = \xi_i$ ($i = 1,2$). The two negative real eigenvalues are $\omega_i = [\rho - (\rho^2 + 4\xi_i)^{1/2}]/2$ ($i = 1,2$). Clearly, $\omega_2 < \omega_1 < 0$. The property $qD_1G_{11} \in (\xi_1, \xi_2)$ can be rewritten as

$$\omega_1(\omega_1 - \rho) < qD_1G_{11} < \omega_2(\omega_2 - \rho). \tag{A.14.3}$$

The number of negative eigenvalues of J (two) falls short of the number of predetermined variables (n, K, F) in the system (E) by one, leaving the stable path of the equilibrium dependent on the initial conditions.

The stable manifold of Y is given by (14.27), where Z_i is the eigenvector of J corresponding to ω_i and is given as follows:

$$Z_i = \begin{pmatrix} z_{i1} \\ z_{i2} \\ z_{i3} \\ z_{i4} \end{pmatrix} = \begin{pmatrix} \dfrac{-qG_{11}}{\xi_i - qD_1G_{11}} \left[\dfrac{\beta}{q\phi} + \left(\kappa + \dfrac{B'}{m} \right)(\rho - \omega_i) \right] \\[4mm] (\omega_i + \theta)/m' \\[2mm] 1 \\[2mm] \dfrac{1}{\xi_i - qD_1G_{11}} \left[qD_1G_{11} - \dfrac{B'}{m'}\xi_i + \dfrac{\beta}{q\phi}\omega_i \right] \end{pmatrix}. \tag{A.14.4}$$

To determine (b_1, b_2) in (14.27), set $t = 0$ and use (14.29). We have

$$\begin{pmatrix} b_1 \\ b_2 \end{pmatrix} = \frac{(n_0 - n^*)}{z_{14} - z_{24}} \begin{pmatrix} \kappa - z_{24} \\ z_{14} - \kappa \end{pmatrix}. \tag{A.14.5}$$

Thus, (b_1, b_2) are uniquely determined for any given ϕ if and only if $z_{14} \neq z_{24}$. Compute

$$z_{14} - z_{24} = -\frac{(\omega_1 - \omega_2)}{(\xi_1 - qD_1G_{11})(\xi_2 - qD_1G_{11})}$$

$$\times \left\{ qD_1G_{11} \left[\left(\kappa + \frac{B'}{m'} \right)(\rho - \omega_1 - \omega_2) + \frac{\beta}{q\phi} \right] + \omega_1\omega_2 \frac{\beta}{q\phi} \right\}.$$

This is positive, because $qD_1G_{11} \in (\xi_1, \xi_2)$ and $0 > \omega_1 > \omega_2$. Therefore, the system (A.14.1) is stable for any given ϕ.

To find the stable path for F, linearize the F equation in (E), substitute the stable manifold (14.27), and integrate. Imposing the condition $\lim_{t\to\infty} F(t) = F^* < \infty$ yields (14.28), where

$$\Gamma_1 = \frac{(z_{24} - \kappa)z_{11}}{(z_{14} - z_{24})(\rho - \omega_1)} \left[c \left(p_{12} - \frac{\sigma p_1 p_2}{p} \right) - (x + qx') \right],$$

$$\Gamma_2 = \frac{(z_{14} - \kappa)z_{21}}{(z_{14} - z_{24})(\rho - \omega_2)} \left[c \left(p_{12} - \frac{\sigma p_1 p_2}{p} \right) - (x + qx') \right].$$

The path (14.28) at $t = 0$ also provides a condition that helps to determine ϕ.

To verify the features of $(\delta, \Gamma_1, \Gamma_2)$, note that $z_{11} < 0$, $z_{21} > 0$, and $z_{14} > \kappa > 0 > z_{24}$. Then, $\Gamma_1 > 0$ and $\Gamma_2 > 0$. Substituting $(z_{11}, z_{21}, z_{14}, z_{24})$ and using the notation $\delta = \Gamma_1 - \Gamma_2$ yields

$$\delta = \frac{[c(p_{12} - \sigma p_1 p_2/p) - (x + qx')]}{(-D_1)\left[\kappa + \dfrac{B'}{m'} + \dfrac{\beta}{q\phi}\left(1 + \dfrac{\omega_1\omega_2}{qD_1G_{11}}\right)\Big/(\rho - \omega_1 - \omega_2)\right]}$$

$$\times \left[\frac{\beta}{q\phi} + \left(\kappa + \frac{B'}{m'}\right)\Big/(\rho - \omega_1)\right]\left[\frac{\beta}{q\phi} + \left(\kappa + \frac{B'}{m'}\right)\Big/(\rho - \omega_2)\right]. \tag{A.14.6}$$

Since $p_{12} > p_1 p_2/p$, $\sigma \le 1$, $x + qx' < 0$, and $D_1 < 0$, we have $\delta > 0$. Similarly one can verify $\omega_1\Gamma_1 < \omega_2\Gamma_2$. QED.

Appendix 14.3. Proofs of Proposition 14.4 and Other Statements in the Fourth Section

In this appendix, I verify the following results used in the fourth: (1) The HH schedule is negatively sloped, whereas the FF schedule may be either positively or negatively sloped; (2) The HH schedule is steeper than the FF schedule when the latter is negatively sloped; (3) $dq^*/d\tau > 0$ and $d\phi/d\tau < 0$; (4) Proposition 14.4: $dv^*/d\tau < 0$ and $dn^*/d\tau < 0$; (5) $q(0) < q^*$; and (6) The dynamics of (n, K) are as described in the text and illustrated in figure 14.6.

To show (1)–(5), differentiate (14.20) and suppress the asterisk associated with the steady state:

$$dv = \frac{\gamma v}{G_2 q\phi\beta^{-1} - 1}\left(\frac{dq}{q} + \frac{d\phi}{\phi}\right). \tag{A.14.7}$$

Denote

$$E_1 = \frac{\gamma v[Gm'/(n\theta) - B']}{G_2 q\phi\beta^{-1} - 1}, \quad E_2 = \frac{\gamma v\rho\delta m'/\theta}{G_2 q\phi\beta^{-1} - 1}.$$

Differentiating (14.30) and (14.31), substituting (A.14.7), we have:

$$\begin{bmatrix} E_1 - q\left[x' + c\left(p_{11} - \dfrac{\sigma p_1 p_2}{p}\right)\right], & E_1 + \sigma c p_1 \\[2ex] E_2 + q\left[c\left(p_{12} - \dfrac{\sigma p_1 p_2}{p}\right) - (x + qx')\right], & E_2 - \sigma c p_2 \end{bmatrix}\begin{pmatrix} dq/q \\ d\phi/\phi \end{pmatrix}$$

$$= c\begin{bmatrix} p_{12} - \dfrac{\sigma p_1 p_2}{p} \\[2ex] \dfrac{\sigma p_2^2}{p} - p_{22} \end{bmatrix}d\tau.$$

Since $p_{12} > p_1 p_2/p$, $\sigma \leq 1$ and $x + qx' < 0$, it is clear that the elements of the above 2-by-2 coefficient matrix are positive, with the only possible exception for the element $E_2 - \sigma c p_2$. Thus, the *HH* schedule is negatively sloped. The *FF* schedule is also negatively sloped if and only if $E_2 > \sigma c p_2$.

Denote the determinant of the above 2-by-2 coefficient matrix by *DT*. When the *FF* curve is negatively sloped, the *HH* curve is steeper than the *FF* curve if and only if $DT < 0$. To verify $DT < 0$, notice that $qp_1 + p_2 = p$, $qp_{11} = -p_{12}$ and $qp_{12} = -p_{22}$, all from the homogeneity of the price index p. Then we can compute

$$DT = -\sigma c \left[c p p_{12} - q(px' + p_1 x) \right] + \frac{\gamma v}{G_2 q \phi \beta^{-1} - 1} \Delta,$$

$$\Delta = \rho \delta \frac{m'}{\theta} \left[c \left(p_{12} - \frac{\sigma p_1 p_2}{p} \right) - qx' \right] - \left(\frac{Gm'}{n\theta} - B' \right) \left[c \left(qp_{12} + \frac{\sigma p_2^2}{p} \right) - q(x + qx') \right].$$

A sufficient condition for $DT < 0$ is $\Delta < 0$, which can be verified using the following relations:

$$D_1 = x' - \frac{c}{q} \left(p_{12} + q \frac{\sigma p_1^2}{p} \right); \quad \frac{Gm'}{n\theta} - B' = \frac{\rho m'}{\theta} \left(\kappa + \frac{B'}{m'} + \frac{\beta}{\rho q \phi} \right);$$

$$\delta < \frac{1}{(-D_1)} \left[c \left(p_{12} - \frac{\sigma p_1 p_2}{p} \right) - (x + qx') \right] \left[\frac{\beta}{q\phi} + \left(\kappa + \frac{B'}{m'} \right) \right] \Big/ (\rho - \omega_1). \quad \text{(A.14.8)}$$

With (A.14.8), one can also show that $dq^*/d\tau > 0$ and $d\phi/d\tau < 0$. Furthermore,

$$\frac{d(q\phi)}{d\tau} = \frac{cq^2 \phi}{(-DT)} \left[\sigma p_2 x' - x \left(p_{12} - \frac{\sigma p_1 p_2}{p} \right) \right] < 0.$$

Thus, $dv^*/d\tau < 0$ and $dn^*/d\tau < 0$.

The inequality $q(0) < q^*$ can be verified directly using the equation for q in (14.27). This completes the proofs of (1)–(5).

For (6), differentiating the equations for (n, K) in (14.27) with respect to time yields

$$\begin{pmatrix} \dot{n} \\ \dot{K} \end{pmatrix} = \frac{1}{z_{14} - z_{24}} \begin{pmatrix} \omega_2 z_{14} - \omega_1 z_{24} & \omega_1 - \omega_2 \\ -(\omega_1 - \omega_2) z_{14} z_{24} & \omega_1 z_{14} - \omega_2 z_{24} \end{pmatrix} \begin{pmatrix} n - n^* \\ K - K^* \end{pmatrix}.$$

Notice that $z_{14} > 0$ and $z_{24} < 0$. It is then evident that the $\dot{n} = 0$ and $\dot{K} = 0$ schedules are both positively sloped. Since the above coefficient matrix has two negative eigenvalues (ω_1 and ω_2), its determinant is positive and so the $\dot{n} = 0$ schedule is steeper than the $\dot{K} = 0$ schedule. The $\dot{n} = 0$ is steeper than the line $G_1 = \rho$ if and only if

$$-\frac{\omega_2 z_{14} - \omega_1 z_{24}}{\omega_1 - \omega_2} > -\frac{G_{12}}{G_{11}} = \kappa,$$

which can be verified by substituting z_{14} and z_{24}. However, the $\dot{K} = 0$ schedule may or may not be steeper than the line $G_1 = \rho$. QED.

Notes

In honor of Robert Mundell this chapter was presented at the Festschrift conference at the World Bank in 1997. I thank Melanie Cao, Raquel Fernandez, Gregor Smith, and a referee for comments and Maury Obstfeld for encouragement. An earlier version of this chapter was also presented as a paper at the Society for Economic Dynamics (Mexico City, 1996). Financial support from the Social Sciences and Humanities Research Council of Canada is gratefully acknowledged.

1. For example, van Wijnbergen (1987) shows that, if the nominal wage is instead fully indexed to a consumer price index and hence responds to a tariff in the same proportion as does the price index, it increases by more than do the terms of trade when the tariff increases. Thus the product wage, which is measured in the domestic good only, rises and employment falls. Other counterarguments to the positive employment effect of tariffs include Mundell 1961, which argues that an improvement in the terms of trade induced by tariffs reduces aggregate demand and output via the Laursen-Metzler effect (see Eichengreen 1981 for more discussions), and Sen and Turnovsky 1989, which argues that tariffs induce a substitution toward leisure and hence reduce employment.

2. If preferences are not time-additive but instead recursive in the Uzawa-Epstein fashion, a tariff will create an incentive to accumulate foreign assets to meet the long-run "target" level of consumption. Long-run output and employment will decrease by even more than in a time-additive model. See Obstfeld 1982 and Shi 1994 for applications of the Uzawa-Epstein preferences in open economies.

3. The exogenous matching function and Nash wage bargaining in the Mortensen-Pissarides model and in this chapter are simple but not necessary elements for the existence of unemployment. Shi and Wen (1999) analyze endogenous matching functions and alternative wage determination schemes.

4. Linear homogeneity of H implies that the two goods are complementary in the sense that $H_{12} > 0$. This implication is plausible and used by Sen and Turnovsky (1989).

5. The approach is also common in other well-known macroeconomic models. For example, in a monetary model, Lucas (1990) assumes that household members go to different markets and pool their receipts.

6. In a search model without tariffs (an earlier version of Shi and Wen 1997), it is shown that, if the search effort is much more elastic than job vacancy, a permanent productivity increase generates the counter-factual result that the ratio of vacancy to unemployment immediately falls.

7. Equivalently, the increased income $\hat{w}(t)q(t)dn$ can be used to purchase $\hat{w}(t)q(t)dn/p(t)$ units of the consumption bundle and so yields utility $u'(t)\hat{w}(t)q(t)dn/p(t)$. Since $u'(t)/p(t) = \phi(t)$, this utility is $\hat{w}(t)q(t)\phi(t)dn$.

8. In a stationary environment, the Nash bargaining solution coincides with the solution to some noncooperative sequential bargaining games (Wolinsky 1987). Coles and Wright (1998) discuss the relationship between the two solutions in a nonstationary environment.

9. The condition required for the left-hand side of (14.25) to be increasing in v^* is $\alpha/(1-\lambda) > 1 - \beta/(q\phi G_2)$, which is satisfied if the firm's bargaining power in the wage determination $(1-\lambda)$ does not exceed its contribution to the match (measured by α) by too large a margin. Such a condition is maintained here (see Hosios 1990 for more discussion on the difference between $1-\lambda$ and α).

10. Throughout this chapter, I will examine only permanent changes in tariff. Transitory changes can also be examined but omitted here.

11. Precisely, the FF curve shifts downward to the left if and only if $G^* - B(v^*) > (1-\sigma)d^*$, or equivalently, $x + \sigma d > 0$, which is easily satisfied if the country exports a positive quantity of goods.

12. To show that the dynamics of (E) approach the true dynamics when $Q'' \approx 0$, one can start with $Q'' > 0$, linearize the dynamics of $(r, \Omega, q, v, n, K, F)$ and then take the limit $Q'' \to 0$ to show that the locally stable path of (q, v, n, K, F) in this dynamic system approaches that of system (E).

References

Andolfatto, D. 1996. Business cycles and labor market search. *American Economic Review* 86:112–32.

Blanchard, O. J., and P. A. Diamond. 1989. The Beveridge curve. *Brookings Papers on Economic Activity* 1:1–60.

Brecher, R. 1992. An efficiency-wage model with explicit monitoring: Unemployment and welfare in an open economy. *Journal of International Economics* 32:179–91.

Coles, M., and R. Wright. 1998. A dynamic equilibrium model of search, bargaining, and money. *Journal of Economic Theory* 78:32–54.

Cripps, F., and W. Godley. 1978. Control of imports as a means to full employment and the expansion of world trade: The UK's Case. *Cambridge Journal of Economics* 2:327–34.

Eichengreen, B. 1981. A dynamic model of tariffs, output and employment under flexible exchange rates. *Journal of International Economics* 11:341–59.

Epstein, L. G., and S. Zin. 1991. Substitution, risk aversion, and the temporal behavior of consumption and asset returns: An empirical analysis. *Journal of Political Economy* 99:263–86.

Fernandez, R. 1992. Terms-of-trade uncertainty, incomplete markets and unemployment. *International Economic Review* 33:881–93.

Fleming, M. 1962. Domestic financial policies under fixed and floating exchange rates. *IMF Staff Papers* 9:369–79.

Hall, R. E. 1988. Intertemporal substitution in consumption. *Journal of Political Economy* 96:339–57.

Hansen, G. 1985. Indivisible labor and the business cycles. *Journal of Monetary Economics* 16:309–27.

Hayashi, F. 1992. Tobin's q, rational expectations, and optimal investment plan. *Econometrica* 50:213–24.

Hosios, A. 1990. On the efficiency of matching and related models of search unemployment. *Review of Economic Studies* 57:279–98.

Johnson, H. G. 1951–1952. Optimum welfare and maximum revenue tariffs. *Review of Economic Studies* 19:28–35.

Layard, R., S. Nickell, and R. Jackman. 1991. *Unemployment: Macroeconomic performance and the labour market*. Oxford: Oxford University Press.

Lucas, R. E. Jr. 1990. Liquidity and interest rates. *Journal of Economic Theory* 50:237–64.

Matusz, S. 1986. Implicit contracts, unemployment and international trade. *Quarterly Journal of Economics* 96:307–22.

Merz, M. 1995. Search in the labor market and the real business cycle. *Journal of Monetary Economics* 36:269–300.

Mortensen, D. T. 1982. Property rights and efficiency in mating, racing, and related games. *American Economic Review* 72:968–79.

Mundell, R. 1968. *International economics*. New York: Macmillan.

Mundell, R. 1961. Flexible exchange rates and employment policy. *Canadian Journal of Economics* 27:509–17.

Neary, P. J. 1982. Intersectoral capital mobility, wage stickiness, and the case of adjustment assistance. In ed. J. N. Bhagwati, *Import Competition and Response*, 39–67. Chicago: University of Chicago Press.

Obstfeld, M. 1982. Aggregate spending and the terms of trade: Is there a Laursen-Metzler effect? *Quarterly Journal of Economics* 97:251–70.

Obstfeld, M., and K. Rogoff. 1995. Exchange rate dynamics redux. *Journal of Political Economy* 103:624–60.

Persson, T., and L. E. O. Svensson. 1985. Current account dynamics and the terms of trade: Harberger-Laursen-Metzler two generations later. *Journal of Political Economy* 93:43–65.

Pissarides, C. A. 1990. *Equilibrium unemployment theory*. Cambridge, Mass.: Basil Blackwell.

Rogerson, R. 1988. Indivisible labor, lotteries and equilibrium. *Journal of Monetary Economics* 21:3–16.

Sen, P., and S. Turnovsky. 1989. Tariffs, capital accumulation, and the current account in a small open economy. *International Economic Review* 30:811–31.

Shi, S. 1994. Weakly nonseparable preferences and distortionary taxes in a small open economy. *International Economic Review* 35:411–28.

Shi, S., and Q. Wen. 1999. Labor market search and the dynamic effects of taxes and subsidies. *Journal of Monetary Economics* 43:457–95.

Shi, S., and Q. Wen. 1997. Labor market search and capital accumulation: Some analytical results. *Journal of Economic Dynamics and Control* 21:1747–76.

van Wijnbergen, S. 1987. Tariffs, employment and the current account: Real wage resistance and the macroeconomics of protection. *International Economic Review* 28:691–706.

Wolinsky, A. 1987. Matching, search, and bargaining. *Journal of Economic Theory* 42:311–33.

**The Policy Rule Mix:
A Macroeconomic
Policy Evaluation**

John B. Taylor

I had the privilege of being a colleague of Bob Mundell at Columbia University during the 1970s when I was starting out in macroeconomics. I am grateful to him for the discussions we had about the workings of international markets, key events in monetary history, and ways to anchor expectations in designing monetary policies, as well as for wise advice over the years since then. This chapter builds on several of his seminal research contributions to monetary policy, fiscal policy, and international linkages between countries.

Research on monetary policy rules has expanded rapidly in the last few years, both in academia and at central banks (see McCallum 1999 for a recent review). Much of this research has focused on examining the properties of simple feedback rules that describe how the instruments of monetary policy react to variables such as inflation, real output, or the exchange rate. Despite this large amount of research there has been little research on how monetary policy rules *interact* with fiscal policy.

The purpose of this chapter is to examine several practical aspects of the interaction between monetary policy rules and fiscal policy rules. The interaction is especially important in situations where the central bank does not, or cannot, react to real variables, thereby creating the potential need for fiscal policy to take up an additional stabilizing role. In particular, this chapter addresses the following two questions about monetary and fiscal policy rules: First, should a central bank's monetary policy rule for the interest rate react to real variables such as real GDP or the unemployment rate? Some argue that the answer to this question is no; for example, some argue that the central bank should not react by raising interest rates if real economic growth accelerates unless there is also a visible increase in inflation. Second, if for institutional, legislative, or political reasons, the central bank's monetary policy rule is restricted so that it cannot react to real variables (but only to inflation or the price level), then is it possible for the government's fiscal policy rule (e.g., automatic stabilizers) to compensate for this absence of a monetary policy reaction to real variables? In other words, is it possible to design a well-functioning "policy rule mix" of monetary and fiscal policy rules in which the monetary policy rule reacts only to inflation and the fiscal policy rule reacts only to real output?

The analysis of the policy rule mix in this chapter builds on the research of Robert Mundell on the fiscal-monetary policy mix, as exemplified by Mundell 1971, one of the most influential of Mundell's many contributions to macroeconomics. The main difference between the question addressed in this chapter and that in Mundell's research is that the focus here is on the variables—inflation or the state of the business cycle—that the instruments of monetary and fiscal policy *react to*, rather than on the targets—again inflation or the state of the business cycle—that the monetary and fiscal policy instruments are *aimed at*, as in Mundell's work. This focus on what the appropriate variables should be in policy rules is characteristic of much of modern macroeconomic policy evaluation research and contrasts in an interesting way with Mundell's early work on the fiscal monetary policy mix.

The analysis of this chapter assumes that the central bank has a target (explicit or implicit) for inflation and that there is no long-run trade-off between inflation and unemployment. The first section starts with a "baseline" monetary policy rule that describes the reaction of the interest rate to deviations of real GDP from potential GDP and to the deviations of rate of inflation from the target rate of inflation. It then considers the arguments for and against a monetary policy rule that reacts only to inflation, a restriction of the baseline policy rule. Considering both theoretical and empirical evidence, the case for including a reaction to real variables in the policy rule seems strong even if the goal of monetary policy is solely to target inflation. This suggests that if for some reason monetary policy cannot react to real variables, it may be advisable to have fiscal policy compensate. Since the automatic stabilizers already represent a rule-like response, the question boils down to how much that response might be changed.

Numerical simulations of a multicountry econometric model (Taylor 1993a) with rational expectations are used to help answer this question. The financial market linkages in this econometric model are based on the Mundell-Fleming approach to modeling exchange rates with perfect capital mobility and represent another way in which this chapter builds on Mundell's contributions to macroeconomics.

The question about the policy rule mix addressed in this chapter is the mirror image of another important policy rule mix issue in which the restrictions on, and compensating adjustments of, fiscal and monetary policy are reversed. This other question is: Suppose that the fiscal policy rule is restricted—as it is in the European Monetary Union (EMU) through the Stability and Growth Pact, which limits cyclical fluctuation in the fiscal deficit (or as it would through a balanced budget amendment)—so that the deficit cannot react fully to real variables such as real GDP and unemployment; then how might the monetary policy rule be adjusted to compensate for the absence of a fiscal policy reaction to real variables? This "mirror image" question about the policy rule mix was addressed in an earlier paper (Taylor 1995) and is reviewed in the final section of this chapter.

The model simulations in this chapter focus on policy rules in the United States, but the results should apply more broadly, certainly to countries or regions similar in size and openness to the United States.

Baseline Monetary and Fiscal Policy Rules

Consider a simple baseline monetary policy rule and a baseline fiscal policy rule of the form

$$r = \pi + g(y - y^*) + h(\pi - \pi^*) + r^f, \tag{15.1}$$

$$s = f(y - y^*) + s^*, \tag{15.2}$$

where

r = short-term interest rate,

s = budget surplus as a percentage of GDP,

π = inflation rate,

y = real GDP ($100 \times \log$),

y^* = potential GDP ($100 \times \log$),

π^* = target inflation rate,

and where r^f, s^*, f, g, and h are all constants (f, g, and h are nonnegative). The term r^f represents the central bank's estimate of the equilibrium real rate of interest. The term s^* is the structural budget surplus.

Displaying equation (15.1) and equation (15.2) together highlights the question of the appropriate mix of fiscal and monetary policy rules. Terms involving real output appear in both rules with coefficients g and f. Here I will consider restrictions on the parameter g and compensating changes in the parameter f. In Taylor 1995, I considered restrictions on the parameter f and compensating changes in parameter g.

Numerical examples of these types of policy rules with the parameter values $f = 0.5$, $g = 0.5$, $h = 0.5$, $r^f = 2$, $\pi^* = 2$, and $s^* = 3$ are discussed in Taylor 1993b. For these parameter values, equations (15.1) and (15.2) describe actual U.S. monetary and fiscal policy reasonably accurately since 1987 on a quarterly average basis.

The absence of the exchange rate in equation (15.1) does not mean that I have a closed economy in mind; it simply means that the exchange rate is not a major determinant of interest rate setting. In fact, the estimated multicountry model simulated below as part of the macroeconomic policy evaluation incorporates exchange rate equations that capture the financial interaction between countries. Clarida, Gali, and Gertler (1997b) show that monetary policy rules similar to (15.1) also describe the behavior of Germany and Japan with the exchange rate playing a surprisingly small role.

Using the notation in equations (15.1) and (15.2) we can restate the questions mentioned in the introduction of this chapter as follows:

1. Should the parameter $g = 0$?
2. If so, can the parameter f compensate for setting $g = 0$.

To be sure, the first question is stated more starkly than necessary. A close, but less extreme, formulation of the question would simply be to ask: How large should g be?

The Case against Monetary Policy Reacting to Real Variables

The central *technical* argument against a monetary policy reaction function with real variables such as $y - y^*$ is that such a reaction requires policy makers to have knowledge of potential GDP and its growth rate. Potential GDP is difficult to estimate. Both its growth rate and its level are uncertain and always subject to an active debate. Some may argue that we are in a "new economy" with real GDP well below potential GDP. Others may warn that real GDP is above potential with a rise in inflation imminent. A related problem is in projecting potential GDP in the future. Conceptually, potential GDP is the aggregate supply of the economy, depending on available labor, capital, and technology. Even if labor supply and capital could be forecast reasonably well, total factor productivity growth is very difficult to forecast accurately. Alan Greenspan (1997) refers explicitly to uncertainty about potential growth as a disadvantage of monetary policy rules that react to deviations of real GDP from potential GDP. He refers to the "current debate between those who argue that the economy is entering a 'new era' of greatly enhanced sustainable growth and unusually high levels of resource utilization, and those who do not," and notes that policy rules like equation (15.1) "depend on the values of certain key variables—most crucially the equilibrium real federal funds rate and the *production potential of the economy*" [italics added].

The fact that there is a close association between the GDP gap (the deviation between real GDP and potential GDP) and other measures of utilization, including the deviation of the unemployment rate from the natural rate, provides some help in measuring the GDP gap. However, there is also great uncertainty about these other measures of capacity utilization. For example, the current level of the natural unemployment rate is the subject of as much debate as is potential GDP.

If g were equal to zero, uncertainty about the level of potential GDP would not be a problem, for the obvious reason that the monetary policy rule would not depend on potential GDP. Hence, if it could be established that macroeconomic performance did not deteriorate if g were zero, a policy rule with $g = 0$ would be very attractive.

A theoretical rationale for lowering the value of a policy reaction coefficient like g because of uncertainty is that put forth by Brainard (1967). Brainard's theoretical rationale distinguishes between multiplicative and additive uncertainty. Only multiplicative uncertainty calls for a reduction in reaction coefficients in fully optimal rules. The uncertainty concerning the level of potential GDP is most likely additive. For example, the intercept coefficient in an aggregate price adjustment equation would be uncertain if potential GDP, the natural rate of unemployment, or the sustainable growth rate of real GDP were uncertain. None of these types of uncertainty seems to add multiplicative uncertainty to the policy optimization problem. If this is so then the reference to the Brainard uncertainty model as support for making g small (or setting it to zero) is incorrect. However, as pointed out by Smets (1998), many *simple* policy rules are only approximations to more complex fully optimal rules; within the class of simple rules, the level of additive uncertainty does matter for the size of the reaction coefficients. Hence, uncertainty about the measurement of potential GDP would in general reduce the size of the coefficient g in equation (15.1).

Another argument against a monetary policy rule that reacts to real variables is that such variables are not subject to monetary control, at least not in the long run. However, such arguments confuse the goals of monetary policy with the strategy for achieving the goals. As I show in the next section, even a central bank that had the single goal of targeting inflation, with no stated goals about unemployment or real GDP, would find reacting to real variables helpful in achieving those goals.

A related reason for not reacting to real variables is the time-inconsistency argument. Because of the time-inconsistency bias toward monetary policies that pay too much attention to real variables, it is preferable to appoint central bankers that pay too little attention to real variables. (See Rogoff 1987.) Such central bankers may indeed argue that g should be zero even though it is not optimal for stabilizing both inflation and output.

The Case in Favor of Monetary Policy Reacting to Real Variables

There are several theoretical and empirical reasons why a monetary policy that reacts to real variables would improve macroeconomic performance, both in terms of more price stability and more output stability. The argument I discuss first is also related to uncertainty, but about the "equilibrium real federal funds rate" (to use Greenspan's term) rather than about potential GDP.

Uncertainty about the Real Interest Rate

The intercept term in equation (15.1) represents the central bank's estimate of the real interest rate. There is, of course, much uncertainty about the level of the real interest rate. Although the parameter g does not seem to interact with r^f in equation (15.1), one can show that setting $g = 0$ can actually increase the impact of this uncertainty greatly. Hence, uncertainty about the real interest rate is a reason for not setting g to zero.

To show this I first derive a useful short-run relationship between the rate of inflation and real GDP. Assume that real GDP depends negatively on the interest rate according to the equation

$$y - y^* = -\beta(r - \pi - r^*), \tag{15.3}$$

where r^* now represents the equilibrium real rate of interest. With $r - \pi = r^*$ we have $y = y^*$.

Substituting equation (15.2) into equation (15.3) gives

$$\pi - \pi^* = -((1 + \beta g)/\beta h)(y - y^*) - (r^f - r^*)/h. \tag{15.4}$$

Equation (15.4) is a negatively sloped "aggregate demand" relationship between inflation and real GDP with inflation $(\pi - \pi^*)$ on the vertical axis and real GDP $(y - y^*)$ on the horizontal axis. The slope of the relationship is important. It determines whether a given shock to inflation will be translated more into inflation or more into real GDP. For example, if the relationship is very flat, then a shock to inflation will cause a large decline in real GDP, which in turn will tend to reduce the inflation increase and thus the variability of inflation. On the other hand, if the relationship is very steep, then a shock to inflation will not have much effect on real GDP, but will result in a large and persistent swing in inflation.

Observe that the slope of this relationship depends on both g and h. Higher values of h (larger reactions of policy to inflation) flatten the relationship. Higher values of g (larger reactions of policy to real GDP) will make the relationship steeper. For a given value of g, including $g = 0$, one can choose h to obtain any desired value for the slope. For the same value of the slope, low values of g will require low values of h.

The second term on the right-hand side of equation (15.4) represents the effects of uncertainty about the equilibrium real interest rate. If the central bank's estimate of the equilibrium real interest rate (r^f) is not equal to the actual equilibrium real interest rate, then the inflation rate will deviate from the target. Note that the interest rate error is multiplied by $1/h$. For example, if $h = 0.5$, the multiplier is 2, so the error in the inflation rate is twice as large as the error in the real interest rate estimate. How does the choice of g affect this error multiplier? The smaller g is, the smaller h has to be for the same slope of the relationship between aggregate demand and inflation. For g close to zero, h would have to be very small to keep the curve from becoming too flat. Such a small value of h could cause small errors in the estimate of the equilibrium real interest rate to translate into large deviations from the inflation target.

Real Variables as Guides to Preemptive Strikes against Inflation

The above argument in favor of reacting to real variables implicitly assumes that one of the goals of policy is to keep the fluctuations in output small. Otherwise one would not be concerned if the inflation-output relationship in equation (15.4) got too flat. However, there are reasons for monetary policy to react to real variables even if they are not part of the goal of policy.

The monetary policy rule in equation (15.1) does not have expectations of future variables in it. This may seem like a defect because policy works with a lag, and it is therefore necessary to be forward looking. However, real variables such as $y - y^*$ are helpful in forecasting future inflation. There is strong time series evidence that real output "Granger-causes" inflation. Thus, an increase in real GDP above potential GDP is an indication that inflation is likely to rise and that an increase in the interest rate to *preempt* that rise in inflation would be appropriate. Similarly, a decrease in real GDP below potential GDP would signal a future fall in inflation and call for a preemptive reduction in interest rates.

Clarida, Gali, and Gertler (1997a) show that equation (15.1) is the implication of a monetary policy rule that reacts only to expected inflation, if lagged output and inflation are sufficient statistics for forecasting future inflation. More generally, real output will appear in a reaction function (perhaps along with other variables) as long as it Granger-causes inflation. Preemptive strikes—increases or decreases in the federal funds rate before there is a visible sign of an increase or decrease in inflation—can be guided by factors in addition to real output, but the strong Granger-causality of output to inflation suggests that output should always be one factor.

Analogy with Money Growth Targets

A third argument in favor of real variables in the monetary policy rule comes from noting the similarity between fixed money growth rules and interest rate rules that incorporate real output. Money growth rules work well (most likely with feedback) when it is possible to measure the money supply accurately. One of the advantages of money growth rules is that they provide an automatic stabilizing effect on both real output and prices. If real output rises, the demand for money rises relative to the quantity supplied, and the interest rate rises, attenuating the real output increase. Similarly, if real output falls, the interest rate automatically decreases, stimulating output. Some research has questioned whether these increases or decreases in the interest rate are large enough, but I know of no research that shows they are too large or should not occur at all.

The presence of the output variable in equation (15.1) for the interest rate policy rule results in exactly the same interest rate movements as a fixed money growth rule, or a money growth rule with feedback from other variables. An increase in real output causes the interest rate to rise, and a decrease in real output causes the interest rate to fall. These changes in interest rates offset the fluctuation in real output and the fluctuations in inflation that they cause. By mimicking this valuable feature of money rules, an interest rate rule with real output improves macroeconomic performance.

Simulations with an Econometric Model

These arguments in favor of a policy reaction to real output are supported by calculations with estimated econometric models as in Taylor 1993a and Bryant, Hooper, and Mann 1993. The model described in Taylor 1993a, for example, is a detailed empirical version of the simple abstract equation (15.3). The model includes exchange rate effects, explicit differences between long-term and short-term interest rates, forward-looking consumption and investment behavior, and perfect capital mobility. It is fit to quarterly data. The simulations of policy rules are stochastic with the shocks to all the equations drawn from the estimated variance-covariance matrix of the shocks.

To assess whether policy reaction to real output adds to the performance of the macroeconomy, one can simulate these models with two versions of policy rule 1, one with real output and the other without real output. The simulation results with the Taylor 1993a multicountry model uniformly favor including real output in the reaction function. I focus on the variability of real output and the aggregate price level. When real output is a factor in the reaction function, both price stability and real output stability are greater (or can be made greater by adjusting the parameters) than when the policy rule is restricted to exclude real variables. In other words, it would be inadvisable to ignore real output whether or not real output is an explicit goal of policy.

This finding about the superiority of rules with feedback from output is true for the seven largest industrial countries in the model, regardless of whether the exchange rate regime involves fixed or flexible exchange rates. In the case of fixed exchange rates the policy rule is a function of a weighted average of real output and aggregate prices in each country in the fixed exchange rate system. All countries within the fixed exchange rate system have a common short-term interest rate because of the rational expectations and perfect capital mobility assumptions in the model. However, given the choice between fixed and flexible exchange rates, the flexible exchange rate system is preferred according to these criteria.

Compensating for Restrictions on the Monetary Policy Rule

The previous two sections have summarized key arguments for and against a monetary policy rule that reacts to real variables. My assessment of these arguments is that a monetary policy rule that reacts to real variables would improve economic performance compared with a monetary policy rule that does not respond to real variables. Uncertainty about the economy's potential growth is a serious problem for interest rate rules such as (15.1), which depend on potential GDP, and is unlikely to be large enough to imply a zero value for the reaction coefficient (Smets 1998). The optimality of reacting to real output is based on four arguments: uncertainty about the real interest rate, the need for preemptive monetary strikes, analogies with fixed money growth rules, and simulations with empirical models.

However, even a strong set of economic arguments does not preclude the possibility that limitations on monetary policy might be imposed externally or even be adopted internally by a central bank for political or time-inconsistency reasons. For example, in an effort to convince market analysts that it is targeting inflation, the central bank might not increase interest rates when real output is above potential if there is no sign that inflation has risen. An interest rate increase in this circumstance could be thought to confuse the market, which would interpret it as a sign that the central bank is actually targeting real variables.

Could the fiscal policy rule in equation (15.2) compensate for such a restriction by having a larger reaction to real GDP? How large would the coefficient have to be? To see the theoretical possibilities we can modify equation (15.3) by adding in a fiscal variable (the deviation of the fiscal surplus from the structural surplus) to get

$$y - y^* = -\beta(r - \pi - r^*) - \delta(s - s^*) \tag{15.5}$$

and then substituting for both the interest rate r and the budget surplus s from the policy rule equations (15.1) and (15.2) to get

$$\pi - \pi^* = -((1 + \beta g - \delta f)/\beta h)(y - y^*) - (r^f - r^*)/h. \tag{15.6}$$

Equation (15.6), like equation (15.4), represents a key negative relationship between inflation and real GDP, but now with the added fiscal policy rule parameter f. The slope of the relationship in equation (15.6) depends on both g and f. Hence, the slope can be held constant by adjusting f to compensate for setting g equal to zero. And because f does not appear elsewhere in the equation, there is no possibility of any side effects. To the extent that equation (15.6) captures the effects of monetary and fiscal policy rules on economic fluctuations, it appears possible in theory to use this fiscal policy rule to offset the restriction on the monetary policy rule.

Simulations of Econometric Models

Although these simple equations are useful for discussing policy issues, they do not come close to describing the full dynamic structure of the economy that is relevant for policy evaluation. A more detailed and theoretically complete model is needed. Hence, to get a better assessment of the possibility of using fiscal policy rules in conjunction with monetary policy rules, I conducted several stochastic simulations of the multicountry econometric model of Taylor 1993a. Three different "policy rule mixes" were considered:

• *Policy rule mix I*: Baseline monetary and fiscal policy rules (equations (15.1) and (15.2)) (parameter values: $g = 0.5$ and $f = 0.5$)

• *Policy rule mix II*: Restricted monetary policy rule and baseline fiscal policy rule (parameter values: $g = 0$ and $f = 0.5$)

• *Policy rule mix III*: Restricted monetary policy rule and more reactive fiscal policy rule (parameter values: $g = 0$ and $f = 1$)

An example of a typical stochastic simulation is shown in figure 15.1. The three policy rule mixes were simulated for the same set of stochastic shocks to the equations of the model over a period of forty quarters; figure 15.1 shows an example of the resulting percentage deviations of real output from potential output for the three different policy rule mixes. The stochastic simulation clearly indicates a deterioration of output stability for policy rule mix II compared with policy rule mix I; this finding corresponds with the results of the simple model discussed above. Figure 15.1 also indicates that the performance of policy rule mix III results in smaller output variability than policy rule

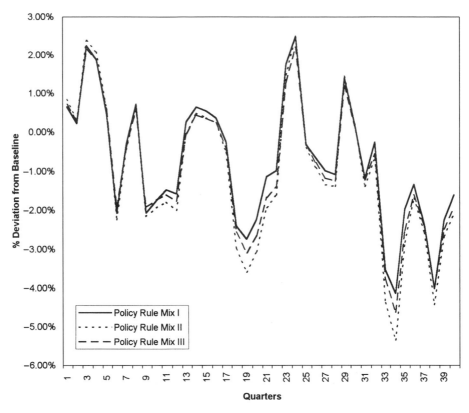

Figure 15.1
Simulation of alternative policy rule mixes. Mix I: both fiscal and monetary policy react
to output; Mix II: only fiscal policy reacts to output; Mix III: only fiscal policy reacts but
with a reaction coefficient that is twice as large

mix II. With the fiscal policy parameter $f = 1$, the degree of output stability is still not quite as good as that for policy rule mix I, suggesting
that a fiscal policy parameter greater than $f = 1$ would be necessary to
fully compensate for the restriction on monetary policy.

Averaging the standard deviations of the differences between output
and baseline over five simulations like that in figure 15.1 shows that
real output stability is 28 percent worse when policy rule mix II is used
instead of policy rule mix I, but only 12 percent worse when policy rule
mix III is used instead of policy rule mix I. Hence, the simulation results
show that values of the fiscal reaction coefficient f in excess of 1 are
needed to give the same amount of stability as the baseline monetary
and fiscal policies. Because a parameter value of f equal to 1 is already

twice as large as the current automatic stabilizers, it seems unlikely that changes in the automatic stabilizers could in reality fully compensate for such a restriction on monetary policy.

These results have some similarity with the "mirror-image" policy rule mix analysis in Taylor 1995, which address the possibility of monetary policy compensating for a restriction on fiscal policy due to a balanced budget amendment or a restriction like that in the Stability and Growth Pact in the European Monetary Union. In that evaluation I also considered three policy rule mixes:

• *Policy rule mix A*: Baseline monetary and fiscal policy rules (equations (15.1) and (15.2)) (parameter values: $g = 0.5$ and $f = 0.5$)

• *Policy rule mix B*: Restricted fiscal policy rule and baseline monetary policy rule (parameter values: $g = 0.5$ and $f = 0$)

• *Policy rule mix C*: Restricted fiscal policy rule and adjusted monetary policy rule (parameter values: $g = 1.0$ and $f = 0$)

In this case, performance of policy rule mix B was worse than policy rule mix A. The adjustment in policy rule mix C improved performance relative to B, but was not enough to bring performance all the way back to the level under policy rule mix A. Hence, monetary policy had to change quite a bit to offset the restriction on fiscal policy.

Conclusions

The main conclusions of this chapter are as follows: First, a monetary policy rule in which the interest rate instrument of policy adjusts to both inflation and real GDP works better than a policy in which there is no instrument reaction to real GDP. Second, it is possible to design a mix of monetary and fiscal policy rules in which monetary policy has the job of reacting to inflation and fiscal policy has the job of reacting to real output. In other words, fiscal policy could adjust to compensate for a restriction on monetary policy. Third, the adjustment of the fiscal policy rule would probably be very large and therefore difficult to make in practice. Hence, although a one-on-one pairing of monetary policy with reactions to inflation and fiscal policy with reactions to real output may seem attractive, a monetary policy rule that reacts both to real output and inflation—despite the uncertainty about potential— makes more practical sense according to empirical evidence on the monetary and fiscal policy transmission mechanism.

Note

The research was supported by the Stanford Institute for Economic Policy Research. I wish to thank Jeffrey Frankel and Akila Weerapana for helpful comments and assistance.

References

Brainard, W. 1967. Uncertainty and the effects of monetary policy. *American Economic Review, Proceedings* 57:411–25.

Bryant, R., P. Hooper, and C. Mann. 1993. *Evaluating policy regimes: New empirical research in empirical macroeconomics.* Washington, D.C.: Brookings Institution.

Clarida, R., J. Gali, and M. Gertler. 1997a. The Science of Monetary Policy: a New Regression Perspective. *Journal of Economic Literature* 37(4):1661–1707.

Clarida, R., J. Gali, and M. Gertler. 1997b. Monetary policy rules in practice: Some international evidence. Economic research report no. 97-32, C. V. Starr Center for Applied Economics, New York University.

McCallum, B. 1999. Issues in the design of monetary policy rules. *Handbook of macroeconomics*, ed. J. B. Taylor and M. Woodford, 1483–1530. Amsterdam: North-Holland.

Mundell, R. A. 1971. The dollar and the policy mix: 1971. Essays in International Finance no. 85, International Finance Section, Princeton University.

Rogoff, K. 1987. Reputational constraints on monetary policy. In *Carnegie-Rochester Conference Series on Public Policy*, vol. 26, ed. K. Brunner and A. Meltzer, 141–182. Amsterdam: North-Holland.

Smets, F. 1998. Output gap uncertainty: Does it matter for the Taylor rule? Working paper no. 60 (November), Bank for International Settlements, Basel, Switzerland.

Taylor, J. B. 1995. Monetary policy implications of greater fiscal discipline. In *Budget deficits and debt: Issues and options*, ed. S. Weiner, 151–170. Kansas City: Federal Reserve Bank of Kansas City.

Taylor, J. B. 1993a. *Macroeconomic policy in a world economy: From econometric design to practical operation.* New York: W. W. Norton. On-line version available at *www.stanford.edu/~johntayl/MacroPolicyWorld.htm*

Taylor, J. B. 1993b. Discretion versus policy rules in practice. In *Carnegie-Rochester Conference Series on Public Policy*, vol. 39, ed. A. Meltzer and C. Plosser, 195–214. Amsterdam: North-Holland.

Name Index

Subject Index